A

D1062949

BIOGRAPHICAL HISTORY

OF

LANCASTER COUNTY:

BEING A HISTORY OF

EARLY SETTLERS AND EMINENT MEN OF THE COUNTY;

AS ALSO MUCH OTHER

UNPUBLISHED HISTORICAL INFORMATION, CHIEFLY OF A LOCAL CHARACTER.

BY

ALEX. HARRIS.

LANCASTER, PA.:
ELIAS BARR & CO.
1872.

– Notice –

The foxing, or discoloration with age, characteristic of old books, sometimes shows
through to some extent in reprints such as
this, especially when the foxing is very severe
in the original book. We feel that the contents of this book warrant its reissue despite
these blemishes, and hope you will agree and
read it with pleasure.

Entered according to Act of Congress, in the year 1872,

By ELIAS BARR & CO.,

In the Office of the Librarian of Congress, at Washington, D. C.

Facsimile Reprint

Published 1989 By
HERITAGE BOOKS, INC.
1540E Pointer Ridge Place, Bowie, Maryland 20716
(301)-390-7709

ISBN 1-55613-245-X

PEARSOL & GEIST, PRINTERS,
LANCASTER, PA

PREFACE.

A Biographical History of Lancaster county is such a one as has not heretofore been attempted to be executed in our midst. That a very general desire existed amongst the intelligent citizens of our county, that a work of this character should be produced, the undersigned has had, since the undertaking of his enterprise, the most abundant evidence. It was owing to this fact that he received the assistance, from the announcement of his enterprise, of a number of intelligent and leading men, who, busied themselves in the collection of all the information in their power, in order to aid him in the preparation of a history of personages whose lives, acts and doings were worthy of being recorded, for the interest of the present and future generations.

That his work will be entirely satisfactory to the people of the county, he cannot have the presumption to anticipate, for it is far from being what he himself would have desired to render it. Instead of being a complete Biographical History of the county, he rather is disposed to regard it as a fragmentary contribution to its history, of which the collected facts may serve as material for a more systematic and complete history at some future day.

The undersigned, in setting out with the proposal to produce a Biographical History, had nothing further in view, save the presentation of brief sketches of the leading citizens of the county, and this it will be perceived he has chiefly kept in view. In this particular, he hopes to be excused when he says that, in his opinion, his work cannot but prove acceptable to a large class of our intelligent readers. Surely an interest must be felt to know the history of those citizens, born, reared, or who have lived in our midst, whose works have enrolled them amongst the famed men of our

nation. Even of the lesser lights, whose rays were more cir-
cumscribed, it is also a matter of interest to have some
knowledge. Of men who are the leading citizens of a community, we always feel an interest in knowing something as
to their history, and this is the main aim of the work now
presented to the people of our county.

As regards the history of early settlers, their descendants
must ever feel a lively interest in ascertaining all that they
may be able to learn of them. Although beyond the scope
of the work, as originally contemplated, yet in deference to
suggestions frequently made, the undersigned has incorporated several of the leading family histories, and such as, in
an especial manner, have contributed largely towards the
development of the county, and in rendering it "the garden
of America." Some other family histories were sought in
vain to be obtained, which would have given additional interest to the production. Reasons, unnecessary to name,
thwarted the obtaining of several such family histories.
This, however, is the less to be regretted, as all this part of
the history was foreign to the original programme. Especial
anxiety, however, was felt to obtain family histories of that
class of our people who have, up to a very recent period,
(and many of them yet), shunned all participation in political life, and as a consequence not obtained that deserved
recognition to which their deserts entitled them. To have
given a history of every family in the county, volumes would
have been required instead of a work of the moderate compass intended. As it is, the author has been compelled
to omit much other interesting matter, in order not to allow
the work to go beyond its proposed bulk.

Without here enumerating the names of the many generous and enterprising gentlemen who rendered cheerful assistance in the collection and transmission of material for
the work, the undersigned now takes occasion to sincerely
thank such, one and all, for their efficient aid and services; and
he will see to it that they each receive due credit in the work,
for the respective articles and biographies they may have
severally furnished him.

And in conclusion, the undersigned commits his work to

the judgment of the intelligent readers of Lancaster county, simply as a contribution to local history; by no means claiming it as anything save a collection of plain sketches that may prove, from the facts recorded, interesting to the people of the county. As to its composition, he has not sought to render it ornate, the generality of our readers preferring plain Anglo-Saxon to the most polished language. That all will be pleased with his production, the undersigned does not anticipate, nor does he hope to escape all adverse criticism; but he will be content if he shall be able to satisfy the reasonable and reflecting, that he has produced a work of moderate interest for his readers. Trusting that a not too critical public may so view his effort, he submits it in the hope that some one vastly more competent than himself, may be incited to undertake a work that may ultimate in a much more brilliant success than can be anticipated for the present humble production.

ALEXANDER HARRIS.

LANCASTER, October, 1872.

BIOGRAPHICAL HISTORY

OF LANCASTER COUNTY.

A.

AGNEW, Robert, a physician of Sadsbury township. He was elected a member of the Legislature in the years 1826 and 1827. His son, David H. Agnew, was born in Sadsbury township, where he practiced medicine for a number of years. He is now a distinguished professor of surgery in the University of Pennsylvania.

ALBRIGHT, Jacob, was born June 26th, 1791, in Lancaster city, Pennsylvania. He received a fair education, and when a young man, taught school for some time in the old Lancaster Academy, in North Queen street, between Lemon and James streets. He was united in marriage with Mrs. Susan Sherer, on the 25th of November, 1847. For some years he was engaged with Dr. Benj. Sherer, in the forwarding and commission business. Mr. Albright was elected Mayor of the city of Lancaster, in the year 1855, on the ticket commonly known as the Know-Nothing ticket, and held the office for one year. He was an official member of the Moravian church, and also a member of the Masonic Order. He was a man of quiet and retiring disposition, very amiable and agreeable in his manners, and was highly respected as a citizen. He died shortly after his retirement from the Mayoralty, March 18th, 1856.

*ALBBIGHT, Rev. Jacob. The father of Rev. Jacob Albright, (Albrecht in German), was John Albrecht, who emigrated from Germany to this country and settled in Douglas

*Contributed by J. B. Good, esq.

township, Montgomery county, Pennsylvania. His domicile was at or near a mountain ridge, known as Fuchsberg (Fox Mountain), about ten miles southeast of Pottstown. In this obscure spot his son Jacob, the subject of this sketch, was born on May 1st, 1759. The house which sheltered his infant head, and where he spent his childhood and youth, is still standing; it is a one-story stone building, of solid but plain architecture.

His parents were poor, and compelled to struggle hard to provide for themselves and their children the necessaries of life. The neighborhood, in its social, moral and religious aspects was then, and is now of such a nature, that one is forcibly reminded of the place where the founder of our religion was brought up, and of which it was said, "Can there any good thing come out of it?" However, the poverty and privations of his youth, served as a rugged school to prepare him for the severe and almost superhuman labors of his later years.

Like most men of his early surroundings, hardly anything is known of his boyhood. His parents belonged to the Evangelical Lutheran Church, whose minister baptized him in his infancy, and gave him the usual catechetical instruction when he arrived at the proper age. He also received such instruction as the schools of his time afforded. Our beneficent common school system had as yet no existence. In rude log cabins, unworthy of the name of school-houses, the simplest rudiments of education were imperfectly taught. Rev. H. Harbaugh, in the Pennsylvania German vernacular, says of these schools :

> Inwennig, um der Offe rum
> ․ Hocke die kleene Tschäps,
> Sie lerne artlich hart, verschteh,
> Un wer net wees sei' A B C—
> Sei' Ohre kriege Räpps.
>
> Die arme Drep! dort hocke se
> In Misserie—juscht denk !
> Es is kee' Wunner—nemm mei Wort—
> Dass se so wenig lerne dort,
> Uf selle hoche Benk.

In one of these unpromising institutions, young Albright acquired the art of reading and writing the German language, and also the first principles of Arithmetic. He never enjoyed the advantages of an English education. Of the German, he acquired a correct knowledge, by reading Luther's translation of the Bible, as also other books written in pure German. Among the latter was a Commentary on the Bible, which he valued very highly.

In person he was of medium stature, about five feet eight inches in height. He had an aquiline nose, his mouth and chin were exquisitely formed. His eyes were blue, and very bright, his hair was black and his complexion fair. Though in his temperament the sanguine and choleric dispositions predominated, yet his bearing was always graceful and dignified. About his person and dress, he was scrupulously neat and precise. Some persons who knew him but imperfectly, thought he was proud ; those, however, who understood his character better, knew him to be entirely innocent of this charge.

In 1785, when about 25 years of age, he was married to Miss Catharine Cope. Soon after his marriage, he moved to Lancaster county, and purchased a tract of land, eligibly located near Frysville, in the present East Cocalico, but then Earl township. Here, besides farming, he also carried on the brick and tile business. At that time many of the dwellings in Lancaster county were covered with tiles. Some of these antique relics are still in existence.

In 1790 several of his children died of dysentery. At the funeral of one of them, Rev. Anton Hautz, a minister of the German Reformed Church, preached a sermon which touched Albright's heart. Of the state of his mind at this time, he says : "In my early youth I had received catechetical instruction in the doctrines of the Christian religion. I did not then comprehend the great truths I learned, and could not appreciate them; but a feeling of reverence toward God was implanted, which never left me. This feeling was very undefined, but it induced me to regard every place where God was worshipped as sacred, and I could not despise or persecute those persons who engaged in the worship of the Most High, no matter to what sect they belonged. This reverence for the worship of God, induced me to frequently

attend religious meetings, and to listen attentively to the exhortations of the Ministers of the Gospel. * * * I became frightened at myself, the judgments of God stood before my imagination, my spirit experienced a deep dejection,
and at last, on a certain day of July, in my thirty-second year,
it rose to such a degree that it bordered on despair. * * *
I fell upon my knees, tears of bitter repentance coursed
down my cheeks, and a long-continued, earnest and ardent
prayer for pardon and salvation, went up to the throne of the
Most High." In this state of mind he was met by a sincere,
warm-hearted Christian, named Adam Riegel, whose sympathies at once entwined themselves around this sincere penitent. It was in this man's house where they earnestly prayed
together, that Albright experienced the truth, that the Son of
Man has power on earth to forgive sins. Of this experience
Albright says : "All distress of my heart vanished. The
peace of God filled my soul, and the Holy Spirit bore witness
with my Spirit, that I was a child of God."

At this period, the German churches in Pennsylvania
were in a deplorable condition. German adventurers, whose
moral and literary attainments precluded their preferment at
home, hunted their fortunes in America, and presumed to
meddle with holy things among the rude and unlettered col-
onists. Tradition has handed down plenty of anecdotes,
which plainly show the grotesqueness of manners and general uncouthness of the clergy of these times. The old adage,
"Like priest like people," was fully illustrated in this instance. The people were industrious and frugal, but nevertheless ignorant, coarse, intemperate and profane. Church
discipline, if such a thing was ever thought of, was exercised
with extreme laxity.

On this subject Albright says : "At this time I knew no
class of professing Christians that seemed more zealous unto
good works, and who had a better discipline than the Methodists. For this reason I went with them and had opportunity
to obtain great good and many blessings for my soul. As
many things in their exercises were as yet not clear to my
mind, and were conducted in the English language, and as I
was not yet fully conversant with that language, I commenced

its study with great zeal, and soon was enabled to fully understand their book of discipline and their articles of faith, which pleased me very much. I sought to conduct myself precisely according to their rules and regulations."

He joined a class that held their meetings in his neighborhood. Mr. Isaac Davis, whose farm adjoined his own, being their leader.

Albright's talents and zeal were so marked, that an Exhorter's license was soon given to him; and as there was at that time considerable religious inquiry among his German neighbors, opportunities frequently presented themselves to exercise his gifts.

On this point Albright says: " I had no gift of eloquent speech, and I must confess that I was herein less competent than any other man who might have undertaken it." Competent judges, however, assure us that Albright under-estimated his powers, as humility was a marked feature of his character. At this time he had no thoughts of regularly preaching the Gospel, and he passed through great struggles before he could make up his mind to take that step. He clearly foresaw the labors, difficulties and afflictions he would have to endure. And then his keen sensitivness as to his own inefficiency, weighed heavily on his soul. He hesitated until the conviction of his divine call to the ministry became irresistible, and he felt with St. Paul: " Wo is unto me if I preach not the Gospel." He especially felt a deep solicitude for his German countrymen, whose spiritual welfare lay near his sympathetic heart. He soon became known in his neighborhood as a very zealous worker.

As regards his relations to the Methodist E. Church at this juncture, it is difficult to arrive at a correct conclusion. It is doubtless true that though some Methodist ministers occasionally preached in German, there were none that exclusively labored in that language. The impression seems to have extensively prevailed, that the German language would soon die out on this continent, and that therefore it was impolitic to employ German preachers. Albright, however, felt such a powerful internal call to labor among his German brethren, that he could not remain silent or inactive,

but continued zealously to labor in his divine Master's cause.
At first his success was but moderate. From 1796, when
he first set out on his mission, until 1803, when the first Conference was held, the number of his followers did not exceed
forty; and besides him, there were only two preachers,
namely, Revs. Walter and Lieser.

This slow increase was principally owing to the illiterate and
obscure character of the ministers engaged in the work, and
the powerful opposition and persecution which was aroused
against them. Besides this, Albright and his coadjutors had,
up to this time, confined themselves almost exclusively to
the counties of Bucks, Berks and Northampton, emphatically
Albright's home; and a greater than he had said before him,
that "a prophet is not without honor save in his own country and in his own house." Afterwards, when the theatre of
their operations was transferred to distant fields, whose soil
perhaps was more promising, their labors yielded more abundant fruit.

On September 15th and 16th, 1807, at Mühlbach, Lebanon
county, Pennsylvania, they held their first regular annual
Conference. At this meeting five itinerant and three local
preachers, and twenty official lay members, were present.
Here Albright was elected Superintendent of the Society, and
by a resolution of the Conference, he was directed to prepare
rules of discipline for the government of the religious Society
thus organized. This, on account of his declining health and
early death, he was prevented from accomplishing. The discipline was afterwards prepared by Rev. G. Miller, in the
year 1809. The membership at this time numbered two
hundred and twenty.

It was soon apparent that Albright's health was daily
failing; but he still continued to travel and to labor as much
as his impaired strength permitted him to do. During the
winter he traveled with the late Rev. J. Dreisbach, who was
then a young man, but who has recently died at the advanced age of eighty-two years. Their circuit extended
partly over the counties of Dauphin, Lebanon, Lancaster,
Berks, Bucks, Montgomery, Northampton, Lehigh and
Schuylkill. They had about thirty appointments or places

to preach, of which some were from twenty to thirty miles apart.

It was during this season that the Society at Millersville, Lancaster county, received great accessions in numbers, among whom was John Erb, who afterwards became an itinerant minister.

On Easter-day, 1808, a quarterly meeting was held at Albany, Berks county, Pennsylvania, where Albright for the last time, appointed his preachers to their several fields of labor. He now began to sink rapidly. Incessant travel, exposure to the inclemency of every season, the privations incident to the itinerancy, and the almost superhuman labors performed by him, had at last undermined his constitution and broken down his health to such a degree that he was compelled to return home. He was suffering with a pulmonary affection, which, however, had now progressed so far that he never reached his earthly home any more. He remained with Christian friends at Mühlbach, Lebanon county, Pennsylvania, who kindly nursed him during a short illness, being confined to his bed for only a few days. He died on the 18th of May, 1808, in the fiftieth year of his age. His remains were buried on the 20th, in a neighboring burying ground, where, in commemoration of his death and burial, a church has since been erected, which bears the name of "Albright's Church."

Since his death, the religious Society founded by him has enjoyed great prosperity. The number of regular or itinerant ministers, exceeds five hundred, and the lay membership approaches to one hundred thousand. The Society supports several institutions of learning; their book concern is in a flourishing condition; and one of their papers, "Der Christliche Botschafter," is the oldest German religious paper in the country. They support promising missions in Germany and Switzerland, which appear to be destined to exert a great influence in the future.

AMWEG, John Michael, was a native of Prussia, who emigrated to this country and settled in Lancaster county before the American revolution. He settled in Cocalico, at a place near Reinholdsville. He was a man of a good education, and pursued the calling of a school-master. Being industrious and economical, he soon acquired property around him. He was the ancestor of the family name in this county. One of his sons was named Jacob, and his son William, was the father of Jacob B., William S., and John M. Amweg, members of the bar of Lancaster. Wm. Amweg died in 1861.

ANDERSON, JAMES, a citizen of Donegal township, who resided near the borough of Marietta. He was a member of the Legislature in the years 1776, 1778, 1779 and 1780.

ANDREWS, HUGH, a member of the Legislature in 1840 and 1841.

ARMSTRONG, ANDREW, a citizen of East Donegal township. He was elected a member of the Legislature in October, 1866, and served one session. He is a man of considerable intellect and force of character, and entertains very independent and decided opinions. He has been one of the early and firm friends of the Free School System.

ARMSTRONG, ARTHUR, a painter of considerable repute; many of whose paintings are yet preserved by citizens of Lancaster. The following notice of Mr. Armstrong, by a cotemporary, seems to depict his artistic skill in its proper light: "It does not require a connoisseur in the fine arts to discover something remarkable in the style of Mr. Armstrong's painting; he leaves nothing in the dark for the imagination to work out; it is bold and distinct, and yet the distance is kept with such a natural harmony as to give it at once that ease and softness essential to the art. The picture (the one our cotemporary describes), is on a rich blue silk, and is intended as a banner for the Washington Fire Company of Louisville, Kentucky. The back of the canvass represents the Washington family, which is not a mere covering of the bare material, but with a persevering assiduity the artist has left nothing unfinished. The scene is under the portico of the mansion at Mt. Vernon, and consists of the domestic family circle. In the distance is seen the Potomac, studded with sails. In short, the whole is beautifully worked out and more worthy the gallery than the back of a banner.

This splendid piece of workmanship reflects a character of no ordinary degree on its author, and it must be a source of gratification to himself, as well as to his friends, that the reputation he has gained by his late productions, secures for him the patronage which his genius so richly merits. Mr. Armstrong is an eminent artist, indeed."

ARMSTRONG, JOHN, elected County Commissioner in 1869.

ARMSTRONG, THOMAS, a member of the Legislature in 1735 and 1736.

ASH, PHINEAS, elected County Commissioner in 1816.

ATLEE, JOHN L., M. D., eldest son of Col. Wm. Pitt Atlee, and grandson of the Hon. Wm. Aug. Atlee, was born in Lancaster, November 2d, 1799. With the exception of about one year, spent in Gray & Wiley's Academy, in 1813 and 1814, he received his preliminary education in his native city, and entered the office of the late Samuel Humes, M. D., in 1815. He graduated at the University of Pennsylvania in April, 1820, and from that time till the present, has practiced the various branches of his profession in Lancaster. He took an active part in the organization of the Lancaster City and County Medical Society, and has been twice elected its President; of the State Medical Society in 1848, of which he was elected President, in 1857; and of the American Medical Association, of which he was chosen one of the Vice Presidents, in 1868.

At the union of Franklin and Marshall Colleges, he was elected Professor of Anatomy and Physiology, and lectured annually to the classes until within the last three years.

He has always taken an interest in the subject of education in his native city, and for more than forty years was a member of the Lancaster City School Board. As a member of the medical profession, Dr. Atlee is a physician of rare skill, extensive practice, and widely famed as one of the most skillful surgeons of Pennsylvania.

ATLEE, SAMUEL J., was a colonel in the American revolution, and one who did effective service in the emancipation of the colonies from British rule. His father married Jane

Alcock, maid of honor to the Queen of England; and the match being clandestine, they immediately sailed for America. They had three children, William Augustus, Samuel John, and Amelia. Samuel John was born in year 1739. Being a youth of great ambition and daring, he, at the early age of sixteen, obtained the command of a company in the provincial service (war of 1755), in the regiment under Col. Burd, and was present at Braddock's defeat. During the continuance of that war, it was his fate to be taken prisoner twice, once by the Indians, and again by the French. He remained in the service eleven years. After the expiration of this service, he read law, and was engaged in the pursuit of his profession until the breaking out of the revolution. He was married to Sarah Richardson, on the 19th of April, 1762.

At the commencement of hostilities with the mother country, Captain Atlee, being one of two in the county of Lancaster who had any knowledge of military tactics, undertook the duties of the drill, in order to prepare his fellow-citizens to breast the impending storm. His unremitting attention was devoted to this object during the greater part of the year 1775; and in the beginning of 1776, by virtue of an Act of the General Assembly of March 5th of the same year, he raised in the Pequea Valley and in Chester county, the First Regiment of State Infantry, of which he was appointed colonel. Although this regiment was called out simply for the defence of the province, yet Col. Atlee and his command voluntarily marched to New Jersey to coöperate with the American army in that quarter. He achieved imperishable honors with his regiment at the battle of Long Island,[1] on which occasion he was taken prisoner, having only a sergeant and sixteen men left, the rest having been previously killed or taken prisoners. He suffered eighteen months' imprisonment, part of it on board a prison ship.

[1] A very interesting account of the battle of Long Island, in which Col. Atlee was prominent, may be found in the Life of President Reed, by his grandson, Wm. B. Reed, Vol. I., p. 221–224. In the same volume is also published an extract from Col. Atlee's journal, describing the particulars of the battle in a spirited manner, Vol. I., p. 413. See also in the Diary of the American Revolution, by Frank Moore, Vol. I., p. 297, in a foot-note, a sketch of Col. Atlee.

During his imprisonment he lived for two weeks on chestnuts. The British gaolers were in the habit of cutting up raw pork into small pieces and throwing them to the prisoners, calling "pig, pig." The prisoners were so near starved, that they killed their dogs and ate them, and roasted their leather breeches for food.

[1]Col. Atlee was chosen a member of the Continental Congress in 1778, and held a seat in this body up to 1782.

In 1780 Col. Atlee was appointed by the Supreme Executive Council, Lieutenant of Lancaster county. In 1783 he was elected Councillor of Lancaster county, and on the 21st of October of the same year he appeared in the Supreme Executive Council, subscribed the required oath, and took his seat as a member of the Board. He was one of the committee with Gen. Sullivan and Dr. Witherspoon, who were sent by Congress in January, 1781, to endeavor to conciliate the mutineers of the Pennsylvania Line. He was afterwards, in 1784, one of the Commissioners, on the part of Pennsylvania, who ratified the treaties of Forts Stanwix and McIntosh, with the deputies of the Six Nations and the Wyandot and Delaware Indians. The Commissioners each were allowed forty-five shillings per diem for their services, the same as a delegate to Congress at the time received.[2]

[1]About the 20th of January, 1779, he wrote to the Supreme Executive Council of the State, claiming to be appointed a Brigadier General. The Council ordered that the same be transmitted to His Excellency, General Washington, and his opinion requested thereon. In a letter of General Washington to President Reed, dated February 9th, 1779, (Pennsylvania Archives, Vol. VII, p. 181,) he considers the claim of Col. Atlee to rank. He says he has a high opinion of his merits and abilities as an officer, but he does not see that he can, at this time, be promoted to the rank of Brigadier, as the State having only two Brigades in the field, is entitled only to two Brigadiers—that Gen. Wayne was one, and that Col. Morgan and Col. Irwin, being senior officers, have superior pretensions to Col. Atlee.

[2]In a letter of Col. Atlee to President Dickinson, dated Pequea, Lancaster county, November 18th, 1784, he mentions his arrival at his home, and reports that part of their mission to the Northern tribes is satisfactorily concluded. He then claims that notwithstanding his absence in discharging his duties as a Commissioner, he is entitled for two years longer to a seat in the Council, and protests against the election of a

He was elected to the General Assembly of Pennsylvania for the year 1782, and also for 1785 and 1786.

Whilst Col. Atlee was attending as a Commissioner in the ratification of the Indian treaty, he contracted a cold by lying on the damp ground, from the effects of which he never recovered. In November, 1786, whilst walking in the streets of Philadelphia, he was seized with a paroxysm of coughing, ruptured a blood vessel, and shortly afterwards expired.

In personal appearance Col. Atlee was very handsome, with a fresh and ruddy complexion, brown hair, blue eyes, straight and portly, and very military in his carriage.

ATLEE, WM. AUGUSTUS, brother of the above, was born at Philadelphia, July 1st, 1735. He moved to Lancaster at an early day, and read law under the instruction of Edward Shippen, esq. He was admitted to the bar, August 3rd, 1758, and soon became prominent in his profession as one of the leading lawyers of his day. He was elected Chief Burgess of the Borough of Lancaster, September 15th, 1770, to which position he was thrice subsequently chosen, and administered the duties of said office up to September, 1774. Upon the breaking out of the American revolution, he became an active and leading Whig, and in 1776 was chosen chairman of the Committee of Public Safety of Lancaster. He was appointed August 16th, 1777, by the Supreme Executive Council, second Judge of the Supreme Court of Pennsylvania, his associates being Thomas McKean and John Evans. During the years 1777 and 1778, he held the position of Commissary of the British prisoners confined at Lancaster. He was re-appointed Judge of the Supreme Court, August 9th, 1784; and on the 17th of August, 1791,

Councillor from Lancaster county in his stead. This claim seems to have been allowed, as Graydon, in the Memoir of his own Times, p. 384, congratulates himself upon having received the appointment of Prothonotary of Dauphin county, in 1785, and goes on to say: "The Republican party possessed a majority in the *Council*, and Col. Atlee, *who belonged to it*, was designated for the office. He was conspicuous as a party man, and if I mistake not, was at the time a member of the Legislature, and on the scale of services and character no one had better claims. To keep out Atlee the Constitutionalists were disposed to give their votes to any one of his competitors. The President (Dickinson) had probably given a promise to Col. Atlee as well as myself."

he was appointed President Judge of the district, composed of the counties of Chester, Lancaster, York, and Dauphin, which position he filled up to his death, September 9th, 1793. As a member of the Supreme Bench of Pennsylvania he rendered efficient service; and it is somewhat noteworthy, that a remarkable uniformity of opinion is observable in the proceedings of the Supreme Court at that early day. Lord Mansfield, speaking of Dallas' Reports in 1791, used the following language: "They do credit to the Court, the bar and the reporter. They show readiness in practice, liberality in principle, strong reason and legal learning."

In private life Judge Atlee was a man of easy and very gentlemanly deportment, and noted for his high-toned integrity and strong adherence to his sense of right.

ATLEE, WM. A., son of Dr. John L. Atlee, is a graduate of Yale College, of the class of 1851, and a member of the Lancaster bar, admitted in 1854. He was elected District Attorney of Lancaster county, in 1865, and in 1869 chosen Mayor of the City of Lancaster, administering said office for two years.

B

BACHMAN, CHRISTIAN, was for a long time cashier of the old Lancaster Bank. He was appointed Prothonotary of Lancaster county in 1830. His son, Benjamin C. Bachman, was President of the Lancaster Bank at the time it failed, in 1856.

BACHMAN, JACOB, a member of the Legislature, in the year 1823.

BAER, JOHN, was the principal founder of the leading German paper of Lancaster county, the *Volksfreund and Beobachter*. In 1817 he came in possession of the old *Volksfreund*, founded in 1808, subsequently consolidated therewith the *Beobachter*, and made the paper a complete business success. He managed the paper up to the period of his death, November 6th, 1858. It is now conducted by Reuben A. and Christian R. Baer, under the firm name of John Baer's Sons.

*BAILEY, FRANCIS, occupied an old house on the premises of his father, in Sadsbury, which he used for a printing office, and for some time he used the upper part of the spring-house for that purpose. About the year 1800 he erected a large stone printing office on the place, which is standing at the present day, where the business was carried on by him until about the year 1815. He was a zealous advocate of American independence, and his name appears very frequently in connection with the *Freeman's Journal*, throughout five volumes of the Colonial Records ; an order was drawn in his favor on the Treasurer, December 2d, 1779, for the sum of £4,873 7s. 6d., the amount of his account for printing work done for Council.[1] It appears by the records that he executed the public printing for Council up to the year 1790.

An order was drawn in his favor on the 18th of August, 1779, for £5,000, to be forwarded for the purpose of purchasing flour for the army; and September 2d, 1780, an order was drawn in his favor for $12,988, for sundry articles purchased by him and delivered to Col. Ryan for the use of the militia called into service.[2] Large numbers of orders were drawn in his favor at many different times for printing and binding, for copies of the laws and constitutions of the different States, for his *Journal* for the use of the members, &c., and for printing done for the Comptroller General's office, and for printing the tax lists and advertisements in the *Freeman's Journal* up to the year 1790.[3] He executed a large portion of the State printing, at his office in Sadsbury township, from the year 1790 until after the close of the administration of Thomas M'Kean. The pamphlet laws were printed at his office until the administration of Simon Snyder, and within the recollection of our oldest inhabitants. Francis Bailey was a worthy patriot of revolutionary times. He was also a pious and religious man; and about the year 1788, beside Count Buelow and Reichenbach, he and his family were among the first in Lancaster county to receive

*Contributed by Isaac Walker, of Sadsbury.

[1]Col. Rec., Vol. XII., p. 188.   [2]Col. Rec., Vol. XII., p. 467.
[3]Col. Rec., Vol. XVI., p. 526.

the doctrines of the New Jerusalem Church.[1] When far advanced in life, he removed with some of his family to the city of Philadelphia, and his lands and residence were purchased by Wm. Maxwell, the father of the present Robert and Richard Maxwell.

*BAILEY FRANCIS, son of Robert Bailey, was an active young man at the time of the American revolution. He learned the trade of a printer and worked a short time in Lancaster borough. He was appointed in 1777, by the Executive Council, Coroner of Lancaster county. On the 8th of April, 1778, Francis Bailey and Captain Long were appointed to bring seventeen of the leading Quakers in Pennsylvania (who were arrested by order of Congress and supposed to be inimical to the American cause), and convey them to Winchester, Virginia.[2] They were also charged to bring the prisoners home again.

[1]Rupp's History of Lancaster Co., p. 431.

[2]The following is a copy of the order of discharge :

LANCASTER, April 10th, 1778.

EXECUTIVE COUNCIL TO FRANCIS BAILEY AND CAPT. LONG, 1778.

Gentlemen : The enclosed resolves will show that you are appointed and authorized to conduct the prisoners sent from this State from Virginia, from Winchester, the place of their present confinement, to this borough ; and on your arrival here, acquaint this Council thereof. Those of them who are in health, you are to bring with you, treating them on the road with the polite attention and care which is due to men who act upon the purest motives, to gentlemen whose station in life entitles them to respect, however they may differ in political sentiments from those in whose power they are. You will please to give them every aid in your power, by procuring the necessary means of traveling in wagons or otherwise, with such baggage as may be convenient for them on the road. Your own prudence and good sense will direct you, in such incidents as may turn up, in which the Council have no doubt but your conduct will justify their confidence in you."

On the 27th of April, Messrs. Bailey and Long reported to the Executive Council, then sitting in Lancaster, that they had received the following persons from the jail in Winchester, Virginia, agreeably to the orders of this Council, viz. : Israel Pemberton, James Pemberton, John Pemberton, Henry Drinker, Samuel Pleasants, William Smith, Edward Pennington, Thomas Wharton, Owen Jones, Charles Eddy, Charles Gervis, Elijah Brown, Thomas Fisher, Samuel R. Fisher, and Myers Fisher ; and that Thomas Gilpin and John Hunt were dead.

*Contributed by Isaac Walker, of Sadsbury.

*BAILEY Robert, one of the early settlers of Sadsbury township. He purchased 300 acres of land in Sadsbury township, on the road leading from the Gap to the copper mines. At the time of the revolution, although advanced in years, he was an early and influential advocate of American independence. He was, on the 15th of November, 1774, elected by the citizens of Lancaster county one of the Committee authorized to be chosen by resolution of the Continental Congress, which Committee was authorized to watch the conduct of all persons as regards their action and sentiments with reference to the pending difficulties between the mother country and the colonies. He was also entrusted with money by the Council of Safety, to distribute amongst the needy associators of Lancaster county.

He erected the large and commodious residence now owned and occupied by Robert Maxwell, where he spent the balance of his useful life.

BAKER, John, was elected Recorder of Lancaster county, in 1867.

BAKER, Rev. John C., son of Samuel R. and Elizabeth Baker, was born in Philadelphia, May 7th, 1792. Having lost his father when a child of eighteen months old, he was reared under the roof of his maternal grandfather. He was delicate in constitution, but was strikingly precocious,

The case of the prisoners brought from Virginia, and now in this borough, being considered thereupon, ordered that they be immediately sent to Pottsgrove, in the county of Philadelphia, and there discharged from confinement ; and that they be furnished with a copy of the order, which shall be deemed a discharge. And that A. B., of the city of Philadelphia, gentleman, one of the prisoners referred to in the foregoing order of Council, is hereby permitted, with his horses, servants and baggage, to pass unmolested into the county of Philadelphia, agreeably to the said order, which is to be respected as their discharge. Also a pass to Philadelphia, for Mrs. Jones, Mrs. Pemberton, Mrs. Pleasants, and Mrs. Drinker ; and for Israel Morris, who attended them, being requested, was granted. And it is ordered that the whole expense of arresting and confining the prisoners sent to Virginia, the expenses of their journey, and all other incidental charges, be paid by the prisoners, and that an order be drawn on the Treasurer in favor of Mr. Bailey and Captain Long, for the sum of one hundred and fifty pounds, for which they are to account.

*Contributed by Isaac Walker, of Sadsbury.

and was regarded by all as a very thoughtful and conscientious boy. He early evinced a fondness for reading, and made more than ordinary progress in his studies. In 1802 he was placed under instruction in Nazareth Hall, a seminary of the Moravian church, in which institution he remained five years. He early determined to study for the ministry, though his friends had wished that he should succeed his father in the mercantile business. After remaining a short time in Philadelphia, he set out for Lebanon, Pa., and began the study of theology under Rev. Dr. Lochman.

In 1811 he was licensed by the Synod of Pennsylvania, and immediately thereafter accepted a call as an assistant minister of a German congregation in Philadelphia. In the following year the church at Germantown, Pa., having become vacant, Mr. Baker was chosen as the pastor of this church. His charge embraced Germantown, Whitemarsh, Barren Hill, and several other smaller congregations. He labored faithfully in this charge for the period of fifteen years, and, in 1818, chiefly through his instrumentality, the new church edifice was erected, a monument of his zeal and enterprise.

In November, 1827, he received a call from the trustees, elders, and wardens of Trinity Lutheran church of Lancaster, Pa., which he accepted.[1] The principal motive in his accepting this latter call, was the prospect of increased usefulness, and a more extended sphere for his pastoral activity. He entered upon his duties, in this new position, January 27th, 1828, delivering his introductory sermon in German, and on the following Sunday, in English. On February 17th, 1828, chiefly through his efforts, the Sunday School of the church was organized. This school was opened on the 9th of March, with 413 pupils and 63 teachers. Mr. Baker preached in both the German and English languages, in both of which he was equally eloquent.

[1] The call extended to Mr. Baker was signed by the following names : George Musser, President ; George King, Vice President ; Peter Protzman, Christian Swentzel, W. Hensel, G. L. Mayer, Adam Keller, Joseph Hubley, George R. Krug, Jacob Snyder, Joseph Blandford, Henry Eichholtz, David Lebkicher, John Yost, Christopher Hager, F. D. Hubley, Christian Bachman, J. F. Heinitsh, Secretary.

On November 1st, 1852, Dr. Baker tendered his uncondi-
tional resignation of his office of pastor of Trinity Lutheran
church, which, though with the greatest reluctance, was
accepted, and on the 30th of January, of the following year,
he preached his farewell sermon, in the presence of an
immense audience, and thus closed his twenty-five years of
pastoral labor in Lancaster.

He removed to Philadelphia, and took charge of St.
Luke's Evangelical Lutheran church, where he spent the
evening of his days in building up a new congregation in
the city of his birth. To this service he devoted himself
with all his youthful zeal, and labored with great faithfulness without compensation; and even contributing from his
own resources to the support of the church. In this charge
he labored like a faithful steward, until the Master called
him home to his reward. He died April 21st, 1859, and he
lies buried in Woodward Hill Cemetery, in Lancaster.

Dr. Baker was an earnest, enthusiastic and indefatigable
minister of the gospel. He could say, that "I must work
while it is day; the night cometh when no man can work."
This was his motto, and faithfully was it followed. He was
unwearied in his varied ministrations, in his attentions to
the old and young, rich and poor, healthy and sick. In the
labors of the Sunday School he was ever faithful and
attentive.

Dr. Baker was familiar with both the English and German
theological works, and received from Lafayette College, in
1837, the degree of Doctor of Divinity.

He was an influential member of the Lutheran Synod of
Pennsylvania, and for many years filled the office of Treasurer. He also presided as president over the deliberations
of that body. In Missionary operations he took a very
active part, and for many years prepared the annual report.

For a long period he was a leading and influential member
of the Lancaster School Board, and was a most regular and
welcome visitor in all the schools.

His kindness of heart and simplicity of manners endeared him to all classes. He was, in short, a bright and
shining light upon Zion's walls.

BALDWIN, J. C., was elected Clerk of Quarter Sessions and Oyer and Terminer, in the year 1863.

BALDWIN, ROBERT, was elected a member of the Legislature in the years 1849 and 1850. He was also elected to the State Senate in the year 1857.

BALMER, DANIEL, for many years a magistrate of Lancaster county, resident at Elizabethtown. He was elected a member of the Legislature in the year 1842.

BARBER, ROBERT, was a native of Yorkshire, England, emigrated to America, and settled in Chester county, Pennsylvania. He was a Quaker by persuasion; and either in Chester or Philadelphia, married Hannah Tidmarsh, a lady of the same religious principles as his own. Prior to coming to America, he had followed a seafaring life and had been captured and detained as a prisoner in France. He was an energetic man, and in 1721 was appointed Coroner of Chester county. In company with John Wright and Samuel Blunston, he purchased a large tract of land near where Columbia now stands. His tract of land lay on the eastern bank of the Susquehanna, and embraced one thousand acres; bounded on the northwest by Chickies Hills, and to the south by what was afterwards called Patton's Hill. He was the first Sheriff of Lancaster county; appointed October 4th, 1729. While Barber was Sheriff, owing to the belief that somewhat prevailed at the time, that the seat of justice would be established at Wright's Ferry (now Columbia), he built a prison near his house. This prison was a strong log building, and was torn down not many years since. It was in this prison that James Annesley, alias Lord Altham, was confined when he ran away from his master. Robert Barber had several children, the oldest of whom was killed by the Indians near the site of Pittsburg.

BARE, ADAM, was for many years an innkeeper, on the New Holland pike, and also was engaged in agricultural pursuits. He was one of the earliest and most influential members of the Anti-Masonic party of the county. He was elected Sheriff of Lancaster county in the year 1830. He was, in 1834, elected one of the County Commissioners.

*BARTON, BENJAMIN S., son of the Rev. Thomas Barton, was born in Lancaster, February 10th, 1766. His mother was the sister of the celebrated philosopher, Rittenhouse. The death of his parents occasioned his removal, in 1782, to the family of a brother, in Philadelphia, where he spent several years in the study of literature, the sciences, and medicine. In 1786 he went to Great Britain, and prosecuted his medical studies at Edinburgh and London. He, afterwards, visited Gottingen, and there obtained the degree of Doctor of Medicine. On returning to Philadelphia, in 1789, he established himself as a physician in the city, and his superior talents and education soon procured him competent employment. He was, that year, appointed Professor of Natural History and Botany, in the College of Philadelphia, and continued in that office on the incorporation of the College with the University, in 1791. He was appointed Professor of Materia Medica, on the resignation of Dr. Griffiths; and, on the death of Dr. Rush, succeeded him in the department of the Theory and Practice of Medicine. He died December 19th, 1816.

Dr. Barton was highly distinguished by his talents and professional attainments, and contributed much, by his lectures and writings, to the progress of natural science in the United States. He published "Elements of Zoology and Botany," in which he made respectable additions to the zoological science of our country, and displayed a degree of genius, diligence, learning, and zeal, in this pursuit, which do honor to our republic, and which bid fair to place him among the most accomplished and useful naturalists of his time. In 1803 he published "Elements of Botany, or Outlines of the Natural History of Vegetables," &c. Dr. Barton has the honor of being the first American who gave to his country an elementary work on botany; and "if we may judge," says Dr. Miller, in his 'Retrospect of the Eighteenth Century,' "of the subsequent interest from the first fruits, it will be rich, indeed. This work is illustrated by thirty plates, and discovers an extent of learning, and an acuteness and vigor of mind, and elegance and taste highly honorable

*Thatcher's Medical Biography.

to the author. Of the thirty plates that accompany this work, twenty-eight have claims to more or less originality, and many of them are completely original. They are well executed; and most of the subjects selected for delineation are remarkable for their rarity and beauty, or some other peculiarity of character. Every part of this work discovers that the author has not been contented with compiling the facts and opinions of his predecessors, but that he accurately observed and thought for himself. He will, therefore no doubt be pronounced, by the best judges, to have presented his countrymen with the most instructive work of this kind in the English language."

Dr. Barton published "Collections for an essay towards a Materia Medica of the United States," which is the only work, professedly, on the subject of which it treats, that had at that time issued from the American press. In 1810 the author published a third edition of this very valuable production. It is an original work, of great merit, and was peculiarly acceptable to the public, as it brought into notice numerous medical remedies, the production of our own soil, which had been entirely neglected, but which have since augmented and enriched the American Materia Medica. In 1805 Dr. Barton commenced the publication of the "Medical and Physical Journal," to which he contributed many valuable articles.

As a naturalist, the merits of Dr. Barton are of no common kind; and he has deservedly received a large share of praise in his own and in foreign countries, for his many and successful exertions in enlarging the sphere of natural knowledge. He published "Fragments of the Natural History of Pennsylvania," an "Essay on the Fascinating Power ascribed to Serpents," &c., and several memoirs on particular specimens in zoology, in the "American Philosophical Transactions." In his "Views of the Origin of the Tribes and Nations of America," will be found vocabularies of a number of Indian languages that were never before committed to the press; comparing these with languages more generally known, both on the Eastern and Western continents; and thence deducing new evidence in support of the opinion that the nations of America and those of Asia have a common origin, and that all mankind are derived from a single pair. His various works evince a closeness of observation, an accuracy of inquiry, an extent of learning, and a vigor and comprehensiveness of mind, which are equally honorable to their possessor and to his country. It is but just to observe, that American science and literature are indebted to the indefatigable labors of him whose memoirs are here presented.[1]

BARTON, GEORGE WASHINGTON, a grandson of Rev. Thomas Barton, was born in Lancaster, Sept., 1807. When a boy, he was very frolicsome and wild, and it was with difficulty that his attention could be attracted with books. His first instructor in the classics, was a Mr. Shiffer of Lancaster, but his truancy often prevented his appearance at recitation time. After making some progress with this teacher, even against his will, he was next sent to Nazareth, a school of wide repute. His stay at this Seminary of learning was between two and three years. Upon his return he entered a printing office, and began the learning of that trade, as he was altogether averse to the professions. Soon afterwards he went to Philadelphia, and meeting with his cousin, Wm. C. Barton, an eminent Professor of Botany in the Jefferson College, he was by him induced to turn his attention to the study of botany. He returned to Lancaster, discontinued the printing business, and, for a time, pursued with great zeal the new study. Shortly afterwards he concluded to travel, and made several voyages to foreign countries. In one of these voyages he was shipwrecked on the coast of Buenos Ayres; and having made his way to the American Consul, he was furnished a passport, and sailed for New York. At this time he was little, if anything, over fifteen years of age. He afterwards made his way to Nash-

[1]In the year 1785, Messrs. Rittenhouse, Ellicott, Peters, and Nevill, were appointed Commissioners to trace the meridian, northward, for the western boundary of Pennsylvania, beginning at the S. E. corner of the State. In this undertaking the services of Benjamin S. Barton were enlisted, a youth then of but nineteen years of age, but whose scientific acquirements, even at that early period of his life, had rendered a useful associate of the Commissioners.—*Life of Rittenhouse.*

ville, Tennessee, when about seventeen, and remained in that city about four years. During this time he was engaged in a printing office. While in this situation he contributed several articles for the press, which drew the attention of Felix Grundy, who offered to instruct him gratis in the study of the law, as he perceived him to possess talents of a rare order. Having at that time no taste for the legal profession, he declined the liberal offer. Hearing of the ·death of his mother, he concluded to return to Lancaster, and did so, arriving at his home in the midst of the Jackson campaign of 1828. After his return, he wrote some articles for the newspapers, that caused quite a sensation; and among the rest drew the attention of James Buchanan. Mr. Buchanan first met him at a barbecue at Cheves' woods, during a political campaign, and was so delighted with the brilliancy which his conversation displayed, that he invited him to call and see him at his office. He did so, and the result was, that he soon became a student of law in the office of Mr. Buchanan. He was admitted to the bar in 1830. He began the practice of the profession with great eclat, and astonished everybody with the brilliancy of his declamation, which surpassed anything that had ever before been heard at the Lancaster bar. His smooth, graceful and polished oratory, is believed by those who heard him, to have equaled the finest displays of eloquence of the American Congress; and he is remembered and constantly cited by the bar and people who heard him as the finest declaimer who ever spoke before a Lancaster jury.

After practicing law for some years, in Lancaster, with great reputation, he was appointed District Attorney for Philadelphia, where he removed, and was afterwards appointed Judge of one of the courts, by Governor Porter. He presided as Judge for three or four years. He subsequently practised in the profession, in the city of Philadelphia, for some time, and afterwards emigrated to California, and located, as an entire stranger, in the city of San Francisco. An opportunity was but needed to introduce him on the Pacific coast. He tendered his services to an undefended criminal, and the great brilliancy and ability displayed in this defence established him at once, and soon he was over-whelmed with business. He took rank, therefore, as one of the leading lawyers of San Francisco. But destiny reserved but a brief glory for this Achilles of the bar, and death removed the brilliant star of genius on the 25th of December, 1851.

BARTON, MATTHIAS, was a son of Rev. Thomas Barton, and was admitted to the bar in 1778. He was elected from Lancaster county to the Legislature, in the years 1793, 1794 and 1795. In 1796 he was elected to the Senate of Pennsylvania, and reëlected in 1800.

Mr. Barton was a man of superior culture, and possessed a great fondness for natural history. In his travels through Pennsylvania and other States, he made considerable collections of natural history ; and he noted, in an especial manner, the habits of animals; in particular the viviparous quadrupeds, and also of birds and fishes. He was for many years engaged in collecting materials for a work " on the Instincts and Manners of Animals." He also made a large collection of the mineral productions of Pennsylvania. In his collection were many specimens of the ores and clays of his native State.

Without the aid of a master, Mr. Barton excelled as a painter and drawer of sketches from nature. A considerable portion of his leisure time was employed in painting scenes from nature, and the animal productions of our country. Some of his drawings of birds and fishes of Pennsylvania were acknowledged by competent judges to have been amongst the most beautiful found in the department of natural history.

Mr. Barton was a gentleman very amiable in his manners, of unspotted private virtue, and whose charms in society endeared him to all with whom he came in contact. He was a useful citizen, and ranked amongst the ablest men of Pennsylvania. He died January 11th, 1809, in the 47th year of his age.

BARTON, THOMAS, was born in Ireland, in the year 1730. He was educated at Trinity College, Dublin. Shortly after graduating, he came to America, and was for about two years engaged as an assistant teacher in the academy at Philadelphia. In 1755 he returned to England, bearing a recommendation from the Professors of the College, and the clergy of the Province of Pennsylvania, and with an earnest petition from the inhabitants of Huntingdon, Pennsylvania, that he might be appointed their missionary. After the requisite preliminaries he was ordained, and came back as missionary for the counties of York and Cumberland.

He reached Philadelphia, about April 10th, 1755, and immediately wrote to some of the leading men of his mission, who caused a number of wagons to be sent for his effects. He reached the field of his labors about the last of May, and his first care was to make himself acquainted with the condition and members of his three congregations, York, Carlisle and Huntingdon. After he had caused wardens and vestrymen to be established in the different congregations, these met in convention, and it was agreed that he should officiate three Sundays in six at Huntingdon, two at Carlisle, and one at York. The labors devolved upon him in attending three congregations, the extremes of which lay 148 miles apart, can be easily conceived. Besides having learned that there were within the limits of the mission, large numbers of the communion of the Church of England, in Shippensburg, and four or five other settlements, he determined to visit each of these four times in the year, in order to prepare them for the Sacrament of the Lord's Supper, and to baptize their children.

Scarcely had Mr. Barton commenced his labors, before his attention was drawn to the wretched condition of the Indians, some of whom resided at no great distance from the seat of his labors; and having heard that a number of them had come down from the Ohio to Carlisle, to dispose of their fur and deer-skins, he took occasion to go among them, and endeavored to secure their good-will in the hope of making himself useful to them. He invited them to church, and such of them as had any knowledge of English, came and seemed attentive. Subsequently, these brought their brethren to shake hands with him; and the result of the interview was, that he had great hope of being able to bring them under the influence of Christianity. But just at this time, tidings came that the forces under the command of General Braddock had been defeated, as they were marching to Fort Duquesne, (now Pittsburg); and this was soon succeeded by an alienation of the Indians, which put an end to all hope of prosecuting, successfully, any missionary efforts among them.

Mr. Barton now finding himself exposed to the incursions of the French and Indians, was compelled to organize the young men of his own congregations for defense against their enemies; and such was his zeal and activity, that he even put himself at their head, and marched either by night or by day when there was an alarm. In 1758, the young men within his mission offered to join the army if Mr. Barton would accompany them; whereupon he proposed himself to Gen. Forbes, as chaplain of the troops, and his services were thankfully accepted. He was, however, absent from his ordinary duties but a short time, though it was long enough to give him the opportunity of making the acquaintance of Washington, Mercer, and other distinguished officers of the army.

It was during the time that Mr. Barton was engaged in teaching in Philadelphia, in 1751, that he formed the acquaintance of David Rittenhouse, then about 19 years of age. A warm attachment sprang up between Mr. Barton and Esther Rittenhouse, which, in 1753, resulted in their marriage. It was chiefly through the instrumentality of Mr. Barton, that the uncommon ability of David Rittenhouse was first discovered, who afforded him every facility for developing his genius, by procuring him books and asssisting him in the study of the languages. The friendship thus early cemented between the philosopher Rittenhouse and Mr. Barton never ceased; even the unfortunate difference of political opinion, as regarded the propriety of revolution, never marred the kind feelings which the one entertained for the other.[1]

In 1759, Mr. Barton was appointed rector of St. James'

[1] Would that such liberality and high toned feeling would become universal in the hearts of mankind.

Church, and missionary for the congregations of Pequea and Caernarvon. This position he continued to fill for the space of 20 years. In addition to these three charges, he officiated occasionally at the churches of New London and White Clay creek—the one distant 35 miles, the other 50 miles from his residence. So great was the amount of labor he performed, and such the fatigue and exposure to which he was subjected in his missionary excursions, that he became sensible that his constitution was greatly impaired; but he still kept on laboring, to the extent of his ability; and the letters which from time time he wrote to the Society for propagating the Gospel, show that he was resolved to persevere in his labors until his health should entirely fail, or Providence should in some other way hedge up his path.

Mr. Barton had never lost, in any degree, his interest in the Indians; and was actually planning an excursion of a few months among them, in or about the year 1764, when his hopes were again blasted by the breaking out of the Indian war, which rendered any approach to them utterly hopeless.

In 1770, Mr. Barton received the Honorary Degree of Master of Arts, from King's College, New York.

As the difficulties between England and the colonies increased, Mr. Barton, on account of his suspected sympathy for the mother country, found his situation to become more and more embarrassing. He still continued to *pray for the king*, and this created so strong a feeling against him and his congregation, that it resulted in his church being nailed shut, and so remained till the close of the revolution.[1] In a letter, dated November 25th, 1776, he thus describes his situation: "I have been obliged to shut up my churches to avoid the fury of the populace, who would not suffer the liturgy to be used, unless the collects and prayers for the King and royal family were omitted, which neither my conscience nor the declaration I made and subscribed when ordained, would allow me to comply with; and, although I used every pru-

[1] At the breaking out of the American revolution, every Episcopal church in Pennsylvania was closed.—*Documentary History of State of New York*, Vol. IV, p. 241.

dent step to give no offense, even to those who usurped authority and rule, and exercised the severest tyranny over us, yet my life and property have been threatened, upon mere suspicion of being unfriendly to what is called 'the American cause.' Indeed, every clergyman of the church of England, who dared to act upon proper principles, was marked out for infamy and insult, in consequence of which the missionaries, in particular, have suffered greatly. Some of them have been dragged from their houses, assaulted with stones and dirt, ducked in water, and obliged to fly for their lives, driven from their habitations and families, laid under arrest and imprisonment. I believe they were all, or at least most of them, reduced to the same necessity with me, of shutting up their churches. It is, however, a great pleasure to assure the venerable Society that, though I have been deprived of the satisfaction of discharging my public duties to my congregations, I have endeavored, I trust not unsuccessfully, to be beneficial to them in another way. I have visited them from hour to hour, regularly instructed their families, baptized and catechised their children, and performed such other duties as atoned for my suspension from public teaching."

Mr. Barton's connection with the congregation of St. James, in Lancaster, ceased sometime in the year 1777, and near the close of the following year he and his wife went to New York, in pursuance of permission granted by the government of Pennsylvania, under certain conditions, one of which was, that he should not return again. His removal to New York was occasioned by his refusal to take the oath of allegiance to the American government, and a passport was furnished him by the Supreme Executive Council, for his banishment within the British lines. All his children, excepting the oldest, remained in Pennsylvania. For nearly two years he was not permitted to see his children. In 1779 his son returned from Europe, when David Rittenhouse, Col. Samuel J. Atlee, (formerly one of his parishioners), and others, exerted their influence to obtain an interview between the parents and children. In reply to a letter from one of these friends, apprising him of his son's arrival home, after a long absence, dated January 30th, 1779, Mr. Barton thus explains the scruples which actuated his conduct, and reveals the sorrow which worked in the parental heart :

"I am just informed that my son has returned to his native country, after an absence of between three and four years. How melancholy and distressing is my situation! Separated from eight children, and three congregations, to whom I am bound by duty, gratitude, and every tie of affection! A parent only knows a parent's woes; and such will feel for me. You are kind enough to tell me that my son requests me to return to my parish. What he can mean by this request, I am totally at a loss to understand. Could the matter have been determined by my option, I should never have left my parish for any prospect or preferment that could offer. But no choice was left me, but either to take the oath or to suffer a painful separation from my dearest connections, as well as from a country which has always had, since I have known it, my predilections and best wishes; a country to which I can declare (with an appeal to heaven for the truth of the declaration), I never did, or wished to do, any act or thing prejudicial or injurious; and, though my heart assures me that many conscientious and good men have conformed to the test-act, yet my own conscience always revolted at the abjuration part of it, and prevailed with me to surrender every worldly consideration that should come in competition or tempt me to a violation of it. This, sir, was the only crime (if a crime it be) for which I now suffer banishment from all that are most dear to me: with an interdict "*not to return again.*" I cannot, therefore, comprehend how I can, consistently, return before this interdict is cancelled, or some assurance given me that I may again unite and live quietly with my family, without being subjected to an abjuration I cannot take. The proper duties and profession of a minister of the Gospel should, in my opinion, never lead him into the field of politics. In conformity to this opinion, every man who knows me can testify, that I never degraded my profession by intermeddling, directly or indirectly, in this present unhappy contest; so that my own scruples would be a stricter tie upon me than any

that could be made by oaths or tests. You will excuse my
troubling you on this subject, when I tell you that the kind
manner which you addressed me, has drawn it upon you."

In reply to another letter from Rittenhouse, he says : " To
see and be united with my children, is my earnest wish ; but
how that happy event is to be obtained, I know not ; if my
son should choose to come to Elizabethtown, perhaps I
might be indulged with a flag, to have an interview with
him there." This letter, written on the 15th of February, 1779,
in connection with the preceding extract, shows the motives
and emotions by which Mr. B. claimed to have been influenced. To understand the motives which actuated the government in thus separating a father from his family, and a
preacher from his congregation, we will glance at a correspondence then going on between Mr. Bryan, Vice President of the Council, and General Washington. From a letter dated March 5th, 1779, Mr. Bryan writes thus :

" This board, ever watchful of the public safety and happiness, think it behooves them to communicate to you their
suspicion, that Mr. Paul Zantzinger, of the borough of Lancaster, in this State, merchant, who has lately gone hence for
camp, has a design of getting liberty to pass into New York.
For this purpose he will hold forth his desire to visit his
father-in-law, Rev. Thomas Barton, now in that city. When
you know the character and conduct of this divine, your
Excellency will judge better of such a request. Mr. Barton
has long been a missionary stationed at Lancaster by the
society in England for propagating the Gospel. It is believed that he has been very instrumental in poisoning the
minds of his parishioners, who are generally of very dis-
affected principles, as to the present contest with Great
Britain. His late conduct in refusing to give the common
proofs of allegiance to this State and abjure the King of Great
Britain, and in taking the benefit of the indulgence of our
Legislature, which allowed him to sell his lands and retire,
as he said, to Europe ; but above all, his acceptance of a
chaplaincy in a British regiment at New York (as is credi-
bly reported here), and thus actively joining the enemy,
confirm the worst ideas that have been entertained of this

gentleman. I would suggest, that Mr. Zantzinger is a trader, who has never manifested much attention to the present contest, and very likely to be drawn by interested views to a mart where European merchandizes are sold at prices inviting to men who seek profit merely.

"Mr. Z. is probably accompanied by a son of Mr. Barton, a young gentleman lately returned from England, where he has been weaned of all fond attachment to that corrupted country, and brought to see the happiness and independence of North America in their proper light and connection. Young Mr. Barton is a much clearer character with us than his brother-in-law, and as such I venture to mention him."

To this General Washington replied, under date of March 10th, as follows:

"I am much obliged to you for the attention you discover to prevent any intercourse with the enemy, which might be attended with doubtful circumstances. I had taken my measures with the gentlemen who are the objects of your information before I received your letter, and restricted them to our own lines at Elizabethtown Point, where they had liberty to see their friends if they could obtain leave to come over. This I imagined a sufficient security against any consequences which might be apprehended from a more liberal indulgence."

This indulgence was not obtained until in April, 1780, when, chiefly through the influence of President Reed, the Council granted a passport, thus sanctioned by General Washington; in pursuance of which, Mr. Barton met his family at Elizabethtown for the last time on earth. Of course the meeting must have been as affecting as the circumstances connected with it were painful. After the interview, he bade adieu to his children and returned to New York, where he died on the 25th of the following month, in the 50th year of his age. His remains were interred in the chancel of St. George's Chapel in that city. His wife (formerly a Miss Thornbury), to whom he was married in 1776, survived him many years, much esteemed for her many virtues, by Mr. Barton's descendants. His first wife (formerly Miss Ether Rittenhouse), now lies interred under what is known as "the Coleman pew," in St. James' Episcopal church, in this city.*

BARTON, RHEA, son of Wm. Barton, born at Lancaster, was a leading physician of Philadelphia. He graduated with distinction at the University of Pennsylvania, and soon attained position as a surgeon, excelling in the treatment of difficult cases. His treatment of compound fracture of the leg by bran dressing, is still followed in our large hospitals. His name has been associated with a peculiar fracture of the radius, involving the wrist joint, and with an ingenious bandage for dressing a broken jaw. He was married to a daughter of the late Jacob Ridgway, of Philadelphia. Dr. Barton died at his residence on South Broad street, Philadelphia, January 1st, 1871.

BARTON, WILLIAM, the oldest son of Rev. Thomas Barton, was a man of solid ability and great energy of character. In September, 1775, at the suggestion of his father, he left America for England, bearing with him letters of recommendation from Bishop Peters, and other persons. While in Europe, he laid the foundation of his education, and otherwise advanced his literary interests, for which he had a peculiar fondness. He left England in 1778, and returned to America by way of Holland and the West Indies, and landed at Baltimore, January 8th, 1779. On his passage from the West Indies to the continent, he assisted in making prize of a British Privateer, which was brought to Baltimore. Immediately upon landing, he took the oath of fidelity and allegiance to the United States Government. Upon his arrival at Lancaster, he received a letter from David Rittenhouse, dated January 24th, 1779, in which he says: "I most sincerely congratulate you on your safe arrival, and impatiently expect the pleasure of seeing you here. I received yours from Baltimore, ten days after the date, and immediately wrote to your father, supposing him to be still in New York, though we cannot be certain as to that matter." He was shortly afterwards admitted to the Lancaster bar, and also chosen an officer of the militia of the

*Sprague's Annals of the American Pulpit. Documentary History of the State of New York, Vol. IV., pp. 229–240.

borough of Lancaster. His advocacy of the cause of the struggling colonies was warm and enthusiastic. On the 18th of August, 1789, he was nominated by President Washington, one of the judges of the Western Territory, and the Senate ratified the nomination. He was afterwards (with but two exceptions), unanimously recommended by the Lancaster Bar, for the appointment to the President Judgeship of the district, composed of the counties of Lancaster, Chester, York and Dauphin. In 1779, he was an ardent Republican, and a staunch advocate of the election of Thomas McKean, for Governor of Pennsylvania. Being a finished scholar and a fine writer, he was, during that campaign, the one generally selected to draft the Democratic addresses, then a leading feature of political parties. He was, in 1800, appointed Prothonotary of Lancaster county, and this office, together with the commission of Clerk of the Orphans' Court, which he obtained in 1803, he held up to 1809, when he was succeeded by John Passmore. He afterwards removed to Philadelphia, and was chosen Secretary to the American Philosophical Society of Philadelphia. He obtained from the University of Pennsylvania the honorary title of Master of Arts. He is the author of a dissertation on the Freedom of Navigation and Maritime Commerce, and also of a biography of the Philosopher Rittenhouse.

BARTON, WILLIAM, was elected Clerk of the Quarter Sessions and Oyer and Terminer, in the year 1869.

BAUMAN, BENJAMIN, was appointed Register of Wills of Lancaster county, in 1818.

BAUSMAN, REV. B., D.D., son of John and Elizabeth Bausman, was born in Lancaster township, Lancaster county, Pa., January 28th, 1824. The. days of his childhood and youth were spent in the bosom of his parental home. As a youth and young man, he was trained to farm work. In early infancy, he was baptized by the Rev. John Henry Hoffmeier. He was nurtured and brought up according to the customs and faith of the Reformed church. At the age of eighteen he became a member of the (First) Reformed congregation of Lancaster.

After enjoying the educational advantages then usual for boys of his age, he studied for several successive winters, with the late Thomas Yearrel, in the old Quaker meeting house, South Queen street (what has since become the Odd Fellows' Hall). In the winter of 1846 he studied in the old Franklin College, Lancaster. In the following May he commenced his studies in Marshall College, Mercersburg, Pa. He graduated in the college, and in 1852 completed his course of study in the Theological Seminary of the same place. In October, 1852, he was licensed to preach the Gospel, at a meeting of the Synod of the Reformed church, held in Baltimore, Md. Several months later he was ordained to the Gospel ministry, by the Susquehanna Classis, and installed as pastor of the Reformed church, at Lewisburg, Pa.

In April, 1856, his congregation gave him leave of absence, in order to make a tour to Europe and the East. On this tour he visited England, Scotland and Ireland, traversed Europe three times, from the Northern Ocean to the borders of Italy, spent two months in Berlin, visited the leading cities of Italy, and tarried one month in Rome. Thence he proceeded over Naples and Malta to Egypt, visited Alexandria, Grand Cairo, the Pyramids, and the country round about; he proceeded on his journey through the Wilderness of Sinai, to Jerusalem. After visiting the principal sacred places in Palestine, he returned to the United States in the beginning of July, 1857.

In 1858, he was elected by the Synod of the Reformed church, associate editor of the *Reformed Messenger*, then published at Chambersburg, Pa. Subsequently he was promoted to the position of chief editor of this paper. In 1861 he resigned this position, and accepted a call from the First Reformed church, of Chambersburg, Pa. In 1863 he became pastor of the First Reformed church, of Reading, Pa., where he is still laboring.

On the 1st of January, 1867, Dr. Bausman accepted the editorship of the *Guardian*, a monthly magazine, founded some twenty years ago, by the late Rev. Dr. H. Harbaugh, which position he is still holding.

After his removal to Reading, Dr. Bausman felt the want of a religious paper to suit the tastes and wants of the Pennsylvania German class of Reformed people. In 1867 he commenced the publication of the *Reformirte Hausfreund*, with the view of meeting this want. The object was to publish a paper, written, as far as possible, in the simple, transparent style of Luther and Claudius. It was, in a measure, an experiment, and, as the result has shown, a successful one. The *Hausfreund* still has its original editor. It is an unique publication, but one that has many warm friends and considerable influence.

Dr. Bausman is the author of a work, entitled "Sinai and Zion, or a Pilgrimage through the Wilderness to the Land of Promise," a volume of 543 pages, which has reached its fifth edition.

He also edited *Harbaugh's Harfe*, a volume of poems in the Pennsylvania German dialect, written by the late Dr. H. Harbaugh.

At the commencement of Franklin and Marshall College, held in June, 1871, the title of D.D. was conferred on him.

BAUSMAN, John, was born in 1780, in Freilaubersheim, in the Palatinate, Germany. His parents were named Henry and Barbara Bausman. He emigrated to America in 1802, and settled in Lancaster county. In 1805 he married Elizabeth Peters, and raised a numerous and very respectable family.

BAUSMAN, William, was a Justice of the Peace, and acted for many years as a scrivener in Lancaster. He was elected County Commissioner in 1775. In 1777 he was elected Burgess of Lancaster borough. On February 1st, 1809, he was appointed Recorder of Deeds of Lancaster county. He owned considerable landed estate around Lancaster.

BAXTER, James, emigrated from Ireland, and located in Bart township. He afterwards moved to Colerain. He was elected a member of the Legislature in the years 1810 and 1811. He was a pure, honest and upright man, and had the fullest confidence of his fellow citizens.

BEATES, Rev. Wm., was born in Philadelphia, in the year 1777. He served an apprenticeship as a tobacconist, but on arriving at the years of manhood, he became awakened on the subject of religion and studied divinity. After taking orders, he was stationed at Germantown, Pa., where he remained a number of years. Upon the solicitation of the people of Chestnut Hill, near Lititz, in this county, he removed from Germantown, and took charge of the Chestnut Hill congregation. Here he continued to labor for fiffeen years, with great diligence and zeal. He next removed to Lancaster city, and finding the German Lutheran congregation of Lancaster scattered and distracted by dissensions, he at once set to work to reörganize and heal all the differences existing in the congregation, and in this labor he was entirely successful. He found the church groaning under a load of debt, and no means at hand or prospect of its payment. He consented to serve the congregation as their pastor for a stipulated salary. His salary, however, as soon as he drew it, was immediately appropriated by him annually to the liquidation of the debt on the church, and in this manner did he serve his congregation until the whole indebtedness was removed. Thus did this faithful and devoted minister of Christ labor and toil, like his Master, virtually without compensation, but in doing so he raised an imperishable monument in the hearts of his people and of the community, never to be forgotten. Such works as his deserve to be recorded as memorials for all coming time. This genuine servant of Christ was no wolf in sheep's clothing, and for many years of his later life he bore in the community the affectionate name of "Father Beates." Long may he be remembered. He is gone, but his name is gratefully remembered by many.

Father Beates died May 16th, 1867, in his 91st year. He was blessed in the attainment of longer years than is usually allotted to man; and he was doubly blessed in his removal from earth, at a moment when, with sanctified mind, he was piously engaged in the administration of the blessed sacrament of the Lord's Supper to the members of his family. At that moment the angel of peace beckoned the aged and faithful servant to come and sit down in the mansions of bliss, and accept the crown of glory which his life of humility and self-sacrifice on earth had merited.

BECK, JOHN, was born June 16th, 1791, at Graceham, Frederick county, Maryland. In his sixth year he came with his parents to Pennsylvania, who located in the neighborhood of Elizabethtown, Lancaster county, from whence they moved, some years afterwards, to Lebanon county, in the same State. In the district that his parents occupied, there were no schools, and the subject of this notice was sent to Nazareth Hall, in Northampton county, Pa., to receive an education.

Upon the completion of his education he returned home, and was, in accordance with the opinion of his father, (that every boy should be taught a mechanical occupation,) apprenticed in Litiz, in his 15th year, to learn the shoemaking trade. In this avocation the next ten years of his life were spent, as an apprentice and journeyman shoemaker. On the 2nd of January, 1815, he began teaching school in an old building that had been used as a blacksmith shop, and with eminent success. He had now entered the career for which nature had peculiarly fitted him. His efforts to promote the interests of his pupils, and the progress they made under his care, soon become noised abroad, and it was not long till pupils began to come to him from a distance. His reputation was established. Pupils entered his school from all parts of Lancaster county, and scarce a State in the Union but had its representatives in his academy. His eminent success in this line, led to the establishment of his large *Educational Institute*, in which several thousands of boys have laid the foundation of their education, and where students flocked for years from all parts of the United States, Canada, and the West Indies. Among his numerous pupils are men now engaged in various occupations, some as mechanics, manufacturers, lawyers, clergymen and physicians, principals of academies, members of State Legislatures and of the national Congress, and officers in the army and navy. His pupils fill the pulpits of ten different denominations.

After the devotion of fifty years of his life to teaching, he retired from his calling on the 31st day of May, 1865, and now lives in easy and comfortable retirement. And though retired, he is by no means idle, as he is regularly in the habit of visiting schools and witnessing the progress of the pupils. He is, and has been for years, in the habit of visiting schools and institutes of learning in different parts of Lancaster and adjoining counties; and he annually addresses, in his peregrinating tours, thousands of pupils. His life has been one of great activity and usefulness.

BENTZ, CHRISTIAN, was elected a member of the Legislature in the years 1845 and 1846.

BEISSEL, CONRAD, was a native of Germany, and fled to escape persecution in his own land. He arrived in America about 1720, and settled at Mill Port, Lancaster county, in 1729, where he and a companion built themselves a house; they were soon afterwards joined by other early settlers. Wholly intent upon seeking out the true obligation of the word of God and the proper observance of the rites and ceremonies it imposed, stripped of human authority, he conceived that there was an error among the Dunkers as regards the observance of the Sabbath—that it was the Seventh day that was commanded by the Lord to be observed, and that this day having been commanded and sanctified by Jehovah, its observance, in the opinion of Beissel, was a matter of perpetual obligation. No change, nor authority for change, had ever been announced to man by any power sufficient to set aside the solemn decree of the Almighty—a decree which he regarded as sanctified to the end of time. Beissel, therefore, felt it to be his duty to contend for the observance of the Seventh day as the Sabbath, that Christians are under obligation to keep sacred.

It was not long after 1723 that he published a tract, entering into a discussion of this point, which created some excitement and disturbance in the Society at Mill Creek. Upon this account Beissel retired from the settlement, and went secretly to a cell on the banks of the Cocalico Creek, said to have been previously occupied by one *Elimelich*, a hermit. His place of retirement was for a long time unknown to the people he had left, and when discovered, many of the Society at Mill Creek, who had become convinced of the truth of his proposition for the observance of the Sabbath, settled around him in solitary cottages. They adopted the original Sabbath, the Seventh day, for public worship, in the year 1728; and from that period, this day has continued to be observed by their descendants.

When in the year 1732, the solitary life was changed into a conventual one, and a monastic society was formed, the title of *Father* (spiritual father) was bestowed upon Beissel, and his monastic name was *Friedsam*, and to this the brethren afterwards added that of *Gottrecht*, implying therein peaceable and godly. Beissel now devoted with great assiduity his whole time and attention to the spiritual advancement of his flock; the management of his secular affairs were entirely entrusted to others. Thus unencumbered by temporal concerns, he was enabled to consecrate his strength to instructing his followers in the Word of life, and establishing amongst them the gospel in all its truth and simplicity. The titles of *Father* and *Gottrecht* were conferred upon him by his followers, and were not presumptuous assumptions on his part.

Morgan Edwards, in his "Materials towards a History of the American Baptists," published in 1770, gives the following character of Beissel: "He was very strict in his morals, and practiced self-denial to an uncommon degree. Enthusiastic and whimsical he certainly was, but an apparent devoutness and sincerity ran through all his oddities. He was not an adept in any of the liberal arts and sciences, except music, in which he excelled. He composed and set to music (in three, four, six and eight parts), a folio volume of hymns, and another of anthems. He published a dissertation on the fall of man in the mysterious strain, and also a volume of letters. He left behind him several books in manuscript, curiously written and embellished."

Beissel wrote a book on Human Depravity, which is as curious as it is ingenious. He enters into long disquisitions on the nature of Adam and his capabilities before the fall; explaining many things pertaining to the fall, and with it elucidating several parts of the Scriptures which would easily have escaped the attention of men of more profundity of genius. His views are somewhat mysterious, yet deep and ingenious; but, in the present day, would be deemed little more than refined speculations sublimated into visions. Conrad Beissel died July 6th, 1768, aged 77 years and 4 months.

BETHEL, SAMUEL, was born in Columbia, Lancaster county, Pa. He was a sister's son of Samuel Blunston. Having lost his father when young, he, at the instance of Dr. Kuhn, was sent to Philadelphia, where he received a classical education, and graduated with the reputation of being one of the best mathematicians of the country. He was completely master of Euclid, and a case of his mathematical instruments is yet preserved. He read law, and was admitted to the bar in 1795. He inherited a large quantity of real estate in Lancaster county, and the ground upon which Bethelstown now stands, was his property. He married Sarah, a daughter of Gen. Edward Hand, of revolutionary memory. He was elected twice to the Pennsylvania Legislature, and served therein as a member during the sessions of 1808 and 1809. He died in the year 1819, aged about 48 years. He lies buried in the Brick Cemetery, in Columbia.

BILLINGFELT, ESAIAS, was born January 11, 1827, at Reamstown, Lancaster county, of poor parentage. He was left an orphan at an early age. He attended the public schools of his native place, where he made such progress that when twelve years of age he was occasionally employed as an assistant teacher. He was, however, soon compelled to devote his time to hard labor to earn a subsistence. He worked as a day laborer, and also learned the trade of a hatter. From his sixteenth year he taught school almost every winter until 1848. In the fall of the latter year he entered the office of the late Peter Martin, where he studied the art of surveying, and made himself familiar with scrivening and conveyancing. In 1850 the village of Adamstown was incorporated as a borough, and Mr. Billingfelt having previously moved to that place, he was in that year elected

Justice of the Peace, which position he held by repeated re-elections until the year 1863. Meanwhile, in the year 1862, he had been appointed Deputy United States Marshal for Lancaster county. In the fall of 1863 Mr. Billingfelt was elected to the House of Representatives of Pennsylvania, and was in the following year re-elected. His course in this position was so satisfactory to his constituents, that he was, in the fall of 1866, elected to the Senate of Pennsylvania, and at the expiration of his term, in 1869, was re-elected. In this capacity he served, during the session of 1870, as chairman of the Committee on Finance, and in 1872 he was chairman of the Committees on Federal Relations, Retrenchment and Reform, and also chairman of the Committee on Constitutional Reform.

BLACK, JAMES, was born in Lewisburg, Union county, Pennsylvania, September 23rd, 1823. He removed with his parents in 1835 to Lancaster city, which he has since made his permanent home. After the attainment of the rudiments of an English education, evincing a rare fondness for books, he was sent by his parents to the Lewisburg Academy, where he acquired a fair knowledge of the Latin and Greek languages. He next began the study of law in the office of James F. Linn, of Lewisburg, afterwards read with Wm. B. Fordney, esq., of Lancaster, and was admitted to the bar in 1846.

Early in life, conceiving a strong dislike to the fashionable habit of dram-drinking, he joined a temperance organization in 1840, of which cause he has proved himself one of the most ardent and efficient advocates. Since the period of the Maine prohibitory law movement, in 1851, Mr. Black has acted conspicuously as a leading mover in the temperance cause, and his name has become widely known as one of the most sincere and enthusiastic champions of prohibition in America. No State or national temperance movement of importance from that period up to the present time has been held, in which Mr. Black's name does not appear as a conspicuous participant. Always alive to the evils of intemperance, as they presented themselves to his mind, he has ever worked with that glowing enthusiasm which heroism inspires. His is the ardor which the rack and the funeral pile do not intimidate, and though by the unreflecting his zeal may pass for fanaticism, in the eyes of others it is the index of genuine nobility and true manhood.

In politics, Mr. Black was a Democrat until 1854, when the question of slavery began to absorb all others. His bitter hatred of southern slavery, then induced him to yield his adhesion to the Republican party of the country, which first unfurled its national banner in 1856. With this party he has continued to act until a recent period. At the National Prohibition Convention, held at Cincinnati, February 22nd, 1872, Mr. Black was nominated as the candidate of the Temperance party for the office of President of the United States, a marked tribute of respect for the ability and warmth which he had displayed in his humanitarian efforts to elevate his fellow men.

In sincerity, honesty and boldness of purpose, Mr. Black ranks amongst the noblest of his kind, and though his enthusiasm may be criticised, his motives can not be impeached.

BLUNSTON, Samuel, a native of England, was one of the early settlers of Columbia. He was a man of considerable means, and bought in 1728 five hundred acres of land, that had been the year before taken up by Robert Barber. His first house was a log cabin, erected near the spot where the present house of Samuel B. Heise now stands. He imported the bricks from England that were used in the erection of the present house of Mr. Heise, and some of the bricks were used in the construction of the wall of the Brick Cemetery. He was an active, enterprising man, in his day, and the citizens elected him a member of the State Legislature for 1732. He was three times subsequently elected, and served in that capacity during the sessions of 1741, 1742 and 1744. He served as a legislator, in all, four sessions. A Scotch filtering stone, imported by him from England, is yet preserved as a relic, by Mr. S. B. Heise. Samuel Blunston was married, yet left no lineal descendants, and his large estate was divided amongst his collateral heirs. He lies buried in the Brick Cemetery in Columbia.

*BOEHM, REV. HENRY. His grandfather was born in 1693, and emigrated from the Palatinate to America in 1715. He was induced to this step by the glowing descriptions given of this country by Martin Kendig, the head of one of the seven families who had settled in what is now Lancaster county. He landed in Philadelphia, from thence he went to Germantown, then to Lancaster, and finally settled in Pequea, Lancaster county. Soon after his arrival, he married a Miss Kendig, bought a farm, and built himself a house. He was by trade a blacksmith, the first in all that region.

Martin Boehm, the father of our subject, was born November 30, 1725, and married, in 1753, Eve Steiner, whose ancestors were from Switzerland. Having inherited his father's beautiful farm, in 1750 he built a house, in which his children were all born.

Martin Boehm was first a Mennonite preacher, for that was the religion of his fathers. He became conspicuous in the movement which resulted in the organization of the church of "The United Brethren in Christ." Martin Boehm and Asbury were lifelong and fast friends. Asbury preached Boehm's funeral sermon, at Boehm's chapel, April 5, 1812.

Henry Boehm, the subject of this memoir, was born in the old homestead, in Conestoga (now Pequea) township, June 8th, 1775. He was born nine years before the Methodist Episcopal church, of which he is a member, was organized. His memory recurs to the time when persons traveled to Fort Pitt on pack horses. He had a common school education, and the old school-house and the schoolmaster he remembers distinctly. The teacher boarded from house to house. His preceptor, being a fine German scholar, he acquired a correct knowledge of this language. This, in after years, was a great benefit to him when he preached in German, for he was one of the first among the Methodists that preached in that language. This he has done in fourteen different States.

When, after an absence of many years, the aged patriarch paid a visit to his native town, he inquired for his old school-

*Contributed by J. B. Good, esq.

fellows, hoping to find one with whom he could converse about by-gone days, but he inquired in vain. They were all gone, and he found himself alone and lonely. Dilworth's spelling book, from which he learned English, and the knife and fork he used when a little boy, have been preserved as relics of his childhood.

His early advantages for religious instruction were good. He was "brought up in the nurture and admonition of the Lord." Morning and evening the old family bible was read and prayer was offered. His mother, too, had much to do in moulding his character and shaping his destiny. One evening as he returned home, he heard a familar voice engaged in prayer. He listened: it was his mother. Among other things, she prayed for her children and mentioned Henry, her youngest son. The mention of his name melted the heart of the listener. Tears rolled down his cheek, and he felt the importance of obeying God's command: "My son, give me thine heart!"

In 1793 the entreaties and prayers of the father prevailed, and the son's stubborn heart yielded, and he experienced, as he always believed, the forgiveness and pardon of his sin.

The subject of this sketch was born near what is known as Boehm's chapel. It was the first Methodist house of worship built in Lancaster county, about six miles south of Lancaster city. This chapel was erected in 1791. It was called "Boehm's chapel," because it was built on Boehm's land; and the several Boehm families contributed much towards its erection. There were great gatherings at Boehm's chapel. The Bishops and distinguished lights of Methodism found their way there, and preached the Word of life. At quarterly meetings, the people came from Philadelphia and Maryland, and Boehm's chapel was a center of influence. It is difficult now to estimate the position it once occupied in Methodism.

In 1798, during a quarterly meeting held in this chapel, the now venerable subject of this sketch was converted. A few months before his probation expired, they appointed him a class-leader, at Soudersburg.

In 1800 young Boehm attended the general Conference of

the Methodist church, which commenced its session on Tuesday, May 6th, at Baltimore. In the same year Boehm, in company with Dr. Chandler, visited Cape Henlopen, and here he saw the ocean for the first time, and having been sick he tried sea bathing, from which he received great benefit. When he returned home he found his father ready to set out on a ministerial tour, and he accompanied him. His father was then allied with the United Brethren. After attending a Conference of this latter body, at which his father was elected one of the Bishops, he nevertheless resolved to travel as an itinerant Methodist minister, and in the same year began his labors.

There was great political excitement at the time. Federalism and Democracy ran high, and Jefferson and Adams were talked about everywhere. The excitement separated families, friends and church members. Boehm was urged on all sides to join one political party or the other.

Bishop Asbury visited his circuit, and he went with him to the Conference, which met in Philadelphia, on Saturday, May 1st, 1802. At this Conference he was appointed to Kent Circuit. This was the oldest circuit on the Peninsula, being formed in 1774. He traveled this circuit till August, when his presiding elder removed him to Northampton Circuit, Pennsylvania, one embracing several counties, besides Northampton, Montgomery, Berks and others.

Another preaching place was at Smithfield, Northampton county; also at Bristol, on the banks of the Delaware, 20 miles from Philadelphia.

The Philadelphia Conference met at Duck Creek Cross Roads, now Smyrna, in May, 1803, in the Friends' Meeting House, the Methodists using their own for divine worship. During the session of the Conference Boehm, was appointed to Bristol Circuit.

After this, Bishop Asbury visited and asked him to accompany him in his travels. They set out for the west, and arrived in Somerset county. Here Boehm preached in German. The Bishop said: "Henry, you had better return and preach to the Germans, and I will pursue my journey alone." Shortly after this he acquired the ability to preach readily in English.

On October 22nd, the yearly meeting of the United Brethren was held at his father's place. These meetings generally lasted three days, and were seasons of great interest. He says: "I had made an appointment to preach in the Court House at Reading, but the Commissioners refused to give up the key, and a large number who were assembled were disappointed. There was, in this town, a deep-rooted prejudice against the Methodists which continued for years. When I passed through Reading, in 1810, with Bishop Asbury, the boys laughed at us and said: 'There go the Methodist preachers.' They knew us by our garb, and perhaps thought it no harm to ridicule us. In 1823, when on Lancaster circuit, I succeeded in planting Methodism in Reading, and formed the first class there, where I had been shut out a score of years before. This I consider quite a triumph.

"Harrisburg was another of our preaching places. I was in the neighborhood of where Harrisburg now stands in 1793. It was then called Harris' Ferry, from John Harris, its founder. In 1803 it was a small place, and Lancaster was then the capital of Pennsylvania.

"Columbia was another of our preaching places. I was at this spot in 1791, when it was called 'Wright's Ferry,' from John Wright, a Quaker preacher, who came from England, and was the original land proprietor.

"My presiding elder was James Smith, a native of Ireland. We used to call him 'Big Jimmy,' to distinguish him from two other James Smiths. I took a tour with him for several days. He preached in English, and I immediately translated his sermons into German. There was no other way to get access to the people, many of them having never heard a sermon in English."

The Philadelphia Conference of 1804 was held at Soudersburg, commencing May 28th. The place was called Soudersburg, from Benjamin and Jacob Souders, the proprietors. They were both Methodists; Benjamin being a local preacher. Methodism was introduced here in 1791, and a house of worship built in 1801. The Conference was held in a private room, at the house of Benjamin Souders, that the meet-ing-house might be used for preaching. There were 120 preachers present, and Boehm exulted at the idea of a Methodist Conference being held in his native county.

At this Conference he was appointed to Dauphin circuit.

On April 1st, 1805, he attended the Baltimore Conference in Winchester, Virginia, a place where Methodism had early been introduced.

At this Conference there were seventy-four preachers present and here Boehm, for the first time, saw Rev. William Waters, the first American Methodist traveling preacher, and also heard him preach.

The Philadelphia Conference met on May 1, 1805, in Chestertown, Md., in the court house, that the meeting house might be occupied for preaching. Here Bishop What-coat ordained seven deacons, among whom was Henry Boehm, whose father was present, desirous to see his son invested with full ministerial powers.

He was at this Conference appointed to St. Mary's Circuit. In his travels in this circuit, he met Lorenzo Dow, who, he says, was an irregular, eccentric and yet powerful preacher. He heard him several years afterwards, in Camden, N. J., where he appeared quite changed and shorn of his strength.

In 1807 he was, with Wm. Hunter, appointed to Penn-sylvania Circuit, embracing that part of the State which lies between the Delaware and Susquehanna Rivers. "It was not," he says, "till 1807 that we got a permanent foot-hold in Lancaster. It was very hard soil for Methodism. Twice we made a beginning, but failed; and for several years the place was abandoned. We had no preaching there, only an occasional sermon. The introduction of Methodism into Lancaster was providential. The translation of the Metho-dist discipline into German, had something to do with it. In 1807 I went to Lancaster to read the proof sheets of this translation at the printers. After I had read them and was about to return home, it commenced raining hard, and I put up at a public house where I had often stopped. Annoyed by the noise and confusion of the people, I left the public house and took a walk through Lancaster, to while away the time. While going along the street, I met with a woman who had been a member of the Methodist church, in Germantown. She told me there was a man by the name of Philip Benedict, in Lancaster, who had been awakened at a camp-meeting, and he and his wife were seeking the Lord; and she advised me to call and see them, telling me where they lived. I went to their house, pointed them to Jesus, and prayed with them. As I was about leaving they said, 'O that we could have Methodist preaching in Lancaster.' I told them they could have it. So I left an appointment to preach at his house. It became a permanent preaching place. In a little while I formed a class of six members: Philip Benedict and his wife and four others. This was the nucleus of the society, which remained permanent. I am thankful that I had the honor of planting the tree of Methodism in that city. Behold, how many links there are in this singular chain; how many small causes to bring such results."

At the request of Bishop Asbury, and the Philadelphia Conference, Boehm had the Methodist discipline translated into German, in 1807. He employed Dr. Romer, and aided him in the translation. They frequently compared notes and consulted about certain terms. Boehm employed Henry and Benjamin Grimler, printers, in Lancaster, to print 1500 copies. The Germans had an idea that the Methodists had no discipline. This translation corrected the error.

At the Philadelphia Conference, held on the 20th of March, 1808, Boehm, with two colleagues, was appointed to his old field of labor.

After this, Bishop Asbury again chose Boehm as his traveling companion; and he traveled with the latter around a large diocese.

"The venerable Asbury says Boehm was sixty-three years old when I began to travel with him. Having been greatly exposed, he was feeble and suffered from many infirmities. I traveled with him much longer than any of his other companions, and hence survived them all many years."

He left the Bishop infirm at Brownsville, Pa., for a while, and went to preach, or "fill his appointments," while the family where he stayed took care of him. Boehm reached Pittsburg, and preached in the court house to about a thousand people, who came to hear the Bishop, and saw but a plain German youth from their own State.

After the Bishop had recovered his health, they started for Ohio, preaching in various places.

In September 6th, 1808, having spent some time in Cincinnati, they left for Indiana Territory, then a vast wilderness. At that time the Methodist church had but seven Conferences. The Western Conference included all the vast tract of country lying west of the Alleghanies, as far as it was settled, except Monongahela District, which belonged to the Baltimore Conference. The Western Conference met on October 1st, at Liberty Hill, Tennessee. Some of the appointments made at this Conference embraced the territory of whole States.

The day after the Western Conference adjourned, Boehm, in company with two Bishops, started for the South Carolina Conference, which was to meet in Liberty chapel, Green county, Georgia, on December 6th, 1808.

On November 23, 1808, Rembert's camp-meeting commenced, where Boehm for the first time saw the Southern preachers, all of whom have passed away except, Pierce and himself.

On the 28th of November they started for Charleston, where Boehm was delighted with the warm-hearted brethren he met with; but he adds to his reflections, written many years later: "It was a sad day for them when secession was born, and they fired upon Fort Sumpter and the old time-honored flag."

From here they went to Southern Conference, the two Bishops riding in a chaise; Boehm on horseback, as a kind of body-guard. The Conference commenced Monday, Dec. 26th, 1808. Here Boehm witnessed the novelty of seeing a camp-meeting held in winter, between Christmas and New Year, where about a thousand people attended.

After the close of this Conference Boehm started for the North; and towards the end of March, 1809, reached the home of his parents again.

On April 3, 1809, the Philadelphia Conference met in St. George's, Philadelphia, Pa. Bishops McKendree and Asbury were both present. Boehm says: " It may be asked to whom I was amenable when I traveled with Bishop Asbury?" I answer, to the Philadelphia Conference. It may be asked, who represented me, as I had no presiding elder. I answer, Bishop Asbury. When the question was asked, " Is there anything against Henry Boehm?" The Bishop was the only person who could answer it, for he was the only one who knew how I spent the year; and he would answer with great gravity, "Nothing against Brother Boehm." It may be asked how I was supported while I traveled with the Bishop? I answer, I received it from the different Conferences, as the Bishops received their salaries. My salary was one hundred dollars."

At the adjournment of the Conference, Bishop Asbury and Boehm went through New Jersey to Long Branch, Staten Island, and Elizabethtown.

On Monday, May 7th, 1809, they left Newark for the city of New York; and in the evening, Boehm went for the first time to the old church in John street, built by Philip Embury, called "Wesley Chapel;" the first in the world named after Wesley.

On May 10th the New York Conference commenced its session in John street. There were 120 preachers present. Bishops Asbury and McKendree were present.

June 16th, 1809, he, with Bishop Asbury, attended the New England Conference at Monmouth, in Maine. After its close, they traveled through northern New York; and afterwards entered Pennsylvania, reaching the Valley of Wyoming, famed by Campbell.

Their appointments were generally sent forward, and in consequence of heavy rains, swollen rivers and muddy roads, they were eighty miles behind their Sabbath appointments. The Bishop says: "Brother Boehm upset the sulky and broke the shaft."

From what has been said, it is evident that the office of a Methodist Bishop, at the time we speak of, was no sinecure; and that Boehm, in accompanying him, had more to do than play the fine gentleman. It was, indeed, toil, intense toil, as much as body and soul could endure. During this tour Boehm visited all the Methodist Conferences then in existence in the United States, and preached the gospel in fifteen States, and became acquainted with the great men of Methodism in the ministry and laity, East, West, North and South. He says: "Never was a mariner after a perilous voyage more rejoiced to get into harbor than we were to reach the old family mansion of my father. We arrived there on Friday, July 28, 1809; but both my parents were from home; therefore, Mr. Asbury concluded to go right on, while I went to a camp-meeting, near Morgantown, where I met my parents, and they embraced me with joy. I had been in seven different States, besides the Province of Maine, since I saw them. At the camp-meeting I heard my father preach in German. I preached immediately afterwards in English." He now started to overtake Bishop Asbury, and came up with him on August 3, 1809, at Fort Littleton. Soon after, our subject and the Bishop directed their journey westward, through Pittsburg to Cincinnati, where, on September 30, 1809, the Western Conference commenced its session, and from thence to Charleston, South Carolina, where Conference commenced on December 23, 1809.

They next returned to Virginia. Of this journey Rev. Boehm says: "My sufferings can never be told. The day we rode to Petersburg, we stopped to rest in the woods, and I lay down upon a log, for I was too weak to sit up. The time came to start, and I told the Bishops (Bishop McKendree had now rejoined us) to go, and leave me there. I felt as if I would rather die on that log than go on. They lifted me from the log on to my horse, and in this plight I rode to Petersburg. When we arrived there, about sundown, I was so weak they had to lift me from my horse and carry me into the house."

On the way south of Washington, they met that peculiar genius and unequaled orator, John Randolph, of Roanoke. He was riding, and had his dogs with him in the carriage. His complexion was very dark, and his eyes were black. They reached Baltimore, and from here Boehm went to see his

5

father, who returned with him to Baltimore to attend the Conference. The elder Boehm preached in the Rev. Otterbein's church. He, Otterbein, and Asbury, were great friends. Henry Boehm says: "This was my father's last visit to Baltimore, his last interview with Otterbein, and the last time he ever attended an annual Conference. From Baltimore they went to the Philadelphia Conference, which commenced its session April 18, 1810, at Easton, Md. When the appointments were read off, they included the following: 'Henry Boehm travels with Bishop Asbury.' They now visited the Pittsfield (N. Y.) Conference, and from there went to the New England and Genesee Conferences. Boehm says of their journey from the Genesee Conference: "We commenced our Southern and Western tour. Such a doleful, fearful ride, few Bishops ever had; and it was one calculated to make the traveler rejoice when at the end of his journey. Asbury, at that time, in consequence of infirmities, rode in a sulky, and I on horseback. Sometimes I would ride before him, and then in the rear. We would occasionally change when he was tired, or the roads very rough."

Asbury, in his journal, says: "We must needs come the Northumberland road; it is an awful wilderness. Alas! read and prayed in the woods. I leave the rest to God. In the last three days and a half we have ridden one hundred and forty miles. What mountains, hills, rocks, roots! Brother Boehm was thrown from the sulky, but providentially not a bone was broken."

Again, Boehm says: "The road was so rough that Bishop Asbury could not ride in the sulky; it jolted and hurt him, so he and I exchanged, and he rode my horse, and I in his vehicle. If he had been thrown out as I was, he probably would have been killed. No bone of mine was broken, and yet the flesh was torn from my left leg so that I was a cripple for months. I suffered more than if it had been broken. Riding on horseback with that poor leg, no language can describe my suffering."

Boehm and the Bishop reached home again. Mr. Boehm says: "After an absence of months I remained at home one day and two nights, and the Bishop said, 'Henry, we must move.' My father and sister, and many others, went to Lancaster, where, on the 5th of August, we had a great day. The Bishop even felt an interest in this place, where we had such a hard time to obtain a foothold. He preached morning and evening; James Smith at three, and I immediately after him in German. The Bishop rejoiced to see such a comfortable house of worship here, and wrote: ' After forty years' labor we have a neat little chapel of our own.' ' Good-bye,' I said to my friends, and at noon on Monday, we were at Columbia, where the Bishop preached. I was lame, and the lameness was increasing, but I did not mention it to my parents, lest they should urge me to stay at home, or worry about me when I was gone, therefore I bore my sufferings in silence."

Their route now again went through Carlisle, Shippensburg, Chambersburg, Connellsville, Brownsville, to Pittsburg. From Pittsburg they went west, to Chilicothe and Cincinnati, to the Western Conference, which was held in Shelby county, Ky. From there they went south and attended the South Carolina Conference. January 28th, 1811, they started to cross Cape Fear river, and narrowly escaped losing their horses and lives. Boehm says: " Bishop Asbury was much alarmed, far more so than I had ever seen him. Our preservation and that of the horses was providential."

They next attended the Virginia Conference, then the Baltimore Conference, after which Boehm left the Bishop and went home to see his parents, whom he found well. Mr. Boehm, on this trip, preached in Lancaster.

After the sessions of the Philadelphia and New England Conferences, Bishop Asbury and he made a visit to Canada. Boehm says: " We crossed the St. Lawrence in romantic style. We hired four Indians to paddle us over. They lashed three canoes together and put our horses in them, their fore-feet in one canoe and their hind-feet in another. It was a singular load, three canoes, three passengers (the Bishop, Smith and myself), three horses and four Indians. They were to take us over for three dollars."

From Canada they passed through the Genesee country, and then reached home, the elder Boehm and Asbury to meet on earth for the last time.

On August 20th they started for the west and south; attended the Virginia Conference February 20th, 1812. Afterwards, while attending the Baltimore Conference, Bishop Asbury seemed to have a presentiment of the elder Boehm's death, and they reached home and found the aged patriarch no more.

Sunday, April 5th, Bishop Asbury preached his funeral sermon at Boehm's Chapel, to an immense crowd.

On May 1st, 1812, they attended the General Conference in the city of New York. This was the last General Conference Asbury attended.

Boehm soon afterwards ceased to travel with the Bishop. The latter thus spoke of the connection with him in his travels: "For five years he has been my constant companion. He served me as a son; he served me as a brother; he served me as a servant; he served me as a slave."

Boehm was now appointed presiding elder of Schuylkill district, embracing Boehm's Chapel, so that he might be more with his widowed mother.

In 1815 he was appointed to Chesapeake district. On July 4th he visited his mother, and Asbury met him there. They went together to Lancaster, and there parted for the last time. Asbury died at the house of George Arnold, of Spottsylvania, Virginia, March 31st, 1816.

At the Philadelphia Conference, held April 18th, 1816, Boehm was elected a delegate to the General Conference, which met in Baltimore, May 1st, 1816. Bishop Asbury's funeral service was here held, at which Boehm was one of the mourners, and Bishop McKendree pronounced the funeral oration. He left a will, of which Boehm was one of the executors; and now, for a long time, the only surviving one. At the Conference held in Philadelphia, in April, 1817, Boehm was appointed presiding elder of Chesapeake district. He made several tours with Bishop McKendree, and also with Bishop George. In 1819 he was appointed presiding elder of the Delaware district.

In April, 1821, Conference was held at Milford, Delaware; and Boehm was married now and resided there. He was reappointed to the same district.

In 1823 he was on Lancaster circuit. His mother died in November of that year, and was buried beside his father. In 1826–7 he was on Strasburg district. For fourteen years he was on circuits after he left the districts. He got a little home on Staten Island, and took a supernumerary relation. Here his wife died. He was a member of the General Conference of 1832, and was present at the memorable Conference in 1844, when the church South seceded. He had much to do in laying the foundation of German Methodism in New York. In 1856 he visited Lancaster again, where he was heartily welcomed by John Boehm's widow. He spent several weeks in the vicinity in visiting old friends, and preaching. He found Philip Benedict and his wife still living, who are now both dead. They talked over the early struggles and triumphs of Methodism in Lancaster.

He visited Boehm's Chapel, from whose windows he could see the graves of his father and mother. The friends of his youth were all gone. He visited the west again, and wondered at the changes since he had traveled there. In Dayton, in the publishing house of the "United Brethren in Christ," he saw a portrait of his father. Here he also saw an excellent likeness of Father Otterbein.

He visited his relative, Samuel Binkley, who formerly lived near his father. Here a cane was presented to him, which originally belonged to Otterbein, who gave it to Asbury, and he gave it to the elder Boehm. After his return home, he again went west and stayed a year in Cincinnati, where he preached before Conference in Xenia, and was present at the marriage of General Grant's sister in Covington, Kentucky, to a German preacher stationed in Cincinnati.

In 1864 he attended the General Conference in Philadelphia, and addressed it on the topics of the past and present. He brought the tears to many eyes in recalling the hardships he and many of the fathers endured.

During the last few years he has annually made a visit to

Lancaster, where he still preaches the Gospel whenever he comes. His appearance is venerable and commanding, his enunciation plain, distinct and deliberate. His memory is very good, and anecdotes nearly a century old fall from his lips with peculiar grace.

On October 1st, 1871, he was present by special invitation, to lay the corner-stone of the new Methodist church in East King street, Lancaster, where he expressed his gratification in being able to behold the progress of the Methodist churches from their early weakness and struggles to their present position of influence in the community.

At the General Conference of the Methodist Episcopal church, held in May, 1872, at Brooklyn, New York, he was present and addressed the assembled ministers, who heartily welcomed the venerable veteran, and he left them carrying with him their hearty congratulations and many good wishes for his happiness in the deep shades of his far advanced life.

BOMBERGER, George H., was a soldier of the war of 1812, and marched to the defence of Baltimore in 1814. He was, in 1822, appointed Deputy Marshal of the Eastern District of Pennsylvania. In 1823 he was appointed Clerk of the Orphans' Court. He was for many years one of the leading conveyancers and scriveners of Lancaster.

His son, Dr. J. H. A. Bomberger, is President of Ursinus College, Pennsylvania, and a theologian of wide reputation in the Reformed church. He is also editor of the *Reformed Church Monthly*, and the author of several theological works.

BOMBERGER, John, was a merchant tailor of Lancaster, and a man of considerable wealth and standing in the community. He was elected County Commissioner in 1811, and appointed Recorder in 1839.

*BOMBERGER. The Bomberger family of Lancaster county, and in fact mostly all bearing this name in the United States and Canadas, are descendants of Christian Bomberger and Maria his wife, who emigrated from Eshelbrun, Baden, and arrived in this county on the 12th of May, 1722. He took up and settled upon a tract of land in War-

*Contributed by I. F. Bomberger, of Lititz.

wick township, which is now in possession of Christian Bomberger, Jacob Bomberger, and Levi B. Brubaker. It contained 548 acres, the patent of which is still preserved, and bears date May 22nd, 1734.

He had two sons, named John and Christian, and six daughters. John's descendants were five sons, viz : Michael, John, Christian, Joseph and Jacob. Of Michael, John and Joseph, no record can be found. Jacob removed to Dauphin county, and but one of his descendants, Jacob, who at present resides in Harrisburg, is known to exist. Christian had seven sons, viz : Joseph, David, Moses, Peter, Samuel, Christian and John. Moses, Peter and John, had no children. Joseph had two sons, one of which, Elias, removed to Virginia. Samuel and Christian went to Canada; and David had two sons, viz : Isaac and Christian (Doctor). The former had two sons, Cyrus and Isaac, both residing now in Penn township; and the latter, who is still living, has two sons, Isaac F. and Samuel G., all residing in Warwick township.

Christian's descendants were five sons, viz : John, Christian, Jacob, Joseph and Abraham. Of Christian and Abraham, no record is found. Jacob had no children; Joseph had three, Christian, Joseph and John; and John had seven, viz : Christian, John, Jacob, Joseph, Abram, Daniel and Peter. John had two sons, Christian and Jacob, who live upon the old homestead. Christian's descendants are in Cumberland county. Jacob left but one descendant, Henry, who resides in Warwick. Peter's descendants are represented by his grandsons, John B., Elias, Martin E., Christ, and Abram, of Manheim. Joseph, Abram and Daniel, have left descendants in different parts of the county; their exact lineage cannot be traced.

BOWMAN, H. B., was born at Ephrata, Lancaster co., Penna., in the year 1804. He received a good English education, graduated in the Pennsylvania Medical College, Philadelphia, and practiced medicine in the village of Neffsville, Lancaster county, until the autum of 1848, when he was elected Recorder of Deeds in and for Lancaster county, the duties of which office he discharged during his official term with entire satisfaction.   In 1856 he started a woolen mill at Neffsville.   In 1862 he was elected a member of the Legislature of Pennsylvania, and in 1863 was re-elected, serving both terms to the satisfaction of his constituents. Dr. Bowman died July 21st, 1869.

BOWMAN, Joseph, was in 1854 elected Prothonotary of Lancaster county.

*BOWMAN, Samuel. The subject of this memoir is a striking instance of that noblest of all spectacles, a poor and uninfluential young man, making his way in life and struggling for intellectual improvement.   When men born to affluence, and aided by all the appliances of the best academical training, succeed in acquiring knowledge, become useful in their day and 'generation, and gain for themselves position, and succeed in having their names inscribed on the rolls of fame, we cannot withhold our admiration and a just tribute of praise.   What shall we say then, when we behold a young man encumbered by all the impediments that adverse circumstances can interpose, by his energy and indomitable perseverance overcoming them all and becoming a conspicuous and shining light, whose benign influence extends beyond his immediate neighborhood, and lasts long after his earthly career is terminated?

It has been well said, that where there are no examples of excellence there will be no efforts to attain it.   In this instance we have a spirit who finds an ideal character of excellence in the fertile resources of his own mind, and faithfully and to a considerable degree successfully struggles to realize this soul-born ideal of perfection.   Truly he, in departing, left behind him

> —"Footprints on the sands of time;
> Footprints that perhaps another
> Sailing o'er life's solemn main,
> A forlorn and shipwrecked brother
> Seeing, shall take heart again."

Our subject was born at Bowman's Mills, in Berks county, Pennsylvania, on the first day of December, 1789.   His father, Christian Bauman, (as the name originally was written in

*Contributed by J. B. Good, esq.

German), was a Swiss Mennonite, whose ancestors had emigrated to America on account of the religious persecutions that followed the revocation of the edict of Nantes by Louis XIV. His mother was Nancy Huber, of whose relatives a number are still living in this county.

Of his early years little is known except that his mother, in his childhood, perceived that he was different from the rest of her children, and, as it is said, in view of the approach of her death, which occurred when he was still quite young, was much concerned for him, not knowing whether his peculiarities indicated mental vigor or imbecility.

As soon as he was sent to school, however, it became evident that he had a natural fondness for letters, and he soon made such progress that he far outstripped all his schoolmates.

English schools had no existence in those days in the neighborhood where young Bowman was born and raised. In his father's family, and in the whole neighborhood for many miles around, no other language than the Pennsylvania German was in use. He, however, assiduously applied himself to the study of the English language, and for this purpose procured the best dictionaries that he could obtain, and he soon gained considerable proficiency in the language.

After he had attended the schools in the neighborhood, and having nearly attained the years of manhood, he attended a school kept in the neighborhood of Churchtown, Lancaster county, Pennsylvania, where he had the opportunity of conversing in English, with both teachers and pupils.

Here he studied surveying, which he afterwards so extensively and successfully practiced for many years, and in which he attained, perhaps, to as much skill and habitual accuracy as any other surveyor in the State or elsewhere.

His clear head and logical mind were eminently fitted for practical geometry. His love of justice and equity, and his high character for honesty and uprightness of purpose, all combined to make him afterwards the most successful practical surveyor in the whole neighborhood for many miles around.

6

About this time his taste for general literature commenced to develop itself. From the time he had learned to read he continued to manifest a remarkable love for books and a taste for the beautiful. It is in regard to this feature of his character that we have the greatest reason to admire this, in many respects, extraordinary man. Surrounded by those who had no literary taste at all; the ignorant, the illiterate and the bigoted, he not only acquired a just taste for elegant literature, so that he enjoyed the best productions of art, and the creations of the beautiful, especially in poetry, but he also occasionally composed himself. His style was very nervous and clear; his points made with much clearness, force and precision.

In his library were found some of the best classical authors in the English language, and he never bought books for playthings or for show, but he used and studied them till their contents became almost a part of himself.

It was thus that he acquired an almost inexhaustible fund of illustrative anecdotes; and there was no one who knew how to apply them in conversation more opportunely and with finer effect than himself.

Among other authors he used to read and admire, was Pope's translation of the Iliad and Odyssey of Homer. Boswell's life of Dr. Johnson he also enjoyed very much, on account of the sterling character of the great moralist, though he heartily despised the sycophantic biographer. Among the German poets, he especially loved the witty and sarcastic Langbein, whose lively verses he enjoyed with exquisite delight. But he had a clear perception of the excellent and beautiful, and he admired and prized it wherever he found it in his extensive reading.

In 1815 he was married to Elizabeth Bauman, a distant relative, an estimable lady, and one who was possessed of considerable personal attractions. Of this marriage were born several children, only one of whom (a daughter, married to Mr. Isaac Sensenig), is living at this time. His wife survived him a few years.

From 1815 to 1820 he was, during the winter months, engaged in teaching school. During the rest of his time he followed surveying, scrivening, and sometimes ordinary labor. He never considered it beneath his dignity to perform, when necessary, any kind of honorable labor.

In teaching school he exercised a remarkable influence over his pupils. He acquired a wonderful reputation among his neighbors, on account of his great knowledge; for they gazed,

> "And still they gazed, and still the wonder grew,
> That one small head could carry all he knew."

But he was especially famous for his success in keeping good order and governing his school well. To this day there are some of his pupils living, who, when talking about the degeneracy of modern school government, will say: "It was not thus in Sam Bowman's school."

In 1820 he built the first house in the place, which was afterwards named after him, "Bowmansville." This place is situated in the valley of the Muddy Creek, in Brecknock township, Lancaster county, Pennsylvania, about four miles from Bowman's mill, the place of his birth.

The house he built was arranged for keeping a country store. Here he commenced the mercantile business immediately after the building was finished. His means were small, and he had, to a great extent, to begin his career upon borrowed capital. But such were his industry, economy and business qualifications, that he soon became a lender instead of a borrower. His well-known character for honesty and fair dealing, as well as his pleasing social qualities, attracted crowds of customers. His store was resorted to far and near; and it is very remarkable that this man, so different in his views, tastes and habits of thought from those by whom he was surrounded, should yet have maintained their friendship, confidence and esteem in an unusual degree. This fact alone proves the high moral qualities of the man, and his unexceptionable deportment towards all those with whom he came in contact.

In the meantime he also followed the business of a surveyor and conveyancer. He was soon appointed and commissioned a justice of the peace, in which office, however, he did not act, except to take acknowledgments of deeds and other legal instruments of writing, of which he prepared great numbers.

On the first day of April, which is the general moving and settlement day in Lancaster county, his store was the place where the business of the whole neighborhood was transacted. He had to perform not only the duties of a country merchant, but also those of a scrivener, banker and legal adviser. Indeed, his neighbors reposed so much confidence in him, that he was frequently consulted on general matters of private business, and his advice was considered so valuable that it was almost invariably followed.

In 1840 a post-office was established at his store, and was after him named "Bowmansville," and he was appointed postmaster, which position he held for a number of years, and performed its duties to the general satisfaction of his neighbors.

He never held any other office except the two mentioned, justice of the peace and postmaster; and yet his influence was greater than those of many men who have held prominent positions in the gift of the people. He never could condescend to wallow in the mire of political scheming and corruption. His nature was honest and straightforward, and incapable of the mean actions and petty tricks of professional politicians.

From what has been said above, it is evident that his life was one of constant and unremitted labor, both of mind and body. Being rather corpulent, as he advanced in life his aversion to active out-door exercise increased, and the consequence was that his physical constitution suffered, and he was attacked with paralysis. His mental vigor also gradually declined, until he was forced to retire from active business. The transition from constant activity to the confinement of his room affected him unfavorably. His health continued to grow worse, until after a short confinement to his bed he died, January 19th, 1857, at his home in Bowmansville, surrounded by his family, and mourned by a large number of friends and acquaintances.

It is very seldom that the death of a mere private citizen occasions so great a void in the community as did that of the subject of this sketch. His character was altogether pure and his morals irreproachable. His word was never doubted. His advice was doubly valuable, because it came from one whose wisdom, honesty and integrity of purpose were undoubted, quite above suspicion. To his unlettered neighbors his knowledge and general intelligence were matters of wonder. He stood so much head and shoulders above them all, that his attainments were by them supposed to be almost infinite, and his judgment infallible. But he was admired by others than his illiterate neighbors. Intelligent strangers were often surprised to find a man of his superior qualities in a locality where they had not supposed that they should meet with any save the plain and simple.

In his business habits, he was very careful and methodical. The deeds of conveyance and other instruments of writing he prepared, and the drafts of the numerous surveys he made, all attest the anxious care as well as consummate skill with which he performed his work. He had a laudable ambition to be esteemed a correct and competent business man; and all who knew him and had business transactions with him can bear testimony to the ability and honesty with which his affairs were conducted.

In his intercourse with his neighbors he was remarkably genial and social. He seemed to forget his superiority when he came in social contact with those around him, and in every respect identified himself with them.

As regards his religious views and opinions, it is difficult to faithfully portray them. The peculiar circumstances which surrounded him in his early youth, had undoubtedly much to do with his religious impressions. The religion of his parents and relatives was clothed in anything but an attractive garb. Dry dogmas, narrow, bigoted views, and unenlightened sectarian zeal, were elements as unattractive to his mind as could be well conceived. The natural consequence was, that every thing bearing the name and resemblance of religion, became odious to him. The active energies of his mind soon raised doubts as to the truth of a system whose aspect was so uninviting and whose spirit was so uncongenial to his more refined nature. And, when

parental love and solicitude for his spiritual welfare brought
the strongest arguments they could command to bear upon
him, they were so absurdly conceived or so awkwardly
handled, that his clear head and subtle discrimination could
not help but perceive their weakness and absurdity. The
inevitable consequence unfortunately was, that he took for
granted that these were the strongest arguments that could
be advanced in support of the truth of the Christian system,
and he became—a skeptic. In these doubts he became more
confirmed by reading various authors, such as Volney and
others; but such was his modesty and conscientious fear of
injuriously affecting others, that he never openly gave
utterance to his opinions.

These doubts cost him many sleepless nights, and they
followed him more or less from his youth through middle
life; and it was only after his sun had crossed the meridian
and the lengthening shadows of the evening of life closed
around him, that his mind rested in peace upon the truths of
the gospel as revealed in the Bible, and died in full faith
and expectation of a glorious resurrection.

*BOWMAN, Rev. Dr. Samuel, was born in Wilkesbarre,
in the beautiful Wyoming Valley on the 21st of May, 1800.
His father was an officer in the Revolutionary war, and
was an active participant in the battle of Lexington. Educated at an academy in his native place, the law had been
chosen as his profession, but he soon became a student of
divinity, having been brought under deep religious conviction by the sudden death of his father, which resulted from
an accident. He was ordained in Philadelphia, August 25th,
1823, and entered upon ministerial duty in this county; in
the same year preaching his first sermons in Leacock and
Salisbury townships, where he remained about two years.
In 1825 he was stationed at Easton, but in the following
year he returned to his former charges in this county. In
1827 he accepted a call to the Rectorship of St. James'
church, in this city, one of the oldest Episcopal parishes in
the State. Of the acceptable manner in which he more than
discharged the responsible duties of this sacred station, we

*From the Lancaster *Daily Evening Express.*

are not confined in our search for testimony to that of his own branch of the church; nor indeed to the circle of professing Christians of whatever denomination. Dr. Bowman not only had the unlimited confidence of the members of his own congregation, but his friends were legion amongst those of no church connection. The characteristics which so strongly attached him to all who knew him, grew with his growth and strengthened with his years. His attachment to his parish and to the community was so deep, that he would never accept any position which involved the necessity of abandoning Lancaster as his home. In 1845 he was, against his own inclinations, voted for as the candidate of those in convention who opposed Rev. Dr. Tyng for bishop, and was several times elected by the clergy, but the laity refused to concur. The contest was long and exciting, and Bishop Potter was finally elected as a compromise candidate, much to Dr. Bowman's gratification, who would have accepted the office with much reluctance, if at all, for the reason above stated. In 1848 he was elected bishop of the diocese of Indiana, which he declined again, reiterating his desire to remain with the flock between whom and himself there was such a strong attachment.

With regard to the two parties which unfortunately exist in the Episcopal church, Bishop Bowman was a conservative, even to the extent of ignoring the existence of what are called "High" and "Low Church." It was only on the Sunday night previous to his death, while walking home with him from St. John's Free Church, where he preached his last discourse, that he remarked that unrestrained party spirit had brought the existing calamity upon our nation, and that if it were possible to destroy the church of Christ, party spirit would be the instrumentality through which it would be accomplished. He regarded party as the besetting sin of both church and State. This, indeed, had been the spirit of his earnest discourse, at St. John's, that evening, based upon the word of St. Paul, addressed to the church at Corinth—"For I am determined not to know any thing among you, save Jesus Christ, and Him crucified."

And this was the spirit in which he accepted the office of

Assistant Bishop, three years before. The convention failing to make a choice between Dr. Vinton and himself, Dr. Bowman offered a resolution for a committee to report to the convention a candidate, which he advocated with great earnestness and ability, solemnly and emphatically withdrawing his name from the nominations before the convention. He said God brought men together by ways unknown to them. His name had been placed there without any feeling of ambition on his part. His great and only desire was, that he might pass the rest of his days in the humble, yet honorable, station of the ministry, to which he was so sincerely attached. He expressed the hope that the carrying out of this resolution would prove the breaking down of the partition that existed between some portions of the church, in which church all should be of " One Lord, one Faith, and one Baptism." Let the only strife be, he continued, as to who shall expend most labor in the cause of God. Let us no longer array ourselves under party leaders. Let our only motto be, " *Pro Deo, pro ecclesia, et hominum salute !*"

After the election of Dr. Bowman, he was introduced to the convention, by a committee, as the Assistant Bishop. He closed a feeling address with the " fervent hope that the work which the convention had accomplished that day would redound to the unity and advancement of the church, through Jesus Christ our Lord."

In 1861, on the occasion of his thirtieth anniversary as Rector of St. James', Dr. Bowman thus alluded to the changes that thirty years had made in the church and parish: " When he preached his first sermon in St. James', the Episcopal church in the United States had but 10 bishops, and 460 ministers ; now it embraces 39 bishops and 1836 ministers. When he entered the parish of St. James' there were but 50 communicants, only 25 of whom remain, the rest having fallen asleep. Now there are two hundred communicants. During the period of his ministerial labors in the parish, he had solemnized 221 marriages, 648 baptisms, and attended 378 funerals; the rite of confirmation was also administered to 270 persons. About 8 years ago a parochial school was established, in which from 80 to 100 children have been continually educated without drawing upon the public for aid. An Orphan Asylum had been established during the same period, affording a Christian home to many helpless and unprotected children. And more recently still, a 'Home' for the aged and infirm, which had already accomplished great good, and promises still more extended usefulness for the future." The enlargement of St. James' was referred to; and more recently, the establishment of a church (St. John's) on the principle of free seats, which has a'ready been paid for, and which he hoped had a long career of usefulness before it. These were charges which do not attract the gaze and admiration of the world; indeed, it is too often the destiny of those who labor in any good cause to have little sympathy from the world, but "God will not forget their works and labor of love."

The death of Bishop Bowman occurred in this wise. He had left home on a tour of western visitation in his official capacity, and had taken the 6 a. m. train, on the Allegheny Valley Railroad, *en route* for Butler, where he had an appointment to administer the rite of confirmation on the following Sabbath. At Freeport, 24 miles from Pittsburg, he proposed taking the stage to Butler. After proceeding about 19 miles, the train was halted in consequence of a bridge which had been injured by a late freshet, and a landslide nearly 2 miles beyond. Arrangements had been made to convey the passengers over this part of the road in a hand-car, a locomotive and a passenger car being in readiness on the other side to carry them on. Several gentlemen preferred walking, and among them Bishop Bowman.

The workmen having charge of the hand-car when returning to the bridge, found the Bishop lying by the road-side, having fallen upon his face as if seized with apoplexy. His face was buried in his hat, in which was his pocket handkerchief, that he had saturated with water in a small stream a few paces back, doubtless as a prevention against sun stroke.

BOUDE, SAMUEL, a member of the Legislature in the years 1784, 1792 and 1796. He was a leading physician of Lancaster.

7

¹BOUDE, Thomas, son of Samuel Boude, was a native of Lancaster county. He served, with distinction, as a captain during the revolutionary war, at the close of which he received the brevet commission of Major. He was a member of the Society of the Cincinnati. He lived at Columbia, and was engaged in the lumber business for many years, and was an active and energetic business man. He was a prominent politician of the Federal party, and was elected a member of the Legislature in the years 1794, 1795 and 1796. He also represented Lancaster county in the National Congress from 1801 till 1803. He died October 24th, 1822, in the 70th year of his age.

BOYD, S. W. P. was elected Sheriff of Lancaster county in 1860. His maternal grandfather, James Porter, was one of the early settlers of Lancaster county. Nicholas Boyd, his father, died December 22nd, 1840, aged 66 years.

BOYER, Joseph, was elected County Commissioner in 1858.

BRADY, John, was elected Recorder of Lancaster county in the year 1851.

BRANDT, Daniel, was elected one of the County Commissioners in 1855.

BRECKBILL, Benjamin, was elected County Commissioner in 1841.

BRECKBILL, John, was a citizen of Strasburg township, and was a member of the Legislature for the years 1790, 1791, and 1792. He was also a delegate to the convention which amended the Constitution of Pennsylvania in 1789.

BRECKBILL, Ulrich, an early settler of Lancaster county, and one of the compeers of Hans Herr and his companions. He was a minister of the Mennonite faith. He was accidentally killed October 19th, 1739, while driving his

¹Thomas Boude bought the wealthy Stephen Smith (colored), of Philadelphia, when a boy of eight years of age, from the Cochrans, of Dauphin county. He raised him, and after he married, Mr. Boude gave him his freedom and furnished him means with which to go into business, and thus laid for him the foundation of his fortune.

team on the Philadelphia road. His descendants in Lancaster are quite numerous.

BRENEMAN, CHRISTIAN, a member of the Legislature in 1814.

BRINTON, FERREE, was elected Assistant Judge of Lancaster county, in 1856. He was re-elected in 1861, and served two terms with great satisfaction to his constituents. As a judge he was very upright and conscientious, and discharged his duties with great credit. A writer in the *Daily Evening Express* said of Judge Brinton, that he " was a gentleman in his manners and habits, and was the most intellectual looking non law-judge that I ever saw on any bench, and he had more mind and information than any non law-judge I ever knew but one."

BRISBIN, WM., a member of the Legislature in the years 1802, 1803 and 1804.

*BROOKS, PROF. EDWARD. It is yet too soon to write a biography that shall do justice to Professor Edward Brooks, for he is yet a young man, and has not reached the meridian of his powers. Though he has already achieved much— more than enough to satisfy the ambition of most scholars and thinkers—what he has done must be accepted, not as the measure of his usefulness, but merely as a promise of what he is yet to do. And yet, in a life so abundant in fruit and so rich in promise, though it has numbered scarcely more than half the years allotted to man, there must be something worthy of being recorded for our interest and instruction. But in attempting to write the biography of a man of thought, this difficulty meets us at the threshold— a lack of stirring events and striking incidents calculated to awaken and keep alive the interest of the readers. His life may have been one of incessant activity, and may have achieved "victories no less renowned than war;" but his activity has not been that of the forum or the field, nor can his victories be estimated by the number of guns captured and enemies slain. His campaigns have been carried on in the class-room and the study; his battles have been fought

*Contributed by Prof. J. Willis Westlake.

and won, not with cannon balls and bombshells, but with arguments and ideas. Hence the biographies of writers and scholars are rarely popular, being mainly confined to the "audience fit though few" of those who are engaged in similar pursuits. This is to be regretted, for the temple of a good man's character is his greatest work; it is the preacher's most effective sermon, the teacher's most useful lesson. How many poor boys have learned the lesson of self-reliance from the life of Franklin, and of truthfulness from that of Washington! And if all the facts connected with the life of the subject of this sketch could be placed prominently before all the youth of our country, they would do more good than all that he has said and written.

Edward Brooks was born at Stony Point, on the Hudson, January 16th, 1831; and in this picturesque place, rendered forever memorable by one of the daring exploits of "Mad Anthony Wayne," he passed the first fifteen years of his life. It is impossible to measure the effect of early influences, but there can be no doubt that the romantic beauty of the scenery with which he was surrounded in his childhood, operating upon a highly sensitive and finely organized mind, powerfully contributed to the formation and development of that fine poetic taste, that ardent love of the beautiful, for which he is distinguished, and which adds such a charm to his literary productions.

The means of education afforded him during these years were very limited, being merely those furnished by the public schools of the neighborhood; but these he improved to the utmost, surpassing all the other members of the school, so that when, in 1846, he went with his parents to reside in Sullivan county, New York, he already possessed a very good elementary education, particularly excelling in mathematics and literature. The region in which he now lived, being a wild and sparsely populated one, had no public school for him to attend, and as circumstances did not permit his going to an academy he applied himself with his accustomed energy to the learning of a trade, an undertaking which he speedily and thoroughly accomplished. But while manual pursuits thus claimed his attention, they by no means monopolized it, nor could they repress his soaring aspirations. Though fully recognizing the dignity of honest labor, yet he felt that there was for him a higher plane of usefulness than that of the mechanic, and he spared no effort to improve his talents and add to his acquirements. He read and studied incessantly, making for himself a school-room of field and forest, of shop and fireside, of every place to which duty or pleasure called him. Thus he not only obtained a mastery of the branches he had begun in the public schools, but pushed on to higher attainments; while he also improved his taste and formed his style by making himself acquainted with music and with the standard English authors. He wrote with considerable facility both prose and verse; and it may be worth while to mention here, that his first published production was a little poem written at the age of fourteen, and which, being too bashful to hand it to the printer, he pushed under the printing office door. In common with most successful literary men, he early formed a habit which cannot be too highly recommended to young readers—that of reading with pencil in hand, and of noting down for future use the most important facts recorded and thoughts expressed or suggested by the author.

> "As a pebble in the streamlet scant
> Has turned the course of many a river;
> As a dew-drop on the infant plant
> Has warped the giant oak forever"—

so an apparently trifling occurrence sometimes decides a man's destiny. It was one of these momentous trifles that turned his mind about this time in the direction of arithmetical analysis, and thus gave him, to use his own words, "the golden key that unlocks the various complex combinations of numbers." The qualities of his mind were such that he would in any case have become eminent in something —perhaps in natural science, perhaps in music, perhaps in poetry and general literature—but he would not probably have become the distinguished mathematician that he is, had he not received this mental impulse. This was nothing more nor less than the perusal of Colburn's Mental Arithmetic—a little book which revolutionized the study of the science of numbers in this country, and powerfully contributed to the breaking up of the dull routine work of the school-room, and the substitution of more rational and normal methods of instruction. At the same time a powerful coördinate influence was exerted by the little treatise, once so popular, entitled "Watts on the Mind." This he read with the greatest interest, and from it were derived those seed-truths of mental science which, taking root in the fertile soil of his intellect, have developed into the ripened grain of knowledge and brought forth a rich harvest of thought.

His career as teacher had a very humble beginning; his first school being a singing-class, his first school-house a barn. Subsequently, when about eighteen years of age, he taught a school in the village of Cuddebackville, N. Y., with excellent success, at a salary, at first, of eighteen dollars a month and board. Here, for the first quarter, he had an experience—sometimes pleasant, often ludicrous, but always inconvenient—of the "peripatetic" old fashion of "boarding 'round." Having an agreeable tenor voice and a pretty good knowledge of music, he introduced singing into his school, and this greatly enhanced his success and popularity as a teacher. At the end of the second quarter, on account of the ill health of his father, he gave up his school and went home. Here he remained a year, and then left to attend the Liberty Normal Institute, under the charge of Mr. Henry Stoddard (brother of Prof. J. F. Stoddard), to fit himself more fully for the work of teaching. In this institution he greatly distinguished himself, both by his scholarship and social qualities, and at the close of the session was awarded the honor of the valedictory. And thus closed his brief career as a pupil. Thenceforward, though still a learner, a faithful and laborious student of the writings of the wise and good of all ages, and especially of the dual works of God, in nature and Revelation—he devoted himself with all his energy to the work of teaching.

We have dwelt at some length on the earlier and preparatory portion of Prof. Brooks's life, for the encouragement of the young into whose hands this book may fall; to show what may be accomplished by industry and energy, in spite of adverse circumstances, without the help, however valuable, of academies and colleges, and independent of all the advantages that wealth and station can bestow. It thus appears that he is mainly self-educated; and this, coupled with the fact that he is thoroughly well-educated, is something of which he has abundant cause to be proud. Learning that is, as it were, thrust on one by rich and indulgent friends, is not half so much valued, generally not half so valuable, as that which is wrung from the reluctant hand of adverse fate—sought for, sweat for, struggled for.

The subsequent events in Prof. Brooks's life we shall pass over as rapidly as possible, in order to discuss, as fully as space will allow, the qualities of mind and heart that have rendered him so eminent.

On the completion of his course at the Institute mentioned above, he taught for three years in a school of which Prof. John F. Stoddard was principal, at Bethany, Wayne county, Pennsylvania. Probably the most important, as it certainly was the most interesting event of these three years, was the formation of an intimate acquaintance with the pianist of the institution, Miss Marie Dean, of North Stamford, Connecticut, who subsequently became his "true and honorable wife," and who has thus far rendered his life as happy in his private, as it has been useful in his public relations. He next taught for a year in the academy at Monticello, N. Y., and then, in 1855, accepted a professorship in the Normal School at Millersville, Lancaster county, Pa., where he has ever since labored with distinguished success, and acquired an influence as an educator second to none in the State. In 1858 the trustees of Union College conferred upon him the well-merited degree of Master of Arts.. In 1866, on the resignation of Prof. J. P. Wickersham, he was elected Principal of the institution which he had so powerfully contributed to build up; and in this position he has shown administrative abilities of a high order, combined with broad and comprehensive views of the work of public education and the adaptation of the normal schools to that work.

Here, amid his labors as a teacher, he has composed the

works that have given him a prominent place among American educational authors. They are, in fact, an outgrowth of those labors; being a successful attempt to present on paper the philosophical methods of instruction employed by him in the class-room with such excellent results.

Prof. Brooks is known to the public at large chiefly as a mathematician; but his reputation does not in this respect do him justice. To his friends he is known to be equally thorough and original in other departments of knowledge. He is no less a metaphysician than a mathematician; and it may safely be predicted that, if he lives to carry out his designs, he will yet give to the world works which, if not more useful, will contribute far more to the permanence and extension of his fame than anything he has yet published.

PUBLISHED WORKS.—The works published by him to the present time (May, 1873), are the following:

1. An Arithmetical Series, consisting of six books; a Primary, an Elementary, a Mental and a Written Arithmetic, together with two "Keys," each containing many valuable exercises and suggestions, besides the solutions to the problems.

2. Geometry and Trigonometry.

3. Elementary Algebra—his latest publication.

The works named above, though unpretending and apparently unimportant, are the result of much thought and labor. They are not mere compilations, as are many text-books at the present day, but bear on every page the stamp of originality; a statement that is abundantly attested by the fact that other authors have extensively copied from them in the revision of existing works on the same subjects, or in the composition of new ones. In a subsequent part of this sketch a few of their peculiar excellences will be briefly pointed out. The influence that these books exert is incalculable, as they are used very extensively in Pennsylvania and several other States, and are moulding the minds and directing the thinking of hundreds of thousands of children.

PROJECTED WORKS.—Prof. Brooks contemplates the publication, at no distant day, of several other works, some of which are already composed, and require only revision and arrangement to fit them for the printer. The list will embrace, among others, the following:

1. Philosophy of Arithmetic.
2. Methods of Teaching Arithmetic.
3. A series of works on the Science of Education.
4. Educational Addresses.
5. The higher works required to complete his series of mathematical text-books.

Several of his addresses have already been published, and some of them, particularly the one entitled "The Spiritual Element in Education," have been greatly admired, both on account of their freshness and vigor of thought, and the beauty and elegance of their style.

PROFESSIONAL AND LITERARY CHARACTERISTICS.—Prof. Brooks's public life presents itself to us in three aspects: 1. As a teacher; 2. As a lecturer; 3. As an author; and we propose to examine briefly his characteristics in each of these particulars, and discover, if possible, the secret of his remarkable success.

As a Teacher: Of Prof. Brooks's wonderful success as a teacher, not only in imparting knowledge, but in giving power, the thousands of active and intelligent young men and women who have enjoyed the benefit of his instructions, are glad and grateful witnesses. This success is due to several causes, of which the three following seem to us the most prominent:

1. A perfect familiarity with whatever subject he attempts to teach, rendering him to a great extent independent of the text-book, and, indeed, superior to it. Thus his mind resembles not a mere reservoir, but a living fountain, from which streams of knowledge issue forth with all the freshness and sparkle of originality.

2. Natural and philosophical methods of instruction. He is as thoroughly Pestalozzian as Pestalozzi himself, and as analytic as Colburn; and yet he can be deductive as well as inductive, synthetic as well as analytic. He has the clear insight that enables him to perfectly adapt his method to the circumstances of each case. He does not drive pupils, but leads them. He does not do away with the necessity of

8

study and thought, but he makes study attractive, and teaches how to think. He does not remove difficulties from the learner's path, but shows how to surmount them. Thus the student, as he ascends the rugged "hill of science," is forever tempted on by new beauties unfolding before him; like a traveler who, unmindful of the toil, climbs some moss-grown precipice to pluck a rare and beautiful flower that he sees smiling down upon him from its mountain home.

3. The possession, in a remarkable degree, of what may be called inspirational power, by which he is enabled to enkindle the enthusiasm of his pupils, and invest the dryest subject with living interest. Part of this effect is doubtless due to the fact that he is himself interested, both in the subject and in the class; but much of it is due to what, for want of a better name, we may call personal magnetism. He not only interests his pupils in the subject, but in himself personally, so that every one becomes a warm and life-long friend. Thus he is enabled to influence their moral natures, as well as their intellectual, and to awaken in them those emotions, and instil those sentiments that tend to build up a noble character and render knowledge a blessing to its possessor and to society.

As a Lecturer: The same qualities that make Prof. Brooks a successful teacher, make him also a popular lecturer. As an instructor at teachers' institutes he is unsurpassed—never failing to interest his audience and to give them practical and valuable ideas. An apparently dry subject like geometry, he can present so simply as to make it comprehensible by a child, and at the same time he can clothe it with all the beauty and attractiveness of romance. Should the interest flag for a moment, he is ever ready to revive it by a pertinent anecdote or a witty remark. Many speakers will make an interesting lecture from which you can get no definite result—nothing but a general impression; but Prof. Brooks gives such a clear outline of his subject, and states his points so strongly, as to enable the hearer not only to apprehend but to retain what he says. His ascending the platform is always a signal for the sharpening of pencils and opening of note-books; for all are sure that they will hear something worthy of record.

As an Author: Since a person's oral instructions and writings are merely different manifestations of the same mind, it is impossible to describe his characteristics as a teacher without at the same time indicating in a measure his characteristics as a writer. Hence, some of the causes of Prof. Brooks's popularity and usefulness in the latter capacity, may be inferred from what we have already said concerning his labors in the class-room and on the platform. Nevertheless, at the risk of some repetition, we shall endeavor to state what appears to us to be the most important of these causes. They are three in number:

1. An abundance of information—partly the fruit of his own fertile and original mind, partly the result of patient and extensive research. He always has something new and striking to say on every subject of which he treats.

2. A logical arrangement of materials, based on a thorough acquaintance both with the subjects themselves and with the laws by which the mind acts in coming to a knowledge of them. Having a clear perception of the uses and limitations both of the inductive and the deductive methods of teaching, he is able to employ both, as occasion demands, without abusing either—always having reference both to the nature of the subject and the degree of advancement of the learner.

3. A style which in scientific statement or discussion is clear, logical, and direct—the natural result of clear thinking; but which, when the nature of the subject allows, abounds in illustration and imagery—the effect of an active imagination and fine poetic feeling.

As shown above, Prof. Brooks's fame as an author chiefly rests upon his mathematical text-books. It would be both interesting and profitable to subject these to a critical examination, and to call attention to the many valuable additions they have made to our stock of scientific knowledge; but for this work we have neither the requisite time nor ability. We shall attempt nothing more than to state in general terms a few of the features that establish their claim to originality, and make them superior to all books that pre-

ceded them in the same field.   Among these are: 1. Many
improvements in old definitions, and several new' ones; 2.
Several new classes of problems; 3. Many new solutions of
old problems; 4. A simplification of the reasoning in arithmetic, and a reduction of what was awkward and illogical to
a simple, logical, and scientific method; 5. Several new gen-
eralizations and classifications, such as the relations of frac-
tions, " composition" as a process correlative with factoring,
the classification of algebraic symbols, etc.   The algebra is
a model of simplicity, conciseness, elegance, and logical
accuracy; and the geometry is one of the most strikingly
original works on the subject ever published in this country.
In the latter, by a variation and simplification of the theorems
and demonstrations, the subject is presented in about half
the space usually devoted to it, without in the least impairing
the chain of logic.

One of Prof. Brooks's happiest and most original ideas, is
that presented in his " Philosophy of Arithmetic "—one of
his unpublished works.[1]   He therein develops the science of
numbers from three fundamental processes—synthesis,
analysis, and comparison—thereby showing the error of
those who have held that the whole science of arithmetic is
contained in addition and subtraction; and also the mistake
of such logicians as Mansel, who claim that there is no
reasoning in pure arithmetic.

His miscellaneous productions, consisting of poems,
essays, and addresses on various subjects, though well
worthy of being put in book form, are scattered here and
there in newspapers and pamphlets, or hidden away in
neglected piles of manuscript.   As shown above, he possesses invention, fancy, taste, a musical ear, power of expression—all the essential elements of a poet; and at various
times he has sought recreation—nothing more—in poetical
composition.   Perhaps his greatest hindrance to success in
this direction, is the consciousness that he is a teacher, the
tendency to be didactic.   If he would, for once, sink the

[1]Portions of this work were published in the *Pennsylvania School
Journal* in 1861 ; also in the *Mathematical Monthly* (since discontinued),
for March of the same year.

pedagogue in the poet, and devote himself to a work of pure imagination, he would undoubtedly produce poetry worthy of his superior genius.

His little poem of five stanzas, entitled " Be a Woman," published anonymously in 1857, has obtained considerable popularity both in this country and England. It has been printed in thousands of periodicals, and read by hundreds of thousands of people. We quote the last stanza :[1]

> " Be a woman ! on to duty !
>   Raise the world from all that's low ;
> Place high in the social heaven
>   Virtue's fair and radiant bow ;
> Lend thy influence to each effort
>   That shall raise our nature human ;
> Be not fashion's gilded *lady*,
>   Be a brave, whole-souled, true *woman*."

We cannot stop to examine his other miscellaneous writings, having already greatly exceeded the limits prescribed for this sketch. They shall presently be allowed to speak for themselves, as fully as they can do so in a few brief specimens. But first let us see what conclusion we have arrived at.

The author's characteristics, as exhibited particularly in his mathematical books—the only ones yet published—have already been given. A wider survey enables us to give the following as a summary of his qualities of mind and heart : A refined taste; an active imagination; great logical acuteness, enabling him to detect the truth or falsity of a proposition at a glance, and deduce results with ease. and certainty ; a profound and pervading sense of moral obligation ; and a style which, despite a tendency to indulge too much in epigrammatic and antithetical forms of expression and an excess of rhetorical ornament, is clear, pure, strong, and eminently pleasing and attractive.

The following extracts, culled almost at random, will show his peculiarities of thought and expression much better than any words of ours can do it ; and we are sure that they will abundantly sustain the literary judgment pronounced above :

[1]For the whole poem and its history, see *Pennsylvania School Journal* for August, 1871, quoted from the Lancaster *Express*.

"It is better to inspire the heart with a noble sentiment than to teach the mind a truth of science."

"I would rather live in the memory of grateful pupils than be honored in song or story."

"The problem of life is filled with known and unknown quantities which, when compared, give an equation whose roots are determined only in eternity."

"The æsthetic nature is higher than the scientific; art, therefore, it would seem, should be placed above science. Science is the product of mere intellect; art involves and embodies both thought and feeling. To write a poem, therefore, is better than to solve a problem; a great poet has a brighter fame than a great philosopher. I would rather be gentle Will Shakespeare, the author of Hamlet, than Sir Isaac Newton, the author of the Principia. Hamlet will be enshrined in the heart of mankind long after the Principia has ceased to be read or printed. * * Music aids in the work [æsthetic culture] with its melodious voice. A school song in the heart of a child will do as much for its character as a fact in its memory, or a principle in its intellect. The cradle song that fell from a mother's lips becomes a sacred memory that inspires the life."

"Spiritual culture demands the training of the moral nature. The moral nature embraces the activity of our entire spiritual being. It consists in the apprehension of the right, in the feeling of obligation to do the right, and the consequent act of the will to carry out the spiritual imperative. The æsthetic nature is idea and feeling; the moral nature is idea, feeling, and volition. In mathematical phraseology, the æsthetic nature equals the Reason plus the Sensibilities; the ethical nature equals the Reason plus the Sensibilities plus the Will."

"The culture of these three powers—Faith, Love, and Obedience—in their relation to God, is religious culture. Faith in God, love to God, and obedience to God, is religion. The relation is simple and logical. Faith leads to love; we must believe before we can love. Love leads to obedience; that obedience is the most willing and perfect which flows from affection. Faith, then, is the soil in which grows the tree of Love, and Obedience is the ripened fruit. Let us plant the tree of Love in the soil of Faith in God, and it will reward us with the golden fruit of perfect Obedience."[1]

"Life is a product of three factors—nature, self, and destiny; but the central and controling influence is self, the imperial power of the free spirit.

> ' We shape ourselves, the joys or fears
> Of which the coming years are made.'

All true success in life is organic, and follows the law of organic development. Analyze any great character or achievement, and you will find an idea at the centre—an idea which determined its growth, and gave direction to its development. This is the universal law. The

---

[1] It will be observed that the author comprehends all religious duties in these three—Faith, Love, Obedience; a generalization which is philosophical, and, so far as we know, original.

ideal is the germ of the real. Development, everywhere throughout God's universe, is the unfolding of a purpose. The acorn slumbering in the soil through the gloom of winter, contains the plan of an oak, and in the spring-time begins to develop the tree which shall live for a century. The little plant, starting in the dark ground, travels all the way up from a seed, with an idea in its head, unfolding it at the top into blossom and fruit."

" Beauty, purity, and generosity may appear in the external act, whilst the motive prompting it may be mean, ignoble, and selfish. Truth, purity, and all the noble traits of character, may be enshrined within the soul, and the life be so unobtrusive that they may not manifest themselves to the public gaze. When asked why Antipater was not dressed in purple, Alexander replied : ' These men wear purple on the outside, but Antipater is royal within.' Character is being *royal within*. It is a soul throbbing with generous feelings, with noble impulses, a soul loyal to the claims of truth and virtue."

"Man must labor for his best achievements. The duty of industry rests upon us as a responsibility from Heaven. The God who made us is a ceaseless energy, a tireless activity, infinite in His doing as in His being. There is no such thing as indolence in His wide universe. The most peaceful place of the summer landscape is but a veil that covers the incessant and tireless activities of leaf, and root, and sunshine, and dew. And all this activity is not for the end of action. Nature aims at results ; she energizes for products. The dew-drops of the summer night are the tree-builders of the summer day ; and the sunshine of spring pours its golden rays into the green leaf, that it may blush in the rose's petal, or glow in the summer harvest."

The heart prompts us, and truth and justice compel us, in closing this imperfect sketch, to say that Prof. Brooks himself, measured as God measures a man, by his soul, his character, is better and greater than any of his works. Fortunate in having had the benefit, in his childhood, of the counsels and prayers of a wise father and a remarkably gentle and intelligent mother, he has never departed from his early lessons of morality and religion. His sensibilities are tender as a child's and strong as a man's; but the will commands the feelings, and duty dominates the will. Having perfect command of himself, he is therefore qualified to command others ; yet the rod of authority was never wielded by a gentler hand. Naturally of a quick temper, he seldom manifests anger ; fond of ease and pleasure, he yet labors to the full extent of physical endurance. Rapid in all his motions, mental and physical, he is never rash. Amid all his multiplicity of duties—administrative and educational, public and private—there is no confusion, nothing hap-hazard. Method is as prominent in his business as his books. His power of mental concentration is prodigious, but it is fully equaled by his persistence and energy. This is the great secret of his success; this is the golden key that has unlocked for him the temples of Fortune and of Fame.

BROWN, JEREMIAH, sr., a member of the Legislature in the years 1796, 1797, 1798, 1799 and 1800.

BROWN, JEREMIAH, jr., was born in the year 1776. He was elected to the Legislature in 1826. He represented Lancaster county in Congress from 1841 to 1845. He was the first Associate Judge elected by the people, in 1851.

BROWN, WILLIAM, a member of the Legislature for the years 1776, 1778, 1779, 1781, 1782 and 1783.

*BRUBAKER FAMILY. John Brubaker emigrated to this country, from Switzerland, in the year 1710, and settled on the Little Conestoga, about two miles west of the city of Lancaster, where Mr. Samuel Binkley's mill is now located; here Mr. Brubaker built the first grist mill in Lancaster county. He had a large family, consisting of nine sons, viz: John, Daniel, Peter, Abraham, David, Christian, Henry and Jacob. Two of these sons, John and Daniel, settled in Elizabeth township, near Hammer Creek; they married sisters, daughters of Michael Tauner. Peter settled in Rapho township. Abraham settled in Virginia. The rest remained in their father's neighborhood. The above-named John, jr., took the farm owned at the present time by one of his lineal descendants, Jacob E. Brubaker. He, however, before settling, paid a visit to Germany in the year 1750, where he married Maria Newcomer, and returned with his wife and cousin to America. His wife only lived thirty weeks, when she died. He then married his second wife, the above Miss Tauner, and had a family of eleven children. I shall speak only of John, the oldest, he being my direct ancestor. He was born A. D. 1752, was married to Anna Eby, and had a family of four children, viz: Two sons and two daughters; Anna, born 1753, Maria, born 1756. The

*Contributed by M. N. Brubaker.

last mentioned was married to [1]John Bear, from whom Mr. Gabriel Bear, at Mount Joy, has descended. I shall speak more fully of this family hereafter. The son, Jacob Brubaker, who was my great grandfather, was born A. D. 1758. He married Miss Susanna Erb, in 1781, and raised a family of seven children. He died of yellow fever, in 1793, contracted while in Philadelphia, he being engaged in hauling his grain and flour to that place during the prevalence of that disease there. His young widow devoted her time and energies nobly to her family. Previous to this time some members of the "Old Mennonite" church settled in Canada; they had purchased a very large tract of land. After awhile they found there was a mortgage on it of $30,000, which would be foreclosed; they became alarmed and sent a committee to Lancaster county to solicit aid from their brethren; after some labor they succeeded in raising the amount; this young widow contributed a large sum towards it. The committee started back to Canada, through the wilderness, with this money in gold and silver in their saddle-bags, on their horses; they reached home safe and cancelled the mortgage. These events transpired about the beginning of the present century. Those men had nothing to give for security but their word and honor, which they faithfully fulfilled. They surveyed the tract, 60,000 acres, divided it into lots of from 500 to 1,000 acres, and sold tickets to the parties who loaned them the money, held a regular lottery, and so this widow drew a large tract of land, in lieu of her claim against the committee. She traveled out, on horseback, to see her land. In the year 1816 she sent her youngest son, John, out to take charge of this land; he married there and raised a numerous family, who still possess some of the land, which has become very valuable. The widow, Susanna Brubaker, lived 51 years in widowhood, and died in 1844, at an advanced age. This old lady traveled to Canada twice on horseback; one day, while leading her horse across the mountains, she came upon a large rattle-

[1]John Bear, spoken of before, was married to Miss Maria Brubaker, A. D. 1756, and these had a family of nine children, of whom Samuel was married to Miss Weaver. They had a family of eight children, of whom Gabriel was the oldest son, who resides in Mt. Joy at the present time.

9

snake, which was lying across her path; she aimed a blow at it with her walking-stick and killed it. Her oldest son, Jacob Brubaker, who was my grandfather, was born in 1782, and was married to Miss Maria Eby. They started out in life on the farm first spoken of; they had a family of nine children, of which Sem, the oldest son, is my father, who resides near Mount Joy at the present time. Jacob, the youngest son, occupies the old mansion farm at the present time, which has been handed down from generation to generation for a period 160 years. The Brubakers in this county and Canada have all descended from the same stock.

BRUBAKER, GEORGE, was born April 24th, 1817, in Leacock township, Lancaster county. On his father's side he is of German descent, and of Scotch-Irish on that of his mother. His early educational advantages were very limited, the time of his pupilage in the common schools not having exceeded eighteen months. At an early age he began teaching school, and pursued this calling for nine consecutive sessions, running through a period of the same number of years. He was one of the first teachers in the county under the free school system, of which he was one of the earliest and warmest advocates.

In 1848 he was nominated and elected to the position of Register of Wills of Lancaster county, by the Whig party, and for the term of three years faithfully discharged the duties of this office. In 1851 he commenced the study of law, and in the year 1854 was admitted to the bar as a practising attorney, which profession he has since followed with a very considerable degree of success.

In 1868 he was nominated and elected to the office of District Attorney by the Republican party. For four years he held the office of Select Councilman in Lancaster city, and was a prominent mover in the division of the city of Lancaster into nine wards.

George Brubaker, as a business man, is keen and sagacious, and as a citizen, kind, liberal and public spirited.

BRUSH, GEORGE GAMBLE, was born in Oxford township, Chester county, Pennsylvania, on the 10th of August, 1793. He was apprenticed in 1809 to William Hensel, of Lancaster city, to learn the carpenter business, and served four and a half years in his employ. In 1814 he removed to Manor township, Lancaster county, to a small village on the Susquehanna river, which had sprung up during the war of 1812–14. In this village he worked at his trade until 1820, when he began the mercantile business. About this time a post-office was established in Manor township, and he was appointed Postmaster by President Monroe, and held this position under the administrations of Monroe, Adams, Jackson and Van Buren. In 1827 the borough of Washington was incorporated, and Mr. Brush was elected a member of the first Town Council. On the adoption of the Common School System by Manor township, he was elected a school director for three successive terms. In 1841, having been elected a justice of the peace, he resigned the Postmastership. In 1846 he removed to a small farm in Manor township, where he has since continued to reside. In the fall of 1855 he was elected a member of the State Legislature, and served as such during the session of 1856. On the chartering of the Lancaster County Bank, in 1841, he was elected a member of the first Board of Directors, and has served in that capacity up to the present time.

BUCHANAN, JAMES, 15th President of the United States, was born in Franklin county, Pennsylvania, April 23, 1791. The place of his birth is situated about three miles from the village of Mercersburg, and in the midst of a wild and romantic mountain gorge, which, with its beautiful scenery, may have served to arouse in his youthful mind, sentiments of lofty aspirations and fervent patriotism. His father, James Buchanan, was a native of the county of Donegal, Ireland, and was one of the early settlers of Franklin county, having emigrated thither in the year 1783. His mother, Elizabeth Speer, was the daughter of a respectable farmer of Adams county, Pennsylvania. His father was a man of great enterprise and industry, and speedily rose from the condition of an humble emigrant to one of independence and prominence in the community. The mother of Mr. Buchanan was a woman of remarkable native intellect, and although not possessed of more than an ordinary English education, yet she was distinguished for her masculine sense and rare literary taste. The most striking passages in Pope, Cowper, Milton and Shakespeare, she could repeat from memory.

In 1798 the father of Mr. Buchanan removed with his family to Mercersburg, and there the subject of our notice received his first lessons in Greek and Latin. His more than ordinary rapid progress in his studies, indicated to his preceptors a mind of rare strength and vigor; and his father, accepting the suggestions of his teachers, determined to afford him the advantages of a collegiate education. At the age of fourteen, accordingly, he entered Dickinson College, at Carlisle, then a Presbyterian institution, under the presidency of Dr. Davidson. Here he at once took rank amongst the most indefatigable students, and rapidly rose in the estimation of his teachers as a young man of mark and great promise. In the studies of his classes he outstripped all his mates, and on no occasion was he found unprepared in his recitations. Whilst always prepared with his lessons, he was by no means what is known as a close student, but rather ranked with those who indulged most freely in sport and relaxation. His college tasks were no burden to him, being acquired as if by intuition; and his vigorous mind displayed itself in every department. He enjoyed all the honors of the literary society with which he was connected, and was presented by its unanimous vote to the faculty for the highest collegiate honors. He graduated in 1809, at the age of eighteen.

In December of the same year, he commenced the study of law in the office of James Hopkins, Esq., of Lancaster, then recognized as the leading lawyer of that bar. He was admitted to the practice of the profession, November 17th, 1812, when but little over twenty-one years of age. From the day of his admission a tide of success seemed to meet him; and until he retired from the profession his was a series of successive triumphs. There, perhaps, was never an instance of such a rapid rise in the legal profession as that afforded in his case. When a lawyer of four years' standing, he was selected to conduct, unaided by senior counsel, the defense of a distinguished judge, who was tried on articles of impeachment before the Senate of Pennsylvania. His defense on this occasion was a masterly display of legal acumen and forensic ability that at once gave him a State-wide reputation, and ranked him as an intellect fit to cope with the ablest men of the nation. His reputation was fixed in that trial, and business poured in upon him with an increasing flood. So successful was he in his legal business, that by the time he was forty years of age, he had acquired a sufficient independence that enabled him to retire from the profession. During the tide of his practice his name occurs oftener in the Reports of the State than that of any other lawyer of his time.

Mr. Buchanan early displayed his patriotism and love of country. During the progress of the war between Great Britain and America, in 1812–14, the British had taken and destroyed the public buildings at Washington. This act aroused a feeling of indignation throughout the whole United States: A public meeting was held at Lancaster in favor of a vigorous prosecution of the war, which was addressed by Mr. Buchanan, and he was the first to enroll his name as a private soldier in a company raised upon the spot, and which, commanded by Capt. Henry Shippen, marched to the defence of Baltimore. In this company Mr. Buchanan served until the same was honorably discharged.

He was, in October, 1814, elected a member of the lower House of the State Legislature, and in that body maintained the same fearless and patriotic course that distinguished him throughout the war. When Philadelphia was threatened with invasion, and the State was left to its own defence, he urged upon the Legislature in the strongest manner, the adoption of efficient measures of relief. The National Treasury was at this time almost bankrupt, and on account of the opposition which the war encountered in the Eastern States, on the part of the Federalists, (of which party Mr. Buchanan was then a member), the soldiers in the public service were with great difficulty paid. Being re-elected to the Legislature, in 1815, he ardently supported a bill appropriating the sum of $300,000, as a loan to the United States, to pay the militia and volunteers of the State in the government service.

At this time Mr. Buchanan took ground against any unjust discrimination against naturalized foreigners, as compared with the native-born population, except that which relates to the office of the National Executive. The Governors of Massachusetts and Connecticut had transmitted to the Governor of Pennsylvania certain resolutions, recommending changes in the Federal Constitution, and among the rest, one which should render naturalized foreigners ineligible to the Senate or House of Representatives of the United States. This proposition was strongly disapproved of by Mr. Buchanan, and the position thus early assumed by him formed one of his cardinal and life-long principles. It was during the period of his second session in the Legislature, that he became impressed with the danger, the inexpediency, and the unconstitutionality of a United States Bank, an opinion he ever afterwards steadfastly defended.

The next political step in the career of Mr. Buchânan, is his election, in 1820, as a member of the lower House of the National Congress, in which body he took his seat in December, 1821. At the time he entered that body, an array of talent was assembled that would grace the halls of any nation. In the House were the distinguished names of McDuffie, Joel R. Poinsett, John Randolph, Philip R. Barbour, Andrew Stevenson, Louis McLane, and others equally noted. In the Senate, Rufus King, Martin Van Buren, Mahlon Dickinson, Samuel L. Southard, Nathaniel Macon, Richard M. Johnson, and others of equal ability were assembled. Among this assemblage of noble Romans, Mr. Buchanan took rank at once as one of the most industrious and indefatigable members of the House. He was always in his seat, and generally participated in the discussions that arose upon any important public question. His first elaborate speech, delivered January 11th, 1822, was upon a bill making appropriations to the military for deficiencies in the Indian department. So ably did he defend the course of Mr. Crawford, then Secretary of the Treasury, that the *National Intelligencer* departed from its usual course and gave a verbatim report of the speech. This speech at once enrolled him amongst the ablest men of the House, gave him a national reputation, and was an earnest of the future distinction that awaited him.

While Mr. Buchanan was strict in the expenditure of the national money, he was liberal where necessity was evident. When some members of Congress found fault with a bill authorizing the relief of soldiers disabled in the revolutionary war, he met the opposition with the remark, that the amount proposed "was a scanty pittance for the war-worn soldier," and that he was altogether disinclined to oppose a measure that patriotism so imperatively demanded. Other things that early engaged his attention as a national legislator, and upon which he made speeches, were the Apportionment bill, Transactions in Florida, the Appropriation bill, and the Bankrupt bill. The debate upon this latter bill was long and animated, and one that called forth the abilities of the House in a remarkable manner. Many of the most distinguished members of that body were strong advocates of the bill. Mr. Buchanan did not participate in the discussion until near the close of the session, and just before the bill came up for final reading. He then delivered, March 12th, 1822, one of the most powerful and eloquent speeches of the session, and in this took grounds against the passage of so unjust a law, as he conceived. In this he said: " We are now called upon to decide the fate of a measure of awful importance. The most dreadful responsibility rests upon us. We are not now to determine merely whether a bankrupt law shall be extended to the trading classes of the community, but whether it shall embrace every citizen of the Union, and spread its demoralizing influence over the whole surface of society." Immediately after this speech the vote was taken and the bill was defeated.

The question of a tariff was a prominent one before the Eighteenth Congress, and was championed by the dauntless Clay, of Kentucky, who christened it with the captivating name of the " American System." In the discussions on this question, which took place in Congress, we find Mr. Buchanan arrayed on the side of a protective policy, and giving utterance to sentiments that would not have met the approbation of the partisans with whom he afterwards affiliated. We find him thus expressing himself: " But, after all, Mr. Chairman, what do we ask by this bill for the manufacturers of iron? Not a prohibitory law, as the gentleman from Massachusetts (Mr. Fuller) seems to suppose, which will exclude foreign iron from our market. We wish only to infuse into our own manufactures sufficient vigor to enable them to struggle against foreign competition. Protection, not prohibition, is our object." Benton's Abridgment of Debates, Vol. VII, p. 673.

In 1827 he again said: " Can any person really believe that because I supported protection in 1824 I am bound to advocate prohibition in 1827." Benton's Abridgment of Debates, Vol. IX, p. 394.

In 1825, when the election of a President took place before the lower House of Congress, Mr. Buchanan urged that it should be conducted in the presence of the people, with the galleries of the House open to the people, and not in secret conclave, as was urged by some members and Senators. He was opposed to the Panama mission, a project that had been conceived by Mr. Clay, and supported by his flowing eloquence. In the second session of the nineteenth Congress a bill was introduced for the relief of the surviving officers of the revolution, and this Mr. Buchanan sustained in a speech of great eloquence and power, in which he triumphantly vindicated the duty of government in providing for the wants of its defenders.

About this time Mr. Buchanan took occasion to condemn, in Congress, the attiring of our foreign ministers in a military coat, covered with glittering gold lace, and decking them with a chapeau and small sword. Thus early did he give evidence of his republican sentiments; and afterwards, during his residence as Minister at the Court of St. James, he appeared, like Dr. Franklin before him, in the simple and unpretending garb of an American citizen.

In 1828 General Andrew Jackson was elected President of the United States, and Mr. Buchanan aided in this result to the extent of his ability. The majority of 50,000, which

Pennsylvania gave for Jackson, furnishes evidence of the efficiency of his support. He, himself, was re-elected to Congress in the same campaign, and during the following session was placed at the head of the Judiciary Committee, a position that had been filled by Daniel Webster. One of the most famed cases that had ever came before Congress, the impeachment of J. H. Peck, Judge of the District Court of the United States for Missouri, was one in the management of which Mr. Buchanan acted a conspicuous part, and secured himself a national reputation as a barrister of the first order. He, with Henry R. Storrs, of New York, Geo. McDuffie, of South Carolina, Ambrose Spencer, of New York, and Charles Wickliffe, of Kentucky, were chosen on the part of the House, as managers to conduct the prosecution before the Senate. William Wirt and Jonathan Meredith were for the defence. The trial was conducted on both sides with distinguished ability, Mr. Buchanan closing the case and confining himself to the legal and constitutional questions involved. He, in a masterly manner, pointed out the difference between the principles which govern English courts and those which, under the Constitution, must govern those of the United States. The Senate acquitted Judge Peck by a vote of 22 to 21, but shortly afterwards an act was passed obviating whatever technical objections stood in the way of conviction, so that no judge afterwards ventured to commit a similar offence.

On the 3rd of March, 1831, Mr. Buchanan voluntarily retired from Congress, of which he had been a constant member for ten years. He was soon afterwards selected, by President Jackson, as minister to the Court of St. Petersburg. In this position he concluded the first commercial treaty between the United States and Russia, which secured to our merchantmen and navigators important privileges in the Baltic and Black seas. In 1833, upon his return from Russia, he was elected to a seat in the United States Senate, taking his seat in that body December 15th, 1834.

The subject of negro slavery came before the Senate in 1835, from the reference, in the message of General Jackson, in regard to the circulation through the United States mail, of incendiary publications designed to excite insurrection in the Southern States, and upon memorials for the abolition of slavery in the District of Columbia. This aspect of the slavery question was a new one before Congress. How, most judiciously to deal with it, was the question to be decided. Mr. Buchanan saw, that if the question was permitted to come constantly before Congress, it would keep up throughout a never-ceasing agitation, which might, in the end, endanger the stability and perpetuity of the American Union. He, therefore, conceived as the best method to deal with it, that some legislation should be enacted that might stifle the agitation in the bud and prevent the question of slavery from being raised and discussed in that body. He favored the receiving of the petitions or memorials for the abolition of slavery in the District of Columbia, and then declaring, after respectfully considering them, that Congress had no power to legislate on the subject. "I repeat," said he, "that I intended to make as strong a motion in this case as the circumstances would justify. It is necessary that we should use every constitutional effort to suppress the agitation which now disturbs the land. This is necessary as much for the happiness and future prospects of the slave as for the security of the master. Before this storm began to rise, the laws in regard to slaves had been really ameliorated by the slaveholding States; they enjoyed many privileges which were unknown in former times. In some of the slave States prospective and gradual emancipation was publicly and seriously discussed. But now, thanks to the efforts of the abolitionists, the slaves have been deprived of these privileges, and while the liberty of the Union is endangered, their prospects of final emancipation is delayed to an indefinite period. *To leave this question where the Constitution has left it, to the slaveholding States themselves, is equally dictated by a humane regard for the slaves as well as for their masters.*"

About this time Texas was passing through its war of independence, and Santa Anna, the President of Mexico, was using all his efforts to reduce it again beneath his authority. Mr. Buchanan sympathized, as an American, with the struggling Texans, and urged its recognition on the part of the United States as an independent government. He afterwards favored the admission of Texas as one of the States of the American Confederacy.

Towards the close of Gen. Jackson's administration, the French indemnity question rose to one of the first magnitude. The French Chamber of Deputies, by a majority of eight votes, refused to sanction the recommendation of Louis Philippe, who had advised the payment of the American indemnity. This conduct on the part of the French, roused Gen. Jackson to the highest pitch of intensity, and he thereupon demanded an appropriation of $3,000,000 for the increase of the navy and for the defence of the maritime frontier. Mr. Buchanan supported the demand of the President in an able speech, and reviewed the whole ground of difficulty between France and the United States, and clearly established, by the law of nations, the error into which the French government had fallen; and that the money being justly owing to American citizens, it was incumbent upon the government to see that they received their dues. The decided stand taken by President Jackson on French affairs, and the noble support accorded him by Mr. Buchanan and other leading men of the nation, hastened the settlement of the troublesome question.

One of the most important subjects that came before this Congress, was the admission of Michigan and Arkansas into the Union. The subject gave rise to much debate, in all of which Mr. Buchanan bore a conspicuous and distinguished part. It was objected to the admission of Michigan that aliens had participated in the formation of the Constitution; but Mr. Buchanan took the ground that aliens who were residents of the northwestern territory had a right, by virtue of the ordinance of 1787, to exercise the elective franchise. In this discussion Mr. Buchanan made use of the following language : " *The older I grow, the more I am inclined to be what is called a State-rights man.* The peace and security of of this Union depend upon giving to the Constitution a literal and fair construction, such as would be placed upon it by a plain and intelligent man, and not by ingenious constructions to increase the powers of this government, and thereby diminish those of the States. The rights of the States, reserved to them by that instrument, ought ever to be sacred. If, then, the Constitution leaves them to decide according to their own discretion, unrestricted and unlimited, who shall be electors, it follows as a necessary consequence that they may, if they think proper, confer upon resident aliens the right of voting."

Mr. Buchanan was early in his advocacy of specie payments by the general government, instead of depreciated bank paper. In this he went hand-in-hand with Thomas H. Benton, the Ajax of American Democracy. He depicted, in forcible language, the evils that flow from the increase of banking capital to the laboring man, and, indeed, to all classes save the speculators. "Banks," he said, "could make money plenty at one time and scarce at another; at one moment nominally raise the price of all property beyond its real value, and the next moment reduce it below that standard, and thus prove most ruinous to the best interests of the people. The increase of banking capital was calculated to transfer the wealth and property of the country from the honest, industrious and unsuspecting classes of society, into the hands of speculators, who knew when to purchase and when to sell."

Upon the opening of the Twenty-fourth Congress, December 5th, 1836, Mr. Buchanan was chosen to the honorable and responsible position of chairman of the Committee of Foreign Relations. The principal feature of this session was the discussion of Mr. Benton's celebrated " Expunging Resolution," which the indomitable Senator from Missouri had introduced, time after time, for the purpose of having expunged from the journal of the Senate the stain which had been affixed upon General Jackson, for his removal of the deposits from the United States Bank. In this noble effort he had the coöperation of Mr. Buchanan, who, in a speech of masterly power, and of rich and graceful eloquence, defended the hero of Orleans from all unjust aspersion, and proved, by the most convincing logic, that an imperative justice demanded of the American Senate that it erase from its records the base brand of obloquy that had been stamped upon the conduct of the National Executive. His oration upon this occasion has always been considered as one of the finest specimens of eloquence that was ever witnessed upon the floor of the United States Senate. Immediately after the delivery of Mr. Buchanan's speech, the vote on the "Expunging Resolution" was taken, and the odious record stricken from the journal of the Senate.

Martin Van Buren succeeded General Jackson, as President, March 4th, 1837. It was a time of great financial distress; greater, if possible, than that of 1820–21, which followed the war of 1812–14. The general flooding of the country with excessive issues of paper currency had stimulated one of those periods of general speculation which had covered the land with universal desolation. The President summoned an extra session of Congress, in order that measures might be devised to remedy the pressure of the financial crisis. Almost the first bill introduced was the "Sub-Treasury Act." Mr. Buchanan favored the passage of the bill in a speech of great power, and therein explained the causes of the monetary embarrassment in a most profound and statesmanlike manner, and presented a clear conception of the power of the General Government in regard to the question under consideration. His views upon this measure were of the most matured character, and his clear exposition of the powers of government aided greatly in securing the passage of the bill.

In the regular session of 1837, the relations of the American government with Mexico came under consideration. In the course of a debate upon this subject, Mr. Buchanan traced the conduct of the Mexican government towards our citizens, and showed that the American flag was no protection to them, and that after being insulted and robbed, no satisfaction or apology was given. In reply to Mr. Clay, who suggested that owing to our deranged state of the currency we had better avoid war, he indignantly replied: "If the national honor demanded vindication, he would not be deterred by any such consideration. He, for one, would not consent to see American citizens plundered with impunity."

The question of the preëmption right of settlers came up
in the Senate about this time, and Mr. Buchanan defended
this right, and was unwilling that any distinction should be
made between American settlers and those of foreign birth.
It was, as he conceived, a just right that should be accorded
to the hardy pioneers, whether native citizens or those who
braved tide and tempest, in order to seek a home in the
wilds of our western country.

Another important question arose under Van Buren's
administration, in regard to the alleged interference of federal
officers in elections. A bill was introduced which proposed
penalties upon any officer of the United States government,
below the rank of a District Attorney, who should attempt
to persuade a citizen to vote for any person to be elector
of President and Vice President of the United States or for
other certain officers. This measure was opposed by Mr.
Buchanan with all the powers of his mind, and it was soon
thereafter abandoned.

The last Congress, under Mr. Van Buren's administration,
commenced its first session December 2nd, 1839. It proved
a very important session, as business of an interesting character engaged the attention of Congress. On the bill introduced by Silas Wright, of New York, "to more effectually
secure the public money in the hands of the officers and
agents of the government," long and violent discussion was
had. It was the call for marshaling the old warriors of
bank and anti-bank. The contest was again terrific and was
another Trojan struggle renewed.

Mr. Buchanan's speech on the Independent Treasury, of
the 22nd of January, 1840, was able, dignified and profound.
It is considered as containing the best synopsis of the science
of political economy, and the relation between capital and
labor that any American statesman had yet produced. At
least it had never been surpassed. At the period of the delivery of this speech, Mr. Buchanan had been familiar with
the working of the government for twenty years. He had
passed through financial revulsions before, and having
studied the effect of extravagant bank expansions, he was
able to place his finger upon the errors of the past, and like

a skillful mariner, direct how to avoid the shoals and quicksands that might lie in the future. It was out of this speech of Mr. Buchanan's, on the Independent Treasury, that his enemies gathered material which served to fasten upon him the charge of having advocated a reduction of the wages of labor. No charge was ever more unjust. John Davis, Senator of Massachusetts, was foremost amongst those who pursued him with this accusation. The manner, however, in which he defended himself from the justness of this charge, upon the floor of the United States Senate, in reply to Senator Davis, and the rejoinders he administered to the latter, are not yet forgotten by the older of our citizens.

The election of 1840 swept, as by a hurricane, the Democratic party from power. General Harrison was elected President of the United States, and the Whig party had the ascendancy in both houses of Congress. Almost immediately after his election, the new President issued a proclamation for Congress to meet in extra session, May 31st, 1841. Congress met, but Harrison was already in his grave. The first movement was the introduction of a bill for the repeal of the Independent Treasury. Early in the same session Mr. Clay presented his plan of a "Fiscal Bank." The Democracy, though in the minority, fought the friends of the bank again, but in vain would have been their resistance but for the assistance of Vice President John Tyler, now President, who came to their rescue. In opposition to Clay's "Fiscal Bank," Mr. Buchanan made one of his great speeches, and reiterated his constitutional objections to the establishment of a National Bank.

The repeated vetoes of John Tyler of the favorite measures of the Whig party, so exasperated the leaders, that Mr. Clay introduced a proposition to abolish the veto power, conferred upon the President by the Constitution. On the 2nd of February, 1842, Mr. Buchanan made an elaborate reply to Mr. Clay's proposition, reviewing our whole system of government and showing the intimate relations existing between its parts. This logical and profound speech manifested on the part of Mr. Buchanan an accurate knowledge of the fundamental laws and maxims of civil government.

The most important feature of Mr. Tyler's administration consisted in the steps taken for the annexation of Texas. As heretofore stated, Mr. Buchanan was one of the earliest advocates of that measure. In his remarks upon this subject he said: " While the annexation of Texas would afford that security to the Southern and Southwestern slave States which they have a right to demand, it would, in some respects, operate prejudicially upon their immediate pecuniary interests ; but to the Middle and Western, and more especially to the New England States, it would be a source of unmixed prosperity. It would extend their commerce, promote their manufactures and increase their wealth. The New England States resisted with all their power the acquisition of Louisiana ; and I ask, what would those States have been at this day without that territory ? They will also resist the annexation of Texas with similar energy ; although, after it has been acquired, it is they who will reap the chief pecuniary advantages from the acquisition." The admission of Texas was not consummated until after the election of James K. Polk to the Presidency.

The election of 1844 again brought the Democratic party into power. James K. Polk, as soon as he was inaugurated President, selected for the responsible position of Secretary of State, the man whose career we are sketching, James Buchanan. So intimately connected were the actions of Mr. Buchanan and the administration of President Polk, that full justice could not be done the former otherwise than in a complete history of that administration. He was the acknowledged head of the Cabinet Council, and nothing of importance was undertaken without his sanction being had and approbation obtained. Of the many able State papers of which he was author during his premiership, time and space forbid our speaking. At the close of Mr. Polk's administration, he retired to private life, at Wheatland.

Mr. Buchanan, although now basking in the shades of rural life, was by no means an indifferent spectator of public affairs. He still continued to watch the current of political opinions with the same eager eye as ever, and discussed public questions with his friends with the same warmth as in his younger years. After the passage of the compromise measures of 1850, Mr. Buchanan was among the first to endorse them, and to spread throughout Pennsylvania a public sentiment in their favor. In a letter written by him in November, 1850, to a public meeting in Philadelphia, he expressed himself freely upon the compromise, and gave it his full and unqualified approbation.

Franklin Pierce, of New Hampshire, was elected President of the United States in the autumn of 1852. Upon his taking the presidential chair, in March following, one of his first acts was the appointment of Mr. Buchanan as Minister to England. One of the principal questions that engaged his attention in London, was the Central American question, which the Clayton-Bulwer treaty had complicated but not settled. He was also one of the Ministers who conferred together at Ostend, regarding the Island of Cuba, and the result of the deliberations of which Conference has popularly been known as the *Ostend Manifesto.*

The question of slavery was one which James Buchanan ever viewed from a conservative stand-point. From the time he first presented in Congress the petition from the Caln quarterly meeting of Friends, till his death, he regarded the subject of slavery as one over which the National Government had no legitimate control, viewing it as within the sole jurisdiction of the States in which the institution had existence. These views he proclaimed when he presented in Congress the above petition to which allusion has been made, and this conservative attitude he ever afterwards maintained, and which was in unison with the sentiments of the framers of the constitution and the principal statesmen of the old Democratic and Whig parties.

Mr. Buchanan was one of those statesmen who regarded the question of slavery as one that existed by virtue of compromise, and he desired to see nothing done to violate the compacts of faith that had been solemnly ratified between the Northern and Southern sections of the Union. The Compromise measures of 1850 had his hearty adhesion, as in these he seemed to recognize the settlement of the only question that could, perhaps for ages, jeopard the national

10

integrity.   With the greatest anxiety and dread, was it therefore that he heard, whilst in Europe, of the repeal of the
Missouri Compromise in 1854.   In a letter written to a leading statesman of his party, about the time that the repeal
began to be mooted, he uttered solemn words of warning,
and strongly remonstrated against the abrogation of this
time-honored compact.   He depicted in strong colors the
dangers that he apprehended would result, should this unwise
attempt be consummated.   From an intimate knowledge of
the feelings of the people of the North, he predicted the
terrible storm that would be excited throughout the country
by such an opening up of the slavery agitation as this would
occasion.

But the admonitions of Mr. Buchanan were unheeded.
The Kansas-Nebraska act was passed by Congress on the
25th of May, and received the signature of President Pierce
on the 30th of the same month.   The windows of slavery
agitation were thereby all opened. as he had predicted, and
the deluge that began to pour upon the land was frightful
and terrific.   The anti-slavery press of the Northern States
teemed full of abuse of the men who had dared in the glare
of the light and advancement of the nineteenth century, to
attempt to favor the cause of slavery ; for in no other aspect
could the action of the National Congress be viewed.   It
seemed in their eyes an unholy effort to turn back the dial
of the age, and an effort to open up all the territory of the
west to the abomination of slavery.   The storm of abolitionism thus aroused, blew and gathered strength by distance, and the strong oaks of the Democratic party were
bending beneath its blasts.

In the midst of this vast hurricane of partisan fury, the
Democratic Convention assembled at Cincinnati in 1856,
and placed in nomination James Buchanan as their candidate
for the presidency.   By skillful management, the old party
of Jefferson, in the face of all opposition was again victorious,
and its nominee, the subject of our notice, was elected.   On
the 4th of March, 1857, he was inaugurated the 15th President of the United States.

After the repeal of the Missouri Compromise, the Territory of Kansas became the battle-ground between the anti-slavery and pro-slavery parties. Emigrants were hurried into the territory by both parties, each aiming at gaining the ascendancy within its borders; the one party seeking to make it a free and the other a slave State. The one persistently contended that slavery was local in its character, and therefore if a slaveholder brought his slaves with him these became instantly free. The other, quite as strongly maintained that slavery was recognized by the constitution, and therefore the owner of slaves had the same right to carry his slaves with him into the territory as any other property. Without this right the Southern people insisted that the equality of the States would be destroyed, and they would sink from the rank of equals to that of inferiors. In this view the pro-slavery party were sustained by the solemn adjudication of the Supreme Court. They yielded acquiescence in the territorial government appointed over them by Congress; whereas, the anti-slavery party having held a convention at Topeka, formed a State constitution and applied for admittance into the Union. They were, however, rejected. The regular Territorial Legislature, on the 27th of February, 1857, passed an act for the election of delegates in June of that year to frame a State constitution.

This was the condition of affairs in Kansas when Mr. Buchanan was inaugurated President, on the 4th of March, 1857. A majority of the pro-slavery delegates were elected in June, 1857, because the anti-slavery party refused to participate in the election. When the convention assembled, they adopted what was known as the Lecompton Constitution; and as slavery was the main question at variance between the parties, it was determined that this should be submitted to a vote of the people of the State. It was so submitted in December of that year, and the anti-slavery party, still persisting in their refusal to vote, the result was 6226 votes in favor of slavery, and but 569 against it. At the election held on the first Monday in January, 1858, under the new constitution, the anti-slavery party voting, a large majority of the members of the Legislature elected, belonged to this party. On the 30th of January, of the same year, the Lecompton Constitution was transmitted to Mr. Buchanan, as the National Executive, from the president of the convention, with the request that it be submitted to the consideration of Congress. This was done in a message of the 2nd of February, 1858, and therein President Buchanan recommended the admission of Kansas as a State, under the Lecompton Constitution. He said : "The people of Kansas have in their own way and in strict accordance with the organic act, framed a Constitution and State Government; have submitted the all-important question of slavery to the people, and have elected a governor, a member to represent them in Congress, members of the State Legislature and other State officers. * * * For my own part, I am decidedly in favor of its admission, and thus terminating the Kansas question."

This message occasioned a long, exciting and violent debate, in both Houses of Congress, between the slavery and anti-slavery members, which lasted nearly three months. It was but the reëcho of the storm that was raging throughout the land. Mr. Buchanan was bitterly denounced as truckling to the slave power, and as lending the weight of his high office towards fixing upon the people of Kansas the curse of slavery against their will. Members of Congress were classified, during this controversy, as Lecompton and anti-Lecompton, as they favored or opposed the admission of Kansas. A wing of his own party separated from Mr. Buchanan on this point, and among these Stephen A. Douglas, of Illinois. Kansas was not admitted under this Lecompton Constitution, and was only admitted a short time before the close of Mr. Buchanan's administration, with a free constitution.

But events were gradually culminating during Mr. Buchanan's administration towards a catastrophe of one kind or another. The slavery question was now the one all paramount. All other questions merged into insignificance, and it is only in the light of the slavery agitation of the period that his administration is estimated. No other act of his as President is ever remembered, and from that standpoint alone will he ever be judged. In the midst, however, of the terrible commotion of the period, it soon became clear that even in the ranks of the Democratic party a schism, in fact, existed, and but time was required to develop it. This was also occasioned by the slavery question, and by many was considered as occasioned by an effort to compromise on the question. Senator Douglas became prominent as the advocate of what he chose to term squatter sovereignty, but which principle found no sanction in the decision of the Supreme Court in the Dred Scott case. His arguments were, however, very captivating and attractive, and he succeeded in carrying with him a large body of the Democratic party. To this interpretation of the Constitution the Southern people were almost equally hostile as towards the out-and-out principles of the Republican party. They simply regarded Senator Douglas as bidding for the Presidency before the abolition sentiment of the North, and therefore they bore him an unquenchable ill-will and steady opposition.

When the Democratic convention met at Charleston, in April, 1860, it was not long till the want of harmony in the party showed itself in the representative body. An attempt was made to agree upon a platform of principles, but without effect, and therefore the withdrawal of the delegates from the cotton States was the consequence of this disagreement. The convention adjourned to meet at Baltimore, in the hope of yet securing harmony in the actions of that body. It re-assembled in June, at Baltimore, but without any better success than at Charleston. The breach had become too great and could not be remedied. Both wings of the party nominated their candidates, Stephen A. Douglas being the nominee of the one, and John C. Breckinridge of the other. The sympathies of Mr. Buchanan were with the wing of the party that nominated Breckinridge, but no hopes of success could be anticipated by either, and the result was the election of Abraham Lincoln as President.

As soon as the election of Abraham Lincoln was made known, the Southern people prepared to inaugurate the movement of secession. The first to secede were the cotton States, and on the 4th of March, 1861, these organized a government at Montgomery, Alabama, with Jefferson Davis as President. The people of the Southern States had long harbored the belief that the Republican party alone would be unable to prevent a dissolution of the Union, because they did not believe that the Democrats of the North would give their adhesion to the prosecution of a war for the restoration of the Union.

It was one of the cardinal principles of the Democratic party, that States could not be coerced by the general government, and one which had been solemnly reiterated again and again in its conventions, and they did not believe that the party could go back of its pledges and resolutions. The Virginia and Kentucky resolutions of 1798, the one sketched by Madison and the other by Jefferson, clearly denied the coercion of States by the general government. These resolutions had ever formed the political bible, as it were, of the Democratic party. Jame Buchanan, however, better understood the tone of the Northern people, and he frequently assured the Southern leaders that the first gun fired upon Fort Sumpter or Moultrie would heal all political divisions in the North, and render it a unit in support of a war for the preservation of the national integrity. He had mingled so long in politics as to have discovered that the promises of most politicians are unreliable, and therefore was it that he uttered his cautions to those who depended upon aid from the Northern States.

As to the doctrine of coercion, he clearly laid down the correct principle of the party in his last annual message to Congress. In this he says : " The question fairly stated is : has the constitution delegated to Congress the power to coerce a State into submission, which is attempting to withdraw or has actually withdrawn from the Confederacy ? If answered in the affirmative, it must be on the principle that power has been conferred upon Congress to make war against a State. After much serious reflection, I have arrived at the conclusion that no such power has been delegated to Congress, or to any other department of the Federal Government. It is manifest, upon an inspection of the constitution, that this is not among the specific and enumerated powers granted to Congress ; and it is equally apparent, that its exercise is not 'necessary and proper for carrying into execution' any one of these powers. So far from this power having been delegated to Congress, it was expressly refused by the convention which framed the constitution.

" It appears from the proceedings of that body, that on the 31st of May, 1787, the clause 'authorizing an exertion of the force of the whole against a delinquent State' came up for consideration. Mr. Madison opposed it in a brief but powerful speech, upon which I shall extract but a single sentence. He observed : ' The use of force against a State would look more like a declaration of war than an infliction of punishment, and would, probably, be considered by the party attacked as a dissolution of all previous compacts by which it might be bound.' Upon his motion the clause was unanimously postponed, and was never, I believe, again presented. Soon afterwards, on the 8th of June, 1787, when incidentally adverting to the subject, he said : ' Any government for the United States, formed upon the supposed practicability of using force against the unconstitutional proceedings of the States, would prove as visionary and fallacious as the government of Congress,' evidently meaning the then existing Congress of the old Confederation."

The above was the old Democratic doctrine, and when he had given utterance to it, if he believed it, he should have maintained it. But so great at that time was the popular clamor in favor of coercion, that in his special message to Congress of the 8th of January, 1861, he attempts to evade the above, and draws the distinction between coercing a State and the individuals of the State. A weak distinction, indeed. What is the State but the individuals who compose it? If no authority was delegated to the general government to coerce a State, whence is the authority derived to coerce the individuals of the State, the very ones who form a State? In this backing down of Mr. Buchanan from the position first assumed· by him, he exhibited a weakness not creditable to one who filled the exalted position of the Presidency of a nation. If his doctrine as regarded coercion was true, it remained so, though all the North should declare the contrary. Then why not maintain it? Though its maintenance should have been pronounced treason, and death the penalty, he of all others should have defended it. Many brave men before had suffered for opinion ·sake, and did they sink in history on that account? They were only the more remembered and respected for their heroism and staunch defence of principle.

Mr. Buchanan repeatedly asked of Congress additional authority to enable him to collect the duty in the Southern ports, where all the federal officers had resigned, but to this Congress gave no attention. At least the additional authority was not granted. His condition as President at that time was a very trying and perplexing one. Elected as a Democrat, upon principles that always gave satisfaction to the people of the Southern States, it is not to be supposed that he would desire to fight with the South the battle of the Republican party. The genuine Democratic party and the South had no quarrel; and James Buchanan, belonging to that school, had none either. Should he provoke a war with the South during the remnant of his term of office? Surely not. He and his party had done all in their power to avert the calamity then coming upon the country, and were able still to settle the troubles if they had the power. But that had passed from their hands, and it was the new power that the South designed to resist. Not the nation did they mean to resist, but simply the power of the Republican party.

It is no wonder, therefore, if James Buchanan would feel a pleasure in being relieved from an office at a time of such embarrassment. He is said to have remarked to the new President: "If you, sir, feel as happy in entering upon the office of President as I do in retiring therefrom, then you are a happy man to-day."

After the 4th of March, 1861, James Buchanan returned to Lancaster, where he met with a reception befitting his rank and condition, and upon this occasion made his last public address to his fellow-citizens of Lancaster. He reviewed the condition of public affairs at some length, and returned, in conclusion, his warmest thanks for the honors his countrymen had showered upon him. The remainder of his days he passed at his residence, called " *Wheatland*," near Lancaster. During the years he lived in retirement he was frequently visited by his Democratic friends, whom he ever received with great cordiality and friendship. After his retirement he prepared a history of his administration, but did not publish the same until the close of the rebellion. It is entitled, "Buchanan's Administration on the Eve of the Rebellion." In this he essays the task of defending the policy he maintained, especially as regards the slavery question and the rebellion consequent upon its agitation. Of the rectitude of his conduct as regards his attitude on the slavery question, he was ever firmly convinced. In the presence of some friends, after his return from Washington, and after the inauguration of war, he remarked: "Well, gentlemen, I am fully convinced that the American people will yet justify me for the attitude I have maintained as regards the slavery question." Mr. Buchanan enjoyed his usual good health for several years. Even his last illness was short. He died June 1, 1868. His funeral was the largest ever seen in Lancaster.

A sketch of the distinguished subject of our notice would be imperfect unless he would be delineated according to his deserts. As a statesman there is no doubt that Mr. Buchanan is deserving of ranking amongst the ablest to whom America has given birth. The great secret of his success as a statesman, was his sagacity to discover the political current before he too fully committed himself. It was this same trait, however, on the other hand, that has occasioned him more abuse than all else. This was his characteristic timidity, for there is no use in concealing the fact, that Mr. Buchanan was timid to a fault. He was not the bold man who would advance his opinions, let them be popular or otherwise. Had he been a man of that boldness, it is scarcely probable that he would ever have filled the presidential chair; or if he had filled it, his action as President would have commanded more respect than it did.

In private life, even so exceedingly reticent was Mr. Buchanan at all times during the rebellion, that his opinion could not be elicited at any time as to the results of the war.

When an opinion was sought of him, he would usually give an evasive reply, and left it only to be guessed what his real opinion was, and it is doubtful even if his most confidential friends knew whether he favored the prosecution of the war for the restoration of the Union or not. If his sentiments were the same as most of the leading Democrats of his school, he could not have favored what he must have regarded as a violation of the Federal Constitution. Yet if such were his opinions, he chose to conceal them; for otherwise in the inflamed condition of Northern sentiment during the war, he felt that his person and property would have been in jeopardy. Indeed, frequent threats were made against his life, but these were ever regarded as the temporary ebullition of passion that would soon subside. Many were the letters he received denouncing him and threatening vengeance upon his head, but to none of them did he ever give any heed. They may, however, have somewhat more firmly sealed his lips during the rebellion, as during all this period he seemed to be particularly close-mouthed. The great fault of Mr. Buchanan was his extreme timidity, which did not permit him to do sometimes what he desired to do.

As a citizen, Mr. Buchanan had no superiors. He was kind-hearted, generous and humane, and a worthy object would never escape his recognition. He was not one of those who blindly became attached to friends, but he had a universal and sympathetic feeling for mankind. He was regarded by many as cold and phlegmatic, and that he had no regard for friends or enemies. Such was not James Buchanan. Many found fault with him because they had not at his hands received such favors as they had hoped. It was not in his power to favor all his friends, but he did all in that way that he possibly could'; and that he could have done vastly more would have been a great pleasure to him. That he was entirely blameless in all his actions could not be expected. He was human and liable to err, as all are; but that his faults were many, none will contend. He was perfectly honest and upright in all his actions and dealings, and in these particulars he is worthy of imitation by all. But few men live a more irreproachable life than Mr. Buhcanan. He was highly esteemed by men of all parties, and none were so hardy as not to concede him honesty of purpose.

As a lawyer, he ranked amongst the ablest of the whole country; and when engaged in the practice he read little but the books pertaining to his profession. He never was a man of great miscellaneous reading, and save law and politics his knowledge was limited. His extensive intercourse with leading minds and his residences in Europe, had given him a very general information upon all current topics, but he was in no sense either a scholar or a student. His knowledge, which was very considerable, was more what might be called picked-up, than acquired by dint of his own reading. He was an American, fully imbued with American ideas, and he cared little for knowing that which he could not turn to practical account. Indeed, he made no pretensions to scholarship or profundity. He therefore knew nothing of many matters that engage the attention of students who are such from choice. His opinions upon no point except law and politics are therefore to be estimated. He knew much of the world, and for an American, as its society is now constituted, he was the man for the times.

Had he been the stern and outspoken advocate of principle at all times, he would have been left in inglorious obscurity, and would perhaps never have been heard of save in his own county, or at most his State, as a sound, able lawyer. He is simply the production of American life and customs; and what he might have been under another form of government we have no means of estimating. He, however, must remain the type of American statesmen, and other times and regulations, perhaps another form of government, will be required to develop a very different one. That Mr. Buchanan had the ability to achieve distinction in any pursuit, and under any form of government, is readily conceded. His ability was of the very first order, at least in the department of statesmanship.

BUCHANAN, JOHN, was elected a County Commissioner in 1824.

BUCKLEY, DANIEL, was an iron-master of Lancaster

county. He was a member of the Legislature in the years 1794, 1798, 1799 and 1800. He is one of the ancestors of Clement B. Grubb, iron-master, of this city.

BURROWES, THOMAS H., was born in Strasburg, Lancaster county, Pa., November 16th, 1805. He received a liberal education at Quebec and Trinity College, Dublin, Ireland, where his parents resided for some years. Although never matriculated as a regular student of Trinity College, yet he acquired a sound knowledge of the Latin and the French languages, considerable acquaintance with the Greek, and the rudiments of the German. He acquired, however, besides the mere education of a collegiate routine, an enlarged view of the world, and those habits of self-reliance which became to him of more importance than the most scholarly attainments could otherwise have been to him. He became better prepared for the stern battle of American life less by contact with books than by observation of life, from his travels and intercourse with society. Upon returning to Pennsylvania, he chose the law for his profession, and entered, as a student, the office of Amos Ellmaker, of Lancaster, a lawyer of liberal scholarship and of the highest standing at the bar. After reading two and a half years with Mr. Ellmaker, he entered, in 1829, the Yale College Law School, and pursued his legal studies in this institution for some time, and was in the autumn of 1829 admitted to the bar of Lancaster county, and soon after began the practice of law. Being in easy circumstances he did not devote himself to the practice of the profession with that zeal and energy that others of less means are necessitated to employ; but he soon became somewhat active in politics, and in October, 1831, was returned from Lancaster county as a member of the Pennsylvania House of Representatives, and was reëlected in 1832. While a member of the Legislature, owing to his party being in the minority, he did not attain any leading distinction; nor did he seek to render himself particularly conspicuous, but was amongst the most regular in his attendance at his post of duty. Upon the ascent of his party to power in the election of Joseph Ritner, as Governor of Pennsylvania, in 1835, he was called upon to fill the office of the Secretary of the Commonwealth,[1] to which

[1]The State of Pennsylvania, in 1838, was upon the verge of civil convulsion, brought about by a dispute that arose in the city of Philadelphia as regards the election returns of certain aspirants for legislative honors. One party claimed certain members as legally chosen, and their opponents insisted that the opposing candidates had been elected. Two sets of conflicting returns had been made out, and one of these had received the sanction of the Secretary of the Commonwealth and was transmitted to the proper officer. When, therefore, the House of Representatives met at Harrisburg, at 11 o'clock, December 4th, 1838, the Clerk of the old House of Representatives began reading the returns of election for members which had been furnished him by Mr. Burrowes, Secretary of the Commonwealth. As soon as he had reached the returns of the county of Philadelphia, a Mr. Pray (one of the contesting members for the county), arose and handed the Clerk another return, and desired it to be read. Mr. T. S. Smith, another member from Philadelphia, protested against the reading of this return as being illegal and void, and not properly before the House. After some discussion, both returns were allowed to be read, and then the returns for the rest of the State were read without objection. The contestant members from Philadelphia of the opposing political factions being admitted, each party now proceeded to elect a Speaker, the Whigs choosing Thomas S. Cunningham, of Mercer ; and the Democrats, James Hopkins, of Washington. After order became restored, each Speaker proceeded to qualify the member of his own party. After the members of each party had been sworn in, each adjourned to meet the next day.

The Senate was called to order at 3 o'clock, in the midst of much disorder, and after a parlimentary display of partisan tactics, Charles B. Penrose was elected Speaker of the Senate. The public excitement by this time had become intense, owing to a popular impression that a design had been concocted to defeat the election of those fairly entitled to seats in the Legislature. The mass of spectators seemed to believe that the Secretary of the Commonwealth had been tampered with, and that his return was made in the interest of the party with which he was known to be in sympathy.

A Mr. Brown, from Philadelphia, attempted to speak and was called to order as not being a member of the Senate. This excited the populace, and the shout was raised—"hear him," "Brown," "Brown," "you shall hear Brown," and similar outbursts of excitement now rent the halls. All at this moment became excitement and confusion, and a Mr. Rodgers, a member of the Senate, rose and moved that Mr. Brown be permitted to address the Senate. Brown now addressed the Senate, and all the while the tumult was increasing, when Mr. Penrose feeling himself unable to preserve order, yielded the chair to Mr. Rodgers and made his escape. Violent threats were now freely made against Thaddeus Stevens, Penrose and Burrowes, and these gentlemen retired from the assemblage and left their opponents in possession of the field.

The same day, Governor Ritner issued his proclamation, calling upon

the Superintendency of Common Schools was then, *ex officio*, attached. From this time Mr. Burrowes made the work of popular education a subject of the most careful study, and prepared a revised school bill, which was adopted by the Legislature in 1836, and from that time, with great energy, devoted himself to the execution of the law. The years of 1837 and 1838 were periods of much activity in the educational life of Mr. Burrowes. In 1837 he published a plan and drawing for the improvement of school houses and furniture, which was widely used, and which was the first effort of the kind in the State, if not in the Union. In 1839, upon the retirement of Joseph Ritner from the office of Governor, and the coming into power of a different administration, the Superintendency of Common Schools passed into other hands, and Mr. Burrowes returned to Lancaster and devoted the next seven years of his life to agricultural pursuits, on a farm which he owned near the city of Lancaster. He had always been attached, and in his youth somewhat enured to rural affairs, yet he lacked that financial fitness necessary to render the pursuit of hus-

the civil authorities "to exert themselves to restore order to the utmost of their power," and calling upon the military force of the commonwealth to hold themselves "in instant readiness to repair to the seat of government; and upon all good citizens to aid in crushing the lawless mob, and in reinstating the supremacy of the law."

In a day or two, numbers of armed military companies arrived from different sections of the State, and order was speedily restored.

The Senate and the two Houses of Representatives continued to assemble, but without an adjustment of the difficulty being yet effected.

In the meanwhile three members of the Cunningham House of Representatives came into the Hopkins House and took their seats, and desired to be qualified as members of that body. These gentlemen, Messrs. Butler and Sturdivant, of Luzerne, and Montelius, of Union, were sworn and took their seats, and this gave the Hopkins party a legal quorum of the whole number of Representatives.

Mr. Micheler, a Whig Senator from Northampton, on the 25th of December offered a resolution to recognize the Hopkins House of Representatives as containing a quorum of the legally returned members, and this resolution was adopted by 17 voting in the affirmative and 16 in the negative. Several Whig Senators favored the resolution, and thus the difficulty terminated which for a time threatened to drench the land in blood. This period of excitement and tumult has ever since been popularly known as the "*Buckshot War*."

bandry a profitable one. Owing to pecuniary losses, which he about this time sustained, he was compelled to dispose of his farm, and in 1845 he again returned to his profession, in the. city of Lancaster. Immediately afterwards he commenced a series of papers, in the Lancaster *Intelligencer*, on the nature, defects and improvement of the Common School System of the State. These being over his own signature, were made more elaborate than newspaper communications usually are, and went into considerable detail. These articles attracted considerable attention, and were copied or otherwise noticed by papers in different parts of the State, and aided in uniting and directing the public sentiment, then beginning to manifest itself in favor of school improvement.

At the convention of the friends of Education, held at Harrisburg in January, 1850, Mr. Burrowes was chosen temporary President, and acted as chairman of the committee "to consider and report the best means for invigorating the general superintendence of the Common School System, harmonizing its local operations, and spreading the knowledge of its true nature and benefits, its progress and necessities." In the report submitted by him on that occasion, Mr. B. recommended the establishment of a separate State department of education, and the publication of a monthly educational State journal for the dissemination of matters pertaining to the interests of education amongst the friends of the cause in all parts of the Commonwealth. His views met the unanimous endorsement of the convention upon this occasion.

In 1851, a number of teachers, of Lancaster, having met in convention, in the city of Lancaster, chose Mr. Burrowes as their chairman, and measures were adopted for the promotion of a permanent educational association in the county. On this occasion Mr. Burrowes delivered an elaborate address upon the condition of the school system and the duties of teachers, which was printed and largely distributed. At this meeting a resolution was adopted authorizing the President to commence the publication of "a monthly paper devoted exclusively to the spread of information relative to education." This was the origin of the *Pennsylvania School*

Journal, a work that until recently occupied much of the time and attention of Mr. Burrowes, and one that has exercised a very important influence upon the educational affairs of the State. By the act of 1855, the *Pennsylvania School Journal* was made the organ of the school department, and one copy directed to be sent, at the expense of the State, to each school district. In 1854 Mr. Burrowes prepared for the State, descriptive matter for "Pennsylvania School Architecture," a volume of 276 pages. After having written all the important school bills that passed the Legislature after 1836, he crowned this eminent service to the State in 1857, by drafting the Normal School law, which is regarded by its friends as being unsurpassed by any legislation on this subject, either in Europe or America. In February, 1858, the subject of this notice had the honor of being elected Mayor of the city of Lancaster, the duties of which office he discharged for one year. In 1860 he was again called upon to administer the school system of the State; and in 1864 was appointed by Governor Curtin Superintendent of Soldiers' Orphans' Schools, and established these institutions in different parts of the State. In 1869 he was elected President of the Agricultural College, located in Centre county, a position he held until his death. In the latter part of the year 1870 he sold and disposed of his interest in the *Pennsylvania School Journal*, to J. P. Wickersham and J. P. McCaskey. To Mr. Burrowes belongs, we think, fairly, the honor of being entitled the father of the Pennsylvania Free School System. He did more to place it upon a permanent basis than any other citizen of the State, and the present shape that it has been made to occupy is chiefly to be attributed to his studious care and indefatigable management. He was also the author of the "Pennsylvania State Book," a work of much research. Mr. Burrowes died March 25th 1871.

BUYERS, JOHN, a member of the Legislature in the years 1825, 1826 and 1827.

C.

CALDWELL, ANDREW*, was born in Scotland, and emigrated to this country prior to the year 1718. He obtained a warrant for 285 acres of land, which lies on the old Philadelphia road, near the line between Leacock and Salisbury. He was united in marriage in the year 1718 with Ann Stewart. He was a worthy member of the Presbyterian church. It was partly owing to his exertions and assistance that the old Presbyterian meeting-house was first established at Pequea, about the year 1730. He departed this life in the year 1752, and was buried at that place.

*CALDWELL, ANDREW, his son, was born in the year 1722, and was joined in marriage with Isabella Andrews, in the year 1747, and died in the year 1768.

*CALDWELL, ANDREW, his grandson, was born in the year 1748, and in the year 1744 was united in marriage with Ann Buyers, of Salisbury. He died in the year 1825, aged 77 years. His great grandsons, Andrew and William Caldwell, of Salisbury, (who are now far advanced in years), still hold the property. He built the first public house on the old Philadelphia road, called the Hat Tavern, which is standing as a private residence to the present day.

CALDWELL, JAMES A., was engaged in the slate quarrying business, at Peach Bottom. He was elected a member of the State Senate in the year 1837. The senatorial district was at that time composed of the counties of Lancaster and York.

CALDWELL, JAMES, a citizen of Bart township, and a member of the Legislature for the years 1819 and 1828.

*CALDWELL, REV. DAVID, D.D., son of Andrew and Ann Caldwell, was born in Lancaster county, Pennsylvania, in the year 1725. He studied with a Mr. Smith, somewhere in the eastern part of Pennsylvania, who kept a classical school, (and who was probably the father of the Rev. Samuel Stanhope Smith, D.D., afterwards President of the

*Contributed by Isaac Walker, of Sadsbury.

11

College of New Jersey); and for the purpose of accomplishing his object, in the pursuit of knowledge, and in order to complete his studies, which he pursued with much avidity, he relinquished to his younger brothers all claim to any share in his father's estate, on condition that they would furnish him the means to carry him through college, with which proposition they readily complied.

In contemplating the character and tracing the progress of any man who has filled a large share in the public eye, and for a time swayed the destinies of millions, or who has in a more silent and unobtrusive way exerted a salutary and permanent influence over mankind, we feel some gratification in knowing by what reasons he was led to pursue the course which he did, or take any important step in that direction; but in this case we are left to mere conjecture, from which no certain conclusions can be drawn, nor any confirmation of principles derived; but it seems probable that about this time he made a profession of religion. He graduated at the College of New Jersey, in the year 1761, at the age of thirty-six years, and was ordained a minister of the Gospel, at Princeton, the year following, and in the year 1765 was appointed by the Presbytery of Philadelphia to labor as a missionary in the churches of North Carolina, including those of which he soon afterwards became pastor. In visiting the counties lying between the Yadkin and Catawba rivers, as well as in Guilford, he found many from Lancaster county, whom he had known in his youth, and while there he formed, or rather renewed, an acquaintance with Rachel, the third daughter of the Rev. Alexander Craighead, of Mecklenburg, whom he had known in her childhood, in Lancaster county, and they were united in marriage in the year 1766, which had an important bearing on his comfort and usefulness through subsequent life, with whom he lived until his death, and by whom he had eight sons and one daughter, who lived to maturity, and survived him, (besides three or four who died in their infancy), five being born within the space of two years. During the Revolutionary war, part of which time her husband had to conceal himself to save his life, which had been imperiled by the sermons he had preached advocating the Revolution and encouraging the men of his congregations to volunteer in the service of their country. His wife was turned out of the house while it was occupied by British officers, and her only habitation, with her infants, was an old smoke-house, with nothing whatever to subsist upon except a few dried apples and dried peaches, which were found among the rubbish; and in this suffering condition she was treated with great severity and indignity by the inferior officers, until after the battle of Guilford Court-house.

He had been installed pastor of the churches at Buffalo and Alamance, long before the war, and in that station he labored for about sixty years; and in the meantime he labored on his plantation, and ditched and drained the swamps and low lands on his farm with his own hands. The people of his congregations, at the time of their organization, were mostly from his own county of Lancaster, and had removed there before him; many of them had known him from his childhood; they had been taught at the same school and worshipped at the same sanctuary.

A company had been formed in Lancaster and Chester counties, called the Nottingham Company, which sent out their agents and purchased a large area of land, in what is now Guilford county, near the waters of Buffalo and Reedy Fork; and when they were making their arrangements to change their residence, (which was about the time he commenced his education), they made a conditional agreement with him that, if Providence permitted, when he obtained license to preach, he would come out and be their preacher. In connection with the ministry, he established a classical school, and being a thorough scholar himself, many of his scholars became eminent as statesmen, lawyers, judges, physicians and ministers of the Gospel; five of his scholars became Governors of different States, many more became members of Congress, and more than forty ministers were educated, in whole or in part, at his school, which served the Carolinas for many years both before and after the Revolution, as an Academy, College and Theological Seminary. He took an active and leading part in the great struggle for

American Independence, and had to undergo great hardships, suffering and imprisonment, while the British army
was encamped on his plantation, under Cornwallis.

Among the many incidents which have been recorded of
this remarkable man, and the many anecdotes which have
been told concerning him, we may, perhaps, find room for
this one, for the purpose of illustrating the character of the
man, and which called for the exercise of his different qualities. About the time that Cornwallis' army was at one side
of his place and General Greene's forces were passing on the
other side, two of the enemy came to the house of his brother,
Alexander Caldwell, (who was absent with Greene's army),
on a foraging excursion, in the evening about dusk; the
one an officer and the other a common soldier, who commenced acting very rudely, seizing whatever they could
carry away, ordering their suppers, &c. Mrs. Alexander
Caldwell immediately sent over a messenger, requesting the
advice of the Rev. Doctor, who sent her back word that she
must treat them politely and furnish them the best supper
her house could afford, only she must be careful to take
notice where they put their guns, and set the table in the
other end of the house; and in the meantime, he would go
over and conceal himself behind a certain haystack. While
the men were in the other end of the house, demolish-
ing the viands on the table, without fearing any danger, he
went quietly into the other apartment, took up one of their
guns, which was loaded, and stepping to the door of the room
in which they were so comfortably employed, and presenting arms, told them at the same time that if they attempted
to resist or make their escape, that their lives would be forfeited. As neither of them cared to die just at the time,
they surrendered at discretion, and he marched them over to
his own house, where he detained them over night, and in the
morning put them on their parole, by making them take a
solemn oath on the family Bible that they would not again
take up arms against the United States, nor in any way assist the British or the Tories, which promise they kept honorably, and returned to him on the day appointed. After
the war was over, he was chosen a member of the conven-

tion which adopted the Federal Constitution, and also a member of the convention which framed the Constitution of the State of North Carolina; and when the Synod of the Carolinas held its first meeting, which was held at Centre church, in the year 1778, a committee was appointed, consisting of five ministers and five elders, for the purpose of addressing a circular letter to the churches under the care of the Synod, and of this committee the Rev. Dr. Caldwell was appointed chairman. He continued to preach in his congregations until the year 1820, and lived until the 25th of August, 1824, when he bid adieu to earth in the one hundredth year of his age.

CAMERON, JAMES, a brother of Simon Cameron, was born in Maytown, Lancaster county. He was for a time a partner in the Lycoming *Gazette*, and in the year 1829 obtained control of the Lancaster *Sentinel*. In 1839 he was appointed Superintendent of Motive Power on the Columbia Railroad, in room of Andrew Mehaffey. He was in 1843 appointed Deputy Attorney General of the Mayor's Court, in room of S. Humes Porter, resigned. Through various and successive steps, he worked his way in life from orphanage and poverty up to distinction and position in society. He held the position of colonel in the late civil war, and was killed at the first battle of Bull Run. A correspondent, speaking of the repulse of the Union army at Bull Run says: "Col. Cameron, who had repeatedly rallied his men, seemed paralyzed at this new reverse; he dropped his sword from his hand and looked a moment at the retreating mass. Some of his men still fired, and when one of his lieutenants came forward for orders about the wounded soldiers, he turned suddenly towards him, faced the battery, and at the same instant a minie bullet pierced his breast. He fell without a groan. After his fall, the rout became complete, and night saw the disheartened army in full retreat toward Fort Corcoran.

CAMERON, SIMON, was born March 8th, 1799, at Maytown, Lancaster county, Pennsylvania. He traces his descent on the paternal side, from the Camerons of Scotland, who shared their fortunes with the unfortunate Charles Edward, whose star of hope sunk on the field of Culloden. Donald Cameron, his great grandfather, was a participant in that memorable battle, and having escaped the carnage, made his way to America, arriving about 1745-6. He afterwards fought under the gallant Wolfe upon the heights of Abraham. On his maternal side, Simon Cameron is descended from Conrad Pfoutz, one of those sturdy German Protestants whose faith no terrors could conquer. An exile from his native land for conscience' sake, he sought the western wilds, and was for a time the companion of that famed Indian fighter, Capt. Samuel Brady, the history of whose life is more captivating than romance.

When the subject of our sketch was about nine years of age, his parents removed from Lancaster to Northumberland county, and his father dying soon after, he was early cast upon his own exertions. Having an unquenchable fondness for books, young Cameron was able to perceive no other means so likely to satiate his appetite as a printing office, it seeming to him the chief centre of thought in the community in which destiny had fixed his lot. He therefore entered, in 1815, as an apprentice to the printing business in the town of Sunbury, where he continued until 1817. His employer at this time proving unfortunate in a financial aspect, his office was closed, and our apprentice, now being out of employment, was compelled to seek a situation elsewhere. He accordingly made his way, on foot, to Harrisburg, and after considerable disappointment was received as an apprentice in the office of James Peacock, of that place.

On attaining his majority he located at Doylestown, Pennsylvania, and in January, 1821, began the publication of the *Bucks County Messenger*. As editor of this paper he evinced a breadth of information which, in view of his limited advantages, seemed astonishing. In March of the same year he entered into partnership with the publisher of the *Doylestown Democrat*, and the firm merged their papers into the *Bucks County Democrat*, whose publication they continued till the close of the year 1821, when the paper was sold to Gen. W. T. Rogers. Cameron started for Harrisburg, and again obtained employment as a journeyman printer, and the following year we find him in the employ of Messrs. Gales & Seaton, publishers of the *National Intelligencer*, at Washington, D. C.

In 1823 Simon Cameron returned to his native State, and was married to Miss Brua, of Harrisburg. In the same year he became one of the publishers of the *Reporter*, a Democratic paper printed at Harrisburg. He was also elected State printer, and received from Governor Shulze the appointment of Adjutant General of Pennsylvania.

The poor printer was now become a man of mark. His official and business connections introduced him to the leading men of the State, and he soon came to be recognized as one of the shrewdest business men of the whole country. His utilitarian character now unfolded itself, and shortly afterwards he obtained a leading position in the financial institutions with which he was connected."

He early became conspicuous in the public improvement enterprises of the State; and the projection of the Harrisburg, Mt. Joy and Lancaster Railroad, is the excogitation of his brain. His energy and ability vastly contributed towards the completion of this public enterprise. In recognition of his efficiency in this particular, he was chosen President of the road. The Lebanon Valley Railroad was another monument of his sagacity and foresight. The Northern Central Railroad, from Harrisburg to Sunbury, was another of his developed conceptions, which, with the Tide Water Canal and other improvements, are sufficient to give him a front rank amongst the useful and enterprising citizens of the commonwealth.

In 1845, after the inauguration of James K. Polk, the position of Secretary of State was tendered to James Buchanan, then one of the United State Senators from Pennsylvania in Congress. A successor was to be chosen to fill Buchanan's place in the Senate. Simon Cameron was the man who, at this time, in recognized sympathy with the Democratic party, was selected for this position as the representative of the wing of the party which favored the policy of a protective tariff. George W. Woodward was, however, the caucus nominee of the Democrats; this party being at the time strongly in the majority. The Whigs consented to unite their strength upon Cameron, because of his known tariff sympathies. By the union, therefore, of the Whigs and a part of the Democrats, the subject of our sketch was elected to the United States Senate.

In 1857 General Cameron was again a candidate for the United States Senate, and succeeded in being elected over John W. Forney, then universally conceded as one of the shrewdest Democratic politicians in Pennsylvania.

Upon the election of Abraham Lincoln, in the year 1860, the distant sound of an approaching storm became instantly audible in the southern horizon. As soon as the new President assumed the helm of state, on the 4th of March, 1861, and began to look around him for those in whom he should repose his counsels in the troubled state of the nation, he tendered the port-folio of the war department to the subject of our sketch. General Cameron became Secretary of War at a period when all the signs of the times indicated an unprecedented hurricane upon the American continent. It came with the bombardment of Fort Sumpter, on the morning of the 12th of April, 1861, and immediately the bugle-blasts of war arose, both North and South, and the period which followed required of the War Secretary a coolness, sagacity and vigor of will, that the exigencies of the nation had never before demanded. General Cameron at once evinced his appreciation of the magnitude of the difficulties to be encountered, and showed a determination of resistance that the crisis required. In accordance with his plans, an army was soon organized, and the Northern States were placed upon a military footing that amply shielded and assured the perpetuity of the Federal Union. The position was, however, a perplexing one for even the steadiest nerves, and our Secretary retired from the post in January, 1862, and was appointed to the important diplomatic position of Minister to Russia.

In 1867 General Cameron was, for the third time, elected to the United States Senate, a position he still continues to fill.

As a politician, General Cameron ranks as one of the most

shrewd and sagacious in the United States; and for years has been recognized as exerting a powerful influence in the political machinery of the nation. His devotion to his friends knows no bounds; and hence, in a great measure, flows his great strength as a leader in the workings of politics. From this cause is it that he has been able to attach to his interests men of both political parties; and those enrolling themselves under his standard are not forgotten when victory perches upon his banners.

CARPENTER, ABRAHAM, was a citizen of Strasburg township, and an influential and leading man of his time. He was a farmer. He was a member of the Legislature in the years 1790, 1791, 1792, 1793, 1795, 1796 and 1797. He was elected a member of the State Senate in the year 1798. He died March 4th, 1815, in the 57th year of his age.

CARPENTER, CHARLES, was a member of the Legislature in the years 1842 and 1843.

CARPENTER, CHRISTIAN, was elected Sheriff of Lancaster county in 1799. He was the father of William Carpenter, late Prothonotary of the county, who was elected in 1857. Wm. Carpenter has for many years been the leading scrivener and conveyancer of Lancaster city.

CARPENTER, EDWARD, was born in Lancaster county, and emigrated to the northwestern territory about the year 1800. In 1802 he was chosen a member of the Ohio Convention that framed the State Constitution. Afterwards he was appointed a Judge of the Court of Common Pleas of Fairfield county, Ohio, and held this position for several years. He filled many minor positions, and all with great acceptability. He died March 20th, 1822, in the 79th year of his age.

CARPENTER, EMANUEL, was a member of the Legislature in the years 1755, 1756, 1757, 1758, 1759, 1760, 1761, 1762, 1763, 1764, 1765, 1766, 1767, 1768, 1769, 1770 and 1771. He was for many years a Justice of the Peace, and President of the Justices' County Court, a position he held up to his death, in 1780. He was the grandfather of Emanuel C. Reigart. The following shows the manner in which his public services were appreciated by his fellow-citizens :

To Emanuel Carpenter, esq., late one of the Representatives in the Assembly for the County of Lancaster :

SIR : The burgesses, assistants, &c., of the borough of Lancaster met this day, at the request of a number of the reputable inhabitants of the borough, and being sensible of your services as one of the Representatives for the county of Lancaster in the General Assembly of the Province, these seventeen years past, have directed that the thanks of the corporation be offered to you, with the assurance of their approbation of your steady and uniform conduct in that station. And, as you have declined serving your country in that capacity, I am charged to mention, that it is the earnest wish of the inhabitants of Lancaster that you may be continued in the commission of the peace and a judge in our county, where you have so long presided, and deservedly acquired and supported the character of an upright and impartial magistrate, &c.

By order of the Burgesses and Assistants.

[Signed,]   CASPER SHAFFNER, Town Clerk.
Lancaster, October 3, 1772.

CARPENTER, EMANUEL, JR., was a member of the Legislature in the years 1777, 1780, 1784, 1785 and 1786.

CARPENTER, HENRY, a Commissioner of Lancaster county, elected in 1823.

CARPENTER, DR. HENRY, was a leading and prominent physician of Lancaster county. He lived near Lampeter, and established a large botanical garden, into which he introduced a fine assortment of rare and costly plants that were exotics in this section of country.

CARPENTER, DR. HENRY, was born December 10th, 1819, in Lancaster, in the same house he now occupies. His father was named Henry, and he is the great grandson of Heinrich Zimmerman (Carpenter), the first founder of the numerous Carpenter family in Lancaster county. His education was obtained in the select schools of the city, and afterwards he went to the Lancaster County Academy. He read medicine in the office of Dr. Samuel Humes, and began the practice of medicine in March, 1841. He immediately obtained a handsome practice in the profession. He was one of the founders of the Lancaster County Medical Society, in 1844, and its first Secretary, a position he held for several years. In 1855 he was elected President of the Society.

He has been Secretary and Vice President of the State Medical Society, and is now one of the Board of Censors for the Eastern district of Pennsylvania. He was President of the Select Branch of City Councils for nearly twenty years, and has been an active and influential member of the Lancaster School Board for about sixteen years. For many years he has served as one of the directors of the Lancaster Gas Company, and also of the Lancaster County Insurance Company. He has, for a long time, been a director of the Conestoga Steam Mills Company, and since their sale, in 1857, one of the principal owners. He was one of the firm that built No. 4 cotton mill. He was one of the originators of the Conestoga Turnpike Company, and its President since the organization.

He is one of the principal physicians of the city of Lancaster, and enjoys a large and very lucrative practice. He was the chosen physician of the late James Buchanan, Thaddeus Stevens, Col. Reah Frazer, and others of our leading citizens.

CARPENTER, JACOB, a member of the Legislature for the years 1765, 1766, 1767, 1769, 1772 and 1781.

CARPENTER, JACOB, was elected three times Treasurer of Pennsylvania. He was appointed January 13th, 1800, by Governor McKean, Clerk of the Orphans' Court of Lancaster county. He died February 13th, 1803, in the 36th year of his age.

CARPENTER, JOEL, a member of the Legislature in the years 1814 and 1815.

CARPENTER, DR. JOHN, also a leading physician of the county. He lived near Earlville, and his services in his professional line were sought for by persons from a great distance. He lies buried in the old Carpenter graveyard, near Earlville.

CARPENTER, MICHAEL, son of Samuel Carpenter, was born September 22nd, 1796, in Warwick township, Lancaster county, Pennsylvania. He removed with his father to Lancaster, in 1807, and learned the business of a turner. Becoming involved in speculative enterprises in which he met with heavy losses, he turned his attention to the writing of deeds and other instruments of legal transactions; in a word, he became a scrivener. In this career he seemed to have found the business for which he was best fitted; and in the year 1843 he was elected Mayor of the city of Lancaster, and by successive reëlections continued to fill this office up to 1852.

In stature, unlike his father, he was not corpulent, but rather of a spare build. He was of a feeble rather than of a robust constitution. In disposition he was kind and gentle, yet grave and serene in his demeanor. He was a man of a high order of integrity and moral worth, and a devoted and humble Christian. He was of industrious and steady habits, and devoted himself sedulously and constantly to business until overtaken by disease (pulmonary consumption), which caused his death, August 5th, 1861.

CARPENTER, SAMUEL, was born November 11th, 1765, in Lancaster county Pennsylvania. He was brought up to the business of agriculture, which he followed for many years, and up to April 1807, when he removed to Lancaster for the purpose of having better opportunities for the education of his children. Here he engaged for some years in the business of inn-keeping; Lancaster at the time being the seat of the State government, and a great resort for strangers from all parts of the State. He was appointed an Alderman, and not long thereafter was elected Mayor of the city of Lancaster, a position to which he was frequently reëlected.

In appearance he was not tall, but of medium height and quite corpulent. He made an excellent magistrate, being possessed of strong native sense, and a clear understanding of right and wrong. His opinions of law were remarkably accurate. In conversation he was affable and exceedingly friendly, and he enjoyed the high esteem of all who knew him.

CARTER, RICHARD, was one of the early settlers of Warwick township. He was a native of Warwickshire, England, and emigrated to Lancaster county at an early day. It was through his influence that Warwick township was named in honor of his native county in England. He died

July 9th, 1750, aged 81 years. He lies buried at the Union Meeting House, in Warwick township.

CASSEL FAMILY. The first family of Cassels emigrated to this country, from Hesse Cassel, Germany, about the year 1680, and settled at Germantown, near Philadelphia, then a small town; at this place the Mennonites, of which the Cassel family were members, had a church and regular preaching. An incident occurred about this period going to show, in a very striking manner, the simplicity of the church at this time. A letter came from Europe to the Cassels that a large legacy was left them by the death of a relative, amounting to nearly a million of dollars, and that they should send out and get the treasure. A church council was called and the matter freely discussed, when it was decided by a unanimous vote not to receive the money, as it would have a tendency to make them proud. Simplicity of manner, plainness of dress, frugality, honesty and economy were some of the characteristics of this people. Abraham Cassel, with an elder brother, heard that there was fine land in Lancaster county, and about the year 1750 these two emigrated to this county and located near Sporting Hill, in Rapho township, then a wild wilderness. Their fortune consisted of a good axe, strong constitution, and a firm and determined purpose. Trees were soon felled to the ground, and a log house erected on the banks of the Back run, where there was a good meadow, well adapted for grazing and raising stock. Here Abraham Cassel, the second, was born; and on the 18th of April, 1775, was married to Esther Weiss, and from this union the following children were born: Henry Cassel, March 12th, 1776; Maria Cassel, December 13th, 1779; Abraham Cassel, December 14th, 1782.

Henry Cassel, the oldest son, located at Marietta, where he was one of the leading men, and greatly instrumental in building up that town. He was President of the old Marietta Bank. He built the house now occupied by Mr. Watt, then one of the most costly buildings in the county. He had three children; the youngest, A. N. Cassel, who was a member of the Legislature in the years 1838 and 1839, and is now one of the wealthiest and most honored citizens of Marietta.

Maria, the second child, was married to a man named Kauffman, and located near Manheim, in Penn township; they had two children. Abraham, the only son, has been one of the leading men of the county for many years.

Abraham Cassel, the youngest of these three children, owned and conducted a farm in Rapho township, the old homestead. He was a man of very marked character, and a sound and practical thinker. He served in several public positions, and was a director of the poor of Lancaster county. His family consisted of three sons and two daughters. The oldest son, Dr. John H. Cassel, studied medicine with Dr. Washington L. Atlee, and afterwards located at Pittsburg, where he was highly respected. Emanuel Cassel, the second son, is a farmer and resides near Mt. Joy, greatly esteemed by his neighbors for his generosity and kindness of heart. The only living daughter is Hetty Ann, married to John K. Barr. They reside near Salunga. Jacob E. Cassel, the youngest son, was born January 22nd, 1822. He was elected a member of the Legislature in October, 1859. Upon the breaking out of the rebellion he enlisted as a private in Hambright's 79th regiment, P. V., but arriving in camp, he was appointed to the position of Quartermaster, which he held up to October 9th, 1862, when he was captured by the enemy. Upon his release, infirm health induced him to retire from the army.

CASSIDY, DR. PATRICK, was born September 22d, 1810, in Butler county, Ohio, where his early life was passed. While a young man, he spent some time engaged in teaching school. In 1835 he removed to the city of Lancaster, and soon entered upon the practice of his profession. He long maintained the rank of one of the most skillful physicians of the county of Lancaster. During all his lifetime he was a student, and ever awake to all discoveries and improvement in the science of medicine. He kept himself informed as to the invention of new surgical instruments as they made their appearance, or to any new method of treating disease which promised more effectually to relieve suffering or preserve life, thus proving a true physician instead of a mere fossil in the profession. " The older I grow," he once remarked, " the less medicine I prescribe. I have long made it the careful rule of my practice, to give absolutely as little medicine as possible."

Dr. Cassidy was one of the most efficient and active members of the School Board of Lancaster city, and he spent considerable sums of money in the purchase of books on the art and science of teaching. He labored in this sphere out of an abiding love for the system of popular education. He was the Republican candidate for Mayor of the city of Lancaster, in 1862 and 1863, but owing to the popularity of his competitor, was defeated. He died in the year 1864.

CHAMBERS, STEPHEN, was a leading lawyer in his day, and was admitted to the bar in 1780. He was a delegate to the convention in 1787, which ratified, on the part of Pennsylvania, the Federal Constitution. He was killed in a duel which he fought with Dr. Reger.

CHAMPNEYS, BENJAMIN, was born in Cumberland county, in New Jersey. His ancestors came up the Delaware before Penn's Charter, with John Fenwick, the grantee of the province of West New Jersey, and landed at Salem. One of these ancestors, Edward Champneys, was Fenwick's son-in-law, and aided William Penn in establishing a proper and just government, and was instrumental in settling a controversy between the proprietary and Byllinge, who had a large interest in the lands of the province. The father of Benjamin Champneys, an only son, spent his early life and was educated in Philadelphia, graduated at the University, and sailed from that port in the "Philadelphia" as a surgeon under Commodore Stephen Decatur.

The subject of this notice was placed under a tutor at nine years of age, and remained under instruction for several years; subsequently, he entered the Sophomore class at Princeton, where he remained till the decease of his father. He then entered the office of Chief Justice Ewing, of New Jersey, and remained there for six months; and at the suggestion of his guardian, Colonel Potter, of Philadelphia, he removed to Lancaster. He became a law student of George B. Porter, esq., and, after three years of study, was admitted to the bar. He soon established himself in his profession and secured for himself a lucrative practice. In the autumn of 1825 he was nominated by the Democratic party and elected a member of the House of Representatives. He was again elected in the year 1828, and discharged the duties of both sessions with credit to himself and to the satisfaction of his constituents.

In 1839 he was appointed by Governor Porter, President Judge of the Courts of Lancaster county, and discharged the duties of this office for three years and a half. While yet judge, he was nominated by the Democratic Convention of Lancaster county for the office of State Senator, and thereupon tendered his resignation of the President Judgeship, to take effect before the election. He was elected Senator in 1842, and served the usual term of three years. Before the expiration of his Senatorial term, he was appointed Attorney General of the Commonwealth, by Governor Shunk, and held this office until the decease of the Governor.

Benjamin Champneys acted with the Democratic party up to the breaking out of the Southern rebellion, when he ranged himself on the side of those who favored a vigorous prosecution of the war for the suppression of the rebellion, and thus became identified with the Republican party, with which he afterwards acted. In 1862 he was nominated by the Republican party and elected to the House of Representatives, and in 1863 was nominated and elected to to the State Senate. He discharged the duties of these positions with a conscientious regard for what, in his opinion, duty required of him. Since the termination of his official career as a State Senator, he was engaged in no active business.

Benjamin Champneys long ranked as one of the leading lawyers of the Lancaster bar, and for many years the amount of legal business transacted by him was, perhaps, surpassed by no member of the bar in the county. He, indeed, ranked amongst the ablest of his profession in Pennsylvania. He died August 9th, 1871, aged 71 years.

CLARK, BRICE, a native of the county of Derry, Ireland, emigrated to America and first settled in New Castle, Delaware. He moved thence to Leacock, Lancaster county, and afterwards to East Donegal. He was elected a member of the Legislature in the year 1794. He died in 1819.

CLARK, ROBERT, a member of the Legislature in the year 1784.

CLARK, THOMAS, an Associate Judge of Lancaster county, appointed in 1813.

CLARKSON, REV. JOSEPH, was born in Philadelphia, and was the son of Dr. Gerardus Clarkson, a prominent physician of that city, and an influential member of the Protestant Episcopal Church. During the early part of the revolutionary war Mr. Clarkson attended a classical school, then of great repute, kept by Dr. Robert Smith, a Presbyterian clergyman, in Lancaster county, Pa. He graduated at the University of Pennsylvania in 1782, and received the degree of Master of Arts from the College of New Jersey, 1785.

Having studied for the ministry he was admitted to Deacon's Orders in 1789, being the first ordained by Bishop White after his return from England, whither he had gone for consecration. During that year he acted as Secretary to the House of Bishops and began his ministry in Philadelphia, removing thence in about three years to Wilmington, Delaware, where he officiated in the Old Swede's Church until 1799. In April of that year he accepted a call to St. James' Church, Lancaster, Pa., where he remained until the time of his death, January 25, 1830. He was a man well beloved by his parishioners, and had during his long life a very peaceful ministry. His remains lie in St. James' churchyard.

*CLEMSON FAMILY. The Clemson family were amongst the most worthy pioneers who opened up the wilderness north of the Gap mountain and the valley of the Pequea, (now Salisbury township), and they were also among the most eminent members of the Society of Friends, at the time that the old Sadsbury meeting was first established, in the year 1724.

James Clemson, the first, emigrated from Birmingham, England, near the close of the seventeenth century, having embraced the doctrines of the Friends. He purchased 636 acres of land in the valley of the Pequea, on which he

*Contributed by Isaac Walker, of Sadsbury.

12

settled. His warrant bears date the 18th of May, 1716. He left three sons and three daughters, viz: James, John and Thomas; Hannah, (married to Joseph Haynes), Mary, (married to Henry Gest), and Rebecca Clemson. He died in the year 1730, and his lands were divided among his sons. James Clemson, the second, purchased 200 acres of his father's tract, from his brothers and sisters, in the year 1731, on which he erected a three-storied stone dwelling house, lately occupied by his great great grandson, Davis Clemson, now deceased, and which is the oldest residence now standing in Salisbury township. He was for many years a public speaker and a worthy member of society, and his name frequently appears on the records of Sadsbury meeting. In the year 1740 James Clemson and Anthony Shaw were appointed representatives from Sadsbury, to represent that monthly meeting in the quarterly meeting of Friends, at Old Chester.

His son, James Clemson, the third, was born in Lancaster county, in the year 1727, and in 1749 was joined in marriage with Margaret, daughter of Stephen Heard, of Sadsbury. He was an early advocate of American independence, and was commissioned a Justice of the Peace before the Revolution. He was elected a delegate to a general county convention in the year 1774, to take into consideration the resolves of the Continental Congress, and the question being put, for or against resistance to British tyranny, James Clemson, John Whitehill, of Leacock, and Robert Bailey, of Sadsbury, voted in the affirmative. On the 5th of January, 1775, he was elected to represent Lancaster county in the Provincial Convention, at Philadelphia. He was also appointed on the committee of observation and inspection for Lancaster, for the year 1775.*

He was a member of the Legislature of Pennsylvania in the years 1777, 1778 and 1779. He was appointed and commissioned a Justice of the Peace and of the Common Pleas, in and for the county of Lancaster, upon a return made according to law, from the district composed of the townships of Sadsbury and Salisbury, in said county, in 1790. He had two sons, James and John, and seven daughters, all

*Rupp's History of Lancaster county, pp. 384 and 389.

of whom were intermarried into the most wealthy and respectable families of the county. His son, James Clemson, the fourth, served for many years as Justice of the Peace in Salisbury; also, his grandson, the late well-known and highly respected James Clemson, esq., the fifth, served in the same capacity. It was an old saying, that "the Clemsons always keep one squire in the family." His great grandson, James Clemson, the sixth, is now an extensive cattle dealer in the city of Philadelphia, and his descendants in the county are both numerous and respectable, and among their number we find the McCauleys, the McCauslands, the Samples, the Skiles', the Ellmakers, the Hendersons, the Buckleys, the Watsons, of Donegal; the Pattersons, of Mount Joy; the McNeils, and the Buyers, of Salisbury; Isaac Atlee, the son of Col. Atlee; the Whitehills, the Bakers, and many of the most respectable families in Lancaster and Chester counties. Thomas Clemson (or William), the grandson of John Clemson, (and brother of the Rev. Baker Clemson), was an eminent chemist, and was married to a daughter of the distinguished statesman John C. Calhoun, of South Carolina. Davis Clemson, the grandson of Judge Clemson, until his death occupied the old homestead, which was erected by his great great grandfather, about the year 1735.

CLINTON, Joseph, was born February 18th, 1800, in Lampeter township, Lancaster county, Pennsylvania. His father was of English descent, and his mother of German. His education was very limited indeed, he having picked up by degrees all the information by means of which he has been enabled to pass through life. He first learned the hatting business in Lancaster, and worked at the same for near forty years. During part of this time he lived at New Holland and thence moved to Elizabethtown, Lancaster county, Pennsylvania. On the 20th of December, 1824, he married Parmelia, daughter of John and Margaret Diffenderffer, of New Holland. In the fall of 1854 he was elected to the office of Clerk of the Orphans' Court, and discharged the duties of the same for three years. He was, in 1850, appointed Deputy Marshal for taking the census of part of Lancaster county.

COCHRAN, RICHARD E., M. D., was born at Bohemia Manor, near Middletown, New Castle county, Delaware, on the 9th day of September, A. D. 1785. His father, descended of Scotch-Irish stock from the north of Ireland, was a farmer and land-owner in comfortable circumstances. The son, after passing his earlier years engaged in agricultural pursuits on his father's farm, obtained an education, including an acquaintance with the Latin and Greek languages, at an academy at Newark, Delaware; and choosing the medical profession as his pursuit in life, took his degree as doctor of medicine at the University of Pennsylvania, from a board of professors, including Rush, Wistar, Dorsey, Physick and other distinguished men, in the year 1810 or 1811. He commenced practice at Middletown, Delaware; but having married in May, 1812, moved to Wilmington, Delaware, in 1813, and there engaged in mercantile pursuits, during the then pending war with Great Britain, during which he volunteered in the military service on the approach of the foe. In 1817, after his father's death, he became the owner of part of his landed estate, and removed to his place, called Somerton, near Middletown, where he resumed and continued the practice of his profession until May, 1824. In the meantime he took an active part in political life, on the side of the old Democratic party, and besides other mere local positions, was twice, in the years 1822 and 1823, elected a member of the House of Representatives of his native State. In May, 1824, he removed with his family to Columbia, Lancaster county, and there continued in an almost unbroken prosecution of professional labor during the remainder of his life. In 1836 he was nominated and elected a Representative delegate from the county, to the convention called to propose amendments to the constitution of the State, and attended the sessions of that body at Harrisburg and Philadelphia in 1837–38. Besides other duties, he discharged those of chairman of the committee to revise and adjust the several sections of the constitution after the amendments had been agreed upon. His life was closed on the 1st day of September, 1854, when he had nearly attained the 69th year of his age, by an attack of the disease called Asiatic Cholera, which at the time raged in that borough, and of which he was one of the earliest victims, as he had visited professionally and with characteristic fearlessness and devotion the first sufferers. He was a ruling elder, and in that character attended many of the judicatories of the Presbyterian church, whose communion he had joined before he left his native State, and remained in until death.

COCHRAN, LIEUTENANT RICHARD E., JR., was the third son of Richard E. Cochran, M. D., and was born on the 16th day of November, 1817, at Somerton, New Castle county, Delaware. His boyhood and youth passed quietly, and in atttendance upon school in his father's family, in Delaware, and after his removal at Columbia, until the year 1838, when he sought and obtained a commission as Second Lieutenant in the army of the United States, and was assigned to the fourth regiment of infantry. In this service he was ordered first to Florida, and afterwards to the western border in Arkansas, and the territory partly now within the State of Kansas, and among the Indian tribes. When the war with Mexico commenced, in 1846, he joined with his regiment the forces under the command of General Zachary Taylor, in Texas. On their march to the Rio Grande, he took part in the battle at Palo Alto, on the 8th of May, 1846, and was slain the next day in the battle of Resaca de la Palma, sword in hand entering the captured entrenchments of the defeated Mexicans. His body was first interred near the scene of his death, but was afterwards brought home by his father and brothers, and placed for final interment in the cemetery at Columbia, attended by a large military and civic procession. A monument was erected over his grave by the citizens of the town, who honored his patriotism and courage, and remembered his kind and genial conduct and disposition while his early years were passed in their midst. He was married and left a widow and daughter to survive him.

COCHRAN, THEODORE D., was the fourth son of Richard E. Cochran, M. D., and was born at Somerton, Delaware, on the 18th day of January, 1821. Brought by his father to Columbia, he passed his boyhood and youth there, going to school and obtaining a knowledge of the art of printing.

In 1840 he became and continued to be for some time, the editor of the *Old Guard*, then published at Lancaster, and then and afterwards wrote largely for the newspaper press, especially the Columbia *Spy* and York *Republican*. In 1847, the country being then engaged in war with Mexico, he entered the military service and received a commission as Lieutenant in the regular line, being attached to the regiment known as Voltiguers. He marched from Vera Cruz in the force commanded by General Cadwallader, taking part in all its contests and in the subsequent battles around Mexico, conspicuously those of Molino del Rey and Chapultepec. He remained there in the service until the forces of the United States were withdrawn from Mexico at the declaration of peace, and the regiment was disbanded. Previously to that time, his fellow citizens of Lancaster county elected him one of their representatives in the State Legislature, in which he served them during the sessions of 1844 and 1845. He was residing at York when the Southern rebellion broke out in 1861, and, although still suffering from the effects of hurts and disease incurred in the Mexican war, he commenced at an early day to raise a company, which he commanded in a three months tour of duty, and after its close took a commission in a regiment of regular forces, but was compelled by ill health to retire from the service. After a lingering and painful illness he died at the residence of his oldest brother, Thomas E. Cochran, at York, on the 26th day of July, 1863, and his body is interred in Prospect Hill Cemetery, adjoining that borough.

COLEMAN, EDWARD, son of Robert Coleman, was one of the wealthiest and most enterprising citizens of Lancaster in his day, and it was chiefly owing to his enterprise that the Conestoga navigation was made a success. He stood high amongst his fellow citizens, and was honored with numerous public trusts. He was elected a member of the Legislature in the years 1818 and 1819. In 1820 he was chosen to a seat in the State Senate of Pennsylvania, and reëlected to a second term in the same body. A public dinner was given him by the citizens in 1827, before his departure for Europe in that year.

COLEMAN, ROBERT, emigrated from Ireland and came to Lancaster county, and found employment with Peter Grubb, the proprietor of Hopewell forge. The following incident introduced him, as the story goes, to Grubb's favorable notice: One of his fellow employees desiring an order to be written, asked Coleman to write it, and when Grubb saw the order he inquired who wrote it, and being told that it was a man by the name of Coleman, he immediately sent for him and ordered him to be entered as his book-keeper at £100 per year, Pennsylvania currency. Afterwards, when the Elizabeth furnace was sold as the property of Baron Steigel, and was carried on by a company, Coleman was employed as its manager. It was not long till he obtained a share in the furnace, and finally came to possess the whole interest of the same. He became in short, by his energy and perseverance, the most successful iron-master in Lancaster county; and to untiring industry and judicious management, he united the utmost probity and regularity in his dealings. To him is Lancaster county chiefly indebted for the celebrity it acquired from the number and magnitude of its iron works and the excellence of its manufacture. He married a daughter of Robert Old. He was elected a member of the Legislature in 1783, and was one of the associate judges of Lancaster county for about 20 years.

COATES, KERSEY, son of Lindley Coates, was for some time a teacher in the Lancaster high school, afterwards studied law with Hon. Thaddeus Stevens. He moved west about 1856, was Colonel of the 77th regiment of Missouri militia during the rebellion, and was afterwards elected President of the Missouri River, Fort Scott and Gulf Railroad. He now resides in Kansas City, Missouri.

COATES, LINDLEY, was born in Caln township, Chester county, Pa., March 3d, 1794. He married Deborah Simmons, and removed to Sadsbury township, Lancaster county, in the spring of 1820. Lindley Coates was one of nature's noblemen. He was possessed of remarkable natural talents, was an able debater, and a bold and fearless advocate in the cause of the emancipation of the Southern slaves. He was appointed a manager for Lancaster county at the first organization of the Anti-slavery Society, in Philadelphia, December 5th, 1833. He was chosen a member of the Reform Convention of Pennsylvania which was held in 1838. He died June 3d, 1856.

COLLINS, CORNELIUS, one of the early setlers of Colerain township, emigrated from Ireland, and took up land in both Colerain and Drumore townships. He was a farmer and a member of the Associate Reformed Church.

COLLINS, CORNELIUS, son of James Collins, was born July 14th, 1795. He has always been engaged in the avocation of his forefathers, that of agriculture. He was a Director of the Poor during the years 1831, 1832 and 1833. He has been an elder and trustee of the Middle Octoraro church for upwards of forty-five years. He was, without any solicitation on his part, elected to the Legislature in 1836, and reëlected in 1837 as a member of the old Whig party. He has never been an aspirant for public positions.

Mr. Collins belonged to the old style of politicians, being nominated as a candidate for the Legislature whilst following his plow. He is in his sentiments entirely liberal and charitable, and has never been known to attempt to dictate to men under his control for whom they shall vote. He always permits men to exercise their own judgment. As a man he is honest and upright, and has ever maintained an irreproachable reputation.

COLLINS, JAMES, son of Cornelius Collins, was born in Colerain township, and was for a time a private in the American army during the Revolution. He was an intelligent, enterprising and influential citizen, and an elder of the Associate Reformed Church, at Octoraro.

COLLINS, ORESTES, appointed President Judge of the several courts of Lancaster county, in 1836.

COLLINS, THOMAS C., also son of James Collins, is a farmer and an active and influential man in his locality. He was elected County Auditor, and was, in 1863, elected one of the Commissioners of Lancaster county.

[1]COPE, CALEB, was born in Chester county, Pa., in the

[1]Major Andre (then Captain Andre) was captured at St. John's, Upper Canada, on the 3d of November, 1775, by General Montgomery,

year 1736, and removed when a young man to the borough of Lancaster, where he became an influential and leading citizen. He was one of the first surveyors and regulators of the streets appointed for the borough of Lancaster, in 1774. In September of the same year he was elected second Burgess of the borough, and reëlected to the same position in the year 1775. He died in Philadelphia, May 30th, 1824.

CONYNGHAM, REDMOND, was a native of the city of Philadelphia, and was a graduate of Princeton College, New Jersey. He inherited from his paternal grandfather an estate of £2,000 per annum, in the county of Donegal, Ireland, where he spent several years of his early life. Whilst in Ireland he was the companion of Curran, Grattan, and other bright intellects of Hibernian soil. Amongst the most

and with other British officers sent to Lancaster, Pa., as a prisoner of war. Caleb Cope, being a member of the Society of Friends, a non-combatant, was not of those who were fierce in their resistance to the pretensions of the British Crown. Public feeling being greatly inflamed against the prisoners, and the landlords of the borough refusing to entertain them, Mr. Cope extended the prisoners the hospitalities of his house. This act required no small degree of moral courage upon the part of Mr. Cope; and, as a consequence, so embittered the citizens against him that they beat in the windows of his dwelling, which, in the disturbance, accidentally caught fire and was burned. In after years the citizens of Lancaster liberally assisted the unfortunate owner in the reërection of his dwelling.

Major Andre was a skillful painter, and had a great taste for the fine arts. His manners were gentlemanly, and his education and accomplishments procured him admittance to the social gatherings of the elite of Lancaster of that day. Under his instructions the celebrated Dr. Benjamin S. Barton, then a youth, received his first lessons in the art of sketching, and he became no mean draughtsman. His descendants yet preserve specimens of Andre's skill, some of which are of singular merit. One of Mr. Cope's sons had a strong natural taste for painting, and he soon became a favorite of Andre's; so much so that he constantly pressed the father to place the lad in his charge, and suffer him to be brought up to the art. On one occasion he urged that he was anxious to go back to England, but could not do so without a reasonable excuse for quitting the army; that he had now an offer to purchase his commission; and that with this boy to look after, a fair pretext for returning home would be afforded. But the father was inflexible, and in March, 1776, the master and pupil were separated, the former being sent to Carlisle. A correspondence was, however, kept up between Mr. Cope and himself for some time.—*Record of the Cope Family*, pp. 32–3. *Life of Andre*, by Sergeant, p. 89.

brilliant of these was his cousin, Wm. Conyngham Plunket, afterwards Lord Chancellor of Ireland, and who was named after Mr. Conyngham's grandfather.

Mr. Conyngham lived some years in Luzerne county, and whilst a citizen of that county had the honor to represent it for some time in the Legislature. He removed to Lancaster county, Pennsylvania, where he spent the balance of his days. He was married to a daughter of Jasper Yeates, Judge of the Supreme Court of Pennsylvania. He died June 16th, 1846, in the 65th year of his age.

Mr. Conyngham was a great reader, a finished scholar, and evinced an especial fondness for antiquarian research; his contributions to the Historical Society of Pennsylvania, and to the American Philosophical Society, of both of which he was a member, rank him as an explorer of no ordinary measure. His papers are valuable contributions to the historical and philosophical domain of our literature. He wrote much on the early history of Pennsylvania, and the aborigines of Lancaster county. His death was announced in the rooms of the American Philosophical Society by Bishop Potter, who pronounced an eloquent eulogium upon the deceased, and a resolution was passed requesting the Bishop, at a future day, to deliver an address before them on his life and character.

In his deportment Mr. Conyngham was an entire gentleman, and exceedingly interesting and entertaining as a social companion. He was the warm friend of all public enterprises looking towards the melioration and advancement of society. In worthy young men he always took great interest, and especially in those preparing themselves for the christian ministry. He was a great friend of Sabbath schools. As a member of the Protestant Episcopal church, he was frequently a lay delegate to its Diocesan conventions. The church in Paradise, this county, is in a good degree a monument of his liberality and zeal.

Mrs. Elizabeth Conyngham, wife of the above, and a lady of great benevolence, survived her husband many years. She died August 3rd, 1867, at the advanced age of 90 years.

COOKE, SAMUEL, a member of the Legislature in the years

1801, 1802 and 1803. He was a citizen of Donegal township, and died March 6th, 1804. He was an early abolitionist, as the following from his will indicates: "*Item*—Having hired out my black man Bob to Samuel Evans, it is my will that immediately on the expiration of the term for which he is hired, he, the said Bob, shall be set free. *Item*—It is my will that within one month after my decease, my negro Tim shall be set free. And likewise it is my will that my negroes and slaves not yet 24 years of age, shall upon their and each of their attaining to that age be set free."

COWDEN, JAMES, was a member of the Legislature in 1780.

COWDEN, JAMES B., was a member of the Legislature in 1853.

*COOPER, CALVIN, emigrated from Birmingham, England, about the year 1730, and located in Sadsbury township. He purchased the land from Thomas Moore, on which the town of Christiana[1] is built, in the year 1734, (being a part of the

[1] *Christiana Riot Case.*—In September, 1851, was enacted within the limits of Lancaster county a tragedy that attained a national celebrity ; and this owing to the antagonistic sentiments that prevailed throughout the country on the subject of African slavery, as it existed in the southern section of the American Union. At the time of the formation of the constitution, in 1787, slavery existed in all the States of the Confederation, save one ; and yet so considerable an opposition displayed itself towards the institution, that a compromise of conflicting opinions on this question was found necessary in order to induce all the States that had borne the banner of independence through the revolution, to adopt the Federal Union. This compromise was effected, and slavery was permitted to exist in the several States, subject to their laws ; and the Northern States, soon enacted laws for the manumission of the slaves within their borders. Slave labor in the Southern States being considered profitable, especially with the increasing demand for cotton, these States clung to an institution that swelled the coffers of the wealthy and afforded them all the pleasures that life could covet. The Southern States became, therefore, the advocates of slavery, and the Northern, its opponents.

With the growth of the United States, and the march of liberal ideas throughout the civilized world, the opposition to slavery continued to increase in the Northern States, and at the time of the admission of Missouri into the Union, so intense became the feeling that was engendered between the two sections, that another compromise was needed to prevent the disruption of the Federal bonds of nationality. Appa-

*Contributed by Isaac Walker, of Sadsbury.

land confirmed to Philip Powell in the year 1702), and the
following year, 1735, he erected a fulling mill on the Octoraro, between Christiana and the residence of Cyrus Brinton.
The machinery for the mill he brought with him from Eng-

rent harmony between the North and South again unfurled its standard
over the broad domain of the American Union ; but the seeds of opposition to the institution of slavery were already sown and germinated,
and time alone was required to produce the fruit. The efforts that had
been made by Clarkson and his compeers in England, to induce the
British government to put an end to the slave trade, had the effect to
arouse the public mind of the educated world to the enormities and
abuses of an institution that, in its best guise, had a revolting aspect.
The British government emancipated, in the year 1834, their slaves in
the West India Colonies, and this event sent its effect across the waters,
and speedily numerous societies were organized, whose object was the
suppression of slavery in the American Union.

Among the foremost (if not the very first), who arrayed themselves
against the institution of slavery, were the Quakers, a pious and estimable class of Christians, whose virtues adorn the annals of history.
The founder of our State, William Penn, in common with many other
members of his society, was led to believe that the holding of human
beings in slavery was sinful, and in his will he emancipated all his slaves,
and to some of them he gave tracts of land in addition to their freedom.
As early as 1688 a company of German Quakers emigrated from the
fatherland, settled at Germantown and took a decided stand against
slavery. They revolted at the idea of good men buying and selling
human flesh, as it were. Faithful to their convictions, they published
an address to the society in the same year, and from that time forth
these devoted followers of William Ames, their leader, who came over
with them from the Palatinate, bore an uncompromising testimony
against slavery. The subject was annually agitated in the society, and
gradually gained strength until the year 1754, when we find Benjamin
Lay, Anthony Benezet, John Woolman and Ralph Sandiford laboring
in the work of emancipation, the last of whom freed his slaves in the
year 1733. In the year 1774 it was made a breach of the discipline and
a dishonorable offence for members to hold slaves. It was also counseled
against hiring slaves or serving as executors or administrators to estates
in possession of slaves. Thus early do we find this body of Christians
(the Quakers) far in advance of others in their opposition to human
slavery.

Upon the organization of the anti-slavery societies throughout the
northern States, it was to be expected that the Quakers should figure
prominently in these efforts to abolish slavery. All that the Quakers
and the other anti-slavery organizations could effect, was to keep up an
agitation of the slavery question, and thus endeavor to educate the
public conscience up to their principles. In this they were in a very
great degree successful. Their opinions entered others of the American

land. In the year 1746 he purchased a large tract of land in the valley, from James Musgrove, being part of the land which had been sold by the Proprietaries' commissioners of property, to John, the father of James Musgrove, in the year

churches, and divisions of the same followed, marked by the Mason and Dixon boundary. The American Union, in the eyes of many of the leading statesmen of the nation, was again rocking in the throes of disunion or civil convulsion, and another compromise, headed by Clay and Webster, was sanctioned by the national Congress, in 1850, which made it the duty of the Northern States to surrender fugitive slaves to masters where the proper legal demand was made for them. Against the compromise of 1850, and especially against the fugitive slave law, the northern conscience at length fully revolted. Slavery being regarded as a sin by a large portion of the intelligent citizens of the North, that they should be compelled to render aid in capturing the fleeing fugitive from labor, was altogether incompatible with their sense of duty. In their view they would rather bear the penalty of the law than aid in its execution. No law could justly, as they believed, compel them to violate conscience.

In no section of the whole North was there a more determined feeling of opposition or disinclination to the execution of the fugitive slave law, than in the eastern part of Lancaster county, where the citizens were mostly either Quakers or their descendants. For years fugitive slaves had found amongst the people of Sadsbury and Salisbury townships kind treatment, and quite a colony of them had become congregated and settled in the vicinity of Christiana. It was natural to suppose that the fleeing fugitive would direct his steps to a retreat amongst the friends of his liberty, rather than amongst those who were ready to surrender him for pelf or out of hatred towards his race.

Some of the slaves of Edward Gorsuch, of Maryland, had made their escape to the eastern part of Lancaster county, and were living amongst others of their race in that section. On the 9th of September, 1851, Edward D. Ingraham, Commissioner of the United States, issued his warrant to Henry H. Kline, an officer appointed by him under the fugitive slave law of the 13th of September, 1850. The warrant so issued, commanded the officer to apprehend Josh Hammond and three other fugitive slaves, the property of Edward Gorsuch, and which slaves had escaped from Maryland, and were then in Lancaster county. The fact of the issuing of the said writ became known to a colored tavern-keeper in Philadelphia, by the name of Samuel Williams, who, with another colored man, preceded the official party to the neighborhood where the slaves resided, and where the arrests were to have been made, and gave notice that they were coming to execute the writs and reclaim the fugitive property.

The capturing party consisted of Deputy Marshal Kline, Edward Gorsuch, the owner of the fugitive slaves, Dickinson, a son of Mr. Gorsuch, Dr. Thomas Pearce, a nephew, and Joshua Gorsuch, besides two

1713. The citizens of Sadsbury having petitioned for a division of the township in 1743, the Court appointed Calvin Cooper, George Leonard, sr., James Wilson, Samuel Ramsey, Robert Wilson and James Miller, to divide the same. The

neighbors of Edward Gorsuch, all of whom came to assist in making capture of the fugitives. They started from Philadelphia for the place where the fugitives were believed to be living, as soon as the warrant was issued, and taking different modes of conveyance. The party arrived at Christiana early on the morning of September 11th, and having secured the service of one acquainted with the locality, set out on hunt of the fugitives, and when they had neared a house kept by a negro named Parker, about three miles from Christiana, they espied one of the slaves coming down the lane from Parker's house. As soon as the slave saw them he retreated and fled to the house, pursued by the party, but he succeeded in eluding their grasp. From the information that had been given by the negro, Williams, it was soon perceived that the negroes of the neighborhood were upon the lookout, and as the party was approaching the house, a horn was distinctly heard, as a supposed signal for the assembling of the negroes. The slave that had been first seen made his way up stairs, and the party in search of him immediately surrounded the house, so as to prevent escape. Edward Gorsuch, the owner of the fugitive, and the Deputy Marshal, now entered the house, and demanded of the blacks that they surrender, which they refused, and began loading their guns, showing the utmost determination of resistance. Mr. Gorsuch told them if they would come down and surrender themselves, he would overlook the past; but the reply came from the negroes that "they could only be taken over their dead bodies." The Marshal read his warrant, and was proceeding to ascend the stairs when he was struck by a sharp instrument and compelled to desist from this attempt. He read his warrant the second and third time, and advised the negroes of the peril of resisting the authority of the government, and gave them fifteen minutes time to consider whether or not they would surrender. Edward Gorsuch had in the meantime stepped outside of the house and called to his slave, and endeavored to persuade him to surrender himself and submit peaceably to his authority, and while doing so was shot at by one of the negroes from a window, but the shot failed to take effect, the aim being too high.

During this period, two white men, named Castner Hanway and Elijah Lewis, suddenly appeared upon the ground. This was seen to have the effect of inspiring enthusiasm into the negroes in the house, who immediately set up a cheering. By this time a large number of negroes had made their appearance armed with double barreled guns, pistols, corn-cutters, scythes and clubs. The organization had been complete, and as soon as the horn was sounded, as above indicated, the negroes assembled from all directions.

The Marshal now approached Castner Hanway, one of the white men, who was upon horse-back, and asked of him that he render assist-

division was ordered, and the eastern part called Bart, and the western retained the old name, Sadsbury.

Calvin Cooper was elected a member of the Provincial Assembly for six consecutive years, from 1749 till 1755.

ance in making the arrest. Hanway demanded of him his authority, and the Marshal read him his warrant. Hanway then told him that he would meet with difficulty in making the arrest, and advised him to desist from the attempt. At the time the Marshal read his warrant, Lewis, the other white man, was also present, but neither he nor Hanway felt themselves bound to obey a mandate against the execution of which their consciences revolted, and they chose rather to endure the consequences of refusal. Besides, an attempt, at this time, to execute the law seemed hazardous and likely to be attended with fatal consequences. By this time the number of negroes that had arrived has been estimated at from 75 to 100, all armed and evincing the most determined spirit of resistance. To the demand of the Marshal, of Hanway, to assist in making the arrest he remarked, "I will have nothing to do with it."

The negroes in the house, seeing their friends in such abundance, sallied out, and raising a shout, surrounded Edward Gorsuch and his companions, and fired upon them. Edward Gorsuch fell, and his son, Dickinson, running to his assistance, was also shot in the breast and lungs and fell to the ground. Dr. Pearce was likewise shot in several places, but succeeded in making his escape. Deputy Marshal Kline, Joshua Gorsuch and the other two individuals, Nelson and Hutchins, who accompanied the capturing party, all made their escape, speedily, as best they could. Edward Gorsuch was mutilated by the negroes, his pockets rifled of about $300, and left lying dead where he fell. His son, Dickinson, was rescued from death through the influence of an old colored man, who begged of the murderers to spare his life, and he was shortly afterwards removed by some white persons, who visited the scene, to the house of Levi Pownall, where he lay a considerable time before he could be removed.

As soon as the news of this occurrence reached Lancaster, John L. Thompson, then District Attorney, and J. Franklin Reigart, an alderman, accompanied by some of the most resolute citizens, repaired at once to Christiana, and after taking certain legal steps proceeded to arrest the blacks. Nine of them were taken in less than two hours. Castner Hanway and Elijah Lewis, hearing of the warrants, surrendered themselves without resistance. All were committed by Alderman Reigart, and conveyed to the Lancaster jail. The United States Marshal, the United States District Attorney, and the Commissioner, with a strong force of marines, and a detachment of the Philadelphia police, arrived shortly afterwards at Christiana and lent their aid in making arrests of suspected parties. Both parties proceeded to make arrests, and in a short time every section of country was pretty well scoured. A large number of additional prisoners were brought in, and among them two whites, a man named Scarlet, and the other Hood.

The citizens of Lancaster county petitioned the Legislature for the passage of an act that would cause the removal of the French refugees from Nova Scotia, who had been thrown upon them by the English government.   An act was.

A difficulty was like to have occurred between the State and the United States authority, as to which the prisoners should be awarded. Mr. Thompson contended that the prisoners had been guilty of the highest crime known to the law of Pennsylvania, willful and deliberate murder, and that as this had occurred in Lancaster county, the prisoners should be taken to Lancaster for trial. District Attorney Ashmead, on the contrary, insisted that the prisoners had been guilty of treason, in levying war against the United States authorities. In this he was sustained by the Commissioner, E. D. Ingraham, and finally a compromise was effected, by which each party was allowed to dispose of its own arrests.

On Monday, November 24th, 1851, the trial of Castner Hanway for treason, was commenced in the United States Circuit Court before Judges Grier and Kane. The counsel who appeared for the United States, were United States District Attorney John W. Ashmead, James R. Ludlow and George R. Ashmead ; Robert J. Brent and James Cooper for Maryland. The counsel for Castner Hanway, were John M. Read, Thaddeus Stevens, Joseph J. Lewis and Theodore Cuyler. The trial lasted fifteen days and was conducted with masterly ability by the legal gentlemen, both for the prosecution and defense. The jury after retiring from the box, returned after an absence of ten minutes, with a verdict of "not guilty."

Caster Hanway and Elijah Lewis were brought to Lancaster to answer any charge that might be preferred against them. An indictment was laid before the grand jury for murder, but the jury ignored the bill and thus ended the Christiana riot case.

The Christiana riot case is an illustration of an attempt to execute an unpopular law, an undertaking that usually proves abortive. Conscience rules supreme in the actions of men, and the law must succumb. With whom lies the blame in such cases? In the present instance both parties, the slave owners and the fugitives with their friends, had apparent justice on their side. The one owned his property by virtue of law and his education told him he was in the line of his duty in seeking to reclaim it. On the other hand, the instinctive law of liberty induced the fugitives to seek for it and even fight in its defense ; and the friends of the fugitives sympathized with them in their contest for liberty. We can, therefore, condemn neither party, and must be allowed to say that what may be wrong in one, in another is the contrary, and therefore, can see no other rule of rectitude in life than to obey conscience, and if sincerely followed, though it be perverted, we are justified. This safe rule would establish charity, toleration and free opinion, unite mankind in a universal brotherhood, where free thought and free speech would crown the highest aspirations of man.

passed March 5th, 1756, and Calvin Cooper, James Webb, and Samuel Lefevre were appointed to carry its provisions into execution. The act empowered and required them or their survivors, that within twenty days from the passage of the act, they should order and appoint the disposition of the inhabitants of Nova Scotia, imported and permitted to be landed, in such manner and proportions as to them shall appear most equitable under certain limitations, having regard to such lands and plantations, or other employments as they might procure for them towards maintaining themselves and their families, and thereby relieving the province from the heavy charge of supporting them.

Calvin Cooper was appointed one of the Justices of the Peace for Lancaster county, which office he held with satisfaction to the public for many years. His descendants became numerous and respectable, and while some of them settled along the valley, and about Cooperville, others settled at Lampeter and at the borough of Columbia; and the Coopers residing there at the present day, are among his descendants. He was a valuable member in unity with the Society of Friends, and undoubtedly a worthy and serviceable man in the community. He was the grandfather of the late well-known and highly respected Jeremiah Cooper, of Sadsbury, who erected a large woolen factory in the valley, below Cooperville, about the year 1825. The present Coopers of Sadsbury, Bart, Lampeter and Columbia, are his descendants of the 5th, 6th and 7th generations. He departed this life near the close of the Revolutionary war, aged about eighty years.

CRAIG, JOHN, was a member of the Legislature in the years 1782, 1783 and 1784.

CRAIG, ROBERT, was a member of the Legislature in 1784. He was also a Commissioner of Lancaster county in 1778.

CRUMBAUGH, REV. J. C., was born in Frederick county, Maryland. He received his education in the Pennsylvania College, at Gettysburg, and graduated in 1851 with the highest honors of his class. He came to Lancaster and studied theology under the Rev. Dr. John C. Baker, and at the same time served as Principal of the Lancaster High

13

School. He was licensed to preach by the Pennsylvania Synod in 1853, and shortly afterwards he was elected pastor of the new St. John's Evangelical Lutheran Church.[1] With constantly declining health he continued to serve this congregation up to March 19th, 1857, when he resigned, and accepted the office of County Superintendent of Common Schools. It had been the hope of his friends that this new position affording him more out-door exercise, might restore his health, but in this they were disappointed. He died of consumption January 13th, 1859, at the early age of 28. As a student in college, he maintained a reputation for talent of the first order, standing ever at the head of his classes, and carrying away the honors over his mates. As principal of the Lancaster High School, he was a model for imitation, being able to maintain the most excellent discipline and order in the class and study rooms; and as a clergyman, he had the unbounded confidence and friendship of his whole congregation and of the community at large.

CUNNINGHAM, JAMES, was a member of the Legislature in the years 1779, 1788, 1789 and 1790.

[1]In the fall of 1851 a number of the young members of Trinity Lutheran Church, of which the Rev. John C. Baker was pastor, held a social gathering and conversed concerning the propriety of opening a mission school in the northwestern part of the city, and it was resolved to make the attempt, provided they could obtain the sanction of the vestry to their undertaking. This consent having been obtained, March, 1852, a Sunday-school, called the Lutheran, was organized with twenty-two pupils, J. C. Crumbaugh being its superintendent.

With the resignation of Rev. John C. Baker as the pastor of Trinity Lutheran church, in January, 1853, the friends of a new church began to consult among themselves, and a meeting was held on the 2nd of April of that year, when it was resolved by those present to constitute themselves the nucleus of a new Lutheran church. On the 18th of May following, a committee was appointed to draft a constitution and by-laws, and another to solicit subscriptions for the erection of a church edifice. On the 15th of June, on motion of G. M. Zahm, the church was unanimously named "St. John's Evangelical Lutheran Church." The small congregation generally worshiped in Fulton Hall or the lecture room of the Moravian church. On the 9th of October, 1853, the corner-stone of the new edifice was laid, Revs. Harbaugh, Kurtz and Krotel officiating. On the 24th of December following, the entire building having been completed, the consecration took place. The edifice cost over $20,000.

D.

DARLINGTON, EDWARD C., became a partner in December, 1841, with R. W. Middleton, in the publication of the *Examiner and Herald.*[1] Shortly after this, Middleton withdrew from the firm, and Mr. Darlington continued the publication of the paper up to October 20th, 1858. During Mr. Darlington's connection with the paper, it was regarded as the organ of what was known as the Silver Grey Whigs[2] of Lancaster county. Mr. Darlington was elected to the State Senate, in 1851.

Mr. Darlington was a man quite retiring in his disposition, a great reader, and a writer who wielded the editorial pen with considerable ability.

[1] The *Lancaster Examiner* was started in the spring of 1830, by Samuel Wagner, who continued its publication until June, 1834. Wagner sold out his interest to George W. Hamersly and Luther Richards, who united it with the *Herald.* These continued the publication, under the new title, until December, 1838, and then sold their interest to R. W. Middleton. On the 8th of December, E. C. Darlington became a partner of Middleton; but on the 22nd of the same month the latter retired, leaving Darlington sole owner and proprietor of the paper, which he continued to be until October 20th, 1858, when he sold out his interest to John A. Hiestand, John F. Huber and Francis Heckert. This latter firm was dissolved November 4th, 1862, by the death of Huber, one of its members. On the 9th of February, 1863, the interest of Huber was purchased by Edwin M. Kline, and the style of the firm became J. A. Hiestand & Co. On the 1st of January, 1864, T. E. & J. J. Cochran sold out the Lancaster *Union* to J. A. Hiestand & Co., and from that date the latter firm began issuing the *Examiner* semi-weekly, which has been continued up to this time. May 1st, 1864, Mr. Heckert's interest in the paper passed to John I. Hartman, and the firm was named Hiestand, Kline & Hartman. On May 1st, 1868, Mr. Hartman withdrew, and the paper is now published by Hiestand & Kline.

[2] After the adoption of the compromise measures of 1850, during the administration of Millard Fillmore, the Whig party divided into two branches; those who favored the compromises and those opposed to them. In Lancaster county, the friends of the administration or of the compromise measures, received the name of *Silver Greys*, who were advocates of the policy of President Fillmore as regards the compromise measures on the slavery question. Isaac E. Hiester was at once regarded as the leader of the Silver Greys, and with him acted

DAVIES, EDWARD, was elected a member of the Legislature in the years 1834 and 1835. He represented Lancaster county in Congress from 1837 till 1841.

DEERING, HENRY, a member of the Legislature in the years 1788 and 1789.

DENUES, CHARLES, was born August 28th, 1823, in York county, Pennsylvania. In 1835 he removed, with his parents, to Lancaster, and was apprenticed to the turning and powder-horn making business; but the uncongeniality of his master caused our subject to shorten the term of his apprenticeship. When about seventeen years of age, acting on an occasion as cannonier for the Washington Artillery, he lost his right hand from the accidental discharge of the cannon. Being thus disabled for manual pursuits, he now turned his attention to the obtaining of an education, and having made some advance, in the year 1842 he began the

Thomas E. Franklin, esq., Edward C. Darlington, William W. Brown, esq., John Sheaffer, of Manheim, James M. Hopkins, of Drumore, John Steger, of New Holland, Michael Shirk, of West Cocalico, Samuel Worth, of Martic, John J. Evans, of Little Britain, and R. A. Evans, of Lancaster. The other wing of the party was headed by Thaddeus Stevens, Dr. Esaias Kinzer, George Brubaker, Peter Johns, David Bair, O. J. Dickey, George Ford, Alexander H. Hood, Samuel Eberly, and Hiram Erb, of Clay, Anthony E. Roberts, Frederick E. Hoffman, and Frederick Smith, of Conoy.

In the Whig convention of 1851, the Silver Grey wing carried off the victory, nominating all the candidates for office except Esaias Kinzer, who, by a faithful canvass before the convention, had secured enough votes to nominate him to the State Senate, along with E. C. Darlington. The defeat of the Anti-slavery Whigs, was regarded as owing to the influence of the *Examiner and Herald;* and as a counterpoise to this paper, it was resolved to start a paper in their interest. Edward McPherson, of Adams county, was sent for, and he began the publication of the *Independent Whig,* devoted to the advocacy of Anti-slavery principles. In 1852 the Silver Greys were again successful, electing Isaac E. Hiester to Congress.

At the National Convention held at Baltimore in 1852, the Silver Grey element of the country supported Millard Fillmore for President; the distinctive New England element voted for Webster; and the Anti-slavery Whigs united upon General Scott and he was nominated. Scott having been so disastrously defeated in the canvass for President, the old Whig party began rapidly to decline. In 1853 the Native American party that had maintained a feeble existence in the large cities, began to revive under the name of Know

study of law with Hon. Thaddeus Stevens, and was admitted to the bar in 1844. He practiced for a time in Lancaster, a short period in York, Pa., and afterwards removed to Wisconsin, in which place he was attacked with disease, and returned home in 1848.

He now began teaching school, a career he followed, at different places, for a number of years. He was principal of the Millersville graded school for nine years.

In 1859 he entered upon the study of theology, and having preached his trial sermon, served as a supply to a congregation at Columbia.

In 1862 he raised a company for the Union army, and was commissioned captain, August 12th, 1862. His company was assigned as part of the 135th regiment of Pennsylvania volunteers, under Col. Porter. He, with his men, protected two of the Union batteries at the battle of Grey's Farm. He participated with his company in the famed

Nothings ; and lodges were organized throughout the country, which were filled chiefly by recruits from the old Whig party. In 1854 there were, therefore, three tickets in the field in Lancaster county, the Democratic, the Know Nothing, and the Whig.

The party manipulations in the Know Nothing lodges were conducted in secret. In the nominations made in the county convention of the old effete Whig party, the best men in their ranks were selected as their standard bearers, and in the election which followed, some of those elected were Democrats, some Know Nothings and other Whigs. Anthony E. Roberts was elected to Congress on the Know Nothing ticket. The disintegration of the Whig party by 1855 was complete, and in that year the whole Know Nothing ticket in the county was elected. The Whigs remained at that time but a very feeble minority. About this period the Democratic party in Congress repealed the Missouri Compromise, and this had the effect of attracting into the Know Nothing ranks most of the anti-slavery element of the country ; and inasmuch as the secret oath-bound dogmas of the party were offensive to many of the recruits from the Democratic and Whig ranks, and the main principle now being hostility to slavery, the party re-moulded itself into an open organization, under the name of Republicans. A few of the old Whigs of Lancaster county feeling themselves entirely out-generaled in the new construction of parties, and out of an unwillingness to acknowledge the leadership of their opponents, attached themselves to the Democratic party, and thenceforth acted in its ranks. The great mass, however, of the old Silver Grey Whigs united their political destinies to the Anti-slavery wing under whatever name it called itself, and from that time Lancaster county has been overwhelmingly Republican.

conflict of Chancellorsville, after which they were mustered out of service, in May, 1863.

Having returned home, he taught school again in the winter of 1863–4. In October, 1864, he was elected to the Pennsylvania Legislature, and reëlected in 1865. During his last session he acted as chairman of the military committee. In the spring of 1866 he again began the practice of the law in Lancaster, which he yet continues. On January 1st, 1867, he was appointed Notary Public, and reappointed January 12th, 1870.

DICKEY, O. J., was born in Beaver county, Pennsylvania, April 6th, 1823. His father, John Dickey, was a leading politician in the western part of the State, and at one time a member of the board of Canal Commissioners, and represented his district in the State Senate, also in Congress, and was marshal of the western district of Pennsylvania at the time of his death. The subject of our notice received his education at the Beaver Academy and at Dickinson College, Carlisle, passing through the junior class of the latter institution. Having closed his classic career one year short of graduation, he entered as a student in the law office of James Allison, esq., one of the old leading lawyers of Beaver (the father of the present Register of the Treasury), and was admitted a member of the Beaver bar. Designing Lancaster as the place where he should locate for the practice of the profession, he came in 1846, with a letter of introduction to Mr. Stevens, who kindly received him and proffered to him the use of his office. Mr. Stevens having by intuition, as it were, perceived that our young barrister was made of solid material, employed him from the start at a fixed salary to attend to certain parts of his business. Mr. Dickey was thus afforded an excellent opportunity of becoming acquainted with the practical business of the profession, and rapidly did he profit with these advantages,. This was an instance of a rare mind meeting with rare opportunities. His progress in business was a very rapid and successful one. After a few years of steady and gradual rise in his profession, he, at the instance of his benefactor, became a partner with the latter, as to all the current business which presented itself, save where Mr. Stevens was himself specially employed. This partnership continued up till the year 1857, when he found it necessary from the press of business to open an office of his own.

In the fall of 1856 he was elected District Attorney of Lancaster county, an office he filled with great credit and ability. After opening a separate office of his own, he still continued to have charge of all Mr. Stevens' business when the latter was absent or unable to attend to the same.

In the year 1857 Mr. Dickey chose to himself a partner for life, in the person of Miss Elizabeth Shenk, of Lancaster.

Upon the death of Mr. Stevens, in 1868, Mr. Dickey was nominated and elected to fill his unexpired term in Congress, as well as for the subsequent term of two years; and in 1870, after a warm and spirited contest, he was again nominated by his party by an overwhelming majority, over J. P. Wickersham, and again elected to Congress.

As a lawyer, Mr. Dickey ranks amongst the first practitioners of the Lancaster bar; his business being perhaps as lucrative as any that could be named. He is well read in his profession, and in the trial of a cause he has no superior. His arguments before a jury are sound, logical and convincing; and he is able to bring out of his case all that is in it.

As a politician, he has but few equals, having a strength with the masses that few possess. Born to rule, he enters an assemblage of tumultuous partisans and contending political aspirants, and organization follows his word and opposition retires. As by a word, he carries with him the meeting, and the result crowns his banner. He is dexterous in his manipulations, active in circumventing his enemies, and always present in the midst of the political battle, saying in essence to his political friends, "follow me." His word has a charm in it, and he generally leads to victory.

As a man, Mr. Dickey is high-toned and honorable, and his word on any occasion is as good as his bond. He is exceedingly liberal in his opinions, never permitting difference of sentiment to alter his conduct or feeling towards a personal friend. In this particular, he is exemplary. He was one of those of enlarged views who, during the dark days of the rebellion (when partisan hate was visible all around), could accord to individuals of different opinion from his own, the same honesty of sentiment as he himself entertained.

Mr. Dickey is not what might be called a fluent declaimer, but his speeches have the ring of energy, ability and force. His political harangues will, however, excite more applause and enthusiasm than will follow the outbursts of a more impassioned and eloquent orator. His manner of speaking is rather better adapted for juridical than partisan purposes. His strength as a politician lies in his great organizing ability rather than in his oratorical. Since the demise of his great precursor in Congress, he is, perhaps, the leading thinker of his party in Lancaster county.

DICKINSON, JOSEPH C., a member of the Legislature in the years 1846 and 1847. He was one of the first who erected permanent buildings in Christiana.

*DICKINSON, JOSEPH, emigrated to this country from Cumberland, England, by way of Ireland, about the year 1725. The ship on which he came a passenger having struck upon a rock, causing it to leak so rapidly that it was impossible to keep the vessel afloat, and was about given up as lost, and the passengers were preparing to meet their fate, when Joseph Dickinson volunteered to go down under the water, on the outside of the ship, and stop the leak, which hazardous undertaking he accomplished by inserting pieces of dried beef in the crevices. He was united in marriage with Elizabeth, daughter of Guyon Miller, of Kennett, Chester county, in the year 1732, when he removed and settled near the Pequea creek, in Salisbury township. He had two sons, Joseph and Gaius, and seven daughters. His son, Gaius, and his grandson, Joseph, continued to reside on the property, while his son Joseph purchased land and resided in Sadsbury.

Joseph C. Dickinson, Moses Pownall and Joseph D. Pownall, of Sadsbury, and Joseph Hood, of Bart, who were members of the Legislature at different times, were the great grandsons of Joseph Dickinson; also, Jacob T. Gest and Isaac Walker, of Sadsbury. Anna Dickinson, of Philadelphia, and

*Contributed by Isaac Walker, of Sadsbury.

Mary Louisa Walker, late of Richmond, Va., but now Mary Louisa Roberts, of Robertson county, Texas, are both the great grand-daughters of his son, Gaius Dickinson. He was a man well educated, and was an esteemed and valuable member of the denomination of Friends. His great grandsons, James and Lewis Dickinson, still reside on the property in Salisbury; and J. D. C. Pownall, one of his descendants of the fifth generation, holds the property in Sadsbury.

DIFFENDERFFER, and a companion by the name of Stone, were the two first settlers who took up the land upon which New Holland is built, and for a mile around it. They were natives of Germany, and came to New Holland in 1728. David Diffenderffer, a son of the first settler, became early identified with the American patriots in their struggle for independence. He entered the army, and served with credit for several years, bearing his part in several of the hard-fought battles of revolutionary history. He died in New Holland in 1846, at a very advanced age. His descendants are numerous. Dr. W. L. Diffenderffer is one of his grandsons.

DILLER, ADAM, was elected sheriff of Lancaster county in 1827.

DILLER, ROLAND, is a native of Lancaster, and a man of great activity and business perseverance. His educational facilities were superior to the great majority of the young men of his time whose lives were designed for active employments. He engaged in the mercantile business for some time; but, upon the death of his uncle, Frederick Seger, who was a conveyancer, he abandoned merchandising and took up conveyancing, a business he has followed ever since. He has also connected with scrivening that of surveying.

Upon the organization of the anti-Masonic party, Mr. Diller was amongst the most prominent and active in that movement. He contributed actively towards the establishment of the first anti-Masonic paper in the county, and in all the political movements of his party he has ever maintained a leading position. He for many years acted as a magistrate of the county, and perhaps no man ever filled that office who seemed, by intuition, to comprehend the intricacies of law better than the subject of this notice. One knowing Mr. Diller intimately, uses this language of him: "The cast of his mind is eminently legal, and had he read law regularly, and practiced the profession, he would have become one of the best jurists our county ever produced."

He has for years been the legal adviser of his fellow-citizens in and around New Holland, and his advice is anxiously sought in all matters of business where a knowledge of law is required. Mr. Diller has always been a great reader, and his library is said to be one of the best, if not the very best, in Lancaster county. He possessed the basis, beyond all question, for extraordinary achievements, and but an arena was wanting to have rendered him one of the most conspicuous men of the nation. He has been frequently mentioned for Congress; but he rather chose a life of retirement than one that brought with it great sacrifices and responsibilities. His wonderful methodical arrangement, if nothing else, displays a mind of no ordinary compass, and this characteristic has been observed in all his business transactions. He possesses complete files of most of the papers he has ever received. Some years since he donated some of these to the Lancaster Athenæum.

DILLER, Solomon, a brother of the above, was a member of the Legislature in 1836 and 1837.

[1]DIXON, William, was the principal founder of the *Lancaster Intelligencer*, which was started by him and his brother Robert, in the year 1799. The paper was issued regularly as a Republican (Democratic) organ by Dixon until his death in 1823. William Dixon was several times elected Treasurer of Lancaster county. He was a man of great popularity and sterling principle.

[1] William Dixon was, in February, 1806, found guilty of libel on Governor McKean, in that he charged the Governor with having made corrupt overtures to Henry Wertz, a Senator from Bedford county. On account of the contradictory statements made by Wertz, before the trial came off, he was not called as a witness ; and, although Dixon proved substantially all he had charged in his paper, yet he was found guilty, under the law of libel as it then existed. He was sentenced, by Judges Henry and Coleman, to three months' imprisonment in the county jail, and to pay $500 as a fine to the Commonwealth, and the costs of prosecution. He was committed in accordance with the sentence. The fine

DONER, JOHN, was born January 8th, 1818, in Lampeter (now East Lampeter) township, Lancaster county, Pa. His parents were of French descent, and in their religious faith, members of the old Mennonite church. His education was such as the schools of his neighborhood afforded, and he has been all his lifetime engaged in agricultural pursuits. After his marriage he removed to Manor township, where he yet resides. He was elected and served as a director of the Lancaster County Bank for a number of years. In 1860 Mr. Doner was elected a Commissioner of Lancaster county, and served through perhaps the most critical period of the county's history, the beginning and the greater period of the rebellion. It was a period that devolved upon the Board of Commissioners a weight of responsibility that never before had required to be assumed by any Board since the organization of the county. Mr. Doner, as one of the Board during

and costs were promptly paid by his political friends, and he was daily visited by members of the Legislature and citizens of the highest standing, all regarding him simply as the victim of political persecution.

A number of Democratic citizens gave Mr. Dixon a supper in his place of confinement, which was handsomely illuminated on the occasion. Major John Light, and Joseph Lefevre, (afterwards a member of Congress), acted as president and vice president, and numerous toasts were drank in honor of Dixon in his captivity.

Mrs. Dixon, wife of William Dixon, evinced great heroism during the imprisonment of her husband, and refused to ask his release of Governor McKean. When certain influential friends volunteered to accompany her to the Governor and endeavor to obtain a pardon, she replied, "For your friendship, and the offer of your company and intercession, gentlemen, I sincerely thank you; but my husband has committed no crime. Why ask forgiveness? A separation from the husband of my bosom is afflicting, but to supplicate the oppressor (who has torn him from my side) would be base servility."

Dixon's imprisonment was denounced by the whole Republican press of the day. A meeting of the leading Republicans of the borough of Lancaster was held at the house of John Whiteside, and an address was issued suggesting the propriety of changing the day of the county meeting from Wednesday, May 14th, till Saturday, the 17th, in honor of it being the day when Dixon's term of imprisonment will have expired. As he will leave the prison about 12 o'clock, the address urged that the Republicans meet at Whiteside's tavern, at 11 o'clock, in order to give Dixon a fitting reception upon his leaving the prison. On the day of his release, accordingly, a large meeting of Republicans met Dixon at he prison and escorted him to his house.

that period, faithfully and efficiently discharged the duties devolved upon him, and to the entire satisfaction of his constituents. Mr. Doner is at present engaged in agricultural pursuits.

DOUGLASS, JOHN, a member of the Legislature in 1756, 1761, 1762 and 1763.

DOWNING, WILLIAM, a member of the Legislature in 1771.

DUCHMAN, JACOB, elected County Commissioner in 1820.

DUCHMAN, COL. JOHN H., was a prominent citizen of Lancaster city for many years. He was, by occupation, in his younger years, a hatter, and carried on this business for years. He kept for a number of years the Leopard hotel, in East King street. Early in life he became captivated with military glory and volunteered in the war of 1812–14. He served as first Lieutenant of the old Lancaster Fencibles, then under command of Capt. John K. Findley, which was famed for its admirable discipline, and which was disbanded about the breaking out of the Mexican war. Some years after this Col. Duchman raised a new company, also named the Fencibles, of which he was elected Captain. It was this company which escorted James Buchanan to Washington in March, 1857, at the time he was inaugurated President of the United States. This company remained in existence up to the breaking out of the rebellion in 1861, and became Company F of the 1st Pennsylvania regiment. Owing to ill health, Capt. Duchman was unable to march with his company, and 1st Lieutenant Emlen Franklin succeeded to the command. For some years he was clerk in the Lancaster bank. During James Buchanan's administration he held a position in the custom house in Philadelphia. Shortly after the breaking out of the rebellion he raised a company for the 79th Regiment, P. V. of which he was chosen Lieutenant Colonel.

On account of advanced age and the rigors of the field, he was compelled to retire from active service after having served about one year. He died October 8th, 1866, in the 70th year of his age.

DUCHMAN, WILLIAM, elected Recorder in 1845.

*DUFFIELD, George, was the third son of George and Margaret Duffield, who emigrated from Ireland in 1730 and settled in Pequea, Lancaster county. They were descended from Huguenot ancestry, their forefathers having escaped from France on account of religious persecution and settled in England, and afterwards passed over into the north of Ireland. The name was originally *du Fielde*, but became anglicised after the family had settled in England.

The subject of this notice was born October 7th, 1732. He received his academical education at Newark, Delaware, where afterwards he officiated as Tutor. He graduated at Nassau Hall, joined the church under the care of Rev. Robert Smith, of Pequea, and shortly afterwards commenced the study of theology under his supervision. He was licensed to preach the gospel by the Presbytery of New Castle, March 11th, 1756. He received a call from the united churches of Carlisle, Big Spring and Monohan (now called Dillstown), and was ordained at Carlisle, September 25th, 1761.

During the pendency of his ordination and settlement at Carlisle, he was married March 5th, 1759, to Margaret Armstrong, sister of General John Armstrong, of Revolutionary memory. By this marriage he had four children. His youngest son, George, was for many years connected as Register and Comptroller General, with the administration of the State of Pennsylvania under Governor Thomas McKean.

At the time of his settlement in Carlisle and the united congregations, each ten miles distant from the borough, the Indians were numerous in the vicinity and often made hostile demonstrations, which required the body of the male members to arm themselves in self-defense. In all these dangers he participated, cheerfully accompanying his flock to the camp, to administer to them there the consolations of religion. The church at Monohan was in such an exposed situation, that as a protection during the hours of worship, fortifications were thrown around it; behind which, while those stationed on the ramparts kept watch, the congregation might, without distraction or fear, engage in the worship of God. His deep interest in and sympathy with a population thus periled and

*Sprague's Annals of the American Pulpit, Vol. 3.

suffering on the frontiers, rendered him, throughout the whole of that region, exceedingly popular. So strong was the attachment for him, that in all perilous adventures, especially during the Revolutionary struggle, the men who had to take up arms for their homes, their liberties and their lives, always welcomed his visits in the camp with the most cordial good-will.

Mr. Duffield was a bold and zealous assertor of the rights of conscience, an earnest and powerful advocate of civil and religious liberty. During the pendency of those measures which were maturing the Declaration of Independence, while the prospects of the colonies seemed most gloomy, his preaching contributed greatly to encourage and animate the friends of liberty. He was not in the habit of writing out his discourses in full; but, having made a skeleton, and arranged his thoughts, awaited the inspiration of the occasion for the filling up. Several of these unfinished discourses which remain, breathe a spirit of the most pure and lofty patriotism, and withal are strikingly prophetic of the religious scenes which were to open out of all that darkness in which the country was then enveloped.

During his ministry at Carlisle, he was twice earnestly called by the Second Presbyterian church of Philadelphia, then worshipping at the northwest corner of Arch and Third streets, to become their pastor ; and the commissioners with great zeal prosecuted their call before the Presbytery. Both the Presbytery and himself, however, judged that his presence at Carlisle was of more importance at that time than at Philadelphia.

In the year 1766 Mr. Duffield was deputed by the Synod, in connection with the Rev. Charles Beatty, to make a missionary tour and visit the families that had made their way along the great valley that stretches through Pennsylvania, Maryland and Virginia. The object of this mission was to administer the offices of religion to those families which had settled in what is now Franklin county, Pennsylvania, and through the range of country where Greencastle, Hagerstown and other villages now stand, as far as the Potomac, with a view to the organization of churches.

Some time after this, Mr. Duffield was called to the Third Presbyterian church in Philadelghia, where he officiated during the sessions of the Colonial Congress, anterior to and during the Revolutionary struggle. That church had been originally a branch of the First Presbyterian church, under the care of the Rev. Dr. Ewing. A controversy arose between them and the parent church, relative to their independence. Both the Presbytery and Mr. Duffield judged that it was his duty to accept the call and remove to Philadelphia. The circumstances under which he was translated to that charge, in connection with the old feuds that had divided the church, produced obstacles in the way of his labors at the commencement of his ministry. He was greatly admired as a preacher, and was recognized as a bold, animated and decided Whig, resolutely contending against the encroachments on civil and religious liberty made by the government of Great Britain. On an occasion shortly after his appearance in Philadelphia, the large church edifice, then standing on the corner of Third and Pine streets, which the First church claimed to have under its control, was closed and barred against his entrance, by their order, notwithstanding an appointment had been made for his preaching in it for the congregation accustomed to worship there, and by their direction. The house was opened by the officers of the Third church, and Mr. Duffield was assisted through the throng that had assembled to hear him, and introduced through a window. News of the people assembling on Sabbath evening spread, and application was made to Mr. J. Bryant, the King's magistrate, to quell what was called a riot. The magistrate proceeded to the spot, and, shortly after the commencement of public worship, pressed his way into the aisle of the church, before the pulpit, (on the very spot where afterwards Mr. Duffield's remains were interred, and where they yet sleep, and in the name of the King, read the riot act and required the people to disperse. The congregation was composed of zealous Whigs, who could not endure Tory influence or authority. The principal officer of the congregation, a Mr. Knox, rose and ordered the magistrate to desist. He refused and went on with his reading. A second time the

zealous champion of liberty, in hearing of all the congregation, with loud voice, demanded that the magistrate cease
from disturbing the worship of God.   He still refused; when,
without further ado, he seized the magistrate, who was a
small man, and lifting him up carried him through the crowd
out of the house, and ordered him to begone, and not come
back there to disturb the worship of God.   The magistrate
bowed to the stern assertor of popular liberty, and Mr.
Duffield went on with his preaching.   But the next day he
was arrested and brought before the Mayor's Court, and was
required to plead to the charge of aiding and abetting a
riot, and give bail for his appearance for trial.   He politely
and respectfully refused to put in any plea or give the bail,
averring, that as a minister of Christ, he was performing the
duties of his office and was no way accessory to a riot, of
the existence of which there was no proof.   The Mayor said
that such a procedure would greatly embarrass the Court,
who would be compelled to send him to prison if he did not
plead and offer bail.   His brother, Samuel Duffield, M. D.,
or other of his friends whomsoever he might name, would
be accepted by him as bail.   He still, with the utmost courtesy, declined.   After some entreaty, the Mayor offered himself to be his bail, not wishing to commit him to prison.   He
cordially thanked his Honor for his unmerited kindness, but
protested that he stood on the ground of principle, and that
he was called, in the providence of God, to assert the rights
and liberty of a minister of Christ, and of a worshiping assembly, and denied the legitimate interference and cogni-
zance of the King's government in such matters.   The Mayor
delayed for several days deciding in the case, and requesting
him to take the matter into consideration, suffered him to
withdraw to his own house, under the assurance that he must
again appear before the Court and give his definite answer.
The occasion and procedure were productive of great excitement.   The news that the King's government was going to
put Mr. Duffield in prison, spread through the city and into
the country, until it reached the region where he had formerly lived.   Here the excitement became so great that the
volunteer forces, to whom he was well-known, and by whom

he was much beloved, assembled, and resolved to hold themselves in readiness to march, though distant a hundred miles
or more, to the city of Philadelphia, if he should be imprisoned, and set him at liberty in opposition to the King's government. The occasion and opportunity for their valor
were never afforded ; for he was never again brought before
the Mayor's Court. He was allowed to pursue his ministerial duties unmolested, and the First Church settled their
matters with the branch, and recognized their right to call
the minister of their choice without dictation or control.

Attempts, however, were made to prevent his introduction into the Presbytery to which the First Church and their
pastor belonged. He insisted on his right, according to the
social compact, to be received by them, refusing to commence his ministry in Philadelphia with allowed imputa-
tions of his character and orthodoxy. Eventually, when he
had been so received, that his presence might not molest
men who did not sympathize with him in ecclesiastical matters, he voluntarily applied for and received a dismission to
the other Presbytery, with whose members he had more
especial affinity.

During a part of the sessions of the Colonial Congress he
was employed, with the Rev. Mr. (afterwards Bishop) White,
as chaplain to that body. John Adams attended regularly
on his ministry, and communed with his church during the
sitting of Congress in Philadelphia.

Mr. Duffield was eminently a man of devotional feelings
and habits, and was instrumental in establishing the first
prayer-meeting in any Presbyterian church in Philadelphia.
So much did he value prayer, and so important did he feel it to
be to excite and encourage the men that had left their homes
and periled their lives in the cause of freedom, to look to
God and put their trust in Him, that he would occasionally,
in the darkest hours of the Revolution, leave his charge and
repair to the camp, where the fathers and sons of many of
his flock were gathered, and minister to them in the public
preaching of the Word, and in personal converse.

When the enemy were lying on Staten Island, and the
American troops were on the opposite side of the Sound, on

14

a Sabbath day he preached to a portion of the soldiers gathered into an orchard, having ascended into the forks of a tree for his pulpit. The noise of their singing arrested the enemy's attention, who directed several cannon shot to be fired toward the spot whence it proceeded. As the shot came rushing through the trees, he suggested that they should retire behind a hillock, and not remote from the spot where they were, which was done under the enemy's fire, without injury, and there they finished their religious exercises. He was with the army in their battles and retreat through Jersey, during that dark and nearly hopeless period of the Revolution, and was almost the very last man that crossed the bridge over the stream immediately south of Trenton, before it was cut down by order of the American general. For this preservation he was indebted to a Quaker friend, whom he had essentially aided in his hour of trial—though of politics opposed to his own—and whose deliverance he had been the means of securing. The British officers had put a price upon his head, and were particularly anxious to destroy him, because of the influence he exerted among the soldiers of the American army. After the retreat from Princeton, he had retired to a private house in Trenton to seek repose, and was not aware that the American army had taken up their line of march and had nearly all crossed the bridge, until his Quaker friend, having ascertained that he was in the town, sought him out and gave him the alarm, just in time for him to escape before the bridge was destroyed by the retreating army of Washington.

He continued the pastor of the Third Presbyterian church until the day of his death, and was greatly respected and beloved by them. He received the degree of Doctor of Divinity from Yale College, in 1785. He died in Philadelphia, among the people of his charge, February 2nd, 1790, aged 57 years.

DUFFIELD, REV. GEORGE, was born in the village of Strasburg, Lancaster county, July 4th, 1794. His father, also named George, was a merchant, and for nine years Register and Comptroller General, under Governor McKean. His grandfather, also bearing the same name, was chaplain of the Old Continental Congress, an honor he held in connection with Bishop White.

The subject of this notice graduated at the early age of sixteen years, at the University of Pennsylvania, then under the Presidency of S. McDowell, LL.D. He read theology, and was licensed to preach by the Presbytery of Philadelphia, on the 20th of April, 1815. He immediately thereupon entered upon the duties of his profession, in which he faithfully continued to labor up to the day of his death. In 1817 he married, in New York city, Miss Isabella Bethune, a daughter of the well-known merchant, and sister of the Rev. George W. Bethune, D.D. In 1837 he was called to the Broadway Tabernacle as the successor of the Rev. Charles G. Finney. In 1838 he was called to the First Presbyterian congregation of Detroit, a position he at once accepted, and continued as the sole pastor thereof until April 27th, 1865, when the Rev. N. S. McCorkle was installed as associate pastor. The subject of this notice was honored with the title of Doctor of Divinity by the University of Pennsylvania.

Dr. Duffield was very regular and assiduous in his clerical ministrations, preaching regularly to his congregation, except when temporarily disabled, up to the period of his death. Even during the cholera epidemic of 1849, he steadily stood his post, and being severely prostrated by the malady, and from the effects of a chronic disease to which he had long been subject, he, at the earnest solicitation of his friends, accepted a leave of absence and went abroad for a year, and then returned completely restored to health.

In his own denomination, Dr. Duffield's learning and ability made him one of its most eminent divines. He ranked in the same category with Drs. Lyman Beecher, Albert Barnes, S. H. Cox, Bethune, Spring, and Sprague. His influence was long exerted and will be permanent. He died at Detroit, June 26th, 1868.

DUNLAP, JOHN M., is a native of Lancaster county, and a practicing physician in the borough of Manheim. He set out in life as a teacher of a subscription school, but soon after abandoned this for the study of medicine. He entered, as a student of medicine, the office of Dr. F. S. Burrowes, of Lancaster city, and graduated at the Jefferson Medical College, in 1845. He chose the borough of Manheim for the practice of his profession, and he was not long in establishing himself in a lucrative business, in which he is yet steadily engaged. In 1863 he was nominated and elected a State Senator, a position he filled by a courteous and close attention to the duties of the office.

DYSART, JAMES, was elected Clerk of the Orphans' Court in 1851.

E.

EBERMAN, JACOB, son of John Eberman, was elected County Treasurer in 1803. He was also elected Director of the Poor, a position he held for three years. He was commissioned by Governor McKean, a Justice of the Peace, but never acted in that capacity. He was a land agent for many years, and was instrumental in this line in securing and effecting land titles for the owners of property while the land office was located at Lancaster.

[1] EBERMAN, JOHN, was a clock-maker of Lancaster, and the manufacturer of the first town clock in Lancaster, and which is yet in existence.

EBERMAN, JOHN, a brother of Jacob Eberman, was cashier of one of the old Lancaster banks for thirty years.

EBERMAN, PETER G., son of Jacob Eberman, above named, held the office of Commissioners' Clerk for a period of upwards of a quarter of a century and until within the last five years. He is an Alderman of Lancaster City.

[1] The old town clock was made and put up by John Eberman in the old Court House, in 1786, at a cost of £550. About the year 1796 a new steeple was added to the building, the clock taken down and new hands put thereon, which were considerably larger than the old ones, improvements much commended at the time. It was on this occasion that Jacob Eberman, son of John Eberman, lost his hand. The clock was put up on a cold day of February, and his hand being numbed with the cold, was accidentally caught between the large wheel and pinion when the works were in motion, and the fingers literally ground off.

EBERLE, DR. JOHN, was born in Manor township, Lancaster county, in January, 1788. His father was a blacksmith, and designed his son to follow the same occupation, but his nature, fitted for another career, prompted him to make exertions to have his life directed in a different channel. Without more than the ordinary education of the schools of his district, he began the study of medicine under the direction of Dr. Abraham Carpenter, of Lancaster; afterwards he read with Dr. Clapp, in Philadelphia, and graduated Doctor of Medicine, at the University of Pennsylvania, in 1809. The subject of his inaugural address was *animal heat*. He entered upon the practice of medicine first in Manheim, Lancaster county, and after a few years removed to Lancaster city, where, a short time afterwards, he accepted a commission as surgeon to the Lancaster militia, and was present at the battle of Baltimore, in 1814. Whilst in Lancaster he became, for a short period, the editor of a political paper during a stirring gubernatorial election, and was thereby seduced into the meshes of office-hunters and unprincipled demagogues, and led into other kinds of practice, that for a season threatened him with entire ruin. In this way he lost all his practice as a physician in Lancaster, and was obliged to select a new location for the pursuit of his profession, and for this he determined upon the city of Philadelphia.

In 1815 he began the practice of his profession in this new location, where considerable time is usually required to establish an extensive business. Not long after this he wrote some articles which attracted marked attention, and he was thus induced, shortly afterwards, to essay the editorial management of a medical journal. In 1818 the *American Medical Recorder* made its debut, under the editorship of John Eberle, M. D., as a quarterly, and was ably sustained by men who were willing to furnish him their contributions without any pecuniary reward. To the establishment of this journal Dr. Eberle greatly owed his subsequent advancement and reputation; he was soon thereafter elected a member of the Linnæan Society of Philadelphia, and in 1822 the Berlin Medical Chirurgical Society enrolled his name in their list of foreign members. In 1825 he was elected a member of the Academy of Natural Sciences of Philadelphia.

He was active in promoting the interests of the Jefferson Medical College, and may be regarded as one of its most efficient founders. After the establishment of this institution he was appointed professor of the practice of Physic, in 1825, and in 1830 was transferred to the chair of Materia Medica, in the same college. He was lecturer, also, on obstetrics. In the fall of 1831 he removed with his family to Cincinnati, and was elected Professor of Materia Medica in the Ohio Medical College. In the changes which necessarily occurred on this occasion, he was called upon to resume the branch he had formerly taught in Jefferson College, and the practice of medicine again came within the immediate duty of his professional chair. He continued to discharge this responsible trust until 1837, when he was induced, from many circumstances, once more to change the the scene of his labors, and he removed to Lexington, Ky. The professorship of the practice of medicine was now tendered to him in the.medical department of the Transylvania University. He died shortly after his installment in this institution, at Lexington, February 2nd, 1838.

Besides his labors as editor of the *Medical Recorder*, he is the author of several distinct treatises which will long render his name familiar to the medical student. In 1822 his treatise on Therapeutics came before the public, one which was conceded not only in this country, but in distant lands, to be the very best work on the subject ever issued from the American press. As evidence of the high esteem placed upon it, the work was translated into several foreign languages, and has been quoted with marked approbation ever since. No American work on Therapeutics has ever yet been published so full of originality and real excellence. In 1830 appeared his practice of *Physic*, in 2 vols. octavo, a deservedly popular work, and since often re-printed. It was the only Philadelphia issue on practical medicine that had ever appeared, professing to be original to a great extent, and not a mere re-print of a foreign work with the addition of a few brief notes. This, like his Therapeutics, found its way into all the respectable libraries of the profession, and was made a text-book in various colleges. In 1833 he issued the first edition of his treatise on the Diseases of Children, a work of considerable merit, and one which met with a fair sale.

The life of Dr. Eberle was chiefly appropriated to the advancement of the profession he had selected as the business of his existence. His knowledge was the result of great individual effort, often under the most discouraging and adverse circumstances; and, nevertheless, it was various and extensive. To modern science, he added a familiar acquaintance with Hippocratic medicine, and his regard for the ancients led him to estimate somewhat unduly their merits. That he labored not in vain, may be inferred from the extensive circulation of his writings, and the estimation in which they are generally held both by the students of science and by men of clinical experience.

Dr. Alban Goldsmith, who was for five years a colleague of Dr. Eberle in the Medical College of Ohio, in a letter to Dr. Francis, of New York, thus writes of his lamented friend: "In a wide survey of medical men with whom I have had intercourse, I have rarely encountered one who possessed a larger share of professional knowledge in the several branches of healing than Dr. Eberle. To great extent of inf rmation he united a kind and courteous demeanor, and was never obtrusive in enforcing his practical opinions, except when they were assailed by ignorance and unwarrantable assurance. During the period that we labored together, he was a constant and indefatigable student, taking a wide survey of the philosophy of medicine. His lectures were always of a practical nature, and his hospital clinics filled with the most valuable facts, the result of careful observation. His deportment towards the junior members of the profession was universally kind and parental, and he was always ready to offer them aid in their inquiries. He was totally free from all professional envy, and his intercourse with his colleagues was characterized by the strictest laws of etiquette. Medicines or money were dispensed by him with like liberality to remove the sufferings and alleviate the calamities of the poor. In short, he was liberal to a fault and often care-less of his own proper interests. He deserves to be recorded as a successful pioneer in the valuable corps who have pro-moted the diffusion of real science in the great west, and his medical writings I think, may be justly estimated as having added to the claims which indigenous literature and science have upon the Confederation of the American Medical Fac-ulty."

His remains, after being for a time deposited in Lexington, were transferred to the Episcopal Cemetery in Cincinnati, where a monument marks their final resting spot.

EBERLY, SAMUEL, elected Recorder in 1839. He is the father of Adam J. Eberly, esq.

EBY FAMILY. This family is an old and numerous one; its members being scattered over different parts of Pennsylvania, the adjoining States of New York and Mary-land, and likewise reside in Canada and the west.

A perfect list of the individual members could not easily be had. Neither can all of the existing branches be traced to the parent stem.

The ancestor who first came to America, and from whom the greater part of the family has sprung, was named Theodorus.

Theodorus, a Swiss by birth, and a Mennonite in faith, left his native country on account of religious persecution, and resided for awhile in the " Palatinate" or " Pfaltz," an old division in Germany, whose chief towns were Manheim, Heidelberg, Simmern and Zwei Brucken.

When William Penn, by his agents, offered free homes to persons of all religious denominations, Theodorus emigrated to America and settled on Mill Creek, Lancaster county, at a place lately known as Roland's mill, situated south of New Holland, and near the line of Earl and Leacock townships.

It is said he had five or six sons in his family, skilled in the various mechanical arts; so that with their assistance he built a mill, and erected such other buildings as were needed, without employing persons outside of his family, except for the purpose of burning charcoal to supply the smith forge, which they did not themselves sufficiently understand.

The place of Theodorus' birth cannot now be definitely ascertained, there being no record in existence showing the fact. Family tradition has it, that he came from Canton "Schweitz," and must therefore have been of a race of hardy mountaineers.

The date of his arrival in Pennsylvania, is fixed by the Colonial Records, in 1715. And in the same year appears the names of Jacob Hochstetter, Jacob Kreider, Johannes Shenk and others. Five years later, in 1720, the family received an addition by emigration, in the person of Peter Eby, said to have been a relative of Theodorus; and still another much later, whose kinship, however, was never recognized.

In 1728, it appears that two persons were naturalized under the name of "Abye." These may have been sons of either Theodorus or Peter, and their names erroneously spelled by the government agent. It is to be observed that the descendants of Theodorus have always scrupulously adhered to the literal translation of the name, while some of the others have adopted the pronunciation of the German into the English, and wrote themselves "Eaby." So far as can be judged from the oldest known members, they must originally have been an active, quick-tempered, brown-eyed, dark-haired family.

The name of only one of the sons of Theodorus is now certainly known, which was Christian.

CHRISTIAN married a Mayer, and settled on Hammer Creek, in Elizabeth township, about three miles north of Litiz. He died in 1756. His wife died in 1787. They left a family of ten children as follows: Christian, Johannes, Barbara, married to Jacob Hershey, Peter, Anna, married to Christian Stauffer, Andrew, George, Elizabeth, married to Jacob Hershey, Samuel, and Michael.

His oldest son, Christian Eby, who married Catharine Bricker, retained the mansion place on Hammer Creek, which he greatly improved by building a new stone dwelling house, the date of which is 1754, a large barn, and a new mill and a dwelling house and barn for his son John.

He was a large, well-proportioned and athletic man, retaining unusual health and vigor of both body and mind, up to the time of his death. He was elder in the Mennonite church, and wore a long beard, which in his later years had turned white. Regular stated Mennonite meetings were held at his house, until a building for that special purpose was erected in the neighborhood.

He lived during the Revolutionary war, and foraging parties carried off some of his horses and cattle, as also large quantities of flour and grain out of his mill. On one occasion his wife's pewter dishes and spoons, and an' oven full of newly baked bread and pies shared the same fate.

During the winter in which the American army was encamped at Valley Forge, a number of disabled soldiers were quartered in the old Lutheran church, near Brickerville, and were supplied weekly with milk and other necessaries from his and other neighboring farms.

He died in 1807. His wife, who is said to have been an amiable and greatly esteemed person, surviving him several years. He left eleven children, as follows: 1. Elizabeth, wife of Joseph Bucher, resided near Lititz, and left descendants. 2. Christian, who resided on the home-place. 3. Peter, who moved to Pequea valley, and afterwards became a Mennonite Bishop. 4. John, who lived at the mill, adjoining the old place. 5. Andrew, who died, middle-aged, leaving several children, that afterwards moved to the west. 6. Catharine, wife of Abraham Burkholder, resided in Earl township. 7. Barbara, wife of Joseph Snyder, moved to Canada. 8. Anna, wife of Jacob Wissler, resided in Clay township. 9. George. 10. Benjamin, who moved to Canada, was made a minister in the Mennonite church, and succeeded his brother Peter as Bishop of the Mennonites in Canada. 11. Maria, wife of Jacob Brubacher, resided in Elizabeth township.

CHRISTIAN EBY, son of Christian the second, was married to a Hershey, and left the following children: 1. Catharine, died unmarried. 2. Elizabeth, wife of David Gingrich, resided in Lancaster county. Left eight children, among whom are Samuel, Christian, and John, who follow farming, and are useful citizens; the latter being an active school director, and treasurer of the board of East Hempfield. 3. Anna, wife of Samuel Nissley, residing in Rapho township, had a family of children. 4. Maria, wife of Peter Eby, resided in Penn township, and left two sons, Seth and Joel. 5. Barbara, wife of Abraham Reist, resided in Penn township, and had a family of children. 6. Rev. Benjamin, served as a minister among the Mennonites for many years, up to the time of his death. Retained the old mansion place, at Hammer creek, the greater portion of his life, and afterwards moved to Washington county, Maryland, where he died. He left four sons and one daughter, all residing out of the county. 7. Christian resided in East Hempfield township, and left three children. Fanny died unmarried; Ann, wife of John Gingrich, and Elizabeth, wife of Abm. Rohrer, both residing in Hempfield township. 8. Sem resides in Leacock township, follows farming, a worthy man, and father of a numerous family. 9. Susan, wife of Henry Stauffer, resides in Rapho township, and has two sons and two daughters.

PETER EBY, married to Margaret Hess, moved to Salisbury township, near the Gap, in 1791, and followed farming when his time was not taken up by his duties as a minister of the gospel or bishop in the Mennonite church. He was ordained a minister in 1800, and the second among his denomination in that neighborhood. Up to 1814 he preached in private houses; then a school-house was erected, and afterwards a meeting-house for that special purpose.

This member of the family deserves more than a passing notice. His fame as a preacher was widely known, and served to fill the houses to their utmost capacity wherever he was known to officiate.

The ministers in the Mennonite church are not educated for the pulpit, nor adopt the ministry as a profession; they are chosen by lot, whenever a position is to be filled, from a small number of the congregation considered most worthy.

Several ministers usually reside convenient to a particular meeting-house, where they are expected to officiate upon all ordinary occasions. On communion days, and other special occasions, a Bishop is required to be present. The bishops have also certain districts allotted to each, and the privilege of presiding amongst them is generally accorded to the senior in office, or the most eminent in abilities. This position Peter held for many years, up to the time of his death; and his authority also extended over the church in Canada, until he was succeeded there by his younger brother, Benjamin.

To form some idea of his powers as an orator, it is necessary to state that the principal sermon in the Mennonite churches was always prefaced by an introductory discourse from one of the younger ministers present; and that on communion day, the subject invariably used to be Bible history, from Adam down, bringing out the prominent events and prophecies pointing to the new dispensation. The introductory discourse generally brought it down to the time of Noah and Isaac, when it would be taken up by the Bishop and continued to the birth of Christ, His ministry on earth, and His final suffering and death. Old as the story had become, the audience never tired listening to it from the eloquent lips of Peter. When he slowly arose, all noise subsided into an almost painful expectation. Then he would break the silence with a kind and fatherly greeting to his hearers, and glide gently into the course marked out for himself. Proceeding step by step, describing, explaining, illustrating and sustaining his points as he went along, with copious quotations from the Scriptures, for all of which he drew upon his extraordinary memory, he would gradually warm up in his theme, and, when under full sway, his discourse moved along like a deep, clear stream, rolling oceanward, without a break or ripple, grand, majestic, and irresistible. His powers, however, were brought out most fully when he came to portray the acts and sufferings of his Master during his last few days upon earth. The scene in Gethsemane ; the sleeping disciples ; the noise and tumult breaking upon the stillness of the night, when the armed men came to take Him ; the doings before the Jewish and Roman tribunals ; the embarrassment of Pontius Pilate, and his fruitless devices to save Jesus ; the message sent him by his wife ; his last resort, when he gave the Jews to choose between Jesus and Barabbas, and the cries of the infuriated multitude that pronounced his condemnation. Then the sorrowful train moving up Calvary; the preparation to carry the fearful sentence into execution; and lastly, the finishing act in the sublime drama; the Saviour of mankind nailed between heaven and earth, His side pierced, and yet, with parched lips, in the agonies of death, crying to the Father to forgive; the darkening of the heavens, the quaking of the earth, and the elements bearing witness, in thunders and lightnings, to the divinity of Him that was suffering. All this he would portray in a manner so vivid that the speaker would be forgotten in the subject. Then, as his voice, suppressed by emotion, and sinking into silence, would allow the attention of his hearers to return to the speaker, he would stand before them, tears streaming down his cheeks, his countenance glowing, and his raised hands directing the penitent sinner, as it were, to the foot of a visible cross.

His preaching was altogether extemporaneous, and its effect upon an audience great. And yet he was not a sensational preacher; he addressed the judgment as well as the feelings, and his discourses abounded in arguments and reasonings that were listened to with admiration by the most polemical or logical. So much was this the case, that it frequently happened, that strangers hearing him for the first time, although otherwise informed, would not be convinced that he was not a person regularly educated and trained for the ministry.

His personal appearance also was greatly in his favor, being somewhat above medium height, well proportioned and fleshy, with a high, square, even forehead, a finely formed face, that had it not indicated quite as much force, might have been called classic; a deportment easy, grave and dignified. An acquaintance of his, who had heard some of the most noted orators of the state and nation, in and out of the pulpit, gave it as his opinion, that for none of them, it seemed, had nature done so much towards making the "Orator," as for this grand old servant of the church.

In the councils over which he presided as Bishop, his voice was equally potent. His clear intellect enabled him to probe difficulties to the bottom; and his impartial decisions pronounced without fear or favor, were acknowledged to be just, and rarely appealed from.

He died April 6th, 1843, in the 78th year of his age. His family consisted of nine children who arrived to adult age; the names of only three were furnished the author, viz.: Peter, Christian and Henry, and one of the daughters, married to a Stauffer.

JOHN EBY resided at the mill adjoining the old mansion place, and was a quiet, unobtrusive, but prominent man in the community in which he lived. A miller and a farmer by occupation, he dealt extensively in produce, which he had transported to Newport and Philadelphia, keeping a team of his own for that purpose, and also employing teams of his neighbors when they could be spared from the farms.

He was a promoter of improvements. In the day of turnpikes he served as a director; had roads laid out; one to open communication between the town of Manheim and the Ephrata turnpike, at Durlach, and one from his place to Brickerville, besides others. The first school-house in the neighborhood was built on his farm, at his own private expense, where the youth of the neighborhood were educated by teachers procured by him.

It was mostly through his influence that the Mennonites of Lancaster county purchased a large tract of land in Canada, to assist their distressed brethren in that part of the world, and which subsequently became the home of many of their descendants. He left eight children, viz: 1. Catharine, wife of John Hostetter, who resided in Manor township, her family consisting of seven children, John, Elias, Jonas, Abraham D., Martha, Mary and Catharine. 2. Jonas, married to Fanny Nissley, resides in West Hempfield township; family consisted of six children, who arrived to adult age, John N., Elias, (now a school director of Rapho), Samuel N., Simon J., Henry N., and Fanny. 3. Mary, wife of Jacob Yundt, resided formerly in Elizabeth township, but moved to Neipersville, Illinois; family consisting of seven children. 4. Rebecca, wife of John Bomberger, resided near Manheim borough, and left three children, Martha, Christian and Sem. 5. Elias resided at the mill in Elizabeth township, followed farming and milling; was elected sheriff of Lancaster county in 1851, serving three years; died September, 1862, in the 57th year of his age. Left three children, Simon P., a practicing attorney in Lancaster city; Mary, and Eliza. 6. Elizabeth, wife of Samuel Risser, resided in West Hempfield township, now in Mt. Joy borough. Her family consisted of seven children, Ann, wife of Jacob K. Nissley, Mary, Levi, Jonas, Reuben, Samuel and Joseph. 7. Levi resided in Rapho township; followed farming, and left five daughters, Mary, Sarah, Fanny, Fianna and Rebecca. 8. Anna, wife of Rev. Samuel Hershey, resides near Manheim borough. Her family consists of four children, viz: Levi, Henry, Mary and Anna.

CATHARINE BURKHOLDER had a son by the name of Christian. He married Veronica Groff, who resided in West Earl township.

Her grandchildren are: 1st, Seth, moved to Whiteside county, Illinois. 2. Christiana, late wife of John B. Sensenig, resided in Earl township. 3. Elias, moved to Whiteside county, Illinois. 4. Ezra, resides in West Earl township, is a justice of the peace, surveyor and scrivener. 5. Catharine, wife of John Martin, resides in West Earl township. 6. Menno, resides in West Earl township. 7. Frances, wife of Adam Myers, resides in Upper Leacock township. 8. Maria. 9. Groff. 10. Ann. These three reside in West Earl township. 11. Christian, deceased. 12. Peter, moved to Whiteside county, Illinois.

ANNA WISLER'S FAMILY. 1. Andrew, moved to Michigan. 2. Jacob, resided in Clay township, farmer left four children. 3. Christian, resided in Clay township, followed milling, left four children. 4. Martha, wife of Jacob Landis, resided in Ephrata township, left three children. 5. Ezra, resides in Clay township, follows farming, family consisting of two sons. 6. Mary, wife of Levi Erb, moved to Canada, and now resides in Shenandoah county, Virginia, family consisting of two daughters. 7. John, moved to Canada, and afterwards to Shenandoah county, Virginia, where he was engaged in the iron business, and died leaving six children. 8. Samuel, resided in Canada, engaged in the milling and manufacturing business, left family of some five children. 9. Levi, resides on the old Wissler family mansion in Clay township, one of the first places settled in that neighborhood, and originally owned by a person named Groff.

Rev. Benjamin Eby, who succeeded his brother Peter as presiding Bishop of the Mennonites in Canada, was married to an Erb, and left a family of eleven children, one of whom also became a minister of the Gospel.

He moved to Canada in and settled where Berlin, the county town of Waterloo county now stands; but which was at was at that time an unbroken forest. He died in a few years ago. His farm, like many others in that county, afterwards settled upon by Lancaster county people, was a part of the large tract purchased by the Mennonites, as mentioned in the notice of his elder brother John.

Two of his sons became printers, and for many years published a newspaper, as also hymn books and other religious works. The latter being done under the supervision of their father.

Maria Brubaker's Family. 1. Sem, resides in Rapho township; has two sons. Martin N. is a justice of the peace, and follows surveying and scrivening. Rev. Jacob N. follows farming, and is a minister, of much promise, in the Mennonite church. 2. Henry E. resides in Elizabeth township, and is the present owner of the old Eby mansion place, on Hammer creek, follows farming and has a family. 3. Isaac, resides in Rapho, and is a farmer. 4. Jacob E., resides on the old Brubaker mansion place, in Elizabeth township, and follows farming. 5. Maria, wife of John Reist, resides in Penn township. 6. ———, wife of Jacob Brubaker, resides in Lancaster township. 7. Anna, wife of Rev. Horst, resides near Manheim borough.

There was a Christian Eby, who resided near Neffsville, and died in 1867, near Brickerville. He was a descendant of Theodorus by another branch. Left nine children: John, resides in Cumberland county; Eliza, wife of Abm. Metzler; Christian, resides in Conestoga Centre; Mary, wife of Erhard Lutz; Anna, wife of Elias Barr, resides in Lancaster city

Benjamin moved to Ohio; Lydia, wife of E. Pfautz; Ephraim O., resides near Brickerville; Catharine, wife of Daniel Flory.

There was an Ephraim Eby, who lived near Elizabethtown, a much esteemed man. He had seven children; Jacob, merchant and banker, resides in Harrisburg; Ephraim, merchant, resides in Philadelphia; Mrs. Grove, of Columbia, and Mrs. Weaver, of Lancaster city. Three dead. A third brother, Jacob, resides in Ohio.

There was a Jacob Eby, a cousin of the elder Christian, who settled on a farm on Hammer creek, Elizabeth township, now owned by Jacob R. Hess. He left three sons: Abraham married, but had no children; Peter, who lived a hermit (Einsiedler), in a pleasant little home in Elizabeth township; died in 1836, leaving a will, by which he directed all his estate and property, of which he possessed a considerable amount, to be distributed in flour among the deserving poor, irrespective of age, sex, nation, color, or religion. This was faithfully carried out by his executors, such distribution being made gradually, and lasting three or four years; two wagon loads were sent to Lancaster city, and there distributed from the hardware store of Geo. Louis Mayer. He also wrote and published a small religious work, most copies of which were either sold or distributed after his death.

The other son, Abraham, left four children, viz: Abraham, Peter, John and Jonas. Of these the first named lived in East Cocalico township, and had eight children. The second lived near Manheim borough, and had two sons; the third left one son in Iowa, and the last named resided near Shœneck, and left one daughter, wife of Henry B. Erb.

There was a Peter Eby who settled in Upper Leacock township, and married a Roland. His family consisted of eight children: Peter, Samuel, Henry, John, David, Christian, Andrew, Ann, wife of Abm. Wenger. The two oldest, Peter and Samuel, served in the Revolutionary war, under Capt. Roland, and were present in the American army when the British took New York, in 1776. Samuel afterwards married and resided in Leacock township, and followed farming. He left four children, Samuel, Jonas, Barbara, wife of Wm. Good; Elizabeth, wife of John Good.

15

His son, Jonas Eby, married a Line, and his family consists of three children, viz: Samuel Eby, a justice of the peace, surveyor and scrivener, and banker, residing in Elizabethtown; Isaac, and Lavina, wife of Martin Leber.

There was also Isaac Eby, of Leacock township, father of Major Christian Eby, who at one time was the owner of Roland's mill, where Theodorus settled, and adjoining which some of his descendants still live.

Jacob S. Eby, who resides on a farm in Upper Leacock township, that has been in the name for about a century, is the son of Jacob, and a grandson of Daniel Eby.

Moses and Joel Eby, of Intercourse, are said to be of the same branch as Jacob S. Eby, although they write their names Eaby.

There was also Christian Eby, of Rapho township, lately deceased, who followed farming and milling, and who left a family of well-doing children, among whom are Jacob and George.

The only descendants of Samuel Eby, who lived about two miles south of Manheim, are a daughter, married to Henry Kurtz, of Mt. Joy borough, and a daughter married to ——— Eberly, of Clay township.

ECKMAN, JOHN, a member of the Legislature in 1794.

EDIE, JOHN, elected State Senator in 1792.

EDWARDS, THOS., a member of the Legislature in the years 1729, 1730, 1731, 1732, 1735, 1736 and 1739.

EHLER, JOHN, elected sheriff of Lancaster county in 1842.

EHRENFRIED, JOSEPH, was born in the city of Mayence, in Hesse Darmstadt, Germany, on the 25th of December, 1783. His parents were members of the Roman Catholic faith, and designed him for the priesthood, and sent him to school to be educated for this purpose. At the age of nineteen he left his native country, and emigrated to America about 1802. He began his career in this country as a school teacher, in 1803, in the "Grove School House," in East Donegal township, Lancaster county. Not long after this period Mr. Ehrenfried received the situation of translator and book-keeper in Albright's printing establishment, in the city of Lancaster, where he acquired a practical knowledge of the "art preservative of all arts;" and in 1808, in connection with William Hamilton, he established the *Volksfreund*, a German paper, which he disposed of to John Baer, in 1817, by whose sons the paper yet continues to be published. He continued in the establishment of Mr. Baer as editor, translator and compositor for twenty years, during which time he translated into German "Buck's Theological Dictionary," and published in German the works of Dietrich Phillips; wrote and published in German "Ehrenfried's Colloquial Phrases," besides a number of other works.

About 1837 he made two visits to his native country, and after his return he removed to Harrisburg, the capital of the State, and published the *Vaterland's Waechter;* and during the administration of Governor Ritner, he held the office of German State printer. He subsequently established the *Friedensboten*, a German newspaper, at Allentown, Pa., which he disposed of some time thereafter, and accepted the office of Deputy Register of Wills, of Lancaster county, in 1845, which he filled until the autumn of 1860, performing the duties thereof entirely to the satisfaction of his superior officer and the community at large, and retiring only at the dictation of age and increasing infirmity.

In 1809 Mr. Ehrenfried married Mrs. Ann Smith, formerly Miss Ann Hubley, a daughter of Bernard Hubley, esq., of Lancaster city, and had celebrated both his silver and his golden wedding days, an event that happens to so few in proportion to the number of marriages. About the year 1816 he became a receiver of the doctrines of the New Church (Swedenborgian), through the instrumentality of Professor Frederick Damish, a Saxon music teacher, a congenial and intimate friend. In 1835 or 1836 he became connected with the "Lancaster New Jerusalem Society," and held the office of president for twenty years. In the welfare of his church Mr. Ehrenfried always manifested a deep interest, as did he also in that of the church at large. He was cotemporary with Damish, Young, Girling, and Keefer.

Mr. Ehrenfried died March 6th, 1862, in the 79th year of his age. In his conduct and deportment he was one of the meekest of men, was most highly esteemed by all classes of citizens, and we hazard the assertion that he died without an enemy. He was an industrious and working man, and in addition to his usual vocation did much in compiling and translating from the English into the German language. Only a short time before his death he was engaged in the translation of Noble's Lectures, for the *Monatschrift*.

The following, as illustrative of his entire rectitude of principle, deserves to be recorded. Having proved unfortunate, he became involved in debt, and all his property passed from his hands. After living in Harrisburg and having regained a footing, he visited Lancaster and gave public announcement in the papers, that he would meet his creditors on a certain day, and pay them his indebtedness, at a place specified. He met his creditors, according to announcement, and paid all his debts, great and small, and from that day forth acted upon the scriptural injunction, " Owe no man anything."

EICHHOLTZ, HENRY, was, in September, 1818, appointed Prothonotary of the Supreme Court of the Lancaster district, in the room of John Hoff, deceased.

EICHHOLTZ, JACOB, was born in the borough of Lancaster, in the year 1776, and shortly after the declaration of American Independence. He, in after years, congratulated himself in having the fortune to be born an American instead of a British subject. His parents were of German ancestry, and having a large family, were not in circumstances to afford the subject of our notice more than a limited English education. His father and three of his brothers bore arms in the struggle of the American Colonies for independence. At the early age of seven years, he showed signs of that inborn trait which, in after-life, enrolled him as a painter of wide repute, and rendered him a marked man in his day. It was as a child up in his father's garret with a piece of red chalk, that he was in the habit of delineating the infantile specimens of his art upon the walls; but his father was unable to appreciate the budding genius, and little heeded these monitions of superior intellect. Besides a few lessons obtained from a sign painter, young Eichholtz received no instruction in that art for the knowledge of which his whole soul was aspiring; and he, in after years, was in the habit of remarking the intense agony that seized him when the sad tale of the sign painter's suicide was brought to his ears, occasioned by unrequited love. All the bright hopes that had dawned upon his youthful vision seemed in this occurrence as buried forever. Sadness for a time seated itself upon the throne of his spiritual existence, and but blank grief seemed to be invited in the prospect of his future career. The instruction in painting he had already received was but as nothing, but the little seed had been sown in a fertile soil.

He was next apprenticed by his father to learn the coppersmith business, and whilst engaged in this business, his predilection was still showing itself in the sketches of his fellow apprentices pictured on the walls of the shop with charcoal. After the expiration of his apprenticeship, he began business as a coppersmith upon his own account; but ever and continually the ruling passion of his inner life was manifesting itself. Chance, as it were, brought a painter to Lancaster, and this formed a pivot of his after career. He now had an opportunity to gather from this painter all the information of which he was in possession as regards the art of his aspirations. Prior to this period, he says: "I had made some rude efforts, with terrible success, having nothing more than a boot-jack for a palette, and anything in the shape of a brush, for at that time brushes were not to be had even in Philadelphia. At length I was fortunate enough to get a few half-worn brushes from Sully, when on the eve of his departure for England. This was a great feast for me, and enabled me to go on until others were to be had."

Having by this time a family of several children, he hesitated the abandonment of the coppersmith business for that of painting, not being fully convinced of the pecuniary result that might follow such a step. To attempt to support his family by painting, seemed hazardous, and his prudent nature forbade a doubtful enterprise. He therefore still carried on the business of his trade, and alternated his time between coppersmithing and painting. The specimens of his skill as a painter went forth, and his reputation steadily grew. His shop became the resort of the fashionable and wealthy. It was no unusual thing for him to be called out of his shop to see a fair lady who desired her picture painted. The coppersmith immediately became the face painter. At length his patronage in the career of his choice enabled him to abandon the coppersmith business and devote all his time to painting. His fame as a painter spread, and he was called upon by the highest magnates of America to have their likenesses painted. Among others he painted a portrait of Nicholas Biddle, President of the United States Bank.

He was now urged by a friend, who appreciated his superior abilities, to visit Boston, then the seat of the American fine arts. He resolved to act upon this suggestion. He visited Boston, and was accorded a handsome reception by gentlemen who were able to appreciate his skill. He took with him a specimen of his workmanship, and called upon the eminent painter, Stuart. Of this interview, Eichholtz says: "Here I had a fiery trial to undergo. My picture was placed alongside of the best of his hand, and that lesson I considered the best I had ever received. The comparison was, I thought, enough; and if I had vanity before I went, it all left me before my return." Stuart, however, assured him that he should not be discouraged, and that the specimen of his skill warranted his perseverance.

Upon his return, finding his native town too small to support a painter, he removed to Philadelphia, where, by an incessant practice of ten years and constant employment, he gathered a competence, and afterwards returned to his native town. He died May 11th, 1842.

The following is a copy of Sully's account of his first meeting with Mr. Eichholtz:

"When Governor Snyder was elected I was employed by Mr. Binns to go on to Lancaster and paint a portrait of the new chief magistrate of the State. Eichholtz was then employing all his leisure hours, stolen from the manufacturing of tin kettles and coffee-pans, in painting; his attempts were hideous. He kindly offered me the use of his painting room, which I readily accepted, and gave him, during my stay in Lancaster, all the professional information I could impart, (in that interim he had visited and copied Stuart). I was much surprised and gratified.

I have no doubt that Eichholtz would have made a first-rate painter, had he begun early in life, with the usual advantages.

In my intercourse with Eichholtz I have admired in him a man of frank, simple and unpretending manners, whose conversation marked his good sense, and whose conduct evinced that propriety which has led to his success and ultimate independence. Mr. T. B. Freeman informs me that, in 1821, he saw at Harrisburg a portrait, by Eichholtz, which excited his curiosity; and going to Lancaster, called upon him and invited him to Philadelphia, where the first portrait he painted was Freeman's, and soon afterwards Commodore Gales." *Dunlap's History of the Arts of Design*, Vol. II, p. 228.

EICHHOLTZ, LEONARD, was an innkeeper, and kept the tavern with the sign of the "Bull's Head." He was father of Jacob Eichholtz, the painter, and died April 26th, 1817, in the 67th year of his age. He had been for many years an elder of Trinity Lutheran church, and a highly esteemed and respected citizen.

ELLMAKER, AMOS, son of Nathaniel Ellmaker, was born February 2nd, 1787, in New Holland, Lancaster county, Pa. Giving early indications of marked ability, his father determined upon giving him a first-class education, and for this purpose sent him to Yale College, where he finished his collegiate career; afterwards he completed his law studies at the celebrated law school, under Judge Reeves, at Litchfield, Connecticut.

He began the practice of his profession at Harrisburg, and was not long in establishing himself in his profession. In 1816 he married Mary R., daughter of Thomas Elder, esq., of that place. He was an officer in the army that marched from Pennsylvania to the defence of Baltimore, in the war of 1812. He was appointed Prosecuting Attorney for Dauphin county, and was elected three times from the same county a member of the House of Representatives. In 1814 he was elected a member of Congress, but declined to take his seat, having been appointed President Judge of the district composed of the counties of Dauphin, Lebanon and Schuylkill. He resigned his judgeship and was appointed Attorney-General of the Commonwealth of Pennsylvania, which position he also resigned, and afterwards, in 1821, removed to Lancaster, where he began the practice of his profession. Here, as a lawyer, he met with extraordinary success, and retired from his labors in independence. He was the candidate of the Anti-Masonic party for Vice President of the United States, in 1832. In 1834 he received the next highest vote to James Buchanan for United States Senator, when the latter was elected. He died November 28th, 1851.

Amos Ellmaker possessed, in a considerable degree, the particular characteristics of his father. He was no courter of popular favor, but on many occasions, when proffered, he refused to accept distinguished stations. Upon the accession of James Monroe to the Presidency, Mr. Ellmaker was tendered the appointment of Secretary of War, a post for which he was admirably qualified, but which he promptly declined, notwithstanding the urgent solicitations of his friends to accept the same. He preferred the quiet enjoyments of private life to all the pomp and consequence of official position.

Mr. Ellmaker possessed, in an eminent degree, those characteristics that go to make up the soul of a great man. In addition to a vast fund of information on all subjects, he possessed a lively, social disposition, that made his presence pleasing to all; and no one had more of that elevation of mind and generosity of soul which distinguish men of rare endowments, than he.

In all the relations and positions of life, he was a model worthy of imitation. He was distinguished for great courtesy to the younger members of the profession, and was ready at all times to take by the hand young men struggling to rise by their own industry and merits. As a lawyer, he always advised the settlement of differences by amicable adjustment, without resort to legal means; and many there are who, having taken his advice, escaped the costs and harassing attendance upon courts from protracted and ruinous law-suits. As counsel, his effort always was to have the parties to settle their differences among themselves, although such advice was against his interest as an attorney. But he took it be his duty to guard the interests of his client, and not look upon him as a bird caught in a snare to be plucked.

He entertained the highest regard for strict integrity, and no one devoid of this trait of character could secure his confidence or friendship. His associates must be free even from the suspicion of a lack of principle. He regarded honesty as the foundation of human excellence, but with those lacking this ingredient of character, he chose to have little intercourse, as they were unable to command his esteem.

He took a lively interest in all the political movements of the day; and although not conspicuous as a politician, yet his views and opinions had great weight in controling the course of public affairs. Indeed, his sentiments in all the movements of the Anti-Masonic and Whig parties were anxiously sought for and highly respected. His judgment was rarely at fault, and his inflexible honesty and steadiness of purpose caused his counsels always to be regarded as wisdom. He continued to enjoy the esteem and high consideration of his numerous friends unimpaired until his death. Nathaniel Ellmaker, esq., son of Amos Ellmaker, has for many years been one of the leading lawyers of Lancaster. His Orphans' Court business is, perhaps, the largest of any lawyer at the Lancaster bar.

ELLMAKER, LEONARD, emigrated from Germany and settled in Earl township, in 1726. His son, Nathaniel Ellmaker, was elected a member of the Pennsylvania State Senate in 1796. He was noted for his indomitable perseverance, independence, integrity and love of truth, and bore the reputation of being a man of considerable ability.

ENGLE, HENRY M., a leading farmer and fruit grower of East Donegal township, Lancaster county. He was one of the first in the county who began fruit growing as a business pursuit. He was elected President of the Agricultural and Horticultural Society, in January, 1869, a position he has held by annual reëlections up to the present time. He was elected a member of the Legislature in 1870, receiving the support of both political parties. Mr. Engle bears an unimpeachable reputation for honesty, entertains no political aspirations, and became a candidate for office, on the occasion above referred to, simply in deference to the wishes of friends.

*ERB FAMILY. Nicholas Erb, the first known ancestor of this name, came to America with his family in the year 1722. He was a Swiss by birth, and, it is said, his father desired him to become a Catholic priest, but he joined the Mennonites and left his native country on account of religious persecutions. He resided for some time, before emigrating to this country, at a place called "Wester Walter Hoff." Where this place of temporary residence was located, is not known. In all probability it must have been a farm on the outposts of some province in Germany that had dangerous neighbors, and the time must have been somewhat turbulent, as it is known that he lived under the promised protection of his Lord or Superior, and in case of an unexpected attack, it had been agreed that he should give notice by firing a gun. It is also related that, either to try the efficiency of the signal or the faithfulness of his landlord, he fired the gun, and in a short time had the satisfaction of seeing his protector, with his retainers, coming to his assistance as fast as horses could bring them.

He settled on Hammer creek, in Warwick township, near where the mill, lately owned by David Erb, one of his descendants, now stands. He was a farmer by occupation. He had a family of five children—four sons and one daughter; the latter married to a Johns.

John, eldest son of Nicholas Erb, came to America with his father, married a Johns from Leacock township, lived for some time with his father, but subsequently moved near to Manheim, where he died. His children were: Jacob, John, Christian, Daniel, Peter and Magdalena.

Nicholas Erb, second son of Nicholas Erb.

Christian Erb, third son of Nicholas Erb.

Jacob Erb, a prominent clergyman in the United Brethren congregation, stationed at the Otterbein church, in Baltimore, and frequently presiding elder, is a descendant of either Nicholas or Christian.

Jacob Erb, fourth son of Nicholas Erb, resided on Hammer creek, in Warwick township, where Erb's mill now stands. He was a leading man among the German popula-

*Contributed by Levi Reist, esq., of Warwick.

tion in the northern part of this county from 1760 to 1790. He was a member of the Legislature when it sat in Philadelphia in 1787, 1788, 1789, and 1790. He had two sons, John and Christian.

Magdalena Erb, daughter of Nicholas Erb, married to a Johns, of Leacock township.

Jacob Erb, son of John, and a grandson of Nicholas Erb, resided near the Mouth of Cocalico creek ; had three sons, John, David and Emanuel. The two former settled in York county, Pennsylvania, and Emanuel kept the homestead. He had one son, Jacob, who still owns the home place, together with some five or six hundred acres of land in Warwick and West Earl townships, and is extensively engaged in farming and stock-raising.

John Erb, son of John and grandson of Nicholas Erb, had one son also named John, who settled in Conoy township, from whence he moved to Linn county, Indiana, with all of his family except Christian S., who now resides in Conoy ; a business man, justice of the peace, and bank director.

Christian Erb, son of John and grandson of Nicholas Erb, born February 6th, 1755, died August 1st, 1812, resided in Warwick township, about one mile north of Litiz ; and was married to Anna Bomberger, born February 8th, 1752, died September 17th, 1823. She is reputed to have been a stately and prim old lady, who, being a Mennonite, wore her dresses plain, but of rich materials, with a snowy kerchief and cap. She was well versed in the Scriptures. They had two sons : Christian and Jacob, between whom their father's place was divided—and a daughter, married to Henry Hostetter, who moved to Hanover, York county, Pennsylvania. Christian, the eldest son, moved to the neighborhood of Dayton, Ohio, having sold his part of the farm.

Jacob Erb, the younger son of Christian, and great grandson of Nicholas Erb, born March 7th, 1781, resided the greater part of his life on the old farm, subsequently moved with his son Henry to Penn township, and afterwards into Manheim township, about one mile north of Lancaster, where he died. He was an active business man in the earlier part of his life and carried on farming and distilling. He was married to Elizabeth Becker, who, dying young, left him a family of seven small children to raise, which parental duty he performed in the most commendable manner, never marrying the second time. He no doubt inherited his mother's taste as to dress, and was known as " gentleman Erb." He became a member of the Legislature in 1833–34 and 1834–35, serving two terms. He was elected on the Anti-Masonic ticket, but declined to follow the ultra men of that party in their extreme measures (of whom Thaddeus Stevens, at that time also in the House, was one), and became classed with those calling themselves National men. His children were Ann, married to Christian Kauffman, moved to Ohio, who had four sons in the Union army. Henry, married to Elizabeth Spickler, now living in Manheim township with his son-in-law, Jacob Myer. Sarah, married to Joseph Bomberger, lives in Cumberland county, Pennsylvania, and whose son, Jacob Bomberger, was a member of the Legislature from that county in 1872. Eliza, married to Elias Eby, ex-sheriff. Catharine, married to David Witwer, moved to Franklin county. Levi, married to Mary Trissler, now residing at Columbia furnace; Virginia, and Mary, married to Elias Bomberger, living in Maryland.

Daniel Erb, son of John, and grandson of Nicholas Erb, had four sons: John, Joseph, Daniel and Jacob. The first named was a minister of the old Mennonite persuasion, and moved many years ago to Cumberland county. Joseph had one son, Daniel S., who resides in Penn township, and follows farming. Daniel has three sons, David W., Daniel W., and John. The old home place that has been in the family for over a century, is owned by Daniel W.; and Israel G. Erb, esq., a rising young man in the neighborhood, is the son of David W.

Peter Erb, son of John, and grandson of Nicholas Erb, had four sons: Isaac, Jacob, Christian, and another who moved to Canada. Isaac had three sons: Henry, Samuel and Isaac, who live in Lebanon county.

Magdalena Erb, daughter of John, and grand-daughter of Nicholas Erb, married a man named Gingrich, whose family moved to Erie county, Pa.

John Erb, son of Jacob, and grandson of Nicholas Erb, had several sons; one of them, named after himself, who lived in Elizabeth township, near Durlach, was a miller and farmer, and kept the tavern where, for many years, the elections were held; was a prominent politician from 1825 to 1840; filled the office of County Commissioner from 1833 to 1836, where his economical management of county affairs made him popular. He was also a candidate for sheriff in 1833 on the same ticket with Gen. David Miller. He had four children: Hiram, now residing in Lebanon county; John B., residing in Litiz; Henry B., residing near Schœneck; and a daughter, married to Geo. Steinmetz, residing on the old place, now in Clay township. His sons are all intelligent and well to do men; John B. follows surveying and scrivening, and served many years as a justice of the peace while living in Clay township.

ESHLEMAN, DAVID G., was born and raised in Strasburg township,[1] Lancaster county. He graduated at Dickinson College, Carlisle, in the year 1840. He entered, as a student of law, the office of John R. Montgomery, esq., and was admitted as a member of the bar in 1842. After coming to the bar he was not long in establishing himself in his

[1] *Strasburg township* was established before or about the time of the creation of the county of Lancaster. As it was established, it included the township of Paradise, which has since been cut off. The part that still retains the original name was settled chiefly by Swiss Mennonites, who emigrated by way of Holland, from 1710 to 1725. The descendants of the early settlers are still to be found in the township, such as the Herrs, Groffs, Eshlemans, Brenemans, Neffs, Lefevres, Kendigs, Brackbills, Brubakers, Buckwalters, Leamans, Howrys, Millers, Lantzs, Hostetters, Myers, &c., &c.

The buildings and improvements of all new communities seem to pass through formations similar to the geological primary, secondary, and tertiary, before they become permanent. In this county we have pretty generally reached the tertiary period. Many buildings of the secondary period remain, however, and occasionally we find remaining one of the primary period. Of this class there are several of minor importance in the township of Strasburg, three of which are deserving of notice.

One of them, perhaps the oldest large house in the county, is situate about a mile east of the borough of Strasburg, and in the occupancy of Dr. Abraham Eshleman. The old portion of the house was finished in the first decade of the last century, and the "new end" was finished in

profession, to the duties of which he has applied himself with great assiduity up to the present time. He was one of the representatives from Lancaster county, in the Legislature, during the sessions of 1848 and 1849.

Mr. Eshleman has always been a close and industrious student, and he justly ranks amongst the best read members of the Lancaster bar. His mind is of a juridical cast, and his opinions upon critical points of law are frequently sought by the other members of the profession. In 1871 he was the Democratic candidate for judge of the several courts of Lancaster county.

EVANS, DAVID, was born in Manheim township, February 21st, 1827. His father was of Irish, and his mother of German descent. He was sent by his parents to the common schools of the neighborhood, and acquired a knowledge of the branches then customary to be taught, viz.: reading, writing and arithmetic. When about thirteen years of age, he attended a quasi select school, taught by a man named Sutherland, and here he began the study of the advanced branches of an education. He worked on the farm and also aided in the butchering business, which was the trade of his father.

He early evinced a great fondness for reading, and pro-

1741. It is at present occupied by the fifth generation, as a family residence, of the family now represented by Jacob Eshleman, of Paradise, Dr. Isaac S. Eshleman, of Philadelphia, Dr. Frank Eshleman, of Downingtown, Dr. Abram Eshleman, of Strasburg, Benjamin Eshleman, of East Lampeter, and David G. Eshleman, esq., of Lancaster.

On the adjoining farm stands an old mill, one and a half stories high, with a saw-mill attached. The first pair of French burrs introduced into Lancaster county are still in use in that mill. The mill was built in the early part of the last century, by Jacob Eshleman, and although of such diminutive and insignificant appearance now, that it would scarcely attract the notice of a traveler, it was considered of sufficient consequence, at the time of its erection, to be called "Eshleman's big mill."

About one and a half miles south of the borough of Strasburg, on the road to New Providence, just beyond the residence of the late Jacob Neff, stands the old mansion house of the Neff family. This house was erected in the second decade of the last century. It stands up on a knoll, which rises abruptly from the banks of Beaver creek, and is remarkable on account of its position and its antiquated and venerable appearance.

cured for himself and read some of the most valuable and useful books. When about twenty years of age, he began teaching common schools, which pursuit he followed for some years. Not long after this, he entered as a student, the Strasburg academy, then taught by Rev. D. McCarter. The last year he attended at this institution, he was employed in the capacity of an assistant teacher, and taught the lower classes. After leaving this place, he attended for some time at the White Hall academy, in Cumberland county, Pennsylvania, and next entered the Sophomore class in Franklin and Marshall college, where he graduated in 1858, obtaining a division of the Marshall honor with a classmate named Theodore Fisher. His theme on commencement day, was "the Constitution of the United States."

He began teaching in Perry county, Pennsylvania, in September of the same year in which he graduated. He was married in the following month, and in February, 1859, was appointed County Superintendent of Common Schools of Lancaster county, in the room of Rev. John S. Crumbaugh, deceased. He was elected to the same office in May, 1860, by the Directors' Convention, and thrice reëlected in the years 1863, 1866 and 1869. He held the office up to the 1st of June, 1872.[1]

EVANS, JAMES, was born in Little Britain township, Lancaster county, in 1791. In 1812 he moved to the borough of Lancaster, and in 1814 entered into partnership with his brother, Robert, in the dry goods business, and so continued to act as partner with him up to 1824. Prior to removing to Lancaster he had himself engaged, in the vicinity of his birth, in the mercantile business, individually, for about one year and a half. In 1824, having established a wide reputation for business sagacity, he was elected cashier of the Lancaster Bank. Dr. F. A. Muhlenberg was at that time President of the Bank. This position of cashier Mr. Evans held for a number of years. March 7th, 1842, he was elected President of the same Bank, and this office he held

[1] When Mr. Evans entered upon the duties of his office, in 1859, the average salary of male teachers in the county was $27.37, and of female teachers $24.18. In 1870 the average salary of males was $38.85, and of females 34.44.

until November 22d, 1849. During the time he officiated as President of the institution, he managed its affairs with great financial success; all this time it was in the highest degree of credit, and its notes passed at par throughout the whole country. Indeed, it is but the truth when it is said, that to him the institution owed its prosperity, credit and financial success. From the time Mr. Evans ceased to be the head of the institution, the downfall of this old and reliable bank dated its origin.

James Evans was a man of strict integrity, of irreproachable and upright conduct, and universally esteemed and respected by his fellow citizens. He was a man of a very generous nature, liberal in his charities when worthy objects presented themselves; yet he gave in no ostentatious manner, and sought rather that his gifts should be known only by the recipients thereof.

As a man of business, he was shrewd and penetrating; and it is not too much to say, that he had no superiors as to business qualities in the county, and but few, if any, in the State. In his opinions he was very liberal and high-toned, and never permitted difference of views to mar social relations between himself and his associates. He was no aspirant for public office, and though this was within his reach, he rather shrunk from cares of this character, devoting his attention simply to business affairs. He died October 12th, 1864.

EVANS, ROBERT, brother of James Evans, was born in Little Britain township, October 4th, 1791. His father, John Evans, was one of the early settlers of Lancaster county, having emigrated from Wales about the year 1740. Having received the rudiments of an education, customary in his day, he was apprenticed, on the 24th of November, 1807, to Michael Gundaker, (a leading merchant of Lancaster), to learn the mercantile business; and, after serving three years, he married Anna Margaret, a daughter of Mr. Gundaker. He set up as a merchant in Lancaster, and continued to follow this business to the end of his life. In 1819 he was appointed by Phineas Ash, Wm. B. Ross and Peter Holl, Commissioners of Lancaster county, to the office of

County Treasurer, and was twice re-appointed to the the same office, in the years 1820 and 1821. Amongst those recommending Mr. Evans to the office of Treasurer, we find the names of several of the principal leading citizens of Little Britain township, viz: Jeremiah Brown, sr., William Brown, Jeremiah Brown, jr., John Kirk, Nicholas Boyd, (father of the late sheriff Boyd), Timothy Haines, Isaac Stubbs, William McCulloch, and Slater Brown. Mr. Evans served for many years as a director of the old Farmers' Bank of Lancaster, and acted besides in many fiduciary positions of trust and responsibility, and was esteemed as one of the most useful and influential citizens of his day. He died November 2nd, 1831, aged 40 years and 29 days. The present Robert A. Evans and Walter G. Evans, esqs., of Lancaster city, are sons of Robert Evans.

EVANS, SAMUEL, elected Clerk of Quarter Sessions and Oyer and Terminer, in 1857.

EWING, A. SCOTT, a member of the Legislature in 1849.

EWING, GENERAL JAMES, was born about the year 1736, in Manor township, Lancaster county. His father had emigrated from Ireland at an early day, and settled in Manor township, and when the subject of this notice was but a boy they removed to Hellam township, York county. At the age of eighteen he was engaged with his associates in repelling the incursions of the Indians. He served in the campaign under General Braddock, and was a participant in the action near Pittsburg, in which that brave but ill-fated officer was killed and his army routed. James Ewing served his country in the capacity of a brigadier general, attached to the flying camp during the Revolution.

In the character of civilian, he was also a prominent and influential member of society. He was a member of the Legislature for several years, and filled many other positions of public trust. He was a man highly esteemed by his fellow citizens, and died in March, 1806, aged seventy years.

EWING, THOMAS, a member of the Legislature in 1739, 1740, 1741 and 1742.

16

F.

FAHNESTOCK FAMILY.* The Fahnestocks are descendants of one Dietrich Fahnestock, who came from Prussia in the year 1724. He had seven sons, viz: Casper, Peter, Dietrich, John, Benjamin, Daniel, and Borieus; of the two latter no record can be found. Benjamin had two sons, George and Dietrich, from whom the druggists of Pittsburg have descended. John had two sons, Jacob and Henry. Dietrich, who was a physician, had three sons, Samuel, Daniel and John, who were all physicians. Casper had three sons, Charles, Dietrich and Daniel. Peter had five sons, Samuel, Obed, Peter, Conrad and Andrew; the latter has been a Seventh-day Baptist minister, living at times at Antietam, and latterly at Ephrata. Conrad was a printer, and published a paper at Harrisburg, during the alien and sedition acts, and being a warm supporter of Mr. Jefferson, was outspoken against the administration of Mr. Adams. He was, in consequence, arrested, with others, and thrown into prison. It was, however, just upon the eve of the election, and he was released a few days afterwards. He had but one son, Peter, who resides at present at Ephrata. Peter has three sons, Samuel and Reuben, both residing in Ephrata township, and John, residing in Ohio.

There are Fahnestocks residing in Lancaster, and also in Lebanon county, who are no doubt descendants of the same family.

FAHNESTOCK, Dr. Samuel, a leading physician of Lancaster for many years. He practiced medicine in Lancaster for nearly forty years.

In the autumn of 1777, when the wounded soldiers were transferred from Brandywine to the village of Ephrata, the subject of this notice, being about fourteen years of age, by his unwearied attention and the coolness he displayed, attracted the attention of General Hand, himself an eminent physician, who advised his father to educate him for a physician. The father accepted the suggestion, and his

*Contributed by I. F. Bomberger, of Lititz.

future career fully justified the prophetic spirit of General Hand.

As he increased in years and practice he became especially distinguished for his treatment of fevers, and the remarkable success that attended the exercise of his skill throughout the prevalence of an eventful epidemic, won for him the most flattering encomiums of the distinguished Dr. Rush. His practice, for many years, extended far beyond the limits of Lancaster county. He died December 8th, 1836, in the 73rd year of his age.

FAHNESTOCK, WILLIAM M., was a man somewhat fond of antiquarian research. In 1835 he published a historical sketch of Ephrata, together with a concise account of the Seventh-day Baptists.

FERREE, ISAAC, a member of the Legislature in 1793, 1794, 1802, 1803 and 1804.

FERREE, JOSEPH, a member of the Legislature in 1770, 1771, 1772, 1773 and 1774.

FERREE, JAMES B., elected Register in 1839.

FISHER, JOSEPH W., was born October 16th, 1814, in Northumberland county, Pennsylvania. He received the simple rudiments of an English education, and when quite young was hired out by his parents to work upon a farm till about the age of fifteen, when he was apprenticed to learn the tailoring business. In this occupation he spent the early years of his manhood. In the year 1840 he removed to Columbia, Lancaster county, where he pursued his trade for several years. In 1848 he was nominated and elected a member of the House of Representatives. In 1850 he was elected a justice of the peace, and so entirely did he satisfy his constituents, that he was reëlected to the same office in 1855, receiving every vote save six. During the time he was acting in the capacity of justice of the peace he read law, and was admitted to the Lancaster bar in 1856, and was not long in stepping into a fair practice.

He was always an active and leading politician; a Whig during the existence of that party, and upon its dissolution he became a Republican. In the campaign of 1860 he took a very active part, and assumed the ground that if Lincoln was elected and war resulted, he would enter the ranks in defence of the flag of the nation. Upon the bombardment of Fort Sumter, therefore, although over age, he enlisted as a private, and was immediately elected Captain of what was afterwards Company K, of the Fifth Pennsylvania Reserves. When the regiment was organized, he was elected Lieutenant Colonel, and served with the regiment through the campaign of 1862, and afterwards participated in the engagements known as the seven days' battles before Richmond, also at Bull Run, South Mountain and Antietam. He led the heroic charge, consisting of a part of the Fifth and Eighth regiments of the Reserves, and killed, wounded and captured the Seventh and Seventeenth Virginia regiments, in which engagement Col. Simmons was killed. Col. Fisher was complimented by Gen. Lemoyne, commanding the division, and recommended for promotion by Gens. McCall, Meade, Reynolds and Lemoyne, to a Brigadier Generalship.

Becoming Colonel, in course, upon the death of Colonel Simmons, at the second battle of Bull Bun, he was not able to command the same, owing to injuries received from the fall of his horse. At the battle of South Mountain he left a sick bed to lead his regiment, and he charged with it up the northern slope of the mountain, and drove the enemy from the summit down the southern and western slopes, and captured a large number of prisoners. He was complimented by Gens. Meade, Lemoyne and Duryea for the undaunted heroism displayed by him in this engagement, and was again strongly urged by them as worthy of promotion. Being with his regiment in the battle of Antietam, he repulsed an attack during the night, of the Fourth Texas regiment, and drove them in utter confusion.

He was transferred by Gen. Meade from the first to the third brigade, to take command of the latter, which command he retained until the close of the third year for which he had enlisted. He participated in nearly all the battles of his division until the close of his term of service. At the battle of Gettysburg he led his brigade up and took what is known as Round Top Mountain, and held it. From Gettysburg he crossed, with his brigade, the Potomac, Rappahannock and Rapidan; and left his sick bed, against the protests of his surgeon, to participate in the battle of Mine Run, in November, 1863.

After this battle the army went into winter quarters, and he had command of the post at Manassas Junction, and remained there till April. After the army got in readiness he moved his brigade from Culpepper, and was in all the battles of the Wilderness, and closed his term of service on the 30th of May, 1864, with a brilliant victory at Bethesda church, near where he had participated in his first engagement.

He then left for home, where he arrived about the middle of June, intending to remain. However, upon the invasion of Maryland and Pennsylvania by the rebel forces, under Generals Early and Breckinridge, at the urgent solicitation of Governor Curtin, he raised and took command of the 195th regiment, and aided in the defence of the Border States, during the one hundred days. He moved with his regiment up the Baltimore and Ohio Railroad, as far as Hedgesville, in West Virginia. Upon the expiration of the one hundred days period of service, he urged his men to reënlist, and succeeded in inducing about 300 of them to do so. He then returned home in November, 1864, and in the following February, was solicited by Governor Curtin to take command of the 300 men, (before stated to have reënlisted) and to raise, if possible, sufficient recruits to complete the full strength of the regiment. This he did, and succeeded in swelling the regiment to 1300 men, of which he was commissioned Colonel on the 25th of February, 1865. He was with this regiment in the Shenandoah valley, up to August of that year, and being transferred to Washington, there remained in command of his regiment up to January 31st, 1866, when the regiment was mustered out and discharged from service.

During the time he was in the Shenandoah valley, in 1865, he had the command of a brigade, composed of the 192d, 195th and 214th regiments, and also the 192d and 193d regiments of New York. Being recommended for promotion by all the superior officers under whom he served, he was raised to the rank of Brigadier General, in 1865.

General Fisher participated in about thirty different engagements of the war. He was never absent from service without leave of his superior officer, and was never reprimanded for dereliction of duty. In all things he was a faithful and efficient officer, and won the esteem of both officers and men. He was frequently detailed to sit upon courts martial, and was for six weeks president of a board of examiners, to examine officers for promotion. His highest ambition, as an officer, was to save his men, and he had the good fortune to secure their unlimited confidence and esteem. Although one of the strictest disciplinarians in the army, he nevertheless uniformly treated the men under his command with kindness and respect, and his men were ready to obey and follow him through every danger.

In the fall of 1866 General Fisher was nominated and elected a member of the State Senate of Pennsylvania, from Lancaster county. He removed to Lancaster city during his term of Senator, and again actively engaged in the practice of his profession. In 1871 he was appointed Judge of the District Court for the territory of Montana, for which place he left, with his family, about the first of April, 1871.

[1] FOGLE, GEORGE. The late well-known and highly respected George Fogle, of Sadsbury, was captain of a company of the Lancaster county militia, in the war of 1812. He resided on the land of the well-known Francis Bailey, (the printer), and farmed the land. He first volunteered as a private soldier, under James Caldwell, esq., of Bart, but when the company received marching orders, Captain Caldwell was on the retired list, and George Fogle was chosen to take his place, in marching the company to Baltimore. After the close of the war he purchased a farm in Bart

[1] George Fogle was the son of Jacob Fogle, who emigrated to this country from Germany about the year 1765; whose son, Adam, was the well known Adam Fogle, esq., who served many years as justice of the peace in Sadsbury. George Fogle was united in marriage with Barbara, the daughter of Simon and Margaret Geist, of Bart, about the year 1796, and died in the year 1854, aged 84 years. J. M. W. Geist, esq., of Lancaster, is the grandson of Simon and Margaret Geist, of Bart.

township, on which his grandson, Joseph Fogle now resides. His son, John G. Fogle, now resides in Christiana. Jacob S. Fogle, the eldest son, is a respected citizen of Columbus, Ohio, where he emigrated many years ago. David H., another son, is a citizen of Berrien county, Michigan. Other descendants of George Fogle are numerous and respectable citizens of the neighborhood.

FONDERSMITH, JOHN, elected Clerk of Quarter Sessions in 1842.

FOREMAN, JACOB, a member of the Legislature in 1840, 1841 and 1842.

FORD, GEORGE, was a leading lawyer of the Lancaster bar. He was elected to the Legislature in 1836, 1837 and 1839.

FORDNEY, WILLIAM B., a retired lawyer, and one who, whilst in practice, ever ranked amongst the ablest of his profession. After his admission to the Lancaster bar, in 1829, his superior abilities soon gave him a front rank in the profession, which he held until his retirement from practice some years since. For several years he acted as prosecuting attorney of Lancaster county. In intellectual capacity he ranked with Gorge B. Porter, Gorge W. Barton, Thaddeus Stevens, Reah Frazer, Benjamin Champneys, and other brilliant stars of the old Lancaster bar.

FORNEY, COLONEL JOHN W., was born in Lancaster, Pennsylvania, in the year 1817. His parents occupying an humble grade in society, were not in possession of the means to afford him more than an ordinary English education. At the early age of thirteen, he obtained employment in a store of his native town for a short time, and then entered as an apprentice the office of the *Lancaster Journal*, at that period one of the most influential papers published in Pennsylvania. Hugh Maxwell, the proprietor of the *Journal*, was a man of remarkable ability, and one who wielded the editorial pen with singularly rare force. In this office, the subject of our notice remained until he attained his twentieth year, when he purchased the Lancaster *Intelligencer*, [1] a strong

[1] The Lancaster *Intelligencer* was first issued in 1799 by William and Thomas Dixon, as a weekly paper, being at first only a small four column sheet. It was regularly published up to 1823, the time of William

Democratic paper of the county, from Thomas Feran, esq. A few years afterwards he bought out the *Journal* and consolidated the two papers, and made the new paper one of the ablest and most influential sheets of the county, and one that exercised a powerful influence not only in Lancaster county but throughout the whole State. In 1839 he was appointed Prothonotary of the Court of Common Pleas of Lancaster county, a position he held for a short time. He remained in Lancaster, absorbed in his editorial duties, up to the year 1845, when he received the appointment of Deputy Surveyor of the port of Philadelphia, from President Polk, and removed to the last named place, the better to attend to the duties of the office.

Soon after his location in Philadelphia, with that enthusiasm for journalism which has ever seemed in him a leading characteristic, he purchased a one-half interest in the old *Pennsylvanian* newspaper, then the leading Democratic organ of the State. This was in the year 1845. He remained associated with the *Pennsylvanian* until the year 1853.

In December, 1851, he was elected Clerk of the House of Representatives, and removed with his family to Washington. This important and influential position he held during the memorable struggle of 1855 and 1856, for the election of Speaker of the House, and which terminated in the election of Nathaniel P. Banks. During those exciting times Colonel Forney was the presiding officer of the House, and the highly satisfactory manner in which he performed his duties, is attested by a resolution offered by Hon. Joshua R. Giddings, tendering him the thanks of the House, for the ability and impartiality with which he had presided over the House during the contest. The resolution was passed without a dissenting voice.

Dixon's death, and was continued afterwards by Mrs. Dixon, assisted by her son-in-law, Mr. Bedford, and subsequently by Thomas Feran, esq. In March, 1837, the paper passed into the hands of James H. Bryson and John W. Forney, the latter of whom obtained the whole control and ownership within the year. In September, 1839, Mr. Forney bought out the *Journal*, first established in 1794, and united it with the *Intelligencer*, under the title of the *Intelligencer and Journal*, at the same time considerably enlarging it. When, in 1845, Mr. Forney left Lancaster for Philadelphia, the paper passed into the hands of Marcus D. Hol-

Subsequently Col. Forney became one of the editors of the Washington *Union,* and remained in that position until James Buchanan received, at the Democratic Convention held at Cincinnati, in 1856, the nomination for the Presidency. He was then elected Chairman of the Democratic State Central Committee of Pennsylvania, and threw himself into the campaign with all his vigor and energy. By this time Col. Forney had become, and was generally regarded, as one of the shrewdest and most sagacious politicians in the Democratic party; and located at Washington, as he was, in the midst of the leading political minds of the nation, his influence was of the greatest account in the Presidential contest. He wielded one of the most fertile pens in the whole country, and his efforts were all powerful in behalf of the Democratic nominee. It is, perhaps, but the truth when it be said, that to J. W. Forney, more than to any other man, was James Buchanan indebted for the electoral vote of Pennsylvania, and with it his elevation to the Presidential chair of the United States.

In 1857 Col. Forney was nominated by the Democratic members of the Pennsylvania Legislature, as their candidate for the Senate of the United States, his competitor being Simon Cameron, a politician of great sagacity and adroitness. The contest on this occasion was that of Greek meeting Greek, and the subject of our notice through the political treason of three Democratic Representatives—Lebo, Waggonseller and Manear—was defeated.

brook, as its manager. In the following year, the latter became sole publisher, but in a few months transferred the paper to Franklin G. May. On January 1st, 1848, May transferred his interest in it to Edwin W. Hutter, who continued his connection with it until July, 1849. Hutter was succeeded by George Sanderson, who afterwards associated his son Alfred with him in the publication, and these continued it up to July 18th, 1864. It was then sold to John M. Cooper, H. G. Smith, William A. Morton and Alfred Sanderson, who published it under the firm title of Cooper, Sanderson & Co. November 1st, 1866, it passed into the hands of H. G. Smith and A. J. Steinman, the present editors and proprietors. August, 1864, the *Daily Intelligencer* was started by Cooper, Sanderson & Co., which, with the *Weekly Intelligencer,* passed into the hands of H. G. Smith and A. J. Steinman. The *Daily and Weekly Intelligencer* yet continues to be published by them. The *Intelligencer* is Democratic in politics.

It was not long after James Buchanan was inaugurated President, that a coolness between Col. Forney and himself became distinctly perceptible. The rupture was by no means complete, however, for a considerable time, Col. Forney still according to Mr. Buchanan his friendship and sympathy. Indeed, in the first number of the *Press*, issued August, 1857, he openly and warmly advocated the administration policy. It was not until the Kansas question became prominent, that any serious difficulty took place between them. It was only when, as he conceived, Mr. Buchanan was lending the weight of his official position towards the establishment of slavery in Kansas, that Col. Forney took issue with him, and at once expressed his views of the measure and the questions it involved, in his usual forcible manner.

In December of 1858, Col. Forney was a second time elected Clerk of the House of Representatives. During his residence at the National capital, he started a weekly paper, entitled the *Sunday Morning Chronicle*, which was subsequently turned into a daily paper, and was one of the most successful journals ever printed in that city.

In 1861 he was elected Clerk of the Senate, a position he accepted and filled with great credit for several years.

During the rebellion Col. Forney was a stern advocate of the principles of the Union party, and a warm supporter of the administration of President Lincoln. Upon the death of the latter, he gave his influence and support to his successor, Andrew Johnson. This course he continued until upon the veto of the Freedman's Bureau bill by President Johnson, it became apparent that the new Executive was swerving from the principles of the party to which he owed his election.

In March, 1871, he was offered by President Grant the position of collector of the port of Philadelphia, which he at first positively declined, but which at the urgent request of leading men of his party in this and other States, he was afterwards induced to accept. He discharged the duties of this office with marked ability and success. The opinion entertained amongst the business men generally, is, that Philadelphia never before had a more efficient Collector.

In personal appearance, Col. Forney is a fine-looking man, of medium height, dark brown hair, piercing eye and prominent features. He has a deep, full voice, which never fails to command the attention of his hearers. He is not an impassioned orator, but he is calm, fluent, logic and emphatic —qualities of which all others are desirable in a political speaker. When rising to address a mass meeting, during a political campaign, his air is imposing and his flowing strains of eloquence and captivating declamation leave the impression that he is a man of brilliant conception and rare intellectual ability.

As a journalistic writer he is smooth, elegant and ornate, his sentences presenting a polish and roundness almost rivaling those of a Gibbon; and yet, at the same time, showing that they are the unstudied first effusions of his pen, no indications of the midnight oil being at all visible in his composition. But few writers equal Col. Forney in this particular. He seems, in a word, to have reached the acme of style most captivating and best adapted for the journalist and newspaper writer. He is a tower of strength in the editorial profession, and his rare mental vigor and complete mastery of the pen, justly entitle him to be regarded and styled the journalistic Achilles of the Western Continent.

FORREY, JOHN, was a member of the Legislature in the years 1816, 1817, 1823, 1825, 1827 and 1828.

[1] FOSTER, REV. WILLIAM, was born in Little Britain township, Lancaster county, in 1740. He was a son of Alexander Foster, who emigrated from the north of Ireland and settled in that township. He graduated at Princeton College, New Jersey, in 1764—having as his cotemporaries in that institution, David Ramsey, the historian. Judge Jacob Rush, Oliver Ellsworth, Nathan Niles and Luther Martin.

[1] Mr. Foster was succeeded as pastor of Upper Octoraro and Doe Run, by the Rev. Alexander Mitchell, who was born in 1731, graduated at the College of New Jersey, in 1765, was licensed pastor in 1767, and was installed at Octoraro, December, 14th, 1785. He had formerly resided in Bucks county, and came from thence to Chester county. He was pastor of Octoraro until April, 1796, when his connection with the church was dissolved. During the last of his time, troubles arose in the congregation which continued for several years. He died December

He was licensed to preach by the Presbytery of New Castle, April 22nd, 1767, and was installed pastor of the Upper Octoraro church, October 19th, 1768. He also, about the same time, became pastor of the Doe Run Presbyterian church, on the Strasburg road, in East Fallowfield township, where he preached one-fourth of his time. He married Hannah, a daughter of Rev. Samuel Blair, of Fagg's Manor, and owned and resided on a farm a short distance east of Upper Octoraro church. This farm he purchased December 15th, 1770.

In the Revolution Mr. Foster engaged heartily in the cause of civil liberty, and encouraged all who heard him to to do their utmost in defence of their rights. On one occasion he went to Lancaster to preach to troops collected there previous to their joining the main army. The discourse was so acceptable that it was printed and circulated, and did much to arouse the spirit of patriotism amongst the people.

Indeed, nearly all the Presbyterian clergymen in this State, at that time, were staunch Whigs, and contributed greatly to keep alive the flame of liberty which our disasters had frequently caused to be well-nigh extinguished in the long and unequal contest; and but for them it would often have been impossible to obtain recruits to keep up the forces requisite to oppose the enemy.

It was a great object with the British officers to silence the Presbyterian preachers, as far as possible; and they frequently dispatched parties into the country to surprise and take prisoners unsuspecting clergymen. An expedition of this kind was planned against Mr. Foster.

The British were in possession of Wilmington, Delaware, and sent a party of light-horse from thence one Sunday

6th, 1812, at the age of eighty-one years, and was burried in Upper Octoraro. He left no descendants. The Doe Run church, to which Mr. Foster and Mr. Mitchell had ministered one-fourth of their time, was made a distinct congregation in 1798.

From 1796 until 1810, the Upper Octoraro church was without a regular pastor, and received supplies from Presbytery.

September 25th, 1816, a call was presented to Rev. James Latta, which he accepted. He had been licensed at New London, December 9th, 1809, and was ordained and installed pastor of Octoraro church, April 12th, 1811. He maintained that relation until October, 1850, a period of forty years, and then resigned.

evening, to take him prisoner and burn his church. Mr Foster received word of it on the morning of that day, at Doe Run, and hastening home collected his neighbors, who removed his family and library into a house remote from the public road. The expedition after proceeding twelve miles on their way, were informed by a tory that their purpose was known, and that parties of militia were stationed to intercept them, and they returned to Wilmington without accompanying their object.

Mr. Foster died September 30th, 1780. He had a high standing as a minister, and was held in much estimation by his congregation. They procured a tombstone to be erected over his remains in Upper Octoraro burial ground.

He occasionally received under his care theological students. The Rev. Nathaniel W. Sample, who was the esteemed pastor of several churches in Lancaster county for forty years, was one of his students. After his death, his family continued for a time to reside on his farm already referred to. It was sold by his widow on September 4th, 1790, to Joseph Park, esq., and the family removed to western Pennsylvania. Henry D. Foster, the Democratic candidate for Governor of Pennsylvania in 1860, is a grandson. He is a son of Samuel B. Foster, the eldest son of Rev. William Foster.

FRANKLIN, COL. EMLEN, youngest son of Judge Walter Franklin, was born in Lancaster, April 7th, 1827. After passing through the select schools of Lancaster, he entered Yale College in 1845, and graduated in 1847. He thereupon entered the law office of Nathaniel Ellmaker, esq., and after the usual time of study, was admitted to the bar, May 15th, 1850. He immediately began the practice of his profession, and in the autumn of 1854 he was elected a member of the House of Representatives at Harrisburg; and having served one term, declined a reëlection, owing to the shape that parties had, in the meantime, assumed.

In 1859 he was elected District Attorney of Lancaster, and discharged the duties of his office, during his term, with credit to himself and to the satisfaction of his constituents.

Upon the breaking out of the rebellion, being at the time

the Captain of the old "Fencibles," he volunteered with his company for the three months' service. In 1862 he raised the 122d Regiment of Pennsylvania volunteers, of which he was chosen Colonel, and which he commanded for nine months, the period for which the regiment had been raised. During this period of his service he participated, in command of his regiment, in the battles of Fredericksburg and Chancellorsville. He returned with his regiment on the 16th of May, 1863; and in June, of the same year, upon the invasion of Pennsylvania by Gen. Lee, in obedience to the urgent solicitation of Gen. Couch, then commanding the department of the Susqnehanna, he immediately raised the 50th regiment of Pennsylvania militia, and in command of one of the brigades, participated in the movements of that campaign. With the restoration of quiet along the borders, these troops were discharged, and Col. Franklin resumed again the practice of his profession. During the fall of 1863 he was nominated and elected register of wills of Lancaster county, which position he filled during his term of three years. During the period of his official service, and up to this time, he has been, and is now, engaged in the pursuits of his profession.

FRANKLIN, THOMAS E., a member of the Lancaster bar, and a brother of Emlen Franklin, has for many years been recognized as one of the leading members of the profession in Lancaster county. He was appointed Attorney-General of Pennsylvania, by Governor Pollock, in 1855. In 1860 and 1861 he was a leading member of the National Peace Convention, convened in order to endeavor to avert the calamities of the impending civil war, which finally deluged American soil with blood.

[1] FRANKLIN, WALTER, was born in the city of New York, in February, 1773. His father having removed, during his minority, to Philadelphia, he there read law, and was admitted to the bar in 1794. In January, 1809, he was appointed, by Governor Snyder, Attorney-General of Penn-

[1] Upon the breaking out of the war of 1812, with Great Britain, the public mind, as always happens in such cases, became instantly crazed, and insults and contumely were heaped upon those who had the courage

sylvania, which position he held until January, 1811, when, upon the death of Judge John Joseph Henry, he was appointed President Judge of the Courts of Common Pleas of the second judicial district of Pennsylvania, which comprised the counties of Lancaster, York and Dauphin, and to which afterwards were added Cumberland and Lebanon. This office he continued to fill until his death, February 7th, 1838.

As a judge he was distinguished for clearness of conception, vigor of mind, and eminent integrity. He discharged the duties of his position with great satisfaction to the public. As a jurist, he ranked among the ablest in the State. He was marked by uniform dignity of manner; was in deportment unvaryingly correct and courteous; and his rare gentlemanly bearing rendered him a favorite with all classes of his fellow-citizens.

*FRAZER, BERNARD, was born in Dublin, Ireland, about 1755. When only eleven years old he left his father's house for the purpose of coming to some friends in America, whom, it appears, he never found. Being well educated for a boy of his age, he found employment in a country store, owned by a family in Chester county, named Witherow, with whom he had his home for several years. During this time he acquired a knowledge of surveying and scrivening, a business

to raise their voices against the war. The civil authority was in many places prostrated, and mob law ruled supreme ; the most respectable citizens were insulted, and the offices of the press, opposed to the war, were in many places destroyed. In the midst of this state of excitement and feeling Judge Franklin delivered a charge to the grand jury of York county, of which the following is an extract :

"The existing state of our foreign relations, and the sensibility of the public mind on all questions connected with it, call for peculiar care in those who are concerned in the administration of justice, to guard against every occurrence which may have a tendency to promote a spirit of popular tumult, or of lawless violence.

"A disposition to riot and commotion may in general be easily suppressed, in its first stages, by a proper firmness and decision on the part of the magistrate ; but if neglected, and suffered to gain ground and extend itself, it soon grows too powerful for the ordinary exertions of civil authority, and bears down everything before it in a resistless torrent of rage and desolation. Fear is said to be the basis of arbitrary govern-

*Contributed by Alex. H. Hood, esq.

which he practiced to a considerable extent in after-life. In 1776 he volunteered in a Pennsylvania regiment, and was present at Brandywine, where he received a bullet in his leg which lamed him for life, and which he carried with him to his grave. In 1786 he came to Strasburg, and was employed as a clerk in a store. Soon after this he married Elizabeth, the daughter of Philip Kessler, the result of which marriage was a numerous and highly intelligent family. He died in 1817, and lies in the Lutheran churchyard at Strasburg. His widow died in 1855, aged nearly ninety years. His sons, John, Samuel and Philip, died while yet young men, leaving families. Warren never was married, and died when about twenty-five years old. William lived to be over sixty, and left a family. Of his daughters, Hannah died unmarried in 1845; and Mary, the wife of Alex. H. Hood, esq., died in 1851. Two of his daughters, Elizabeth, the widow of Captain Christian Sherts, resides in Lancaster; and Angelica, a single lady, resides in Strasburg.

Mr. Frazer was a very useful man in his day. He, and all his family, were remarkable for the beauty of their penmanship; and in his section of the county, when anything in that line was to be done, he was always employed. In hunting up old titles, his deeds are often to be found, and they fully justify his traditional reputation. The few who still remember him, speak of his ability as a teacher, a surveyor and a scrivener, in the highest terms. Philip Frazer, of Philadelphia; Christian Frazer, of Austin, Texas; and David T. Frazer, of Venango, Pa., are the grandsons who inherit his name.

ment, and virtue the ruling principle in republics. Laws, and not faction, should bear the sway in every free country. No condition is more deplorable than that produced by anarchy; and experience has abundantly proved, that of all governments, a mob is the most despotic and sanguinary.

"We are, each of us, deeply interested in avoiding a state of things so awful and calamitous. Let us unite then in our endeavors to prevent the most distant approaches towards it, and let us evince our reverence for the principles of the institutions of republicanism, by a faithful adherence to the law, and a strict and impartial execution of it against offenders of every description."

The above are the utterances of sound wisdom, and such as should be observed in all civil commotions. Unfortunately, however, the mass of mankind never are able to live up to them.

FRAZER, COL. REAH, was, in his day, one of the leading lawyers of Lancaster, and a politician who exerted a controlling influence in his party. He read law in the office of Amos Ellmaker, one of the luminaries of the bar, and was admitted a member of the profession in the year 1825. Being possessed of a very buoyant and impulsive temperament he was not long in establishing himself as one of the most conspicuous attorneys of Lancaster, and for many years, and indeed up to a short time before his death, he was employed in most of the important cases that came before the courts of his native county.

He was ardent and enthusiastic in all he undertook, and he brought the whole power of his impassioned nature to the investigation and trial of his cases; evincing during the whole of the proceedings the same zealous and passionate ardor as were he advocating or defending his own individual case. His was a nature which knew no moderation. In his speeches in Court he seemed to have the power to carry the day, from his faculty of being able to convince the jury that he himself fully believed all he uttered and advocated. This, in short, was one of the great secrets of his success as a legal practitioner.

For many years he was the leading Democrat of Lancaster county, and was known throughout Pennsylvania as the "Lancaster War Horse." As a politician he was all powerful with the masses, who are ever more swayed by passion than by argument. Wherever he presented himself during a campaign, the occasion was a signal that called forth the huzzas and plaudits of the congregated multitude. He died December 30th, 1856.

In the business of his profession, he was very industrious and persevering; and he prepared and tried his cases to the utmost of his ability. He would seem, however, to a critic witnessing his impassioned displays before a jury or a political meeting, as unhewn intellectual marble, lacking symmetrical precision and connected systematic cohesion. His efforts were terrific and applause-producing; and he simply bore off the victory by the herculean might of his inflammatory declamation.

17

FREY, JACOB F., elected Commissioner in 1856. He was elected sheriff of Lancaster county in 1866.

FRY, SAMUEL, was born February 12th, 1809, in Ephrata township, Lancaster county. He was a miller by trade, and carried on the Millport mill for many years. He was a man of rare business capacity, and was often by his neighbors employed in fiduciary trusts. In 1840 he was elected a justice of the peace, and after serving that office for ten years, he was, in 1850, elected Commissioner of Lancaster county. He was one of the board of Commissioners when the new Court House was erected. For many years he stood at the head of the Lancaster County Corn Exchange. He was, for a time, engaged in the commission business, in Market street, Philadelphia, in the firm of Fry, Acheson & Rommel. He died October 23d, 1868, and he lies buried at the Union meeting-house, in Warwick township.

* FULTON, ROBERT. The aid of the historian, or biographer, is hardly necessary to preserve the name of Fulton. He is identified with the age in which he lived, and so long as a knowledge of the power of steam remains, tradition will perpetuate the character and exertions of him who, by his successful application of its power to the purposes of navigation, defied alike wind and tide, and compelled the elements to bow to the genius of man.

Yet, although his memory exists, and will exist until the unsparing hand of time shall have swept away alike the records of his fame and the knowledge of his triumphs, and mental darkness shall again obscure the earth, it becomes not less our duty to render him the praise which is his due, and to enroll his name in our humble volume among the illustrious worthies of our native land. Lowly in his origin, needy in circumstances, and devoid in his youthful career of the appliances of wealth and the patronage of friends, he possessed a mind and temperament that enrolled him in the ranks of genius, and by his self-dependence enabled him to command the one and disregard the other.

He smoothed for himself the rugged road to power, and

* National Portrait Gallery.

when standing on its lofty eminence, he relaxed not the toils
by which he had attained his elevation, but

——"gazing higher
Purposed in his heart to take another step."

The father of Robert Fulton was an emigrant from Ireland
to this country. He married Mary, the daughter of Irish
parents by the name of Smith, then settled in Pennsylvania,
and from this union Robert was born in the township of
Little Britain, (now Fulton township,) Lancaster county, in
the year 1765, being the third child and oldest son. His
father dying when Robert was little more than three years
old, his means of instruction, which during the lifetime of
his parent were small, were still more reduced, and to the
town of Lancaster he was indebted for the rudiments of a
common English education. The early bent of his genius
was directed to drawing and painting, and such was his proficiency that, at the age of seventeen, we find him in Philadelphia pursuing this avocation for a livelihood, and with a
success that enabled him, by strict frugality, by the time he
had arrived at the age of twenty-one, to acquire sufficient
means for the purchase of a small farm in Washington
county, on which, with filial affection, he settled his mother.

In 1786 he embarked for England and became an inmate
in the family of his distinguished countryman, Benjamin
West, where he remained several years, and with whom he
formed an intimacy which death alone dissolved.

For some time after leaving the family of Mr. West, he
devoted himself chiefly to the practice of his art, and during
a residence of two years in Devonshire, near Exeter, he became known to the duke of Bridgewater and the earl of
Stanhope, with the latter of whom he was afterwards for a long
time in regular correspondence. About this period he conceived a plan for the improvement of inland navigation, and
in 1794 he received the thanks of two societies for accounts
of various projects suggested by him. In 1796 he published
in London his treatise on the system of canal improvement.
The object of this work was to prove that small canals navi-
gated by boats of little burthen, were preferable to canals
and vessels of larger dimensions; and to recommend a mode

of transportation over mountainous regions of country without the aid of locks, railways and steam engines. This he proposed to accomplish by means of inclined planes, upon which vessels navigating the canals should be raised or lowered from one level to another through means of some ingeniously contrived machinery placed on the higher level, by lifting and lowering the vessel perpendicularly. The only ideas in these projects claimed by him as original, were the perpendicular lift and the connection of the inclined planes with machinery.

From England, in 1796, Mr. Fulton proceeded to France and took up his lodgings at the same hotel with his celebrated fellow-citizen, Mr. Joel Barlow. Mr. Barlow afterwards removing to his own house, Mr. Fulton accepted an invitation to accompany him, and continued to reside in his family for seven years. In this period he studied several modern languages and perfected himself in the higher branches of mathematics and natural philosophy.

The attention of Mr. Fulton appears to have been early directed to the application of steam to the purpose of navigation. It is not claimed for him that he was the originator of the idea, nor that he was first to make the experiment, but it is affirmed, and justly, that he was the first who successfully applied this powerful engine to this branch of human industry, and by his genius and perseverance removed the incumbrances which had hitherto obstructed the path and contributed to those splendid results which we are daily witnessing, and in which its saving of time has shortened space, and by bringing the various sections of our beloved country into more frequent intercourse, has strengthened the Federal compact and joined more closely the bonds of union. This important object was, however, temporarily suspended, and in the meantime, in addition to various other scientific projects, Mr. Fulton embarked in a series of experiments, having for their object the destruction of ships of war by submarine explosion. The situation of France at this period, engaged in a war with nearly all the powers of Europe, and compelled to succumb on the ocean to the naval superiority of Great Britain, gave a universal interest to his scheme, and at once invited the attention of the French government to the suggestion. A commission was appointed by Napoleon, then first consul, to examine the plans and report upon the probability of their success. Accordingly, in 1801 Mr. Fulton repaired to Brest, and there commenced the experiment with his plunging boat, the result of which we find detailed by himself in an interesting report to the committee, from which, as related in Colden's memoir, we gather the following facts:

"On the 3rd of July, 1801, he embarked with three companies on board his plunging boat, in the harbor of Brest, and descended with it to the depth of five, ten, fifteen, and so on to twenty-five feet, but he did not attempt to go lower, because he found that his imperfect machine would not bear the pressure of a greater depth. He remained below the surface one hour. During this time they were in utter darkness. Afterwards he descended with candles, but finding a great disadvantage from their consumption of vital air, he caused, previously to his next experiment, a small window of thick glass to be made near the bow of his boat, and he again descended with her, on the 24th of July, 1801. He found that he received from his window, or rather aperture covered with glass, for it was no more than an inch and a half in diameter, sufficient light to enable him to count the minutes on his watch. Having satisfied himself that he could have sufficient light when under water, that he could do without a supply of fresh air for a considerable time, that he could descend to any depth and rise to the surface with facility, his next object was to try her movements as well on the surface as beneath it. On the 26th of July he weighed his anchor and hoisted his sails; his boat had one mast, a mainsail and jib. There was only a light breeze, and therefore she did not move on the surface at more than the rate of two miles an hour, but it was found that she would tack and steer, and sail on a wind or before it as well as any common sailing boat. He then struck her mast and sails, to do which and perfectly to prepare the boat for plunging, required about two minutes. Having plunged to a certain depth he placed two men at the engine, which was intended to give her progressive motion, and one at the helm, while he, with a barometer before him, governed the machine, which kept her balanced between the upper and lower waters. He found that with the exertion of one hand only, he could keep her at any depth he pleased. The propelling engine was then put in motion, and he found upon coming to the surface that he had, in about seven minutes, made a progress of four hundred meters, or about five hundred yards. He then again plunged, turned her around while under water, and returned to near the place he .began to move from. He repeated his experiments several days successively, until he became familiar with the operation of the machinery and the movements of the boat. He found that she was as obedient to her helm under water as any boat could be on the surface, and that the magnetic needle traversed as well in the one situation as the other.

"On the 7th of August Mr. Fulton again descended with a store of atmospheric air compressed into a copper globe of a cubic foot capacity, into which two hundred atmospheres were forced. Thus prepared, he descended with three companions to the depth of about five feet. At the expiration of an hour and forty minutes he began to take small supplies of pure air from the reservoir, and did so as he found occasion, for four hours and twenty minutes. At the expiration of this time, he came to the surface without having experienced any inconvenience from having been so long under water.

" Mr. Fulton was highly satisfied with the success of these experiments; it determined him to attempt to try the effects of these inventions on the English ships which were then blockading the coast of France and were daily near the harbor of Brest.

" His boat at this time he called the submarine boat, or the plunging boat; and he afterwards gave it the name of the Nautilus ; connected with this machine were what he then called submarine bombs, to which he has since given the name of torpedoes. This invention preceded the Nautilus. It was, indeed, his desire of discovering the means of applying his torpedoes that turned his thoughts to a submarine boat. Satisfied with the performance of his boat, his next object was to make some experiments with the torpedoes. A small shallop was anchored in the roads; with a bomb containing about twenty pounds of powder, he approached to within about two hundred yards of the anchored vessel, struck her with the torpedo and blew her into atoms. A column of water and fragments were blown from 80 to 100 feet in the air. This experiment was made in the presence of the prefect of the department, Admiral Villaret, and a multitude of spectators."

The experiments of Mr. Fulton with his torpedoes were subsequently renewed in England, where, in 1805, he blew up in Walmer roads, near Deal, a Danish brig of two hundred tons, provided for the purpose.

On his return to this country he continued his experiments, and in 1807 blew up a large hulk brig in the harbor of New York. These experiments, however satisfactory to himself, were not so to the various governments to which he had offered his services, and his efforts were therefore productive of no further immediate results than to demonstrate the effect of submarine explosions.

We now recur to an important period of Mr. Fulton's life, for the purpose of tracing in a connected point of view those labors, the successful result of which has exercised so beneficial an influence on the destinies of the world and on which rest his own claims to imperishable renown. As early as 1793, as appears by a letter addressed by him to Lord Stanhope, his attention had been drawn to the practicability of steam navigation. It does not appear that any experiments were made by him until the year 1803.

"Among his papers," says Colden, "are a variety of drawings, diagrams and innumerable calculations, which evidently relate to the subject; but they are imperfect; most of them are mutilated, and they are without dates, so that they cannot with certainty be assigned to any period. They render it very evident, however, that the application of water-wheels, as they are now used in the boats which he built in this country, was among his first conceptions of the means by which steam vessels might be propelled."

It is not our intention to enter into an examination of Mr. Fulton's claims as an originator of this idea; he made no such pretensions. Experiments had been made again and again by different individuals, but without success; in some instances, indeed, vessels had been moved by the power of steam, but they had only served to prove the fallaciousness of each invention, and to confirm the ignorant in their belief of its impracticability; and until the attempt of Fulton, we unhesitatingly assert that the practical establishment of navigation by steam was wanting, and that to him is the world indebted for its advantages.

How contemptible is that narrow-minded sectional feeling which in its desire to give credit to natives of a particular country, would descend to calumny and falsehood for the purpose of robbing another of his well-earned laurels, merely because his birth-place was on a different soil.

Genius belongs to the earth at large. It is the property of the universe. It disdains conventional trammels, and like our own free eagle, it soars in the boundless space far above the clouds of prejudice and envy, regardless of the petty storms beneath.

As well might the claims of Watt, as an inventor, be disputed, because steam engines were in operation before his day, as those of Fulton, because others had unsuccessfully attempted similar experiments; and yet we are told by Stuart, in his "Anecdotes of Steam Engines and of their Inventors and Improvers," that "there is probably no one whose name is associated with the history of mechanism and whose labors have received so large a share of applause, who appears to have less claim to notice as an inventor than Robert Fulton."

So also in another part of his work, in speaking of Mr. Fulton's publication on the subject of canals, before adverted to, he says: "The character of this book was that of its author, it contained nothing original either in matter or manner." We can hardly return the compliment of Robert Stuart, in reference to his production, as he is certainly entitled to the credit of originality for his idea of Fulton's character, and we may add that in this thought he stands alone. While Mr. Fulton was yet in France engaged in his experiments with the Nautilus, Robert R. Livingston, esq., arrived in that country as an American minister, and an intimacy at once commenced between them. Chancellor Livingston had previously been engaged in some experiments in that country, and in 1798 had procured from the Legislature of the State of New York, the passage of an act vesting him with the exclusive right of navigating all kinds of boats which might be propelled by the force of fire or steam on all the waters within the jurisdiction of that State for the term of twenty years, upon condition that he should within one year build such a boat, the mean rate of whose speed should be at least four miles an hour.

A boat was accordingly constructed by Mr. Livingston, in accordance with this act, but not meeting the condition of the law, the project was for the time abandoned. His acquaintance with Fulton was the commencement of a new era in the history of science. It was the union of congenial spirits—a junction of minds alike distinguished for capacity, energy and perseverance, and bent upon the same grand design, and from whose embrace sprang into being the mighty improvement which, in its influence on human affairs, has outstripped all other efforts of modern times.

The mind of Fulton was of an order which peculiarly fitted him for this undertaking; active, inventive and unyielding, towering in stature, it may be aptly compared to that of the bard who saw

——" The tops of distant thoughts,
Which men of common stature never saw."

Possessing a keen penetration, a mind also of superior mechanical order, and thorough theoretical knowledge of the laws of mechanics, Mr. Livingston was deficient in that practical information which, with the other qualities, was united in Fulton; and on meeting with him, he at once perceived the man through whose talents he might hope to accomplish his valuable designs.

It was immediately agreed between them to embark in the enterprise, and a series of experiments were had on a small scale, which resulted in a determination to build an experimental boat on the Seine. This boat was completed early in the spring of 1803; they were on the 'point of making an experiment with her, when one morning as Mr. Fulton was rising from a bed in which anxiety had given him but little rest, a messenger from the boat, whose precipitation and apparent consternation announced that he was the bearer of bad tidings, presented himself to him and exclaimed, in accents of despair, "O, sir, the boat has broken to pieces and gone to the bottom!" Mr. Fulton, who himself related the anecdote, declared that this news created a despondency which he never felt on any other occasion; but this was only a momentary sensation. Upon examination he found that this boat had been too weakly framed to bear the weight of the machinery, and that in consequence of an agitation of the river by the wind, the preceding night, what the messenger had represented had literally happened. Without returning to his lodgings he immediately began to labor with his own hands to raise the boat, and worked for four and twenty hours incessantly, without allowing himself rest or taking refreshment, an imprudence which, as he always supposed, had a permanently bad effect on his constitution, and to which he imputed much of his subsequent bad health.

The accident did the machinery very little injury, but they were obliged to build the boat almost entirely anew. She was completed in July; her length was sixty-six feet, and she was eight feet wide. Early in August Mr. Fulton addressed a letter to the French national institute, inviting them to witness a trial of his boat, which was made in the presence of a great multitude of the Parisians. This experiment was so far satisfactory to its projectors as to determine them to continue their efforts in that country; and arrangements were accordingly made with Messrs. Watt & Bolton to furnish certain parts of a steam engine according to the directions of Fulton. Mr. Livingston also procured a reënactment of the law of 1798, extending the provisions of that act to Fulton and himself for the term of twenty years from the date of the new act. In 1806 Fulton returned to this country, and at once commenced building his first

American steamboat. In the spring of 1807 the boat was launched from the ship-yard of Charles Brown. The engine, from England, was put on board, and in August she was moved by the aid of her machinery from her birth-place to the Jersey shore. Great interest had been excited in the public mind in relation to the new experiment; and the wharves were crowded with spectators, assembled to witness the first trial. Ridicule and jeers were freely poured forth upon the boat and its projectors, until, at length, as the boat moved from the wharf and increased her speed, the silence and astonishment which first enthralled the immense audience was broken by one universal shout of acclamation and applause. The triumph of genius was complete, and the name of Fulton was thenceforth destined to stand enrolled among the benefactors of mankind.

The new boat was called the Clermont, in compliment of the place of residence of Mr. Livingston, and shortly afterwards made her first trip to Albany and back, at an average speed of five miles an hour. The successful application of Mr. Fulton's invention had now been fairly tried, and the efficacy of navigation by steam fully determined. The Clermont was advertised as a packet boat between New York an Albany, and continued, with some intermissions, running the remainder of the season. Two other boats, the Raritan and Car of Neptune, were launched the same year, and a regular passenger line of steamboats established from that period between New York and Albany. In each of these boats great improvements were made, although as yet imperfect.

In 1811–12 two steamboats were built under the superintendence of Mr. Fulton, as ferry-boats for crossing the Hudson river, and shortly after another of the same description, for the ferry between Brooklyn and New York. These boats consisted of two complete hulls, united by a common deck, moving either way with equal facility, and thereby saving the necessity of turning. A painful incident as regards the starting of this boat is as follows: The boat had made one or two trips across the river, and was lying at the wharf at the foot of Beekman street. Some derangement had taken place in the machinery, which the chief engineer was engaged in rectifying, when the machinery was set in motion, and coming in contact with the engineer, mangled him in a manner that produced his death the next day. He was removed to the house adjacent to that occupied by the author of this sketch, and well does he remember the conversation between Mr. Fulton and the attending surgeon in reference to the unfortunate man. After some conversation in relation to the prospect of his recovery, Mr. Fulton, much affected, remarked, "Sir, I will give all I am worth to save the life of that man." When told that his recovery was hopeless, he was perfectly unmanned, and wept like a child. It is here introduced to show, that while his own misfortunes never for a single moment disturbed his equanimity, the finer feelings of his nature were sensitively alive to the distresses of others.

It is hardly necessary to trace the further progress of Mr. Fulton's career in regard to steam navigation. Altogether thirteen boats were built in the city of New York, under his superintendence, the last being the steam frigate which, in compliment to its projector, was called Fulton the First. The keel of this immense vessel was laid on the 20th of June, 1814, and in little more than four months she was launched from the ship-yard of Adam and Noah Brown, her architects, amid the roar of cannon and the plaudits of thousands of spectators. From the report of the commissioners appointed to superintend her construction, we extract the following description of this magnificent vessel: "She is a structure resting on two boats and keels, separated from end to end by a channel fifteen feet wide and sixty-six feet wide; one boat contains the cauldrons of copper to prepare her steam. The cylinder, of iron, its piston, levers and wheels, occupy part of the other. The water-wheel revolves in the space between them. The main or gun-deck supports the armament, and is protected by a parapet four feet ten inches thick, of solid timber, pierced by embrasures. Through thirty port holes, as many thirty-two pounders are intended to fire red-hot shot, which can be heated with great safety and convenience. The upper or spar deck, upon which several thousand men might parade, is encompassed with a bulwark which affords safe quarters. She is rigged with two stout masts, each of which supports a large lateen yard and sails; she has two bowsprits, so that she can be steered with either end foremost; her machinery is calculated for the addition of an engine which will discharge an immense column of water, which it is intended to throw upon the decks and through the port-holes of an enemy, and thereby deluge her armament and ammunition."

Before the conclusion of this mighty undertaking, it pleased the Almighty to remove Mr. Fulton from the scene of his labors. He died in the city of New York, on the 24th of February, 1815, after a short illness, consequent on severe exposure. The announcement of his death was accompanied with all those tokens of regret which mark the decease of a great public character. His corpse was attended to its last resting-place by all the public officers of the city, and by a larger concourse of citizens than had ever been assembled on any similar occasion. Minute-guns marked the progress of the procession, and every testimonial of gratitude and respect was lavished upon his memory. Mr. Fulton left four children, one son and three daughters, and we regret to add, in the language of Colden, with no other "patrimony than that load of debt which their parent contracted in those pursuits that ought to command the gratitude as they do the admiration of mankind." In person Mr. Fulton was about six feet high, slender, but well proportioned and well formed. In manners he was cordial, cheerful and unembarrassed; in his domestic relations eminently happy. A kind husband, an affectionate parent, a zealous friend, he has left behind him, independent of his public career, an unsullied reputation and a memory void of reproach.

G.

GARA, Isaac B., was born near Soudersburg, Lancaster county, Pennsylvania, October 28th, 1821. At the age of sixteen he entered the *Examiner and Herald* office as an apprentice to learn the printing business, the paper at that time being under the ownership of Hamersly & Richards. After remaining in the employ of this firm for about three years, the paper passed into the hands of other proprietors, and the subject of this notice passed out into life and began the publication of a paper in Bellefonte, and afterwards in Lock Haven. For about nine months he edited the semi-weekly *Gazette*, at Galena, Illinois. The climate of this part of Illinois not agreeing with him, he returned to Pennsylvania and became associate proprietor and editor of the Erie *Gazette*, a position which he held up to May 4th, 1865. In January, 1867, he was appointed by Governor Geary Deputy Secretary of the Commonwealth, and retained the same up to May 1st, 1869, when he resigned the Deputy Secretaryship to accept the office of postmaster of the city of Erie, a position voluntarily tendered him. Hugh S. Gara, of Lancaster city, is a brother of Isaac B. Gara.

GARBER, CHRISTIAN, (Carver) emigrated from Germany sometime between the years 1700 and 1720, and settled in West Hempfield township, near where the present Jacob B. Garber, his great grandson, resides. He took up and settled a tract of land, and obtained a deed in 1735 for 236 acres, with the usual allowance of 6 acres to the 100 for roads, &c., from John, Thomas and Richard Penn, true and absolute proprietors of Pennsylvania and the counties of New Castle and Sussex, on the Delaware. For this tract of land he paid £46, 11 shillings and 8 pence. The original tract has remained in the family until the present time, and is yet in the possession of Jacob B. Garber and Jonas Garber, also a descendant of the original settler. Jacob B. Garber says : " The house I live in was built by my father in 1812, and is the third dwelling house erected on this farm, besides the squatter's cabin first put up in the wilderness. Previous to the time of my forefather's locating on this farm, several families had penetrated as far as the Susquehanna river and took possession of the ground whereon Columbia is now located." The Garbers have all been of a retiring disposition, devoting their time and attention to farming. The name has been spelled differently—as Karver, Carver, Gerber, Garber.

Jacob B. Garber is an old, estimable citizen, noted for the leading position he has for many years held in county and State Agricultural Societies. He has been a contributor for many years to agricultural journals.

GATCHELL, J. C., a member of the Legislature in 1868 and 1871.

GALBRAITH, ANDREW, a member of the Legislature in the years 1731, 1732, 1733, 1734, 1735, 1736 and 1737.

GALBRAITH, BARTRAM, a delegate to the convention in 1776 which ratified the first Pennsylvania Constitution. He was a Colonel in the Revolutionary war.

GEIST, J. M. W., one of the editors of the Lancaster *Express*, was born in Bart township, Lancaster county, on the 14th of December, 1824. His parents being persons in straitened circumstances, and having the burden of a large family devolving upon them, the subject of our sketch had not the advantages of more than an ordinary education afforded him. Being, however, of a delicate constitution, superior educational training was given him over and above that received by the rest of his brothers and sisters. He early gave evidence of superior ability in the rapid acquisition of knowledge, and soon distanced his youthful competitors in the various branches of learning then taught in the schools. Finding himself competent to impart instruction, he taught school for some time in Chester county and elsewhere. Whilst engaged in teaching, at the suggestion of friends he read medicine, and in 1843 visited Philadelphia in order to attend medical lectures in that city. An opportunity now presented itself to him to learn the trade of his early choice —printing and stereotyping—and he abandoned medicine, having little taste for this profession. In 1844 he began his editorial career in charge of the *Reformer*, a temperance paper of Lancaster. Prior to this he had contributed considerably as a writer for newspapers. His enterprise in Lancaster proving a financial failure, and inducements being held out to him by the State temperance organization to essay the establishment of his paper at Harrisburg, he accepted the offer. The promised aid not being furnished him, he was again unsuccessful, and was involved in difficulties which required years of patient toil amidst great discouragement to surmount. · In 1846 he edited an anti-administration paper called the *Yeoman*, supported by a wing of the Democracy in opposition to the administration of Francis R. Shunk, Governor of Pennsylvania. Some time after this, we find him employed in Philadelphia, in the *Quaker City* newspaper office, for which paper he afterwards contributed a serial story, entitled the "Prayer of Love," supposed to embody much of his own life experience. After this he became editor of the *Sunday Globe*; next one of the publishers of the *Sunday Mercury*. In February, 1852, he accepted the proposition of John H. Pearsol, came to Lancaster and assumed the editorial management of the *Weekly Express*, then the organ of the temperance sentiment of the county. In 1856 Mr. Geist purchased an interest in this paper, and with his partner, the original proprietor, established in connection with it the *Daily Express*, and has succeeded in building it up as one of the most influential and independent newspaper organs in eastern Pennsylvania. As an editor of a newspaper, Mr. Geist wields a fertile and vigorous pen, his style being free, easy and euphonious. Although a Republican in principle, he is independent, and no party fealty checks his pen when truth demands the exposure of political corruption. It is this cause which has rendered his paper the powerful moulder of sentiment it has become.

GEIST, PHILIP, elected Commissioner in 1853.

GETZ, GEORGE, was born in the city of Lancaster, July 18, 1789. He learned the printing business in the Lancaster *Journal* office, under Hugh Hamilton. Afterwards he entered the service of the United States, as midshipman in the navy. He took part, under Captain James Lawrence, in the memorable engagement between the Hornet and the Peacock, and performed active duty in several minor naval engagements. In the latter part of the year 1813 he resigned his post in the navy, and was appointed by President Madison, a lieutenant in the army, in which capacity he served until the close of the war. In 1816 he removed to Reading, Berks county, Pa., where he established the *Berks and Schuylkill Journal,* a paper which he conducted for over sixteen years. In March, 1850, he was elected Mayor of the city of Reading, and was twice reëlected, in the years 1851 and 1852. He died February 10th, 1853.

GEST, JOSEPH, born at Bethel, (now Delaware county), in the year 1722, was the son of Henry Gest, who emigrated to this country from Birmingham, England, about the year 1700, and who was married to Mary, the daughter of James Clemson. While yet a boy, Joseph removed to Lancaster county, and resided with his uncle, Thomas Clemson; here he learned the trade of a carpenter, and soon became an extensive contractor, and was engaged in erecting some of the finest buildings among the early settlements. In the year 1764 he purchased 300 acres of land from William Webster, the original patentee, on which his grandson, Jacob T. Gest, now resides; and in the following year he was joined in marriage with Deborah, the daughter of Joseph and Elizabeth Dickinson. His son, John Gest, was appointed to the office of Recorder of Deeds, for the city and county of Philadelphia, under the administration of Governor Ritner, in the year 1835; and his son, Joseph Gest, was, for many years, county surveyor for Hamilton county, Ohio, and for the city of Cincinnati. He lived to the age of 92 years, and his descendants are among the most intelligent and respectable personages in the eastern section of Lancaster county.

GETZ, PETER. The following notice of Mr. Getz we extract from Barton's Life of Rittenhouse: "Peter Getz was a self-taught mechanic of singular ingenuity in the borough of Lancaster, where he exercised the trade of a silversmith and jeweler, and was remarkable for the extraordinary elegance and beauty of the workmanship he executed. He was, in 1792, a candidate for the place of chief coiner or engraver in the mint."

GIBBONS, ABRAHAM, elected Commissioner in 1824.

GIBBONS, MRS. PHOEBE EARLE, a lady of literary tastes, was born in Philadelphia, August 9th, 1821. Her father, Thomas Earle, was a man of great note in his day, and in 1840 was the first candidate of the Liberty party for

18

Vice President. The subject of this sketch was well educated in select schools in Massachusetts, and taught in Mr. Picot's French school in Philadelphia and elsewhere for some years. In 1845 she was married to Dr. Joseph Gibbons of Lancaster county. In 1861 she began the study of Greek, with Professor William M. Nevin, of Lancaster. A portion of the Odyssey, translated by her was published in the *Ladies' Friend* of Philadelphia. A small medical work was translated by her from the French, for Lindsay and Blakiston, which was published in 1866. She has also translated a portion of the Herman and Dorothea of Gœthe. At different times she has written articles for magazines. In 1872 she published a small volume, entitled "Pennsylvania Dutch," a portion of which originally appeared in the *Atlantic Monthly.* Mrs. Gibbons is an active member of the Lancaster Linnæan Society. She is a lady of varied acquirements and marked intellectual capacity.

GIBSON, GENERAL JOHN, was born in Lancaster city, Pennsylvania, on the 23rd of May, 1740. Having received an excellent education, at the age of eighteen he made choice of a military career as the most congenial to his tastes. His first service was under Gen. Forbes, in the campaign that resulted in the capture of Fort Duquesne (now Pittsburg), from the French. When the peace of 1763 was concluded between the French and English, he settled as a trader at Fort Pitt. Shortly afterwards, war broke out anew with the Indians, and he was taken prisoner by them at the mouth of Beaver creek, while descending the Ohio river in a canoe, together with two men in his employ, one of whom was immediately burned, and the other suffered the same fate on reaching the mouth of the Kanawha river. Gibson, on this occasion, owed his life to the partiality of an aged squaw, who chose him as her adopted son, in lieu of her own whom she had lost in battle. He was necessitated to remain many years with the Indians, where he became immediately conversant with their language, habits, manners, customs and traditions. It has been a subject of extreme regret by many, that he should have held these matters in such slight esteem as to deem his collections unworthy of being transmitted to posterity; for it is evident that in the present state of antiquarian research, they would throw light upon many questions that are now agitated among scientific men. No man of his attainments and ability to set forth his observations, has had equal opportunities for coming to a correct knowledge of the Indian character, unless his friend, the Rev. Heckewelder, is to be excepted. Upon the termination of hostilities, he again settled at Fort Pitt.

In 1774 he acted a conspicuous part in the expedition against the Shawnee towns, under the command of Lord Dunmore, and was particularly active in the negotiation of the peace that followed, and which restored many prisoners to their friends after long years of anxious captivity. It was on this occasion that the celebrated speech of Logan, the Mingo chief, was delivered, and the circumstances connected with its delivery are of sufficient interest to account for their recital in this sketch, such as they were detailed by Gen. Gibson himself a short time before his death. When the troops had reached the principal town of the Shawnees, and while active preparations were being made to put everything in readiness for the attack, Gen. Gibson, with an escort and flag of truce, was despatched to the Indians with authority to treat for peace. As he approached he perceived Logan, (whom he had previously seen), standing in the path, and he addressed him with the familiar greeting: "My friend Logan, how do you do? I am glad to see you." To this, Logan, with a coldness of manner and brevity of expression which clearly betokened his feelings, replied: "I suppose you are," and immediately turned away. After explaining the object of his embassy to the assembled chiefs, (all of whom were present except Logan), he found them all sincerely anxious for peace. Whilst the terms of reconciliation were being discussed he felt himself plucked by the skirt of his capote, and turning around he saw Logan at his back, standing with his face convulsed with rage, and by signs beckoning to follow him. What to do he was at first in doubt, but reflecting that he was at least equal to his antagonist, being armed with dirk and side pistols, and in muscular strength his superior, and considering, above all, that any betrayal of fear in this emergency, might prove detrimental to the negotiation, he followed in silence, while Logan with quick steps led the way to a copse of woods at some little distance. Here they seated themselves, and the stern and fearless chief was instantly suffused in a torrent of gushing tears, but as yet no word was uttered, and his grief appeared inconsolable. As soon, however, as he had regained the power of utterance, he delivered the speech in question, and desired it to be transmitted to Lord Dunmore, in order to remove all suspicion that might be entertained in reference to a treaty, in the ratification of which a chief of his importance had not participated. Accordingly, the speech was translated and sent to Lord Dunmore without delay. Gen. Gibson could not positively say that the speech, as given by Jefferson in his Notes on Virginia, was *verbatim* as he had penned it; but he was inclined to think from certain expressions which he remembered, it was so; that it gave the substance, he was confident. Gen. Gibson, however, believed that it was not in the power of a translation to do justice to the speech as delivered by Logan; a speech to which the language of passion, uttered in tones of the deepest feeling, and with gestures at once naturally graceful and commanding, together with a consciousness on the part of the hearer that the sentiments proceeded immediately from a desolate and broken heart, imparted a grandeur and force inconceivably great. Indeed, as compared with the original, he even regarded the translation as but lame and insipid.

On the breaking out of the revolutionary war, Gen. Gibson obtained the command of one of the Continental regiments, and was with the army at New York and during its retreat through New Jersey; but during the remainder of the war he was detailed on the western frontier, a service for which his long sojourn among the Indians had peculiarly qualified him. In 1776 he was a member of the convention which framed the Constitution of Pennsylvania, and was afterward appointed a judge of the court of common pleas of the county of Allegheny, and a major general of the militia. In the year 1800 he received from President Jefferson the appointment of Secretary of the Territory of Indiana, and this position he retained until the territory was admitted as a State into the Union. Laboring under an incurable cataract, which had for a long time afflicted him, he now retired to Braddock's Field, the residence of his son-in-law, Geo. Wallace, esq., and there died April 10th, 1822, having sustained through life the character of a brave soldier and an honest man.

GILCHRIST, JOHN, was a member of the Legislature in the years 1778 and 1779.

GISH, JACOB, was a member of the Legislature in the years 1805, 1806, 1807, 1808, 1809 and 1824.

GLEIM, WILLIAM, was elected Register of Wills in the year 1845.

GOOD, ANTHONY, was elected Recorder in the year 1857.

GOOD, DANIEL, elected Commissioner in 1854.

GOTSCHALK, ABRAHAM, was a member of the Legislature in the years 1867 and 1869.

GRAFF, HANS, (John), a native of Switzerland, born in 1661, was one of the first pioneers of Lancaster county, who settled in it as early as the year 1717, when the district in which he chose his future home was comparatively a howling wilderness, still inhabited by the tawny races of the new world. He belonged to the pious but persecuted sect of religionists in Europe, the Mennonites, against whom the sword of intolerance was unsheathed; and it was to escape the destruction that seemed to threaten the devoted followers of Menno Simon, that the subject of our notice was induced, together with his fellow-religionists, to select some portion of the new world as their place of refuge. About the year 1695, Hans Graff had fled from his native home in Switzerland, and taken up his abode in Alsace, a district of France, where he remained until he emigrated to America, and settled at Germantown, Pa. His stay in this latter place was of some duration; but finally, induced by glowing descriptions of the fertility and excellence of the soil of the Pequea valley, he removed thither and chose it as his abode, unless one more adapted to his tastes should come to his knowledge. In his wanderings through the new territory he came into a

finely timbered district of country; and embowered in the
midst of beautiful and majestic oaks, he saw a gushing stream
of limpid water issuing from its fountain in all its native
purity. Fascinated with this delightful elysium of nature,
this exiled wanderer for conscience resolved to select the
lovely spot upon which his eyes then for the first time
rested, and the place where, in coming years, he and his
successors might pour out their adorations to the God of
their fathers, with none to fear nor make them afraid. His
resolution was fixed. Returning to his home at Pequea, he
disposed of his effects and immediately took up his journey
for the place which he had chosen as his future home and
abode. Here he erected a cabin under a large white oak
tree, in which he, the partner of his bosom and an only
child, spent the first winter. In the following spring, in
order to secure himself in this the territory of his choice,
he took out a warrant for a large tract of land, and then
built for himself a house of more commodious dimensions
and near to the site of his first rude and homely cabin.
Fortune favored, in a remarkable degree, this early pioneer
of Lancaster's wilds; and it was not long till his prosperity
attracted others of his countrymen, who came and settled
around and near him; and in this manner the nucleus of a
flourishing settlement was in a short time formed. For
many years, however, the principal persons with whom Hans
Graff had intercourse, were the red men of the forest, and
this accounts for his great knowledge of the Indian tongue,
in which he is said to have discoursed as fluently as in his
vernacular German. He was not slow in taking advantage
of the circumstances by which he was surrounded, and with
the Indians he soon established a trade that resulted to his
great profit and advantage. He sold to the Indians milk,
vegetables, blankets, and other articles of merchandise
which he could purchase in Philadelphia, and obtained in
exchange for them furs and other objects of trade, for which
he could secure a ready sale, and which, to him, were equivalent to cash. In this way Hans Graff laid the foundation
of a princely fortune; and by the time that Lancaster was
organized into a separate county, he was already one of the

most independent and influential of its citizens. The township in which he had selected his abode, was named Earl (Graff) in honor of him, as its most respected inhabitant. He was an active and energetic man in his day; useful as a counsellor amongst his neighbors and fellow-citizens; and no business of importance was transacted at that early period unless his judgment was first consulted and his consent obtained. Despite the jealousy of race, that in those early times inflamed the antagonistic Irish and German elements of the county, we find the name of Hans Graff often conspicuously appearing in positions of official trust, to which he had been assigned by the Governor and Board of Council of the province; and by the judges of the court of his county. After having served his day and generation, he was followed to his last resting-place by his numerous friends and descendants, who have erected a shrine to his memory more enduring than the lofty marble monuments reared to princes, kings and emperors.

Hans Graff raised six sons: Peter, David, John, Daniel, Marcus and Samuel. David was married to a Miss Moyer, and died at the age of sixty-two years. His wife attained the age of ninety-two years. David, son of the last named, married Barbara Hirst, and built the house in West Earl township where Levi W. Groff now resides. He died at the age of twenty-seven, and his widow married David Martin. John, (gross Johnny), son of the last, was married to a Miss Wenger. Levi W. Groff is one of his sons, and David G. Swartz, esq., of Lancaster, is a grandson.

GRIEST, ELLWOOD, was born in Chester county, Pa., June 17th, 1824. His parents belonged to the Society of Friends. After receiving an ordinary English education, he was apprenticed to the blacksmithing business, and having learned this trade, he worked in the capacity of a journeyman in Lancaster, Chester and Delaware counties. He carried on this business in Bart township, and afterwards in Christiana, up to the breaking out of the rebellion. He entered the service of the United States in December, 1862, as a clerk in the subsistence department, in the Third Division, Sixth Army Corps, Army of the Potomac. In this capacity

he served up to October, 1863, when he was captured by
Moseby's guerrillas, and sent to Richmond. Here he was
detained for some months, and after returning home, was
detailed for duty to Johnson's Island, in Lake Erie, a depot
of rebel prisoners. In August, 1864, he was commissioned
commissary of subsistence, with the rank of captain. He
was ordered to Gen. Sheridan's army, and placed on his
staff as issuing commissary at headquarters. He remained with Sheridan till February, 1865; and when the
latter went on his raid in the Shenandoah Valley, Captain
Griest was left as post commissary at Winchester.

During the time that Captain Griest was connected with
Sheridan's staff, General Alexander Shaler, who knew him
well in the Army of the Potomac, and was now commanding
the post of Columbus, Kentucky, made repeated applications
to have him assigned to duty on his staff. These applications were at length referred by the Commissary General of
Subsistence to General Sheridan, who returned them with
the following endorsement:

HEADQUARTERS MIDDLE MILITARY DIVISION, WINCHESTER, Va.,
December 14th, 1864.

Respectfully returned to the Commissary General, with the remark
that Captain Griest is an intelligent and efficient officer, whose services
at this time, in this department, cannot very well be dispensed with.

By order of   MAJOR GENERAL SHERIDAN.

JNO. KELLOGG, Col. and Chief C. S.

He was afterwards detailed with Sheridan to New Orleans;
next to Jacksonville, Florida, at which latter place he remained till mustered out of service in April, 1866, with the
brevet rank of Major. Before returning home a lieutenant's
commission in the United States infantry was tendered him,
which he declined accepting. In the following September,
upon his return home, he was appointed County Treasurer
by the county commissioners, in room of Samuel Ensminger,
deceased. Whilst acting as Treasurer he was engaged by
S. A. Wylie to edit the *Lancaster Inquirer*, then published
by the latter. In 1868 he entered into partnership with the
latter, a position he retained till the death of Mr. Wylie, in
June, 1872. He is still editor of the *Inquirer*.

GREY, HENRY, was a member of the Legislature in the years 1852 and 1853.

GRIMLER, BENJAMIN, the editor of the *Wahre Americaner*, a German newspaper published in Lancaster during the period that it was the seat of government of Pennsylvania. The paper was published by himself and his brother, Henry Grimler. Benjamin was the youngest of a considerable family. His father had emigrated from Wirtemberg, Germany, at an early day, and his mother was a native of Charleston, South Carolina, and an intimate acquaintance of the celebrated Benjamin Franklin, having boarded in the same family with him for some time. *Der Wahre Americaner* was for a long time the leading Democratic paper of Lancaster county, and looked upon as the political bible of that party. The Messrs. Grimler were employed by the Legislature to do the German printing as long as the sessions of the body were held in this place. Benjamin Grimler went out as lieutenant of a company, raised in Lancaster, to Elkton, Maryland, to assist in keeping at bay the British, who were cruising around the coasts under Admiral Cockburn. His service was not of long duration, and after his discharge therefrom he returned to Lancaster and resumed again the business of civil life. In 1824 he was elected to the lower house of the Pennsylvania Legislature. Benjamin Grimler was a ready writer, in either German or English; and could deliver an impromptu address or pen an editorial upon any occasion. At the time when Captain George Hambright was defeated by the delegates of the Federal party for the office of sheriff, and ran afterwards in opposition to the settled ticket of his party, Benjamin Grimler was successful in inducing the Democratic party to support him, and he was elected. Hambright was supported by the plebeian wing of the Federal party, and also by the Democrats. During this campaign Grimler issued in his paper one of his masterly addresses, which aroused the masses of the people to the support of his candidates, and insured their triumphant election. He died in 1832, and lies buried in the graveyard of Trinity Lutheran church. The mother of Hon. Henry G. Long was a sister of Benjamin Grimler.

GRIMLER, HENRY, brother of the above and co-editor with him in the publication of *Der Wahre Americaner*. He was a man of much greater brilliancy of intellect than his brother, and possessed a great fondness for writing blank verse. Some of his productions of this kind evince a high order of intellect. He died at the early age of 36 years.

GROFF, JOHN, a member of the Legislature in 1812.

GROFF, SEBASTIAN, was elected State Senator in 1790. He was, in 1787, a delegate to the convention to ratify the Federal constitution, and was again a delegate in 1789 to the convention held to amend the constitution of Pennsylvania.

GROH, C. L., elected a County Commissioner in 1831.

GROSH, JACOB. In 1745 two families of the name of Grosh, emigrated to this country from Manheim, Germany. On landing at Philadelphia, two of the children were indentured as "Redemptioners," to aid in paying their passage money.

Valentine Grosh, the grandfather of the subject of this sketch, settled in East Hempfield, on wild lands purchased on credit from the government, at a shilling (13⅓ cents) per acre. The houses being built of round hickory logs, the neighborhood was called Hickorytown; afterward Snufftown. After a time Valentine removed to Litiz, being a member of the Moravian church, and gave up the farm to his son John, the father of Daniel and Jacob, and their sisters.

Jacob Grosh, the youngest of these children, was born January 25th, 1776. Between the ages of eight and twelve years he was sent to school in Litiz—three months each summer—a daily walk of ten miles. The teacher was Rev. Mr. Grube, grandfather of John Beck, the founder, and for fifty years the principal of the Boys' Academy in Litiz. This twelve months of schooling, all he ever received, was in German; nor did he learn to read and write English until aided by his second wife. At 12 years of age he was put to "man's work," plowing, felling trees, &c. At 20 he married, and was disowned by his father. He soon went to work, and thus describes his establishment: "Our house (rent $7.00 a year,) was built of round logs, the crevices filled with clay mortar. It was 15 by 16 feet, of one-story, (6 feet in the clear,) roofed with straw, and had one window of four panes, 6x8. My wages were good, and we had everything we really needed, a bed, two chairs, two pewter spoons, two knives and forks, two plates, a table of rough boards, a few pots, pans, &c., and suitable clothing in a chest. We were really comfortable and contented, and happy in each other. I had a tender, loving wife, of my own choosing, a healthy, virtuous and agreeable woman." His wife died on Christmas eve of 1796.

His father having married again, came and thus addressed him : "Jacob, your new mother, and, I may add, your new father, want you to come home again. Next Sunday I wish you to go to church with your mother, brother and sisters, and I will acknowledge you as my son as publicly as I disowned you." Their mingled tears washed away all unkind recollections.

In 1799 he made his home with Daniel, his brother, whose wife, "Gretel," (Margaret) was always a beloved sister; laboring on the farm, where he became acquainted with Margaret, daughter of George Gutedel, (anglicised into Gooderl); but as he could understand no English, and she no German, their intercourse was confined to looks and dumb show. But a marriage resulted, June 13th, 1799. His father now gave him the tenancy of 100 acres of wild land, and became security for necessary stock and utensils. He cleared ten acres, and built a two-story log house, 28 by 30 feet, and a double barn, himself felling and preparing all the timber for buildings and fences. His energetic wife was his helper in nearly all the labors in field and barn, in dairy and household, as was then the country custom. Here were born to them Hannah, (who died, aged four years), and Aaron Burt, (Mr. G.'s mother's family name); and afterward, in Marietta, Rufus King, C. C. Pinkney, J. A. Bayard, Malvina, Magdalena, and B. Franklin.[1] Hard labor, exposures, and the anxieties of debt impaired his health, and finally compelled a change. The farm, stock and utensils were sold,

[1] Of these seven children, only the first and third sons survive (1872.)

debts paid, and a surplus of $1,000 obtained. The towns of Waterford and New Haven (now Marietta), had just been laid out at Anderson's ferry, on the Susquehanna, and thither they moved in March, 1806, and built (of brick) the seventh house in the place, and opened it as a tavern. The land-lady's tact and skill made it successful, but it was disagree-able to him. One day while his wife was on a visit, he cut down the sign-post, and closed the tavern. Thus ended a few brief months of tavern-keeping. He entered next into the lumber business, which he continued for fifty-three years. This led him into new associations, and somewhat into dissi-pation.

In 1811 he was nominated for the House of Representa-tives, and having overheard his wife and a friend expressing their fears of the result, he inwardly resolved that hence-forth he would not forfeit the public confidence, nor blast the hopes of his family and friends, and from that day to the close of his life he never gambled in any way. And during his first winter at Harrisburg, by the representations of an aged room-mate, (Col. Erwin, Senator from Bucks county,) he vowed that he would never taste intoxicants while en-gaged as a legislator. In after-life he often gratefully re-viewed the many snares he had escaped by observing these resolutions. He was reëlected to the Legislature for the sessions of 1813, 1814 and 1816. In 1818 he was elected to the State Senate, and served four years, making his legis-lative service eight years, four in the House and four in the Senate.

As a legislator he was noted for his close attention to his duties, his intimate acquaintance with rules and usages, his sound judgment, strict integrity, and readiness to attend to all proper calls for aid and information. He was conscien-tiously opposed to the war of 1812–15. He believed that it should not have been declared until the country was put into a condition to make it effective. The early disasters of our army and pecuniary distress of the government confirmed these views; but when Washington city was captured, the capitol and its records burned, and other cities threatened, his blood boiled within him and he contributed liberally to send a company of drafted men to Baltimore. Soon after, Governor Snyder issued a proclamation calling for volunteers, and sent a copy with a letter, appealing to Mr. Grosh to give it his influence. He at once hired the town-crier to go through the streets, read the proclamation, and call a town meeting that evening. At the meeting he made a warm appeal and called for volunteers. Over eighty gave their names on the spot, uniform and name ("Marietta Greys") were agreed on, and money subscribed to equip the men and provide for needy families. The principal work and cost soon rested on Mr. Grosh, who was unanimously chosen Captain; John Pedan, 1st Lieutenant; John Huss, 2d Lieutenant; and J. Albright, Ensign.[1] On the fourth day after receiving the Governor's proclamation, 107 men[2] were uniformed and marched for their destination. They were mustered in as "9th Co., 2d Reg., Pa. Vols., L. Inf.," commanded by Col. Lewis Bache. As cold weather came on the captain purchased 100 blankets at $8.00 a pair, for which he never made any claim on the government. While in camp, commanding men who were associates and friends, and some his social superiors, he lived on the same fare and bore the same privations and restraints, and thus secured their cheerful obedience to his orders and submission to the hardships of camp.

During the speculation[3] fever Mr. G. (in 1813) bought 48 acres of land, east of (now in) Marietta, at $13.00 per acre, and laid it out in lots. In two months all were sold, at $500 each, and, in February following, when titles were given, were held at $600 and upward. He bought back many lots at these prices, and a farm of 133 acres, seven miles from town, at $250 per acre—merely to invest his money. He also built a first-class three-story brick house

[1] The women of Marietta assembled in a school-house, and made garments and knapsacks for the volunteers in Captain Grosh's company, so that when the men left their homes to march to Marcus Hook, they went fully equipped.—*Sypher's History of Pa.*, pp. 239, 240.

[2] Of these 107 men but one now (1872) survives, Jacob Jones, of Delaware.

[3] Few persons now living have any definite idea of the speculations that desolated so many homes and ruined so many fortunes in Marietta during and after the war of 1812–15, when property fell in successive

in the new town, costing over $10,000. In those days of abundant paper money, all felt rich, and indorsing was "a mere form," for every man was "abundantly able to meet all his engagements;" so that when Mr. G. went to camp, in 1814, he was bail and indorser for more than $55,000, beside his own heavy debts. By 1819 every man for whom he had indorsed, was bankrupt; his absence had necessitated new indorsers, and thus saved him! On his return, he freed himself from other entanglements, barely in time to meet the coming storm. For when his property fell to one-tenth in price, while debts contracted in paper money had to be paid in coin at about quadruple value, he found himself utterly bankrupt—save that no one knew it—only his wife suspected it. Once, when sued as bail on a bond, for $2,960, by selling his entire stock of lumber at a sacrifice, he escaped an execution; and the free use of his brother's credit stocked the yard again. In the family, the merest and cheapest necessaries only were used.[1] Thus through ten years of agonizing debt, Mr. G. slowly emerged into comparative comfort, still limited in means, but free from fears of the sheriff.

His faithful wife sunk into consumption, and died December, 1823, aged 36 years, leaving six children, the youngest about five years old.

When the Marietta Bank became insolvent Mr. Grosh and six others were appointed trustees to settle its affairs. Its notes were bought up at a heavy discount by brokers, who hoped to sell them at great profit when the bank's debtors values and debts pressed inexorably, until everything except indebtedness went down under the sheriff's hammer for almost nothing; and fathers and husbands were dragged to jail by unsatisfied creditors, leaving families without the necessaries of life, which the imprisoned men were thus prevented from earning. Nor were the sufferers few. Up to 1822, out of 2,000 souls in Marietta, only four men escaped insolvency! Houses sold for less than the cost of the mortar in and on their walls; one, that cost $16,000, sold for $1,100; lots brought one per cent. of former prices; even farms, five or six miles from town, sold for only one-sixth of their cost!

[1] Rye coffee, without sugar; rye, corn and potato bread, generally without butter; cheap meat, twice a week; home-spun clothing for the children's every-day wear, &c.

were pushed for payment. But in 1823 the bank was robbed of all its evidences of debt, and its notes rendered worthless, unless the trustees could be made liable for them, or responsible for the robbery. Hence, civil suits were commenced against them for over $400,000, the U. S. Bank leading the way, and the Legislature of 1824–5 was induced to cite them to appear before it for trial. Mr. Grosh promptly refused to appear, and Mr. Shannon, Sergeant-at-Arms, was sent to compel attendance. He found Mr. Grosh entrenched in his chamber, armed for resistance unto death. In vain Mr. Shannon urged (among other considerations,) that a refusal would be considered proof of guilt. Mr. Grosh acted on principle, and was therefore regardless of people's opinions, and Mr. Shannon went to summon a *posse*. He returned after a time, saying that not a man would aid him, even as Mr. Grosh had predicted. So, after dinner, (which Mr. Grosh had ordered prepared, but did not preside at!) he departed, bearing to the Legislature Mr. Grosh's protest, which stated—that the Constitution vested all government in three departments (legislative, executive, judicial,)—that neither department could exercise powers vested in the others- -that in citing the trustees for trial the Legislature usurped judiciary powers, in violation of the Constitution and of the right of citizens, for if it had a right to try the trustees for alleged bank robbery, it had a right to try any other person for any other alleged crime, (robbing a hen-roost, for instance !) He concluded with assurances that he refused, not out of disrespect, nor fear of conviction, but out of duty to resist a precedent so dangerous to the prosperity of government and the rights of its citizens, and pledged ready obedience to the summons of any lawful criminal court. These events excited much feeling and various comments on all sides ; but the result was, that the Legislature dropped the matter, and never afterward undertook any similar affair ; no criminal suit was ever brought ; and, after much manœuvering and costs, even the civil suits were decided against the plaintiffs or quietly dropped. Many years afterwards a worthy townsman, on his death-bed, informed Mr. Grosh that he and others had robbed the bank to save themselves from the utter ruin which must have ensued had the bank collected its claims.

He found, in the Litiz "Sister House," a lady every way suited to make him happy, and was married November 2d, 1824.

In 1822 his oldest son embraced Universalism. Owing partially to surmises long entertained, he was induced to consider the subject of religion more earnestly, reading books and periodicals on both sides, and studying the Scriptures so thoroughly that few were better acquainted with their contents, and thus he became (as he afterward lived and died) a Universalist Christian.

Mr. Grosh had been reared a Federalist. But the war of 1812–15, and the Presidential contest between five candidates in 1824, gradually effaced party lines. He voted for Mr. Adams in 1824 and 1828; but before 1832 Gen. Jackson's views on nullification and the United States Bank so fully accorded with his own, that he thenceforward acted with the Democratic party, until, in 1857, his life-long hatred of slavery led him to vote with the Republicans. In 1832 he again became an active politician. In 1840 Governor Porter nominated him to the Senate for Associate Judge. Both Lancaster Senators being ardent Whigs, opposed the nomination, alleging that he was incapable, superannuated, an infidel, (because a Universalist), and a Sabbath-breaker, in that he held Universalist meetings in his house, and attended temperance meetings on Sundays. Only 101 persons could be induced to thus remonstrate, but he was rejected, 15 to 18, by a strict party vote. In 1841 Governor Porter again nominated him, stating that many of both parties desired it; that careful inquiry proved him fit and capable; and that religious prejudice should not be heeded, &c. He was confirmed—18 Democrats and 4 Whigs for, and 9 Whigs against. When, five years later, he was again nominated, nearly all of the bar requested it, and the Senate *unanimously* confirmed it.

Shortly after Mr. G.'s appointment, Judge Dale died, and Judge Champneys resigned his seat upon the bench. Before Mr. Shaeffer had taken Judge Dale's place, Judge Grosh was alone on the bench. Yet he opened the court, qualified the new associate, charged the juries, and presided at trials; the first instance an associate judge had so officiated in the county. On the first day he thus presided, Thaddeus Stevens, who had lately removed to Lancaster from Adams county, came to him, at noon, and said, "The settling of the docket was forgotten this morning." The judge replied that that would be attended to next Monday, the first day of Common Pleas. Mr. Stevens remarked, "This is the proper day;" and added that he had taken judgment in two cases, naming them. The judge said that where both terms were held the same week, (as in Adams county,) the first day might be proper, but if Mr. Stevens would consult some old member of the bar he would find that it was not the rule here. Mr. Stevens fiercely replied that he knew his own business, and would impeach any judge who dared alter that entry on the docket. When the court opened the judge calmly said, "Mr. Prothonotary, Mr. Stevens (in a mistake, the Court presumes,) entered judgments by default against ———— and ————; and, as he declines striking them off, the Court now directs you to do it." It was done, amidst great suppressed excitement in the bar, Mr. Stevens looking pale and vexed, but from that day he and Mr. Grosh were friends, despite their political differences.

Another lawyer, presuming on Mr. Grosh's timidity, was unruly and speaking "out of order." He was told to take his seat, but heeded it not. The judge mildly said, "Sit down, or the Court will be compelled to commit you for contempt," to which the lawyer saucily replied, "Your Honor had better try your hand at that!" "Sit down, sir!" said the judge, in such stern tone and with flashing eye, that the lawyer literally *dropped* into his seat. That was the last attempt to browbeat him on the part of any attorney at the bar. The greatest pain was suffered in deciding cases of fugitives from slavery, not one of whom, however, was ever remanded into bondage by him or Judge Shaeffer. One case only is here noted. Before the law of 1848, which debarred all State officers from acting in slave cases, fugitives could be tried by a single judge, "in chambers."

Thus, Henry Johnson, kidnapped by slave catchers, and rescued, was brought to the judge's residence for trial. The crowd and excitement were so great that the strong front door was forced from its hinges. As Johnson desired a lawyer, the case was adjourned to the court house, on the ensuing Saturday, when Judge Shaeffer assisted by taking down the testimony, and Mr. Stevens appeared for the defendant. The proof of identity, and that Johnson had run away from the claimant, was clear, and Mr. Stevens, seemingly paralyzed, could only express suspicions of forgery, &c. Judge Grosh, also in deep distress, asked time for consideration. The claimant's lawyer, with much heat, exclaimed, "Why, judge, a plainer case could not come before you;" when the judge interrupted him with, "I generally do my own thinking," and ordered the case adjourned till Monday, at 2 o'clock, p. m. Leaving the crowded court house he went to Hinkletown, where his wife was on a visit. On seeing him she cried out, "Good God! what ails you? how wretched you look!" He told her all, and asked to be alone that he might *think*. He read the testimony again and again, and worried through the weary hours, till with Monday morning came a ray of hope. He reached Lancaster at noon on Monday, and Judge Shaeffer almost leaped with joy as he related his plan. At 2 p. m. the court house was so full that the judges had to get in through a window. After the opening Judge Grosh asked the claimant's attorney, "Can a person be legally a slave, unless born in a slave State, and of a slave mother?" "If a free woman were kidnapped and carried into slavery, would her progeny be legally slaves?" The answers were, "Certainly not." "Then (said the judge) the case is clear. In all cases where freedom and slavery are at issue, all constructions, all doubts, must enure to the advantage of freedom. So I should charge a jury, so I must govern myself. I doubt whether Johnson's mother was a slave. I will adjourn the court for one week, if you claim that you can remove that doubt." A dead silence, no motion for such adjournment, and he proceeded, "No answer! I therefore decide that you, Henry Johnson, are a free man," &c. Shouts rent the air, and it was some time before order could be restored. Toward the close of his second term, by the amended constitution, the office became elective, and Judge Grosh declined candidacy.

In 1842 his wife was taken ill and lingered along, until he, too, was prostrated by a fever, from the delirium of which he awoke to find that his affectionate wife had died August 26th, 1842, aged 58 years. He next married Miss Leah Bushong, of Reamstown, in 1843. She died October 15th, 1847. A fifth marriage was entered into with Mrs. Sarah Albright, on May 24th, 1849, who survived him. The close of his long life was quiet and peaceful. The deaths of many children, grandchildren and friends often excited the wish, that " these young plants could have been spared, and the old, useless trunk been taken in their stead," but he did not repine at Providence. His two sons aided him in his business, and, with their families, cheered his lonely hours. His general health continued good, and his faculties active, for one of his years, until his last comparatively brief illness, which terminated his life on November 4th, 1860, in his 85th year. Judge Grosh, though of quick temper, never bore malice; and though he reared a large family of children and dependents, he never but once inflicted corporal ·punishment on any of them. Indeed, most of "his failings leaned to virtue's side;" and many portions of his life furnish interesting examples to encourage the poor and erring amongst mankind.

GROSH, SAMUEL, a member of the Legislature in 1823.

GRUBB, HENRY, emigrated from Wales to Lancaster county at an early day. His son, Peter, obtained possession of the Cornwall ore banks, and built a furnace as early as 1725. The title of the property was confirmed to Peter Grubb by the proprietaries, in 1732. Peter Grubb died in 1745, leaving two sons, Curtis and Peter, the former inheriting two-thirds, and the latter one-third of the estate. The estate in 1783 consisted of Cornwall furnace, the Hopewell forges, and Union forge, on the Swatara, at the foot of the Blue Mountains. Curtis Grubb was a member of the Pennsylvania Assembly for the years 1775, 1777, 1778 and 1782.

He died in the year 1788. His son, Peter, was Colonel of the 8th battalion of Lancaster county militia. He was a member of the Legislature in the year 1784.

H.

HAINES, HENRY, was born near Columbia, Lancaster county, Pa., December 8th, 1759. His parents being in very humble circumstances, he was apprenticed at an early age to the tailoring business, and his education was entirely neglected. All the little learning he acquired was picked up by him after his marriage, in a German night school. At the early age of eighteen he evinced his patriotism by enlisting as a soldier in the revolutionary army, in which he bore his part heroically. He was chosen as one of the guards to the Hessian prisoners, captured at Trenton, and assisted in their removal to Lancaster. Afterwards he was attached to Col. Bole's command in his expedition up the Susquehanna to subdue the Indians. After the revolution he settled in Maytown, where he spent the balance of his useful and active life. In 1797 he was appointed a justice of the peace, the duties of which position he discharged for many years. Some time after this he was elected and commissioned a captain of militia by Governor Simon Snyder. Being a warm and ardent Democrat, he was nominated and elected to the Legislature in 1804. He was reëlected again in 1810, and also in 1811, serving his constituents with great satisfaction. In 1825 he was again elected, and also in 1828; but owing to ill health, was obliged to retire before the close of the session. The Anti-Masonic party,[1] about this time coming

[1] The political complexion of Lancaster county has, from an early period of its history, been moulded to a certain extent by the religious sentiments of the people. The bulk of the early settlers being non-resistants, a line of division soon manifested itself which never ceased to be visible. Even an earlier difference than this separated the German and Scotch-Irish elements of the county. This was the earliest line of distinction, and it was some generations before it disappeared. Before its disappearance the difficulties between the Quakers and Scotch-Irish arose, chiefly brought about by the Quaker policy of Pennsylvania with reference to the Indians within the State. The Scotch-Irish, being the

OF LANCASTER COUNTY. 253

into power, and Mr. Haines being a man of wide influence, was tendered by this party the position of Senator if he would attach himself to the new organization. So fixed, however, was he in the principles of Jefferson, that he spurned the offer with contempt. He never further took an active frontier settlers, were about the time of the outbreak consequent upon the French and Indian war, and afterwards in the conspiracy of Pontiac, subjected to be the victims of the most inhuman murders and tortures of every description that can be conceived; and being so situated they implored the Governor and assembly of the province to remove the Indians that they were harboring, and also vote supplies for their defence. Deaf ears were turned by an assembly, the majority of whom were Quakers, and non-resistance their religious policy. Out of religious sympathy the Mennonites of Lancaster county, and other non-resistant sects sided with the Quakers against the Scotch-Irish. This was the first line of political distinction that divided the people of Lancaster county.

Upon the breaking out of the revolution the old division was not obliterated. As is well known, the Quakers, Mennonites, and other non-resistant sects felt averse to the war, because of religious scruples. They were stigmatised as Tories and adherents of the British crown. In nowise did they side with the British government, but their conscientious scruples would not allow them to favor any war, defensive or otherwise. They chose therefore to remain quiescent and participate with neither party in the struggle. Non-resistant sects are in all countries found loyal to the powers that be. They paid their taxes and assessments the same as other citizens, and followed the employment of their lives, farming. The Mennonites, in particular, were no politicians then, nor are they yet, such at least as remain truest to the faith of their fathers.

After the achievement of American independence the Quakers, Mennonites, and other non-resistants, still clinging together out of old sympathy, and feeling the necessity of aiding, as speedily as possible, in the solidification of a new government, gave their early and hearty adhesion to that party which favored the new constitution and the establishment of the Federal Union. Being of those classes that are ever averse to revolution and change in government, they were not slow to perceive that the Federalists, in their view, was the party to which their adhesion should be given. Early, therefore, having attached themselves to this party, (and at a time, too, when the ablest men of the nation were arrayed under its banners), it is in accordance with experience that they should remain faithful to their new allies, now become the representatives of the government. They thus early became and remained the devoted advocates of the party of their first choice throughout the changing phases of its history. In other German counties of Pennsylvania, the early settlers of which did not belong to non-resistant sects, a marked difference of political attitude has been observed. The people of Lancaster county, for the reasons stated,

part in politics; but so steadfast was he in his principles, that at the age of 83, when blind and feeble in health, he could not be induced to abstain from voting, inasmuch as he regarded the liberty of his country as resting upon the free exercise of this invaluable privilege. He deposited what, being the great majority of them of German non-resistant sects, early became members of the Federal party, and not giving that attention to politics as many others did, even the unpopular measures of John Adams were not sufficient to wean them from their early choice.

The large majority of men of position in the county, from the origin of the government, continued the advocates of the measures of this party. The great Democratic victory in Pennsylvania, which carried Thomas McKean into the gubernatorial chair in 1799, and which broke the strength of the Federal party, had none of its laurels in Lancaster county. His competitor carried the county by a considerable majority. Thus we find parties at this early period. Occasionally a Mennonite, or his descendant, gave his adhesion to the Democratic party, but the great bulk of them remained attached to the old opinions of their fathers. When the Federal party became more and more unpopular in public estimation, the non-resistant sects chiefly abstained from the polls, and the Democrats (then called Republicans), occasionally carried the day in the county. Thus, in 1802, 1803 and 1804, the Democrats carried the county by small majorities. In 1805 the Federals gained, and likewise the following year. In this manner elections somewhat alternated; one year the Federals carrying the victory, and another their opponents. A marked feature is, that the Democrats never carried it by a large majority, as would occasionally the Federals, showing that Democratic success was rather to be attributed to the apathy of their opponents than to their own numbers. The Federals carried the county in 1814 by about 800 majority ; in 1815 by 650 ; in 1816 by 460, and in 1817 by 1,000 majority. About this time the financial bubble burst, and with it collapsed the Federal party. From that time up to 1828 the Democrats occasionally carried the county, or elected a part of their ticket. Andrew Jackson, in 1828, carried the county for President by over 1,500 majority. But the movement, of all others, that made the county of Lancaster the strong citadel of Democratic opposition, was the Anti-Masonic crusade that took its rise from the abduction of Morgan, in New York State, in the year 1826. Morgan's abduction was seized hold of by politicians, and by the fall of 1828 a considerable party was already organized upon principles of opposition to the Masonic order. It was a very captivating question with which to make capital for a party. A jealousy always exists in the human mind against that which is exclusive, and towards secret societies this feeling is ever alive. Particularly amongst the people of the rural districts does this jealousy exist the strongest; and with many religious bodies secret societies receive no favor. The Mennonites, Omish, and other such German sects, were not hard to be persuaded into a party that had for its object

as he surmised, proved his last ballot, with the remark:
" Let it be so, this may be my last vote and I must cast it
for my children's children." He died February 1st, 1842,
highly esteemed and respected by all who knew him. He
was a man of great firmness, purity of principle, and one
the overthrow of Masonry, and they therefore welcomed the crusade
that was being preached against the murderers of Morgan and the
advocates of the Masonic iniquity, as they regarded it.

An organ of the new party was started in June of the year 1828, at
New Holland, entitled the *Anti-Masonic Herald*, with Theo. Fenn as
its editor. This sheet was widely circulated through the county, and
the effect was tremendous. Quite a number of those who had hitherto
acted with the Democratic party received the new paper, and became
converts to the new cause. The party grew with great rapidity. The
most of the German non-resistants warmly espoused the cause. In the
election held in 1829, the Anti-Masonic party swept the country with a
considerable majority. From that time for several years Anti-Masonic
principles in Lancaster county were in the ascendant. Masonry sank
rapidly below par. No longer was a member of the Order free from
insult, and they mostly ceased all connection with their lodges. These
were closed one after another, and every lodge in the county remained
closed for some years. Most of the rural lodges were never again re-
opened. Lecturers passed through the country detailing the horrors of
Masonry ; exhibitions were given in which the different scenes of Masonic initiation were said to be represented upon the stage ; and
almanacs, both English and German, were filled with cuts representing
Masonry in the most ludicrous light. Feeling became more and more
intense against the Order ; and he was a bold man, indeed, who any
longer owned himself the member of an organization resting under such
public odium. Most members of the Order denied that they were
Masons, and it even become matter of insult to charge a man as being a
Free Mason.

Jarvis F. Hanks, a Mason of ten years' standing, and eighteen degrees, from New York State, began on Monday, May 4th, 1830, holding
exhibitions in Lancaster, representing the various initiations of Masonry.
He exhibited first in Lancaster, and afterwards in Mt. Joy, Strasburg,
New Holland, Manheim and other places. He carried with him tools,
implements, robes, &c., by which the better to illustrate the Masonic
initiations. He charged twenty-five cents admittance to his exhibition.
He represented himself as an artist by profession, a member of church
in good standing, and an editor of the *Investigator*, an Anti-Masonic
paper. He began his exhibitions and illustrations by introducing "*a
poor, blind candidate*," with a bandage over his eyes, and a rope around
his neck ; "*neither naked nor clothed, barefooted nor shod.*" His exhibitions purported to represent the oaths, mysteries and ceremonies of
Free Masonry, and to display before the eyes of his audience the spectacles and workings of a Masonic Lodge. His exhibitions were numer-

ever resolved to stand by what his conscience dictated as duty.

HALDEMAN FAMILY. In Rupp's History of Lancaster county, p. 397, a list of citizens is given who were chosen in 1775 as a Committee of Public Safety, in the ously attended. In his exhibitions Hanks generally represented the first evening the Entered Apprentice and Master Mason's Degree ; the next evening the Royal Arch Degree, and on the third, the Templar Degree. At Mt. Joy he exhibited in the school-house ; but great opposition was made to his exhibiting in the public building. He also exhibited to audiences of ladies the initiations into the Entered Apprentice and Master Mason's Degree ; and at Mt. Joy a lady of standing received the "Heroine of Jericho," or lady degree. He exhibited to the ladies without compensation. These exhibitions were held all over the county, and were designed to bring the Masonic Order into public contempt. Anti-Masonic papers were full of prospectuses and announcements of the publication of books and rituals exposing the secrets of Masonry. One writing in 1830 says : "The developments and exposures of Masonry have already thrown the institution into disgrace. Five years ago no one dared to speak against it, but now its members become angry if called Masons, and publicly talk against it. No public parades are any more held, and no initiations are made into the Order. The Democratic party found itself obliged to exclude all Masons from its ticket."

Lancaster Lodge, No. 43, after being closed for a considerable time, was again opened, and members stealthily began to visit it in small numbers, few members of respect, for a long time, frequenting any of the meetings. Robert Moderwell, esq., Mayor Albright, and Dr. Geo. B. Kerfoot were amongst the most respected and influential Masons who helped to lift the Order again to respectability. In 1837 the meetings of the Lodge were small, and those who visited them sought access so as not to be seen by their neighbors. An odium hung over the Order even for years later, and it was not much before 1850 that Masons felt bold enough to hold their public processions as in times prior to the Anti-Masonic excitement. It soon became clear that the Anti-Masonic party could never become national, its strength being confined very generally to the North. Although it had already lost its distinctive importance, the election of Ritner as Governor, in 1835, was regarded as an Anti-Masonic triumph. About this time, however, the Anti-Masonic party in Lancaster divided, a part calling themselves Whigs. Fromt his time Anti-Masonry continued to decline in the county until Stevens came to Lancaster from Adams county, in 1842, and attempted, but unsuccessfully, to revive it. The leading Anti-Masons were Amos Ellmaker, Isaac Burrowes, Thos. H. Burrowes, Roland Diller and Samuel Parke. The leaders who brought up the Whig party in Lancaster county. were Christopher Hager, John Shaeffer, John F. Long, Wm. Gleim, Geo. W. Hamersly and Luther Richards.

troubles which resulted in the war with England, and among numerous German names, that of Jacob Haldeman [1] appears as one of three for Rapho township. To his grandson Henry Haldeman, a similar trust was confided at Harrisburg during the so-called Buckshot War in 1838. Jacob Haldeman was the father of John Haldeman, (1753–1832) of Locust Grove, near Bainbridge,[2] on the Susquehanna, who lived in the house now occupied by his grandson John (son of John B.) Haldeman, about two miles below Bainbridge. The elder John was married to Maria Breneman, and they brought up a large family, most of whom were sons, and became successful business men.[3] After a prosperous career, John Haldeman and wife left their homestead to their oldest son, John B., (1779–1836) and retired to a life of leisure in Columbia. The large stone mill at Locust Grove (subsequently transferred to his fourth son, Henry), was built by him and bears the inscription—ERBAUET BEI JOHN HALDEMAN AND MARIA HALDEMAN, 1790.

About the year 1795 he was a member of the State Legislature for two terms at Philadelphia, where he made the acquaintance of various distinguished men of the period. He was well informed, fond of reading, and a subscriber to works like 'Guthrie's Geography,' 2 vols. 4to. 1794, and 'The World Displayed,' 8 vols. 8vo. 1795, both of which he presented to S. S. Haldeman when a boy. These imparted a taste for geography and travel to the recipient, who in 1837, when engaged in the geological survey of the State in the vicinity of Hummelstown, remembered the exaggerated description in Guthrie, of the cave on the Swatara. Upon visiting it he discovered the main cave, (pre-

[1] Born in German Switzerland, October 7th, 1722; died December 3d, 1783. General Haldeman, a native of French Switzerland, and the first British Governor of Canada, visited Lancaster county in 1773, and offered to adopt one of Jacob Haldeman's sons, as he had not a family of his own. The celebrated scientific writer, Mrs. Marcett, was related to this family.

[2] This town was founded by his sons John B. and Henry Haldeman.

[3] Particularly the second Jacob M. Haldeman, (1781–1857) of Harrisburg, whose son Jacob S. was Minister to Sweden in 1862, and another son, (Richard J.) is now (1872) a member of Congress from Cumberland county, Pennsylvania.

viously unknown), by climbing to a small hole into which he crept, and found a descent where a rope was required to reach the floor. In the apartment thus entered for the first time, every delicate stalactite was perfect; there was not a foot-print in the soft clay floor, and the bones of bats were the only signs of previous visiters.

HALDEMAN, S. S., was born at Locust Grove Mills in 1812; the oldest son of Henry Haldeman (1787–1849) and his wife Frances Steman, (1794–1826). The house of his parents was well supplied with books, a pair of globes, &c., which afforded indoor occupation. He went to the local schools until the age of thirteen, and as there was little or nothing required of him in the way of employment, his time in the vacations was spent in the use of tools, in the shops on the premises, in shooting, fishing, boating, trapping, riding and swimming, thereby securing a good constitution and founding habits of observation which were afterwards applied to the study of the sciences. Scott's beautiful map of Lancaster county (published about the year 1824), had great attractions for him, and taught him the local geography; and as a boy he studied natural history, wading in the Susquehanna for shells, collecting plants, and traversing the river shore for minerals, Indian arrowheads and stone axes. He formed a little museum on the loft of the carriage house, where among other things, he had rude anatomical preparations made from rabbits, possums, muskrats, and other animals; and a traveling Methodist preacher taught him how to stuff birds. From his father's house an eagle's nest was visible, upon a large buttonwood, on an island a mile distant, and it was easy to observe the eagle chasing and robbing the fish-hawk, and to ascertain that when he cannot thus get fish, he will dive for them himself—a fact first put on record by Mr. Haldeman, who also published the fact that the peregrine falcon nests in rocks, as in Europe, and not in trees, as Wilson and others had supposed. He had in reality procured young ones from a nest in the cliff (Chickies Rock) which rises behind his present residence.

In the spring of 1826, when nearly fourteen years of age, Prof. Haldeman was sent to the Classical Academy of Dr.

John M. Keagy,[1] at Harrisburg, where he remained for two years, and then went to Dickinson College, Carlisle, where he was a student for two years more. Here he took lessons in French as an extra study, a language to which his attention had been turned by the grammar used by his mother when a pupil at Litiz; and his taste for natural science was encouraged under Prof. H. D. Rogers, subsequently the distinguished geologist. Preferring to direct his own studies, he returned home at the age of eighteen, and while occasionally assisting his father in the saw-milling business at Chickies, he continued his studies and gradually accumulated cabinets of geology, conchology and entomology, and a scientific and linguistic library.

In 1835 he published his first communication of a scientific character in the Lancaster *Journal*, being a refutation of Locke's "Moon Hoax," in which it was pretended that with a telescope twenty-four feet in diameter, animals had been observed in the moon.[2] At this period he was interested in education, and was ready to lecture before lyceums, which came into vogue about that time; and subsequently before educational conventions, on scientific and linguistic subjects, taking care to expose the scientific errors which are so often present in educational literature. To one of these books he devoted an entire pamphlet, ('Notes on Wilson's Readers'), of which the revised edition has the date of 1870. When editing the '*Farm Journal*,' (1851, p. 2 and 66,) he ridiculed the 'Paine Light;' and when 'spirit rappings'

---

[1] See Mombert's History of Lancaster county, 1869, p. 398.

[2] The following paragraph will give an idea of this refutation: "The magnifying power of the new telescope is said to be 42,000 times, and capable of distinguishing objects of a few inches in diameter on the lunar surface. Now this power is much too great for an instrument twenty-four feet in diameter, and still not great enough to distinguish objects of *eighteen* inches. The unassisted eye, when viewing the moon, can distinguish a spot of about seventy miles, and of course with a telescope magnifying seventy times, one mile of lunar surface would just be visible. According to the rule for calculating the power of telescopes, it would require a magnifying power of 37,000 to distinguish *ten feet* of lunar surface, and a lens to produce this power could not be less than *sixty feet* in diameter, with a focal distance of three hundred feet. From this, we may judge to what an extent the powers of a twenty-four foot diameter telescope have been overrated."

came up, they received like attention. On one occasion a
a speaker spoke of the sciences as leading to skepticism,
when he replied, that if it had not been for physical science
we would probably have been executing witches to this day.

In 1835 Prof. Haldeman married Miss Mary A. Hough,
and removed to the residence which they still occupy, at
Chickies, where he was subsequently joined by his brothers,
Dr. Edwin Haldeman and Paris Haldeman, in the iron business. In this connection he published a paper, in 1848, on
the construction of blast furnaces; in 1855 he edited the.
second edition of Taylor's "Statistics of Coal," and for many
years he has been an officer of the State Agricultural Society. In 1841 his "Freshwater Univalve Mollusca" of the
United States was commenced, a work which had no superior
in the style and finish of its plates.[1] About the period of
1855–8 he was professor of agricultural chemistry and
geology in Delaware College, confining his course to several
months of each year, without residing permanently at the
college. His paper "On Species and their Distribution,"
(1851), opened a question which has been more recently developed into what is now called Darwinism, and Darwin
himself makes favorable mention of this article in his later
editions.

As language is a characteristic of mankind, his attention
was drawn to it as an aid to ethnology; he studied it as a
natural science, and the first result was his "Elements of
Latin Pronunciation," (1851), in which the attempt is made
to ascertain the ancient pronunciation.[2] Professor Haldeman subsequently lectured on the "Mechanism of Speech"

[1] The original shells figured have been presented to the Academy of
Natural Sciences, Philadelphia; and those of the continuation, published in Paris, were given to the celebrated Delessert-Lamarck collection in that city.

[2] That philosophical talent and tact so essential for investigations in
natural science, which he is well known eminently to possess, he has
here brought to bear on the elements of the Latin language with peculiar success. His conclusions, we fancy, are generally, if not always,
correct, as they are founded on philosophical principles, having been
drawn from various reliable materials, both ancient and modern, in a
manner almost as satisfactory and as safely to be trusted as the deductions of mathematics.—*Mercersburg Review*, March, 1852.

before the Smithsonian Institution, and in 1858 his "Tre-velyan Prize Essay" was successful in England, against six-teen competitors. This essay was published in 1860, by J. B. Lippincott & Co., Philadelphia, under the title of "Ana-lytic Orthography," and it contains specimens of about seventy languages and dialects, as heard from the lips of the natives themselves. In 1865 his 'Affixes to English Words' appeared, which claims to be the key to the analysis of 100,000 words;[1] and in the *Southern Review* (Baltimore, July, 1869), he has an article on American Dictionaries.[2]

Of late years the advance of learning has required an increase of professors in the large colleges, and among these the University of Pennsylvania stands in the front rank, its location in a large city like Philadelphia affording facilities for getting instructors in the various sciences. The last professorship added to the list in this institution, was that of Comparative Philology, in 1870, to which Prof. Haldeman was elected. Studying language as a natural science, and simultaneously with it, he often gives definite information upon points which his predecessors had attributed to 'acci-dent' or 'euphony;' and studying the vocal elements of many languages by ear, he ascertained, for example, that a certain sound of Arabic and Hebrew occurs in Wyandot, another in Esquimaux, while another is common to Cherokee and Welsh. It is obvious that to ascertain such facts, the same person must *hear* the sounds compared, and from native speakers. Comanche was thus heard in Washington, Ha-waian at Liverpool, and from Queen Emma in London, Gud-jerati from a Parsee in Paris, and the language of the Tonga Islands, and Coordish, at the missionary college of the Propaganda at Rome, at which many languages are spoken.

At school and in college the subject of this notice was an

[1] Mr Haldeman has compressed in an elegantly printed octavo volume, * * a collection more rational, complete, and exhaustive of the com-ponent parts of our language, than we have had any good right to hope for within the present century; * * a most practical, useful work, * * absolutely indispensable to systematic and thorough students of language.—*Contemporary Review*, London, July, 1867.

[2] It is a learned and exhaustive examination of the respective merits and demerits of Worcester's and Webster's dictionaries.—*Trubner's Literary Record*, London, September, 1869.

average student, acquiring knowledge slowly; and had he remained to graduate, he would probably not have taken any of the honors. His success is to be attributed to facility in determining the proper line of inquiry, caution in adopting results, and persistent industry in research; traveling to observe, but living the life of a hermit when working up his materials, and thus producing a series of from eighty to one hundred communications in the scientific journals, causing Dr. Hitchcock, the distinguished geologist, to express surprise that he should "find time to make and bring out so many new discoveries." As work produces fatigue, rest is required, and as rest may be secured in a change of study, the "Tours of a Chess Knight," (1864, illustrated with 114 figures) was the result of such a change.

Acknowledgments for his aid, or for suggestions, are given in various American works of science, such as Lynch's Dead Sea Expedition; and he has been honored with membership in a number of learned societies, American and foreign. One of his latest labors has been an essay on that curious dialect of German spoken among us, and called " Pennsylvania Dutch," which he was requested to prepare for the Philological Society of London, and which is now in their hands.

HAMBRIGHT, GEN. HENRY, was a member of the Legislature in the years 1813, 1814, 1816, and 1817.

HAMBRIGHT, GEORGE, elected sheriff of Lancaster county in 1815.

HAMBRIGHT, HENRY A., now Major of the 19th United States Infantry, brevet Colonel United States army, and brevet Brigadier General United States Volunteers during the late rebellion, was born at Lancaster, Pa., on the 24th day of March, 1819, and was the third son of Major Frederick Hambright and Elizabeth Shaeffer, his wife. The family of Hambrights were always fond of military life; in fact they were natural born soldiers; his father and uncle, Col. George Hambright, both of whom were highly popular men, not only served as captains of our old-time volunteer companies, but during the war of 1812–14 marched to the battle-field and defended their country. The father of Henry A. Hambright was Major-General of the militia of Lancaster county, and was a soldier in reality. Henry A. Hambright, after commanding a fine and spirited volunteer company, (as his father and uncle had done before him), in which he had served under his father as second sergeant, no sooner heard of the declaration of war between the United States and Mexico, in 1846, than he volunteered and entered into the service of his country. His company had been previously twice called upon by the then Governor of Pennsylvania, David R. Porter, and marched to Philadelphia to quell the riots there taking place, and it rendered efficient service. He early felt the necessity of learning the "school of the soldier," and the efficiency of discipline. Giving proper attention thereto, he became a good soldier, and marched as First Lieutenant of a company in the 2d regiment of Pennsylvania volunteers, commanded by Colonel William B. Roberts, to the Mexican war. He served throughout the whole war in the valley of Mexico, from Vera Cruz to the City of Mexico, and was consequently present in the battles of Cerro Gordo, La Hoya, Contreras, Cherubusco, Molino del Rey, Chepultepec, Belen Gate, and the taking of the City of Mexico. After his return with the regiment to the United States, which was mustered out of service at Pittsburg in 1848, he resumed his business as a contractor on public works, and afterwards was an efficient officer on the Pennsylvania Central Railroad, stationed at Lancaster.

It was in this capacity that he was serving when the rebellion became a "*fixed fact*," and having reorganized his old volunteer company, the "Jackson Riflemen," and tendered its services with his own to the Governor of Pennsylvania, was received and marched to Harrisburg. He was mustered into service in the 1st Pennsylvania volunteers, under Colonel Samuel Yohe, for three months, and participated in all the actions of the campaign under Gen. Robert Patterson. On the discharge of this three months' regiment, he immediately raised a new regiment and offered its services to the government to serve for three years, which offer was accepted, provided he had it ready for service in thirty days, and to report to the Adjutant General, U. S. A., at Wash-

ington city. This order was promptly complied with, after
a short extension of time. The regiment proceeded to Pittsburg, and was organized October 18th, 1861, with its full
complement of officers and men, and a fine regimental band.
It was afterwards known throughout the whole war, as the
gallant and efficient 79th Pennsylvania regiment, and Col.
Hambright continued in its command until it was finally
mustered out of service at the conclusion of the war. On
the 7th day of June, 1865, *"for meritorious services in the
field,"* he was commissioned by the President " brevet Brigadier General of volunteers." While serving in the three
months' service as Captain, he received the commission of
Captain in the 11th regiment United States Infantry, of the
regular army ; this appointment he accepted ; but his higher
temporary rank as Colonel of a brave regiment of volunteers
where he was doing his whole duty, at times being in command of a brigade, kept him in full employment, and he continued in command as Colonel of the 79th, and brevet Brigadier General in the army of the Ohio, and that of the Cumberland, and formed part of Sherman's grand corps in the celebrated march to the sea. Under all circumstances he brought
into service those active and energetic powers with which
he was naturally gifted, and participated in all the actions
and battles of the campaigns under Generals Buel, Rose-
crans, George H. Thomas, Sherman and other commanders,
which ended the war ; eliciting from them all high com-
mendations.

Colonel Hambright, since the close of the war, has served
in Texas and other parts of the south, and is at present
commanding officer at Fort Jackson, Louisiana, together
with Fort St. Philip, lying adjacent thereto on the other bank
of the Mississippi river, near its mouth. He is an honor to
the army and a credit to his native State. His actions and
meritorious conduct speak for themselves, and need no
eulogy.

HAMBRIGHT, MAJOR FREDERICK, son of John and
Susanna Hambright, was born at Lancaster, Penna., November 22d, 1786. Early in life he displayed a taste for military affairs, and in 1810 became a member of the Lancaster

Phalanx. As fourth corporal of this company he marched to Elkton, Md., in 1813, under Captain James Humes. In 1814, when Baltimore was threatened with destruction and pillage by the British, the Phalanx again mustered for the defence, and on this occasion the subject of this notice accompanied it in the capacity of ensign. The company was now under the command of his brother, George Hambright. After going into camp for three months the Pennsylvania troops were discharged, and returned to their respective homes. In the year 1815 Mr. Hambright was elected captain of the Phalanx, a position he held up to 1838, when the company disbanded. During the afore-mentioned period he had several times been elected major of a battalion, composed of different volunteer companies of Lancaster county, in which position he was highly esteemed and gave very general satisfaction.

In the year 1839, at the request of the "Jackson Rifle-men," a very spirited company, composed chiefly of young men, he became their captain, and many new names having been added to the roll, he commenced a series of instructions that made it one of the best military companies in that branch of the service anywhere to be found. In 1840 he marched his company to Camp Wayne, Pa., and at the request of a regiment there assembled, composed of volun-teers from various sections of the State, among which was his own company, he assumed the command. In July, 1841, Captain Hambright was called upon by a committee from York, Pennsylvania, to take command of all the volunteers to assemble at Camp Lafayette, in the following month; he accepted and marched to York with his riflemen, on the 23d of August, and organized the brigade. This is said to have been one of the handsomest displays of volunteers ever witnessed in Pennsylvania, and gave Capt. Hambright great credit for the discipline of the entire command. He won golden opinions from all assembled, as he, on this occasion, displayed a knowledge of military affairs inferior to none, and ranked himself as a commanding officer of rare military attainments. He continued in command of the Riflemen until 1846, when they disbanded their organization.

20

On the 4th of July, 1842, he was elected Major General of the 4th division of the Pennsylvania Militia by the officers thereof. In the year 1824 Major Hambright marched two companies—the "Lancaster Phalanx" and the " City Guards" by invitation, to participate in the reception of the nation's guest, General La Fayette, on his arrival in this country. This, at that time, was one of the most brilliant receptions witnessed in the United States. Major Hambright also marched a command to Philadelphia on two several occasions when riots were taking place in that city, in obedience to the call of David R. Porter, Governor of the commonwealth. On those occasions Major Hambright was the recipient of much applause for the high state of discipline which his command exhibited, and for the very efficient services which he so cheerfully rendered. As a civilian, Major Hambright held a prominent and influential position amongst his fellow-citizens. In the fall of 1821 he was elected High Sheriff of Lancaster county, an office previously filled by his brother, Col. George Hambright. As an evidence of the esteem in which he was held by the people, upon the termination of his office of Sheriff he was elected a member of the State Senate of Pennsylvania, the duties of which he discharged honestly and faithfully. About twenty years ago he removed to Allegheny, where he resided up to the time of his death, which took place March 17th, 1872, at the residence of his daughter, Mrs. Charlotte Kennedy, in the 86th year of his age.

As a testimony of the regard in which Major Hambright was held by those under his command, the following certificates are appended, one signed by the officers of the "Lancaster Phalanx" which he so long commanded, and the other signed by the Lancaster city Battalion.

"I, Peter Reed, jr., First Lieutenant of the Lancaster Phalanx, a volunteer corps belonging to the city battalion of volunteers in the 1st Brigade, 4th Division, Pennsylvania militia, do certify that Major Frederick Hambright became a member of said corps at the organization, on the 18th day of July, 1810 ; and in the year 1813, when the said corps marched to Elkton, in the late war, he was appointed a corporal ; in the year 1814, when said company marched to the defence of Baltimore, he was elected ensign in the corps ; in 1815 he was elected captain, which command he still holds ; and in the various duties of private, officer and commander, for twenty-five years, his conduct has been that of a gentleman, a soldier and a patriot, alike anxious for the honor of his corps and the welfare and prosperity of the strong arm of our country's defence, the volunteer system.

Given under our hand this 4th day of May, A. D. 1835.

(Signed)   PETER REED, Jr.,
1st Lieut. Lancaster Phalanx.

We, the undersigned officers of the Lancaster city battalion of volunteers, in the 1st Brigade, 4th Division, P. M., do hereby certify that Major Frederick Hambright was elected and commissioned Major commanding said battalion on the 12th day of May, A. D. 1826, which command he yet holds, and has conducted himself as an active disciplinarian, vigilant officer, and honorable gentleman, beloved and respected by his soldiers, and enjoying their highest confidence as a gallant commander, ever ready to defend the rights of freedom and the welfare and glory of his country.

Given under our hands this 4th day of May, A. D. 1835.

(Signed)   CHARLES NAUMAN, Adjutant.
JOHN LEONARD, Surgeon.
JACOB KAUFMAN, Quartermaster.

HENRY PINKERTON, Captain City Guards.
GEORGE HAUGHMAN, Captain Jackson Riflemen.
PETER REED, JR., 1st Lieut. Lancaster Phalanx.
CHAS. NAUMAN, 1st Lieut. City Guards.
MICHAEL TRISSLER, 1st Lieut. Jackson Riflemen.
PHILIP PYLE, 2d Lieut. Lancaster Phalanx.
JACOB FOLTZ, 2d Lieut. City Guards.
GEORGE EAGLES, 2d Lieut. Jackson Riflemen.

HAMILTON, JAMES, a member of the Legislature in 1734, 1735, 1736, 1737 and 1738.

HAMILTON, JOHN, elected State Senator in 1825.

HAMILTON, WILLIAM, was born in the city of Philadelphia, and learned the business of printing in the office of Benj. F. Bache. In the winter of 1794–5 he came to Lancaster, and entered into partnership with Henry Wilcox to publish the *Lancaster Journal*, a newspaper which the latter had started. The partnership was not of long duration. Hamilton purchased the interest of his partner, and published the *Journal* from June, 1796. He continued its publication until 1820, when he sold out his interest to Huss & Brenner. During the year 1796 Hamilton favored the election of Thomas Jefferson for the next President, and so strongly that he alienated certain Federal leaders from him, and they withdrew their support from the paper. Among those who did so, were Robert Coleman and Charles Smith, esq. His paper had ostensibly set out in its publication as a neutral in politics, but by 1799 it donned the full Federal uniform, and continued to wear this garb as long as Hamilton controlled it. He was elected a member of the Legislature in 1810 and 1811, and a State Senator in 1812. Hamilton was captain of a rifle company, raised in 1814, in Lancaster, and he marched with his company to Baltimore on the 3d of September, 1814. He was elected Treasurer of Lancaster county, in the year 1816, and twice reëlected, in 1817 and 1818. He became a defaulter to a large amount of money, upwards of $20,000, and his securities became responsible therefore. His securities were Geo. Musser, Wm. Cooper, and John Bomberger. The securities paid the interest on the defalcation debt for some years, and finally the County Commissioners exonerated them from the debt. Hamilton, after his failure, became so distressed in mind that he was believed by many to have become insane, and he was removed to the almshouse, where he died April 10th, 1820, in the 49th year of his age.

HAMILTON, WILLIAM, elected a member of the Legislature in 1855 and 1856. In 1860 he was elected to the State Senate.

HAMAKER, DANIEL, elected a member of the Legislature in 1829 and 1830.

HAND, GENERAL EDWARD, was born December 31st, 1744, at Clydaff, Kings county, province of Leinster, Ireland. He received in 1807 the appointment of surgeon's mate, or surgeon to the 18th Royal Irish regiment of foot, and sailed with the regiment from Cork, May 20th, 1767. He arrived at Philadelphia, July 11th. He was ensign of the same regiment, his commission bearing date in 1772. He went with the 18th regiment to Fort Pitt, and returned to Philadelphia in 1774, resigning his commission and receiving a regular discharge from the British service. In the same year he came with recommendations to Lancaster, in order to practice his profession. The following year he married. In 1775 he entered the Continental service, his first commission bearing date in June of that year.   In 1777 he was chosen Colonel of the 1st regiment of Pennsylvania riflemen, one famous for its exploits during the Revolution.   He was raised to the grade of Brigadier General and subsequently to that of Adjutant General.   He was the Adjutant General at the battle of Yorktown, and marched with his troops back to Philadelphia, where they were dismissed.   Upon the close of the war he resumed the practice of medicine in Lancaster. In 1798 he was appointed Major General in the Provisional army.   In 1785 he was elected a member of the Pennsylvania House of Representatives.   In 1789 he was a delegate from Lancaster county to the Convention that amended the first State Constitution.   He was a member of the Continental Congress in 1784 and 1785.   In politics he was a Federalist.   He died September 3rd, 1802, in the 58th year of his age.   As a citizen he was highly esteemed, and as a physician greatly sought after and beloved, especially by the poor, to whom he was in the habit of rendering his services gratuitously.

HARBAUGH, Rev. Henry, an American clergyman and author, was born in Franklin county, Pa., October 28th, 1817.   His great grandfather emigrated from Switzerland about the year 1736.   His father was a farmer, and the subject of this notice spent his youth working on the farm until the 19th year of his age.   Being very fond of reading, he was in the habit of saving all the spare money he could, and therewith buying himself books.   In 1836 he started west, with the design of learning the carpentering trade.   He followed this occupation for some time, still using his spare moments in reading.   For three years he taught school in winter and went to an academy in summer; and in the year 1840 he entered Marshall College, at Mercersburg, and at the same time read divinity in the Theological Seminary at the same place.   He was licensed and ordained in 1843, and became pastor of the German Reformed congregation in Lewisburg, Pa., still continuing his literary studies with unabated interest.   In 1848 he published "Heaven, or an Earnest and Scriptural Inquiry into the Abode of the Sainted Dead."   This work was well received, and has passed through numerous editions. In January, 1850, he commenced the publication of the *Guardian*, a monthly magazine, still continued. In 1850 he received a call from the First German Reformed church of Lancaster, which he accepted and entered upon his duties April 1st, 1850. Being a strong advocate of total abstinence, and having in his congregation a few liquor dealers and many more who did not disapprove of the moderate use of intoxicating drinks, considerable opposition soon manifested itself against him. He, however, overpowered the opposition, the Consistory sustaining him. The congregation, through his instrumentality and influence, began in 1852 the erection of a new church, which was completed in 1854. A committee of the Eastern Synod having recommended for the use of the Reformed church a provisional liturgy, Mr. Harbaugh gradually and cautiously introduced it during the morning service, without exacting the responses from the congregation; but even this partial leaning to what was termed "high churchism," created decided dissatisfaction. An attempt made shortly after to define the limits of membership, and admonish irregular members, created further trouble. Several of the members slackened their attendance, or ceased attending church altogether. The secret of opposition was their dislike to the liturgy, and this continued to increase until it culminated one Sunday morning in the Consistory locking him out of the church. For this offence they were arraigned before Classis, deposed from office, and suspended from the benefits of communion. This led to another secession of twenty or thirty members, most of whom connected themselves with St. Paul's church. He still continued to serve the balance of the congregation until September, 1860, when he resigned. He accepted a call from St. John's church, Lebanon, where he served for three years, and was then elected Professor of Theology in the Seminary at Mercersburg, Pa., which position he held at the time of his death, December 28th, 1867. In 1851 he published "The Heavenly Recognition, or an Earnest and Scriptural Discussion of the Question, ' Will we know our Friends in Heaven.'" In 1853 he published "The Heavenly Home, or the Enjoyments of the Saints in Heaven." In 1854 he published " The Birds of the Bible." In 1857 appeared his life of Michael Schlatter, and in 1857–58 the "Fathers of the German Reformed Church in Europe and America," in 3 volumes. Shortly after this he issued "The True Glory of Woman, as portrayed in the Beautiful Life of the Virgin Mary." He is also the author of " Union with the Church," and the " Plea for the Lord's Portion of a Christian's Wealth, in Life by Gift, in Death by Will." Dr. Harbaugh deservedly ranks as a man of high order of intellect. As a clergyman, he spoke with considerable force, being solid, weighty and emphatic in his delivery. As an author, his works give evidence of great industry, rather than profundity. His writings are chiefly of the popular order. He no doubt possessed the ability to become a theologian of eminence, but perhaps it may be suggested that his attention was too much dissipated in the collection of his material for and in the writing of his histories to allow him to bestow such attention upon theological questions as would have rendered him profound. As a poet, he showed some ability in the Pennsylvania German, his native vernacular.

HARTMAN, DAVID, was elected Sheriff of Lancaster county in 1845.

HARTMAN, JOSEPH, elected Commissioner in 1837.

HAVERSTICK, GEORGE, elected Commissioner in 1828.

HAWTHORNE, GEO. C., elected Register in 1860.

HAWTHORNE, SAMUEL, a member of the Legislature in 1829 and 1830.

HAYES, ALEXANDER L., was born in Kent county, in the State of Delaware. He was educated in the Southern Boarding School, in Smyrna, afterwards studied in the Newark Academy, and graduated at Dickinson College, Carlisle, in 1812. He began the study of law in the office of Hon. Henry. M. Ridgely, of Dover, where he continued to read for three years, the period prescribed for law students in that State, and was then admitted to the Delaware bar. He commenced the practice of the profession in Dover, but afterwards removed to Philadelphia, and was admitted as a practitioner before the District Court, Court of Common

Pleas, and the Supreme Court, in 1820. After practicing his profession for about a year in Philadelphia, he moved to the city of Reading, Pa., where he practiced the profession for about six years. While a resident of Reading he married a daughter of Galbraith Patterson, esq., of Mifflin county, Pa. In June, 1827, he was appointed by Governor Shultz, Associate Judge of the District Court of the counties of York and Lancaster, Judge Bradford being President of the court. He discharged the duties of the office of associate judge for about seven years, when the district of which this court was composed was divided, and a separate district court was formed out of the county of Lancaster. Upon the recommendation of the members of the Lancaster bar, he was, in 1833, appointed by Governor Wolf, president of this court.[1] Judge Hayes held this position by subsequent re-appointments, until 1849, when he resigned the presidency of this court and resumed the practice of the profession. It was not long after this that he became warmly interested in the enterprise, then first beginning to be discussed, of establishing a cotton mill in the city of Lancaster. He was among the first who subscribed money for the new project, and was selected by the stockholders to draft the first articles of the association. He was afterwards selected by the stockholders as one of a committee of five, (Christopher Hager and David Longenecker being part of the number), who should visit the New England States, and make themselves acquainted with cotton manufacture in that section of the Union, and report upon the feasibility of the contemplated enterprise; and if, in the judgment of the committee, the establishment of such a branch of manufacture would seem warranted, then to secure the services of an architect, who should cause the erection of a first-class cotton mill in the city of Lancaster. This committee visited, in 1845, Boston, Newburyport, Lowell, Saco, in Maine, and the principal cotton manufacturing towns of New England. Upon returning, the committee reported in favor of the projected enterprise, which report was unanimously adopted by the

---

[1] The District Court of Lancaster was presided over by one judge alone, and he was entitled the president judge of the district court.

stockholders, and they proceeded immediately to erect cotton mill No. 1, in the city of Lancaster. The report submitted by the committee that had visited the Eastern States, was framed by the subject of our notice, and evinces the great care and observation brought into requisition in the preparation of this document.

Judge Hayes was solicited to become one of the five managers who should superintend the affairs of the new corporation, but declined for want of sufficient time to do justice to the duties of the position. In 1846 or 1847, in consequence of the declination of John N. Lane, one of the five managers, he was again solicited to accept the vacant position, to which at length, with reluctance, he gave his assent, and was thereupon elected to this vacancy, and continued to hold the same until 1854. During this time he was elected general agent of the company, and upon the resignation of Mr. Hager, as president of the board of managers, was chosen President of the said board. In the meantime the company had erected two other cotton mills near the site of the first one, and were employing eight hundred hands in the mills, and running between seven and eight hundred spindles. In 1854 the Legislature having created an associate law judge of the court of common pleas of Lancaster county, Judge Hayes was elected to fill the said position so established, and thereupon resigned his position in the cotton mill company. The duties of this position he continued to discharge up to 1864, a period of ten years, when he was again reëlected to a second term of the said office, which position he yet continues to fill.

HEINITZSCH, CARL HEINRICH, is the earliest settler of the Heinitsh family in Lancaster. He emigrated from Leipsic, in Saxony, in the winter of 1781, and located in Lancaster and established the first drug store west of the Schuylkill. The business thus established by him has been carried on by his son, and is still continued by his grandson, Charles A. Heinitsh. He died in 1803, and lies buried in the burying ground of the Trinity Lutheran church.

HEITLER, RICHARD R., appointed Register in 1839.

HENDERSON, JAS., a member of the Legislature in 1839.

HENDERSON, Mathew, was born about 1770, in Salisbury township, where his parents resided. He was of Scotch-Irish descent. His grandfather, Thomas Henderson, emigrated from Ireland about the year 1727. The subject of this notice having received a classical education, studied medicine and practiced his profession for many years with fine success. In 1820 he was elected a member of the Pennsylvania House of Representatives, and in 1821 reëlected. In 1822 he was elected a member of the State Senate. After the expiration of his legislative career he retired from the practice of his profession and lived upon his farm. He died about the year 1830.

HENDRICKSON, George R., son of Okey Hendrickson, was born June 2d, 1826. After receiving an education he taught school for a number of years. In the autumn of 1851 he was nominated and elected Clerk of quarter sessions and oyer and terminer, and discharged the duties of that office in person for three years. He was the last clerk in the old court house, in Centre Square, and the first in the new one, and officiated at the court when held at Fulton Hall. He was, during the rebellion, elected quartermaster sergeant to Company F, of the 15th regiment Pennsylvania three months' volunteers. He was, in 1868, elected a justice of peace.

HENDRICKSON, Okey, a descendant of a Dutch-Swede family, emigrated from New York to Lancaster county about the year 1815. He was a man of unusual enterprise and public spirit for his time. He was instrumental in the establishment of a post-office in Mount Joy, and was appointed the first postmaster, which position he held for many years under different administrations, until 1837, when on account of the active support he gave the Anti-Masonic party, he was succeeded by a Democrat. He was re-appointed to the same position in 1841, under President Harrison, with whom he enjoyed a personal acquaintance, and whom he had entertained in his house, but died before entering on the duties of the office. Out of respect for his memory, the appointment was promptly conferred upon James, his oldest son. The project of a railroad, connecting

Lancaster with the State Capital, originated in the town of Mount Joy; and Okey Hendrickson, who was one of the incorporators, was influential, in concert with Jacob Rohrer, esq., Dr. Simon Meredith, Abraham Harnley, Henry Musselman, and Samuel Smith Patterson, in procuring a charter for the road, and the capital for its construction.

*HENRY, JOHN JOSEPH, was born November 4th, 1758, at Lancaster, Pennsylvania. He was apprenticed by his father, Wm. Henry, at the age of 14, to an uncle, who was a gunsmith, then a resident of Lancaster, but who after some time removed to Detroit, taking his nephew, John Joseph, with him. At that place his stay was but short, on account of the scarcity of business. He returned on foot with a single guide, who died in the wilderness which lay between Detroit and his home. It was here that hardships and misfortune first were felt, and which were his future companions during a length of years. Young Henry returned to his parents and home, dissatisfied with the employment a judicious father had pointed out for him to gain a future subsistence. His arduous mind panted after military glory; the troubles of his country, which was then making vigorous and ultimately successful struggles for a total emancipation from slavery, wrought strongly upon one, the acme of whose hopes and wishes was to be one of those who contended most for freedom. In the fall of 1775 he clandestinely joined a regiment, raised in Lancaster county, for the pnrpose of joining Arnold, who at that time was stationed at Boston. After enduring all the fatigues of a veteran soldier they entered Canada on his birthday, he being then but 17 years of age. He endured hardships here which he has enumerated in his history of the campaign against Quebec. It was in prison, where he lay for nine months, that he contracted a disease, (the scurvy), which at that time did not make its appearance; but six weeks afterwards, on his return home, at a time when least expected, it made its appearance under its most malignant form; it was at a time when it became a duty for him to continue in the army. ·A captaincy had been procured for him in the Virginia line,

*History of the Campaign against Quebec.

and a lieutenancy in that of Pennsylvania. He had designed to accept of a command under the hero, Gen. Morgan, that of captain, but the disposer of all events arrested his career, and instead of his fond expectations being accomplished, all his hopes were blasted, his high prospects thwarted, and his life became a dreary blank, by the order of that Omnipotence which furnished him with the fortitude which enabled him through all his misery to kiss the rod that chastised him. It was after two years' continuance on the couch of sickness, that his leg, which was the unfortunate cause of his illness, began to heal, and renovated health gave brighter hopes for him.

His lameness precluded all possibility of his again entering the army. He had, however, by a disregard of parental authority, at least so far as concerned his trade, forfeited his claim to his father's exertions to place him in such a situation, such as would make him capable of rendering himself useful to society. A vigorous effort on his part was necessary; resolution was not wanting; it was made. He bound himself an apprentice to John Hubley, esq., Prothonotary of the county of Lancaster, as a clerk in the office for four years; he pursued his business with the closest application, and discharged the duties of that office with unabated care and strictness, and when the labors of the day was over his nights were consumed in study, endeavoring to make up in some measure for the neglect that his education had suffered by his becoming a soldier. His frame, still somewhat debilitated by his illness, was not capable of sustaining the fatigues of office, his health suffered much from labor so severe and application so intense. The time of his indenture having expired, he commenced the study of law under Stephen Chambers, esq. Here he became acquainted with his future companion in life, the youngest sister of Mr. Chambers. He was admitted to the bar in 1785, and began the practice of his profession, which he continued to pursue until 1793, when he was appointed by Governor Mifflin President of the second judicial district of Pennsylvania.

A number of years had now elapsed, and his family was large. By an unfortunate removal to a district, at a sickly period, he was attacked by the gout, which from inexperience, and owing to his having no knowledge as to the consequences that would necessarily ensue, he did not take proper precaution so as to thwart the disease. Under that deceptious name, numerous disorders invaded his frame, and at times with so much severity that he was necessitated to continue at home, and he was thus prevented from executing his official duties as a judge. It was during some long years of bodily suffering that his mind and memory reverted to those scenes (more forcibly than ever) which formed so eventful a field in a life of misfortune and vicissitude. The interesting narrative of the sufferings of that band of heroes, of which he was the youngest, is a simple tale of truth, which he undeviatingly throughout his book adheres to.

He is supported in all his assertions by the testimony of a number of his companions in that arduous campaign, men of character and respectability—his relation of incidents, his descriptive accounts of the country they passed through, the situation of Quebec and the disposition of the army, all mark him to have been a youth of accurate observation, of a comprehensive and intelligent mind. Possessing, as he must necessarily have done, activity of spirit and contempt of fatigue, he gained the approbation and esteem of his seniors. The buoyant spirits of youth rose high over misfortune; under the pressure of that severest distress, vivacity was still retained and burst forth at intervals to cheer his hopeless companions.

Disease had now made rapid progress on a constitution weakened by repeated attacks and accumulation of disorders which no skill could counteract or remedy. The non-performance of his duties caused petitions from the several counties to be presented to the Legislature for his removal; nothing was alleged against him but absence. That honorable House having examined and considered the charges, acquitted him with honor. His commission he retained for the space of two years afterwards; but illness and debility increasing, and a knowledge of his infirmities being incurable, compelled him to resign that office which he had held with integrity for seventeen years. Four months succeeding, his worn-out frame was destined to feel the stroke of death, and his freed soul to seek refuge in the bosom of his father and his God. He died at Lancaster, April 15th, 1811. The history of the campaign against Quebec was written by Judge Henry, who often compared it in many respects to the celebrated retreat of the ten thousand Greeks, and said of it that it would require the talents of a Xenophon to do it real justice.

HENRY, WILLIAM, was an ingenious and successful mechanic of Lancaster, and for many years conducted a large gun manufactory and iron-mongery, at the southeast corner of Centre Square. He was inventor of the screw auger, which, previous to 1777, could be had only at his store. His discovery of the principle of the auger is thus said to have been suggested to his mind : He was at a time sitting on his porch and twisting thoughtlessly, with his fingers, a piece of lead, and this he bored into a turnip, and he observed that the twisted lead threw out chips, and this suggested to him the idea of the screw auger. He sent a sample of his invention to England and obtained a patent therefor. He acted as a justice of the peace for many years before the breaking out of the revolution. In 1772 he was appointed one of a committee, with John Lukens, Surveyor General, David Rittenhouse, and others, to survey the route of the Susquehanna and Lehigh rivers, in order to ascertain the best location for a canal, to be constructed through the interior of the State of Pennsylvania.

Mr. Henry was one of the most active men of the borough of Lancaster who espoused the cause of the colonies in their opposition to Great Britain. He was immediately engaged by the general committee of safety of the province of Pennsylvania, to manufacture and repair arms for the continental army, and the privilege was accorded him by the executive council to choose such workmen as he might deem proper to be engaged in his employ, and that these men, so selected, should be exempted from draft in the army. He was, on July 4th, 1777, appointed by the executive council of Pennsylvania, a justice of the peace under the new constitution. This position he held continuously up to his death, and he was president of the county court from 1781 up till 1786. He was also chosen a member of the Pennsylvania council of safety, by act of assembly of 13th October, 1777. For some time during the revolution he was treasurer of the county of Lancaster.

Wm. Henry was one of the first who recognized in the youthful Benjamin West a genius of a high order, and his first master-piece, the " Death of Socrates," was painted at the former's suggestion. Young West, about 1749 being in Lancaster, and some of his paintings having met the eyes of Mr. Henry, the latter suggested to him that instead of wasting his time upon portraits, he should turn his attention to historical painting. He, at the same time, mentioned the death scene of the great Grecian philosopher as affording one of the best topics for illustrating the moral effect of the art of painting. Upon the painter's confessing that he knew nothing of the philosopher, Mr. Henry went to his library, and taking down a volume of the English translation of Plutarch, read to him the account given by the writer of this affecting story. The young painter said he would be happy to undertake the task, but having hitherto painted only faces and men clothed, he should be unable to do justice to the figure of the slave who presented the poison, and which he thought ought to be nude. Mr. Henry had among his workmen a very handsome young man, and without waiting to answer the objection, he sent for him. On the young man entering the room, he pointed him out to West, and said, " there is your model." The instruction at once convinced the artist that he had only to look into nature for his models. The Death of Socrates was finished, and the fame of the artist was from that time established.

During the Revolution the house of Mr. Henry was somewhat a place of resort for men of culture and intellectual standing. The host being a man of acknowledged ability and well-known reputation, naturally attracted others of like grade around him. Whilst the British held possession of Philadelphia from September 1777 till June of the following year, David Rittenhouse, the philosopher, (then being State Treasurer), Thomas Paine, author of the Rights of

Man, and John Hart, a member of the Executive Council, were inmates of the house of Mr. Henry. The biographer of Rittenhouse, the philosopher, speaking of this period of life, says: "While he continued in the borough of Lancaster, he made his home in the house of Wm. Henry, esq., at that time treasurer of the rich and populous county of the same name; a situation which at that time was very commodious for the business of his office, from its connection with that of the County Treasurer, and one which was also the more agreeable by reason of Mr. Henry being a person of very considerable mechanical ingenuity." It was during the time that Thomas Paine was stopping at the house of Mr. Henry, that he wrote No. 5 of his celebrated political treatise, the Crisis. Mr. Henry was for many years one of the most active and influential assistant burgesses of the borough of Lancaster. He was commissary of the regiment of troops raised in Lancaster county in 1775, and which was destined to reinforce Arnold at Boston. All through the Revolution he was very active on the side of the colonies, and his correspondence in 1779, as chairman of the committee on the supply and regulation of the flour market, shows him to have been a good writer and a shrewd practical business man. He was a member of the Continental Congress from 1784 till 1786. Mr. Henry was a man of the strictest honesty and known probity. He was possessed of a strong and independent mind, and yet his conscience was one of the most tender. He had a full and abiding faith in revelation, and his trust in the Redeemer seemed to him all-assuring in his later years. He was a strict and consistent member of the Moravian church. Ever of a benevolent and unsuspecting mind, Mr. Henry acted through life upon the principle, "that we should consider every one as possessing probity until we discover him to be otherwise." He died December 15th, 1786.

HERR, BENJAMIN, a member of the Legislature in 1843 and 1844.

HERR, BENJ. G., a member of the Legislature in 1837, 1838 and 1839.

HERR, CHRISTIAN, a County Commissioner in 1812.

HERR, DANIEL, a member of the Legislature in 1852 and 1853.

HERR, DR. ELIAS B., was born the 1st of May, 1833, in Manor township. His descent may be traced down from one of five brothers who came from Europe prior to 1710. He was educated in the schools of John Beck, Litiz, and also in the York County Academy. At the age of eighteen he commenced the study of medicine with Dr. F. A. Muhlenberg, of Lancaster, and graduated at the New York University in March, 1854; he immediately followed his profession, and at the same time took a great interest in the cause of education, especially in his native district. Politically, he has always been an active Republican, and was elected to the Legislature of Pennsylvania in 1869.

*HERR FAMILY. John Herr came to this country in 1710, from Switzerland, bringing with him his four sons, and others of his friends; he had five sons married, Abraham, Christian, Emanuel, John and Isaac. Christian had come to this country before the rest of the family.

ABRAHAM HERR was the oldest, and came with his father in 1710. He was married in Europe, and had a large family, some of his children being grown and married. He settled near Wabank, on the west side of the Conestoga creek. He was the only one of the family that settled in Manor township, and having several children grown when he came there, the family became very numerous.

CHRISTIAN HERR was a minister of the Mennonite church, and was the first of the family in this country. He came with Martin Kendig, John Mylin, and others, in the year 1709. They were pleased with the country, and concluded to send for the rest of their friends. They therefore cast lots who should go, and the lot fell on Christian, their minister; they not wishing him to go, Martin Kendig offered to go, and in 1710 brought over the rest of the Herr family, and others. Christian built a house of sandstone in 1719, half a mile east of Willow Street, where it stands yet, with his name and the date upon it, now in possession of David

*Contributed by Christian Herr (farmer), West Lampeter.

Huber. Christian had three sons, John, Christian and Abraham.

John lived on the farm now owned by John Musselman, about one mile from Willow Street, on the road leading from Willow Street to Strasburg, and part of the original tract owned by his father, Christian. He had five sons, named Abraham, John, Benjamin, Christian and David.

Christian lived on the farm now owned and occupied by David Huber, a half mile west of where his brother John lived; and also part of the original tract owned by his father, Christian. He had two daughters—both married Kendigs; one afterwards married Michael Withers. Her daughter, by the first husband, married George Withers, the brother of Michael. George was the father of Michael and George, living in Lancaster.

Abraham lived on the farm and in the mansion house built by his father, he falling heir to the home division of the original tract. He had four daughters—two married Barr brothers; one married a Huber, grandparent of David Huber, now owning said property; the other married a Shaub. The family name expires with Abraham.

REV. CHRISTIAN'S SON JOHN'S FAMILY. Abraham carried on milling on Pequea creek, on the road from Lampeter Square to Strasburg, where Daniel K. Herr now resides. He had five sons, and one daughter, married to John Huber. Their names were Abraham, John, Tobias, David and Emanuel.

John carried on milling on Pequea creek, near Soudersburg, now in possession of Benj. Herr, a grandson of said John. He had two children, one son and a daughter. The former, named John, also a miller. The daughter married Samuel Herr, grandson of Emanuel.

Benjamin lived where John Holl lives now in Strasburg. He died without issue.

Christian (Big) lived on the farm now owned and occupied by the author of this sketch, C. Herr, (farmer). He had two sons and five daughters. The sons, named Benjamin and Christian. The daughters married Jacob Breneman, Christian Snavely, Martin Mylin (blacksmith, and grandson of old

John or Hans Mylin), Martin Light and Martin Herr, (grandson of Emanuel, one of the sons of the original John or Hans Herr).

David lived on the farm occupied by his father, John. He was the youngest of the family. He had two children, both daughters, named Betsy and Martha. The former married Adam Herr, (a grandson of Emanuel and a brother of Martin, who married Big Christian Herr's daughter). The other married Christian Brackbill. Here David's family name ends. This also ends the record of John's family. I shall now take their children, beginning with Abraham's (miller) children.

ABRAHAM'S (MILLER) CHILDREN. Abraham lived on the farm occupied by his son a few years ago, adjoining his father's mill property, situated on the west side of Pequea creek. He had three children, all sons. Henry, (who died single), John and Abraham.

John lived on the homestead occupied by his father and carried on milling; he had one son, Samuel.

Tobias lived near Strasburg, on property now owned by John Book. He had four sons and three daughters. Benjamin, John, David and Tobias. Nancy married John Shenk; Betsy married a Hoffman, and she dying, he married Hettie, the youngest.

David lived near his father, on part of the homestead, in what is now called Turniptown. He had one son, Benjamin, who was killed in his grandfather's mill, then in possession of to his cousin, Samuel (John's son). He went to the cog-pit start the hoisting apparatus, and while doing so accidentally fell and was crushed to death; stopping the mill, the gearing had to be taken apart to get him out. This occurred in 1830. He had also two daughters; one married Adam Beck.

Emanuel settled somewhere in the vicinity of Martic Forge, and reared a family there. One of his sons was named Levi.

JOHN'S (MILLER) FAMILY. John lived on the place occupied by his father. He carried on milling, and was a justice of the peace. He had three sons and four daughters; namely, Benjamin, (miller), John and Henry; Maria, who died single; one married to Henry Witmer, one to Amos Witmer, and one to George Lefever.

CHRISTIAN'S (BIG) FAMILY. Benjamin lived on the farm formerly occupied by his father, Christian, (big). He sold his farm and went west, leaving some of his children married here. He had six sons and three daughters, viz: Anna married John Bachman, Lizzie married John Herr, her second cousin, son of Tobias Herr, and grandson of Abraham Herr, (miller), but Lizzie dying, he married her sister Maria. The sons were Martin, Rudolph, David, Benjamin, Christian and George.

Christian lived on the road leading from Willow Street to Martic Forge, about one mile south of Willow Street. He here carried on the distilling business. Afterwards he went west with his family. One of his daughters married her first cousin, George, a son of Benjamin.

John, also a grandson of Abraham, was married and lived as a renter, here and there. Two of his sons live in the eastern part of the county.

Abraham, also a grandson of Abraham, lived by the side of his uncle John's mill. He lived there and raised a family of three sons and four daughters. One daughter married Aaron Witmer. Abraham has two children; Christian has one, and Elam two children.

Henry, Abraham's son, was a grandson of old Abraham, the miller, and died single.

JOHN'S FAMILY. Samuel carried on milling where his forefathers before him carried on the trade. He was married, but died without issue.

TOBIAS' CHILDREN. Benjamin studied law and practiced in Lancaster.

John lives on the road from Willow Street to Conestoga Centre, in Pequea township.

David lives in Lancaster.

Tobias lives above Lancaster.

JOHN'S (SQUIRE) CHILDREN. Benjamin lives on the homestead of his forefathers, and also is a miller. He is married.

John lives on the road from Strasburg to Paradise, at Fairview.

Henry lives in Lancaster.

EMANUEL HERR, one of the five sons that came to Lancaster in 1710, pitched his tent on the bank of the Pequea creek, on the road from Strasburg to Lancaster, where John Musselman now resides. It was he that built the first mill there, ran the burrs by water and the bolt by hand. He was married and had three sons: Rev. John, Martin and Emanuel, and one daughter, who married a man named Carpenter; they were the parents of Christian Carpenter, and grandparents of Israel and William Carpenter, of Lancaster city. Hon. John W. Forney's (editor of the *Press*) mother, was a sister of Christian Carpenter.

Rev. John built his house and farmed the property now owned by Henry Keener, about one mile southwest from Strasburg. He was twice married and had two sons by his first wife: John and Francis; and by his second wife three sons: Henry, Martin and Adam; and four daughters; two of these daughters married Witmers, one married Tobias Herr, and the other married David Strohm, father of Hon. John Strohm.

Emanuel lived on the place owned now by Mrs. John Brackbill, near that of John Musselman's. He built the house there, was married and had one son, Samuel, and three daughters; one married Henry Miller and another John Kendig.

JOHN'S (MINISTER) CHILDREN. John carried on milling at the mill formerly occupied by his father and built by his grandfather, now owned by John Musselman. John rented this mill to Mr. Gray; Gray put in a conveyor to carry the ground wheat to the bolt; when Gray's time had expired John took out the conveyor and said that this made lazy millers, and made them carry it by hand again. He married and had one son, John.

FRANCIS'S FAMILY. Francis built the house torn down a few years ago by Gabriel Wenger, and farmed that property, owned by him now. He married Fanny Barr, a daughter of Mr. Barr; who married a daughter of John's one of the five brothers. He had three sons: John, Francis and Martin; and five daughters: Anna married Henry Mylin (a great grandson of the original Hans Mylin who came in with the five Herr brothers); Esther married Martin Eshleman, Francis married Benjamin Eshleman, Martha married Abraham Groff (saw miller), and Lizzie died single.

Henry lived on the farm owned by Jacob Rohrer, in Strasburg township, north of Bunker Hill.

Martin lived on the farm now owned by his son Abraham, alongside of his father and grandfather's mill, across the creek. He was married three times; his first wife was a daughter of (Big) Christian; the third wife was Susan Buckwalter. With the last wife he had ten children: Four boys, Abraham, Adam, John and Henry; six daughters, Esther was married to Mr. Metzler, Lizzie married Mr. Kreider, Mary married Jacob Huber (a grandson of the original Christian, one of the five brothers), Susan married Rev. John Kinports, Anna to Abner Rohrer, and Martha married Christian Miller.

Adam lives on the home-place, where his father lived, which property his father obtained with his last wife. He was married to Elizabeth Herr, (a daughter of David Herr, and great grand-daughter of the original Christian, one of the five brothers). He had five sons, viz: Daniel, Adam, Christian, David and John. He had three daughters, viz: Martha married David Herr, (whose mother was a sister of Martha's father, and from his father's side he was great-great grandson of the original Christian, one of the five brothers.) Elizabeth married Levi Lefever.

EMANUEL'S FAMILY. Samuel lived close by the mill formerly owned by John Herr, (Squire). The farm lay east or southeast of the mill. He was married to John Herr's (squire) sister, (great grand-daughter of the original Christian, one of the five brothers). He had three sons, viz: John, Benjamin, and Emanuel; and two daughters; Anna married Frank Kendig, and Sarah married Abraham Keagy.

REV. JOHN'S GRAND-CHILDREN. John lived at the mill formerly owned by his father, his grandfather, and his great-grandfather, Emanuel, one of the five brothers. He married Christiana Mylin, (who was a great grand-daughter of Hans Mylin, who came with the five Herr brothers). He had two sons, Francis and Martin; and one daughter, Lizzie, who married a man named Zercher.

John lived on the farm now owned by his son, John F. Herr, one-half mile north of Strasburg. He married

Elizabeth Groff, (who was a grand-daughter of Mr. Forrer, who married the daughter of John, one of the five brothers). He had two sons, Benjamin G. and John F., and six daughters; Mary was married to Christian Herr, Elizabeth to Rev. Daniel Musser, Anna to Henry Frantz, Martha to Dr. Jacob Musser, Naomi to Dr. Benjamin Musser, and Fanny, died single.

Francis' father divided the homestead, and gave the eastern half to him; he lived on it; it is now owned by his son Francis. He married Fanny Neff, whose father, Jacob Neff, married a grand-daughter of John Herr, one of the five brothers. He had three sons, Amos, Cyrus and Francis, and five daughters. Elizabeth married Adam Herr, who was a great grandson of Emanuel; Anna married Martin Weaver, Charlotte married Henry Herr, (who was son of Martin and great grandson of Emanuel); Fanny and Amanda are single.

Martin lived on the home-place with his father, Francis. He married Polly Herr, (daughter of John Herr, granddaughter of Abraham Herr, great grand-daughter of Rev. John, and great-great-grand-daughter of John, one of the five brothers). He had two daughters; Mary married John Kendig, and Martha married Gabriel Wenger.

MARTIN'S FAMILY. Abraham lives in Lampeter Square, and married Susan Hess.

Adam died single.

John lives also in Lampeter Square. He married Fanny Kreider, and has two sons and three daughters.

Henry now lives in Lampeter. He, previous to this, carried on milling, where his son, Rev. Daniel K. Herr, carries on now. He was married three times. He had one son, D. K. Herr, (Rev.) and two daughters; Susan, married to Daniel Musser; and Lizzie.

ADAM'S (BROTHER OF MARTIN) FAMILY. Daniel Herr lives on the Philadelphia pike below Greenland. He was married to Sarah Strohm. He has three sons and three daughters.

Adam lives on a part of the farm now farmed by his son Alpheus, and formerly owned by Abraham Groff (saw miller). He married Elizabeth Herr (daughter of Francis and great-grand-daughter of Emanuel.) He has one son and one daughter.

Christian lived on the farm now owned by David Kendig, in West Lampeter township. He married Maria Light, whose father was married to (Big) Christian Herr's daughter. He had two sons and two daughters.

David kept store in Lampeter Square; afterwards went to Ohio. He was married to Mary Landis. He had six children, two sons and four daughters

John lives on a property close to the Green Tree Hotel, on the Beaver Valley turnpike. He was married to Anna Herr, daughter of the Rev. Christian Herr, of Pequea, and has but one son, Benjamin.

SAMUEL'S FAMILY. John lived below Strasburg, and died there in 1871.

Benjamin died single.

Emanuel lived on the place now owned by John B. Herr. He went to Maryland 25 years ago.

JOHN'S (MILLER) FAMILY. Francis received the mill from his father, but traded it with Michael Musselman for a piece of land in Paradise township. He was married to Lydia Barr, and had two daughters; one married Henry Stehman, and the other Nathaniel Mayrs.

Martin lives on the farm alongside of John Musselman's mill. He was married to Eliza Snavely, and has one son and one daughter, both single.

REV. JOHN'S FAMILY. Benjamin G. lives on the farm alongside of that on which his father lived, and he devotes his time principally to literature; has written some eight or ten books of poems. He was a member of the Pennsylvania Legislature for three years, 1836, 1837 and 1838. He was married to Mary Emma Witmer, and has five sons and three daughters.

John F. lives on the homestead occupied by his father, Rev. John, and farms his father's farm. He was a member of the Pennsylvania Legislature for one term. He was married to Martha Musser, and has three sons and two daughters.

FRANCIS'S CHILDREN. Amos lives at Longenecker's meeting-house, and on the farm formerly occupied by John Longenecker. He was married and has four sons and five daughters.

Cyrus lives on the farm formerly occupied by David Miller, and adjoining the land south of the homestead of his father. He was married to Mary A. Brackbill, and has four sons and one daughter.

Franklin lives on the home-place occupied by his father before him. He was married to Sarah Frantz and has eight children; three sons and five daughters.

REV. D. K. HERR (MILLER) grandson of Martin and son of Henry, lives on the mill property owned by his father, Henry. He was married to Susan Musser, and has one son.

JOHN HERR, one of the original five sons that were the first settlers of the Herr family in Lancaster county, built a homestead on a tract of land of 530 acres, which he bought of William Penn for £30 6s., with a rent of a silver English shilling yearly for every hundred acres; his title was dated July 3, 1711. He built his house of sandstone; said house being on the same site of Jacob Herr's present house, who resides therein; said house being some five miles south of Lancaster, on the road from New Providence to Lancaster, in West Lampeter township. John had six children; two sons and four daughters, named John, Christian; Anna married a Forrer; one was married to a Burkholder; one to a Barr, and one to Ulrich Brackbill. All the Brackbills in the county come from this family—Ulrich being the only son; he (Ulrich) had one sister named Barbara, who married a Groff; they being the father and mother of my grandmother on my father's side. This Brackbill family came to America in 1717.

John was born in Europe, came in with his father, was a small boy at the time of his father's coming in. He married and lived in the house built by his father, which was torn down by the Rev. Benj. Herr, a new house being on the same position, and occupied by Christian B. Herr, (Benjamin's son), said house being about three-fourths of a mile south of where his father lived, on the same road. He had three children, two sons and one daughter, named Abraham, Christian, (Pequea); the daughter married a Bachenstose.

Christian lived on the homestead where his father lived before him; he was married twice; first to Anna Kendig, then to Fanny Groff. He had one son and five daughters, Christian, Fanny, Anna, Mary, Elizabeth and Barbara; the three older daughters by the first wife, and the two other by the last, Christian being the youngest child. Fanny married G. Bressler; Anna, Benjamin Herr, grandson of Christian, one of the five brothers; Mary married Abraham Witmer, who built the bridge across the Conestoga, near Lancaster, on the Philadelphia turnpike road. The two of the second wife were married; first, Elizabeth, to Jacob Neff; and Barbara, to John Neff, two brothers.

Abraham lived on the homestead, and married a Barbara Weaver, and had five sons, named Jacob, John, Abraham, Martin and Joseph.

Christian lived on the place and in the same house now occupied by the Rev. Amos Herr. He married Miss Bowman; had one son, Christian, and six daughters; one married to George Diffenbaugh; one to John Funk; one to Christian Rohrer; one to Henry Bowman; one died single. As Christian lived close to Pequea creek, he received the name Pequea, which has ever since adhered to his family.

CHRISTIAN'S CHILDREN. Christian built a house across the road from where his father lived; this house was torn down a few years ago, and a new one erected by his daughter, Elizabeth. He had four sons and three daughters; Christian, John, Benjamin and Jacob, Fanny, Susan and Elizabeth. He was married twice; first, to Elizabeth Withers; second, to Mary Rohrer; two daughters, Fanny and Susan, by the first wife, and the rest by the latter. Fanny married Samuel Herr, son of John (miller), grandson of Abraham, (miller), great-grandson of John, and great-great-grandson of Christian, one of the five brothers; Susan married Benjamin Breneman, and Elizabeth remained single.

ABRAHAM'S FAMILY. Jacob bought a tract of Martin Kendig, adjoining the home-place of his father. He here built his house upon it, now occupied by John Tout, and owned by Jacob Herr. He had one child, Jacob.

John lived on the home-place, formerly occupied by his father, Abraham. He was married twice; first to a Miss Shultz, and then to the widow Stauffer, formerly Miss Brackbill, a grand-daughter of Ulrich Brackbill. He had six children; one son, John, and five daughters; Susan, Polly, Barbara—these were of the first wife; then Elizabeth and Fanny, of the second wife. Susan married John Barr (he a grandson of the Barr who married John's daughter, one of the five brothers); he died; she then married Hon. John Strohm; Polly married Martin Herr (son of Francis, grandson of Rev. John, and great-grandson of Emanuel, one of the five brothers); Barbara, married to David Strohm, (cousin to Hon. John Strohm); Elizabeth, to Henry Hess; Fanny, to Benjamin Snavely, whose mother was a daughter of (big) Christian, who was a son of John, himself a son of the Rev. Christian, one of the five brothers.

Abraham lived south of New Providence, and was married to a Shaub, who was a daughter of Abraham Herr's, (son of the Rev. Christian, one of the five brothers) daughter, who married Henry Shaub. He had three sons, Abraham, John and Martin; and one daughter, Polly, who married Jacob Groff.

Martin lived near New Providence, afterwards owned by Mowrer. He had three children, two sons, Benjamin and Martin; and one daughter, Barbara, who married Simon Groff.

Joseph settled on a farm now owned by Mr. Myers, situated near the termination of the turnpike leading from the Lamb Tavern, on the Willow Street pike, to Marticville. He married Maria Forrer, (who was a grand-daughter of the Forrer who married the daughter of John Herr, one of the five brothers). He had eight children, five sons, viz: Abraham, Christian, Joseph, Martin and David; he had three daughters; Nancy, who married a Stoner; Barbara, who married Isaac Houser; Maria, who married John Harnish. This ends the children of Abraham.

Christian lived in the house and farmed the place which

his father, Christian, (Pequea), occupied before him. I
married Nancy Forrer, a sister of Maria Forrer, who ma
ried his cousin Joseph. He had eight children, six so1
and two daughters; Benjamin (Rev.), Elias, Christian, Josep
Amos (Rev.), and Daniel; Maria married John Brackbill,
descendant of Ulrich Brackbill; Anna, who married Jol
Herr, who was a great-grandson of Emanuel, one of the fi'
brothers.

Christian, son of Christian, grandson of Christian, a1
great-great-grandson of John, one of the five brothe1
lives on the farm formerly occupied by (big) Chri
tian, one mile southeast of Willow Street. He marri
Mary Herr, daughter of the Rev. John Herr, (she bei1
great-great-grand-daughter of Emanuel, one of the fi'
brothers). He had two sons, Amaziah and Ezra, and thr
daughters, Lizzie (dead), Louisa and Addie; the daughte
all single.

John lived on the farm formerly owned by Joseph Le
mon, and adjoining, on the north that of his father's hom
stead, the whole being a part of the original tract of 5£
acres. He was thrown from his horse crossing the creek
Herr's mill, formerly owned by Samuel, married to his sist
Fanny. He was married to Susan Rohrer, daughter
Christian Rohrer. He had five children, two boys, Ald1
and Henry; Fanny, who married John Brackbill, jr.; Sar£
Ann and Lizzie, both single.

Benjamin lives on the place formerly owned by Mart:
Kendig, who came in with the five brothers. The old hou;
which Martin built, was used by Benjamin until he built
new one by the side of it. The old house was then used :
a private school house for several families. Benjamin w:
married twice. First to Catharine Bair, by whom he h£
two children, Christian S. B., and Mary Ann, who marri
Christian Witmer, (minister). By his second wife, An1
Sener, he had three sons, Sanner, Millo, and Aldus.

Jacob lives on the old homestead where his father, gran
father and great-grandfather lived. He married Anna Mu
ser, and has seven children; five sons, viz: Benjami
Hebron, Jacob, Francis and Amos; two daughters, o1

married David Hess, the other is single. Here ends the record
of Christian's children ; we now recur to that of Abraham's
(who married Barbara Weaver), descendants.

Jacob lived on the farm of his father. He married Martha
Forrer, and had four children, three daughters and one son;
Jacob F., who married Barbara Witmer, and has seven children, five sons and two daughters; Mary and Anna died
single; Barbara married Tobias Kreider, (minister).

John lived on the old home-place with his father, John,
but went to Ohio some 37 years ago, and settled near Columbus. He had four sons, Levi, (a noted horse trainer and
dealer, living at Lexington, Kentucky), Christian, Francis
and John, all in Ohio.

Abraham is dead, and his family is scattered.

John, his son, married a Miss Bartholomew, and had two
daughters, Susan and Lizzie; the former is single, and the
latter is married to Henry Miller.

MARTIN'S FAMILY. Benjamin was a fuller by trade, and
carried on the fulling business at Martin Huber's, below the
Valley tavern.

Martin was married to Jacob Martin's daughter.

JOSEPH'S FAMILY. Abraham lives with his brother Christian at Groff & Landis's mill on the Willow Street pike. He
married Miss Stoner. He had four children, two sons named
Abraham and Isaac, (and this Abraham is married and has
five children, two sons and three girls).

Christian lives on the farm spoken of in my last record of
Abraham. He was married to a Hess, and has six children:
four sons.

Joseph, a carpenter by trade, lives in Willow Street, on
the road from Lancaster to Marticville. He married Miss
Snavely, and has three children.

Martin Herr married a Miss Miller, and left four daughters.

REV. CHRISTIAN'S (PEQUEA) FAMILY. Benjamin lives on
the property where the original John, one of the five brother's sons, John (the minister) lived. He married Nancy Bren-
neman, and has two children. He is a bishop of the Mennonite church.

Elias lives on a farm now belonging to his son Elias, and
22

lying over east from where his father lived.   He has been married three times.   He has five children; four sons: Jeremiah, Andrew, Elias, and Benjamin; and Mary Ann, married to Elias Groff.

Christian (Pequea) lives adjoining farm to his brothers Elias and Benjamin.   He married Susan Breckbill, sister to John Breckbill, who married his sister Maria.   He has four children; three sons, John, Levi and Christian (Pequea), and one daughter.

Joseph lives on the property formerly owned by his aunt Barbara Forrer.   He was married to Hetty Stauffer, and has two daughters.

Rev. Amos lives on the old homestead owned by his father and grandfather.   He was married to Elizabeth Rohrer, and has one son, Christian, and three daughters; one married to Benj. Snavely, one to Mr. Ronk; the other is single.

Daniel lives about half a mile down the pike from where his brother Amos lives.   He carries on the lime-burning business extensively.   He was married to Anna Breneman, and has two sons, Enos and Reuben; and Lizzie, a daughter, who was married to Christian S. B. Herr.

HERR, JOHN, was a member of the Legislature in 1838.

HERR, JOHN F., was a member of the Legislature in 1854.

HERR, JOHN, the founder or organizer of the New Mennonite church, was born in Lancaster county, Pennsylvania, September 18th, 1781.   His father, Francis, was the son of Emanuel Herr, one of the five sons of Hans Herr, who emigrated to Lancaster county in the year 1710.   Hans Herr was the pastor and spiritual leader of a large colony of emigrants who made their way into the bounds of Lancaster county, and settled in what was known as the Pequea valley, and which is now included in the townships of Strasburg, Lampeter, Conestoga and others.   The subject of our sketch belonged to a family noted in the early history of our county as leaders in religious opinions, many of whom were clergymen of the Mennonite persuasion.   It would seem somewhat appropriate in this connection, to glance at the causes which induced the important movement in the Mennonite church, which ultimated in its division into the old and new communions. It is an event of august concern in our county's history; one which deserves some consideration, and would space warrant, (which it does not) it should be treated in full detail. The inceptive impulse which led to the separation of the church was given by Francis Herr, the father of our subject. For sufficient reasons, Francis Herr became disunited with the old Mennonite church[1] of his fathers, and so remained till the period of his death. Being a man of considerable intellectual vigor, he was able to attract a number of followers who sympathized with him in his views, and who were in the habit of meeting together for spiritual conversation and edification of each other. In these meetings of Francis Herr and his followers nothing seems to have been further in view than to endeavor to act in accordance with Christ's promise, that he would be in the midst of two or three of those who should meet together in his name. These small assemblies were congregated in the name of the Redeemer, and His promise was fervently invoked upon their meetings. The design of founding an antagonistic church to that to which his ancestry had belonged, never perhaps entered the thoughts of Francis Herr or any of his followers. He was an earnest investigator of the doctrines of Menno Simon, and he critically compared them with the teaching of the gospel and the whole of the New Testament. This

[1]The Mennonite Christians exhibit a simplicity of faith and worship that serves to call to mind the early days of the reformation epoch. Deducing their views from the literal sense of Scripture, they have not been seduced into the reception of new-coined and rationalistic theologies that have since the beginning of the eighteenth century been steadily making their way into the other churches of England, Holland, France and Germany. They may, (especially in America), therefore, be regarded as presenting the faith-type which most clearly portrays that which obtained in Europe in the sixteenth century. They have successfully resisted the insinuating currents of free thought that have been creeping into many of the other churches of Europe and America during the last one hundred and fifty years, and on this account they stand nearer than most others in accord with the views of the Reformed fathers. Perched upon the mount of Gospel faith, the rippling brook of deistic unbelief, the encyclopedic stream of French infidelity, and the surging flood of German rationalism have passed by scarcely noticed by the inerudite followers of Menno Simon; and the opinions of this early

investigation served but to convince him that the teaching of that reformer was fully supported in the discourses of Christ and his apostles, and his chief aim seemed simply to be to aid in building up life-examples as the gospel enjoined. Doctrine, without a corresponding walk and conversation would, in his view, be of no avail. In all his exhortations to his small flock of followers, he urged upon them in the most emphatic manner, holiness of life and uprightness and godliness in all manner of conversation. What should it benefit him to be a full believer in the tenets of Menno Simon if his action did not conform thereto, and his walk be upright and pure. In a holy life, therefore, as he thought, did all Christian godliness consist.

In all this he had before him the example of the reformers of the sixteenth century. With them he agreed in endeavoring to bring back the purity of the early ages. Nothing further was his aim than the rejuvenation of Christian simplicity and piety in the life and actions of his small band of faithful followers. All this, in his estimation, was attainable outside of nominal church organization; and the communion of the spirit of Christ and his fellowship was all that was desirable. This could be secured in the bosom of his small company of sympathizers, who were in the habit of meeting together for mutual consolation.

But at length the winged arrow of death bore Francis

reformer yet shine in the vales of the fatherland and on the American continent in all their pristine purity.

The important movement in the Mennonite church, the establishment of a theological seminary in Europe in 1735, was an event that occurred after their early settlements had been made in America. This has given to the European church an educated ministry, and an array of distinguished Mennonite clergymen stand conspicuous in modern ecclesiastical history. Their brethren in America prefer, on the contrary, pastors of apostolic simplicity, and as yet maintain with a tenacious grasp the uncorrupted creed of their fathers.

The American Mennonites see in Christianity a perfect system as it flowed forth from the mouth of the Redeemer of mankind, instead of being a progressive science as is contended by learned modern expositors. Little else in their view is required of the ministers of Christ, save that they shall be able to read the Scriptures of the Old and New Testament. The critical acumen of a Reimarus, Wolff, Ernesti, or Semler, is not desired by these plain followers of the ancient doctrines.

Herr from the scenes of his life's activity and from the companionship of his faithful circle of followers, and his freed spirit took its flight to regions beyond the skies. His mantle, however, fell upon worthy shoulders—upon him whose task it should become as the master workman to polish the unhewn material that his father had been gathering, and therefrom erect a living temple fitted to resist the adverse blasts of persecution, and which is being constantly increased, enlarged and beautified. The architect of the Christian edifice referred to is the subject of our notice.

Of the youthful career of John Herr, whose sketch we pen, little data exist. Having never preserved any diary of his labors, all that can be gathered of his career comes through tradition. It is, however, inferable from the career in which his father was engaged, that our subject was trained in the fear and admonition of the Lord, and that the lessons of truth and morality were taught him by his pious mother. It is said of him that in youth he was of a gay and lively disposition, fond of society, and that he engaged in the sports of his comrades to a great extent. His conscience was, however, cast in a tender mould, and his horror of sin was so acute that he frequently lamented with tears during the night, the follies of which by day he had been guilty. In these secret hours of the night, when all around him was hushed in sleep, he would deplore his imperfections and promise to the Saviour an amendment of his course of life. But these, like the ordinary evanescent promises of youth, were forgotten. The dawn of day and the appearance of his youthful comrades, again dispelled the good resolves, and carnal desires and natural enjoyments soon seated themselves in his affections.

His educational attainments were of limited scope. Besides the acquisition of the simple elementary branches of reading, writing and arithmetic, he as a youth was not favored. Being possessed of a very retentive memory, he exhibited a great taste for reading, and was remarkably fond of investigation. He seldom accepted anything without prior careful study, and the reason of everything must be apparent. What little spare time he was able to snatch from the labors of the farm, he sedulously devoted to the reading of such works as came within his reach. His father's library, however, being composed of but few books, save of the religious and devotional kind, it is reasonable to suppose that he should become well versed in the Bible and works of a religious character. In his youth, therefore, he perused works on Church History and the Reformation, the lives of the Martyrs, writings of Josephus and those of Menno Simon, besides others; and his inquisitive mind led him thoroughly to investigate the doctrines of the Mennonite church, which he found, like his father before him, to accord with the Gospel. It is doubtful at this time whether he had access to any works on profane history, biography, travels or polite literature. The only works of fiction, indeed, that he ever read, were the writings of John Bunyan; and he uniformly condemned the practice of devoting valuable time to the reading of modern novels. Poetry he appreciated very highly, especially if of a devotional character; and in his mature years he composed hymns on frequent occasions. As regards science, art and rhetoric, he had no opportunities whatever in his youth to acquire a knowledge of them; and yet in his old age he had attained a fund of general information upon all these subjects. His extensive intercourse for many years with various classes of society, some of them the best scholars in the country, his great powers of observation, his faculty for minute analysis, his extraordinary memory and his extensive reading, caused him to become in his latter years, if not profound, at least well informed upon all ordinary topics.

As above stated, John Herr's youth was chiefly spent in the reading of the Bible and other religious works, and in hearing the important question of the soul's salvation and the scheme of redemption discussed by his father, and by those he met in argument. His naturally bright mind availed itself of the opportunity thus afforded, and he soon became well trained in this particular field which so admirably qualified him for the great work for which he was destined. When the period arrived for him to begin the work, his preparation had been of such a character, that he entered thereon, not simply as in the performance of a duty, but with the greatest of pleasure and zeal did he inaugurate the great work of his life.

Upon the death of his father, being painfully exercised by the conviction of sin, he took occasion to reveal the state of his feelings to some of his father's friends, who were also similarly concerned for their own salvation. But owing to the increase of worldly cares devolved upon him by the death of his father, he permitted himself again to grow languid in his love for Christ, and for a time seemed to regret that he had revealed his spiritual emotions to his friends. This state of feeling having continued for some months, an incident occurred in his career that served to lead him back to God. He now resigned himself wholly to the Lord, and soon found comfort. The friends who had sympathised with his father, were still in the habit of meeting together and mutually comforting each other in spiritual converse. John Herr now became a constant attendant at these meetings. At one of these, held during the year 1810, Mr. Herr was requested to give his experience upon the all important question of the soul's salvation. This was an important epoch in the life of Mr. Herr. Clothed, as he felt, in the garb of truth, and mailed in the armor of righteousness, with the sword of the spirit in his hand, he stepped forward ready to battle and die, if need be, in the cause of the Redeemer. Animated by sympathy for lost humanity, and gratitude to God for His merciful plan of salvation, he addressed the small auditory in words of peace and comfort. Then it was that the firm resolve was made, that come what might, while life would last, his time and talents should be devoted to the cause of Christ; that he would mete out to his fellow-men the consolations of redemption, warn them of their folly and the wickedness of sin, and point out the way of truth as God should vouchsafe to instruct him. In spite of his comparative youth, being but as yet in his twenty-ninth year; in spite of adverse surrounding circumstances, he nevertheless dared the scorn of the ungodly, met the jeers of his associates, and openly braved the opposition of the whole unchristian world. His remarks, altogether

impromptu, breathed severe denunciations of sin and all un-
righteousness. And at the same time in burning strains of
eloquence he presented to his hearers a vivid delineation of
the great richness of divine grace and the wonderful sublimity and awful grandeur of the God-conceived plan of
salvation for the souls of miserable and fallen men.

The sermon of Mr. Herr, delivered on that occasion, was, as
tradition tells us, an extraordinary effort, in the opinion of
his illiterate and simple-minded hearers. In their opinion, it
surpassed anything they had ever heard. For profundity of
sentiment and eloquent invective, poignancy of grief at the
wickedness of the age; for clear, logical elucidation of man's
requirements; for sublime invocations for mercy and aid, it
could not, as his auditors conceived, be surpassed. The effort
must have been indeed extraordinary. No sooner was the
news spread abroad that Mr. Herr had preached such a
powerful sermon, than applications poured in upon him to
preach in various parts of the county. His services came in
great demand on funeral occasions. He was at once chosen
the leader of the new flock. The tree which his father
Francis had planted and nursed so carefully for many years,
now began to bear its fruit under the auspices of John Herr.
The soil was well watered by the penitent tears of himself
and co-laborers.

The fact that Mr. Herr was a decided radical on religious
subjects; that he would not compromise his views and thereby
sacrifice his sense of right, soon brought him into controversy with clergymen of different denominations. Many
were the foul charges and false slanders that were heaped
upon his head. His motives were impugned and his views
misconstrued. Ridicule and derision were hurled at him in
great abundance, but they fell harmlessly at his feet. The
envenomed shafts of calumny that poured in upon him from
every side, never ruffled the serenity of his disposition, or
excited in him anything save emotions of pain and sorrow;
and in return he simply offered up prayers for the souls of
his calumniators. He veritably fulfilled the scripture injunction, in praying for those "*who despitefully use you and
persecute you.*" Nothing, however, debarred his onward

progress; the more he was maligned and persecuted, the more strenuous were his exertions; and in spite of the most untoward circumstances, his influence steadily extended. New accessions were constantly being made to the ranks of his sympathizers. In the month of April, 1811, the ordinance of baptism was first administered in the new body. On this occasion Mr. Herr was baptized by Abraham Groff, who, in turn, in company with Abraham Landis, was baptized by Mr. Herr. The organization known as the "Reformed Mennonite," or "New Mennonite" church, was instituted by this trio. They commenced by holding regular meetings at stated periods; instituted the regular church ordinances, such as baptism and the breaking of bread; established a regular system of rules of church government in accordance with the injunctions of the apostles. Mr. Herr was at once recognized as their pastor, and was subsequently elected bishop. Their proceedings occasioned great excitement in the community, and, as a consequence, their meetings were attended by numbers prompted by mere curiosity. Mr. Herr's labors were soon heavy and exacting; he not only preached regularly and attended frequently at funerals, but was continually sought by individuals at home and abroad to offer the consolations of religion at the bedside of the sick and the dying. His time was so largely occupied in duties of this kind, that he was unable to devote much time to his private affairs. In this he greatly sacrificed, as regards pecuniary matters, for he was unwilling to receive any compensation in lieu of his time and services, feeling that the ministrations of the gospel should not be made a means of worldly accumulation; and he from the first, made up his mind to look for his reward in the blessings promised to the faithful who labor in the vineyard of the Lord. Nor did his temporal affairs fail him. Indeed, to such an extent did they flourish, that he had always sufficient to live upon and rear his family in comfort and independence.

In the autumn of the same year, Mr. Herr baptized fifteen penitent souls, among whom was included his wife, who stood by him faithfully in all his trials and tribulations, and his venerable mother. He proceeded in his undertaking in the even tenor of his way, exhorting, preaching and discussing at times with those that disagreed with him in opinion, and all the while was steadily gaining new converts to his opinions. His object was not, however, to build up a large congregation, merely for the purpose of being their leader. If such had been his design, he might have secured many more followers than he did. He admitted none as members of his congregation without the most thorough examination, and unless ample proof existed of sincere repentance. Candidates, therefore, who desired admission as members of his church, must undergo a searching ordeal and a trying examination in order to test their fitness for such communion. All this he knew was necessary to keep the church pure and uncorrupted. It must be preserved free from all corruption and impurity so far as was possible. He was determined that, so far as lay in his power, no hypocrite, with assumed Christian habiliments, should obtrude himself and interfere with the successful working of the new organization; and when, unhappily, a few such were admitted, and a few fell from grace, he obeyed the apostolic injunction, and of them made stern examples, and treated them as " publicans and heathen." By this constant care and vigilance which he exercised, was he enabled to prevent schism from entering the organization, and likewise rendered it out of the power of pride, worldly allurements and vanity to prevail against it.

The services of Mr. Herr all this time were coming more and more in demand, and many invitations came to him from abroad to preach for them. He visited and preached in the neighboring counties of York, Cumberland, Franklin, Lebanon, Bucks, Montgomery, and others, in most of which he organized congregations and ordained pastors over them, who constantly kept him advised of their proceedings. As a consequence, his correspondence became very large; so much so, indeed, that nearly all his time unoccupied in preaching was required to reply to his correspondents. Nor were his labors by any means confined to the localities above named; he made repeated visits to New York and Canada, when traveling was not a matter of the ease and convenience of the present day. His mode of conveyance was either on horseback or in those heavy two-horse wagons made use of by emigrants before the spring carriage was invented. On his route he preached at various points, and planted the nuclei of various congregations, that bore in after years abundant fruit. He also made several trips to Ohio and Indiana, when those States were but little reclaimed from their primitive condition of a wilderness, and when the crossing of the Alleghenies was regarded as quite an adventure. He established congregations in both the above named States, as he did also in later years in the State of Illinois. As he became advanced in years, and the fruits of his labors were ripening in distant and more extended regions, his correspondence grew still more voluminous, so much so that it became necessary for him to call in aid to assist him in his labors. His prayers for aid in his arduous work were not in vain. A band of laborers grew up around him who were able to challenge the world for piety, disinterested benevolence and purity of life. Though not of the refined and educated, nevertheless, like the humble fishermen of Galilee, they were mailed in the holy armor of gospel truth, and with devoted hearts and heroic spirits they were amply qualified to fight the battles of the Lord. These came to Mr. Herr's aid, and largely relieved him of the details of superintendence. But never, until the day of his death, did anything important or unusual transpire in church affairs, either at home or abroad, without his knowledge and never did an important question arise in the whole church of his organization, wherever scattered, that was not referred to him for solution.

Notwithstanding Mr. Herr's great correspondence and other labors connected with the ministrations of church affairs, he still found time to write several volumes and pamphlets upon religious topics. They were all written in German, with the exception of that entitled, his "Remarkable Vision," which he wrote in English. The others were all translated into English, and passed through several editions. In this brief sketch we are unable to analyze his writings, and speak of them all severally as they deserve. Of his "Vision," this, however, may be said: that it is a remarkable work in every sense, and one that indicates a genius of a high order; and the little work will not suffer when placed in comparison alongside of the " Pilgrim's Progress."

Mr. Herr maintained an epistolary controversy with a pastor of the Moravian church of Litiz, which finally resulted in a pamphlet, entitled "a brief and apostolical answer,' which was published in the year 1819. It is clear, at this late day, that Mr. Herr had the best of the argument; and his clerical antagonist seemed to think so himself, as he never saw proper to reply. This was not the only instance that Mr. Herr had such correspondence with clergymen, but it is the only one that was published.

Had John Herr received the culture of a classical education and made politics his study, he could have become a leader in spite of all opposition. He was an admirable judge of mankind, and could intuitively almost, as it were, select those who should execute what he desired to be accomplished. It is not known, indeed, that he was ever deceived in a single instance in any of his appointees, whether for the transaction of church or business matters. And it is somewhat remarkable that, as in accordance with his religious opinions, a resort to legal tribunals was not warranted; yet in business affairs he became the dupe of sharpers and knaves to a much less extent than is usually the case with business men.

He was a natural born orator. His oratory was both emphatic and persuasive. He was grandly eloquent when he wished to enforce a truth or depict the evils of sin. A leading feature of his character was his earnestness and sincerity. His reasoning powers were of a high order, and in argumentative discourse he had few if any equals. He had a fine voice, and when appealing to sinners to turn from their evil ways, (and on such occasions made use of his persuasive powers,) the effect was electrical. He was a sound logician, and fortified his arguments by appropriate quotations. He never spoke from notes, and his impromptu efforts on the spur of the occasion were frequently his most successful ones.

He was a radical in religion, and would have been in politics had he given it any attention; but his mind was so equally poised, that he never would have become agrarian. His mind was so well balanced, that under no circumstances did he despond or become unduly excited. He possessed extraordinary good judgment, was frequently an arbiter between neighbors, when a dispute arose between them, and his decisions were always satisfactory. His disposition was mild and childlike in simplicity ; the pauper and degraded had as free access to his attention as the most respected. His kindness of heart was so proverbial, that he never could gainsay a legitimate request; but when anything was demanded contrary to his principles, no inducement could swerve him from his course. Except in his religious views, it is doubtful if John Herr ever had an enemy; his business transactions were of such a nature that no one ever took umbrage thereat; on the contrary, all his acquaintances were so attracted by the excellency of his conduct, the unselfishness of his motives, and by the unostentatious benevolence that characterized all his labors, both temporal and spiritual, that they became his devoted friends.

Mr. Herr's sole and only aim in this life, seems to have been to prepare himself, and point out the way to others, for a life in the future. And as every person with whom he came in contact soon became convinced of his sincerity, they respected him on account of his motives, even though they differed with him in opinion. In the family relation he was a perfect model as a son, husband and father. He filled all these relations creditable to human nature. That he had his failings in temper and desire, no one was more conscious than himself; and of this he gave frequent evidence in the pulpit and his writings. But take Rev. John Herr all in all, and it may be said of him by one who knew him for many years, that " his like will not soon be found again."

John Herr was married in 1808, to Elizabeth Groff, a descendant of Hans Groff, the head of one of the surviving families who accompanied Hans Herr from Switzerland. They had ten children, two of whom died in infancy. In accordance with his sense of duty, Mr. Herr took his last trip to Canada in 1850. He preached a sermon in the evening, traveled to a neighbor's house to spend the night, and died on the 3d of May, 1850, far from his wife, his kindred and connections, and at peace with all the world. He calmly and willingly resigned his soul into the hands of his Creator, in the firm and abiding hope that he should receive the crown of glory prepared for the faithful in the mansions of eternal rest.

HERSHEY, CHRISTIAN, elected Commissioner in 1836.

HERSHEY FAMILY. Andrew Hershey was born in Switzerland in the year 1702, and moved with his father to the Palatinate. In the year 1719 he and his brother Benjamin sailed for America and settled in Lancaster county. His brother Christian also came to America, settling in Lancaster in 1739. The three brothers were each of them chosen ministers in the Mennonite church. Andrew died in the year 1792, aged ninety years. He left twelve children, viz.: Christian, Andrew, John, Benjamin, Jacob, Abraham, Isaac, Henry, Catharine, Maria and Odti.

Andrew Hershey, second son of Andrew, one of the first settlers, was born in Lancaster county in the year 1734, and died July 16th, 1806. By his first wife, named Bachman, he had one daughter, Catharine, born in the year 1760. His second wife, Maria, whose maiden name was Acker, was born September 26th, 1743, and died September 13th, 1831. By his second wife he had the following children : Anna, Jacob, Maria, Andrew, Henry, Elizabeth and John. Anna was born February 27th, 1762 ; Jacob was born October 2nd, 1765, and died May 30th, 1821 ; Maria was born May 23d, 1768 ; Andrew was born September 14th, 1779, and died August 1st, 1835 ; Henry was born December 19th, 1772 ; Elizabeth was born December 5th, 1775 ; John was born March 31st, 1783, and died July 16th, 1831.

Andrew Hershey, one of the family last named, married Esther Kauffman, who was born May 31st, 1770, and died March 3rd, 1829. By her he had the following children, viz.: Christian, born December 28th, 1796, and died September 5th, 1834 ; Anna, born July 15th, 1799 ; Andrew, born January 15th, 1802 ; Maria, born December 9th, 1804 ; Catharine, born January 15th, 1809 ; Esther, born September 11th, 1811 ; Barbara and Elizabeth, born December 9th,

1814; John, born March 14th, 1818; and Magdalena, born March 20th, 1821.

HESS, CHRISTIAN, elected Commissioner in 1851.

HESS, MARTIN D., Recorder in 1857.

HERTZ, REV. DANIEL, was born in Susquehanna township, Dauphin county, April 23d, 1796, where he grew up to manhood. His parents were named Lewis and 'Rosanna Hertz. In youth he learned, in Harrisburg, the printing business, but this not agreeing with his health, he abandoned it for brick-laying, a trade which he learned with his brother. In the winter months, not being busied in the business of his trade, he engaged at intervals in teaching school, and so continued until having made the acquaintance of Rev. Isaac Gerhart, he was induced to prepare himself for the ministry. He began his preparatory studies to this end, under Rev. Gerhart, and closed them under Dr. Helfenstein, of Philadelphia. He entered upon the duties of the ministry somewhere about the year 1821, and after preaching somewhat desultory for some time, received a call to Ephrata, which he accepted and entered upon duty at this place in the spring of 1823. His charge at Ephrata embraced several congregations; and his trial sermon was preached at Muddy creek, in the same church in which he closed his labors, forty-five years and six months afterwards. His was a long and faithful pastorate, and his name remains enshrined in the memories of those who oft listened to the words of truth that flowed from his pure and mellowed lips. In his long and dutiful service to the congregations of his charge he preached 10,028 regular Sabbath and week-day sermons; 1,776 funeral discourses, and united in the bonds of matrimony 1,136 couples. After his long and faithful stewardship he resigned his charge into other hands, and peacefully breathed out his soul into the bosom of his Redeemer, September 22d, 1868. In the words of Rev. J. V. Eckert, the subject of this notice as a pastor, "was laborious and faithful in his ministry. He pursued his calling with almost unexampled devotion. He was instant in season and out of season. Like his heavenly master, he went about doing good. He was systematic, conscientious, and particular in his calling. His manner and

deportment was high-toned and manly; and never com
plained, nor allowed any one to trifle with his ministeria
character."

HIBSHMAN, HENRY, was elected a member of the Leg
islature in the years 1811, 1815 and 1821. He was electec
to the State Senate in 1833.

HIBSHMAN, JACOB, was a native of Lancaster county
and a citizen of great prominence and respectability in the
community. In 1810 he was appointed one of the associate
judges of Lancaster county, the duties of which office he dis
charged for nine years. In 1818 he was elected a membe
of Congress for the district composed of the counties of Lan
caster, Lebanon and Dauphin. He filled the office of Dep
uty Surveyor for the county of Lancaster, for a period o
upwards of twenty years. He was appointed by the Gover
nor Appraiser of Damages, suffered by land-owners in con
sequence of the public improvements. He served the offic
of justice of the peace for many years under the old consti
tution; and after the adoption of the new one, was continuec
in office by the suffrages of the people. He held the offic
of Major General of the 5th Division of Pennsylvania Militi:
for twelve years. He died at his residence in Ephrata, Ma
19th, 1852, aged 80 years, 4 months and 19 days. In publi
as well as in private life, Jacob Hibshman was esteemed fo
his integrity, ability and high sense of honor. In him wer
united a sound understanding and a kindness of heart whicl
endeared him to all who knew him. In his entire characte
he was well worthy of imitation. He left behind him a
unspotted reputation.

HIESTAND, JOHN A., editor of the *Examiner and Her
ald*, was admitted as a member of the Lancaster bar in th
year 1849. He was elected to the Legislature of Pennsylva
nia in the years 1852, 1853 and 1856. In 1860 he wa
elected to the State Senate, and served one term in that body
He was appointed in 1871, by President Grant, to the posi
tion of Naval Officer in the city of Philadelphia.

HIESTAND, JOHN M., elected Commissioner in 1852.

HIESTER, ISAAC E., son of William Hiester, and grand
nephew of Governer Joseph Hiester, was born in New Hol

land, Lancaster county, in May, 1824. At an early age he was sent to the Moravian school for boys, at Litiz; afterwards to the Abbeville Academy, and subsequently to Bolmar's Institute, at West Chester, where he was prepared for college. In 1838 he entered Yale College, and after pursuing a full course of studies in that institution, graduated with high honors. He entered and read law in the office of Thomas E. Franklin, esq., and was admitted to the bar in 1845. Coming to the bar well fitted for the duties of the profession, and his family ties being amongst the most influential in Lancaster county, he speedily rose in the legal ranks. In 1848 he was appointed District Attorney for the county, by the Attorney General of the State. In 1852 he was elected to Congress by the Whig party, and though young, made his mark in that body, delivering a brilliant speech against the Kansas-Nebraska bill. Upon the organization of the Know Nothing party, Mr. Hiester chose not to go with the majority of his party, and with a small wing of followers, united himself to the Democratic party. He was again nominated by this party for Congress in 1854, but was defeated. With the Democratic party he continued to act as long as he lived, but by no means sympathized fully with it. In 1856 he was again the candidate of the Democratic party for Congress, but his popularity was by no means sufficient to overcome the great opposition majority in Lancaster county. In 1868 he was elected a delegate to the Democratic National Convention, and was chosen to represent the State of Pennsylvania in the Democratic National Executive Committee. He died February 6th, 1871.

On the question of the prosecution of the war for the suppression of the rebellion, Mr. Hiester seemed not materially to differ in sentiment with the other recognized leaders of the Democratic party; but after the close of the war his opinions showed a restiveness in Democratic harness. His views by no means harmonized with those of his party, and he was zealous and outspoken for a dissolution of the Democratic organization, a change of name and an entire remodeling of principles. By instinct he belonged, as it were, to the Republican party; and although at times he must and did oppose them, yet it is very doubtful if he did not oft regret his abandonment of the old party in which he had been reared, and to which he was indebted for his most substantial honors. He believed that the attitude of the Democratic party, as regards the Southern rebellion, had ruined it, and he regarded, therefore, a defence of dead principles as useless. In other words, in his judgment, the Democratic party had been weighed in the scales of American public opinion and found wanting.

As a lawyer Mr. Hiester was conceded talents of a high order. From the analytical character of his mind, he was able to grasp legal questions and unfold them before the court and jury in a very happy manner. He always had his cases well prepared, and in their trial was fully equal to any member of the Lancaster bar. He enjoyed a large and profitable practice. In all his relations with the members of the profession his conduct was exemplary, and his word when given, equalled his bond. He was purely a business man. Save political distinction, he had no other ambition than to shine in the ranks of the profession, and in this latter aspiration he was worthily gratified. With his immense wealth, his talents might have secured him eminence in other careers than business, but his mind never seems to have been aroused to anything except the career in which he spent his days. He appears to have had no taste for travel, science, or literature, any of which might have served to occupy his time quite as pleasantly as the legal profession. As a citizen he was kind and courteous to all. He possessed, however, a dignified reserve that gave no room for familiarity, and even in the midst of his most intimate friends this was not laid aside.

HIESTER, William, was born in Berks county, Pennsylvania, October 10th, 1790. He removed to Lancaster county when a young man, located at New Holland, and married Lucy E. Ellmaker, a daughter of Isaac Ellmaker of that place. He early became known as a politician, and first took a prominent political part in the movements in Lancaster county that gave shape to the Anti-Masonic party of the county in 1828. He acted as secretary of the great

Anti-Masonic meeting, held at New Holland in 1828, which passed resolutions refusing to support any man for office who was a member of the Masonic order. Mr. Hiester was nominated in the campaign of 1828 for Congress on the Anti-Jackson ticket against James Buchanan, but was defeated. He was again nominated in 1830 for Congress, and elected. He was twice reëlected to Congress, and served as a member of that body from 1831 till 1837, and rendered general satisfaction to his constituents. He was, in 1836, elected a member of the Convention to revise the Constitution of Pennsylvania. In 1840 he was nominated and elected a member of the State Senate, and during the session of 1842 was chosen speaker of that body. Whilst a member of Congress, Mr. Hiester advocated and voted for a tariff that should ensure a sound national currency; as a member of the Reform Convention he advocated an amendment to the Constitution, which, if adopted, would have prevented an excessive increase of the public debt; and whilst a Senator, he was ever the rigid advocate of reform, and desired even to commence with the reduction of his own compensation.

During all his public service, he was remarkable for his attention to the interests of his constituents, and for his regular attendance at his place of official duty. His career of official life secured for him the lasting confidence of his constituents, and many of them, against his earnest protests, still desired to crown him with yet higher honors. He was president of the great Whig meeting, held at Lancaster, July 29th, 1843, which advocated the claims of Henry Clay for the Presidency in 1844. He was the unanimous choice of Lancaster county for Governor, in 1844; and although the delegates were instructed for him, he declined allowing his name to come before the convention. Physical infirmity, he felt, would not permit him to undertake a trust of such importance, especially as he had for some years been in declining health. He was the Whig Presidential Elector in 1844.

Mr. Hiester was a German by birth, a farmer by occupation, and a gentleman well informed upon all the current topics of the day. He spoke the German as fluently as the English. In private life he was a man of unblemished

moral character and integrity, of winning manners and easy
address. He was respected and esteemed wherever known.
He died at New Holland, Oct. 13th, 1853, in the 63d year of
his age.

HIPPLE, FREDERICK, was elected a member of the Legislature in 1833 and 1834. He was also elected Commissioner
in 1842.

HOFF, JOHN, was appointed Clerk of Orphans' Court in
1817.

*HOFFMAN, GEORGE, was born in Strasburg, March 9th,
1784. He must have been quite a student in his youth,
and, without doubt, improved all his opportunities to their
utmost extent. He obtained the first rudiments of education from an old German schoolmaster, named Buch, of
whom but very little is known, but who, according to Mr.
Hoffman's recollection, must have been a man of considerable knowledge and ability. Of Mr. Hoffman's parents but
little is known. His father died when George was quite young,
and his mother, whose maiden name was Drum, did not live to
be old. Old people, who had any recollection concerning
her, always said she was a woman of good sound sense, a
fact which all who knew her son were free to confess. Such
a man could not have been the son of any other than a
woman of first-rate natural abilities.

When George was about fifteen years old he was placed
in the store of James Whitehill, then the most considerable
of the Strasburg merchants. Here he remained till he was
over twenty-one years old. For the next eight or ten years
he was employed as clerk in other stores, all the while retaining his studious habits and love of knowledge. In 1809
he was married to Mrs. Barbara Maynard, of Safe Harbor,
and went into the mercantile business on his own account.
About five years afterwards he removed to Strasburg, where
he continued to reside and keep store till the time of his
death.

In 1816 he was appointed by Governor Snyder a justice
of the peace, an office which he held till the winter of 1827–8,
when he ceased any longer to perform its duties, he having

*Contributed by Alexander Hood, esq.

been, at a special election held in December, 1827, elected to the Legislature over the regular Jackson Democratic nominee. Being a supporter of Adams, in 1828, he could not be reëlected.

At this time Mr. Hoffman stood very high in the party which opposed Jackson in this county. True, it was but a small party in the State, but it contained all the wisdom and most of the political honesty of the time. The cry of corruption raised against Clay and Adams, swept everything before it. In the small vote which the State then polled, Jackson had more than fifty thousand majority. In Lancaster county, owing to the exertions of Mr. Hoffman and others, the disproportion was not so overwhelming. Buchanan's majority for Congress, in 1828, was 1,299, smaller by about 200 than that which William Hiester, as an Anti-Mason, received two years afterwards.

As a magistrate Mr. Hoffman was one of the most useful and upright men who ever filled that office. His aim was never to make money for himself, but to do good to those around him. No civil case that could be amicably adjusted, did he ever push onward to a suit, for the sake of making costs for himself or the constables. In all cases of misdemeanor, where the law permitted an amicable arrangement, he never failed to exert his good offices towards that end. He was emphatically, a peace-maker; and many had cause to bless him for his efforts in that direction. Nor did his good offices as an adviser end with his magisterial career; to the end of his life he was the friend and counsellor of all who applied for his advice, the great merit of which was, that he was almost invariably right in his views of what was most proper to be done in all cases of difficulty. He had, in an eminent degree, the rare faculty of making persons who were wrong and angry, perceive their error and the folly of their ill temper; and this he could do without giving them the least offence. He seemed to know, by intuition, how to treat every person with whom he came in contact, and this in all cases without the least departure from his habitual dignity. The writer of this knew him perfectly well, and now, twenty-seven years since his death, upon an impartial view of his

23

character, comes to the conclusion that Mr. Hoffman was so nearly devoid of all prejudice, that his judgment was never in the least influenced thereby; that, with the greatest kindness of heart, he had the clearest perceptive power of any man of whom he has ever had any personal knowledge.

His friendship for the young was at all times remarkable. No man ever took a stronger interest than he did in young people who fell in his way. To them he was like a father; and his advice was always given with so much good feeling that no one could ever take offence, even when the admonition took the form of reproof. It was this feeling which gave rise to the sentence uttered by him, which led to the first effort to found a system of public schools in Pennsylvania. In January, 1831, in consequence of a sentence uttered by him, a discussion took place in his store, which ended in the call of a meeting, of which George Diffenbach was the chairman, and James McPhail, esq., secretary. This meeting, which was held in the Jackson street school house, and which was attended by about forty persons, sent the first petition to the Legislature in favor of general education, resulting in the passage of the act of 1831, appropriating certain funds towards the establishment of public schools at some future time. From this time till the school system was firmly established, in 1835, Mr. Hoffman, with other friends of education, never lost sight of the grand movement to which in our State they had given the first impetus. To the day of his death he was always one of its firmest supporters.

It has already been said that Mr. Hoffman was strongly opposed to the election of Andrew Jackson. Being a very quiet member of the Masonic order, in 1829, when Anti-Masonry swept over this country like a deluge, he was forced back into the Democratic party, the ticket of which he voted till his death, except when Henry Clay was a candidate for the Presidency, for whom he always cast his vote and influence. He was at all times a firm believer in the protection of American industry, and an ardent supporter of the rights of man, without distinction of color or race. When Charles Burleigh delivered the first anti-slavery lecture in

Strasburg, Mr. Hoffman was one of the few who stood by him at all hazards. He always was a decided abolitionist, and hated slavery in all its forms. Had he lived till the great contest between liberty and slavery had developed itself, only so far as in its form of free soil against slavery extension, there is no doubt as to where he would have been found.

His whole nature revolted against wrong and oppression in every shape; but he was not permitted to see the political salvation of a down-trodden race, nor to look upon the red, white and blue, untarnished by the blackness of slavery.

In 1845 he was attacked by typhoid fever of the most malignant type. From this he never rallied, and on the 30th day of June he breathed his last. No man within the circle of those who knew him, was ever more sincerely regretted. He left three children, Barbara, the widow of Jacob Erb, who resides in Conestoga township; Ann, the wife of B. B. Gonder, esq.; and Jesse Hoffman, who resides in Strasburg.

HOFFMAN, VALENTINE, was a superior manufacturer of edge tools and cutlery in Lancaster at an early day. He was a highly respected citizen.

HOFFMEIER, J. L., was elected Clerk of the Quarter Sessions in 1839, being the first elected under the new Constitution. After serving this office he was engaged in various clerkships until 1858, when he was appointed clerk and salesman of the Lancaster County Prison, a position he retained up to April, 1863. He was reëlected in March, 1864, and held the office up to April, 1872, with the exception of a brief interval.

HOLL, PETER, was a resident of Warwick township, owner of a mill on Litiz creek, and a man of influence in the community. He was elected Commissioner of Lancaster county on the Federal ticket in 1819. Shortly after the expiration of his term of office, he left Lancaster county and settled in Cumberland county, Pa.

HOOD, ALEXANDER. In 1696 an Englishman, named John Hood, with his wife, settled within a few miles of where Norristown now stands. This man, it seems, when quite young, had been concerned in some plot against the government and fled to Holland, afterwards going back to England as a soldier in the army of William III. A grandson of this man, Rev. Philip Hood, had a numerous family, among whom was a son named Gerhart, born in 1756, who married Mary, the daughter of Philip Wentz, of Skippach, at whose house General Washington had his headquarters before and after the battle of Germantown. About 1792 Gerhart and his brother John removed to Chester county, not far from Andrew's Bridge, the place being now known as Homeville. John remained there till his death, in 1832, but Gerhart removed to Lancaster in 1795, remaining there till 1802, when he removed to Philadelphia, and died there in 1814.

Gerhart Hood had three sons: Frederick, born near Norristown, June 14th, 1779; George, born at the same place, about 1783; and Samuel, born at Lancaster in 1796. George moved from Philadelphia to Lancaster, Ohio, in 1816, and died there a few years afterwards. Samuel died in Philadelphia, unmarried, in 1822.

Frederic Hood learned the trade of a hatter at Lancaster, and afterwards worked in various places, till he married Margaret, the daughter of John Higgins, of Chambersburg, Pa. After the war of 1812, in which he participated in several battles and was taken prisoner, he removed to Philadelphia, and in 1819 removed to Strasburg, where he followed his trade for several years. He died at Soudersburg, October 14th, 1865, in his 87th year. His two sons, Alexander H. and John Gerhart Hood, reside in Lancaster.

Alexander H. Hood was born at Chambersburg, Pa., and when a small boy came to Strasburg with his parents, as above stated. When about sixteen years old he was apprenticed to a shoemaker, and worked at that business till he was over twenty years old. He then became a teacher of a public school, and in 1837 was appointed a clerk in the office of the Secretary of State, at Harrisburg, where he remained till the close of Ritner's administration. In April, 1839, he became the editor and proprietor of the *Lancaster Union*, which he conducted with marked ability till October, 1842, when he sold out to R. W. Middleton. In 1839 he was elected Clerk of the Orphans' Court of Lancaster county, and before his term expired he was elected to the Legislature, in which, owing to a split in the party, he remained but one session. While serving in this capacity, John Mathiot, who for several years had been Mayor of Lancaster, died. Mr. Hood, on the petition of many Whigs and a few Democrats, introduced and had passed into a law, a bill making the Mayor elective, though it was covertly opposed by all the leading Democrats. After the defeat of Clay, in 1844, he took but little part in politics for some years. In 1844, having read law under the direction of the late Hon. Thaddeus Stevens, he was admitted to the bar, and soon became one of its most prominent members. In 1847 he identified himself with the free-soil movement, voting for Van Buren in opposition to Taylor. When the Republican party was formed, he was one of the very few who held the first meeting in Lancaster county. From that day to the present time he has always been prominent in the Republican ranks. At the outbreak of the war, all his energies were exerted in behalf of the Union cause. In 1861 he received the regular Republican nomination for President Judge of this district, but was defeated by a coalition of dissatisfied Republicans with the Democrats, who put the old incumbent, then regarded as a Republican, in the field against him. The majority of the successful candidate was very small, and Mr. Hood could have been easily elected had he not refused to take any part in his own behalf.

In August, 1862, he was appointed Collector of Internal Revenue of this district, by President Lincoln, a position which he held till September, 1866, when he was removed by Andrew Johnson for refusing to contribute funds towards the formation of Johnson's new party. Since that time Mr. Hood has been steadily engaged in the practice of his profession.

As to social science, Mr. Hood can scarcely be said to be either conservative or progressive, though his mind tends most strongly in the latter direction. He is the furthest possible remove from an old fogy, but he does not like to go ahead without being sure he is right. His opinions are all formed after patient investigation, and when his mind is once made up on any question, he has full confidence in the result at which he has arrived. From his boyhood he was a decided abolitionist, and was never afraid to express his views, even when such expression was attended with considerable danger. He has at all times been the friend of the oppressed, without regard to race, color, or condition.

As one of the few who at Strasburg put the ball in motion, which resulted in the school system of Pennsylvania, it was natural that when an attempt to destroy that system was made, he should oppose it with all his force, though the attempt was sanctioned by the most of the party to which he belonged. In truth, it may be said, that in all cases where the contest has been between the strong and the weak, the powerful and the oppressed, he has always been found on the side of justice and right.

Mr. Hood's mind is eminently mathematical, and in this department of science he is said to be proficient. His arguments all indicate study in this direction, and it is this faculty of mind which prevents his impulses from getting control of his judgment; and it is this which imparts to him that full confidence he has in all his conclusions. As a speaker, he is logical and argumentative rather than flowery or fluent; yet in many of his speeches there are touches of pathos which go directly to the hearts of his hearers. His illustrations are always apt and forcible, but, like the drawings of Michael Angelo, a few touches tell the whole story. On the stump he always takes the crowd along with him, and the effect of his speeches all tell upon the majorities where he speaks.

HOOD, Joseph, was a member of the Legislature in 1860.

HOLLINGER, Isaac, was elected Recorder in 1866.

HOPKINS, George Washington, son of James Hopkins, was one of the brilliant lights of the old Lancaster bar, whose great oratorical powers and splendid declamation have associated his name with John R. Montgomery and George W. Barton. These three names are ever associated together as the bright trio of intellectual stars of the first magnitude, that shone with such dazzling splendor on old

Lancaster, the remembrance of which will never perish whilst memory endures.

HOPKINS, JAMES, for many years was the most eminent lawyer of the Lancaster bar, and ranked amongst the most noted in the whole State. His business in the profession was immense, and he accumulated a vast fortune in the practice. With him studied many of the old able attornies of the country, and amongst these James Buchanan. He was employed in the trial of important causes in different counties of the State. On one occasion he was selected by the Legislature, with Ross, of Pittsburg, to try a case calling for great legal ability. He was purely a lawyer, mingling little in politics, but was elected a member of the Legislature in 1821. He died whilst engaged in the trial of a case in Lancaster.

HOPKINS, JOHN, brother of James Hopkins, was a member of the Legislature in the years 1787, 1788, 1789, 1796, 1797, 1798, 1799 and 1800. He was also elected to the State Senate in 1814.

HOPKINS, W. W., grandson of James Hopkins, and a member of the Lancaster bar, was elected to the Legislature in the year 1868.

HOSTETTER, HENRY, a citizen of Ephrata township, was elected to the Legislature, on the Democratic ticket,[1] in 1828. He was a farmer, and a minister in the denomination of the Seventh-day Baptists.

HOUSEKEEPER, W., was a member of the Legislature in the years 1855 and 1856.

HOUSTON, SAMUEL, one of the early settlers in Lancaster county, emigrated from Scotland to America with five sons, prior to the Revolution. He purchased a large body of land in Pequea valley, a few miles northwest of the Gap. He at once espoused the American cause and rendered impor-

---

[1] The Democratic success in Lancaster county in 1828, was its last victory in the county. Prior to that time it had been somewhat alternately successful in the elections, but with the coming into power of the Anti-Masonic party, the Democratic party sunk. Many Democrats became Anit-Masons, and the Democratic party has been in a miserable minority in the county ever since.

tant service. Four of his sons joined the army and served during the war. He was a valuable and influential member of the Associate Presbyterian church.

HOUSTON, SAMUEL, son of the above, was born in Scotland, and removed with his father to this country about the year 1769. He married Sarah, daughter of John and Mary Hopkins, in the year 1787. He was for many years engaged in mercantile pursuits at the Gap, in Salisbury township, and was appointed a justice of the peace by Governor Mifflin, which office he held with satisfaction to the public for more than forty years. He was, in 1829, elected a member of the State Senate of Pennsylvania, which position he held for three years. He was honored by the people with many other important trusts. Mr. Houston was a man of great usefulness in the community, and by his persevering industry and business activity, he acquired a handsome independence, among which were included several fine farms, Houston's mill, the hotel at the Gap, besides several store houses. He was a worthy and esteemed member of the Presbyterian church. He died in the year 1842, aged seventy-five years. His youngest son, Benjamin F. Houston, is among his surviving descendants; and the late John Houston, of Washington city, who held a situation in the Treasury department uninterruptedly for more than fifty years, was the eldest son of Samuel Houston, esq.

HOWELL, CHARLES M., was born in Philadelphia, April 24th, 1814. He received his education in the schools of that city, and was a student of the Plainfield Academy, in Connecticut, for some time. At the early age of fourteen he was apprenticed to Gen. Peter Fritz, to learn the marble mason business, and served with him till he was twenty-one years of age. Upon the close of his apprenticeship he continued to work as a journeyman for several years. In the spring of 1838 he set up for himself in his business in Philadelphia, and carried on till September, 1841. Having married into a Lancaster family, he, in 1841, removed to and began business in Lancaster, in East King street, on property of John N. Lane, where he carried on with excellent success. A few years afterwards he purchased the old Gompf property, on the west side of North Queen street, where he has since carried on his business. In 1863–4 he erected a handsome new building on the site of the old property purchased by him. Mr. Howell was elected County Treasurer, on the Democratic ticket, in the fall of 1856, which office he filled with entire satisfaction to the public. He was also elected City Treasurer by the City Councils, in 1865. He has frequently been a member of both branches of City Councils, and also for some time a member of the City School Board. Mr. Howell is emphatically a self-made man, and has from an humble grade in society arisen until he is a man of considerable wealth and influence. He became a member of the Masonic fraternity in Philadelphia, in 1835, and since 1853 has been District Deputy Grand Master of District No. 1 of Pennsylvania; and he was also Grand Generalissimo of the Grand Commandery of the Order of Knights Templar of Pennsylvania. A new Masonic Lodge, founded in 1871, was named Howell Lodge, in honor of the subject of this notice.

HOWER, J. W., elected a member of the Legislature in 1848.

HUBER, John, one of the early settlers in Warwick township, and the principal contestant in the dispute with Richard Carter in reference to naming the township. He was a leading man and an iron-master. The following lines were upon his furnace:

"Johan Huber, der erste Deutsche man
Der das Eisenwerk vollfüren kann."

HUBLEY, Adam, a brother of John Hubley, was, in December, 1776, appointed Major of the 10th Pennsylvania regiment in the Continental service. He was a member of the Legislature for the years 1783, 1785, 1786 and 1787. He was also chosen a member of the State Senate in 1790.

HUBLEY, Bernard, was born in Germany, October 18th, 1719. He emigrated to America when a boy of about sixteen years of age, and settled in Lancaster. He learned the tanning business with Valentine Krug, and afterwards carried on this business for many years. He purchased and owned what was years ago known as the Brady farm. He ranked in his day as one of the most influential and respected citizens of the community. He was a member of the Board of Assistant Burgesses of the borough of Lancaster for the years 1750, 1757, 1766 and 1767. He was for some years a commissioner of the county of Lancaster. He was a man who exerted considerable influence in political circles, and was a member of the Federal party. He was an active Whig in the Revolution, and was appointed barrack-master of Lancaster county in 1778. By his energy and perseverance he accumulated a considerable fortune, and left his children in easy circumstances. He was twice married, and had twenty-one children, the youngest of whom was Anna, the wife of the late Joseph Ehrenfried. He sustained heavy losses in the depreciation of the Continental currency. He died January 29th, 1803. He was for many years an elder of Trinity Lutheran church.

HUBLEY, John, son of Michael Hubley, was born at Lancaster, December 25th, 1747. He was married to Maria Magdalena, the daughter of Ludwig Lauman. He read law under the instruction of Edward Shippen, and was admitted to the bar in 1769. He was one of the delegates from Lancaster county to the convention which met in Philadelphia, July 15th, 1776, to adopt a State Constitution. August 5th, 1776, he took his seat as a member of the General Pennsylvania Council of Safety which had been established by the first Constitution. On January 11th, 1777, he was appointed commissary of Continental stores, and the stores of Pennsylvania at Lancaster, with the rank of Major, and with authority to appoint such deputies as he might judge necessary. A few days afterwards he was authorized to employ all the shoemakers among the Hessian prisoners at Lancaster, in making shoes for the State. He was for some time a Councillor of the Supreme Executive Council. He was appointed April 5th, 1777, by the Supreme Executive Council, Prothonotary of the Court of Common Pleas, Clerk of the Orphans' Court, Clerk of Quarter Sessions, and also Recorder of Deeds, part of which offices he held for upwards of twenty years. In January, 1777, he was commissioned also a justice of the peace. In 1787 he was a member of the State Convention that ratified the Federal Constitution. He died January 21st, 1821.

HUBLEY, MICHAEL, brother of Bernard Hubley, was born in Germany, February 28th, 1722. On the 2d of October, 1832, he came with his father to America, and landed at Philadelphia. In the spring of 1840 he came to Lancaster, where he continued to reside until his death. On the 6th of August, 1745, he married Rosina, a daughter of Dietrich Strumpf, who was also born in Germany, and who lived with him until her death, June 28th, 1803, at the age of 84 years. He was, in 1777, appointed by the supreme executive council a justice of the peace of Lancaster county, and for some time was the presiding justice of the several courts of the county. He was re-commissioned a justice of the peace in 1784. For some time during the Revolution he held the position of barrack-master of Lancaster county. He was an acting magistrate of the county for the period of twenty-seven years. During the last 43 years of his life he served the Trinity Lutheran congregation as warden, elder and trustee. He died May 17th, 1804.

HUMES, DR. SAMUEL, an eminent physician of Lancaster. He was a graduate of the University of Pennsylvania. He began the practice of his profession about 1812, and was busily engaged therein until his death in September, 1852. Dr. Henry Carpenter being a student of Dr. Humes, and his executor, succeeded him in his practice. Dr. Humes was Treasurer of Lancaster in 1806.

HUNSECKER, C. L., was born in Manheim township, November 1st, 1814. He is a miller by occupation, and a leading, influential and intelligent citizen of the community. He was first elected to the Legislature from Lancaster county in 1850, then quite a young man, and served in the sessions of the Pennsylvania Legislature in the years 1851, 1852, 1854 and 1856. He was reëlected to the Legislature in the year 1871.[1]

[1] By the late apportionment made in 1871, Lancaster county is entitled to but one Senator and three members of the House of Representatives. The first members under the new apportionment for the session of 1872, were David K. Burkholder, Dr. J. C. Gatchell and C. L. Hunsecker.

HURFORD, Lewis, a member of the Legislature in 1849.

HUSS, John, was born in Chester county, Pennsylvania, November 6th, 1790. He learned the printing business in Lancaster, in the office of William Hamilton, and afterwards worked as a journeyman printer with Hugh Maxwell. It was he who began the publication of the first newspaper in Marietta, and which he called the *Pilot*, but afterwards changed its name to the *Pioneer*. He started this paper about the close of the war of 1812–14, and in 1827 sold out his interest therein to Charles Nagle. The vignette of his paper was a steamboat, engraved by J. J. Libhart. The motto of his paper was the following:

> "This world is a bubble, all things show it;
> Once I thought so, now I know it."

He was elected a member of the Legislature for the year 1822 and reelected for 1823. He died July 19th, 1841.

HIGH, George J., was elected Recorder of Deeds in 1870.

J.

JACKS, James, a member of the Legislature in the years 1780, 1781 and 1782. He was appointed Recorder of Deeds in 1783.

*JACKSON, Joel, was born at West Grove, Chester county, in the year 1776, being a descendant of one of the oldest families in that region. At an early age he went to Wilmington, Delaware, and entered into the mercantile business, for which it would seem he was singularly unfitted. Remaining in Wilmington but a short time, he returned to Chester county, purchased, improved, and disposed of a farm situated in London, Britain township. In his 37th year he determined to leave his native county, and with this end in view came to Lancaster and purchased from a family by the name of Coppock's, a large farm, located in the southern part of Little Britain. This land being very poor, Joel Jackson, with untiring industry set to work to improve it, by burning lime and feeding cattle. The place was soon

*Contributed by Charles H. Stubbs, M. D.

rendered quite productive, and the new proprietor well known as a successful and intelligent farmer. As an instance of the general poverty of the soil of the southern part of the township at this period, 1813-14, it might be mentioned that on several occasions, in the first year of his occupancy, he had to haul corn for his stock from the richer central parts of the county.

It is not of him as a successful farmer we would speak, but rather of those marked traits of character before alluded to, and as possessing abilities of the very highest order for the acquisition of science, which, if cultivated, would have placed him in rank with the Cuviers, Farradays or Davys of Europe. Though, doubtless, he was conscious that by nature he was fitted for something higher than the life of toil that laid before him, and as necessary for the welfare of his family. Perhaps no more hard-working, industrious man, one more self-reliant, and one who would permit no person to do for him anything that he thought could possibly be done by himself, and one more strictly honest in his dealings, never lived. His strict integrity and keen sense of the justice due all men, was manifested all his life in the care he would take not to ask too much for anything he had to sell, or above the market price of the article. Though somewhat hasty in temper, he was very kind and courteous in manner. But if he should detect a man in any duplicity or dishonesty, he took no pains to conceal his dislike. This same strict sense of justice led him to forbid his day-laborers to work after sundown ; always having their meals ready for them that they could return home; himself, even when a very old man, doing up the usual chores before coming to the house. If the poet was right, that "an honest man is the noblest work of God," Joel Jackson was emphatically one of Nature's noblemen. In his habits he was very domestic, rarely leaving home unless absolutely necessary ; never going to public meetings of any kind, and only to elections when he thought some question of interest was at stake. His love of science and of nature always remained with him ; and the reading of all works accessible on these subjects, in hours snatched occasionally from labor, and from the time others devoted to slumber, was his greatest delight. This seemed to have rendered his life more endurable, and towards the close cheered its decline. His greatest recreation, in his more advanced years, was the study of botany, the general principles and the more minute details of which it was no trouble for him to master. This was also true of geology, his greatest delight being to receive all the new publications on the subject.

When he found himself unable to conduct his business on the upper farm where he then resided, being about seventy-four years of age, he made such distribution of his property as he thought just, and then retired to a small house near the Rock Springs, in a remote corner of the place, to wait for death as a friend to lead him to rest. Here, in the silence of the solitary hours, cheered, however, by frequent visits from his children and his grandchildren, who kept him well supplied with books and papers, and finding employment in the cultivation of about an acre of land, he awaited with composure the last great change, knowing that death is not only inevitable, but in the great scheme of creation, that it is just as necessary as life. As he felt its near approach by his increasing infirmities, he gave directions that he should be buried in a plain manner, and no notice given, except to some of the nearest of his friends, as he had always disapproved of great expense and large collections of people on such occasions. He desired that no stone be placed over him, but that one should be placed over his wife, who had preceded him to the better land. After a short illness he passed away peaceably from earth, in September, 1857, aged nearly eighty-one years. And there, in a family graveyard, containing some of his children and grandchildren, rests the remains of Joel Jackson. The ground is surrounded on three sides by old forest trees, and there, in the quiet of that nature he loved so well, a quiet unbroken, save by the song of the wood-bird, and with a few wild flowers planted over him by loving hands, life's fitful fever over, he sleeps the sleep of death.

JACKSON, LEAVIN H., was elected a. member of the Legislature in the years 1832, 1833 and 1834.

JACOBS, Thomas B., was a member of the Legislature in the years 1845 and 1847.

JENKINS, Catharine M., a daughter of the celebrated divine, Rev. John Carmichael, was born in Chester county, Pennsylvania, July 23d, 1774. Her mother died when she was but thirteen days old, and her father before she had reached the age of twelve. Not long after her father's death she became the inmate of the family of the Rev. Robert Smith, a relative by marriage. In his house she found a congenial and happy home, and in the learned and devoted pastor of Pequea a friend and father. In the fall of 1792 she became a member of the Presbyterian church of Pequea. Shortly before the death of Rev. Robert Smith, which occurred on the 15th of April, 1793, she accepted an invitation to make her home in the house of Rev. Nathaniel W. Sample, of Strasburg, and after some time accepted an invitation to the like effect from Daniel Buckley, an iron-master of courteous and hospitable manners. In a letter to her half-sister, Phœbe, dated Pequea, June 7th, 1799, she says: "I am no longer an inhabitant of Strasburg. I bade adieu to that place the last week of March, and am now a member of Mr. Daniel Buckley's family, whose forge and farm, you may recollect, we passed in going from Strasburg to Brandywine. It is a charming situation in the summer; and if I am to judge of the time to come by what is past, I have every reason to expect much happiness. Mr. and Mrs. Buckley treat me with all the attention and kindness I could expect from relations, and express the greatest pleasure in seeing and entertaining my friends and acquaintances."

In September, 1799, the subject of this notice was married to Robert Jenkins, and became the mistress of Windsor Place. The first impulse that inspired her after her marriage with Mr. Jenkins, was to render her home the hospitable mansion and favorite retreat for the pious and learned. As soon as she would contract an acquaintance with a clergyman, she never failed to extend to him a cordial invitation to visit the "Preachers' Hotel." In consequence of her great amiability and kindness thus manifested, her house was the constant resort of ministers of every denomination who

passed that way. Catharine Jenkins was very fond of reading, and her centre table presented always a collection of
the best religious and periodical literature of the day.
Scholars and literary men were her especial favorites, and
she ever aimed to render them easy in her presence and feel
at home in her hospitable mansion. She loved to entertain
them in a style becoming their education and attainments.
Mrs. Jenkins was a lady of great spirit and resolution, and
exerted these qualities of her character for the promotion of
truth and the elevation of mankind. She was an implacable
foe to the wine cup and the gaming-table, and the following
may be cited as illustrative of her resolution and stern purpose. In her husband's employ were a large number of
workmen who were greatly addicted to the rum bottle, and as
a consequence entailed misery upon themselves and their families. The hands would frequently come to the table at their
boarding house in a state of intoxication, and this condition
of affairs Mrs. Jenkins endeavored to reform by moral
suasion, and by endeavoring to depict the great sin they
were committing. She now determined to employ more
decisive means. By the aid of one of her servants, she
obtained the bottles in which the men kept their rum. At
dinner time the hands were surprised and mortified to see
their bottles in a row standing upon the table, and their contents visible through the glass. Mrs. Jenkins soon after
entered the room, and in her amiable manner remarked, that
she had in her possession a number of bottles belonging to
them which she desired to return to their respective owners,
and asked of them each to come forward and claim his
property. As none had the hardihood to do this under the
circumstances, she next remarked: "They are now in my
possession, and as you will not take them, of course they are
at my disposal." After that she took them to an open
window, and striking them one by one against the wall, they
fell in shivers to the ground. The bottles and their contents
being destroyed, she addressed the men and said, in a mild
but decisive manner, "if they be replaced by others, they
shall share the same fate." She used all her influence to
oppose vice and immorality, not only among her dependents,

but also amongst those who moved in the higher walks of life. Every sphere in which this pious lady moved, felt her influence. Immorality never escaped her disapprobation, no difference what were the circumstances under which it presented itself. More than once were the cards and wine-cup, with great reluctance, removed from the social circle when the approach of Mrs. Jenkins was announced.

As one whose life had been devoted to the service of Christ, her life was truly an exemplary one. She, on all occasions, labored for the cause of her Redeemer, and liberally gave of her means for the promotion and building up of His church. Upon an occasion when attending a Presidential levee, and the Scripture was sneered at in such a manner as to indicate that the party were largely tainted with skeptical views, she firmly defended and challenged respect for the sacred book, which was not further gainsaid by any present. She died September 23d, 1856.

JENKINS, DAVID, the original ancestor of the numerous descendants of this name, was a native of Wales, who emigrated to America and landed at Philadelphia in the year 1700. His son, John Jenkins, penetrated into the forests, and selected a site on which the Windsor forges[1] were afterwards erected. He erected a temporary residence near where now stands the Windsor Mansion, and entered into a contract with John, Thomas, and Richard Penn for the purchase of 400 acres of land, January 10th, 1733. The land was surveyed, but a patent therefore was not taken out by Mr. Jenkins, and he sold it after some years to William Branson & Co., of Philadelphia, who took out a patent for the tract December 28th, 1742, and erected the Windsor forges and Mansion House.

JENKINS, DAVID, son of John, the first settler at Windsor, was born July 2d, 1731. He purchased from William Branson & Co., the whole of the Windsor property. He

[1] The Windsor Iron Works were amongst the first established in the United States, if not the first in Pennsylvania. They were put in operation by a company upon the lands originally purchased by John Jenkins in 1731. The company sold out their interest about the time of the Revolution, to David Jenkins, who managed the works with skill and economy.

24

was a member of the Pennsylvania Legislature in 1784. He died in 1797.

JENKINS, ROBERT, son of David Jenkins last named, was born July 10th, 1767, at Windsor Place. He inherited from his father the Windsor estate upon the death of his parent, and managed the same with success until the spring of 1848, a period of about fifty years. When a young man, he was a member of a troop of horse that was sent by the government to the northern part of the State to repress Fries' insurrection. He was married in 1799 to Catharine, daughter of the eminent divine, John Carmichael, of Brandywine Forks, Chester county, Pennsylvania. He was a member of the Legislature in the years 1804 and 1805. He represented Lancaster county in Congress from 1807 until 1811, during the stormy period that preceded the war of 1812 with Great Britain. He died April 18th, 1848, and lies buried in the Cærnarvon Presbyterian churchyard.

JENKINS, WILLIAM, brother of Robert Jenkins, was born at Windsor Place, on the 7th of July, 1779. He graduated at Princeton College, New Jersey, in 1797. He read law in the office of James Hopkins, esq., and was admitted to the bar on the 10th of August, 1801. In the winter of 1817–18, he was appointed by Governor Findley Prosecuting Attorney for the county of Lancaster, an office he filled with marked ability and fidelity for the period of twenty-three years. In 1845 he was appointed by Governor Shunk Recorder of the Mayor's Court, the duties of which office he discharged until the abolition of the said court in 1849. From that period he appeared but little in public; declining years and infirmity forbidding it. He died at his residence on Duke street, May 24th, 1853. As a lawyer, Mr. Jenkins stood in the first rank of that list of eminent men who, in the old history of the Lancaster bar, rendered it so celebrated throughout the commonwealth. He was an able jurist, and a well-read lawyer; a safe counsellor and an eloquent advocate, winning his way to the hearts of the jury with a resistless power, and presenting to the court the strong legal points of his case with a tact and energy that seldom failed of its effect. Always courteous to his opponents, he never for a moment, however, forgot the interests of his client, but seemed to become, as it were, identified with his cause. To young men entering upon the profession, his kindness was great, and he was ever ready to instruct or assist them. His mind was eminently a legal one, and a superior knowledge of law may be said to have been his distinguishing characteristic. Never an active politician, he was nevertheless firm and decided in his opinions, yielding to all the privilege of entertaining and expressing their convictions, and never permitting political to interfere with his personal feelings. In the domestic circle Mr. Jenkins was an ornament. As a husband and father he had no superior; and as a hospitable gentleman, his home was proverbial. His hand and heart were open to his friends, as was his purse to the afflicted and needy.

JOHNS, JOHN, elected Register in 1857.

*JONES, JOHN, was born in Chester county, Pennsylvania, in 1756, and died in Little Britain township, February 2d, 1800. In early manhood he removed to the vicinity of Peach Bottom, Lancaster county, where he purchased land and erected thereon a mill and fine mansion—the latter in the old English style of architecture. This building was nicknamed "Jones's Folly," now known as the "Red House." He was the first to have slate taken from the hills on the eastern shore of the Susquehanna. Entering into the manufacture of iron, he built a forge on the Octoraro, called "Octoraro Forge." These buildings, as well as his mansion near Peach Bottom, were covered with roofing slate. John Jones, in addition to being a man of business, possessed a fine literary taste. In early life he was subjected to much bodily affliction as well as severe trials, partly arising from the course of military operations, at that time progressing. These, however, operating on a remarkably susceptible and intelligent mind, were embraced as profitable incitements to seek for a more intimate internal acquaintance with God, the great source of true consolation. Hereby his views of the divine sufficiency became enlarged to the production of an operative faith—his tribulations, agreeably with the apos-

*Contributed by Charles H. Stubbs, M. D.

tolic testimony, working "patience, and patience experience, and experience hope." Continuing his religious progress, he in time became an approved Minister of the Gospel in the Society of Friends ; and as his experience in the spirituality of the Christian dispensation advanced, he was sometimes drawn in the power of divine love to unfold to large congregations to whom he ministered in a very remarkable and impressive manner the deep and solemn mysteries of the Gospel of Christ. His natural disposition was remarkably cheerful, his manners engaging, and his social conversation pleasingly instructive ; his rational faculties were strong and lively, and his judgment in natural things prompt and discriminative.

John Jones, towards the latter part of his life, wrote a religious work entitled, Analysis of Revelation. This volume was published after his death by his friend and admirer, Joseph Churchman.

K.

KAUFFMAN, ABRAHAM, son of David Kauffman, was born in Rapho township, Lancaster county, March 30th, 1799. His father moved to a farm in what was then the southwestern part of Warwick (now Penn) township, where Abraham has lived up to this time. His father died January 15th, 1846, aged 75 years, 1 month and 8 days. His mother died March 11th, 1867, aged 87 years, 2 months and 26 days. He was brought up to agricultural pursuits. He lived chiefly in private life, save his being entrusted with several minor positions, until 1835, when he was elected to the House of Representatives. It was during this session that the first appropriation was made toward commencing the Gettysburg railroad, and here he differed from all his colleagues from the county in taking a stand against it, while they supported it, and continued to do so during the second session he was in the House. After giving his last vote against it in 1838, he put his reasons for so doing on the journal, April 16th, 1838. Page 1156, House Journal.

It may be stated that after the State had expended nearly $1,000,000 on the doubtful project, it was abandoned. He was again elected to the House of Representatives in 1836. It was during this session that the surplus revenue of the United States, by resolution of Congress, (session of 1835–6,) distributing said surplus among the several States, fell into the hands of the Legislature, Pennsylvania's share being nearly $4,000,000, and wishing to secure a portion of it to the people direct, offered a joint resolution, February 20th, 1837, (House Journal, Vol. I, p. 563,) authorizing the State Treasurer to redeem $2,000,000 of the State indebtedness. February 23d, (page 593,) on motion, the said resolution was considered in committee of the whole, when, after considerable discussion, the opposition succeeded in having it postponed to March 13th, when it could not be reached again. At this time there was a strong improvement feeling, and log-rolling the order of the day. The said surplus was all scattered to various projects, excepting $500,000, which was distributed amongst the several school districts of the State. He was again elected to the House of Representatives in 1837, and again under the new constitution, in 1843, and served during the session of 1844. In 1850 he was elected a director of the poor for Lancaster county. He was reëlected in 1853, of which board he was president during the last five years. February 11th, 1865, he assisted in organizing the Manheim National Bank, of which institution he has been president up to this time. In the year 1869 he made a donation to the borough of Manheim, of three acres of woodland, containing a spring of water, near said town, to be used as a public grove. This the town council properly named after the donor.

KAUFFMAN, ANDREW I., a member of the Legislature in 1836.

KAUFFMAN, BENJAMIN, a member of the Legislature in 1801.

KAUFFMAN, BENJAMIN, a member of the Legislature in 1839. He was also elected Clerk of Orphans' Court in 1845.

KAUFFMAN, C. L., elected a member of the Legislature in 1856.

KAUFFMAN, Dr. Michael, one of the five brothers, named Christian, John, Michael, David, and Isaac, sons of John Kauffman, was born March 5th, 1767, near what is now Landisville, in East Hempfield township, Lancaster county, Pennsylvania. His younger years were spent on the farm, when he learned the millwright trade. About 1790 he bought a mill in Rapho township, which business he followed for some years, when he moved to Manheim, where, with his brother John, he went into the hardware business for a few years, when he commenced studying medicine with Dr. Bard, and commenced practicing about 1803 and followed it up to the time of his death. In 1831 he was elected to the House of Representatives and reëlected in 1832; during these several sessions he attended industriously to his duties as a representative. This long usefulness in the vicinity in which he lived, can perhaps not be better described than they are given in the following obituary notice:

"Dr. Michael Kauffman died at his residence in the borough of Manheim, on Sunday morning, July 7th, 1839 aged 72 years, 4 months and 6 days. His earthly remains were interred on the following day at two o'clock, p. m., attended by an unusually large concourse of relatives and friends. Impressive addresses were delivered on the occasion by Revs. Messrs. Jacob Hochstetter and Daniel Fritz, on verse 22d, 16th chapter, Book of Job: 'When a few years are come then I shall go the way whence I shall not return.' It is seldom that one is called from amongst us whose loss will be more extensively felt and more deeply deplored than that of the individual whose name heads this obituary notice. He has been a resident and an extensive practitioner of medicine upwards of forty years; he was liberal and ever ready to render assistance to the distressed. Of him it may be truly said, the poor have lost a friend. After his death many, very many, called to get a last sight of him for whom they had at one time or another, during life, sent in the hour of suffering."

KAUFFMAN, Michael, and family, emigrated from the vicinity of Greenstad, Hesse, on the upper Rhine, and came to this county between the years 1710 and 1719, and settled somewhere not now known. Michael died a few years after their arrival. The widow next died, leaving a son John and a daughter Elizabeth. The guardian of these children bought of William Penn's commissioner a considerable tract of land, in the vicinity now known as Landisville, Lancaster county, Pa., where the said John Kauffman settled. All that is known of Elizabeth is, that she was married to Christian Stoneman, December 12th, 1734. The said John Kauffman had three sons, Christian, Michael and John. John Kauffman lived on the farm now owned by Samuel Nissley, about one mile from Landisville, where he died March 24th, 1776, aged 48 years, 6 months and 12 days. His widow died December 22d, 1806. They had nine children grown up and married, viz: Maria, Anna, Christian, Barbara, John, Michael, Elizabeth, David and Isaac, besides two, Anna and Susanna, who died minors. This family has now all passed away.

KEENAN, REV. BERNARD, was born in the county of Tyrone, Ireland, and was early designed by his parents for the clerical profession. He began the study of the classics in the seminaries of his neighborhood, and as soon as he was qualified, entered the college of Dungannon, where he remained as a student for four years. He was then engaged as a teacher in that institution, and thus occupied for the next seven years, having been the first Catholic who had been known to be employed as a teacher in the Protestant college of Dungannon. Having made up his mind to leave his native home, he proposed going to France; but as the Right Reverend Bishop Conwell was then on his way to London to be consecrated Bishop of Philadelphia, he accompanied him to Liverpool, where he remained until the Bishop returned, and thence sailed with him to the United States. They landed at Baltimore on the 21st of November, 1820, and from thence they proceeded to Philadelphia, where the subject of this notice was ordained priest, having been the first priest ever ordained in the Philadelphia conference. Shortly after his ordination he went to Mount St. Mary's College, near Emmettsburg, Maryland, where he remained until the death of the Rev. J. J. Holland, of St. Mary's church, Lancaster, in the fall of 1823. During the period he spent at Emmettsburg he assisted in giving instruction to young men pursuing their studies, for which his superior linguistic attainments amply fitted him. Before leaving Ireland he had taught for a time in a gentleman's family. He was appointed by the Bishop of the diocese to fill the vacancy existing in St. Mary's Church, a position he has held uninterruptedly up to the present time. While in Philadelphia, and prior to his appointment to the Lancaster charge, he was believed to be in the last stages of consumption, his physicians pronouncing the left lobe of his lungs as entirely gone with that disease.

The duties pertaining to the pastorship of St. Mary's church at the period of his first appointment, were very arduous, and the labors devolving upon him onerous; the Catholic clergymen in America were at that time few in number, and not one-half that were actually needed; it therefore devolved upon him, in connection with his duties at Lancaster, to attend at alternate periods the missions of Harrisburg, Lebanon, Colebrook, Elizabethtown and Columbia. This district now occupies the services of twelve pastors. Catholic clergymen are required to attend in cases of sickness to the calls of any member of their congregations; the Catholic, as is well known, in his last illness in all cases requires the ministrations of his spiritual pastor in order to have the last sacraments of the church administered to him; and this branch of ministerial work devolved upon Father Keenan an immense amount of labor, that we of the present generation can scarcely realize. This was particularly the case during the time that the public works were in progress, and oft was it necessary for him to cross the Susquehanna in a frail canoe, and spend day after day among the poor of his flock, in supplying spiritual food for their souls. For nearly half a century has this devoted servant of Christ labored in our midst in the discharge of his pastoral duties. It would be difficult to cite a similar example, that of a pastor officiating above forty-eight years for one congregation, a circumstance that in itself speaks volumes in his favor. The old stone church in which he commenced his labors still stands, though built more than a century since, (in 1762.) In front of it, however, has been erected one of the finest churches in the State, a lasting monument of the zeal manifested by himself and his congregation. During the absence of Bishop Shannahan at the Ecumenical Council at Rome, in 1870, Father Keenan was designated in lieu of him, the administrator of the Diocese of Harrisburg. He is a fine classical scholar, being master of the Greek, Latin and Hebrew languages, and has also a ready acquaintance with the French. One trait in the character of the subject of this notice which deserves special mention, and that which has endeared him to all classes, both Catholics and Protestants, and which displays itself in all his actions and language, is his " charity," which lies at the basis of all true religion. Bigotry with him never found any countenance. In his discourses, the doctrines of his dissenting brethren were never maligned or impugned. Each individual who at any time has heard any of his sermons, must have felt at its close that although differing in modes of faith, yet that as fellow Christians we should practice the golden maxim, " to love one another."

KEENE, GEORGE W., was elected Clerk of the Orphans' Court in 1869.

KELLER, SAMUEL, a nephew of Peter Holl, was elected County Commissioner in 1825. He was a citizen of Warwick township, and for many years the owner of the well-known Litiz mill. He was an excellent and upright citizen. His sons have emigrated to Virginia, and are now engaged in the iron business.

KEMPER, DAVID, was elected County Commissioner in 1862.

KENDIG, FRANCIS, was a member of the Legislature in 1822.

KENEAGY, SAMUEL, son of Henry Keneagy, was born June 20th, 1820. Having received an education, finishing the same in the Strasburg academy, he began the study of medicine in the office of Dr. F. S. Burrowes, in 1842. He attended the Jefferson Medical College in Philadelphia, and graduated in the spring of 1844. He began the practice of medicine in Strasburg with fair success. He ever took a warm interest in politics, and in 1858 he was nominated and elected to the Pennsylvania Legislature, and reëlected the following year. During the rebellion he was for a short time surgeon in the 50th Pennsylvania regiment, under Col.

Franklin. In 1868 he accepted, for one year, a professorship of anatomy, physiology and hygiene in the State Agricultural College, in Centre county, Pennsylvania. After the expiration of his term, he removed to Lancaster city, and resumed the practice of medicine.

KENEAGY, ULRICH, was born in Berks county, Pennsylvania, and emigrated therefrom in 1795, and settled near Kinzer station, in Lancaster county. His ancestors were of the Omish persuasion, and came from Switzerland about the middle of the 17th century. The name was originally spelled Gnege, afterwards Knege, and now Keneagy. Ulrich, in 1805 moved to near Paradise, then Strasburg township, and followed farming. He had three sons, viz: John, Henry and David. The latter died about 1807. John had one son and a daughter. Henry married Sarah, the eldest daughter of Christian Shertz, in 1809, and had seven sons and two daughters. He died in 1845, aged 63 years.

KENNEDY, MAXWELL, a Lancaster county Legislator, was born in Warren county, New Jersey, May 1st, 1782. He emigrated with his father and his family to Salisbury township, Lancaster county. In the war of 1812 he volunteered as aid to General Watson, and marched to York, Pa., and from there to Baltimore, arriving the day after the battle, in time to assist in burying the dead. His division was sent from there to Elkton, Maryland, and he was appointed Major of one of the divisions. On account of his powerful voice and military knowledge, he was at one time drill officer of the division. The following incident may be mentioned while he was in the army at Elkton: A rumor was put in circulation that the British had landed on the opposite side of the bay, and were marching up towards the town. That night General Watson received orders to take twelve of his most trusty men, cross the bridge, and go down and reconnoitre the enemy. Mr. Kennedy was one of the chosen twelve. They crossed the bridge, expecting every moment to come in contact with the enemy. After marching some distance, the sentinel fired off his gun. All was ordered ready, when the sentinel cried quarters. The General asked where the enemy was, and was told there was no enemy there. When asked why he had done so, he replied that he was so ordered by his superiors. The party returned back to town, and the matter was investigated. There were two reasons assigned for this transaction: One was, that the commander wished to try the bravery of General Watson; and the other was, that the citizens of Elkton, who they were defending, were not supplying them with suitable provisions, and they wanted an excuse to leave. In the morning the place was deserted; the inhabitants, fearing danger, had quit the place; and the soldiers were only retained by fair promises of better accommodations, and which were fully realized until the time of their departure, when affairs at New Orleans rendered their stay no longer necessary, and they were discharged to their homes and families.

Maxwell Kennedy was elected a member of the Legislature in 1835 without any solicitation, and declined being a candidate the next year on account of failing health. Having led a very active life, close confinement did not agree with him. He died from cancer of the stomach, after a lingering illness, August 30th, 1845. He was a member of the Presbyterian Church, and an influential man in the community.

KERFOOT, DR. GEORGE B.,[1] was born in the city of Dublin, June 27th, 1808. He emigrated to America when about 11 years of age, and when aged 15 he entered the employ of Dr. Samuel Humes, of Lancaster, as a shop boy, and the doctor perceiving in him a peculiar brightness, induced him to study medicine. After having studied medicine he took up the study of Latin and Greek, and

[1] December 20th, 1838, Henry Cobler Mussulman, who was under sentence of death for the murder of Lazarus Zellerbach, sold his body for five dollars to Dr. Kerfoot, in order that it might be dissected after he was hung. The assignment of sale is yet preserved, and is in the handwriting of George Ford, esq., and is witnessed by the writer of it and Capt. John Wise.

In this connection the other executions in Lancaster county may be enumerated. Prior to 1770 no record of any such is preserved. From the year 1770 till 1780 several executions took place. During this decade at least five persons were hung in Lancaster county for various offences; other crimes than murder being then punished with death. A man named "Jockey Jones," was hung for horse stealing; Catharine Fisher for infanticide; Capt. Taylor for highway robbery; a colored man for

unaided he made considerable proficiency therein. He also studied the German, and was able to read it with great ease and fluency. He attended the medical lectures of Jefferson College, in Philadelphia, and graduated March, 1830. He immediately began in Lancaster the practice of the profession, and soon succeeded in acquiring a lucrative practice. In a few years he rose to great distinction, and ranked amongst the ablest in the profession. He was one of the main instruments in establishing the Lancaster County Medical Society. He established an anatomical hall, and was in the habit of giving lectures during the winter to numbers of students. At one time the number of his students reached sixty. Dr. John McCalla was numbered amongst his students. The Rev. Mr. Bahnson and many other intellectual men frequented his lectures during the winter season. He was for several years a leading member of the Lancaster school board, and also of the city councils. Dr. Kerfoot died in 1851, leaving a large and lucrative practice, aged 43 years, 3 months and 16 days. Dr. Kerfoot was an ardent and active Democrat, and was a frequent contributor to the Lancaster papers, especially to the *Intelligencer*. He was possessed of a poetic genius, and wrote some poems of great merit. He was frequently summoned as a witness to testify in medical cases before the courts in Baltimore, Harrisburg, and elsewhere, especially where critical questions were to be decided. He, on several occasions, delivered public lectures on the eyes and brain, those parts of the human system to which he had given the most study. On the Haggerty trial

rape, committed upon a white woman ; and Samuel Brandt for killing his own father and setting the dwelling house on fire. From 1780 until 1822 no person was hung in Lancaster county. On the 25th of October, 1822, John Lechler was executed for the murder of his wife, Mary Lechler. Daniel Sheaffer was hung April 13th, 1832, for the murder of a widow, named Bowers, living in Marietta. Sheaffer was convicted upon his own confession, alleging that the reproaches of his conscience no longer permitted him to conceal his crime. He voluntarily surrendered himself, and was committed, tried and executed. Henry Smith (colored) was hung May 11th, 1838, for the murder of Benjamin Peart, of Columbia. This execution took place in the jail yard, and was the first which was carried into execution after the passage of the law abolishing public executions. John Haggerty was, in 1847, executed for the murder of Melchoir Fordney and a woman named Catharine

he was the principal witness. Dr. Kerfoot was a leading member of the Masonic fraternity, being at the time of his death District Deputy Grand Master. He was proverbial for his charity, and but for this trait in his character he might have accumulated a vast fortune from his medical practice.

KEYS, RICHARD, was a member of the Legislature in the years 1795, 1796, 1797, 1798, 1799 and 1800.

KIEFFER, CHRISTIAN, was elected a member of the Legislature in the year 1840, and reëlected in 1841. He was three times elected Mayor of the city of Lancaster in the years 1852, 1853 and 1854.

KIMMEL, JACOB, a member of the Legislature in 1803, 1805, 1806, 1807, 1808 and 1809.

KING, ROBERT, one of the early settlers of Little Britain township, emigrated from Ireland, and came to Lancaster county about 1717. He took up a tract of 150 acres of land and followed agricultural pursuits. His son, John, was a clergyman, and became pastor of the congregation, of which the father of James Buchanan[1] was a member. Robert King, one of the descendants of the first settler of this name, was born January 2d, 1789. He marched in 1814 as lieutenant of a company, under Dr. James McCulloch as captain; and when the latter was promoted to be surgeon of the regiment, Mr. King succeeded to the captaincy of the company. For many years he served as colonel of the Lancaster militia.

Tripple, as also one of her children. Alexander Anderson and Henry Richards (both colored) were executed in April, 1858, for the murders of Mrs. Garber and Mrs. Ream, of Manheim township.

Before the period of the abolition of public executions the executioners wore masks, and the condemned criminals were taken from their place of confinement, placed upon their own coffin in a cart, and driven through the streets, directly under the gallows, often amid the hoots and jeers of the excited populace. The public parade thus made of the prisoner, and the consequent spectacle of the execution, were supposed to be calculated to intimidate offenders from the perpetration of like offences. It came, however, to be believed that the object aimed at was not attained, and public sensibility at length revolting at the idea of public executions, they were discontinued.

[1] Rev. John King was the first to perceive the remarkable ability of James Buchanan, when a boy, and it was he who first suggested to his

*KING, VINCENT, son of Vincent and Mary King, was born in Little Britain township, (in that part now included in Fulton), Lancaster county, in the year 1786. His mother's maiden name was Brown; she was a daughter of Joshua Brown, a distinguished minister among the Friends. Her ancestors have been traced back long prior to the days of William Penn, many of them having come over from England soon after Penn's settlements on the Delaware.

His paternal grandfather was James King, an early settler in this neighborhood. The father of the subject of this sketch had six children, as follows: Joshua, James, Vincent, Jeremiah, Mary and Hannah. Vincent, the third son, in early youth was known as a remarkably active boy, of a kind disposition, and possessed of a lively imagination. His parents being strict Friends, he was sent to Westtown school, an institution under the fostering care of that Society, to receive a thorough English education. He remained at this school several terms, and while there the following incident took place, which may have had a tendency to lead him to pursue the study of medicine and adopt the practice of it as an avocation in after-life. One of the students was attacked with what was then termed typhus fever, and to use a common phrase, was "given up to die" by the attending physician. Vincent King—a brother student—became much interested in the case, and asked permission of the superintendent to nurse and attend upon the pupil, who had now ceased to receive much aid from the physician in charge of the institution. Permission was granted, and young King assumed charge of the patient, watching him night and day, prescribing and caring for his school-mate. Finally, the sick student recovered, and, we are informed, is yet living at an advanced age. This success with his first patient led Vincent parents the propriety of affording him an education. It has been told us, by an aged citizen, that upon one occasion when James Buchanan was dismissed from Dickinson College, for some student delinquency, his parents applied to Rev. King to have him re-instated. This the Rev. King accomplished, he being at the time one of the trustees of the institution, and for this act of kindness Mr. Buchanan ever bore his early pastor a lasting good-will.

*Contributed by Charles H. Stubbs, M. D.

King to inquire further into the mysteries of the healing art, and while he remained at this school he was called doctor, by pupils and teachers.

Leaving Westtown, he at once chose the profession of medicine, and with this end in view, repaired in company with his brother, Jeremiah, to Philadelphia—then, as it is now, the seat of medical science in this country. Here he entered the office of Dr. Houston, an eminent practitioner of that city, and after preparing himself, entered and attended a regular course of lectures in the medical department of the University of Pennsylvania. He graduated in the class of 1807. The same year in which he received his degree of Doctor of Medicine, he was united in marriage to Phœbe Trimble, daughter of William Trimble, of Uwchland township, Chester county. Immediately after marriage he settled in Philadelphia, and practiced his profession in that city for about two years; he then removed to Goshen, Chester county, and while there obtained an extensive practice. Being of an unsettled state of mind, he remained in this location but a short time, and thence migrated to Baltimore, Md., and finally to Columbia, Pa. At the last named place he met with great affliction in the loss of his wife, who was removed from earth after a short illness. Her decease took place in the year 1816, in the 28th year of her age. Dr. King remained a widower five years, and married Patience Wright, in the year 1821. From the time of the decease of his first wife until his marriage with the second, he remained and practiced medicine at Columbia. After the second marriage he removed to Little Britain, near the place of his birth, and resided with his mother and brother. Here he at once entered into a large practice, which continued to increase every year.

Being called to see a patient at Webb's forge, he was suddenly taken ill, and so violently held that he could not be removed to his residence. After lingering a few days, surrounded by friends anxious that he should recover, he departed this life on the 2d of December, 1825, aged 39 years. In his last illness he was fully sensible of his precarious condition, and in answer to some friend who was solicitous of his welfare, he replied, that he "must die as well as others, and that they must be willing to give him up." He was the father of five children, viz: Mary Ann, Lydia T., Jane P., William T., and Jeremiah. All the sons died in infancy— the eldest daughter dying in her thirteenth year; only two survive, Lydia T., and Jane P., now Mrs. Edge.

Dr. King was a man of talent and was well posted in his profession, being on intimate terms with some of the most distinguished medical men of his day. In person, he possessed a fine and commanding appearance; and in his movements was quick and vivacious. Gifted with rare conversational powers, he was well calculated to succeed and become eminent in his profession. While he practiced in different localities, several students, in order to avail themselves of the advantages to be derived from the counsels of so able and worthy a practitioner, studied medicine under his direction. Among the number were Dr. Glatz, of Marietta, and Dr. Jeremiah B. Stubbs, of Fulton. Dr. King was not only learned in his profession, but was familiar with the old English poets, and, to some extent, cultivated an innate taste for the muses. Even when engaged in a laborious practice, he would devote occasional hours to reading and writing verse. On the deaths of his aged mother and his little sons, he wrote several stanzas, filled with sorrowful reflections that pervaded his mind at the time of these afflictions. These we have failed to secure.

In concluding this sketch, we insert two of his poetical productions, one an extempore piece, the other

"A MONODY ON THE DEATH OF HIS WIFE."

Alas! Maria is no more; dread death,
With vengeful ire has hurled his missive dart,
And left me here to languish out my days,
To weep unseen in deepest solitude,
And mourn amidst the giddy scenes of men.
My comfort and my love of life is fled—
In one dread hour was severed from my soul;
Deep consternation, awful reveries flowed
Throughout each day and melancholy night—
Oh! had I met my lasting, final fate,
Ere manhood raised for me her spotted crown,
And fired me with ambition's wild career!

Then had I slept in undisturbed repose,
Unconscious of the sweeping scythe of time.
Dear Maria's image dwells with me,
And may her virtues long vibrate my heart;
Her soothing voice amid afflictions sore,
Buoyed up my soul and checked the rising tear;
When death his double mission had performed
And paralyzed, as with electric flash,
Two blooming boys, just raised to interest dear,
To show their pressing wants and smile assent,
And joyous chatter all the livelong day;
Bereft of these, in deep affliction bathed,
She sighed and with a pious soul resigned,
Proclaimed that God who gave had a right to take,
To call away in youth or hoary age.

EXTEMPORE.

Great Architect of worlds above, below,
Who formed the soul and taught its fires to glow;
Whose mighty fiat rules and reigns above,
Thou Being of all beings, God of love,
Oh teach us to be wise and prize Thee more
Than earthly wealth and all its chequered store.
Without Thee all creation is but dust,
Delivered o'er to death and warring lust,
Confusion dread would overwhelm the whole,
And darkness and despair appall the soul,
But with Thee we are rich without alloy,
All beauty, order and consummate joy.

KINZER, Dr. E., elected to the State Senate in 1851.

KIRK, Jacob, elected a member of the Legislature in 1823 and 1825.

KITTERA, John W., son of Thomas Kittera, was born in East Earl township, Lancaster county. He graduated at Princeton College, New Jersey, in 1776, and afterwards practiced law at Lancaster. He represented Lancaster county in Congress from 1791 until 1801, a period of ten years. He was then appointed United States District Attorney for the eastern district of Pennsylvania, and removed to Philadelphia. He was a man of fine personal appearance, and exceedingly gentlemanly and polite in his intercourse with his fellow-citizens.

KONIGMACHER, Joseph, was a native of Lancaster county, and a man of high standing and influence in the

25

community in which he lived. He was the proprietor of the popular summer resort at Ephrata—the Mountain Springs hotel. In 1837–38 he was a member of the Reform Convention, called for the amendment of the State Constitution, and although at the time young and inexperienced in legislation, he discharged his duties with great credit to himself and his constituents. He strongly opposed the law that compelled the people of any school district to accept the Free School System of education contrary to their wishes, and he favored a system by which the Germans could have their children taught German if they choose. In 1838 he was nominated and elected a member of the Legislature, and was reëlected in 1839. As a legislator, he took an active part in all questions of general and local policy, and distinguished himself by the production of one of the ablest documents that ever emanated from our legislative halls—*The Report on an Asylum for the Insane Poor.* Mr. Konigmacher was, in 1846, recommended by the Whig convention of Lancaster county as a candidate for Canal Commissioner, and he served during that same year as one of the members of the Whig State Central Committee. In 1848 he was nominated and elected to the State Senate of Pennsylvania, the duties of which office he discharged with entire satisfaction. He died at Michael's hotel, in the city of Lancaster, April 4th, 1861. In politics he was a strong and enthusiastic Whig, and always exerted himself—whether in public or private life— to promote the success of the principles of his party. While in office, it was his aim to endeavor to introduce the principles in which he believed, into the administration of the State government. In his youth he had been a mechanic, and in feeling was strongly identified, and always deservedly popular with the laboring classes. In his disposition he was kind, genial, and open-hearted, and was possessed of a singular sweetness in his deportment and great amiability of manners.

*KRAMPH, FREDERIC JOHN, was born near the village of Schleiesbach, in the valley of Auc, about three miles from the city of Heidelberg, in the Grand Duchy of Baden, on the

*Contributed by S. S. Rathvon.

11th of March, 1811. The paternal residence was an humble cottage, about half a mile from the banks of the Necker, and his ancestors were plain, honest fishermen, and members of the German Reformed church, highly esteemed by the community in which they resided. At about six years of age he was placed in an excellent school for children, in Heidelberg, his mother having removed to that place—having lost his father before he was born—where he remained until after the death of his mother, in 1819, when he was just eight years old. He was then placed in the Orphans' Asylum of Heidelberg, where he remained until he had attained his fourteenth year, and where he patiently endured all the deprivations and hardships incidental to such institutions at that period, in a monarchical government. The *curriculum* of the Asylum included among other things, the preparation of its inmates for "confirmation" in the German Reformed church, and after that event was consummated with our subject, he was bound apprentice to Herr Schulemyer, until he was twenty years of age, and taught the art and mystery of the tailoring trade. He was always active, obedient, and intelligent; and in every position he occupied throughout his life, he always shared largely of the popular esteem. Of course, situated as he was, his educational means were very limited, but he was always fond of reading, and availed himself of every opportunity to gratify his love of books. He was religiously predisposed, and in his reading did not forget to include the Bible, and at a very early age possessed himself of a copy. Before he was twenty-one, he had read nearly all of Cooper's novels that had then been translated into German, and the reading of these works gave birth to the *desire* to ultimately emigrate to, and make his home in America. Having neither father nor mother, sister nor brother, nor any more remote relative that manifested any special interest in him, there were, therefore, no special ties of consanguinity to bind him to his fatherland.

He spent about eighteen months in traveling through his own country and adjoining German States, after the end of his apprenticeship, working at his trade at intervals to obtain the necessary means; but as the traveling of journeymen mechanics, at that period, was always performed on foot, his wants were easily supplied. Indeed, there were facilities afforded to pedestrians, in many of the German States at that period, that America has perhaps never known. At the convents, monasteries, and the houses of the rich and the noble along the public roads, a special mug of beer or wine, with a slice of brown bread, was reserved for the way-passer, and which he could claim, and was accorded to him as a *privilege.* Returning to Heidelberg in the early spring, after some preparation he proceeded in company with others to the city of Manheim, where he bid a final adieu to his native land in the blooming month of June, and sailed for America, landing at the city of Baltimore in August, 1832. When he landed at Baltimore he had but a single *Heller*[1] in his purse; all had been exhausted during the long passage. After working about a week in Baltimore, and finding business dull, full of hope and trust in the leadings of Providence —a trust that never forsook him during his entire life—he struck out for the interior of our vast country on foot, and in due time reached the borough of York, Pennsylvania, where he obtained employment. Learning, however, that his employer was *bad pay*, he left his service and demanded the wages that were due him. This being withheld or refused, he was advised to sue him, which he accordingly did, and brought him before a justice "forthwith" on a *capias*, and obtained his money. Being at this time without a Bible, with these wages he immediately purchased a copy, and was again alone in the world with only a few shillings in his purse, and out of employment. Retiring to a wood near the town, he there knelt down under the shade of a friendly tree, and poured forth his fervent thanks to the Almighty for the blessings he enjoyed in a land of liberty, for in his own country justice could not have been thus obtained so speedily.

Returning to the town again, he met Mr. John Bell, of Marietta, in search of a journeyman tailor, and immediately went into his service, and accompanied him to that place, where he remained until January, 1833. We record these

---

[1] Five *Hellers* are equivalent to *one* United States cent.

peculiar events here, because our subject made it a rule of life always to do his whole duty so far as he had an opportunity and ability to do it, and then to "wait patiently on the Lord," feeling assured that " He would bring it to pass," so far as was best for his temporal and spiritual welfare. At Marietta he contracted friendships that continued throughout his entire life, and there he also made progress in acquiring a knowledge of the English language, and in acquainting himself with English literature, and learning the modes and manners of his adopted country. He left Marietta on foot, in mid-winter, and visited Lancaster, Reading, Lebanon, and Hummelstown, in search of employment, but was not successful until he reached the last named place, and his pecuniary means, through a liberality which was a leading characteristic in him, were again nearly exhausted. Here he made himself so useful and was so highly esteemed by his employer, that he offered extra inducements for him to remain and take a partnership in his business, but as those inducements contemplated a contingency not within the category of his immediate future intention, he therefore left this town, at the opening of early spring, and wended his way to Harrisburg, the capital of the State. Here he made application for employment at every tailoring establishment in the place without success. Much exhausted, but still hopeful, he entered a German "Gast-House," near the terminus of the only bridge that then spanned the Susquehanna at that place, and called for a "shepley bier," and the ever accompanying "pretzel," to recuperate his tired energies. Finding the host a native of his own "fatherland," he soon entered into a cheerful and interesting conversation with him, which was only interrupted by the entrance of another visitor.

This visitor was a Mr. Backstresser, from New Cumberland, a village in the southeastern angle of Cumberland county, where the Yellow-breeches creek empties into the Susquehanna river, and he was in search of a tailor to take charge of business in a room next to his store in that place. The host immediately referred him to Mr. Kramph, who still sat at the table sipping his beer, as a person he thought would suit him, and an engagement was soon made with him to go and set up business for himself in New Cumberland. After a visit to a hardware store to procure a tailor's iron, an extra pair of shears, and other necessary implements, he at once accompanied Mr. B. to the village, and began a new and active career of life in America. At this place he remained until the spring of 1840, a period of seven years, during which time he made many warm friends, and accumulated some property. Here he obtained his naturalization papers, identified himself with the interests and policies of our institutions, and entered into the progressive spirit of our country; and, perhaps, few men have become so thoroughly Americanized in so short a time as he was, and no man could possibly have manifested more gratitude than he did for the blessings he enjoyed in a land of liberty. Always of temperate, studious, and industrious habits, he had no idle hours, for those fragments of time not necessarily devoted to business, were employed in the cultivation of his mind; and as aids to this end, he commenced to accumulate English and German books, gave some attention to the natural sciences, and kept up a regular correspondence with a few intellectual friends in his native land. Perhaps the greatest turning point in his life took place during the latter years of his residence in New Cumberland. His religious sentiments had, however, undergone a change, and he became deeply imbued with the doctrines of *Restorationism.* His ultimate aim, also, was a settlement somewhere in the great West, and from causes, real or imaginary, he had made a semi-resolve never to enter into marriage.

During the winter of 1835 or 1836 an exciting religious revival took place at New Cumberland, and many of his friends and neighbors became seriously but too temporarily affected. One evening, after the dismissal of the congregation, perhaps half a dozen of the better class of young men of the town assembled at his shop, and the conversation was on the subject of religion. One said, for his part, he was a Presbyterian, another was a Lutheran, another a Baptist, a German Reformed, and so on until all had expressed their religious preferences, except Mr. Kramph. "Well, Frederic," said one, " What is your faith ?" Being religiously unsettled

in mind, he casually replied, "I am a Swedenborgian."
Now, he had never read a line of Swedenborg in his life, and
never had heard his name until he had heard it mentioned
by a passenger on board the ship during his voyage from
Europe, and then only as a great *seer* in connection with the
"Seeress of Prevorst" and others. "Oh!" said one of the
young men, "We have a book at our house written by
Swedenborg, which we found on taking possession of the
premises sticking under one of the rafters on the garret."
According to promise, the book was brought the next day
to Mr. Kramph. It was "Heaven and Hell," translated from
the Latin by Rev. Thomas Hartly, of England, with a long
preface. Busy as he was, he immediately read the preface
and fell to deeply thinking; then laid it aside for a few
weeks, and read it again and again. He then read the book
itself and reflected, and then read it again. At this second
reading, he drank it in as the ultimatum of theological truth
as fast as he was capable of receiving it. He soon thereafter
made the acquaintance of the venerable Joseph Ehrenfried,
then State printer at Harrisburg, and through him, of
Henry Keffer, and Louis C. Iungerich, of Lancaster city,
and he borrowed or purchased the works of Swedenborg,
and the collateral literature of the church as rapidly as time,
means, and opportunity afforded; and so far as he understood them, he received their doctrines as the truth, without
a doubt, and also tried to the best of his ability to *live* them.

In 1836 a small society of Swedenborgians was formed,
and met for worship in Lancaster city, and Mr. Kramph
became a member of it, and this induced him to visit that
place more frequently and to form a more intimate acquaintance with its members and the church in general, than would
otherwise have existed, which lead to the turning point
before alluded to, and which took place about three years
afterwards, for he had sold his property and had even made
a purchase of some western town lots with a view of settling
there. Whilst on a visit to Lancaster in 1839, his friends
there suggested a settlement in that city instead of the west,
when he accordingly changed his mind and removed thither in
the month of March, 1840, and commenced the business of a

merchant tailor and clothier. He was the first man that gave impulse to merchant tailoring in Lancaster city. Previous to his location there, but one small establishment of the kind, with a very limited stock, existed there, and there was much prejudice against it by those whose interests it seemed to conflict with. At this time there are at least a dozen such establishments in the place, and the stock in them from a few hundreds of dollars has increased to many thousands. His active, energetic mind, found a wider field here for the display of its powers, and he soon commanded a large and a reasonably lucrative business. His affability, his social qualities, and his general integrity was such, that he made many friends, even among those who might otherwise have been his enemies. To him also, perhaps, belongs the credit of stimulating those building improvements which so conspicuously distinguishes the last twenty years of the material history of Lancaster. If the men of ample means in that city had done as much for it in proportion to their abilities, as Mr. Kramph did in proportion to his, perhaps at this day it would not have been so far outstripped in business and population as it has been by its sister city of Reading.

It is true, that other men may have since erected more splendid private residences, made more showy and convenient store improvements, and built a greater number of houses, but they have been but following his excellent and enterprising example, and have been identifying themselves with that spirit of improvement which was developed so largely through his innovations upon the old fossilized order of things, which existed prior to 1840. Nothing gave him more pleasure than to see men engaged in building up and beautifying his adopted city, except perhaps when he himself could be of any assistance to them in doing so; and hence he aided many an honest, industrious poor man, in providing himself a home, which, without his aid, he might never have accomplished. Mr. Kramph was liberal in his donations and support of all worthy enterprises; liberal in the support of religious institutions, and especially those of his own faith; liberal in his sentiments towards those who differed from him in politics and religion; liberal in his contributions to all public and private charities; and liberal in his remembrances of his family and his friends; and yet he was singularly free from ostentation, and never seemed to claim any special merit for any good he may have done. In his estimate of men, he was influenced more by their *actions* than by their *professions;* and if they were honest and pure, they were infinitely more in fraternal harmony with him than if they were intellectual and corrupt, no matter what their social and pecuniary condition may have been. He could not have been called a *wit*, and never indulged in ambiguities and double meanings, and yet he always appreciated pure witticisms in others, and was quick in perceiving their point. He was exceedingly kind, affectionate and forbearing in all his social and domestic relations, and seemed to enjoy no place on earth more than the precincts of his family circle. Although he was interested and actively engaged in the progress of the world, yet he could not, in any sense, have been called "a man of the world."

Mr. Kramph was married three times. His first marriage was in 1841, with Miss Ann, a daughter of Rev. James Robinson, a Swedenborgian minister, formerly of Derbyshire, England. The issue of this marriage was two sons and two daughters, a son and daughter of whom still survive, the other two having died in infancy. His first wife died in July, 1847, much lamented by her family and friends. He entered into marriage a second time with Miss Mary, a sister of his first wife, in October, 1848. The issue of this marriage was one daughter, which died in infancy. His second wife died in November, 1849. After these sad ruptures in his domestic relations, he broke up housekeeping, and placed his two surviving children at a boarding school, in the State of Rhode Island, and spent some months in traveling through the eastern, western and northern States, leaving his business, under his direction, in the hands of his foreman. In the autumn of 1853 he entered a third time into marriage with Miss Sarah M., a daughter of the late David Pancoast, formerly of Cincinnati, Ohio. By this marriage he had no issue. Nothing could possibly have been a truer reflex of the elevated character of the man, than his union with the pure, high-toned and intellectual women he had chosen as his married partners. Perhaps few men have been more happy and better contented, during the continuance of their marriage relations, than our subject, and more sincerely regretted their abrupt termination than he did whilst at the same time he endeavored to yield a willing resignation to the things "which seemed ordained."

Mr. Kramph was of a bilious, sanguine temperament, and perhaps inherited from his mother, a rather delicate physical constitution; and had it not been for the predominating energies of his will, his body might have succumbed long before it did. After an active and useful life in America, of twenty-six years, eighteen of which were passed in Lancaster city, he was "gathered to his fathers" on the 18th of April, 1858, aged 47 years, 1 month and 7 days.

Although Mr. Kramph never *sought* political, civil, social or literary distinction, yet he was identified with many of the progressive movements of his day. He was an active member of the select council of Lancaster city, and for many years a member of the board of school directors, and was serving in that capacity when he died. He was also one of the members of the "Old Lyceum," and nearly eighteen years a member of the "Mechanics' Library Association," and one of the few who assisted in reviving and sustaining that time-honored institution. He was one of the originators and most active sustainers of the "Lancaster New Jerusalem Society," and a life member of the "Swedenborg Printing and Publishing Society," of New York. His sustaining influence was not only exercised towards the persons and institutions of his adopted country, but he also sent liberal annuities to some needy aged friends in his native land, one of whom was his foster-mother, and for whom he always entertained a filial affection. In politics he was rather a conservative, and for twenty years had been a member of the Whig party, but was not a distinctive party man, "right or wrong," but was willing to make some concessions —other things being equal—to friendship and to local pride. Perhaps few men, in his sphere of life, have left such a favorable and lasting impression upon the minds of those who knew them, than he has; and many remember with gratitude the countenance, the encouragement, and the material support he afforded them in the beginning of a subsequent successful career in life. Few men in his circumstances have shared more largely the confidence of the community in which he lived, or have had more deference paid to their judgments on matters in general than he. He died as he had lived, with a full faith in the verities of his church, believing that in the "other life" he would be judged out of the book which he had written by his acts, intents and purposes in "this life," and that as death left him, so would judgment find him.

KREADY, J. C., was elected County Commissioner in the year 1868.

KREIDER, JACOB, the first settler of the numerous family of this name, took up eight hundred acres of land on the north side of the Conestoga, about two miles south of the city of Lancaster. He settled in Lancaster county in 1716 or 1717. His descendants are very numerous.

KREITER, BENJAMIN, was appointed Clerk of the Orphans' Court in 1829.

KRUG, JACOB, was a member of the Legislature in the year 1781.

KUCHER, CHRISTOPHER, a member of the Legislature in the years 1779, 1780, 1781 and 1782.

KUHN, ADAM SIMON, DR., son of John Christopher Kuhn, was a native of a small town of Swabia, near Heilbron, on the Neckar. He came with his father to Philadelphia in 1733. He was a man of bright natural parts, improved by the benefits of a liberal education, and he was considered as a very skillful, attentive and successful practitioner of medicine. He was a magistrate of the borough of Lancaster for many years, and an elder of Trinity Lutheran church. He was exceedingly zealous and enthusiastic in his efforts to promote classical education among the youth of the borough. For this purpose he procured the erection of a school house, in which the Greek and Latin languages were taught by skilled preceptors. There was no one amongst his cotemporaries who had at heart more the spreading of religion, and there was no place of worship throughout the whole county to which he did not liberally subscribe. The utmost pains were bestowed by him on the education of his numerous offspring, in order to enable them to become useful members of society. There is a tablet in the Lutheran church, perpetuating his memory. Dr. John Kuhn, Dr. Frederick Kuhn, and Dr. Adam Kuhn were sons of the above. Dr. John Kuhn graduated at the Academy of Pennsylvania, and afterwards at the University of Edinburg. He was a surgeon in the Revolutionary army. He first located at Reading, and married a Miss Jones of that place, and afterwards returned to Lancaster, where he practiced till his death. He was one of the leading physicians of Lancaster. Dr. Frederick Kuhn was also one of the leading physicians of Lancaster. He served for some time as associate judge of the courts. He died April 1st, 1816, in the 68th year of his age. Dr. Adam Kuhn was professor of botany and materia medica in the University of Pennsylvania.

*KURTZ, JACOB, was elected County Commissioner in the year 1829, on the first Anti-Masonic ticket which was successful. He was the only son of John and Magdalena Kurtz, of Chester county. He was a member of the Omish church. Inheriting a lame foot, his father gave him a fair English education, in order to enable him to make his way the better in life. He followed school teaching till his marriage, and then his father gave him a farm. He carried on farming, and at the same time he engaged himself considerably in conveyancing. Writing a beautiful hand, he soon gained the reputation of being a first-class scrivener, as also a farmer. He was a great friend of the free school system and of temperance. He felt disinclined to sell his corn to distillers, and he advised his neighbors to feed their corn to their stock. When he took his seat as a member of the board of commissioners, he found many things that he condemned. He was in for economy in everything where money could be saved with prudence. He was greatly denounced by those who had been in the habit of getting bargains, in contracts from the old board. His efforts did much to inaugurate a new and better system. He secured the confidence of his fellow-citizens for his vigorous and successful efforts in establishing economy in the board of commissioners. Industry and economy was his life's motto.

KURTZ, JACOB H., was elected Prothonotary in the year 1845.

*KYLE, JOHN, was among the earliest settlers of the western part of old Sadsbury (now Eden) township; and before Lancaster county was organized he had purchased nearly all the land in the western part of the township, extending from the Strasburg township line to Quarryville. He is said to have emigrated from Ireland, and to have belonged to the original Scotch-Irish, and was a man of considerable influence among the early pioneers. He was a member of the second grand jury for Lancaster county, in November, 1730. He was elected to the Legislature from Lancaster county for the year 1731, and reëlected for the year 1733. He was commissioned a justice of the peace at Chestnut Level, by Governor Thomas, in the year 1738. He was re-appointed to the same office a number of times, which office he held with credit to himself and general satisfaction to the public, for the space of about twenty years.

L.

LANDIS, DAVID, a soldier of the Revolution, who enlisted when but 17 years of age, and served faithfully till the termination of the struggle, a period of five years and seven months. He was engaged in agricultural pursuits, and in 1824 was elected from Ephrata township a member of the Pennsylvania Legislature. He died April 7th, 1852, aged ninety years.

†LANDIS FAMILY. All the citizens of a community naturally feel, to a greater or less extent, an interest in the people generally who, generation after generation were in-

*Contributed by Isaac Walker.
†Contributed by Andrew M. Frantz, esq.

strumental in developing their religious, moral and material condition. And in proportion that this instrumentality ex-·erted itself and manifests itself in great and good results, this feeling of interest grows strong and anxious. A large body of people can, however, not be contemplated with the same satisfaction as one may contemptate an individual or a particular family of individuals. Entirely free from any just imputation for invidious distinction between families or individuals, the selection of a particular family under the circumstances of this occasion and for the purposes of this publication, will not be regarded as any breach of propriety. That Lancaster county is foremost in the march of modern improvement and achievement in field culture, in farm buildings, and fences, and in the use of the improved machinery for agricultural purposes and the general comfort, prosperity and happiness of the rural population, is neither doubted nor disputed by any body. The past and present generations have made this county what it is, by their wisdom and virtue, their industry and economy. The present generation owe a debt of gratitude to generations now passing away, and those who have passed away before them. More is owing to certain individuals than others, and more to certain families than to others. It is not necessary to inquire into the causes for this difference, the fact that it exists is sufficient.

There are many families who have, through many generations, been noted for their religious and moral excellence, their sterling character for industry, and economy. There is, however, one family in this county, that is after all, perhaps, entitled to some sort of superiority or preference, not because of anything particularly prominent in individual character of one or more of its members, but rather on account of its numerical strength and steady devotion to the interests of Lancaster county—plain farming. There is no family so closely and so essentially connected with the growth and development of Lancaster county, as the Landis family. It is more numerous, and continued to be through all generations, time and changes devoted to farming, which department of industry made this county what it is, as is well known. The pedigree, or genealogy of this numerous and powerful family, will be herein accurately given to the fifth generation or degree, from the first emigrant, the root of the stock. The biography of the family will be given in a general way, rather than individual. The family are not so much distinguished for producing great public men as for the uniform private worth of all its members; not intending to convey the idea that they would have been less able or competent to fill public positions than others, but that a certain feature of character impelled them always to attend to their own business first. They are not and never have been ambitious for public honors or preferment, except such as naturally spring from good private citizenship. As a family they have maintained, in a very great degree, the genuine Lancaster county character, having been industrious and economical without almost an exception. Modesty, coolness and deliberation are some of the leading characteristics of the stock, and these proved a shield of defence against the allurements and enticements of excitements and speculations, which obtained here and there, and which tempted some others more unstable to follow the delusive phantoms, leading them away from the land of their fathers to seek fortunes elsewhere. The Landis family are nearly all here at this time, and most of them own one or more farms. The propositus or common progenitor of the Landis family, whose descendants are here traced and arranged in order, by branches of families, emigrated to this country in 1718, a native of Switzerland. No one knows, and none can tell anything beyond this. Like most of the early settlers in the wilds of America, this pioneer was of the common class of people, comparatively poor in worldly possessions, and upon arriving here had quite enough to do to provide for himself and his family the necessaries for subsistence; in other words, to keep the wolf from the door. The new and unknown home, with its many privations and wants at first, after awhile the gradual development of goodly prospects in the land of adoption, all combined to preclude all thought, as it seems, of making any note or record of things left behind or transpiring in the present.

These pioneer settlers, in the wilds of America, instinctively became the champions of the great and peculiarly American principle of progress. Onward! upward! has been the motto all along the line of generations that have lived, flourished and passed away. The present generations have literally been helped out of the woods by the past. We have been put in a position that enable us from its eminence to look back, still nothing is to be seen or known beyond the period of ancestral emigration. The dark curtain which time draws over all earthly things, is let down so low and has become so thick that, in the absence of recorded history, we cannot penetrate it; the beginning of our forefathers in this country, is our absolute beginning.

REV. BENJAMIN LANDIS, a Mennonite preacher, accompanied by his only son and child, whose name was also Benjamin, aged eighteen years, came to America from Switzerland in the year 1718, and bought from the Conestogo Indians a tract of about two hundred and forty acres of land, situated in what is now East Lampeter township, about four miles from Lancaster city, at the intersection of the Horse-shoe and old Philadelphia roads. The most part of the original tract is now owned and occupied by Henry N. Landis, in the fifth degree from the propositus.

BENJAMIN LANDIS, the younger emigrant, had four sons, whose names were in the order of their births and respective ages, as follows: Benjamin Landis, Abraham Landis, Jacob Landis, and Henry Landis. The plan adopted to illustrate the pedigree of the family, is to take these four sons, being the first born upon the soil, in the order of their respective ages, and enumerate the descendants of each one of them in regular order to the fifth degree. Counting the senior or older emigrant, the first degree or beginning, will place the four first born upon the soil in the third degree. This plan will bring us to, and stop with, the generation now represented by men all over sixty years of age, but about one-half of them still living, and all of them second cousins in relationship. They being in cousinship one degree nearer than they would be if the progenitor would have had two or more sons with descendants in the male line. With a view to a better understanding of the matter, one of each branch of the family in the degree, marking the stopping place, is here given, beginning with the oldest branch, as follows: John Landis, of Manor township, called Manor John; Benjamin Landis, of East Lampeter township, called big Benjamin; Benjamin Landis, of Manheim township, called rich Benjamin; David Landis, of East Lampeter township, called miller David; Abraham Landis, of Lancaster township, occupying and owning the city mill farm; Abraham Landis, of East Lampeter township, called old road Abraham; Jacob Landis, of the same township, called gentleman Jacob; Henry Landis, residing near New Holland; Benjamin Landis, of East Lampeter township, called little Benjamin; Daniel Landis, now living in Manheim township, near the village of Eden; David Landis, called fuller David; and Henry N. Landis, residing upon the original Landis homestead in East Lampeter township.

Benjamin Landis, the first born upon the soil, and oldest son of the younger emigrant, moved to and settled in Manheim township, in the year 1753, on a farm about three miles from Lancaster city, near the Reading road, and near where the Landis valley Mennonite meeting-house now stands. He had three sons—Benjamin, Henry, and John. Benjamin, the oldest of these three sons, had also three sons —John, Benjamin, and Jacob; and these are the fifth generation. This John Landis resided in Manor township, and was called Manor John, and was elected commissioner for Lancaster county in 1838. Benjamin, the second of these, lived on the old Manheim homestead, and died in 1822. Jacob, the youngest, moved to the State of Ohio a few years ago, where he is still supposed to live.

Henry, the second of the three, had five sons, viz: Benjamin, Henry, John, Isaac and Jacob. Benjamin, the oldest, called rich Benjamin, lived in Manheim township, near Oregon, and died there some years ago, leaving a numerous and prosperous family. Henry, the second son, called drover Henry, now resides in the same township. John, the third son, called miller John, resided in Hempfield township, where he died. Isaac, the fourth son, resided in Manheim

26

township, and was noted for feeding fine cattle. Jacob, the youngest, now resides in the same township, near the Landis valley meeting-house. John, the third son of the three, had also three sons, viz: John, Benjamin and Henry. John, the oldest of these three, resided in the vicinity of Landisville, and was known as swamp John. Benjamin, called big Benjamin, resided in East Lampeter township, on the horseshoe road. Henry, the third and youngest, resided in the same township, on the long lane, and was known as swamp Henry. These are the descendants of Benjamin, the oldest son of the junior emigrant to the fifth generation.

Next in order come the descendants of Abraham Landis, the second son of Benjamin, the younger emigrant. This Abraham had two sons, viz: Benjamin and John. Benjamin, the older of these two, lived in East Lampeter township, and had four sons, viz: John, Abraham, Benjamin and David. John, the oldest of these four, called farmer John, lived in the same township, and was elected commissioner for Lancaster county, in the year 1846; he was the first president of the Lancaster County Bank, after it was chartered as a regular banking institution—elected to that position in the year 1841, and continued to fill the same with honor to himself and advantage to the institution, until February, 1867, a period of twenty-six years. He was buried on the 7th day of February, 1867, in the graveyard belonging to Mellinger's meeting-house, about four miles east of Lancaster city, on the old Philadelphia turnpike road. Abraham, the second of these four, lived and died in East Lampeter township. Benjamin, the third of these four, lived and died in the same township. David, the youngest of the four, now resides in the same township, and is known as miller David, and is at present a member of the board of directors for the poor of Lancaster county.

John Landis, (called Musser John), the second son of Abraham, had three sons, viz: John, Abraham and Emanuel, all of whom resided in East Lampeter township, except Abraham.

John, the oldest of these, died about fifteen years ago. Abraham owns and occupies the farm near the city water works, known as the city mill farm in Lancaster township.

And Emanuel resides near the Pennsylvania railroad bridge on the Lampeter side of the Conestoga.

Next in order come the descendants of Jacob Landis, the third son of the younger emigrant. This Jacob had two sons—John and Abraham. John, the older of these two, called brick John, had eight sons—Jacob, John, Abraham, Benjamin, Christian, Martin, David, and Daniel. Jacob, the oldest, died in East Lampeter township near where Landis's warehouse on the Pennsylvania railroad stands, probably thirty years ago; John lived and died in West Lampeter township, on the Millport and Strasburg turnpike road; Abraham, called old road Abraham, resides on the old road in East Lampeter, about four miles from Lancaster; Benjamin resides in Upper Leacock township, near Bareville; Christian lived in East Lampeter, and died there in 1871; Martin resides in Upper Leacock, near Bareville; David also resides in the same township, a little south of Bareville; and Daniel resides in Hempfield township, near the village of Petersburg. Abraham, the younger of the two sons of Jacob, had five sons—Jacob, Abraham, Benjamin, John, and Adam. Jacob, the oldest of these five, called gentleman Jacob, resides in East Lampeter township, near the old road, about four miles from Lancaster, and was at one time director of the poor for the county. Abraham, the second of these, resides on the old yard occupied by the original emigrant, on the farm adjoining Jacob's, and Benjamin also on the farm adjoining; John, the fourth of these, resides in East Hempfield township, near the village of Petersburg, and is a Mennonite minister of the Gospel; Adam, the youngest, is unmarried, and lives with his brothers in East Lampeter.

We now come next to the descendants of Henry, the fourth and youngest son of the younger emigrant; he had five sons, viz: Benjamin, John, Henry, Peter, and Abraham. Benjamin, the oldest of these five, had four sons, viz: Daniel, Henry, Benjamin, and John; all of these were born and resided part of their time about New Holland; the two older ones died there some years ago; the third one, Benjamin, moved to Adams county, Pennsylvania, many years ago, where he is still living; the youngest one, John, also moved

to Adams county, where he now resides, about five miles
east of Gettysburg. John, the second one of these five, had
two sons, viz : Benjamin and John. Benjamin, the older,
called little Benjamin, resided in East Lampeter, near Miller's store, where he died a few years ago ; John, the second
and younger of the two, died at the age of eighteen, at least
fifty years ago. Henry, the third one of the five, had four
sons, viz : Daniel, Jacob, Henry, and Isaac. Daniel, the
eldest of these four, resides in Manheim township, on the
New Holland turnpike road, about three miles from Lancaster city; Henry, the second one, died some years ago unmarried, in East Lampeter township, where he lived; Isaac
now lives in the same township, near Landis's store; and
Jacob died unmarried in the same neighborhood a few
years ago. Peter, the fourth one of these, had only one
son, whose name was David, and was known as fuller David,
residing in Upper Leacock township, near the village of
Monterey. Abraham, the last of the five and youngest son
of Henry, the youngest son of the junior emigrant, lived and
died upon what is part of the original Landis homestead, in
East Lampeter township. He died in 1861, at the age of
eighty-one years, and was the last connecting link between
the two generations. He was a Mennonite minister of the
Gospel, and a man much esteemed for his goodness as a citizen, a neighbor and a Christian. He had five sons, viz :
Henry N., Abraham, Jacob, John, and Benjamin. Henry
N. Landis, the oldest of these, now occupies and owns the
old homestead in East Lampeter township ; Abraham, the
second one, emigrated to the State of Illinois in 1849,
settled and now resides in Whiteside county, near Sterling;
Jacob also moved to the same State, and died there about
twelve years ago ; John, the fourth of these five sons, also
moved to Illinois, and died there about fifteen years ago ;
Benjamin, the youngest of the five, moved to Franklin
county, Pennsylvania, and died there also about fifteen years
ago. These are the generations of this family of Landis's,
to the fifth degree from the senior propositus. In tracing
the pedigree, it appears that this family embraces all the
Landis's who are now living within eight or ten miles of

Lancaster city, except a very few. There are Landis's living in this county, north of Ephrata, but they are not related to these whose genealogy is herein given. In the third degree, according to the manner of computation, there were four Landis's; in the fourth, twelfth, and in the fifth, forty-seven; in the sixth degree, taking the same ratio of increase, one hundred and eighty; and in the seventh degree, many of whom belonging to the older branches of the family, are now over twenty-one years old, there are certainly not less than five hundred all in the male line. It is perfectly safe to assume, that there are at this time one thousand living descendants, male and female, in Lancaster county, all sprung from Benjamin Landis, junior, who started out a boy eighteen years of age, just one hundred and fifty-three years ago. The writer regrets very much that the name of the woman to whom this young man was married, cannot be ascertained.

The first emigrant, Benjamin Landis, was, as has been stated, a Mennonite minister of the Gospel, and all his descendants to the fifth generation adhered to the Mennonite faith without an exception.

LANDIS, JOHN, a native of Switzerland, emigrated to America in the beginning of the eighteenth century, and located in Bucks county, Pennsylvania. He had five sons, viz: Jacob, John, Martin, George and Samuel; and two daughters, Veronica and Barbara. John, one of the five sons, was born in Bucks county, Pennsylvania, November 11th, 1720, and removed to Montgomery county, in the same State. His son John, and grandson of the first emigrant, was born August 16th, 1776, and emigrated to Lancaster county in 1797. He married a daughter of Michael Kline. the grandfather of George M. Kline, esq., of this city. He was for many years engaged in the mercantile profession.

LANDIS, JESSE, son of the last named John Landis, was born October 15th, 1821. He read law with Emanuel C. Reigart, and was admitted to the bar in September, 1843. Being a very sedulous and attentive student, he has steadily won his way in the profession, until he ranks at present amongst the well-read attorneys of the Lancaster bar. In 1861 he was elected by the county commissioners solicitor of the county, and held the same by annual reëlection until the year 1869. He has written, and is now preparing for publication, a supplement to Linn's Analytical Index.

LANDIS, SAMUEL, a member of the Legislature in 1829 and 1830.

LANE, JOHN N., was a successful merchant of Lancaster city, and the wealthiest of our deceased citizens.

LATTA, REV. JAMES, was pastor of the church at Chestnut Level, Lancaster county, and principal of an academy for many years at the same place. He was called to this charge in 1770, with a salary of £100 Pennsylvania currency, which was never increased nor all paid. Rev. Latta manifested a deep interest in the cause of American independence, and on one occasion actually took his blanket and knapsack and accompanied the soldiers on their campaign. At another time he served for a short time in the army as chaplain. In 1785 a movement was set on foot amongst many congregations, upon the subject of procuring acts of incorporation, and Rev. Latta favoring the proposal, had the misfortune to alienate many of his flock from him. Another subject of alienation between himself and his congregation, was his effort to introduce Watts' Psalmody in his churches. In this, however, he failed; and the new hymns were not accepted until after the death of all the old members who had originally formed the opposition. Rev. Latta published a pamphlet of one hundred and eight pages octavo, in defence of the new hymns, which passed through four editions. The degree of D.D. was conferred upon him by the University of Pennsylvania, about the close of the last century. Dr. Latta died January 29th, 1801. His widow, a lady of great piety and amiability, continued to reside on the family farm, at Chestnut Level, until her death, February 22d, 1810.

LAUMAN, LUDWIG, was born May 5th, 1725. He was a merchant of Lancaster, and a man of influence about the period of the American revolution. He was a very zealous and active Whig, and ranked with Edward Shippen, George Ross, Jasper Yeates, Mathias Slough, and William Henry, in his ardor for the promotion of the American cause. He was elected a member of the Legislature of Pennsylvania in 1776. He was an active and influential member of Trinity Lutheran church of this city, and died March 22d, 1797.

LEBKICHER, DAVID, elected Register in 1842.

*LEECH, FRANCIS, emigrated to this county from Ireland, about the year 1750. He was soon afterwards married to Isabella, the young widow of Christopher Griffith, of Salisbury, and by his marriage acquired a large property. He purchased all the real estate about the Gap, and erected that large hotel (known afterwards as the Henderson property,) about the year 1760, in which a public house was kept for nearly one hundred years. When the road was laid out from the Schuylkill to Strasburg, under the administration of Richard Penn, in 1772, its course was defined to the public house of Francis Leech, and thence to Strasburg.—Col. Rec., Vol. x., p. 218. His son, George Leech, also made many improvements about the Gap. The venerable Thomas Leech, also the very aged Anna and Elizabeth Leech, are the living grandchildren of Francis Leech.

LEFEVRE, JOSEPH, a leading Democratic politician, and member of Congress from 1811 till 1813. He was a citizen of Strasburg township.

LEHMAN, HENRY C., was elected a member of the Legislature in the years 1861 and 1862.

LEHMAN, JOHN, was elected to the Legislature in the year 1836.

LEHMAN, SAMUEL L., was elected Recorder in the year 1863.

LIBHART, JOHN J., was born in York county, August 6th, 1806. He removed with his father to the borough of Marietta when about six years of age, and was educated in the local schools of Marietta and the borough of York. When he was about fourteen years of age, Arthur Armstrong came to Marietta and engaged in portrait painting. An enthusiasm for the new avocation immediately seized

*Contributed by Isaac Walker, of Sadsbury.

young Libhart, and he took up the business and pursued it
with success for several years, executing a number of pieces
with great credit.   After the death of Dr. Glatz, postmaster
of Marietta, he was appointed by James K. Polk to fill the
vacancy, a position which he held for two years.   While he
was pursuing the occupation of artist, he took up the study
of natural science, such as mineralogy, ornithology and
zoology, and made considerable advancement in their study.
He made quite a collection of specimens in natural history,
especially in ornithology, which he donated some years
since to the Linnæan society of Lancaster.   Besides his
great taste for natural history, he has always possessed a
remarkable fondness for history.   His predecessor in the
post-office, Dr. Glatz, having been engaged in the drug business, upon his death his store was purchased by the subject of
our notice, and this business he has carried on up to this time.

He was born and raised a Democrat, his ancestors having
been strong advocates of the principles of Thomas Jefferson.
Upon the breaking out of the late rebellion, favoring a
vigorous prosecution of the war, he became identified in
sentiment with the Republican party, and has acted with it
from that time.   In 1867 he was appointed an associate
judge of the courts of Lancaster county, and in the succeeding election was chosen to fill the same office for a period of
five years.   He has filled all the borough offices of Marietta,
having been burgess, councilman and school director.   In
the latter capacity he served for the period of sixteen years.
He was one of the earliest and staunchest advocates of the
free school system in Lancaster county.   Judge Libhart is
an intelligent, liberal-minded, high-toned gentleman, and as
an officer of the court he is perfectly pure, honest and
upright.

LIGHT, MAJOR JOHN,[1] was a native of the State of New
York, but the greater portion of his life was spent in Lan-

[1] On August 17th, 1798, the clerkship of the Sun engine and hose
company was made a permanent office, and John Light was elected
to this position, who served the same till April 17th, 1824. His grandson,
Dr. John L. Atlee, sr., was elected to the same position, and held it till
October 21st, 1854, when he resigned, and his son, John L. Atlee, jr.,
was elected to the post filled by his great grandfather.

caster. He early entered the American service as a minute man for the Jerseys, in 1775, and participated in the expedition that was made against the Tories on Long Island. He was in the division that invaded Canada, and participated in the battle of Three Rivers. He was a sharer in the privations at the river Sorel, and on the retreat from Canada to Ticonderoga. In the battle of Lake Champlain he was present, and was among those who defended Ticonderoga and other places, until the retirement of the British army to winter quarters. Upon his return home he immediately reënlisted, and was with Washington in his retreat through New Jersey, and fought in the battle of Princeton. He acted as guide to Gen. Washington, and to several of the officers who commanded scouting parties detached from Gen. Putnam's command, when the British possessed Brunswick; and he was among the first of those who entered that place after its evacuation by the enemy. He was a participant in the battle of Somerset Court House, and several other skirmishes about this time. He was in the battle of Monmouth Court House, and also at Germantown. He was one of the light dragoons who guarded Burgoyne's prisoners from New Jersey to the Potomac. In one service and another he acted with the American army, and was present when Lord Cornwallis surrendered his forces at Yorktown. After the revolution he kept tavern in East King street for some years, ceasing this business in 1803. He was inspector of the 1st brigade of Lancaster county militia in 1800. In 1806 he was appointed a justice of the peace. He was a leading Democratic politician of his day, and a man of great influence. In 1818 he was appointed clerk of the orphans' court, of the quarter sessions, and of the oyer and terminer. He was appointed in the room of John Hoff, deceased. He returned again to New York State, where he died about the year 1834.

LIGHTNER, JOEL, a member of the Legislature in the years 1812, 1813, 1815, 1816, and 1817.

LIGHTNER, JOHN, elected a member of the Legislature in 1819, 1821. He was appointed Clerk of the Quarter Sessions in 1836.

LIGHTNER, Nathaniel F., elected a member of the Legislature in 1824 and 1828. He was afterwards Mayor of Lancaster.

LINDLEY, Thomas, a member of the Legislature in 1739, 1740, 1741, 1742, and 1743.

LINVILLE, Benjamin, elected a member of the Legislature in 1829 and 1830.

*LIVINGSTON, John B., was born in the year 1821, in Salisbury township, Lancaster county, Pennsylvania. His father, John Livingston, was a farmer of considerable intelligence, who held the office of justice of the peace. His son, the subject of this sketch, was sent to school at the age of five years, and soon learned to read well for his age. He became so fond of books that they became his constant companions. At the age of seven he was remarkable for his accuracy in spelling. He remained for weeks together at the head of a large class, principally composed of much older pupils. His father being physically disabled by lameness for severe manual labor, and he being the oldest son, his services on the farm were so valuable that his time for attending school was limited to those months in the winter when the duties on the farm were not so exacting. He, however, acquired the habit of improving every leisure moment during the more busy season of the year; and though the work on the farm kept him from school, it did not keep him from his books. His proficiency became so conspicuous, that in 1842 the directors of the common schools, in the district in which he resided, solicited him to engage in teaching school during the winter months. He, however, considered it his duty to consult the wishes of his father, before he consented to accept their proposition. As the younger brothers had now grown up and become capable of working the farm, the father consented, and young Livingston was duly installed into the office of school teacher, which employment he continued to follow during the winter months, for four or five sessions. His time during the vacations being spent in working on his father's farm and teaching private school.

*Contributed by John B. Good, esq.

About the year 1845 he began to think of studying a profession; and it is said for a time his inclination tended towards medicine, and that considerations of the great responsibilities devolving on the physician, when the fate of precious lives depend on his skill, deterred him from choosing that department as his place of activity. He concluded that a slip in the practice of the law is a less serious calamity than a blunder in medicine or surgery, in proportion as a man's pocket is more easily repaired than his life or limbs. He therefore resolved to study law. In pursuance of this resolution, he wrote to Hon. Thaddeus Stevens, inquiring whether he had room for a student, and if so, what his terms were. In due time the answer came in the Old Commoner's laconic style : " Have room. Terms, $200. Some pay, some don't." On the 26th of January, 1846, the young teacher left his parental roof, and the scenes of his boyhood and youth, for the city of Lancaster, to enter upon the stormy mazes of the law. With Blackstone he may have said :

> Lost to the fields, and torn from you,
> Farewell, a long, a last adieu !
> Me, wrangling courts and stubborn law,
> To smoke, and crowds, and city draw.

He applied himself earnestly to his studies, and on the day on which the two years appointed by the rules of Court for initiatory studies expired, he was admitted to the bar of Lancaster county, of which he was destined to become an ornament. He soon gave evidence of a useful career. His industry and wonderful capacity for labor did not permit him to be idle a minute. No one ever saw him idling away his time either on the street or in the office. He believed that no one willing to work need fail, and he acted in accordance with this principle. It is probable that these traits of character, and the facility and taste displayed in his penmanship, attracted the attention of N. Ellmaker, esq., into whose office he moved in 1851, and where he remained actively assisting in the extensive practice in the orphans' court and general law practice in that office up to the time of his election to the office of District Attorney in the fall of 1862.

His election to this public position, and the satisfactory manner in which he performed its duties, caused him to be more extensively and favorably known throughout the community, and from this time his practice commenced to rapidly increase. His mind being familiar with the general practice in the several Courts, and his pen unusually ready, he was able to perform an incredible amount of labor. His charges always moderate, his manners affable and pleasant, his honesty above suspicion, his office was constantly crowded with clients. Under these circumstances, it is not strange that he did not consider the promotion from the bar to the bench a desirable change. When, however, in the fall of 1871, a vacancy was about to take place in the office of President Judge of the second judicial district of Pennsylvania, composed of Lancaster county, the people with unusual unanimity elected him to that office. On December 4th, 1871, he assumed its duties, and has since continued in that position.

LONG, HENRY G., was born in Lancaster, August 23d, 1804. His paternal grandfather, Nicholas Long, a native of Zweibrucken, in Bavaria, emigrated to America, and settled in Lancaster in 1754. Here he married, and reared in comfort a large family. He rose to be a man of standing and influence in the community, and often was a juror in the trial of causes. Jacob Long, the father of the subject of our notice, became a successful merchant and accumulated an independent fortune. He was a sergeant in the American revolution, and saw service therein during a long period of the struggle. He came near being in the battle of Brandywine, arriving on the spot with his company just as the battle was over. He died in December, 1842, in the 82d year of his age. The subject of our notice received his education in the schools of Lancaster. When but seventeen years of age he was appointed clerk in the prothonotary's office, under Dr. F. A. Muhlenberg, and owing to the professional engagements of the latter he was obliged to perform most of the duties of the office. This position he retained for three years. He then, in 1824, began the study of law, in the office of George B. Porter, esq., then the leading lawyer at the bar, and was admitted to the full practice of the profession in 1827. He immediately opened an office and begun the practice of law, and was not long in establishing himself fairly in the profession.

When he left the Prothonotary's office, it was the design of his father that he should succeed him in the mercantile business, and it was only at the suggestion of Mr. Porter that he began the reading of law. When he commenced its study it was rather that he might be profitably employed than with the design of entering the profession. After reading a short time, however, he acquired a fondness for it, and so continued until he was prepared for admission to the bar. Shortly after coming to the bar, he was chosen by the commissioners county solicitor, a position to which he was successively re-chosen and held the same for twenty years. Soon after his admission to the bar, he became active in politics, and being very decided in his political views, he was elected in 1836 a member of the Reform Convention, being one of the youngest men of that body. He was elected in the fall of 1838 to the Legislature of Pennsylvania, and was a member of that body during the buckshot war, a period of great excitement in Pennsylvania. After serving this session, he again resumed the duties of the profession, to which he now steadily gave his attention until 1851, when he was nominated and elected President Judge of the court of common pleas of Lancaster county. His nomination was at this time entirely unsolicited. Learning that his name would be used, he prepared a letter of declination and handed the same to Abraham Cassel, a member of the convention, and authorized him to have his name withdrawn. So fully satisfied, however, was Mr. Cassel, and with him the convention of his eminent fitness for this position, that the letter of declination was not presented, and he was unanimously nominated. Finding himself thus the unanimous choice of his party for this high office, he did not feel at liberty to decline an election, and he therefore deferred to the wishes of his friends, and as a consequence was triumphantly elected. The manner in which he discharged the duties of this office gave entire satisfaction.

Upon the expiration of his ten years term of service as Judge, making no effort to secure a re-nomination for the same, he was defeated by a majority of five in the convention of his party, held in 1861, and Alex. Hood was the successful nominee. This, however, was a period when party lines greatly changed, consequent upon the rebellion then raging, and the result was the holding of a new convention by those of the Republican party dissatisfied with the regular nominations, and the Democrats united with them. This alliance, calling itself the Peoples' party, placed Henry G. Long in nomination for the same position he then held, and for which he had been defeated in the regular Republican convention. His great popularity secured his election, and he has again completed his second term.

Henry G. Long was always a conservative in his opinions, and this trait of his character was exemplified during the period of the buckshot war. In conversation with some of his party friends, he intimated his misgivings as to the propriety of the conduct of certain extreme leaders of his party; and his remarks having been carried to the ears of Governor Ritner, gave the latter much offence. A party friend afterwards remarked to Mr. Long, that the Governor was astonished that a man of his party, and especially one from Lancaster county, should have given utterance to expressions as he had done. Mr. Long, far from being daunted, and true to his convictions, boldly remarked, that what he "had expressed, he believed, and he should not hesitate to give expression to the same sentiments upon any and every occasion."

As a Judge, Henry G. Long was fair and impartial, and his honesty has never been questioned. He sought to decide causes purely upon their merits; and he bore with his retirement the universal esteem of the bar and community. As a citizen, he is kind, courteous and obliging, and he will long be remembered for his bland and amiable manners. In him it may truly be said, that he will, during the remainder of his days, enjoy *otium cum dignitate*.

LONG, JOHN, elected a member of the Legislature in 1829 and 1830. In 1835 he was elected one of the board of county commisssoners.

LOVETT, JOHN, elected a member of the Legislature in 1831.

*LOWERY, COL. ALEXANDER, was born in the north of Ireland, in December, 1723, and came to America with his father, Lazarus Lowery, in 1729, who settled in Donegal township, Lancaster county, and was licensed by the Court in 1730 to sell liquor by the small; and by the Governor, as an Indian trader, which latter occupation he pursued for a number of years thereafter. His sons, John and Daniel Lowery, were also Indian traders. Having made frequent trips to the far west to trade with the Indians, Alexander probably accompanied them. He became a great favorite with the Indians, and exercised an influence over them which he retained during his life.

About the year 1748 he formed a partnership with Joseph Simons, of Lancaster, in the fur trading business, which lasted forty years. The fur traders usually made annual trips to the Allegheny and Mississippi rivers, in convoys, for their mutual protection. The Indians knew about the time they were expected, and brought their peltries from their hunting grounds farther West, to certain points, where they exchanged them for blankets, &c. Col. Lowery was a powerful man, and capable of enduring any amount of fatigue. He was considered one of the fleetest "Indian runners," and was frequently selected by the Government to collect the chiefs of the various Indian tribes at Detroit and other places, to make treaties. The only subsistence he was able to obtain for weeks at a time, was that procured by his trusty rifle. He was taken with inflammatory rheumatism while amongst the Indians along the banks of the Allegheny river, and was carried to a log cabin, situate in a lonely dell, where he was nursed by an aged squaw for several days, when an Indian doctor came along and carried him to the river, where a hole was made in the ice—for it was midwinter—and ducked him in the river. The shock was so great to his system, that he was cured instantly, and never afterwards had a return of it. Col. Lowery accumulated money rapidly, and about the year 1755 commenced purchas-

*Contributed by Samuel Evans, esq., Columbia.

ing large tracts of land. In 1757 he purchased of Joseph Pugh, sheriff, four hundred acres, sold as the property of his father, Lazarus Lowery, (deceased). In this purchase was included the farm lately sold by James B. Clark to Cameron, upon which the Lowerys resided from 1740 to 1758 or '59. In 1759 he purchased of sheriff Smith, four hundred acres, sold as the property of Daniel Lowery, his brother. (Duffy's park farm is a part of this place.) He removed to it in 1760, and lived in a log house—which stood in the meadow south of the barn—a few years. About the year 1762 he commenced to build the present stone mansion. His partner, Joseph Simons, brought carpenters from Lancaster and conducted its erection. Col. Lowery went amongst the Indians, and did not return until the building was completed. In 1763, at the time of the massacre at Bloody Run, Col. Lowery was sent back to Fort Rays, (Bedford,) in the evening, to get something left there by the traders. In the night the Indians murdered many of the traders and their men, (amongst whom was Daniel Lowery, his brother,) and destroyed an immense amount of goods. When he returned, about daylight, he discovered the terrible havoc made by the Indians, who attempted to capture him. He ran for the timber and was hunted for several days amongst the mountains; they finally discovered him when near the river, on the York county side of where Vinegar's Ferry now is, and made chase. He swam the river and made good his escape. This was the only instance in which he was molested by the Indians. He often remarked, that they were so frenzied that they knew not friend from foe.

In 1770 he purchased of sheriff Stone, eight hundred acres, and the ground rents in Maytown, and a tannery adjoining, sold as the property of Jacob Downer. This land ran from Maytown to the river, and was afterwards sold to Alexander Boggs, Longenecker, and others. In 1774, when hostilities broke out with the mother country, Col. Lowery at once became very active on the side of the colonies. In July, 1774, he was placed on a committee of correspondence, to consult with other committees of conference in the province, who met in Philadelphia, July 15th, 1774. December 15th, 1774, he was appointed on a committee. to watch the suspected persons, and prevent, if possible, the purchase and use of tea. Mrs. Lowery, being a member of the Church of England, sometimes induced the teamsters when they went to Philadelphia, to procure her some tea. When Col. Lowery discovered it, he invariably destroyed it. On another occasion, when he was from home, she procured a " Coat of Arms," and placed it upon his carriage; when he returned he destroyed it, and every other emblem of aristocracy. He was elected a member of Assembly in 1775, and served on many important committees. He was also elected colonel of the Lancaster county militia, 3d battalion; and in 1776 a member of the Assembly, and a member of the convention which framed the first Constitution of Pennsylvania. In 1777 he was appointed, with others, by the war office, to supply the army with blankets, the army being entirely destitute of clothing during the winter of that year. He commanded the Lancaster county militia at the battle of Brandywine. He was elected a member of Assembly in 1778–80, and a member of the Senate to fill an unexpired term of one who died. After the Revolutionary war, Col. Lowery retired to his farm at Marietta. August 29th, 1791, Gov. Thomas Mifflin commissioned him a justice of the peace for the townships of Donegal, Mount Joy and Rapho. Maytown being a lively place at that time, fights were a common occurrence. The parties often came to Col. Lowery to settle their disputes. His manner of dealing with them suited the times, and saved the county unnecessary expense. He usually placed the combatants upon the green sward in front of his house and made them fight it out, he standing by to see that there was fair play and no gouging. Sometimes he turned in and whipped both of the parties. This novel and summary way of dealing out justice, put a stop to the quarreling, and especially their complaints before Col. Lowery. Daniel Clark, the father of Myra Gaines, widow of the late General Gaines, was a wagon-boy of Col. Lowery's, and usually accompanied him on his western trips amongst the Indians. After attaining his majority, he went down the Mississippi river and settled at New Orleans. It is said,

27

when trading with the Indians, in the absence of weights, that Col. Lowery used his hand, which weighed two pounds, and his foot, which weighed four pounds.

About the close of the Revolutionary war James Cunningham, of Lancaster city, (who was lieutenant colonel in Col. Lowery's battalion, and served many years in the Legislature with him, and was a companion in his western trips,) died. An express was sent to Col. Lowery, notifying him of the sad event. He hastened to Lancaster, and arrived there just as the remains of his departed friend was about to be placed in the grave. The coffin was opened to permit the friend of his life to gaze once more upon his features. He advanced with tears in his eyes, and grasped the hand of the corpse, and exclaimed, "honest Jimmy Cunningham, that never told a lie, or did a dishonest or mean action, has gone to his fathers." It has been related by those who were at this funeral and witnessed this, that it was a most affecting scene, and drew tears from all present. Col. Lowery was a bluff man, with a commanding voice. He spoke as he thought. When in conversation with a friend, and about to enter the church at Donegal, of which he was a member, he walked in, continuing the conversation, and in the same tone of voice, which was unusually loud, until he had finished what he had to say. When Congress sat in York, Anderson's ferry, now Marietta, was the principal crossing along the river. Often boats were prevented from crossing by reason of the floating ice. Col. Lowery's house during these occasions was filled with officers and members of Congress, who were on their way to York. General Gates and lady, with some staff officers, were thus delayed and invited by Col. Lowery to his home. He placed them in the hall and proceeded to the kitchen, to enquire of Mrs. Lowery whether she could entertain them. She at once declared she could not think of it—when her husband told her to hush, that the party was at his heels and would hear her if she made much noise. Alex. Lowery was married in 1752, to Miss Mary Walters, by whom he had six living children. In 1772 he married Ann Alricks, widow of Hermanus Alricks, who was prothonotary, register, recorder, clerk of the court, and justice of the peace for Cumberland county, and grandmother of Herman and Hamilton Alricks, esqs., of Harrisburg. When he married her, he had been a widower but six months, and she a widow but ten months. He promised to say nothing about the affair, but when they arrived in the vicinity of Maytown, several hundred persons turned out in all sorts of conveyances, and lined the public road for several miles to receive them, to the mortification of his bride. The colonel, being fond of a joke, evidently sent word in advance of his coming. She was a sister of Francis West, the grandfather of chief justice Gibson. Congress having made the continental money a legal tender, Col. Lowery sold the Clark farm to James Anderson, (who sold to Brice Clark,) and most of the Downer lands for that kind of money. When absent from home, James Polk, uncle of the late President Polk, a resident of Sherman's valley, Cumberland county, Pa., came and offered to pay a judgment note, held by Col. Lowery against him, in continental money. Mrs. Lowery, who was a spirited woman, refused to take the money, when Polk deliberately put his horse in the stable and declared his intention of staying until the colonel came home. He actually remained several days, and badgered and annoyed Mrs. Lowery so much, that she took the money, and bade him clear out and never show his face there again. Frances Evans was the only child by this marriage; she married Samuel Evans, a member of the Legislature from Chester county. John Evans, his ancestor, a native of Wales, landed in Philadelphia in 1690, with a family consisting of seven persons, viz: his father, mother, wife and daughter, brother and sister. In the spring of 1696 John Evans purchased a tract of land in the State of Delaware, called the "Welsh tract." In 1715 he purchased four hundred acres on the white clay creek, in Chester county, Pa., now owned by Esquire Niven. In 1718 John Evans, jr., married Reynold Howell, a native of Wales, who came to this country the same year. They left a family of six children, all of whom died young, except Evan, George and Peter. Evan was the father of Samuel Evans; Evan had three sons and three daughters. George served as a sergeant in Bailey's regiment during the Revolutionary war, and was wounded at New York, by a bayonet which was thrust through his body; he lived many years thereafter. His daughter married Johnson, the Napoleon of the turf in this country. The first fee received by the late Judge Yeates, was from Col. Lowery. He had a wonderful memory, and was frequently called upon in different parts of the State to settle disputes about the title of lands. A few years before his death, he and Joseph Simons selected referees, one of whom was the late Adam Reigart, to settle the partnership affairs, which ran through more than forty years. Strange as it may appear, there was not a solitary record or scrap of paper to show the transactions between them, which must have amounted to many thousand pounds. Colonel Lowery would call Mr. Simons' attention to an amount of money paid him on a certain log, perhaps thirty or forty years before, when Simons would give his assent thereto, and in return remind Col. Lowery that he paid him a certain sum of money at a certain spring many years before, and thus these honest men recapitulated circumstances which covered forty years of time, without one word of dispute, and settled up their affairs. Mr. Reigart often remarked, that he never saw or heard of such a settlement.

Col. Lowery was married a third time to Sarah Cochrane, a widow, who lived near York Springs, in 1793. Samuel Eddie wrote the marriage contract. Col. L. had been on a visit to the Gibsons, in Sherman's valley. On his way home he stopped at York Springs; some of his friends, whom he met there, intimated to him that there was a spry widow, named Cochrane, at the springs, for whom he had better "set his cap." He hastened home and returned with his carriage, and at once proposed to the widow to marry; promptly she responded that she would. While crossing the mountain, on his way home, she manifested great fears lest the carriage would be overturned, and intimated that she would rather walk. The Colonel told Sammy, her son, who was driving, to stop and let his mammy out; he drove on and halted at the foot of the mountain, and remained there until his wife came up. She was a large woman, and suffered very much; she carried her shoes in her hand; she never thereafter manifested her fears by expressing a desire to walk. It turned out that a trick had been played upon the old man, who was nearly seventy years of age. This Mrs. Cochrane was not the widow of that name who was first at the springs, but a very inferior woman. When he discovered the trick which had been played upon him, he built the house, (afterwards owned by Duffy), and placed her there, and never afterwards lived with her. Her sons, who were sporting men, robbed the old man of many hundred pounds, which they squandered at the races, &c. He died January 31st, 1805, leaving a large landed estate in different parts of the State. Col. Lowery was in the habit of saying that James Wilson, a member from Pennsylvania, of the convention which framed the Constitution, was the author of it. He knew the persons engaged in the murder of the Conestoga Indians, at Lancaster, and told his daughter, Mrs. Evans, that many of those engaged in it died a violent death.

M.

MACKEY, JAMES, was elected a member of the Legislature in the years 1831 and 1832.

MARSTELLER, PHILIP, a member of the Legislature in 1776. He was also a delegate in 1776 to the convention which adopted the first State Constitution.

MARTIN, B. F., elected a member in the Legislature in 1851.

MARTIN, DAVID M., elected Clerk of Quarter Sessions in 1848.

MARTIN, GEORGE, elected Sheriff of Lancaster county in 1854.

MARTIN, HUGH, was a farmer of Drumore township, and was elected to the Legislature on the Federal ticket in 1816 and 1817. His brother, Samuel Martin, was a clergyman, who had received his education at the Rev. Mr. Latta's academy, at Chestnut Level. He ministered at the Presbyterian church, at Chanceford, in York county. He was a man of good ability and ripe scholarship.

*MARTIN, HON. PETER, was born in January, 1805, in that part of Elizabeth township which, since its division, is called Clay township, Lancaster county, Pa. He was of Swiss descent. His grandfather, John, or Johannes Martin, immigrated from Switzerland, and settled about two miles from Woodstock, Shenandoah county, Va. Here his father, Peter Martin, sr., was born, and resided until the Indians became very troublesome and rendered the residence of white settlers utterly unsafe. The subject of this sketch frequently listened to the relation of his parents concerning nightly surprises, habitations in flames, murdered husbands and fathers, and women and children hiding in grain fields, seeking safety from the murderous savages. These dangers induced his grandfather to remove to a place more remote from the Indian frontier. He chose the quiet and peaceful scenes of old Ephrata, Lancaster county, Pa. Here, after the grandfather's death, Peter Martin, sr., the father of the subject of our sketch resided for a number of years, following the business of a shoemaker and country merchant. He was appointed a justice of the peace by Governor Findlay, and afterward moved to Elizabeth township, Lancaster county, where he acted as justice of the peace, and followed the business of a surveyor and conveyancer, and also kept a country store.

Here his son, Peter Martin, jr., was born. Concerning his early years little is known. He received such education as the schools of his time and neighborhood afforded. It is well known that the facilities for obtaining a good common school education were, at that time, far inferior to what they now are. He assisted his father in his store, and also in his business as a surveyor and conveyancer. His father's instructions and training, in a great measure, supplied the want of early education. He acquired the facility of handling his pen rapidly, and of drawing an article of writing with care and skill. He was frequently heard to talk of his youthful ex-

*Contributed by J. B. Good, esq.

ploit of drawing an executor's deed for his father, without a
blot or flaw on its face. The achievement was considered
by him as a great triumph, on which his memory in after
years delighted to dwell.

As his father advanced in years, the weight of business
gradually shifted on his son's shoulders. The Governor
appointed the son a justice of the peace, in the room and
stead of his father, whose mantle thus fell on worthy shoulders. To the new incumbent the ordinary business of a
magistrate's office had no attractions. In fact, he scarcely
transacted any criminal business at all. This resulted partly
from the moral condition of the community around him, and
partly because his time was occupied with business more
congenial to his taste. In his extensive practice as a surveyor and scrivener, he was constantly consulted in regard
to the many legal questions which continually arise in the
course of its pursuit. He was the friend and guide of executors, administrators, guardians and trustees of every kind.
His mind became familiar with the statutes relating to these
subjects, and with the decisions of the courts made under
them. Whenever his advice was desired, he was indefatigable in examining the point in question in order to reach a
correct conclusion. Although he never pursued a regular
course of legal study, yet such was his industry and natural
acumen, added in later years to his extensive experience,
that his opinion was generally entitled to a great deal of
respect. This was more especially the case in that branch
of the law relating to the practice in the orphans' court and
the settlement of estates of decedents. Every change in the
acts of Assembly, or a new ruling of court, was watched by
him with an eagle eye, as he took a laudable pride in keeping up with the times, and having his mind amply stored
with useful knowledge. It has been objected to his method
of drawing instruments of writing, that he was unnecessarily
prolix, and more especially in drafting wills, too circum-
stantial in detail. His own apology for this was, that if you
confine yourself strictly to the truth, you cannot say too
much, and that it is better to be tedious than ambiguous.
In the latter years of his life he frequently declared, that he

knew of no instance in which a law suit originated out of any ambiguous or uncertain directions contained in a last will drawn by him.

He held his commission as a justice of the peace till the amended constitution came in force, under whose provisions he was twice reëlected, although the party with which he acted was in a minority in the district where he resided. In 1850, however, he declined a reëlection, and he never afterwards held a magistrate's commission. He had early identified himself with the Democratic party, and always claimed that, however party names and circumstances had changed, he still remained faithful to his old political principles, and that he never was or had been anything but a genuine Jackson Democrat. In the local politics of Lancaster county he soon succeeded in obtaining a very prominent position, which he maintained for a long time. He, at several times, was the Democratic candidate for Congress, but on account of his party being in a hopeless minority in the county, always failed of an election. In the fall of 1843 he ran the last time for Congress on the Democratic ticket. The late Jeremiah Brown was the Whig candidate, and the Hon. A. E. Roberts the Anti-masonic standard-bearer. Mr. Brown was elected in this triangular contest. Upon the inauguration of the American, or Know-nothing movement, he identified himself with that party, and was their candidate for prothonotary in the year 1854, when Joseph Bowman, the Whig candidate, was elected, B. F. Holl having been the Democratic candidate for the same office.

Mr. Martin always was a friend of the late Col. Reah Frazer, familiarly known as the " Democratic War Horse." When the anti-Lecompton or Kansas troubles commenced, which culminated in the organization of the Republican party, it was natural that he should cast his lot with them, and oppose the election of Buchanan to the Presidency in 1856. In this step, those of his friends who knew him best, believed he acted conscientiously and from principle, however his notions may have been impugned by his old friends, whose party he left, or by his political enemies, with whom he now affiliated. The Republican county convention, which met at Lancaster in the fall of 1857, nominated him as their candidate for the office of prothonotary. It may easily be imagined that this action of the convention was not approved by a great number of the old line Whigs, with whom Mr. Martin had fought so many political battles. The consequence was, that William Carpenter, one of their number, received and accepted the Democratic nomination for the same office. A very spirited and somewhat acrimonious canvass ensued, and when the election was over and the votes counted, Mr. Carpenter was returned as having a small majority. As usual, each party accused the other of fraud. The election was contested, and the Court, after a patient investigation, decided that Mr. Carpenter was elected by a majority of ten votes.

To most men such a series of political defeats would have proved so disastrous that their prospects would have been irretrievably ruined. But such was not the case with Mr. Martin. He himself attributed his recuperative powers to the fact that he constantly retained the esteem and support of his neighbors, and never committed any act by which he forfeited their confidence and friendship. He understood the local politics of his county as well, perhaps, as any other man living at that time. His policy was to concentrate several of his neighboring districts, so that their weight and influence should go together. His next step was to seek alliances with other candidates in different parts of the county who controlled similar powers, thus effecting what he was accustomed to call "a concentration of strength." The practical result of these tactics was, that Peter Martin and his friends were all but irresistible in county conventions. The most difficult part of this, as of many other programmes, was to begin right—that is, to have the votes and influence of your neighbors; thus illustrating the wisdom of one of Mr. Martin's favorite maxims, that to a politician it was important, above all other things, to be "right with his neighbors at home."

From what has been said, it may be inferred that he had not much apparent trouble in obtaining his nomination for the office of prothonotary by the Republican county convention of 1860; but there were still some of his party who objected to his nomination, and when his name was announced as the successful candidate in the convention, it induced the Democrats to nominate Mr. Gerardus Clarkson, who had previously always been regarded as a Republican, as their candidate for the same office, hoping that the result of the election held three years before might again be realized. In these expectations, however, Mr. Clarkson and his friends were disappointed, and Mr. Martin was elected by a large majority. He served the office of prothonotary for the term of three years, to the satisfaction of his constituents and with honor to himself. After its close he retired to his home at Lincoln, where he remained in private life until the fall of 1866, when he was elected associate judge of the several courts of the county of Lancaster. This position he held at the time of his death, which occurred rather suddenly, on the 16th of August, 1867, at his home, having been sick only for a few days previous to his death. In person Mr. Martin was of medium height, inclining to corpulency. He had fine eyes, beaming with intelligence. He wore his hair short, which in his later years was entirely white. His face and chin were smoothly shaved. Though his manners were simple and unaffected, there was a certain native dignity in his bearing which at once impressed the beholder that he was a person of more than ordinary force of character.

MATHIOT, JOHN, was elected sheriff of Lancaster county in the year 1818. He was an alderman of Lancaster and carried on the business of a scrivener. He was elected in 1831, by city councils, Mayor of the city of Lancaster, and eleven times reëlected. He died January 22d, 1843, in the 58th year of his age.

MAXWELL, HUGH, was born in Ireland, December 7th, 1777. When quite a youth he came to Philadelphia, and at the age of nineteen he entered in partnership in the book publishing business with Matthew Carey, and with him published one of the first literary magazines in the city of brotherly love. He afterwards edited the *Port-Folio*, a magazine of some repute in its day. Whilst in the book publishing business, he cast his own type and made his own wood-cuts. Having met with severe losses in the financial crisis that succeeded the war of 1812–14, he for a time abandoned the editorial career and followed agricultural pursuits. His active temperament, however, soon introduced him into other editorial enterprises. In 1817 he removed to Lancaster and established the *Lancaster Gazette*, which he conducted with decided ability for several years. He next purchased the *Lancaster Journal*, one of the oldest Democratic papers of Pennsylvania, and this he published up to 1839. As a citizen, he ever ranked amongst the most active and enterprising in all projects looking towards the establishment and promotion of public improvements. He was one of the most active members of the company organized in 1820 for the improvement of the Conestoga navigation; and he it was who called the first meeting at Columbia, which discussed the project of uniting that place and Philadelphia by a railroad. He was gratified to live to see this enterprise completed in spite of much opposition and ridicule. The " Mechanics' Literary Association" of Lancaster, of which he was the first president, greatly owed its foundation to his spirit and enterprise. Hugh Maxwell was a man of considerable mechanical ingenuity, and among his inventions the " printer's roller," patented in 1817, was a fruit of his genius. He drew such attention to the cause of boiler explosions as elicited great praise in his day. With Wm. White, ex-sheriff of Lancaster, he discovered the Lykens Valley and Short Mountain coal fields, and shipped the first coal to market from those mines. As editor of a newspaper, Mr. Maxwell had few superiors in his day. He was a vigorous writer, and could pen an editorial of great power, and withal, couched in smooth and graceful language. He was a bold and independent thinker and fearless leader in public affairs. He died November 1st, 1860.

MAXWELL, ROBERT, was a citizen of Drumore township, and died November 6th, 1819, in the 80th year of his age. He was elected county commissioner in the year 1798. He was elected to the Legislature of Pennsylvania in 1806, 1807, 1808, 1809, 1812 and 1813.

MAY, DAVID, elected Clerk of the Orphans' Court in 1848.

MAYER, CHRISTIAN, was elected State Senator in 1804, and reëlected to the same position in 1808.

MAYER, GEORGE, a merchant of Lancaster, and brother of Dr. Mayer. He was possessed of a fine memory, and when a member of the Legislature in 1835, he took quite an active part in legislative proceedings. Abraham Kauffman, who was cotemporary with him in the Legislature, speaking of him said: "I once heard one of the canal commissioners remark of him after he had given some testimony before the House : what a mind and memory Colonel Mayer possesses; his language is fit for the press just as he speaks from recollection." He died September 9th, 1862, in the 82nd year of his age.

MAYER, REV. DR. LOUIS, an able divine, was born in the city of Lancaster, March 26th, 1783. His father was a gentleman of liberal culture. After he had made such proficiency in education as boys of his grade usually obtained, he resolved upon business, and made the experiment in Fredericktown, Maryland; but having no aptitude for secular pursuits this result was not flattering. About this time his mind became aroused as to spiritual affairs, and he seemed to recognize in his internal feelings a call to the ministerial career, for which he cherished a peculiar fondness. He now entered upon the preparatory studies necessary as a preparation for this field of service. His mind being formed of solid material, he made rapid progress in his classical and theological studies, and he was licensed to preach in the year 1807, by the Reformed Synod of Pennsylvania. In 1808 he accepted a call from the Shepherdstown charge, including Martinsburg and Smithfield congregations. Here he labored with great zeal and efficiency for twelve years. Whilst serving these congregations several efforts were made to obtain his services, but without success. In 1821 he was induced to accept a call from the Reformed church of York, Pa., where he continued to officiate until he was called upon to preside over the theological seminary of the German Reformed church. In 1825 he resigned his charge in York, moved to Carlisle, Pa., and began his duties as professor in the seminary. The new institution was fortunate in obtaining the services of Dr. Mayer, at a time when everything depended upon those interested with its control and management. The new professor was popular and discharged his duties with great fidelity. The infant institution, however, was but poorly endowed, and this, in connection with other circumstances needless to detail, proved very embarrassing to the incumbent of the theological chair, and indeed to the Synod itself. In 1829 the seminary was removed to York, Pa. A second professor of the seminary was found necessary, and it was also resolved to connect a classical school with the seminary. This latter department was committed to Frederick A. Rauch,[1] a distinguished German scholar, and afterwards President of Marshall College, in Mercersburg, Pa. Dr. Mayer faithfully served the church in the capacity of professor in the seminary, until 1835, when it was removed to Mercersburg. Not choosing

[1] A few remarks and reflections will not be untimed as regards the career and influence of Dr. Frederick Augustus Rauch, who, although never living in our midst, yet whose ashes lie amongst us, and whose influence is felt swelling the intellectual gales of our country. His monument reared on Franklin and Marshall campus, will, in coming time, be one of the objects of interest for visitors to the inland city of Lancaster. In the coming of Dr. Rauch to the United States, there was freighted into our country a cargo of philosophical thought that, in a great measure, has served to arouse American life to the existence of the gigantic intellectual revolution that had been fought across the waters in the fatherland. Prior to the arrival of this scholar in America, little was known as regards the state of opinion in Europe, and the little that it was came by way of England, that had itself scarcely waked up to a knowledge of the great world-battle that had been fought on German soil. From the time that Dr. Rauch was made President of Marshall College in Mercersburg, in 1835, a new era dawned upon the American mind, and a tide of thinking set in which from that period has flowed onward with gathering strength. The names of Kant, Jacobi, Fichte, Schelling, Hegel, Schleiermacher and Daub, are familiarized to a circle of American auditors, and the thoughts of these world-famed thinkers are made to take hold upon our cis-Atlantic intellect. Dr. Rauch, in the works he brought with him, was as by charts enabled to point out the respective positions of the contending hosts of European thought, and as one who had surveyed the whole field of the contest, could say what had been severally gained by the one, and lost by the other.

America, at that time, was still adhering to the nude dogmatism of

to leave York, he resigned his professorship in the seminary, but upon the earnest solicitation of Synod, was afterwards prevailed upon to resume his professorship. He did so, however, with the distinct understanding, that his services should simply be regarded as temporary. In October of the following year, at the meeting of the general Synod, Dr. Mayer again tendered his resignation, which was accepted. From that time till his death he continued to reside in York, and was engaged, as far as health would permit, in preparing several works for the press.

As a preacher, Dr. Mayer was learned and faithful. In the early part of his ministry it was his custom to write and commit his sermons; but in his later years he preached chiefly extemporaneously. His preaching was plain, practical and impressive. In the delivery of his sermons he was measured, earnest, and always very serious. His style was clear, chaste, and adapted to the comprehension of his auditors; often argumentative, and at times very powerful. Being possessed of a clear, logical mind, he was very happy in his

creeds, abandoned by the philosophic mind of the world for near a century. Its intellectual status at that period, was but little developed in the direction of metaphysical inquiry and philosophical research; and, indeed, the grade of collegiate training seemed to aim at nothing higher than a preparation for practical life and the distribution of inherited opinions. That, it must be confessed, is too truly even yet the case; but with the meeting of Drs. Rauch and Nevin at Mercersburg, a new spirit arose upon American soil. It was the spirit of inquiry, and the same that served in Descartes for the complete overthrow of scholasticism. The new spirit grew and advanced, and some years afterwards found its main foothold in Lancaster county. It germinated in what is known as the Mercersburg school of theology, but that is simply one phase of the influence following the dissemination of the new principle.

The war of the American scholastics against the new school of thought was commenced, and, with scarce an intermission, has been continued up till the present. Our county in the removal of the Theological seminary of the German Reformed church, during 1871, from Mercersburg to Lancaster, has become a centre of thought-distinction, whose existence dare not be unrecognized. From it will continue to emanate an influence potent on American life and thinking, towards the building up of a clear systematic and rounded philosophy which can turn all the weapons of a puerile scholastic dogmatism.

The man from whom, in a large measure, this influence has flown, Dr. Frederick A. Rauch, and whose remains lie in Lancaster, was born

explanations of the Scriptures, and in setting forth their true sense. He had somewhat a taste for lecturing, and his expositions of the sacred oracles were, in general, very clear and forcible.

As a professor, Dr. Mayer was eminently qualified. For thirteen years he filled the chair of professor of theology, and a part of this time gave instruction also in the Hebrew language and church history. Like many of our eminent men, he was chiefly indebted to his untiring industry for his ripe scholarship. He was a fine linguist, and had made himself familiar with the various European systems of theology and philosophy. He was a fine German scholar, and he perused many of the works which emanated from that land of scholars and deep thinkers. His mind was admirably adapted to the study of biblical antiquities, hermeneutics, exegesis, and didactic and pastoral theology. Few, perhaps, surpassed him in sermonizing, and in preparing and dictating skeletons of sermons. If a skeleton prepared and read by a student was not *au fait*, it underwent a remodeling immedi-

in Hesse-Darmstadt, July 27th, 1806. At the age of fifteen he became a student of Marburg, where he took his diploma in 1827. Afterwards he spent some time at Giessen and Heidelberg. Upon leaving Heidelberg he became professor extraordinary in the university of Geissen, being at the time twenty-four years of age. Possessing a temperament that could ill repress real sentiment, he gave utterance to views offensive to the governing powers, and his safety required on his part a voluntary self-expatriation. He came to America in the fall of 1831, having just completed the twenty-fifth year of his age. He spent his first year in Easton, Pa., where he applied himself assiduously to the learning of the English language. His stores of classical and philosophical learning were at this time of little avail, and he derived the most immediate advantage to himself from his knowledge of music, of which he was a master. He procured his support by giving lessons on the piano. In June, 1832, he went to York, Pa., and took charge of the classical school, then an appendage of the Theological seminary, in which capacity he labored up to 1835. In this latter year he moved to Mercersburg, and was chosen president of Marshall College. In this responsible position he continued to labor, in the midst of great difficulties and discouragements, up till the time of his death, which occurred March 2d, 1841. His remains, after resting in Mercersburg for eighteen years, were brought to Lancaster in 1859, and now lie in front of Franklin and Marshall college edifice. Lancaster you should be proud that your earth forms the urn of one of Germany's noble band of philosophic thinkers.

ately, or was altogether laid aside and another dictated at once. To his class he seemed always prepared on the topics of the recitation, and perfectly at home on all collateral matters claiming attention. On subjects connected with personal piety, he was in the habit of speaking to the students, and embraced every fitting opportunity to give them counsel and to urge upon them the importance of a prayerful and holy life.

Dr. Mayer edited for many years, with great acceptance, the *Magazine and Messenger* of the German Reformed church, and occasionally contributed ably written articles for some of the leading American reviews. Among his published works, are those on the *Sin against the Holy Ghost; Lectures on Scriptural Subjects*, and his *History of the German Reformed church.* He died August 25th, 1849.

MAYER, NATHANIEL, was elected a member of the Legislature in the years 1862 and 1863.

McALISTER, ARCHIBALD, was a member of the Legislature in the year 1820.

McALISTER, JACOB, was elected County Commissioner in the year 1832.

McCAMANT, JOHN, was a member of the Legislature in the years 1824 and 1827. In 1826 he was the Democratic competitor of James Buchanan for Congress.

McCLEERY, CARPENTER, was elected Clerk of Quarter Sessions and Oyer and Terminer in the year 1845.

McCLURE, JOSEPH, was elected to the Legislature in the years 1840 and 1841.

McCULLOCH, WM., was a member of the Legislature in the year 1820.

McEVOY, PATRICK, an extensive contractor and banker, was born at Millick, Queens county, Ireland. He emigrated to America friendless, and found employment with a railroad contractor in a subordinate position. Having shown a rare acuteness in business, he was encouraged to embark in contracting, and in this he proved remarkably fortunate. In a few years he became one of the most extensive contractors in the country, and had large contracts in the construction

of the Pennsylvania railroad, the New York and Erie railroad, and the Susquehanna and Tide Water canal; he was
also a contractor on a railroad in New Jersey. It was he
who built the section of the Pennsylvania Central railroad
at Kittaning point, which is regarded by railroad men as one
of the finest pieces of work in the United States. Mr. Mc-
Evoy lived many years near the city of Lancaster, and was
a man highly esteemed and respected. In 1864 he was the
Democratic elector for this district on the Presidential ticket.
He was a director of the old Lancaster bank, and filled
numerous other official positions of trust. At the time of his
death he was engaged in completing a very heavy contract
for the Philadelphia and Erie railroad company, in construct-
ing Bennet's branch railway, eighteen miles in length, at
Driftwood. He died February 1st, 1870, in the sixty-fifth
year of his age.

*McGOWAN FAMILY. John McGowan emigrated from
Ireland about the time of the last war with England, when
quite young. He was an enterprising and intelligent man,
and by his persevering industry and good character, rose
from being a clerk to an extensive manufacturer of iron in
Sadsbury township. He was united in marriage about the
year 1830 with Catharine, the daughter of William and Sarah
Knott, and settled on a farm which he purchased in the
valley. He died in the year 1851, leaving his widow with
nine sons and five daughters, who are all living at the present time (except one which died in infancy.) The family
now own most of the original tract of Moses Musgrove in the
valley. They are the well-known, highly respectable Mc-
Gowan family, among whom are William McGowan, esq.,
John McGowan and Joseph McGowan, late assistant assessor of internal revenue.

McGRANN, JOHN, brother of Richard McGrann, was an
enterprising business man and contractor.

McGRANN, RICHARD, a prominent contractor, who died
October 14th, 1867, aged seventy years. The following is
from the Philadelphia *Press :*

"Richard McGrann was well known in Pennsylvania as one of the
*Contributed by Isaac Walker, of Sadsbury.

28

most enterprising and courageous contractors in the State. The elegant bridge which spans the Schuylkill at the end of Chestnut street, Philadelphia, is a lasting and most creditable monument of his labor. The Pennsylvania and Northern Central railroads, as well as many other lines testify to his energy and success. At the time of his death he was engaged on a large and handsome railroad bridge near Easton. He came from Ireland when a young man, poor and friendless. He was a man of controlling weight in his county, and the head of a large and substantial family connection. He was a gentleman of warm impulses, unimpeachable integrity, and great public spirit."

He was a delegate to the Democratic State Convention in 1863.

McLENEGAN, ZEPHANIAH, appointed Prothonotary in 1839.

McMILLAN, JOHN, a member of the Legislature in 1776.

McSPARREN, JAMES, elected Commissioner in 1806.

MEHAFFEY, GEORGE W., was elected Commissioner in 1871.

MEHAFFEY, HUGH, was appointed Register of Wills in 1836.

MERCER, CAPT. J. Q., was born in Sadsbury township, and belongs to Quaker ancestry. He was engaged in teaching school when the firing upon Fort Sumpter roused the country to arms. He immediately enlisted for the three months' service in company K, of 20th regiment (Scott Legion). Upon the expiration of this service he reënlisted as 3d duty sergeant in company P, 28th Pennsylvania volunteer infantry, and served in the same until after the battle of Antietam, when the company was transferred and made a part of the 147th volunteer infantry. His company afterwards formed part of the army of the Cumberland, under the command of Gen. Hooker. He was with his company and a participant in many of the hard fought battles of the rebellion, and amongst these, Lookout Mountain, Antietam, Mission Ridge, Chancellorsville, Ringgold, Resaca, Gettysburg, Snicker's Gap, and Pine Knob. In the latter engagement he was wounded in the right leg above the knee, June 16th, 1864, having been previously commissioned captain of his company, June 8th of the same year. On account of this wound he was necessitated to suffer amputation of his right leg, and after a hospital confinement of some months was discharged from service, March 2d, 1865. In October of 1866 he was nominated and elected clerk of the orphans' court of Lancaster county, the duties of which office he discharged to the satisfaction of the public.

MERCER, JAMES, was a member of the Legislature in the years 1781, 1782, 1783 and 1784.

MICHAEL, WILLIAM, was elected clerk of the Quarter Sessions in the year 1830.

MILLER, DAVID, was elected Sheriff of Lancaster county in the year 1785, and held the same for three years. He was elected to the Legislature in 1789. He was also elected to the State Senate in 1794, and in 1801 returned again to the Legislature.

MILLER, GEN. HENRY, a native of Lancaster county, was a conspicuous officer of the American army during the Revolutionary war. He was engaged in many of the hard fought battles of that stirring period. He was born in the year 1741, and died at Carlisle in the year 1824.

*MILLER, HENRY, was born in Reading, Berks county, Pa., December 18th, 1774, came to Manheim in 1803, where he carried on the hatting business. During life, being of a domestic, quiet disposition, he meddled little with public affairs. In 1826 the Federal party, to which he belonged, nominated him for a seat in the Legislature without his knowledge or consent. When apprised of it, he first declined ; after considerable persuasion, his friends succeeded in having him accept the nomination. He was elected and served the session of 1826–27. In 1827 he was again nominated for the same position. At this time parties were closely divided between Democrats and Federals. General Jackson being nominated for President, strengthened the Democratic party considerably in the county, and he was this time defeated. He spent the remainder of his life in private, much respected in the community in which he was so well known. He died May 11th, 1847, aged 73 years, 7 months and 21 days.

*Contributed by Abraham Kauffman.

MILLER, JOHN, a farmer of Manheim township, was elected County Commissioner in the year 1839. He was one of the early anti-slavery men of his district; a great friend of the free school system, when his township was opposed to it; and an advocate of the cause of temperance. He was one of the most devoted friends of Thaddeus Stevens in the county. Besides agricultural pursuits, he latterly carried on the business of milling.

MILLER, MARTIN, was elected County Commissioner in the year 1843.

MILLER, TOBIAS H., was elected Recorder of Deeds in the year 1854.

MILES, COLONEL DAVID, is a native of Franklin county, Pa., born in 1831. In his youth he worked upon a farm, then learned the tin and sheet-iron business, which he followed till the breaking out of the rebellion. He went out as orderly sergeant of the Lancaster Fencibles in the three months service, and after this term of duty had expired, he again marched as First Lieutenant of company B of the 69th regiment of Pennsylvania volunteers, under Captain Duchman. Upon the promotion of Captain Duchman to be Lieutenant Colonel of the regiment, Lieutenant Miles took his place as Captain, and afterwards succeeded him as Lieutenant Colonel when the former left the army. He participated in the battles of Perryville, Stone River and Chickamauga, in which last he was taken prisoner, and was detained as such in Libby Prison, Richmond, at Macon, Georgia, and at Charleston, South Carolina. After being exchanged, he served in Sherman's famous march to the sea in command of a brigade, and fought in the battle of Bentonville, where he was wounded, besides many other minor engagements. He was discharged from service with the rank of Colonel by brevet. In 1866 he was nominated and elected register of wills of Lancaster county, the duties of which he discharged for three years.

MITCHELL, JAMES, was elected a member of the Legislature in the years 1729, 1744, 1745 and 1746.

MOHLER, JOHN, was a member of the Legislature in the years 1801 and 1802.

MOHLER, Samuel, was a member of the Legislature in the year 1827.

MONTGOMERY, John R.,[1] was one of the ablest lawyers and finest pleaders that ever practiced at the Lancaster bar. A cotemporary, writing of him, says: "His mind was well schooled and disciplined in a knowledge of all of our political institutions, in the varied systems which prevail under the constitutions and legislation of the different States; with a thorough knowledge of the adjudications of the national and State tribunals, and with all these qualifications he possessed, in an eminent degree, that untiring assiduity, energy and integrity which are necessary to discharge the high responsibilities that devolve upon the profession. In the inferior and in the superior courts, in every position in which he was placed in the profession, he displayed that legal learning that marked him as one of the ablest men of the State and nation." James Buchanan, in speaking of the case of Reichenbach vs. Reichenbach, which was the last in which he ever appeared as an attorney, and which had been prepared for trial by John R. Montgomery, said it was the best prepared case he had ever known. On another occasion he remarked to a legal friend, that "of all the lawyers he had ever encountered in the trial of a cause, John R. Montgomery seemed to him the weightiest." He died November 3d, 1854. The subject of our notice yet lives fresh in the memory of the members of the profession and people of Lancaster city and county, and throughout Pennsylvania; and whenever ability with oratory combined are being estimated, as to members of the Lancaster bar, amongst groups of legal gentlemen, a trio of brilliant names always associated are sure to be mentioned, those of John R. Mongomery, George Washington Barton and Washington Hopkins.

MONTGOMERY, Joseph, the father of John R. Montgomery, esq., was a member of the Legislature in the year

[1] When, in September, 1824, Gen. Lafayette visited Lancaster, John R. Montgomery engrossed much of his attention; and when he left Lancaster the latter escorted him in his carriage, drawn by match greys, as far as Port Deposit, Maryland. On their way they stopped at the Black Bear tavern, and at that place met with several of his old soldiers of the Revolution, and he shook hands with them for the last time.

1782. He carried on the busines of blacksmithing, and also farming. The following anecdote is told as regards him : Being a strict Presbyterian, his family had been in the habit of never preparing supper on Sunday. Having an Irishman as a journeyman blacksmith in his employ, the latter was told that it was the custom of the family to have no supper, as there was no work going on. The journeyman had been used to Sunday suppers, and, going out to the blacksmith shop, he began work hammering upon the anvil as usual. Mr. Montgomery going to the shop, asked the Irishman what all that meant, as he did not allow working on Sunday. The Irishman replied, that he had been told that he could get no supper unless he worked, and that he desired. The journeyman had no occasion further to begin working in order to get his Sunday supper.

MOORE, ANDREW, brother of John and Thomas Moore, came from Ireland in the year 1723, and settled near Sadsbury township, Lancaster county. He was a man of great piety, of indomitable courage and energy of character, and was in possession of considerable means. He purchased large tracts of lands lying on both sides of the Octoraro, and shortly after his arrival built the first mill in the southwest, near Penningtonville, Chester county, the old remains of which are yet visible. Although his own residence was on the Chester county side, yet his improvements extended into both counties. He erected another mill on the west side of the creek, and other substantial buildings, some of which are yet standing. He was chiefly instrumental in establishing the Friends' meeting-house, at " Old Sadsbury," in 1724, and his descendants stood at the head of the society for upwards of one hundred years.* He had seven sons and two daughters, all of whom reared families. His sons were James, David, John, Robert, Andrew, William and Joseph ; and his daughter, Sarah, married to William Truman, and Rachel, the wife of John Truman. Andrew Moore lived to a very advanced age, and left sixty-seven grandchildren, several of whom attained to the age of 100 years. The only survivor among the grandchildren, is Phœbe Wicker-

*Retrospect of early Quakerirm, by Dr. Michener.

sham, who, in 1870, was in the 85th year of her age. Andrew
and Isaac Moore, of Sadsbury, Lancaster county, and Henry
Moore, of Chester county, are amongst his descendants, who
still own and occupy parts of the original purchases of land
made by their early ancestor.

*MOORE, JAMES, son of Andrew Moore, was born in Ire-
land, 1716, and came over with his parents in 1723. He
married Ann, daughter of Jeremiah and Rebecca Starr, about
1740. He was among the leading pioneers in the settlement
of Sadsbury,[1] and was a very pious and worthy man. The
old mill below Christiana was re-built by him, and he erected
those substantial stone dwellings along the Octoraro which,
together with the mill, have been standing in good condition
for more than one hundred years. Most of the old improvements in that neighborhood were built by himself and his
family. James Moore was a minister in the society of
Friends, and labored greatly for the advance of truth and
righteousness, not only among those of his own society, but
amongst others. He contributed largely for the purpose of
erecting the present meeting-house at Sadsbury, about the
year 1760, and afterwards bequeathed a large sum of money
in care of the society, the interest of which was to be applied

[1] The first land purchased from the proprietors in Sadsbury township,
and perhaps within the present limits of Lancaster county, is part of
what is known at present as the " Pownall tract," lying west of the
Octoraro, in the great valley about one mile south of Christiana, and
containing about 300 acres. It was conveyed by William Penn to John
Kennerly, of Shawangta, (or Shawanatown), and the deed bears the
date of the year 1691. The deed is still retained in the Pownall family
with the name of William Penn attached thereto. This tract was afterwards purchased from Kennerly by Constantine Overton in the year 1796,
and by him re-sold in the year 1708 to George Pierce, of Concord, Chester county. The latter, in company with Robert Pyle, was appointed
by the quarterly meeting at Chester, to go down to Nottingham for
the purpose of establishing a meeting there. Retrospect of Early
Quakerism, p. 254. While at Nottingham he met with friends who
expressed a desire to visit the Indians in the western parts of Chester
county and at the Susquehanna, and he accompanied them. They
traveled through the woods and were kindly received by the Indians at
Conestoga.

At that time the Shawanese had wigwams along the banks of the

*The sketches of the Moore Family were contributed by Isaac Walker,
of Sadsbury.

to the education of the children of members in low circumstances; but provided it was not needed in the society, then
it should be appropriated for the education of others who
were not members, without regard to *color ;* this money remains a school fund in the hands of the society to the present day. Mr. Moore was a man of herculean strength, who
was able to carry nine bushels of corn up the mill steps at
one time. He was able to take a fifty-six pound weight on
each of his little fingers and touch them together over his
head.*

He married his fourth wife when 75 years of age, and also
survived her. He died in the year 1810, aged 94 years, and
his descendants comprise a large and respectable portion of
the citizens of Sadsbury, Lampeter, Columbia, and many other
places. James Moore had, by his first wife, four sons and
two daughters, all of whom attained to considerable age and
raised families. His sons were Andrew, Jeremiah, John,
and Doctor James Moore; and the daughters, Rebecca intermarried with John Cooper, the father of Calvin, Jeremiah,
James, John, and William Cooper; and Ann, who was married
to Asahel Walker, the grandfather of Joseph C. Walker, of
Salisbury, and of Isaac Walker, of Sadsbury.

MOORE, JOHN, brother of Andrew and Thomas Moore,
Octoraro, and an Indian village called "Old Shawana town." Rupp's
History of Lancaster, p. 42. It was probably on this visit that George
Pierce first discovered this tract of land, which he purchased and settled
on two years afterwards. He was among the very first pioneers who
made a substantial settlement in Lancaster county. Meetings of worship were held at the house of George Pierce, near the residence of the
late Joseph Pownall, many years before the meeting at "Old Sadsbury"
was established, and these meetings were attended by the Musgroves,
the Leonards and other early Quakers. The old grave yard which had
been laid out on land now owned by Levi Scarlet, 4 rods square, was reserved in the patent given by William Penn to Moses Musgrove, (the
original patent is now in the hands of the McGowan family.) At the
time of the organization of Lancaster county, Caleb Pierce, son of
George Pierce, was appointed one of the associate justices of the Lancaster county Court, and held other important trusts. Some years afterwards they sold out to the Musgroves and removed to Fallowfield, Chester county, and their descendants in both counties are numerous and
respectable ; among the number is the well known George Pierce, of
Bart township.

*Friends Miscellany, vol. vi., p. 45.

purchased the Christiana tract in the year 1727, which had been patented by Philip Howell in 1702 and 1703. John Moore left no children, and willed his property to Thomas Moore, his brother, in 1728, who sold it to Calvin Cooper about six years afterwards.

MOORE, THOMAS, brother of Andrew and John Moore, was an early pioneer in the settlement of the eastern section of Lancaster county. He came from Ireland and settled in Sadsbury township, at a very early day. He had erected the first grist mill on the Brandywine creek before the year 1718, from which a public road led to Philadelphia, called the King's highway.* At a council held at Philadelphia, May 29th, 1718, a petition of several of the inhabitants of and near Conestoga, was presented, setting forth the great necessity of a road to be laid out from Conestoga to Thomas Moore's mill and the Brandywine; and the board having taken said petition into consideration, appointed Isaac Taylor, John Taylor, John Cartlidge, Ezekiel Harlen, Thomas Moore, Joseph Cloud, (of Pequea), and William Marsh, to lay out said road, and make report thereof to the Board, in order to be confirmed.†

MORRISON FAMILY. Samuel and James Morrison, brothers, settlers originally in Drumore township, about 1717 or 1718. They emigrated from the North of Ireland. Each of them took up considerable tracts of land. Samuel lived with his brother and his family, and died leaving no heirs. James Morrison had two sons, named James and Daniel, both of whom were prominent men in their day. James Morrison, jr., was a captain of the militia, and served for a time as a soldier of the Revolution. He was a member of the Legislature in the years 1791, 1792, 1793, and 1795. His son, Daniel, was also a member of the Legislature in the years 1818 and 1819. Samuel Morrison served in the Legislature in the years 1822 and 1824 ; and George Morrison in the years 1845 and 1846. George was born in 1789, and died in 1860. George Morrison was an extensive cattle and sheep grazier, and an influential man in the community.

*Col. Records, vol. iii., p. 142.   †Col. Records, vol. iii., p. 43.

MOSHER, JEREMIAH, a blacksmith in Lancaster for many years. He served under Arnold in the attempt to storm Quebec, and was one of the forlorn hope which penetrated to the works in what was called the lower town. All his companions were killed or wounded but himself, and being taken prisoner, was afterwards released, and served in the American army till the close of the Revolution, and then retired covered with honorable scars. He carried on black-smithing extensively in Lancaster, and did most of the work for the different stage lines running from Philadelphia through Lancaster to Pittsburg. He was a man of excellent character and good judgment. He was a member of the Legislature in 1815 and in 1818. He was elected colonel in 1812. He was buried with the honors of war, and a horse upon which his regimentals were placed, was led in his funeral procession.

MUHLENBERG, FREDERICK AUGUSTUS, M. D., was born in Lancaster city, Pa., March 14th, 1795. Having attained an education, he studied medicine under the instruction of the celebrated Dr. Rush, and graduated with high honors at the university of Pennsylvania, April 9th, 1814. He immediately began the practice of his profession in Lancaster, being but 19 years of age; and he was not slow in winning his way to public confidence, and establishing for himself a large and lucrative practice. In 1821 he received from Governor Hiester the appointment of prothonotary of Lancaster county, an office he held until succeeded in 1823 by N. W. Sample. He was for many years president of the old Lancaster Bank, and to himself and James Evans, cashier of the institution, was it owing that the old corporation enjoyed for a long time a high degree of popularity and business prosperity. He served as trustee and treasurer of the old Franklin. college for many years, and exerted the weight of his influence in securing the removal of Marshall college to this place, and the consolidation of the two institutions into the present Franklin and Marshall college. Upon the establishment of the State Lunatic Asylum at Harrisburg, he was named as one of the trustees, a position he held until relieved at his own request. He had no political aspirations, but owing to his great personal popularity, he was often urged to become the candidate of his party for office, but usually declined. On one occasion he was the candidate of the Democratic party against Thaddeus Stevens for Congress. He gave his steady attention to the business of his profession for a period of over fifty years, and for a long time ranked as one of the two leading physicians of Lancaster. Even in his later years, when physical infirmity required of him to relinquish the most of his business, a large number of his old patients still clung to him, and anxiously sought his professional advice.

Upon the breaking out of the Southern rebellion, he gave his adhesion to the war party in favor of the restoration of the Union of the States, and thenceforth acted with the Republican organization. He lent his influence towards the establishment of the Union League in Lancaster, and acted as its first President. For many years he was, perhaps, the leading member of the Trinity Lutheran church, of which he was a steady and consistent member. In all charitable and benevolent movements, Dr. Muhlenberg always bore a prominent part, and but few enterprises of importance were inaugurated unless he was first consulted. He died July 5th, 1867, in the 73d year of his age.

MUHLENBERG, HENRY ERNST, the youngest son of Henry Melchoir Muhlenberg and his wife, Anna Maria, (a daughter of the celebrated Conrad Weiser,) was born in Montgomery, Pa., November 17th, 1753. He attained the rudiments of an education in his native village, and after his parents removed to Philadelphia, he attended the schools of that city. In 1763 he and his elder brothers were sent to Europe, and were entered as pupils in the orphan house of Halle. He here pursued his studies, and obtained a knowledge of the Latin, Greek, Hebrew and French languages. In 1769 he entered the university, where he remained for one year, and returned to America in September, 1770. In the following month he was ordained by the Synod of Pennsylvania, at Reading, and became his father's assistant, preaching in Philadelphia, Barren Hill, and in the churches on the Raritan. On the 4th of April, 1774, he was elected minister of the Philadelphia congregation, which position he held until the British obtained possession of Philadelphia, when he retired to New Providence. During the period of the Revolution his situation was transitory for a time, and until he accepted the charge of the Trinity Lutheran Church in Lancaster, in 1780. Here he spent thirty-five years of useful and active life in ministerial duty, and until the shaft of death removed him from the sphere of his usefulness, May 23d, 1815. The University of Pennsylvania conferred upon him the degree of doctor of divinity, a merited tribute to his learning and varied attainments. As a theologian, he ranked amongst the ablest in the Lutheran church of America. In the study of natural science he evinced a great fondness, especially in botany, and was named by Dr. Baldwin, the *American Linnæus*. He was, in 1804, honored by a visit from the distinguished scientist and traveler, Alexander von Humboldt. He prepared and published an English and German lexicon and grammar, in 2 vols. He wrote the "Catalogus Plantarum" and the "Descriptio Uberior Graminum," works frequently quoted by botanical writers in Europe and America. He has also left considerable manuscript materials on theology and ethics.

*MUSGROVE FAMILY. John, Aaron, Moses, Thomas and Abraham Musgrove, were the first settlers in the valley of Sadsbury, Lancaster county. Their warrant bears date in the year 1713. They purchased nearly all the land in that rich valley from George and Caleb Pierce, cleared off their land, and erected themselves residences, some of which stand to the present day. They were members of the society of Friends, and attended the meetings for worship at the house of George Pierce for many years before the establishment of the meeting-house at old Sadsbury. The old Musgrove burying ground was expressly reserved by Moses Musgrove, when, in 1747, he sold the land to Samuel Williams. It was on the southeastern part of the place, and is now on the land of Levi Scarlet. It was kept enclosed with a fence within the recollection of the oldest inhabitants, but having fallen into sacrilegious hands, it was plowed up long since with the cultivated field.

*Contributed by Isaac Walker, of Sadsbury.

JOHN MUSGROVE, sr., was a valuable and worthy member of society, and stood among the most prominent of the early pioneers in the settlement of Lancaster county. At a council held at Philadelphia,. October 15th, 1726, a petition of divers inhabitants about Pequea, in the county of Chester, was presented, setting forth that, by an order of Chester court, a road had been laid out through the township of Pequea, over hills, swamps, rocks, &c., to the great inconvenience of travelers and the said inhabitants, which road is that which leads from Thomas Mill's place towards the township of Donegal, and therefore the petitioners pray, that six good men may be appointed to view the said road, and make such alterations therein as may be necessary for the public service. This petition being considered, it was ordered that John Wright, George Aston, Samuel Blunston, Samuel Rutt, John Musgrove and Edmund Cartlidge, or a majority of them, view the same road, and particularly that part leading through the township of Pequea, (now Strasburg, &c.) and make such alterations therein as may seem to them most just and reasonable for the public service, and make return of their proceedings herein to this board. Colonial Record, Vol. iii, p. 263.

John Musgrove was appointed a commissioner in the year 1728–29, to divide the county of Chester, at the time that Lancaster county was stricken off from Chester and organized. He was elected a member of the general Assembly for the years 1730–31. His son, John Musgrove, sr., served on the first grand jury in Lancaster, November, 1730. After having conveyed his lands to his sons, the old homestead to his son James Musgrove, he died about the year 1737, and was buried in the valley, at Musgrove's old burying-place. He was in all respects one of the most worthy and exemplary men of his time.

AARON MUSGROVE was also a worthy and serviceable citizen among the early settlers of Sadsbury. He was the original purchaser of a large tract of land in the valley (including that now owned by Levi Pownall.) He was one of the most influential men in that early settlement, and was greatly instrumental in procuring roads to be laid out, some of which yet bear his name. In the year 1738 he became a member of the Sadsbury meeting of Friends. In 1754 he sold his lands and removed and settled at New Garden, Chester county, Pa. His son, Aaron Musgrove, was married to Ann, the daughter of James and Alice Smith, of Lampeter township, in 1757. His grandson, Aaron Musgrove, was the leader of the party that captured, in the year 1788, those notorious desperadoes and outlaws, Abraham and Levi Doane, who were hanged at Philadelphia on the 24th of September of that year.[1] See Col. Record, vol. xv., p. 502.

MOSES MUSGROVE was also a valuable member of society among the first settlers of Sadsbury. He was well educated and did much to render the wilderness a fit dwelling-place for civilized men. After he had labored for more than thirty years in the settlement of Sadsbury, in his declining years he sold his estate to Samuel Williams, and removed to Fallowfield, in Chester county. It is now owned and occupied by Levi Scarlet, and that large and respectable family of the McGowans.

THOMAS and ABRAHAM MUSGROVE were also valuable members of the Friends' society, about the time Sadsbury monthly meeting was first established; and after having the names of their sons and daughters enrolled in the records of that meeting, they removed and settled at Darby, near Philadelphia, in 1749. Their lands are now owned by Truman Cooper, J. D. Carothers, esq., William Spencer, esq., Levi and Henry Pownall, the McGowans, John Allen, Calvin Carter and others. But a small remnant of their descendants reside at the present time in Lancaster county.

MUSSER, GEORGE, was born July 11th, 1777, and died May 26th, 1868. He went out as a Lieutenant in the war

---

[1] Philadelphia, Thursday, July 31st, 1788, before the Hon. Peter Muhlenberg, esq., Vice President, and the Board : Upon the opinion of the Attorney General, now received in favor of the claim of Aaron Musgrove and others, to the reward offered by proclamation of Council, dated the 26th of July, 1784, for apprehending and securing Abraham Doane and Levi Doane. Resolved, that two orders be drawn on the Treasurer in favor of Aaron Musgrove, Thomas Taylor, Benjamin Miller, William Webb and John Morrison, for the sum of one hundred pounds each, being the reward offered as aforesaid, for apprehending and securing Abraham and Levi Doane.

of 1812, and was promoted to the rank of Captain. He was for many years a director of the branch bank of Pennsylvania, located at Lancaster. He was elected one of the board of county commissioners in 1814. He was, with Wm. Cooper and John Bomberger, security for Wm. Hamilton, when he was elected treasurer of Lancaster county. He served for many years as an alderman of Lancaster. He was for nearly sixty years a member of the vestry of Trinity Lutheran church, and for a number of years one of the three trustees, an office only bestowed upon the oldest and most respected members.

MUSSER, HENRY, elected Clerk of Quarter Sessions in 1860.

MUSSER, JOHN, a member of the Legislature in 1820.

MUSSER, MICHAEL, elected County Commissioner in 1802.

MUSSELMAN, HENRY, elected County Commissioner in 1848.

MUSSELMAN, MICHAEL, elected County Commissioner in 1830.

MYERS, FREDERICK, elected Sheriff of Lancaster county in 1869.

MYERS, JAMES, is a leading citizen and iron-master of Lancaster county, and widely reputed for his benevolence and Christian charities. His sympathies have ever strongly manifested themselves in behalf of the poor and down-trodden. He has on several occasions been spoken of as a candidate for Congress, but has informily declined a nomination for this position. He was elected to the Legislature of Pennsylvania in 1861.

MYERS, SAMUEL M., was born in Rapho township, Lancaster county, October 24th, 1824. He is of German descent. His great grandfather emigrated from Germany at an early day, and settled in the northeastern part of the county. He served about six months as an apprentice to the tailoring business, and afterwards went into the mercantile business, in which he continued up to 1860, when he was elected Clerk of the Orphans' Court.

N.

NAUMAN, Col. George, U. S. A., was born in Lancaster, October 7th, 1802. He entered the U. S. Military Academy at West Point, as a cadet, in 1819; in 1821 was acting assistant professor of French in that institution; in 1823 he graduated, and the same year was appointed second lieutenant of the first regiment of artillery; was assistant instructor of French at West Point, from September, 1828, to August, 1829; promoted first lieutenant, May, 1832. He served continuously in the Florida war from February, 1836, to May, 1838, and was distinguished particularly in the battle of Wahoo Swamp; captain of first artillery, February, 1837; served through the Mexican war under Generals Taylor and Scott; brevet-major for gallant and meritorious conduct at the battle of Cerro Gordo, April 18th, 1847; brevet-lieutenant colonel for gallant and .meritorious conduct at the battles of Contreras and Cherubusco, August 20th, 1847; and was wounded in the battle of Chapultepec, September 8th, 1847. He commanded the first regiment of artillery, and was commissioner of prize, at Vera Cruz, at the close of the war, and conducted the evacuation of that city by the U. S. army. He served on the Pacific coast from May, 1854, to January, 1861; was promoted major of the third regiment of artillery, December 24th, 1843, and commanded that regiment from May, 1854, to March, 1857, and for seven months in 1860; was inspector of artillery for the department of Oregon and California, from 1859 to 1861, and conducted the artillery school at Fort Vancouver in 1860. He was promoted lieutenant-colonel of the first artillery, July 23d, 1861, and was chief of artillery at Newport News, in March, 1862, during the engagement with the Merrimac, Yorktown, Jamestown, and other rebel steamers, on which occasion he was favorably mentioned by General Mansfield, in his report of the affair. He was stationed at Fort Warren, in the harbor of Boston, in 1863, engaged in placing that important work in a proper state of defence.

He was promoted colonel of the fifth artillery, August 1st, 1863, and died in Philadelphia, August 11th, 1863, of sun-stroke, his health having been much impaired by exposure and hardships incident to his long and faithful services.

For forty years he served the United States, and had been stationed in every section of the Union, participating in three wars, and in every capacity acquitted himself with honor and distinction. He had just left California, and was with his family, then residing in Florida, when the rebellion broke out. He was offered high rank and command by the men then organizing the new confederacy, but he spurned the offer, preferring to stand by the flag under which he had so often fought. As a compliment to his long and distinguished services, the war department issued the order promoting him colonel of the fifth artillery, after they had received official notice of his death.

NEALE, THOMAS, was a member of the Legislature in 1835.

NEVIN, JOHN WILLIAMSON, D.D., was born February 20th, 1803, in Franklin county, Pa. He is descended from Scotch-Irish ancestry, and one conspicuous in statesmanship and literature. His paternal grandmother was a sister of the distinguished Hugh Williamson, LL.D., one of the framers of the United States Constitution, and a man noted in the re-public of letters. His parents were strict members of the Presbyterian church, and the subject of this notice was early indoctrinated into the religious principles of this influential and respectable body of Christians. His father was a farmer and a man of strong native ability, who had received a liberal education, having graduated at Dickinson college, Carlisle, Pa., then under the presidency of the celebrated Dr. John Nesbit. The subject of this notice being designed by his father for one of the learned professions, he was early intro-duced by that parent to the knowledge of the Latin and Greek languages, preparatory to his entering upon a college career. In the autumn of 1817 he was matriculated as a student in Union college, New York, then under the presi-dency of Dr. Nott. Although the youngest in his class, he was able to rival in study any of his classmates, and gradu-

29

ated with honor in 1821. His college course was a severe ordeal for him. Owing to his youth and the close application he had given to study (for his ambition would not allow him to be outstripped by his classmates), he left his Alma Mater with health prostrated, and for the next two years was sickly and unable to engage in any avocation. When at college, he attended a series of revival meetings conducted by a Mr. Nettleton, and professing a change of heart, he united himself as a member of the visible church of Christ.

The bodily prostration that followed his classic career, was accompanied with dyspeptic ailments, and being advised to take plenty of exercise upon his father's farm in his wanderings amongst the fields and woods, he acquired for a time a taste for botanical pursuits. He was in the habit of perambulating for days upon horseback and upon foot in search of plants and flowers; and of these, in a short time, he acquired quite a collection. This course of life was at the time just what was required; and as health began to return, his thoughts recurred to the fancy scenes of Greece and Rome once more. Gradually the study of Cicero and Homer was again taken up; and the sweet flowing language of Fenelon and Bossuet, for which he had an especial taste, was now prosecuted with greater zeal than ever. Martial arder came in for a share of recognition also from our youthful *ad libitum* student, and having united himself in a military company, he was unanimously chosen orderly sergeant.

After his health was found to be quite well restored, and it was perceived that he was again giving much of his attention to study, he was induced, in conformity with the wish of his father, to take up the study of theology. This had from the first been the wish of his parent, but was abandoned when he returned from college, utterly bankrupt in health, and for a long time showed scarcely any signs of returning strength. Accordingly, in pursuance of this view, he entered the theological seminary at Princeton, in the fall of 1823. Ever impelled with a longing and thirst for knowledge, he felt an inexpressible pleasure as soon as the consecrated walls of the seminary had enclosed him. He thereupon made no haste to prosecute his career with great celerity through the seminary, feeling that in this institution a more congenial home existed for him as a student than might be found in any other pursuit of which, as yet, he had any knowledge. In the regular theological course of the seminary, he took a special interest in oriental and biblical literature, and made great progress in the study of Hebrew, outstripping in this branch all his classmates. Before the close of his seminary course, he had read the whole Bible in Hebrew, and secured the flattering distinction of being universally admitted as the best Hebrew scholar in the institution. This distinction in Hebrew scholarship was what formed the turning point in his life, and contributed to mould his whole subsequent career. It was owing to this distinction that he was, in 1826, invited to supply the place of Dr. Hodge, who had gone on a visit of two years to Europe for the benefit of the institution. This occupied his attention for the next two years, at the small salary of $200 per annum, and it was during this period that he wrote his Biblical Antiquities, an excellent hand-book of Bible knowledge, and one which has obtained an extensive circulation, not only in America but also in Europe. Upon the return of Dr. Hodge from Europe in 1828, his duties expired at Princeton, and in October of the same year he was licensed to preach the Gospel by the Carlisle Presbytery; and to this he now devoted himself for the next year in a more or less itinerant manner.

Before leaving Princeton, he had been selected as the person who should fill the chair of biblical literature in the new Western Thelogical Seminary in Allegheny city, which the general assembly of the Presbyterian church were taking steps to establish. During this time he became enlisted in the cause of temperance, and, as a consequence, his sermons breathed more or less frequently denunciations of the sin of manufacturing and selling intoxicating liquors. He became exceedingly ardent and condemnatory at times of the dram-shops, and he was by no means careful to discriminate whether his remarks might occasion offence, should some be present whom his castigation might personally affect. This proved to be the case in fact, and in one instance turned out to his disadvantage. A call of a large and wealthy congregation was about being extended to him, but because he had preached a sermon which inflicted severe censure upon the liquor-selling members, these feeling themselves personally aggrieved, exerted their influence in preventing the call being made. In the spring of 1829 he set out *au cheval* to see after the theological seminary in Allegheny city, and so shaped his arrangements that he should return in the fall and undertake the duties assigned for him in the new institution. On returning home he became stated supply to the congregation at Big Spring, Cumberland county, for four months, and was strongly urged to become the pastor of this congregation. He also, about this time, received a pressing invitation to return to Princeton and become a writer of books for the Sunday School Union ; but his mind was now fully made up to go to Allegheny city.

The father of the subject of our notice died in 1829, and this devolved on him, as the oldest of the family, a weight of responsibility he had not heretofore felt. This necessitated him to give some of his time to business affairs, although up to the present period he had charged himself little with matters of this kind. In consequence of the new relations thus devolved upon him by the death of his father, he was not in condition to set out for Allegheny until the beginning of December of this year. When he entered upon the discharge of his duties as instructor in the Western Seminary, he was in the twenty-seventh year of his age. At the time Dr. Nevin entered upon this field of labor, the Western Seminary was but a feeble institution. It " had no buildings, no endowments, no prestige from the past, and only doubtful and uncertain promise for the future." The movements that had secured the establishment of this seminary had met with great opposition ; the affections of the east were wedded to Princeton ; and in the west great dissatisfaction was felt in its being thought not sufficiently central to meet western wants. Upon western Pennsylvania, as a consequence, devolved the whole responsibility as to the support of this institution. Prof. Luther Halsey and Dr. Nevin labored in the building up of this seminary, and their labors were crowned with good success. The Western Theological Seminary, which has now become a power in the Presbyterian church, owes much of its prosperity to the assiduity and ability of the subject of our notice. For the three first years of his life in Allegheny, Dr. Nevin made his home in the house of Dr. Francis Herron, president of the board of trustees, and until his mother and her family removed thither.

In 1835 Dr. Nevin was united in marriage with Martha, the second daughter of Hon. Robert Jenkins, of Windsor Place, in Lancaster county. During his whole ten years connection with the Western Seminary, Dr. Nevin continued to preach in different churches, almost as regularly as if in charge of a congregation. At first he officiated simply as a licentiate, but after some time was ordained in full to the ministry by the Presbytery of Ohio. During part of the time he preached with considerable regularity at a young ladies' seminary, at Braddock's Field, near Pittsburg, and afterwards served as stated supply for the congregation of Hilands, some miles out of Pittsburg. He frequently appeared as contributor to the press during his connection with the Western Seminary, and many sermons, delivered by him on special occasions, were published by request of the congregations before whom they were delivered. In 1833–34 he conducted the editorial management of the *Friend*, a literary and weekly journal in the service of the young men's society of Pittsburg and vicinity. This journal, while under the guidance of Dr. Nevin, was the unreserved opponent of infidelity, fashionable amusements, ladies' fairs, and theatrical entertainments; and the views of the editor upon these topics proved the occasion of considerable offence. On account of the opposition made by this journal to the movement set on foot to get up a theatre in Pittsburg, he was threatened with cowhiding; and on another occasion fears of a mob were apprehended, on account of the supposed incendiarism of the *Friend* upon the subject of slavery. For no other reason than the pro-slavery proclivities of the community at that time, was the journal obliged ultimately to succumb, the last issue appearing March 12th, 1835.

Dr. Nevin was ever the staunch and outspoken opponent of slavery in every form, and battled in favor of abolitionism in a truly Christian spirit. He, however, never sympathized with the so-called abolition party of the North, and openly condemned Garrison and his followers as irreligious in spirit and unpatriotic. But the system of slavery, as it existed in the southern States, was, in his opinion, a vast moral· evil, and one especially deserving criticism and censure. He never spared the institution in his articles in the *Friend;* and on one occasion he was denounced for this cause by a prominent physician of the place, as "the most dangerous man in Pittsburg." That his opinions upon this point may appear, some extracts from the *Friend* are here adduced. In the journal of April 17th, 1834, he speaks as follows: "We trust that the time is not far distant when, what has been rashly spoken by abolitionists and colonizationists may be forgotten, and the friends of humanity will find themselves able to stand on common ground in regard to the great evil of slavery, without denouncing either the one interest or the other. That abolitionism has exhibited, in some cases, a wildly extravagant form, we have no doubt; but we have just as little doubt that great and powerful principles of truth have been all along laboring underneath its action, and struggling to come to clear and consistent development by its means." In the valedictory issue of the *Friend,* Dr. Nevin thus discourses: "Slavery is a sin as it exists in this country, and as such it ought to be abolished. There is no excuse for its being continued a single day. The whole nation is involved in the guilt of it, so long as public sentiment acquiesces in it as a necessary evil. That which is absolutely necessary for its removal, is the formation of such a public sentiment throughout the country as will make slaveholders ashamed of their wickedness, and finally reform the laws under which the evil now holds its power in the different States. Such a sentiment has not heretofore existed, and it is plain that much discussion and thought are needed to call it into being. There is, therefore, just the same reason for the system of action pursued by the abolition society, with reference to this subject, that there is for the system of the temperance society with regard to the curse of ardent spirits. The institution and the effort are among the noblest forms of benevolent action witnessed in the present age. We glory then in being an abolitionist, and count it all honor to bear the reproach for such a cause. It is the cause of God, and it will prevail."

When the above sentiments were penned by Dr. Nevin, the Presbyterian church, along with the other churches of the country, was fully committed to the southern side of the slavery question, and considered it a religious, as well as a moral wrong, to meddle in the discussion of this question. The leading religious newspapers were, likewise, hostile to the anti-slavery movement in every form. All the ecclesiastical judicatories, as well as the anniversary meetings of all the great national religious societies, made it a point from year to year to ostracise and repress, by all manner of means, every attempt to get the question of slavery before them. The merest whisper of abolitionism was enough to throw a whole general assembly into agitation. In 1837 Dr. Nevin was unqualified in his dissent from the ecclesiastical policy which divided the Presbyterian church. In the struggle between the two great parties in the church, his sympathies were upon the side of the old school; but he nevertheless entertained the opinion, that the controversy on that side was in certain quarters urged forward in an extreme way. He deprecated especially, the idea of the Pittsburg Synod being forced to take part in the eastern quarrel with regard to Mr. Barnes; and he went so far as to urge seriously, through the *Christian Herald*, Dr. Alexander's plan of relatively independent Synodical jurisdiction. It was during Dr. Nevin's connection with the Western Seminary that he began the study of the German language, which he has succeeded in mastering, and now reads with equal ease and satisfaction as his vernacular. This study he undertook in order to reach the contents of the theological and philosophical works of the deep thinkers of Germany, the land of profound erudition and ripe scholastic attainment. The first work read by him in the German, was Neander's "Geist des Tertullianus." Dr. Nevin by this time had become a man widely reputed for his attainments in biblical science, and as a theologian of rare penetration and deep philosophical mind. His reputation had far passed the boundary of his own religious persuasion. His services, therefore, became a prize in the eyes of many, and he was tendered on the part of the Synod of the German Reformed church, the professorship of theology in the theological seminary at Mercersburg, Pa. In this call Dr. Nevin seemed to recognize the summons of his Divine Master, to a field in which he might be able to perform more effective service than in the one where he then labored. Accordingly, after mature and serious deliberation, he concluded to accept the position tendered him, and entered upon the duties thereof in May, 1840.

This change of position was not considered to be of itself any change of denominational faith. It was simply a transition from one section of the general *Reformed Confession* to another, and took place accordingly with the full approbation and favor of the friends of Dr. Nevin in the Presbyterian church. It was under the advice and recommendation in particular, of his former theological instructor, the late venerable Dr. Archibald Alexander, of Princeton. Still, like change of position in all cases, it exerted a material influence on the subsequent progress of his spiritual life, and became thus a central epoch for his history. Without taking him out of the Reformed church, it widened his view of its proper constitution and history, enlarged the range of his German studies, brought him into new and closer communication with the theological life of the Lutheran Confession, and in this way made room in his mind more and more for a sense of the catholic, the historical, the objective in Christianity, which may be taken as the key to the whole course of his thinking and working in the church afterwards, down to the present time.

In the theological seminary at Mercersburg, he found himself associated with the well-known German scholar, Frederick Augustus Rauch, who was at the same time president of Marshall college in the same place. The death of Dr. Rauch, March 2d, 1841, left Dr. Nevin in sole charge of the seminary, and made it necessary for him besides to assume the presidency of the college also; a provisional arrangement in the first place which, however, the wants of the infant institution converted into a permanent one; the office being held by Dr. Nevin, in fact, for ten years afterwards without any salary.

In 1843 Dr. Nevin became involved in what has been known as the "anxious bench controversy," through the publication of his tract called the *Anxious Bench*, directed against the use of certain means and methods (new measures), employed extensively at the time among different denominations in the service of religious revivals. This may be looked upon as the beginning of the movement which has since come to be spoken of as the Mercersburg theology; a movement whose ultimate bearings and consequences were not dreamed of at the time by either side in that first controversy, while they can easily be seen since, nevertheless, to lie all in one and the same direction. The controversy, while it lasted, was carried on with great activity, partly within the German Reformed church itself, but mainly in the end, as between this body and surrounding religious communions.

The same view of Christianity which led to the publication of the Anxious Bench, appears also in Dr. Nevin's opposition to another new measure, as we have it represented in his tract on *Religious Fairs*, published towards the close of the same year. This, however, was in the main but little more than what he had published on that subject ten years before, in Pittsburg.

In the fall of 1844 Dr. Nevin received as his colleague in the seminary, Dr. Philip Schaff, who had been brought by special call from Germany to fill the place whose name has since become famous throughout the world, and who is now honored as professor of church history in the Presbyterian theological seminary of New York. On the 25th of October this gentleman delivered his inaugural address at Reading, in the German language, a truly able discussion of the distinctive, original and fundamental meaning of the great Reformation of the sixteenth century. It was the first fair attempt to vindicate the historical right of Protestantism in

this country, and went full against the unhistorical spirit
which has all along formed the life and strength of our
American sectarianism. This work Dr. Nevin translated
and published in 1845, under the title, *The True Principle of
Protestantism as related to the Present State of the Church*,
with an introduction from his own pen, and by Dr. Schaff's
particular desire, with the appendage also of a sermon on
Catholic Unity, preached by Dr. Nevin the previous year,
before a convention of the Dutch and German Reformed
churches in Harrisburg, the whole forming a volume of more
than 200 pages. Here, of course, was new offence to the
general sect-spirit of the land. Anti-popery began to take
the alarm, and a formal attempt was made in a Synod held
at York, to make out a charge of heresy against the Mercersburg professors, particularly Dr. Schaff, but the result was
their triumphant vindication.

The following year, 1846, Dr. Nevin published the "*Mystical Presence;* a vindication of the Reformed or Calvinistic
doctrine of the Holy Eucharist." This also led to controversy. Strangely enough, Lutheranism, in certain cases,
contended against it by openly forsaking Luther, while
Presbyterianism did the same thing, by trying grossly to
falsify Calvin.

Looking in the same general direction, we have from the
pen of Dr. Nevin, in 1846, *The Church*, a sermon preached
at the opening of the German Reformed Synod, at Carlisle ;
in 1847, *The History and Genius of the Heidelberg Catechism ;*
and in 1848, a tract, entitled *Antichrist, or the Spirit of Sect and
Schism*. From January, 1849, to January, 1853, he edited
the *Mercersburg Review*, published by the alumni association
of Marshall college, being himself, during all this time, the
chief contributor to its pages. And he has written largely
since, also, for the same periodical, as well as for the *Reformed
Church Messenger*.

At the close of 1851 Dr. Nevin, much against the wish of
the church, resigned his situation as professor in the theological seminary, continuing however to act as president of
Marshall college until its removal to Lancaster, in 1853,
when it became consolidated with Franklin college, under

the title of Franklin and Marshall college. He was offered the presidency of this new institution, and the place was kept vacant for a whole year, with the hope of his being induced to accept it ; but in conformity with his previously declared intention he declined the service, and withdrew into private life, being now in truth much worn out, both in body and mind, and not expecting to take upon him again any public charge. He delivered, however, by special request, a baccalaureate address to the first graduating class of the new college, on the 31st of August, 1853, which was published as a tract, under the title of *Man's True Destiny*.

Leaving Mercersburg, after the removal of the college, Dr. Nevin lived for a year in Carlisle, where he stood in close and pleasant social relations with the professors of Dickinson college. He then came to Lancaster county, residing for a year first in the city ; in the next place, from the fall of 1856 to the spring of 1858, making his home, for domestic reasons, at Windsor Forge, near Churchtown, the old mansion property of his wife's father ; and finally settling himself permanently, where he has since continued to reside, in the immediate neighborhood of Lancaster city, at Cærnarvon Place. Through these years he still continued to preach frequently, and also to perform occasional work with his pen. He had much to do, in particular, with the long and difficult task of bringing to completion the new *Liturgy*, which engaged for so many years the best energies of the Eastern Synod of the German Reformed church.

In the end, as advancing age seemed to bring with it for him a renewal rather than a decline of health and strength, Dr. Nevin yielded to the desire there was to have him back again in the college, and in the fall of 1861 took upon him partial service in its faculty, as professor in particular of History and Æsthetics. Five years later, in 1866, he became once more president of the institution, with full charge, a position which he has continued to occupy since with all the vigor of his best days. In connection with the Sunday services, which devolve upon him as the pastor of the college church, his department of instruction embraces now, mainly by lectures, the Philosophy of History, the Principles of

Mental, Moral and Social Science, and the Science of Æsthetics in its modern German character and form.

No biographical account of Dr. Nevin, however brief, can be complete without some notice taken of the so-called Mercersburg system of theology, which it has been common on all sides to associate with his name. This has never claimed to be an original system or rounded whole in any way; neither has it owed its existence to any spirit of philosophical speculation, as has sometimes been imagined. It has grown forth historically from an interest in the felt needs of the Christian life itself. Without going into details, let it suffice here to present the following comprehensive outline of the system, taken from an article on the subject in vol. xii. of the new *American Encyclopædia*, published in 1863.

" The cardinal principle of the Mercersburg system, is the fact of the incarnation. This, viewed not as a doctrine or speculation, but as a real transaction of God in the world, is regarded as being necessarily itself the sphere of Christianity, the sum and substance of the whole Christian redemption. Christ saves the world, not ultimately by what He teaches, or by what He does, but by what He is in the constitution of His person. His person, in its relations to the world, carries in it the power of victory over sin, death, and hell, the force thus of a real atonement or reconciliation between God and man, the triumph of a glorious resurrection from the dead, and all the consequences for faith which are attributed to this in the Apostles' Creed. In the most literal sense, accordingly, Christ is here held to be ' the way, the truth, and the life,' ' the resurrection and the life,' the principle of ' life and immortality,' the ' light' of the world, its ' righteousness,' and its ' peace.' The ' grace which bringeth salvation,' in this view, is of course always a real effluence from the new order of existence, which has thus been called into being by the exaltation of the Word made flesh at the right hand of God. It must be supernatural as well as natural, and the agency and organs by which it works, must, in the nature of the case, carry with them objectively something of the same character and force. In this way the church is an object of faith; the presence of the new creation in the old world of nature; the body of Christ, through which as a medium and organ He reveals Himself and works until the end of time. It mediates with supernatural office, instrumentally, between Christ and His people. Its ministers hold a divine power from Him by apostolic succession. Its sacraments are not signs merely, but the seals of the grace they represent. Baptism is for the remission of sins. The eucharist includes the real presence of Christ's whole glorified life, in a mystery, by the power of the Holy Ghost. The idea of the church, when it is thus held as an object of faith, involves necessarily the attributes which were always ascribed to it in the beginning, unity, sanctity, catholicity, and apostolicity. The spirit of sect, as it cleaves to Protestantism at the present time, is a very great evil, which is of itself sufficient to show that if Protestantism had any historical justification in the beginning, its mission thus far has been only half fulfilled, and that it can be rationally approved only as it is taken to be an intermediate preparation for some higher and better form of Christianity hereafter. The distinguishing character of the Mercersburg theology, in one word, is its Christological interest, its way of looking at all things through the person of the crucified and risen Saviour. This, as the world now stands, embraces necessarily all that enters into the conception of the church question, which this system holds to be the great problem for the Christianity of the present time."

These views in the nature of the case, could not be otherwise than distasteful to much of the popular religionism of the country. For years, accordingly, as is well known, it has been the fashion in certain quarters to stigmatize them in the most contradictory terms of reproach, as rationalism, mysticism, pantheism, transcendentalism, Romanism, Irvingism, Swedenborgianism, and much else of like bad sound. By Dr. Nevin himself the system has been maintained all along as being, in his view, neither more nor less than the simple theology of the Apostles' Creed. Among his more important publications relating to it, and not yet named, may be mentioned the following: 1. *The Doctrine of the Re-*

formed Church on the Presence of Christ in the Lord's Supper;
an extended answer to Dr. Hodge's review of the "Mystical
Presence" in 1848. 2. *The Apostles' Creed: Its Origin, Constitution and Plan,* 1849. 3. *Early Christianity,* 1851. 4.
Cyprian, 1852. 5. *The Dutch Crusade,* 1854. 6. *Review
of Dr. Hodge's Commentary on the Ephesians,* 1857. 7. *The
Liturgical Question,* 1862. 8. *Christ, and Him Crucified;* a
concio ad clerum, preached at the opening of the first general Synod of the German Reformed church in Pittsburg,
1863. 9. *Vindication of the Revised. Liturgy,* 1867. 10.
Answer to Professor Dorner, of Berlin, Germany, 1868. 11.
Once for All; based on a sermon preached before the Synod
at Danville, Pa., 1869. 12. *Revelation and Redemption;*
opening sermon before the Synod at Mechanicsburg, 1870.
13. *The Revelation of God in Christ;* anniversary discourse
before the theological seminary at Mercersburg, 1871. 14.
Christ and His Spirit, 1872. 15. *Baccalaureate Discourse on
John iii: 13,* 1872.

Dr. Nevin, as a theologian, is one of no ordinary cast.
His strong dialectic acumen has led him far beyond the
range of mere theology, and has enabled him to unravel the
mazes that metaphysical subtilty has drawn around the
Christian faith. His own mind is a deeply metaphysical one,
and his profound inquiries into this department have led him
to scan the whole range of philosophy, and to investigate it
on the metaphysical side from Aristotle to Hegel, as well as
on the metaphysico-theological side, from Plato to Schleiermacher. The argumentations and reasonings of an Origen,
an Augustine, an Anselm, and an Aquinas, are to him no
longer mysteries. The thoughts of these world-renowned
thinkers he has made his own. Nor is he unfamiliar with
the range and results of modern German metaphysical ratio-
cination. He has, although an American, after having made
himself familiar with ancient forms of thought, and, after
grasping the results of the Kantian problems, kept pace with
the latest developments of the German mind. Like Jonathan
Edwards, unfavored with European university culture, who,
by his own innate strength of intellect, could grasp and
solve the problems of the philosophers of whom he had

never heard, and who ranks as the first metaphysician of his century, the subject of our notice has also probed the depth of the human understanding; and to his comprehensive mind metaphysical difficulties retire, and faith and reason stand harmonized in gospel revelation. To Dr. Nevin will history also accord, if not the highest niche in the temple of the metaphysical fame of the century, at least a very high one.

It is because he has made the different theological and metaphysical systems so thoroughly his own, and has by long usage and reading acquired their entire terminology, (which has now become a part of his own thinking), that his sermons and writings appear to those unfamiliar with such forms of thought, mazy and unintelligible. Often will his auditors confess that they do not comprehend his ideas. This is not strange. Whoever comprehends in a remote degree the vast revolution that theology has undergone in Germany during the last one hundred years, will not be surprised at this terminology made use of by Dr. Nevin. It is necessary if he be true to the feelings of his own soul, that he use no other manner of expression, for no other language conveys the deep import of evangelical truth as illuminated by the christological and philosophical developments of later ages. Not that any new truth is thereby promulgated, but modern thought is but fully awakening to the full comprehension of the great truths of revelation; those truths that ages ago to the mental eye of a St. Anselm and a Duns Scotus were looming into view. These intellectual giants were simply ages in advance of their times, and the moderns are but beginning to recognize the truths they so fervently attested.

Later ages, as they will come to take up in their conscience-preceptions, the discoveries of those now standing upon the highest pinnacles of mental vision, will see the rectitude of doctrines that are being promulgated and that are now so seemingly obscure. And in the march of ages, instead of Dr. John W. Nevin being found to have been the advocate of pantheistic absorption, he will gradually be elevated upon a pedestal in the Schleiermacherian school along with the brave leaders who strove to turn aside by the light of scientific and philosophical progress the stream of humanitarian error, and enable the faithful soldiers of the cross to capture the great Babylon of modern infidelity.

Dr. Nevin, as a critical scholar, has but few equals. He reads the Greek, Latin, Hebrew, French and German, with ease. Before taking up the study of German, he chiefly read theological works in the Latin; but for many years past, since his mastery of the German, he reads the most theological works in this latter language. In this he has perused the master-pieces of modern composition. He has a fine memory, and therefore retains most that he reads. His articles upon "Cyprian and His Age," published in the *Mercersburg Review*, evince his deep study of ancient christianity, and are of themselves sufficient to give him a high rank in the theological world. They are quoted and cited as standard authority even in Europe.

Dr. Nevin, deservedly, is entitled to rank amongst the first, if not as the very first theologian and metaphysician of America, after Jonathan Edwards. Had circumstances thrown him in a different sphere, where vast libraries would have surrounded him, and should he have chosen the field of history, he might have ranked with Mosheim and Neander. Choosing, however, to keep aloof from great metropolitan centres, he has attained to the merited distinction of being intelligently ranked amongst the first thinkers of his age; and after generations will universally concede to him a place in the category of a De Wette, a Dorner, a Daub, and at Marheineke.

In conversation, he is exceedingly entertaining, especially when the subject turns upon metaphysical questions; for in this department he seems especially at home. Any question propounded in theology or metaphysics will receive a minute and lengthy explanation, which serves more than all else to show the great depth and wonderful profundity of his mind. German, French and English schools of philosophy and theology will be cited, their diverging opinions presented and compared, and the correct conclusions of reason educed therefrom. In his lectures to the students of his classes, his breadth of mind and comprehensive grasp of the subject in hand are constantly apparent. In his deportment no triviality is ever perceptbile, but a gravity upon all occasions marks his demeanor.

In personal appearance Dr. Nevin is tall, spare and slender, and in the pulpit is not at once attractive. In his delivery of a sermon no indications of oratory appear. He is by no means fluent, and none but those who can follow an argument are much attracted by his preaching. His sermons, however, are pregnant with thought from beginning to end, showing complete mastery of his subject and great research. He has ever been a close student, and this his appearance indicates. Thought is marked upon every lineament of his countenance.

NISSLEY, C. H., elected County Commissioner in 1866.

NISSLEY FAMILY. Jacob Nissley, the original settler of this family, came to this country at an early day and settled in Mt. Joy township. He had five children—two sons and three daughters, viz: John, married a Sechrist, Martin, a Snyder; the daughters married, one a man named Buhrman, another an Eversole, and the other a Steward. John had six sons and one daughter, viz: Michael, Abraham; John, married to a Hertzler, born 1746 and died 1825; Jacob, father of Martin, of Conewago, died 1796; Rev. Samuel, his wife a Kreider, born 1761, died 1838; Martin, his wife a Lehman, born 1763, died 1825; and Fanny, her husbands, a Frantz, a Long, and a Hiestand, born 1759, died 1813. The children of Rev. John, of Paxton, were: Jacob, his wife, a Nissley; John, his wife, an Ober; Martin, his wife, a Landis, born 1786, died 1868; and Maria, her husbands, a Frantz and Rudy Martin. Jacob Nissley's children were: Martin, married to a Kreider; Fanny, to C. Mumma, born 1789; Elizabeth, to Long and Hershey, born 1794; and Maria, to a Bear, born 1784. The family of Rev. Samuel Nissley were: John, (Rapho), married to a Hershey, born 1786, died 1847; Martin, married to a Bomberger, born 1788; Sem, married to an Eby, born 1792, died 1868; Rev. Christian, married to a Bomberger, born 1794; Jacob, (Sporting Hill), married to a Witmer; Henry, married to a Nissley; and Fanny, married to Jonas Eby, born 1798, died 1839. The

30

family of Martin Nissley, (of Paxton), are: John, married to a Rupp; Samuel, married to a Wissler; Maria, married to a Heiges; and Catharine, married to an Overholt. The family of Martin, (of Middletown), are: Nancy, born 1808, died 1841; John, married to a Heiges, born 1811; Martin, born 1812; Felix, born 1814, died 1864; Mary, born 1816, died 1847; Fanny, born 1820; Isaac, born 1822; Solomon, born 1825; Jacob, born 1828; and Joseph Herman, born 1831. The family of John, (Rapho), are: Elizabeth, married to C. Newcomer, born 1808; Nancy, married to Levi Eby, born 1810, died 1866; Fanny, married to C. Nolt, born 1812; John, married to B. Gerber, born 1819; Catharine, married to John Musser, born 1827; Sarah, born 1829, and died 1843. The family of Martin Nissley, (Rapho), are: Martha, married to Sem Brubaker, born 1814; Barbara, married to J. W. Nissley, born 1818, died 1868; Nancy, married to Emanuel Cassel, born 1819, died 1845; Fanny, married to J. W. Snyder, born 1821; and Maria, married to Benjamin Musser, born 1824. The family of Sem Nissley, (Rapho), are: Henry, married to Ann Hostetter, born 1814, died 1851; Fanny, married to Samuel Snyder, born 1816; Christian, married to a Breneman, born 1818; Samuel, married to Long and Hershey, born 1818; Jonas, born 1821, died 1848; Benjamin, married to Susan Stauffer, born 1823; Catharine, born 1826; and David, married to a Rutt, born 1829. The family of Rev. Christian Nissley, (Chiques), are: Samuel, born 1817, died 1824; Joseph, married to Martha Sherch, born 1821; Christian, born 1825, died 1844; Martin B., born 1829; Martha, married to Andrew Gerber, born 1818. Abraham Nissley moved from Conoy to Franklin county in 1800, and died in 1823. He had six children—three sons and three daughters, viz: Elizabeth, married to Samuel Ott; Jacob, married to Susanna Rutt; Mary, married to Jacob Leidig; Herman, married to Elizabeth Witmer; Joseph, married to Sarah Schwartz; and Fanny, married to Abraham Metz, born 1800, died 1838. The family of Martin Nissley, (Mt. Joy); he had two wives, the first a Snyder, and the second a Stauffer; and eight children—four sons and four daughters, viz: Jacob, married to a Detwiler;

Martin, married to Barbara Reist, born 1747, died 1799; John, married to Gertrude Shearer; and E. Neff, born 1750, died 1819; Christian, married to a Stauffer, and Catharine Bossler, born 1759, died 1822; Barbara, married to a Shelly; Anna, married to Abraham Stauffer, of Fayette county, born 1752, died 1817; Fanny, married to J. Shallenberger, of Ohio, born 1756, died 1840; Maria, married to Christian Musser, born 1763, died 1811. The family of Jacob Nissley, (Dauphin county), are: Martin, married to a Rutt; Barbara, married to J. Hershey, of Swatara, born 1773, died 1823; Esther, married to Jacob Nissley, of Highspire; and Fanny, married to Joseph Bossler. The family of Martin Nissley, (Dauphin county), are: Jacob, married to Charlotte Books; Martin, married to E. Mumma; Esther, married to Abraham Long, of Franklin county, born 1799, died 1865. The family of Martin Nissley, jr., (Mt. Joy township), are: Anna, married to Jacob Stauffer, born 1774, died 1856; Rev. Christian, married to Maria Kreybill, born 1777, died 1831; Rev. Martin, married to Anna Witmer, born 1784, died 1834; Peter, born 1787, died 1799; Barbara, born 1780, died 1799; Veronica, born 1792, died 1799.

The family of Rev. Christian Nissley and of his wife, Maria Kreybill, are: John, married to Barbara Snyder, born 1800; Rev. Peter, married to a Witmer, a Kreider, and a Sherch, born 1802; Jacob, married to Elizabeth Kreybill, born 1808, died 1862; and Barbara, born 1812, died 1812. The family of deacon John Nissley, sr., (Mt. Joy,) and his wife, B. Snyder, are: Henry S. Nissley, married to Anna B. Reist, born 1827; Mary S., married to Martin W. Nissley, born 1828; Fanny S., married to C. K. Hostetter, born 1832; Christian S., married to Mary N. Eby, born 1835; Sarah S., born 1837; John S., married to Sarah N. Eby, born 1839; and Barbara S., married to Samuel S. Garver, born 1843. The family of Rev. Peter Nissley, of East Donegal, are: Mary K., married to Solomon L. Swartz, born 1830, died 1856; Esther K., born 1832, died 1853; John K., married to Maria B. Reist, born 1834; Leah K., married to David L. Miller, born 1835; Christian K., born 1838, died 1867; Barbara K., married to C. F. Hostetter, born in 1840;

Catharine K., born 1844, died 1862; Anna K., born 1848; died 1850. The family of Jacob Nissley, of Mt. Joy township, and Elizabeth Kreybill, his wife, are: Christian, born 1830, died 1833; Jacob K., married to Anna Rissor, born 1831; Martha, married to Elias Eby, born 1833; Amos, born 1835, died 1843; Barbara, married to Jonas E. Hostetter, born 1837; Mary, born 1839, died 1842; Catharine, married to Michael H. Engle, born 1840; Elizabeth, married to David Rutt, born 1843; Anna, married to Jacob Good, born 1845; Samuel, born 1847, died 1855; Rebecca, married to Jacob Mumma, born 1848; and Simon K., born 1854. The family of Hans or John Nissley, who lived on the first mansion farm, his first wife being Gertrude Shearer, born 1754, died 1794; and his second, Elizabeth Neff, born 1757, died 1815, are: Martin, (miller,) married to E. Hershey, born 1784, died 1854; Henry, married to Elizabeth Hershey, born 1795, died 1860; Abraham, married to Nancy Wissler, born 1798; Samuel, married to Mary Hershey, born 1800; Barbara died single; Fanny, married to C. Witmer, born 1779, died 1807; Gertrude, married to David Eversole, born 1780, died 1821; Anna, born 1782, died unmarried, 1861; Elizabeth, married to Peter Kreybill, born 1787, died 1826; Mary, married to Christian Kreybill, born 1790. Family of Martin Nissley, (miller,) of Mt. Joy township, are: Elizabeth, married to Jacob Rutt, born 1813, died 1858; Anna, married to Christian Mumma, born 1815; Maria, married to Christian Rissor, born 1816; Barbara, married to Joseph Wolgamuth, born 1819; Fanny, married to Joseph Rissor, born 1820; Susan, born 1823, died 1823; Christian H., married to Barbara Lindemuth, born 1824; Martin, born 1826, died 1843; Catharine, married to Jacob Rissor, born 1828, died 1852. The family of Henry Nissley, of Mt. Joy township, and his wife, Elizabeth Hershey, born 1795, are: John H., married to Anna Gisch, born 1820, died 1867; Henry H., married to Jane Wolgamuth, born 1822; Christian, married to Anna Wanner, born 1824, died 1866; Isaac, born 1825, died 1850; Abraham H., married to Susan Garber, born 1828; David, born 1831, died 1852; Mary, married to Abraham Rissor, born 1819; Elizabeth, married to

Jacob Shenk, born 1825. The family of Abraham Nissley, of Mt. Joy township, and his wife, Nancy Wissler, born 1800, died 1867, are: John W., married to Elizabeth Berry, born 1823; Jacob W., married to Mary Lindemuth, born 1825; Anna, married to Henry Breneman, born 1827; Mary, married to Peter Gisch, born 1831; Fanny, married to Abraham Bachman, born 1833; Henry W., married to a Miss Horst, born 1835; Abraham W., born 1838; Daniel, married to Elizabeth Musser, born 1840, died 1867; and Sarah, married to Henry Heisey, born 1842. The family of Samuel Nissley, of Mt. Joy township, and his wife, Maria Hershey, are: Joseph H., married to Mary Brubaker, born 1826; Samuel H., born 1831; Elizabeth, born 1835, died 1867; Mary, born 1837, died 1848. The family of Christian Nissley, (above Maytown), first married to a Stauffer, and next to Catharine Bossler, are: John, married to Mary Hershey, born 1788, died 1823; Christian, married to Fanny Hershey, born 1790, died 1822; Jacob, married to Mary Miller, born 1797, died 1869; Martin, married to Anna Bachman, born 1798, died 1833; Joseph B., married to Mary Snyder, born 1804, died 1857; Nancy, born 1791, died 1809; and Barbara, married to Jacob Kreybill, (miller), born 1795, died 1814. The family of John B. Nissley, near Bossler's meeting-house, are: Catharine, married to John Engle, born 1809, died 1871; Rev. Jacob H., married to a Brubaker, born 1810; Elizabeth, married to Benjamin Martin, born 1811; Barbara, married to an Eshleman, born 1813, died 1841; John, married to a Brubaker, born 1815, died 1849; Christian, married to a Musser, born 1820, died 1849; and David, born 1824, died 1824. The family of Jacob Nissley, of Cumberland, and his wife, Mary Miller, born 1802, are: Elizabeth, married to an Eberly, and afterwards a Sener, born 1819; Benjamin, married to a Felsenhard, born 1821; Jacob, married to Leah Fetroe, born 1824; David, married to Anna Brintle, born 1827; Maria, married to a Belshoffer, born 1829; and Christian, married to Mary Markle, born 1834. The family of Martin Nissley and his wife, Anna Bachman, born 1799, are: Peter B., married to ι Huffman, afterwards a Huffert, born 1823, died 1869;

Nancy, born 1825, died 1830; Christian, married to Christiana Hilty, born 1827; Daniel B., married to Sallie Lindemuth, born 1829; and Jacob, born 1831, died 1851. The family of Joseph B. Nissley, (Donegal meeting-house), and his wife, Mary Snyder, born 1808, are: Samuel S., married to Martha Kreider, born 1830; John S., born 1832, died 1839; Joseph S., married to Maria Stauffer, born 1834, died 1861; Catharine, married to Christian Stauffer, born 1838, died 1863; Mary, married to Abram Ruth, born 1842, died 1869; and Elizabeth, born 1849, died 1850. The family of Rev. Martin Nissley, of Donegal, and his wife, Anna Witmer, are: Anna, married to Joseph Eversole, born 1811; Joseph W., married to Barbara Nissley, born 1813; Barbara, married to Daniel Heisey, born 1816, died 1862; Fanny, married to Jacob Snyder, born 1818; Maria, married to Philip Greiner, born 1820; and Martin W., married to Mary Nissley, born 1824.

NISSLEY, JACOB, elected a member of the Legislature in 1849 and 1850.

NOBLE, WILLIAM, elected a member of the Legislature in 1835.

NORTH, HUGH M., was born in Juniata county, Pa. He read law in New Berlin, Union county, in the office of Hon. Joseph Casey, Chief Justice of the Court of Claims at Washington city, D. C. He was admitted to the bar in 1849. He located at Columbia, Lancaster county, Pa., about the year 1850, and engaged in the pursuits of the profession in which he has been employed up to this time. He was elected to the Legislature in 1854, serving one session. He was delegate to the National Democratic Convention at Charleston and Baltimore in 1860, and represented Pennsylvania on the committee of credentials. He was the Democratic candidate for Congress in 1864. He has served as a member of the Columbia school board for upwards of thirteen years, and for a time filled the position of president of that body. He has been for years the confidential solicitor of several banks and other corporations, and has for some time been the solicitor of the Pennsylvania Railroad company. Mr. North is an assiduous, industrious and persevering business man, and has at this time a large and lucrative practice, and can be regarded as a man of means and independence. He is a sound, well-read lawyer, and prepares and tries a cause well.

O.

OBER, MICHAEL, was elected a member of the Legislature in the year 1860.

OLD, JAMES, was one of the early iron-masters of Lancaster county, and an influential and leading man in his day. He was elected a member of the Legislature in the years 1791, 1792 and 1793.

ORTH, ADAM, elected a member of the Legislature in 1783–84.

OVERHOLTZER, HENRY D., a member of the Legislature in 1826.

OWEN, BENJAMIN, a member of the Legislature in 1821.

P.

PARKE, SAMUEL, was a member of the Lancaster bar, admitted in the year 1820. He was a leading lawyer for many years, and was a man of considerable influence in political movements. He was elected a member of the Legislature in the years 1829–30. We find the following notice of him, written February 18th, 1840:

" The lecture of Mr. Parke on ' Matter,' delivered before the Mechanics' Institute on last Thursday evening, was listened to with profound attention. The originality of his remarks respecting the formation of coal beds, mountains and valleys, gave this production a degree of interest of which lectures in general are not possessed. The subject throughout was managed in the most skillful manner, fully sustaining the high reputation which Mr. Parke enjoys as an able writer."

PARR, WILLIAM, was a native of England, who emigrated to America at an early day, and settled in Lancaster. He read law, and was admitted to the bar in 1752. He was elected a member of the Legislature in the year 1783. He was a man of considerable ability, and was noted in his day as a skilled marksman.

PASSMORE, JOHN, a citizen of Lancaster, and a man of remarkable corporeal proportions, weighing about 450 lbs. He was appointed by Governor Snyder, in 1809, prothonotary of the Lancaster district of the supreme court, comprising the counties of Lancaster, Berks, York and Dauphin. He was, in 1818, appointed one of the aldermen of the city of Lancaster, and the same year was elected the first mayor of the city, a position to which he was twice reëlected, discharging the duties of the office for three years.

PATTERSON, ARTHUR, a member of the Legislature in years 1743, 1744, 1745, 1746, 1747, 1748, 1749, 1750, 1751, 1752, 1753 and 1754.

PATTERSON, D. W., is a native of Lancaster county, and a graduate of Washington College, Pennsylvania. He read law, and was admitted to the bar in the year 1842. He was elected a member of the Legislature in the year 1846. In the year 1853 he was elected District Attorney of Lancaster county, the duties of which he discharged for three years. He is engaged in the pursuits of his profession.

PATTERSON (JAMES) FAMILY. James Patterson was born in the north of Ireland in 1708, and emigrated to America in 1828, and settled in Lancaster county. He was a farmer by occupation. He married Mary Montgomery, and had the following children, viz.: William, born March 14th, 1733, died June 29th, 1818; John, Hannah, Mary, Samuel, Jane, Isabella, James, born November 14th, 1745, died August 17th, 1825; Elizabeth and Thomas, born February 1st, 1754, died March 28th, 1829. James Patterson, the first settler, died in Little Britain township in 1792.

WILLIAM PATTERSON, son of the first settler, married Rosanna Scott, by whom he had the following children: Mary, born January 7th, 1759; Moses, born October 16th, 1760; Samuel, born October 7th, 1762; Thomas, born October 1st, 1764, died November 17th, 1841; and James, born March 1st, 1767. He, after the death of his first wife, married

Elizabeth Brown, born March 16th, 1747, died January 30th, 1826. With his second wife he had the following children: John, born February 10th, 1771; Rosanna, born December 31, 1772; William, born April 8th, 1775, died September 20th 1844; Nathaniel, born 1777; Rachel, born June 3d, 1778, died January 9th, 1817; Elizabeth, born January 8th, 1781; Josiah, born November 10th, 1783, died February, 1843; Hannah, born May 22d, 1786; Nathan, born September 11th, 1788, died February, 1846; and Eleanor, born October 17th, 1792. William Patterson settled in Washington county, Pa. Two of his sons, John and Thomas, were members of Congress during the contest between Jackson, Adams, and Crawford for the presidency.

JOHN PATTERSON, second son of the first settler, was a farmer in Little Britain township, but late in life removed to Ohio. He was married to Eleanor Milligan, and had the following children: Mary. born April 24, 1765; James, Martha, John, Hannah, Eleanor, William and Elizabeth.

SAMUEL PATTERSON, third son of the first settler, lived in Little Britain township, where he also died. He married Mary Wylie, and had two children, Elizabeth and Mary. The first married Dr. Smith, of Westmoreland county, Pa., and left a large family.

JAMES PATTERSON, fourth son of the first settler, lived in Little Britain township, and was a member of the Legislature in the years 1802, 1803 and 1804. He married Letitia Gardner, and had the following children: Isabella, born April 29, 1783; died December 24, 1818; Francina, born May 17, 1785; died December 1, 1823; Robert, born March 21st, 1787, died March 31, 1861; Mary, born April 17, 1789, died May 1, 1848; Elizabeth, born April 26, 1791, died July 26, 1830; Jane, born February 28, 1794; James, born March 7, 1796; Letitia, born May 29, 1798, died November 12, 1823; Rachael, born May 20, 1803.

THOMAS PATTERSON, fifth son of the first settler, married Mary Tannehill, by whom he had the following children: Rebecca, born August 13th, 1778; Elizabeth, born March 18th, 1780; Samuel, born March 3d, 1782; Nathan, born

February 20th, 1784; died January 24th, 1792; Mary, born March 3d, 1786; died June 5th, 1854; Margaret, born June 10th, 1788; died March, 1821; Thomas, born February 13th, 1790; died July 30, 1857; James, born January 11th, 1792; and Jane, born May 10th, 1796.

PATTERSON (ARTHUR) FAMILY. This branch of the name in Lancaster county, all descended from Arthur Patterson, who emigrated from the north of Ireland in 1724, and settled, with his wife, (who was Ann Scott,) the same year, on the banks of the Big Chiquesalunga, in Rapho township, Lancaster county, then a wilderness. He purchased and located a large tract of land and commenced farming. He had acquired in the old country the trade of blacksmithing, and which trade he found almost indispensable to the success of farming, after coming to this country. Mechanics of all kinds were then very scarce here, not less so the blacksmith; and Arthur Patterson, at first for his own convenience and economy, performed his own smithing; afterwards the wants of his neighbors and the settlements, still farther west of him, demanding it, he carried on the blacksmithing very extensively, in connection with his farm-. ing. Often did it occur that the farmers composing the settlement in Cumberland valley, in the vicinity of Carlisle, sent their plow-irons, &c., on pack-horses, all the way down to Arthur Patterson's, to be sharpened and repaired, the messenger waiting until they were done, then would return, taking them with him. Arthur died leaving nine children, four sons and five daughters. One son, Arthur, the youngest, died while quite young; Samuel, James and William grew up to manhood, and all served their country in the war of the Revolution. The latter was taken prisoner by the British, and died while held a prisoner in the prison-ship, on Delaware bay, the fate of many of our patriotic army who were unfortunate enough to be taken prisoners, and where the American officers openly charged the British with deliberate murder, by means of supplying their prisoners with unhealthy and spoiled food. Samuel and James both survived their campaigns; the last severe conflict they participated in being the battle of Princeton, after which James returned home, having in charge the prisoners taken by our forces in that engagement. They were also members of the committee of safety for Lancaster county, in 1775, a body chosen from the several townships to concert measures to defeat the machinations of the tories, and to resist the unjust and tyrannical edicts of the British Parliament. James also served several sessions in the Provincial Assembly of Pennsylvania.

SAMUEL PATTERSON, son of Arthur, married Martha Agnew, and died November 15, 1820, at the advanced age of 93 years, having left four children, Arthur, Rebecca, James and Samuel. Arthur married Elizabeth Moore, and died, leaving two daughters, one of whom married Benjamin Osbourne; and left two sons, James and Patterson Osbourne, who reside now in Ohio; the other died young. Rebecca married Rev. Matthew Henderson; James married Elizabeth Witherow, and died near Mount Joy, October 29, 1852, and left two children, viz: Sarah, who died in her 18th year, and Samuel Smith Patterson, who is still living, and now a citizen of Sterling, Illinois, where, by engaging first in merchandizing and latterly in banking, he has acquired large wealth, and is much respected for his amiable qualities of character. He had married Mary McJimsey, by whom he had a large family, six of whom still survive, viz: five sons, all successful business men, Joseph M., James B., Smith, Frank and John; and one daughter, Martha Rebecca, who married Doctor Thos. Galt, once a citizen of this county, and now residing in Rock Island, Illinois. Samuel Smith Patterson succeeded his father, Major James Patterson, at farming, near Mount Joy, and spent a large part of his life there, taking an active part in local and State civil affairs. He ably represented Lancaster county in the State Legislature for two successive sessions, in the years of 1834–35. His son, Samuel, married Mary Ann McJimsey, and died October 27th, 1831, at his farm, below Mount Joy, leaving ten children, six sons and four daughters. Of the sons, Samuel Patterson, now a successful merchant of Marietta, is the sole survivor. John Patterson, late of Mount Joy, and a successful and much-esteemed coal and lumber merchant there, was another son; also James M., and Thos. Jefferson Patterson, formerly of Mount Joy. Robert died young, as did S. Alexander and Elizabeth. Martha intermarried with Thomas Sterrett, Mary Ann with Jas. B. Ferree, and Rebecea Jane with William Spangler.

WILLIAM PATTERSON, son of Arthur, who died a prisoner, had married Elizabeth Dysart, and left three children; one a daughter, Eleanor, who married Alexander Dysart, and settled in Huntingdon county, where some of her descendants still reside, respected by all who knew them; and two sons: Arthur, the father of William, Douglass and Alexander Patterson, the two latter now residents of Mount Joy, the former residing in the west, and several daughters; and Alexander, who died February 2d, 1842, and who intermarried with Jane Pedan, leaving three children, two of whom died young; and one, a daughter, Sarah, grew up to womanhood, and married Abrm. Hatfield, both now residing in Chester county, Pa. The daughters of Arthur were five: Catharine, married Robert Hays; Elizabeth married Mr. J. Thomas; Eleanor married Ephraim Moore; Jane and Rebecca died unmarried.

JAMES PATTERSON, son of Arthur, intermarried with Margaret Agnew, by whom he had nine children, viz: Arthur, who married Mary Witherow, died September, 1822, leaving seven children, and whose three sons located in Franklin county, Pa.; Rebecca intermarried with James Scott, and again as a widow, married Col. James Agnew, of Bedford county, Pa.; James, who married Mary Watson, died May 30th, 1863, leaving seven children; Martha, who intermarried with John Scott, lived and died in Washington county, Pa., where she left a large family; Samuel, who married and resided in Steubenville, Ohio, where he died, leaving one child, Samuel; Margaret, who married John McConaughy, a lawyer of Gettysburg, Pa., had five children, viz: Robert and David, both of whom studied and practiced law in Adams county, the latter of whom represented that district in the Senate of Pennsylvania for three years, commencing in 1868. James resides in Johnstown, Pa., and successfully carries on a large steam tannery.

Hannah Mary intermarried with the Hon. Moses McClean, an attorney of Adams county, who represented that district in the United States Congress. Elizabeth married Prof. M. S. Stoever, late of Gettysburg college; and Emeline married the Rev. D. Wilson; the three remaining children of James, Ann, William, who was a physician; John died unmarried. The foregoing constitute the greater portion of four generations, descending from their ancestor, Arthur Patterson.

PATTERSON, COL. JAMES, the subject of this sketch, was born in Rapho township, Lancaster county, Pennsylvania, on the 7th day of October, 1775, and died, after a brief illness, in Mount Joy, where he spent his last years, after retiring from farming on the 30th of May, 1863, in the 88th year of his age. He was the son of James Patterson of revolutionary times, who was a devoted soldier in that war in behalf of the colonies. His grandfather was Arthur Patterson, who emigrated from Donegal county, Ireland, in 1724, and settled in Rapho township, Lancaster county, where he afterwards lived and died. Col. James, therefore, sprang from Scotch-Irish ancestors, and was one of a family of nine children. His father being a farmer, his son James was reared to out-door labor and exercise, and in consequence grew up to manhood with a strong and vigorous constitution. In the days of his boyhood there were no common schools, and the opportunities to obtain even a good common school education, were exceedingly limited. The entire time afforded to him to acquire learning in school, was all embraced in the short period of ten months. At the age of about fifteen years, and just on the eve of the troubles incited by the whiskey insurrection in Western Pennsylvania, his father died, and he was left without the directing hand and cherishing culture of paternal affection. His older brother, Arthur, and the adult population generally of his native section, being shortly after called out to military service by the United States government, to quell the whiskey insurrection, James was left to take the sole charge and direction of a large farm, and to manage it the best he could. This, and the many incidental responsibilities, threw him quite young in life on his own resources, and gave him a maturity in experience and a decision of character, long before he attained to years of manhood. As may be supposed, therefore, when he arrived at adult age he had acquired an enviable reputation amongst his neighbors for good practical common sense, and fearless candor in expressing his convictions. These traits, united with a natural cheerful disposition and genial social qualities, caused him to be held in high esteem by all his neighbors. Although deprived of school privileges, and his time devoted to constant labor, his love of learning made him seek opportunities for acquiring knowledge. This, added to fine natural abilities, gave him great success in acquiring information on all topics. His stock of knowledge and experience made him a wise counsellor and a judicious adviser; and on many occasions, both of public and private interests, his counsel was sought and obtained. On attaining to his majority he took charge of his own farm, and commenced clearing away the heavy timber and erecting the necessary buildings. In the year 1805 he was united in marriage to Mary Watson, a daughter of the late Dr. John Watson, of Donegal. By her he had seven children. One, a son, died in his youth; another, a daughter, died just as she verged into womanhood. The five remaining children grew up to mature years, four of whom still survive—James A. Patterson, whose occupation was that of a farmer, but now retired and residing in Mount Joy; David W. Patterson, a member of the legal profession at the Lancaster bar; Harriet B., now the wife of Dr. J. L. Zeigler, of Mount Joy; Rachel J. Patterson, and the remaining daughter, Anna Mary, who was intermarried with Robert S. McIlvain, of Paradise township, and died in the year 1855. No man excelled Col. Patterson in public spirit and disinterested sacrifice for the public good. He occupied important positions, both civil and military. When the war of 1812, between this country and Great Britain broke out, he immediately left his farm and family and volunteered for the war. A battalion of troops having been raised by his exertions, Gen. Nathaniel Watson, major-general of the division, composed of Lancaster and York counties, commanding, made Col. Patterson (then major) one of the aids on his staff. He remained in the service until peace was declared, having most of that time commanded a regiment of Pennsylvania volunteers as lieutenant-colonel, and returned home holding that commission. For a decade of years after that war, the whole country, encouraged by liberal legislation, were active in developing the militia system, then high in popular favor, for home defence. Col. Patterson took a prominent part in organizing and commanding that strong arm of the Republic. While his taste led him to take part in military matters, a pure patriotism seemed to be the motor of his action. An instance of that may be remembered by many yet living. When the South inaugurated the late unnatural and terrible rebellion, Col. Patterson, although then in his eighty-sixth year, said with all seriousness, "I wish I was a little younger, I would go out myself and defend the life of our government."

In the civil affairs of his native State, he always took a deep interest. Feeling the want of educational advantages in his youth, he expressed the deepest anxiety to see those advantages placed within the reach of all. These convictions made him a warm and active supporter of our beneficent common school system, declaring that school-tax was the cheapest tax that any citizen could pay. As all know, the school system was at first left to a vote of the people of the several townships. This feature caused many warm contests at the polls, in which Col. P. always took the side of free schools, although his own children were at the time all advanced in their studies beyond the then standard of common school education. Col. P. represented Lancaster county in our State Legislature in the session of 1817–18, and again for two successive sessions of 1832–33 and 1833–34, taking an active part in the political questions of that period. But the occupation of his life—farming—was his favorite pursuit. He largely gave his personal attention and labor to his farms; read extensively on the subject; studied the nature of the soil, and the character of the fertilizers best adapted to produce the highest state of cultivation. And his neat farming and abundant crops, showed the wisdom of his conclusions. With him has gone another of the landmarks between the present and the past, and he is no longer seen amid his native and long-life familiar surroundings. His last days, as well as his last moments of dissolution, were calm and peaceful, for the well-grounded faith of the Christian believer did not forsake him. His remains rest in the old Donegal churchyard, with the dust of his fathers; and a long, honorable and useful life is at an end. Our forefathers are at rest, a worthy band whose fine virtues, honest purpose and high-toned morality make their memories a richer legacy to their children than gold or silver, or even the daring deeds of heroism.

PATTERSON, JAMES, was elected County Commissioner in 1809.

PATTERSON, THOMAS, elected County Commissioner in 1845.

PAXSON, JOSEPH, was elected County Commissioner in 1838 and 1840. He was also elected a member of the Legislature in 1844.

PAXSON, REV. WILLIAM, was born in Lancaster county, April 1st, 1760. He devoted the early part of his life to agricultural employments, and served in two companies at different times during the revolutionary war, in one of which he was present, and participated in the battle of Trenton. His love for knowledge afterwards induced him to seek the advantages of a liberal education, and he began his preparatory course when twenty-four years of age, in the Strasburg academy, then taught by the Rev. Nathaniel W. Sample. He never obtained the advantages of a collegiate education, but by diligent study he laid a foundation upon which he accumulated a more than ordinary amount of knowledge, literary, scientific and theological. He was taken under the care of the New Castle Presbytery, April 29th, 1789, and having passed, with great credit, through the several trials assigned him, he was licensed on the 8th of April, 1790, as a candidate for the gospel ministry. On the 6th of October following he was appointed stated supply to the churches of West Nottingham and Little Britain. In this service, having continued about six months, he received a call from these

congregations to become their pastor, which, after deliberation, he declined. In his probationary visitations and preaching, he accepted an invitation to preach to the congregations
of Lower Marsh creek and Toms creek, in the Carlisle
Presbytery. They had recently become vacant by the transfer of the Rev. John McNight, their late pastor, to the
collegiate Presbyterian churches of the city of New York.
Mr. Paxson's services were so acceptable to those vacant
congregations, that they promptly and unanimously gave him
a call to become their pastor. He accepted the call on the
4th of April, 1792, and was accordingly dismissed from the
Presbytery of New Castle to put himself under the care of
that of Carlisle. This took effect on the 7th of June, 1792,
and on the 3d of October following he was installed as pastor
of the churches above named.

On the 20th of January, 1794, he was united in marriage
with Miss Jane Dunlap, daughter of Col. James Dunlap,
then residing near Shippensburg. He ministered to the
united congregations composing his charge for several years,
until Lower Marsh creek congregation became desirous of
securing his entire services. To this change the other congregation submitted with deep regret, and from that time
until his death his labors were devoted to Marsh creek alone.
His service to this congregation was a devotion, indeed, being
one of larger duration than falls to the lot of most clergymen, and extending over a period of forty-nine years. Very
rarely, indeed, was he absent from the public duties of the
Sabbath, unless to assist a brother in the administration of
the Lord's Supper, and in one or two instances when, by
sickness, he was for a short time unable to render his
ordinary services. His ministrations were always characterized by decided ability and great faithfulness. By his congregation they were always appreciated, and their attachment
to, and estimation of him, suffered no abatement. To relinquish him as their pastor, was very unwelcome, even when
his bodily infirmities rendered it not only expedient, but
absolutely necessary. In 1826 the degree of doctor of
divinity was conferred upon him by Dickinson college. He
severed his long connection with his congregation by resign-

31

ing his charge on the 19th of October, 1841. He, however, afterwards preached to them occasionally, until they obtained a successor. He died April 16th, 1845.

As a preacher, Dr. Paxson was highly interesting and acceptable. His sermons were distinguished for appropriate and well-digested thought, natural and lucid arrangement, and thorough discussion. Far from being dry and merely intellectual, they were lively and impressive; and a well-regulated imagination often added force and beauty to his scriptural illustrations. In preparation for his public services, he was conscientiously careful and punctual. His manner of preaching was what is usually denominated extempore; but the matter was the result of mature thought and exact preparation. In manner he was solemn, dignified, commanding, graceful, without any theatrical effort, and with only those gestures which his feelings naturally prompted him. As a pastor he was affectionate and faithful. In the exercise of church discipline, he was strict and conscientious, yet considerate and wise. In his habits, he was very domestic. He was, however, eminently social in his disposition, and fond of the society of his brethren.*

PEARSOL, John H., one of the editors of the Lancaster Daily and Weekly Express, was born January 12th, 1818, near Waynesburg, Chester county, Pa. His parents belonged to the humblest of society. From Chester county they removed to Sporting Hill, and from thence to Marietta, Lancaster county. In this place, when he was but four years of age, he had the misfortune to lose his mother, who was shot by a drunken man, named Hamilton.[1] At the age of

[1] William Hamilton, more familiarly known, subsequently, as "Billy Hamilton," was a North-Irelander, who had settled in Marietta at an early period of its history, and followed the occupation of hand-weaving. Under ordinary circumstances he was regarded rather as a useful and industrious citizen, but somewhat irritable and obstinate, and, when under the influence of liquor, a man of almost ungovernable passions. Mr. Pearsol's mother was his nearest neighbor, and was known as a remarkably mild and benevolent woman, who often acted as a peace-maker between belligerent neighbors, and possessed marked influence as such. She had often used her influence previously in pacifying Hamilton in his stormy moods, when they were directed against his

*Sprague's Annals of the American Pulpit, vol. 3.

seven he was placed in the employ of Hugh Maxwell, publisher of the Lancaster *Gazette*, as errand boy, and continued in his service for seven years, and so long as to partially acquire a knowledge of printing. Having left Mr. Maxwell, he worked in Philadelphia several years, and made himself fully master of his trade. When twenty-one years of age he returned to Lancaster, and Bryson, Pearsol & Wimer started the *Semi-Weekly Gazette* as a literary paper. With this firm he continued for about a year and six months, and then sold out his interest, losing in non-payments all the products of the sale. On a borrowed capital of $500 he began, February 10th, 1843, as a temperance organ, the

wife, his neighbors, or other members of his family. On the unfortunate occasion which so suddenly and so violently resulted in Mr. Pearsol's early orphanage, Hamilton was under the influence of strong drink, and had an altercation with some one, and as is usual on such occasions, when he came home he directed his ire against his wife and other members of his family. Mrs. Pearsol, either voluntary or through solicitation, attempted to administer the oil of peace which she had so successfully administered on former occasions, but her benevolent mission only seemed to have chafed him the more, if he did not come to regard it as an impertinent interference ; he therefore ran up stairs into a room, and *declared he would shoot the first person who entered it.* His terrified family would fain have persuaded her not to approach him in his present frame of mind, but she, perhaps, not *knowing* that he had a deadly weapon, or fearing he might do violence to others if his stormy passion was not allayed, nevertheless entered his room, when the phrenzied man immediately shot her dead, and escaped from the house. It was some days before Hamilton was arrested, and having some very warm friends in the place, who connived at his concealment, it was considered hazardous to attempt his arrest, even if his whereabouts had been known.

At length suspicion fell upon the house of his friend, James Kane, or McKane, familiarly known as "Jimmy Kane," and the "Marietta Blues," a volunteer company, then under the command of Lieut. Elijah Russel, was called out, to assist in making the arrest. The company proceeded to the house aforesaid, and after a feeble resistance on the part of the inmates, entered it with charged bayonets ; where, after a thorough search, they found Hamilton concealed under the flooring of the cellar. Kane, having been discovered with a gun in his hand, which he had threatened to use, before Hamilton was discovered, was, with another of his friends, also arrested as *accessories after the fact*, and the three men were immediately lodged in the Lancaster jail. At the trial which followed, his two friends were discharged, but Hamilton was convicted of murder in the *second degree*, and sentenced to *eighteen years' imprisonment* in the old Arch street prison, in Philadelphia.

Weekly Express,[1] and continued its publication up to 1856, it being the longest instance of the connected publication of a temperance paper as yet known in Pennsylvania. During 1856 he associated with him Mr. J. M. W. Geist, and the firm started the *Daily Express,* (and also continued the weekly), which they have published up to this time. In the subject of this sketch, we have an instance of a man rising from the humblest origin to respect, influence and independence, by dint of determined energy and steady perseverance, qualities always sure to win when properly observed. The early event that deprived him of his mother, was that which originally gave him his first bias in favor of temperance, and

Hamilton became very penitent, and his conduct in prison was very meek, exemplary and praiseworthy, so much so that the usual rigor of the prison rules were relaxed in his case, and he was entrusted with many minor duties, all of which were faithfully discharged. After serving nine years in prison he became a subject of executive clemency, and, accordingly, received a free and full pardon from Governor George Wolf, in 1831.

After his discharge from prison he returned to Marietta, where he married a widow Coble—his former wife having died in the meantime, if she had not been released by his diabolical act and criminal conviction—and led a rather quiet and industrious, if not a religious life, and died in 1847. Notwithstanding his religious professions, the odium of having committed a murder, ever attached to Hamilton—whether justly or unjustly, he never outlived it—and, doubtless, on a multitude of occasions, he realized that "the way of the transgressor is hard." Many people imagined that they could read *murder* in the lineaments of his face, and herein perhaps consists as solemn a warning as the indulgence in inebriation. Every indulgence in violent anger leaves not only a scar upon the moral character, but also more or less impresses itself ultimately upon the facial angles of a man. Intoxication, therefore, only relaxes the bonds of moral and civil restraint, a violent breaking down of these barriers, and letting the habitual inner man recklessly rush forth in some act of violence. Early impressed with the fact, that it was through the instrumentality of ardent spirits, as a primary cause, that Mr. Pearsol was wantonly deprived of a kind and affectionate mother, at the very period when he most needed a mother's care, it is not surprising that he should have devoted the best energies of his life to the advancement of the temperance cause.

[1] When Mr. Pearsol published the *Express,* as a temperance organ, the tone of society was very different towards the temperance cause from what it afterwards became, and has been for years. During the thirteen years of its temperance career, he was prosecuted eight times for libel, found guilty in every instance, and mulcted in fines and costs. In

the same which has ever intensified his support of this cause. No more worthy instance of genuine worth and steady adhesion to principle, triumphing over poverty and all accompanying obstacles, is presented in our county's history than is afforded in the career of the man whose sketch we have penned.

PEELOR, JOHN, appointed Recorder of Deeds in 1830.

PENNEL, BENJAMIN, was born in Chester county, Pa., June 26th, 1787. He served as a soldier of the war of 1812, and was present at the battle of Baltimore. He was a wool-carder and fuller by occupation. He settled in Warwick township, being induced thither chiefly through the influence

every case he had simply published what he stood ready to prove, but this the law forbade, and for publishing the truth he was obliged to endure the penalty. On one occasion he was found guilty of libel, and sentenced to pay a fine of $200 and the costs, which nearly equalled the fine; and not having the means to liquidate the penalty, he was committed to prison in compliance with the sentence of the court. So great, indeed, was the the antipathy towards the temperance sheet, that some of the leading business men of Lancaster refused to have the name of the temperance editor stand as an imprint upon their business bills. The cause of temperance was in the lowest repute, and it even required a man of courage to avow himself as its supporter. Mr. Pearsol was often threatened with cowhidings for his support of the cause. This was the passage through the fiery ordeal that tries the metal of which men are composed. Such, to the unreflecting, however, would seem the lowest ebb in one's career, but in this instance, as is often the case, it proved the turning point in his life. The determined effort to ruin the *Express* and its owner, roused the friends of the cause, of which it was the organ, and funds were immediately raised, the editor released, and during the same year the list of subscribers was increased from 500 to 3,500. The struggling paper was at once placed upon a permanent and enduring basis. It had passed the turning point, and its success was established. Since the year 1856 many prosecutions have been instituted for libel, but all have uniformly been withdrawn and none prosecuted to judgment, with the exception of one case, in which a verdict of not guilty was rendered.

It may be here added, that the lager beer trade was first started up in Lancaster about the year 1843 or 1844. One of the first lager beer saloons opened in Lancaster city was kept near where the Pennsylvania railroad depot now stands, and the beer was named Bavarian beer, (bierish). Henry Franke was one of the first in the business in this city, and afterwards went into its manufacture, which, in late years, has developed into a large and profitable trade. It is now one of the growing branches of manufacture.

of Jacob Reist, and he followed his trade there for some years. He was appointed a justice of the peace by Governor Shultz, under the old Constitution, and served until the adoption of the new. In 1840 he was elected to the House of Representatives, and reëlected in 1841. He died August 12th, 1865, aged 78 years. Mr. Pennel was a man of a remarkable memory, and was able in citing events that had transpired, to name the year and day of its occurrence. He was a strong friend of the temperance cause. He was perfectly honest and upright, and no man could sway him in any manner from what he regarded as right. Any corrupt overture to him, when a member of the House, would have been spurned, and would have received a fitting rebuke. He chose to remain poor and leave an untarnished reputation in preference to the accumulation of pelf by base and dishonorable means. Poor Benjamin Pennel was a man of honor, and highly esteemed where honor is respected, and by the few who appreciated his inner worth. Raise an humble monument to his memory, for mausoleums have decked less worthy ashes.

PETERS, ABRAHAM, was born August 29th, 1791, near Millersville, Lancaster county, Pa. His father, of the same name, emigrated from Alsace, in France, (now Germany), about nine miles from Strasburg, when nineteen years of age, and located in the vicinity of Millersville,[1] then called Millersburg. He purchased ten acres of land, for which he paid £270 in the year 1777. He died February 5th, 1818, aged 77 years. He kept tavern in an old log house, in which the subject of this notice was born, and also carried on a distillery. Abraham Peters, after the death of his father, still continued the distilling business, and did so up to 1853. He was, at the same time, engaged in farming. Up to 1851 he also kept

---

[1] Millersville, originally called Millerstown, afterwards Millersburg, derives its name from the founder of the village, John Miller, who owned a large body of land upon which the village now stands. He sold five-acre lots, reserving ground-rent. John Miller erected a large brick house, composed of extremely thick walls, and displayed his taste in having one of his rooms covered with beautiful and artistic carvings. Miller, in after years failed, and his property passed into other hands. His large house was torn down some thirty years since.

tavern. He was married on the 16th of October, 1825, to Miss Fanny Gamber. Abraham Peters was one of the leading movers with B. B. Martin, Lewis M. Hobbs, John Brady, Jacob K. Shenk and others, in the establishment of the Millersville Normal School. Mr. Peters was elected the first president of the board of trustees, a position he has held up to this time. The meetings that led to the foundation of the Normal School, were held in the years 1853–54. The institution was opened in 1855, as the Millerstown Academy. After Mr. Peters retired from the distilling business in 1853, he prosecuted the business of farming up to 1862. For many years he had carried on the business of saw-milling, at Petersville, on the Conestoga Navigation. In 1861 Mr. Peters was nominated and elected on the Union ticket, a member of the House of Representatives, and discharged the duties of this position with credit to himself and to the satisfaction of his constituents. Since 1862 he has retired from active pursuits, and resides on his place in Millersville.

PETERS, JACOB G., son of Abraham Peters, was born September 4th, 1834, in Millersville, Lancaster county, Pa. He was educated at the schools of his district, and afterwards pursued a collegiate career in Franklin and Marshall, in the first years after the college was removed to Lancaster. He was going to Marshall college, in Mercersburg, and was the student selected by the faculty of the college to have charge of the transportation of the college fixtures from Mercersburg to Lancaster. After graduating at college, his father having been engaged in the lumber business, and wishing to retire therefrom, Jacob G. Peters continued the same steadily up to 1866. From that time he has chiefly devoted his attention to agricultural pursuits. When the Farmers' Mutual Insurance Company of Lancaster county was re-organized in 1870, Mr. Peters was elected as the general agent of the company, with full power to remodel the same, and he is clothed with authority to issue new policies to insured. During 1870 he acted as superintendent of the Lancaster and New Danville Turnpike Company of Lancaster county; also as superintendent for the erection of a bridge across the Conestoga creek.   Up to the breaking out of the war, Mr. Peters was an active and influential Democrat, but since that time he has operated with the Republican party.   He was, by this latter party nominated in 1868, and elected a member of the House of Representatives.   He has been a frequent delegate of his party to the nominating conventions, and was a member of the State Convention at Philadelphia, which placed Gen. Grant in nomination for the Presidency.   Mr. Peters has for several years been an active member of the board of trustees of the Millersville Normal School, and acts as chairman of the household committee.

PORTER, GEORGE B., a son of General Andrew Porter, of revolutionary memory, was born in Lancaster, February 9th, 1791.   He read law and was admitted to the bar in the year 1813.   He speedily won a front rank in the profession, and was for several years one of the leading lawyers at the Lancaster bar.   He was, in April, 1818, appointed prothonotary of Lancaster county, succeeding J. Passmore.   He was a leading Democratic politician, and was recommended by the convention of his party in Lancaster county as a candidate for Governor of Pennsylvania.   In 1824 he was appointed adjutant-general of the State.   He was an eloquent speaker, and was chosen by the city of Lancaster to make the reception speech to General Lafayette,[1] when he visited it in 1824.   He was selected as the attorney to defend Walter Franklin, when the latter was impeached before the Senate of Pennsylvania.   He was elected a member of the Pennsylvania Legislature in the year 1827.   He was appointed Governor of Michigan territory, the duties of which office he discharged for three years.   He died at Detroit, July 6th, 1834, in the 44th year of his age.

PORTER, JAMES, was a delegate from Lancaster county to the Reform Convention of 1837–38.

PORTER, JAMES, was one of the early settlers of Lancaster county.   He owned a large body of land in the south-

[1] At the time Lafayette visited Lancaster, a ball was given in honor of the nation's distinguished guest, which eclipsed everything which up to that day had been seen in the old inland city.

ern section of the county. His son, William Porter, was a member of the Legislature in the year 1779.

PORTER, JOHN J., was elected Clerk of Quarter Sessions in the year 1854. David Fulton filled the last year of his office by appointment.

PORTER, THOMAS, was a member of the Legislature in 1775. He was also a delegate from Lancaster county to the convention of 1776, which framed the first State Constitution.

POWELL, REV. WALTER, a native of New York State, and pastor of the Presbyterian church in Lancaster city, from the year 1857 up to his death, in 1858. Rev. Powell was a man of rare intellectual capacity, and one who had caught the new spirit of liberal christianity[1] which has so thoroughly made its way into the churches of New England and some other sections of America. His sermons to the old members of the congregation seemed entirely strange, and many of his congregation were unable to become reconciled to his style of preaching. He was a close student, a deep reasoner, and one who (had years been spared him) would have left a

[1] The religious tone of the people of Lancaster county, is a matter of all others that deserves some consideration. It may be said, perhaps, without exaggeration, that there is no inland county in Pennsylvania where a greater variety of religious sects exists than in Lancaster. It is owing to this great commingling of sects and interchange of opinions, that Lancaster county has risen to so comparative a height in the scale of toleration and liberality of sentiment, compared with many other sections of our country ; for, it is a fact well known, that the entertaining of no religious opinions (those of any sect) serves to arouse antagonism or ill-will upon the part of any of opposite sentiments. Perfect harmony and good-will prevail amongst all denominations ; even Roman Catholics and those of the different Protestant sects live in the best social relations toward each other. The liberalizing sentiments of modern theological views have silently insinuated themselves, to a certain extent, into the midst of all the various religious denominations of the county, and the harsh visage of the olden times has been driven in the background. A large number of intelligent and influential citizens of the county are scarcely nominally attached to any precise faith or mode of worship, and yet many such rank amongst the most respected of our people. Such are, nevertheless, benevolent, humane and charitable to an extent that may cast the virtues of professors in the shade; but a wide tolerance is entertained by all such for opposite opinions, and with these sincerity is accepted as the all-justifying requisite. Indeed, this sentiment, originally emanating from this independent class, has made its

marked impress upon his age.   He, however, for this locality
was beyond his time, but his spirit yet lives amongst us, and
will grow until in time it shall have reached its full developed
stature in the current and progressive movement of our age.

POWNALL FAMILY. Levi Pownall, sr., of Salisbury,
was born in Bucks county, in the year 1755. He was the
son of Simeon Pownall, and the great-grandson of George
and Eleanor Pownall, who emigrated to this country with
William Penn, in the year 1682, and whose son, George
Pownall, jr., was born in Bucks county in the same year.
Levi Pownall was united in marriage with Elizabeth, the
daughter of Joseph and Martha Buckman, in the year
1782, and having removed to Lancaster county in the year
1784, he first erected a tannery at Simmonstown, (in Sadsbury township,) where he carried on the manufacture of
leather for some years. He next purchased what is known
as the Christiana tract, which had been patented by Philip
Pownall in the year 1702, on which he resided a number of
years, and was engaged in agricultural pursuits; and in the

way into churches; and it would be difficult to-day to find an intelligent
churchman who would not concede that conscience is the guide of man.
This might be regarded as a vast innovation upon the opinions of the
past. The world moves, and we move with it. Opinions also move
steadily onward, and the views of one age are no special index of what
those of the following age may be. The case cited, is but one of the instances of the rise of the human mind over the inherited beliefs of the
past, and the banishment of the same amidst the superstitions of dark
ages. Rationalizing influences are felt and prevalent all around upon
men of every class and grade in society, and are heartily cherished by
those still clinging to the truth of revelation. But with all this liberalizing movement that falls in with the current of the age, there is in our
county but few who feel bold enough to step aside from the cherished
faith of the church, and avow themselves unbelievers in revelation. To
do so, requires more than ordinary courage, especially in view of the fact
that the American mind has not yet attained to that *ultima thule* of
toleration which will even be willing to extend equal respect and honor
to the Christian, Mohammedan, Jew and Infidel. An intelligent class
exists, however, amongst us, many of whom, members of our churches,
have already touched this height of toleration, and are ready to accredit
equal honesty, candor and respect to all sincere opinions that may be,
and are entertained. When all our people reach this, a progress will
have been made, indeed, and one that should seem as likely to usher in
the halcyon days of the long delayed millennium.

year 1803 he purchased what is known as the Pownall tract, comprising about three hundred acres of land in the valley, about one mile south of Christiana, a large part of which land was purchased from William Penn, (in England), by John Kennerly, in the year 1691. The original patent for this tract was signed by William Penn, and is now in the possession of Joseph D. Pownall, esq., of Sadsbury, and is beyond question the oldest title in Lancaster county. He was a liberal-minded and generous man, and a worthy and exemplary member of the society of Friends. He had three sons, Joseph, Levi, and Simeon, and two daughters, Elizabeth and Catharine. His son Joseph was joined in marriage with Phœbe, the daughter of Joseph, and grand-daughter of Joseph, sr., and Elizabeth Dickinson. Levi and Simeon were united in marriage with Sarah and Maria, the daughters of Thomas and Eleanor Henderson, of Sadsbury, and the grand-daughters of Hattil and Abigail Varman, of Leacock. He departed this life in the year 1840, in the 85th year of his age. His grandsons, Moses and Joseph D. Pownall, have served at different times in the Legislature of Pennsylvania, and held various other public trusts. George Whitson, late recorder of deeds for Lancaster county, and Thomas Griest, late assistant assessor of internal revenue, were both married to the grand-daughters of Levi Pownall, sr.; and his grandsons, Levi, Ambrose and Simeon, still hold the original properties in the valley, where he spent the remainder of his useful and eventful life. His grandson, Henry Pownall, one of the present prison inspectors of Lancaster county, was married to Deborah, the daughter of Isaac and Deborah Walker, of Sadsbury. Moses Pownall, the son of Joseph and Phœbe Pownall, and the grandson of Levi Pownall, sr., was born in Sadsbury township, in the year 1815. He inherited from his ancestors the old homestead at Solesbury, in Bucks county, which had been purchased from William Penn before his first arrival to the province, in 1682. He was married in the year 1838, to Susannah, the second daughter of Asahel and Sarah Walker, of Sadsbury. He purchased the homestead of his grandfather Dickinson, in Sadsbury, and was commissioned a justice of the peace in 1846. He was elected a member of the Legislature in the year 1851, and reëlected for 1852. He was the Whig candidate for canal commissioner in 1853. He was an enterprising and serviceable man in the community, and did much to improve the neighborhood. He and Wm. Noble established the town of Christiana. He died on the 13th of February, 1854, in the 38th year of his age. His only son, J. D. C. Pownall, still holds his property in Sadsbury.

PRICE, S. H., a member of the Lancaster bar, admitted in 1852. He was elected to the Legislature in the years 1857-58.

PYFER, COL. FREDERICK S., was born November 24th, 1832, in Martic township, Lancaster county. His father, also named Frederick, was by birth a Prussian, and his mother a descendant of one of the oldest families of the county. After passing through the schools of his district, he went to the Marietta Academy, taught by Prof. Wicker-sham, where he continued two years and six months. He went for a short time afterwards to the Normal School at Millersville. He taught the boys high school at Columbia for three years, at the same time reading law, and completed his legal studies in the office of Issac E. Hiester. He was admitted to the bar in 1857. He began the practice of the profession in 1860, and was chosen chairman of the Democratic county committee, a position he retained up to the breaking out of the rebellion. Upon the breaking out of the war, he enlisted as a private in April, 1861, for the three months service. The company in which he was serving being soon afterwards attached to the 1st Pennsylania volunteers, he was commissioned Regimental Quartermaster, with the rank of First Lieutenant. He served the period of enlistment, (three months) and then returned home. He immediately set to raising a company for three years, which formed a part of the 77th Pennsylvania volunteers, and he immediately was chosen captain of the same, it being company K of the regiment. The regiment was sent west to the army of the Cumberland, and participated in all the battles of that division, from Shiloh till the battle of Chickamauga, in September, 1863, when he was taken prisoner with nearly the whole regiment. He was in the battles of Shiloh, Chaplin Hills, Murfreesboro, Laverque, Liberty Gap, besides numerous minor engagements. After the battle of Murfreesboro he was unanimously elected Lieutenant-colonel of his regiment by the officers, and commissioned by the Governor of Pennsylvania. He was at the time the junior captain of the regiment. He was confined in Libby Prison for nearly nine months, suffering all the privations incident to such a condition, and coming away with a broken-down constitution, not yet recuperated. He was released on parole until exchanged in June, 1864. Upon resuming his command it was found that his health was too much impaired to be able to endure the hardships of the active campaign then in progress under General Sherman, in his march to the Atlantic. He was therefore detailed by general orders to preside as president of a general court-martial at Nashville, Tennessee, in which capacity he acted until he was mustered out of service upon the expiration of his term of enlistment, February 4th, 1865. Upon returning to Lancaster, he resumed again the practice of his profession, in which he has since been steadily engaged. In October, 1871, he was elected Mayor of the city of Lancaster, a position he now holds.

R.

RAMSEY, DR. DAVID,* was born in Lancaster county, Pennsylvania, on the second day of April, 1749. He was the youngest child of James Ramsey, a respectable farmer, who had emigrated from Ireland at an early age, and by the cultivation of his farm, with his own hands, provided the means of subsistence and education for a numerous family. He was a man of intelligence and piety, and early sowed the seeds of knowledge and religion in the minds of his children. He lived to reap the fruit of his labor and see

*From National Portrait Gallery.

his offspring grow up around him, ornaments of society and props of his declining years. The early impressions which the care of this excellent parent made on the mind of Dr. Ramsey, were never erased. He had the misfortune to lose an excellent and amiable mother very early in life; but that loss was in some measure repaired by his father, who took uncommon pains to give him the best education that could then be obtained in this country. He was, from his infancy, remarkable for his attachment to books, and for the rapid progress he made in acquiring knowledge. At six years of age he read the bible with facility, and it is said was peculiarly delighted with the historical parts of it. When placed at a grammar school his progress was very remarkable. It was no uncommon thing, says a gentleman who knew him intimately at that time, to see students who had almost arrived at manhood taking the child upon their knees in order to obtain his assistance in the construction and explanation of different passages in their lessons. Before he was twelve years of age, he had read more than once all the classics usually studied at grammar schools, and was in every respect qualified for admission into college, but being thought too young for collegiate studies, he accepted the place of assistant tutor in a respectable academy in Carlisle, and notwithstanding his tender years acquitted himself to the admiration of every one. He continued for upwards of a year in this situation, and then went to Princeton. On his examination he was found qualified for admission into the junior class, but in consequence of his extreme youth, the faculty advised him to enter as a sophomore, which he did, and having passed through college with high reputation, he took the degree of bachelor of arts, in the year 1765, being then only sixteen years of age. Having completed the usual college course at sixteen, he was enabled to devote some time to the general cultivation of his mind before he commenced the study of physic; and he spent nearly two years in Maryland as a private tutor in a respectable family, devoting himself to books and enriching his mind with stores of useful knowledge.

He then commenced the study of physic, under the direction of Dr. Bond, of Philadelphia, where he regularly attended the lectures delivered at the college of Pennsylvania, the parent of the celebrated medical school which has since become so distinguished. Dr. Rush was then professor of chemistry in that college; and this led to a friendship between Dr. Rush, the able and accomplished master, and Ramsey, the ready, ingenious and attentive student, that was fondly cherished by both, and continued to strengthen and increase to the latest moments of their lives. For Dr. Rush, young Ramsey felt a filial affection; he regarded him as a benefactor, while he entertained the highest veneration for his talents. He never had any hesitation in declaring himself an advocate of the principles introduced by Dr. Rush in the theory and practice of medicine; and in his eulogium on Dr. Rush, a last public tribute of respect to the memory of his lamented friend, he declares that "his own experience had been uniformly in their favor ever since they were first promulgated;" and adds a declaration, that in his "opinion Dr. Rush had done more to improve the theory and practice of medicine than any one physician either living or dead." Dr. Ramsey was graduated bachelor of physic—a degree at that time uniformly conferred—early in the year 1772, and immediately commenced the practice of physic at the "Head of the Bohemia," in Maryland, where he continued to practice with much reputation for about a year, when he removed to Charleston. Dr. Rush, in a letter written September 15th, 1773, after stating that he would recommend Dr. Ramsey to fill the opening which then existed at Charleston, thus proceeds: "Dr. Ramsey studied physic regularly with Dr. Bond, attended the hospital and public lectures of medicine, and afterwards graduated bachelor of physic with great eclat. It is saying but little of him to tell you, that he is far superior to any person we ever graduated at our college; his abilities are not only good, but great; his talents and knowledge universal. I never saw so much strength of memory and imagination united to so fine a judgment. His manners are polished and agreeable, his conversation lively, and his behavior to all men always without offence. Joined to all these, he is sound in his principles; strict, nay, more, severe in his morals; and attached, not by education only, but by principle, to the dissenting interest. He will be an acquisition to your society. He writes, talks, and what is more, lives well; I can promise more for him, in everything, than I could for myself." Such was the character of Dr. Ramsey at the commencement of his career in life.

On settling in Charleston he rapidly rose to eminence in his profession and general respect. His talents, his habits of business and uncommon industry, eminently qualified him for an active part in public affairs, and induced his fellow-citizens to call upon him on all occasions when anything was to be done for the common welfare. In our revolutionary struggle he was a decided and active Whig, and was one of the earliest and most zealous advocates of American independence. On the 4th of July, 1778, he was appointed to deliver an oration before the inhabitants of Charleston. In this oration, the first ever delivered on the anniversary of American independence, he bodly declares that "our present form of government is every way preferable to the royal one we have lately renounced." In establishing this position, he takes a glowing view of the natural tendency of republican forms of government to promote knowledge, to call into exercise the active energies of the human soul; to bring forward modest merit; to destroy luxury and establish simplicity in the manners and habits of the people; and finally to promote the cause of virtue and religion. In every period of the war Dr. Ramsey wrote and spoke boldly and constantly; and by his personal exertions in the Legislature, and in the field was very serviceable to the cause of American liberty. The fugitive pieces written by him from the commencement of that struggle, were not thought by himself of sufficient importance to be preserved, yet it is well known to his contemporaries that on political topics no man wrote better than Dr. Ramsey, in all the public journals of the day. For a short period he was with the army as a surgeon, and he was present with the Charleston ancient battalion of artillery at the siege of Savannah. From the declaration of independence to the termination of the war he was a member of the Legislature of South Carolina. For two years he had the honor of being one of the privy council, and with two others of that body was among those citizens of Charleston who were banished by the British authorities to St. Augustine. In consequence of an exchange of prisoners Dr. Ramsey was sent back to the United States, after an absence of eleven months. He immediately took his seat as a member of the State Legislature, then convened at Jacksonsboro. It was at this assembly that the various acts confiscating the estates of the adherents to Great Britain, were passed. Dr. Ramsey being conciliatory in his disposition, tolerant and humane in his principles, and the friend of peace, although he knew well that the conduct of some of those who fell under the operation of these laws merited all the severity that could be used towards them, yet he remembered also that many others were acting from the honest dictates of conscience. He could not, therefore, approve of the confiscation acts, and he opposed them in every shape. Dr. Ramsey continued to possess the undiminished confidence of his fellow-citizens, and was in February, 1782, elected a member of the Continental Congress. In this body he was always conspicuous, and particularly exerted himself in procuring relief for the Southern States, then overrun by the enemy. On the return of peace, he returned to Charleston and commenced the practice of his profession; but was not permitted long to remain in private, and in 1785 was again elected a member of Congress from the Charleston district. The celebrated John Hancock had been chosen president of that body, but being unable to attend from indisposition, Dr. Ramsey was elected president, *pro tempore*, and continued for a whole year to discharge the important duties of that station with much ability and impartiality. In 1786 he again returned to Charleston and reëntered the walks of private life. In the State Legislature and in the Continental Congress, Dr. Ramsey was useful and influential. He was a remarkably fluent, rapid, and ready speaker; and though his manner was ungraceful, though he neglected all ornament, and never addressed himself to the imagination or passions of his audience, yet his style was so simple and

32

pure, his reasoning so cogent, his remarks so striking and original, and his conclusions resulted so clearly from his premises, that he seldom failed to convince.

He was so ready to impart to others his extensive knowledge on all subjects, that whenever consultation became necessary, his opinion and advice were looked for as a matter of course, and it was always given with great brevity and perspicuity. Thus he became the most active member of every association, public or private, to which he was attached. In general politics he was thoroughly and truly republican. Through the course of a long life his principles suffered no change; he died in those of his youth. Always disposed to believe his opponents to be the friends of the country, he endeavored by his language and example, to allay party feeling, and to teach all his fellow-citizens to regard themselves as members of the same great family. Through the whole course of his life, he was assiduous in the practice of his profession. Whenever his services were required, he never hesitated to render them promptly at every sacrifice of personal convenience and safety. In his medical principles, he was a rigid disciple of Dr. Rush, and his practice was remarkably bold. Instead of endeavoring to overcome diseases by repeated efforts, it was his aim to subdue them at once by a single vigorous remedy. This mode of practice is probably well adapted to southern latitudes where disease is so sudden in its approach and so rapid in its effects. In the treatment of the yellow fever, Dr. Ramsey is said to have been uncommonly successful; and it is well known that he effected several remarkable cures in cases of wounds received from poisonous animals. Those who knew him best, and had the experience of his services in their families for forty-two years, entertained the most exalted opinion of his professional merits. His widely-extended reputation induced many strangers, who visited Charleston in search of health, to place themselves under his care; and they always found in him the hospitable friend as well as the attentive physician.

We proceed to consider Dr. Ramsey as an author. It is in this character he is best known and most distinguished.

His reputation was not only well established in every part of the United States, but had extended to Europe. Few men in America have written more, and perhaps no one has written better. The citizens of the United States have long regarded him as the father of history in the New World; and he has always been ranked among those on whom America must depend for her literary character. He was admirably calculated by nature, education and habit, to become the historian of his country. He possessed a memory so tenacious, that an impression made on it could never be erased. The minutest circumstances of his early youth, facts and dates relative to every incident of his own life, and all public events, were indelibly engraven on his memory. He was, in truth, a living chronicle. His learning and uncommon industry eminently fitted him for the pursuits of an historian. He was above prejudice, and absolute master of passion. "I declare," says he in the introduction to his first work, "that embracing every opportunity of obtaining genuine information, I have sought for truth, and have asserted nothing but what I believe to be fact. If I should be mistaken, I will, on conviction, willingly retract it. During the whole course of my writing, I have carefully watched the workings of my mind, lest passion, prejudice, or party feeling should warp my judgment. I have endeavored to impress on myself how much more honorable it is to write impartially for the good of posterity, than to condescend to be the apologist of a party. Notwithstanding this care to guard against partiality, I expect to be charged with it by both of the late contending parties. The suffering Americans, who have seen and felt the ravages and oppressions of the British army, will accuse me of too great moderation. Europeans, who have heard much of American cowardice, perfidy and ingratitude, and more of British honor, clemency and moderation, will probably condemn my work as the offspring of party zeal. I shall decline the fruitless attempt of aiming to please either, and instead thereof, follow the attractions of truth whithersoever she may lead." From these resolutions the historian never departed.

From the beginning to the close of the war, Dr. Ramsey

was carefully collecting materials for this work. After it was completed it was submitted to the perusal of General Greene, who having given his assent to all the statements made therein, the history of the revolution in South Carolina was published in 1785. Its reputation soon spread throughout the United States, and it was translated into French, and read with great avidity in Europe. It was ever the wish of Dr. Ramsey to render lasting services to his country; and being well aware that a general history of the Revolution would be more extensively useful than a work confined to the transactions of a particular State, want of materials alone prevented him in the first instance from undertaking the former in preference to the latter. When, therefore, in the year 1785 he took his seat in Congress, finding himself associated with many of the most distinguished heroes and statesmen of the Revolution, and having free access to all the public records and documents that could throw light on the events of the war, he immediately commenced the history of the American Revolution. Notwithstanding his public duties, he found time sufficient to collect from the public offices, and from every living source, the materials for this valuable work. With Dr. Franklin and Dr. Witherspoon, both of them his intimate friends, he conferred freely and gained much valuable information from them. Anxious to obtain every important fact, he also visited Washington, at Mt. Vernon, and was readily furnished by him with all the information required relating to the events in which that great man had been the chief actor. Dr. Ramsey thus possessed greater facilities for procuring materials for the history of the Revolution than any other individual of the United States. He had been an eye witness of many of its events, and was a conspicuous actor in its busy scenes. He was the friend of Washington, Franklin, Witherspoon, and a host of others who were intimately acquainted with all the events of the war; and it may be said with perfect truth, that no writer was ever more industrious in collecting facts, or more honest in relating them. The history of the American Revolution was published in 1790, and was received with universal approbation. It is not necessary to analyze the character of a work that has stood the test of public opinion and passed through the crucible of criticism.

In 1801 Dr. Ramsey gave to the world his life of Washington; as fine a piece of biography as can be found in any language. It will not suffer in comparison with the best productions of ancient or modern times. Indeed, our biographer had one great advantage over all others—we mean the exalted and unrivaled character of his hero—a character "above all Greek, above all Roman fame." In 1808 Dr. Ramsey published his history of South Carolina, in two volumes, octavo. He had, in 1796, published an interesting " sketch of the soil, climate, weather, and diseases of South Carolina ;" and this probably suggested the idea of a more minute history of the State. No pains were spared to make this work valuable and useful. The author was himself well acquainted with many of the facts he has recorded ; and by the means of circular letters addressed to intelligent gentlemen in every part of the State, the most correct information was obtained. Many important facts thus preserved, must otherwise have been soon forgotten ; and by this publication the author fully supported the reputation he had so justly acquired. The death of his wife, in 1811, induced him to publish a short time afterwards, the memoirs of her life. This interesting little volume, which, in addition to the life of Mrs. Ramsey, contains some of the productions of her pen, is very generally read, and has been extensively useful. In addition to the works already mentioned, Dr. Ramsey published " an oration on the Acquisition of Louisiana ;" " A review of the improvements, progress, and state of medicine in the eighteenth century," delivered on the first day of the new century; "A Medical Register, for the year 1802 ;" "A dissertation on the means of preserving health in Charleston ;" " A biographical chart, on a new plan to facilitate the study of history ;" and " A Eulogium on Dr. Rush." All these works have merits in their several departments; and particularly the Review of the Eighteenth Century, which contains, perhaps, as much medical information in a small space as can be found in any production of the kind. He had also committed to the press, a short time before his death, " A

Brief history of the Independent or Congressional Church in Charleston." To this church he had from his youth been strongly attached, and this little work was meant as a tribute of affection.

The increasing demand for the history of the American Revolution induced the author, several years before his death, to resolve to publish an improved edition of that work. In preparing this, it occurred to him that a history of the United States, from their first settlement as English colonies, including as much of the Revolution as is important to be known, brought down to the present day, would be more interesting to the public as well as more extensively useful. After completing this up to 1808, he determined to publish it in connection with a universal history, hereafter to be mentioned. Had not death arrested his progress, he would have brought this work to the end of the late war. But the last and greatest work of the American historian yet remains to be mentioned. He had for upwards of forty years been preparing for the press a series of historical volumes which, when finished, were to bear the title of "Universal History Americanized, or a historical view of the world from the earliest records to the nineteenth century, with a particular reference to the state of society, literature, religion and form of government in the United States of America."[1] The mind of Dr. Ramsey was perpetually grasping after knowledge; and the idea so well expressed by Sir Wm. Jones, "that it would be happy for us if all great works were reduced to their quintessence," had often occurred to his mind. It was a circumstance deeply lamented by him that knowledge, the food of the soul, should be in such a great measure confined to literary and professional men; and he has often declared, that if men of business would only employ one hour in every twenty-four in the cultivation of the mind, they would become well informed upon all subjects. It had also forcibly suggested itself to his mind, that all of the histories that had been written were chiefly designed for

[1] This work was published after his death, by Carey & Lee, in nine volumes, in connection with his history of the United States, in three more, making in all twelve volumes.

the benefit of the old world, while America passed almost unnoticed, and was treated as unimportant in the scale of nations. With a view, therefore, of reducing all valuable historical facts within a small compass, to form a digest for the use of those whose leisure would not admit of more extensive reading, this great work was undertaken.

The labor of such an undertaking must have been great, indeed; and when we remember the other numerous works which occupied the attention of the author and the interruptions to which he was constantly exposed from professional avocations, we are at a loss to conceive how he found time for such various employments. But it has been truly said of him, that "no miser was ever so precious of his gold as he was of his time;" he was not merely economical, but parsimonious of it to the highest degree. From those avocations which occupy so great a proportion of the lives of ordinary men, Dr. Ramsey subtracted as much as possible. He never allowed for the table, for recreation, or repose, a single moment that was not absolutely necessary for the preservation of his health. His habits were those of the strictest temperance. He usually slept four hours, rose before the light, and meditated with his book in hand until he could see to read. He had no relish for the pleasures of the table. He always ate what was set before him; and having snatched his hasty meal, returned to his labors. His evenings only were alloted to recreation. He never read by the light of a candle; with the shades of the evening he laid aside his book and his pen, and, surrounded by his family and friends, gave loose to those paternal and social feelings which ever dwell in the bosom of the good man. The great merit of Dr. Ramsey as a writer, is now generally acknowledged. We are sure that we but embody the opinion of literary men in this country when we say, that as an historian Ramsey is faithful, judicious and impartial; that his style is classical and chaste; and if occasionally tinctured by originality of idea or singularity of expression, it is perfectly free from affected obscurity or colored ornament. Its energy of thought is tempered by its simplicity and beauty of style. As a man, the mind of Dr. Ramsey was cast in no common mould; his virtues were of no ordinary stamp. He was distinguished for philanthropy, enterprise, industry and perseverance. He was altogether regardless of wealth and free from ambition; and his active philanthropy only made him an author. He was an enthusiast in everything which tended to promote the moral, social, intellectual and physical state of his country.

Want of judgment in the affairs of the world, was the weak point of his character. In common with most eminent literary men, he had studied human nature more from books than actual observation. Hence, resulted a want of that sober judgment and correct estimate of men and things so essentially necessary to success in worldly pursuits. This was the great defect in his mind; as if to show the fatal effects of a single error, this alone frustrated all his schemes, and through the whole course of a long and useful life, involved him in perpetual difficulties and embarrassments from which he was never able to extricate himself. As illustrative of this part of his character, it will be sufficient to mention the zeal and perseverance with which he proposed and urged the promotion of a company for the establishment of the Sumter Canal in South Carolina, a work of great utility, but attended with the most ruinous consequences to the individuals who supported it. In society he was a most agreeable companion; his memory was stored with almost an infinite fund of interesting and amusing anecdotes, which gave great sprightliness and zest to his conversation. He never assumed any superiority over those with whom he conversed, and always took peculiar pleasure in the society of young men of intelligence and piety.

Dr. Ramsey was killed with the bullet of a maniac, and the narrative of this occurrence is thus detailed: A man by the name of William Linnen having been thrown into prison, it was on his trial represented to the court, that he was under the influence of mental derangement. Dr. Ramsey and Dr. Benjamin Simons were appointed by the court to examine and report on his case. They concurred in opinion that Linnen was deranged, and that it would be dangerous to let him go at large. He was therefore removed to prison, where he was confined until exhibiting symptoms of returning sanity he was discharged. He behaved himself peaceably for a time, but was heard to declare that he would "kill the doctors who had joined in that conspiracy against him." On Saturday, the 6th of May, Dr. Ramsey was met in Broad street, about one o'clock in the afternoon, within sight of his own door, by the wretched maniac who passed by, and taking a large horseman's pistol, charged with three bullets out of a handkerchief in which it was concealed, shot the doctor in the back. The perpetrator was arrested, committed to prison, where he remained confined as a maniac until his death. Dr. Ramsey lingered two days, and died on the 8th of May, 1815.

RAMSEY, WILLIAM, a member of the Legislature in the years 1805, 1806, 1807 and 1808.

RATHVON, GEORGE, a lieutenant in the army of the American Revolution, born 1750; mustered into the service under Capt. Nathaniel Page, in Colonel Mathias Slough's battalion of Lancaster county militia, August 24th, 1776. Being a superior mechanic, he was detailed in 1777 to make guns for the army, in the factory of William Henry, esq., at Lancaster. Died in 1819.

RATHVON, LEONARD, a colonel in the Revolutionary army. Born in 1748. Chiefly employed in the commissary and mustering service in Lancaster county, during the war. Died in 1814.

RATHVON, SIMON S., was born at Marietta, Lancaster county, April 24th, 1812. His father was Jacob Rathvon, a gunsmith, who settled in that town in 1810, and died there in 1839. His mother was Catharine Myers, of York county, who died at Marietta in 1825. His grandfather was George Rathvon, the subject of the above sketch, and his grandmother was a Kramer, of Warwick township. His great grandfather was Christian Rathvon, who, with a brother, named George, emigrated from South Germany, or Switzerland, about the year 1740, and settled in Conestoga township, near Conestoga Centre, where the original residence is still pointed out, and from whom all in this country of that name have sprung. It may be necessary here to say, that the name was originally spelled *Rathfong*, and that it has no relational affinity with the Rathbones, Rathburns, Rathbuns, or Ruthvens, which are of English or Scotch origin, unless one may have been derived from the other in Europe before their migration to America. The *g*, at the end of the name, is now universally disused, although many retain the *f* in preference to the *v*. It is stated, on the authority of an emigrant from the canton of Berne, in Switzerland, that the name still exists there, and this is the only accessible evidence, in support of the supposition, that that country is the fatherland of the subject of this sketch and his progenitors.

There was nothing in the early career of the subject of this sketch to distinguish particularly him from the other boys among whom he mingled. Inheriting a delicate constitution from his mother, at the age of eight years he was sent to a day-school, kept by a John Smith, in his native town, where he continued two quarters, learning the alphabet and spelling in one syllable. After an interval of three months, he was sent two quarters to Samuel Ross of the same place, but did not make more than a very ordinary progress. In the winter of 1821–22 he attended two quarters at the school of George Briscoe, where he made more progress in one month than he had during the whole previous periods put together, and left school in the spring, able to "read, write, and cypher"—at least as far as *compound-addition*. Although possessed of industrious habits, a retentive memory and ordinary perceptions, he did not seem to have a very clear appreciation of the advantages of an elemental education, until too late in life to avail himself of the usual opportunities of obtaining it, and therefore, at ten years he hired himself to different farmers in east and west Donegal and Rapho townships, among whom he spent five years doing farm work, alternating it during the spring season with working along the Susquehanna river at such labor as boys of his age could perform. On the 9th day of July, 1827, he bound himself an apprentice to John Bell, tailor, of Marietta, for five years—without stipulating for any schooling—and served him to the best of his ability to the end of the term. Bell was by no means a man of letters, and therefore his immediate opportunities for intellectual culture were very limited. Moderately fond of reading, he was kindly furnished with books by Jacob Grosh, esq., and Mr. Abraham N. Cassel, from their private libraries, which was continued for two or three years.

A few weeks after the expiration of his term of service with Mr. Bell, through a combination of circumstances which he could not resist at the time, he commenced the tailoring business on his own account, in his native town, on the first of September, 1832, although he was not yet twenty-one years of age. In a month or six weeks after this event, he became a member of a thespian society, and was elected its secretary, and also took a prominent part in its representations on the stage. Here he came in social contact with some of the literary men of the town and vicinity, and then, too, he became conscious of his own literary deficiencies, and he availed himself of all the opportunities for intellectual improvement which it afforded. Perhaps his whole subsequent scientific and literary advancement, received its first impulse from his connection with this society, and his social intercourse with these men. New planes of thought, new avenues of intelligence, and new standpoints for meditation seemed to be opened to him, and without always possessing the discriminating ability to sift the wheat from the chaff, still he made progress in intellectual culture, at least. This relation continued until the first of November, 1833, when he disposed of his establishment, and went to reside in Philadelphia, where he remained, principally in the employ of Thomas McGrath, until May 20th, 1834, when he returned to his native place, and reëstablished himself in business. At Philadelphia he fortunately fell into good hands, by the selection of a boarding house conducted by three intelligent Quaker ladies, who were sisters. The house contained none but orderly inmates, and these were of different degrees of intelligence, but from all of whom our subject was enabled to learn something, or to receive a valuable impression. On the 27th of May, 1834, Mr. Rathvon was married to Catharine Freyberger, whose family had only been removed two generations from the fatherland, (the Grand Duchy of Baden,) in the vicinity of Heidelberg, being the consummation of a long prior engagement.

Commencing married life with little more than twenty dollars in his purse, and with no dependencies, save Providence and his own energies, many of its earlier years were but a series of struggles to sustain a family—which ultimated in seven sons and four daughters—and to maintain an intact integrity. On the 1st of September, 1839, he discontinued business again in Marietta, and took a situation in the store of a brother who was in the dry goods business in Lancaster city, where he continued until the 1st of March, 1841, when he returned to his native place and commenced business there for the third time. He continued in business with reasonable success until the 1st of November, 1848, when he removed with his family and located permanently in the city of Lancaster, and went into the employ of Mr. F. J. Kramph, merchant tailor, on the corner of North Queen and Orange streets, as foreman and book-keeper, and continued in his employ until his death, on the 18th of April, 1858. In the summer of 1842, at Marietta, he commenced the collection of insects and the study of entomology, so far as it was compatible with his attention to his usual occupation, which was his sole reliance for the support of his family. Prior to that period, however, as early as 1837, under the inspiration of Josiah Holbrook, a Lyceum of Natural Science had been established in Marietta, and our subject became a member of it, and made a collection of minerals and a small one of birds. Trifling as these things may seem, yet they were valuable intellectual and moral aids in elevating his mind above mere sensual indulgence. In 1844 his first literary composition was published in the columns of the *Argus*, a weekly newspaper of the place. While in the employ of Mr. Kramph, he became a writer of moral and miscellaneous essays, and also of practical contributions to entomology, which were published in the *Farm Journal*, the *Marriettian*, and various other papers.

In March, 1859, he purchased the stock in the establishment of his late employer, and commenced the business of a merchant tailor on his own account, devoting such intervals from labor as he could conveniently command, to the pursuit of his specialty in natural history, and in various literary pursuits; and his miscellaneous writings, over the pseudonym of GRANTELLUS, as well as over his own proper signature or initials, have appeared from time to time in the various newspapers of Lancaster city and county. He has for years been in the habit of contributing articles for many of the leading scientific and literary journals of the country. Several of his papers upon entomology have been published in the State and national departments of agriculture.

Near the close of 1850, and after a conflict with the merely worldly man, Mr. Rathvon identified himself, through re-baptism, with the New Jerusalem church—perhaps better known outside of that organization, as the "Swedenborgian church"—having for some years previously been, to some extent, a reader and *receiver* of its fundamental doctrines. His father was of Moravian stock, his mother of Lutheran, but his own *earliest* religious instruction was in the Presbyterian church. It was not *common* in his childhood and youth, for parents to inculcate any special doctrinal truths. That was left to the Sunday-schools and the church. But before reaching any definite theological conclusion, he passed over what he has always since considered a rugged, a dark, and a dangerous way. Indifference, "nothingarianism," nominal universalism, skepticism, pantheism, deism, and so-called rationalism, all, by turns, suggested themselves to his mind as the *ultimatum* of religious truth. But his mental organization was such, that he could not divest his mind of the doubts usually involved in these and many other forms of mere materialism. He was also more or less influenced by that superficial and uncharitable assumption which condemns a *creed* because its receivers are faithless to its teachings. If the sentiments involved in the various *isms* were unsatisfying to his mind, so were also those of popular orthodoxy. Therefore, when the doctrines of the new church were presented to him, his first impression was that they were beautiful, if true; and then that if they were not true, they *ought* to be true; and, finally, that they *were the truth,* so far as he was able to comprehend the truth. Although convinced that they *are the truth*, without qualification, yet he is just as fully convinced that no man rationally and practically *believes* any farther than he truly *understands*.

Our subject, on his own individual account, has never solicited social or political position, power or place, and, indeed, through deafness, which gradually came upon him after 1841, he has felt himself quite incompetent for the discharge of many duties which otherwise he might discharge with ability. Nevertheless, he has for forty years been a member of different organizations, and has been honored with the confidence and respect of his fellow-citizens. In 1831, and while he was yet an apprentice, he was elected a member of a volunteer company, and served in that capacity for eight years, during the last four of which he was its commander, holding his captain's commission from Joseph Ritner, Governor of Pennsylvania. He was, in addition to others named, a member of the borough council, and secretary of the thespian society, the amateur band of Marietta, and a performing member in both the latter; a member of the board of common schools, of the select council, a trustee of the Children's Home, in Lancaster city. He is now professor of entomology in the "Pennsylvania Horticultural Society," corresponding member of the "Academy of Natural Sciences" of Philadelphia, and of the "American Entomological Society;" honorary member and entomologist of the "Fruit Growers' Society" of Pennsylvania, and of the "Agricultural and Horticultural Society" of Lancaster county; an honorary member of the "Diagnothian Literary Society" of Franklin and Marshall college, and of the "Page Literary Society" of the State Normal School, at Millersville; secretary and leader of the New Jerusalem Society," chairman of the library committee of the "Mechanics' Society," and treasurer of the "Linnæan Society"[1] of Lancaster city. In several of these he is an

[1]Mr. Rathvon was one of the founders and incorporators of the "Linnæan Society" of Lancaster county, and was one of its most active and punctual members, never having been absent from a single meeting since its first organization in 1861. No other member has been instrumental in contributing so largely and so continuously to its museum, its

active working member.   He is also a member of Lodge No. 43, A. Y. M.; of Chapter 43, R. A. M.; of "Goodwin Council," No. —; and of "Lancaster Commandery," No. 13, of Knights Templar, and of the "Empire Hook and Ladder Company." If wealth and political or social distinction, however, be the only evidences of a successful career in this world, then the life of the subject of this memoir can scarcely be claimed as a success.

He is still delving quietly and unostentatiously, in his professional calling, and in his usual literary and scientific pursuits, making no higher pretension than a mere amateur in these.   He is now in his sixtieth year, with his usual energy and health, and has seen most of the companions of his youth one by one pass away; himself, his wife, and eight children, still surviving—five sons and three daughters.

Without any very special patronage, and with nothing but untiring industry, he has not only supported and moderately educated his large family, but has accumulated a library of nearly a thousand volumes, costing nearly two thousand dollars; a clever mineralogical collection, and nearly ten thousand species of insects of different *orders*, but mainly *coleoptera;* besides a comfortable home.   Perhaps, after all, such an example from the lower walks of life, will be as a beneficial to posterity as one of more transcendant talents and a higher social and pecuniary position.   Those in humble life are often overawed by the commanding abilities of many occupying positions so far above theirs, and they are also often deterred from making any attempt to

archives, and its library; scarcely a month passing in which he has not read one or more papers on natural science before it, or in some way contributed to its material support.   Much of that persevering thought and carefulness of details so necessary in sustaining a society of this kind, and the patient labor of carrying its resolves into effect, has devolved on him, and perhaps no society has made any more cheerful, constant, and unselfish working member.   He was also one of the founders of the "Lancaster County Agricultural and Horticultural Society ;" and of the *Lancaster Farmer*, a monthly periodical established under its auspices, and devoted to its interests.   He was its senior editor from its very beginning, and no number of that journal has appeared in which he has not been a contributor to its columns.   Although, professedly, neither an agriculturist or horticulturist, and without any immediate

alter or better their condition, simply because they have not a more advantageous starting point. If it is impossible for all men to *distinguish* themselves, at least all may be better than they are, and achieve more if they *will*. Perhaps nothing has contributed more to the success of our subject, so far as his life has been a success, than his industry and perseverance, supported by an integrity that never repudiated or evaded a pecuniary, social or domestic responsibility, or an obligation; and that alone ought to infuse into others, in like circumstances, sufficient encouragement to " go and do likewise."

As a scientist, S. S. Rathvon is an ardent student and lover of nature. In the department of entomology he is especially distinguished, as he is also in the kindred sciences. As a writer upon entomological subjects, he is justly entitled to rank amongst the first investigators of the science in the whole country. He is diligent and devoted in the pursuit of his favorite studies, and perhaps there is no instance in America of such an incessant, self-sacrificing pursuit of knowledge, under adverse circumstances, as his has been. After the ordinary business labors of the day are past, he spends every night almost in his study until twelve, two, three, and four o'clock in the morning enveloped in study; and then retiring for a few hours he rises and breakfasts, and is at his place of business by the usual hour in the morning. His are the ardor and application of a Cuvier, or a Humboldt, and but for his surroundings and obstacles, a high niche in the temple of fame could have been achieved.

pecuniary interest in these vocations, yet he has always given the weight of his influence, so far as it might be useful to every enterprise that had for its object the welfare and the advancement of these departments of human labor; and this, too, without any pecuniary reward. He has been for more than twenty years a member of the *New Jerusalem Society* of Lancaster, and for two-thirds of that period has been its "leader" in public worship and the superintendent of its Sunday-school; and has uniformly been punctual in the discharge of the duties devolving upon him in these capacities. Seeing that, for the greater part of the time, he stands almost isolated in this community, deprived of the sustaining influence of larger religious communities, our subject exhibits a consistent adherence to religious principle, that is not always met with where there are no ulterior worldly ends to accomplish.

Fortune seems not to have bestowed upon him the conditions necessary for the highest scientific attainment, yet he has far outstripped others more favorably circumstanced.

His has been the school of difficulties, and nobly has he risen, despite his surroundings, and achieved a higher degree of moral worth than otherwise he might have been able to attain. It is in this latter particular that he has risen to the perfection of manhood, and exhibits a shining example of high moral tone but seldom attainable by man. In this he is a nobleman, indeed; and but few know the great superiority and high moral sublimity of this true example of Christian manhood. Nobler sentiments than imbue his whole life and conversation, never influenced a Socrates, a Seneca, or a Confucius; and not in act only, but in thought does this high moral standard pervade his feelings. No action that he feels to be wrong, could he be induced to commit. Unkind feelings he entertains towards no specimen of mankind; no slander ever falls from his lips; nor does he give utterance to any ungenerous remarks, it matters not how any one may have injured him. Perfectly unselfish in all his actions, his efforts instead of being incited by sinister motives, are prompted alone by a desire to elevate mankind, and diffuse generally the principles of morality. If there be one man in our county who has endeavored with all his soul to take up into the whole substance of his being, constitution and actions, the moral excellence of Christ's teachings and example, as recorded in the Evangelist, that man is the subject of our notice. He has done this so far as weak and erring humanity is capable. Not for the applause of the world is his conduct shaped; his own internal sense of right is his guiding star. What popular opinion may be, he cares not; only so far as it accords with the promptings of that informed monitor of his bosom, does he give it audience. He, however, condemns no man who may differ with him in opinion, freely permitting others to enjoy their own sentiments as their consciences may dictate. His example and life are worthy of imitation, and if a higher reward than mere earthly be the lot of devoted aspiration to the subject of our notice, a large inheritance will be his portion.

33

RAUCH, RUDOLPH F., was elected Prothonotary of Lancaster county in the year 1842.

RAWLINS, JOHN, elected a member of the Legislature in 1853.

REED, ELIAS, emigrated from Germany about the year 1761, and first settled with his family in Bucks county, Pa. A few years afterwards he removed with his family to the valley of the Wyoming, where he took up four hundred acres of land. He did little more, however, than build a log cabin for himself and family, and a stable for his horses and cattle, when he was compelled, by the hostility of the Indian savages, to return to Bucks county, leaving behind him his horses and cattle. His log cabin and stable were burned as soon as his family had fled to save their lives. He had four sons, one of whom enlisted under Gen. Wayne, and served under him during the whole period of the Revolution.

REED, JOHN K., a banker of Lancaster city, and a man of estimable and highly honorable character. He was in 1851 elected prothonotary of Lancaster county, and in October, 1870, elected one of the board of county commissioners. He was elected commissioner by the vote of both political parties.

REED, PETER, youngest son of Elias Reed, came and settled in the town of Lancaster, (now city), about the year 1783. As a citizen he was highly honored and much respected, and held several important offices in the county of Lancaster.

REED, PETER, jr., son of the last named, was elected high sheriff of Lancaster county, in 1836, and held the same for three years.

REED, THOMAS, one of the first legislative delegates from Lancaster county in 1829.

REDDIG, JACOB, of West Cocalico township, was born October 7th, 1794. His grandfather emigrated from near Manheim, in Germany, and settled in Lancaster county at an early day. His father was named Jacob, and died in 1854, aged 84 years. The subject of this notice followed the mercantile business from the age of eighteen years up till

1862, when he retired and has since been living in retirement upon one of his farms. He was elected a member of the Legislature in the year 1837.

*REICHENBACH, JOHN CHRISTIAN WILLIAM, was born January 26, 1749, in Swartzburg-Rudolstadt, Upper Saxony, Prussia. Little is immediately accessible in reference to either his ancestry or his youth, but from the fact that he received a liberal scientific and classical education, for that period, the inference is, that his family occupied an easy, if not a distinguished social position in his native country. This is rendered further probable from the fact that he graduated, or at least attended the university at Marseilles, in France. In 1785 he left Germany, and spent some years in travel, or engaged in some learned occupation. At all events, he reached Lancaster, Pennsylvania, about 1780, and was immediately appointed professor of mathematics and German literature in Franklin college, then just going into operation. Soon thereafter he married Mrs. Elizabeth Graeff, formerly Miss Schwartz, by whom he had a number of children, all of whom are dead, and some of whom he survived. In addition to his duties as professor in the college,[1] and also for some years subsequently, he practiced surveying and gauging, in the county of Lancaster. He was originally a member of the Moravian denomination, and sometimes preached lay sermons in their church in Lancaster, and otherwise made himself generally useful.

About the same time that Reichenbach arrived in Lancaster, Henry von Beulow, a German nobleman, and a native of Prussia, who in his early years had adopted the military profession, also arrived there, and spent some time in it. Von Buelow had embraced the peculiar theological and philosophical views of Emanuel Swedenborg. Reichenbach and Buelow soon became acquainted, and socially and intel-

[1] Franklin college was originally located in North Queen street, Lancaster, near James street, and for many years was known as the "barracks," the "old stone house," and subsequently as "Franklin row." It was suspended finally for the want of pecuniary resources, and it is probable that Reichenbach only engaged in the occupation of surveyor and gauger after its suspension.

* Contributed by S. S. Rathvon.

lectually affiliated, and this soon led to a theological and philosophical affiliation. The latter had brought with him from Germany a number of the works of Swedenborg, for gratuitous circulation and for sale. On examining these doctrines, Reichenbach embraced them and avowed them openly. He afterwards translated and published several works on the doctrines of Swedenborg—otherwise called the "New Church,"—one of which was entitled *Agathon*, which was published in both English and German, from the Latin manuscripts of Von Buelow, copies of which are still extant. Reichenbach was an extensive writer, and at his death left a large mass of manuscript, which never was subsequently utilized, and finally became extinct through age, mould and mice. These consisted of theological and philosophical speculations, Latin and Greek translations, solutions of mathematical problems, and sacred and sentimental poems. It is fair to infer, that some of his compositions must have been published under pseudonyms, not now recognizable in the *Halcyon Luminary*, the *Dawn of Light*, and other new church publications of his day. He led a peaceable and useful life, universally respected, in the companionship of Damish, Eckstein, Carpenter, Bailey, Ehrenfried and others, who composed the little band of " Receivers," after the return of Von Buelow to Europe, and at last was gathered to his fathers on the 15th of May, 1821, in the 73d year of his natural life. How deeply impressed he was with the Swedenborgian doctrine of the resurrection, may be inferred from the inscription on his tombstone :

"By a process which they call death, the earthly part sunk here precipitated;
The nobler part, by our good Lord, rose heavenly sublimated.

REIGART,[1] ADAM, was an innkeeper during the American Revolution, keeping his house on the west side of North Queen street, near Centre Square. His hotel was the Whig headquarters during the Revolution, and here the supreme

[1] It was at the house of Adam Reigart that the lots were drawn in order to determine upon which one of the British officers, held as prisoners of war at Lancaster during the Revolution, the execution of the *lex talionis* should take place in retaliation for the murder of Captain Hudy, who had been executed at New York in violation of military law.

Executive Council held its sessions when in Lancaster. He was Lieutenant-colonel of a regiment under the command of Colonel George Ross, and marched with his regiment to Amboy, in New Jersey, and served with it until the regiment was discharged. He was in various encounters which his regiment had with the British during his service as one of its commanding officers. He was elected a member of the Legislature for the year 1780.

REIGART, EMANUEL, son of Adam Reigart, was a tanner and currier by occupation, and carried on this business quite extensively. He was elected repeatedly a member of the Legislature, being a member during the sessions of 1813, 1814, 1815, 1817. He was cotemporary as a legislator in 1814–15 with James Buchanan, when the latter was making his first debut in political life. In 1821 he was elected sheriff of Lancaster county. He also served once in the office of coroner.

REIGART, EMANUEL C., son of Emanuel Reigart, was born in Lancaster in the year 1797, and was for many years one of the leading and influential men of the city. He read law with Amos Ellmaker, and was admitted to the bar April 19th, 1822. Belonging to one of the old and influential families of the county, Mr. Reigart soon took a leading rank in his profession, and for many years was recognized as one of the ablest lawyers of the city. In 1834 he was nominated and elected to the Legislature, on what was known as the Anti-Masonic ticket. While in the Legislature he submit-

The drawing of the lots was conducted by Colonel George Gibson, and the lot fell upon Captain Sir Charles Asgill. As soon as Gibson perceived upon whom the lot had fallen, he remarked to Captain Stake (pointing to Asgill), there is your prisoner. Asgill was immediately ordered under the command of Captain Stake, who, upon the solicitation and pledge of honor of Major Gordon, another British officer, surrendered Asgill to his keeping for a few days. When Major Gordon was conducting Asgill away from the place where the lots had been drawn, the latter partially fainted and fell prostrate. Major Gordon upbraidingly remarked to him : " For God's sake don't disgrace your colors." Through the interposition of lady Asgill, the mother of Sir Charles, the French Minister used his influence with Washington and obtained his release, and thus rescued him from being executed, as otherwise he would have been, in obedience to the *lex talionis*.

ted a minority report in favor of the school law of 1809, instead of that of 1834. On the 24th of February, 1835, he delivered a speech, favoring the resolution offered by Mr. Stevens for the suppression of Masonic oaths.[1] On November 14th, 1843, Emanuel C. Reigart addressed a letter to Henry Clay (then the prominent candidate of the Whigs for the presidential nomination), interrogating him as to his connection with the institution of Free Masonry. To this Clay replied, that he had joined the order in early life, but that he had entirely retired from connection with the lodge for upwards of nineteen years. In 1837–38 Mr. Reigart was a member of the State Constitutional Convention and took a prominent part therein, generally coöperating with Thaddeus Stevens—also a member of the Convention—on important questions. With him were associated in this convention, from Lancaster county, Henry G. Long, William Hiester, Lindley Coates, Jeremiah Brown, James Porter, Dr. Cochran, and Joseph Konigmacher. In 1846 Mr. Reigart was the Native American candidate for Congress from Lancaster county, and in 1847 he was the Native American candidate for Governor, against Shunk, Democrat, and Irwin, Whig, and received 11,000 votes in the State. When a young man, Mr. Reigart enlisted in 1814 in the company raised by Captain Edward Shippen, which marched for the defense of Baltimore. In the same company were James Buchanan, Molton C. Rodgers, Dr. F. A. Muhlenberg, and in fact the *elite* of Lancaster. At a mass meeting held in Lancaster in 1848, Mr. Reigart nominated Thaddeus Stevens for Congress, which was the first public nomination Mr. Stevens had ever received for that position.

In the year 1848 Mr. Reigart retired permanently from the practice of the profession. In 1851, having been appointed commissioner by President Fillmore, to attend the

---

[1] The Anti-Masons were opposed to the administration of extra judicial oaths, such as were alleged by them to be imposed upon Masons, and they desired the enactment of a law that would prevent such oaths from being administered. They feared that these oaths would come in conflict with the administration of justice. No oaths, they argued, should be allowed to be administered that might in any wise conflct with those of a judicial character.

World's Fair in London, he fulfilled the duties of this appointment, and next made a tour of the continent, visiting all the places of interest that delight the intelligent tourist. The latter part of Mr. Reigart's life was spent in retirement, and in the management of his extensive estate. A few years before his death he was appointed by Judge Cadwallader, United States Commissioner for this district, a position he held at the time of his death. He died December 20th, 1869. Mr. Reigart was a man of considerable benevolence. He was the founder of the Lancaster Athenæum, having endowed the institution with $2500. A few years before his decease he gave to the Howard Association $1000, to be used for the relief of the poor of the city of Lancaster.

REIGART, HENRY M., was elected commissioner of Lancaster county, in the year 1822. He was afterwards postmaster of the city of Lancaster.

REIGART, FRANKLIN, J., a native of Lancaster, and a man of considerable intellectual vigor. He studied civil engineering, and served in this business under Mr. Gay, from 1834 till 1836, on the Columbia and Philadelphia railroad. He aided in the location of the Harrisburg and Lancaster railroad. He was surveyor for Lancaster, and published the first map of the city. He was the first to get up meetings to start the Lancaster gas works, and also for the new markets. He was appointed clerk of quarter sessions in the year 1839. He served for some years as an alderman, and also for some time as recorder of the city of Lancaster. He is now engaged as patent agent in Washington city.

REINHOLD, JESSE, was elected a member of the Legislature in the year 1855.

REINOEHL, A. C., is a native of Lancaster county, and a graduate of Franklin and Marshall college, Pennsylvania. He served with credit to himself in the war of the rebellion. After retiring from the army he read law, and was admitted to the bar in 1866. In 1867 he was elected a member of the Legislature, and twice reëlected in the years 1868 and 1870. In the year 1871 he was appointed deputy secretary of the commonwealth.

REIST FAMILY. Peter Reist, the founder of this family, was a native of Switzerland, whom religious persecution first drove to the Palatinate, and afterward to America. While in the Palatinate he married his wife, whose maiden name was Anna Clara Boyer. He arrived in Lancaster county in the year 1723, and became a convert to the Mennonite faith. He built himself a cabin near Kissel Hill, which was claimed by a man named Witmer. He relinquished possession of this and went about two miles northwest, where he took possession of six hundred acres of land. Two hundred acres of this tract is yet in possession of John and Jacob Reist, great-great-grandsons of the first settler. Peter Reist had five sons and two daughters. The sons were Peter, Christian, Abraham, Jacob and John. Peter settled in Lebanon county, Pennsylvania, and Christian died without heirs. Abraham acquired considerable property and left numerous descendants. Abraham H. Reist, of Lancaster, is his great-grandson. Among his descendants are the Reists of Shaefferstown, Lebanon county, and those in Linglestown, Dauphin county, and in Canada are also of them. His blood flows in the Reigarts, Swarrs, Bears, Stauffers, Hostetters and Hersheys, of Lancaster county. Jacob Reist was killed on Braddock's field, July 9th, 1755.

JOHN REIST retained the old homestead, with four hundred acres of land, on which John Reist, his great-grandson, yet resides. John had five sons and three daughters, viz: Christian, Abraham, Jacob, John, and Peter. Christian retained the old homestead, and Abraham procured an adjoining tract of land. Ezra Reist, prison inspector, is the latter's grandson. Jacob died unmarried; and John left a son in Erie county, New York, named John Reist, a Reformed Mennonite clergyman. Peter settled between Oregon and Millport. One of Peter's sisters was married to a man named Kauffman, and settled in Virginia; another was married to a man named Bomberger, grandfather of Rev. Christian Bomberger. The other sister married a Hostetter, the father of Henry Hostetter, a member of the Legislature in 1827. Rev. Charles Hostetter, a Mennonite clergyman, is a grandson of Hostetter, first named.

PETER REIST[1] had two sons, John and Jacob, and one daughter, the mother of the wife of Greybill Bear, of Mount Joy, and Joseph Brubaker's wife, of Warwick. John was a well educated and talented young man. He was commissioned a justice of the peace of Manheim township, and died at the early age of thirty-two years. He was a surveyor, and with Jacob Hibshman and Charles Montelius, laid out the towns of Warwick and New Ephrata, now called Lincoln.

Joseph Ritner, afterwards Governor of Pennsylvania, was a hireling for some time in the employ of Peter Reist, then being a poor young man. When he became Governor he paid his old friends in Warwick township a visit, and spent a night with Jacob Reist, who had been oft his playmate when in the employ of Peter, his father. He made numerous observations, and remarked the great changes that had taken place on the farms since he had lived in that section. Ritner,[2] on that occasion conversed freely on politics. Having been for years a prominent Democrat, he remarked the great strength of the Masonic order, and said that he believed, had he been a Free-Mason, he would have been nominated for Governor by the Democrats at the time Wolf was made their candidate. His conscientious scruples, however, prevented his being a Free-Mason.

The Reists were all originally Democrats, but left the

[1] Peter Reist was an ardent Democrat, and when the news came that Jefferson was elected President over Burr in 1800, happening to be in Lancaster, and expressing his joy at the result, the Federalists fell upon him, and he with difficulty made his escape to his home.

[2] When Joseph Ritner was elected Governor in 1835, being free and untrammeled of pledges, he chose his cabinet officers without any previous bargaining. He had concluded in his own mind to tender the Secretaryship of State to Amos Ellmaker, of Lancaster. Mr. Ellmaker declined the position, but at the same time recommended Thomas H. Burrowes, who had studied law in his office, and to whom he felt attached. He assured the Governor that Mr. Burrowes was fully competent for the position, and if any assistance would be needed he would cheerfully render him any aid. This recommendation of Mr. Ellmaker made Thomas H. Burrowes Secretary of State, and was the foundation of his prominence as a Pennsylvania school man. Had Mr. Ellmaker recommended Henry G. Long or Emanuel C. Reigart, Mr. Burrowes would never have been Secretary of State. The word of an influential man is therefore potent.

party at the same time that James Buchanan joined it.
Simon Reist, grandson of Peter, was one of the nine men in
1855, who organized the Republican party in Lancaster
county.

Jacob Reist was somewhat an active politician in his day,
and is now living, a man of advanced years, in Petersburg,
Lancaster county. He had four sons, Simon, Peter, Levi
and Isaac; also, five daughters, Elizabeth, married to Samuel
Royer; Anna, married to Greybill Bear; Catharine, married
to Henry L. Landis; Barbara, married to A. D. Greybill, and
Levina, married to H. H. Oberholtzer. Isaac died single,
and Simon died in 1862, near Lancaster, leaving four sons,
Henry, Linnæus, John and Simon.

REIST, Levi S., of Warwick township, was born April
13th, 1817. He was raised upon a farm, and has been engaged in agricultural pursuits all his lifetime. In politics
he has always been a leading man in his district, and in 1848
was one of the delegates from Lancaster county to the State
convention of the Whig party that nominated a canal commissioner, and chose presidential electors which elected
General Taylor President of the United States. In 1851 he
was elected a justice of the peace for his township, a position
he filled for ten years. He was elected in 1859 one of the
board of county commissioners,[1] a position he held for three
years. In 1866 he was one of three who signed a call for a

[1]The office of county commissioner was, during the rebellion especially, one of grave responsibility. New duties devolved upon the
board which required rare judgment to discharge with entire satisfaction. The commissioners, together with two of the judges of the court,
were constituted a board of relief for distributing aid from the
public funds to the widows and families of soldiers in destitute circumstances. The commissioners were required to procure arms, and have
them in readiness for defense along the border, if occasion should
require. The first muskets received by them, were old flint-locks that
were lying idle in the State arsenal at Harrisburg, and which they had
altered into percussion locks by Henry E. Leman, gunsmith, of Lancaster. They were furnished at another time with one thousand new
muskets, for which the county gave bonds. They were frequently
solicited to furnish quarters for soldiers in the national service, and on
several occasions did so; at one time on the fair grounds, and on other
occasions soldiers were quartered in the court house and in the churches
of the city. In the beginning of the war the commissioners offered a

meeting, which laid the foundation of the Lancaster Agricultural and Horticultural Society, and was the first president of the same. He aided actively in the establishment of the Lancaster *Farmer*, in January, 1869, and during the first year was on the editorial corps, and has ever since been one of its leading contributors.

REITZEL, JOHN, was appointed Recorder of Deeds in 1821.

REYNOLDS, JOHN, a native of Lancaster county, was the editor of the *Journal* for many years before its union with the *Intelligencer*. After his retirement from editorial life, he moved to Cornwall, and assumed the management of the iron works at that place. He was chosen guardian of the minor children of Thomas B. Coleman. He remained the manager at Cornwall until about 1847, when he returned to Lancaster. In 1822 he was elected a member of the Legislature, and reëlected in 1823. He died in Baltimore, May 11th, 1853, in the 67th year of his age. He is the father of General John F. Reynolds and James L. Reynolds, esq.

*REYNOLDS, MAJOR GENERAL, JOHN FULTON, was born in Lancaster, Pa., on the 21st of September, 1820. He was educated in the schools of his native city, and in 1837 was

bounty of fifty dollars for one regiment of ten companies for nine months. Instead of ten companies fourteen companies were raised.

Muskets were distributed to the citizens by the commissioners, who were enrolled *pro tempore* for the preservation of law while the drafting process was being performed at the court house, in Lancaster, during the year 1863. This was deemed necessary on the part of the authorities, in order to repress strong indications of riot that were manifesting themselves upon the occasion referred to. The reason of this was, that as great difference of sentiment prevailed amongst the people of the North as to the justice of the war against the South, many were unwilling to be compelled to fight in a cause that they regarded unjust and unconstitutional. Those amongst whom the riotous proceedings were manifested, were generally the German inhabitants of the city, many of whom were in principle opposed to the war policy of the government. A few citizens were arrested, but order was again restored, when a number of the inhabitants of the city were armed with muskets, and so detailed about the court house as to intimidate an outbreak.

*Contributed by J. M. W. Geist.

appointed a cadet at West Point. He graduated from the Military Academy in 1841 ; in July of the same year he was appointed brevet second lieutenant in the Third Artillery, and was ordered to Fort McHenry, Baltimore ; three months later he was promoted to a second lieutenancy ; early in 1843 he was ordered to St. Augustine, and at the close of the year was transferred to Fort Moultrie. In 1845 he was sent to Corpus Christi, and afterwards to Fort Brown. In June, 1846, he was promoted to first lieutenant, and marched with his battery, accompanying General Taylor's army, into Mexico; was engaged at the battle of Monterey, and two days thereafter was breveted captain for gallant conduct. On the 21st of February, 1847, he was in the battle of Buena Vista, and received the brevet of major for meritorious services. At the close of the Mexican war he was sent to the forts on the coast of New England, where he remained four years, when he was appointed a staff officer to General Twiggs; and in 1853 went to New Orleans, but in the following year returned to the east, and was stationed at Fort Lafayette, until he was attached to an expedition which was sent across the plains to Utah. He reached Salt Lake City in August, 1854 ; in March, 1855, he was promoted to a captaincy, and sent across the mountains to California. During the year he remained on the Pacific coast, he engaged in expeditions against the Indians, commanded posts, and at one time was on a board to examine candidates for admission into the army from civil life. In December, 1856, he arrived at Fortress Monroe, and in the summer of 1858 was placed in command of battery C, of the Third regiment, and was ordered to cross the plains with his command, to Utah. The battery was one of the most efficient in the service, and hence Secretary Floyd sought to destroy it, by mounting it and sending it across the Rocky Mountains. The company, however, arrived in safety at Fort Vancouver, in December, 1859.

In September, 1860, Major Reynolds was appointed commander of cadets at West Point ; in May, 1861, he was appointed lieutenant-colonel of the Fourteenth Infantry, and sent to New London, Connecticut, to recruit his regiment to its maximum strength for service in the rebellion.[1] In August he was promoted to the rank of brigadier-general of volunteers, and was ordered to command Fort Hatteras; but, at the request of Governor Curtin, General Reynolds was assigned to the command of the first brigade of the Pennsylvania Reserve Corps. He marched and fought with his brigade on the peninsula, and in Pope's campaign. General Pope says in his report:

"Brigadier-General John F. Reynolds, commanding the Pennsylvania Reserves, merits the highest commendation at my hands. Prompt, active and energetic, he commanded his division with distinguished ability throughout the operations, and performed his duties in all situations with zeal and fidelity."

After the retreat of General Pope to the defences around Washington, it became apparent that the enemy contemplated an invasion of Maryland, and probably of Pennsylvania. Governor Curtin, therefore, on the 4th of September, 1862, issued a proclamation calling out 75,000 of the State

[1]The period of the Southern rebellion was one that called forth a tone of sentiment in Lancaster county which cannot, with due propriety, as it seems to us, be passed over in silence. A state of feeling existed, that it is to be hoped will never again be experienced. After the election of Abraham Lincoln to the presidency, in 1860, the Southern States, one after another, prepared to put their long asserted resolves into execution; and in December of that year, South Carolina passed an ordinance of secession, severing her allegiance from the Federal Union. This step was looked upon by our people as an ebullition of anger that would amount to nothing; and when any one happened to express his fears that the event betokened something serious, he was met by the remark, "*O this will soon blow over,*" or, "*we can whip them in two weeks,*" and language of that character, all going to show that no adequate idea was entertained of the magnitude of the difficulties that were threatening the country.

When at length the bulletin board, on the morning of April 13th, 1861, told the sad news that Fort Sumter had been fired upon, it was surrounded by a crazed multitude, as it would have seemed, and threats were in every mouth almost, that the Southern States should be wiped out of existence. Even to intimate a doubt of the speedy downfall of the rebellion, was accepted by the infuriated as evidence of treasonable sentiments; and a remark made by an individual in presence of some citizens: "Gentlemen, this will be a three years war," was met with such replies as, " *Why, man, you are crazy,*" or, " *O my God, this means nothing, it will be all over in a month.*"

The feelings of those favorable to the war, became speedily embittered towards such as intimated the least doubt as to the success of the

militia, and on the 12th General Reynolds was relieved from the command of the Reserve Corps, and ordered to proceed to Harrisburg, at the request of the Governor, to organize and command these forces. He received the men, who were pouring in incessant streams to the Capital, organized them into brigades, and marched them up the Cumberland valley to protect the borders of the State. After the battle of Antietam the militia was disbanded, and General Reynolds rejoined the Army of the Potomac, and assumed command of the first corps; he rendered distinguished service at the battle of Fredericksburg, and carried the enemy's works on the left. He was appointed military governor of that city, and his administration of affairs was so vigorous and equitable, that the loyal citizens rejoiced in the establishment of the authority of the United States in their midst. His troops were present, but were not called into action at the battle of Chancellorsville. When General Meade moved the army

struggle. The great majority of the people appeared, and were in reality, in favor of the prosecution of the contest for the restoration of the Union. No intimation that the abolition of slavery was an object, was made by any of the war partisans; and when one opposed to the war would claim that it was prosecuted for the purpose of freeing the negroes, this was ever indignantly denied. The fact need not be concealed, that a considerable number of the people felt averse to the prosecution of such a war, as they regarded all difficulties between the two sections as capable of being settled without a collision of arms. But the larger number of those who entertained such opinions were careful to conceal them, as it was perceived that in the midst of the excitement their persons and business were in jeopardy by the expression of opinions then very unpopular. The people were speedily divided into those favorable to and those opposed to the war. The shrewd and designing of the latter division, simply allowed their opinions to be known by those who agreed with them. They, as a consequence, were popular with both parties, for they could easily vary their sentiments to suit the company in which they might happen to be. But there are always those who are bold enough to express their real opinions, whether they be popular or the contrary. Upon this small band the popular venom poured itself. All who as a consequence expressed any sentiment that did not accord with the popular opinion, were denounced as traitors, and deserving of being executed. They were required to meet frowning looks in all their meanderings, and hear offensive and insulting remarks at many a corner as they passed the streets. Oft would the man of honest opinions cross the street sooner than encounter one whose hatred of him and his opinions he felt was intense. Men that had been bosom friends for

from Frederick into Pennsylvania, expecting each hour to encounter the rebel force, he selected General Reynolds, his bosom friend, and the man of all others in whom he reposed the most implicit confidence, to lead the advance wing, composed of three corps, the First, Third, and Eleventh. Morning and evening, frequently during the day, and in the still hours of night, these two distinguished soldiers, Pennsylvania's noblest contributions to the army, could be seen in close consultation and earnest discussion. The commanding general communicated fully all his plans and intended movements to his companion, and heard with deep interest the comments of the great soldier. Reynolds, in turn, with the whole ardor of his noble nature, entered into the work assigned him; he led forth his troops, marching at the head of the great army as a patriot going out to battle for the honor of his country and the liberty of his race.

When, on the morning of the 1st of July, he rose to the summit of the hills in front of Gettysburg, he saw at a glance,

years before the war, would pass and repass without exchanging recognitions, because of diversity of political sentiment. Relations, and even members of the same family, quarreled over the question of the war. After an election, the vulgar of the winning party were always loud in their taunts and insults of their discomfited partisans. A member of the defeated party, on a morning after the election, was sure to hear plenty of such remarks as : "the copperheads hang their heads this morning." This condition of feeling continued during the whole war, and had the mob in some cases been permitted to have taken their way, the houses of citizens who did not favor the war would have been burned over their heads. But there were always men of influence in the war party who prevented acts of this kind from being perpetrated.

They knew the obnoxious individuals, and felt convinced that their sentiments were as honest and equally patriotic as their own. They simply differed as to the manner of settling the national difficulties. At a time during the rebellion when a couple of regiments were encamped near Lancaster, loud threats were made against ex-President Buchanan, and had not a few leading citizens interposed, his residence might have fallen a victim to the rage of a heated soldiery, and himself subjected to such indignities as have disgraced the annals of history. This long period of war was sufficient to unfold to an observer almost a complete philosophy of democratic society. Before the breaking out of the war, Democratic leaders hastily penned resolves for conventions, denouncing all coercion of the Southern States. They stood upon the Kentucky and Virginia resolutions, and no coercion should be sanctioned. But no sooner was the call for soldiers issued, than these same leaders were mustering in

as his practiced eye viewed the country around him, that there, on the rocky hills, must be fought the great battle, which was to decide whether the honor of the Northern people should be preserved inviolate, or whether their cities, and country, and villages should be sacked and destroyed by the invading foe.

Arriving nearer the town, at eleven o'clock in the forenoon, he found General Buford's cavalry division already skirmishing with the Confederate troops, who appeared two miles to the westward. Reynolds, with his accustomed boldness to attack, did not hesitate as to his duty, or wait for instructions; he was an accomplished soldier, and knowing that it was Meade's determination to fight the enemy on the first advantageous ground in his front, immediately advanced to the support of Buford's cavalry, and engaged the enemy. The First corps pushed forward through the town to occupy a hill on the west side, near Pennsylvania college, where it encountered Heath's division of Hill's corps of Con-

men for the conquest of the South. Unfortunate is that country that can have no better class of leaders. Again the oaths went up, loud and long, upon the part of many of the mob, that they would not go to the war " to fight for negroes." The next news, however, that came was, that these same swaggering oathsmen were drilling and enlisted for the struggle. All this is simply evidence of the value of the asseverations of that class of people. Again, it was but a common occurrence to meet one high in standing and authority denouncing the abolition crusade to his friends, and the same day addressing a company of departing soldiers for the war, and urging upon them to press forward in the holy work in which they were engaged. Fame should, as it ever does, consign the names of all such, to the lowest depths of infamy, despite the miserable honor that they may conceive attaches to their palty posts or official positions. The stern vindicator of right implanted in the breasts of true humanity, measures out deserved honor, regardless of the mob's disapprobation or approval, and the tribute so awarded is genuine and enduring.

Time, however, moved onward, and the war closed. Instead of being of three years' duration, it lasted over four years. Entire alienation between individuals and friends continued up to that period and for some time afterwards. But owing to the pressing business of society (the war being no longer the engrossing subject of conversation,) the old remembrances gradually became effaced, old friendships were renewed, and the hatred that had been felt by one towards the other, vanished and passed away, it is hoped, forever. The war is now over for some years, and all the hatreds engendered in the commotions, are forgotten. May such a time never again overtake the American republic.

federate troops. The battle opened with artillery, in which the enemy at first had the advantage. Reynolds rode forward to change the position of the batteries; the rebel infantry immediately advanced, pushing forward a heavy skirmish line, and charged upon the guns, expecting to capture them. General Reynolds ordered up Wadsworth's division to resist the charge, and rode at the head of the column to direct and encourage the troops; but his gallantry made him a conspicuous mark for the deadly bullets of rebel skirmishers, and he was shot through the neck, and fell mortally wounded, dying before he could be removed from the field. The loss of their brave leader, personally the most popular officer of his rank in the army, might well have seriously affected the behavior of the men, but the spirit with which his presence had inspired them did not perish at his death; his corps, led by the senior officer, General Doubleday, repulsed the enemy in a gallant charge, while the fighting for a time became a hand-to-hand struggle, during which the rebel General Archer and his whole brigade were captured and sent to the rear.

General Reynolds was charged by some military critics with rashness in prematurely bringing on the battle of Gettysburg; but it would, perhaps, be more just to say, that he had but little direct agency in bringing it on; that it was unavoidable; that it was forced upon us by the rebels; that if they had not been held in check that day, they would have pressed on and obtained the impregnable position which our troops were enabled to hold; and that, most of all, the hand of Providence, who gave us at last a signal victory, guided the arrangements of that memorable day.

General Reynolds was one of America's greatest soldiers; the men he commanded loved him dearly; he shared with them the hardships, toil, and danger of the camp, the march, and the field; devoted to his profession, he was guided by those great principles which alone can prepare a soldier to become the defender of the liberties of a free people. He nobly laid down his life a sacrifice on his country's altar, at the head of his brave corps, that victory might crown the efforts of those who followed him to fight the great battle of the Nation. He fell, valiantly fighting for his country. Still more, he died in the defence of the homes of his neighbors and kinsmen. No treason-bleeding soil drank his blood, but all of him that was mortal is buried in the bosom of his own native State. His body was carried to Lancaster and buried in the family enclosure in the Lancaster cemetery, on the 4th of July, 1863.

Over his remains the family have erected a handsome and substantial marble monument, commemorative of the patriotic services of the deceased. On the south side, surmounted by the military emblem of the sword and belt, is the inscription—" John Fulton Reynolds, Colonel of the Fifth Infantry United States Army, and Major General of Volunteers. Born September 21st, 1820. Killed at the Battle of Gettysburg, while commanding the Left Wing of the Army of the Potomac, July 1st, 1863." On raised panels immediately below, are the words " Chancellorsville," " Gettysburg." On the north, under the national coat-of-arms, are the words " Rogue River" and " Mechanicsville." On the west, the American flags, crossed over " Gaines' Mills," "Second Bull Run" and " Fredericksburg." And on the east, the military emblem of the cannon, with the Mexican battle-fields on which the deceased won promotion, " Fort Brown," Monterey," and " Buena Vista."

REYNOLDS, SAMUEL H., was born at Brier creek, in Columbia county, Pa., November 20th, 1831. In the spring of 1832 his father, Thos. Reynolds, left his farm and removed to Danville, to engage in the mercantile business with his older sons. The subject of our notice being too young to enter the store, was sent to school, and soon afterwards admitted to the Danville academy. At the age of fourteen he entered the Freshman class at Dickinson college, Carlisle, Pa., where he graduated in 1850 with honor. In the fall of 1850 he went to Bellefonte, and took up his residence with his brother, W. F. Reynolds, a wealthy bachelor, to whose generosity and wise counsel he owes much of his success in life. Here he began the study of law under the instruction of Hon. James T. Hale, and was admitted to the bar in 1853. In 1854 he made a tour of inspection through the West, in order to look out a suitable location for the practice of his profession. A short residence in St. Louis convinced him that his native State afforded as fair an opportunity for a lawyer as the far-famed El Dorado of the West, and he returned to Bellefonte to decide upon some new departure. A friend suggested to him that Lancaster city, although crowded with legal ability, was a place where he might succeed. Accordingly, he prepared himself with letters of introduction to leading men, and set out for his new home. He reached Lancaster an entire stranger, (he knew no one in the city or county,) and reconnoitered the situation, and but for the friendly advice and sincere words of encouragement which he received from the late Hon. Thaddeus Stevens and Col. Reah Frazer, it is doubtful if he would have remained. His choice, however, was fixed; and accordingly, on the first of September, 1855, on motion of Reah Frazer, he was admitted to the bar at Lancaster, and at once commenced the practice. During the winter of 1855–56 he lost no time in making acquaintances in the city and county. His sparkling oratorical powers, together with his amiable manners, shrewd sagacity and business tact, soon attracted clients around him, the numbers of which have, year by year, rolled in upon him in an augmenting column.

In 1856 the great political battle between Buchanan and Fremont was fought. Mr. Reynolds being an enthusiastic Democrat, rallied to his party standard, and being an eloquent speaker, was called upon to address meetings all over Lancaster county, and also in other sections of the State. The acquaintance thus made, and the brilliancy exhibited by him in the campaign, proved of immense value to him in his subsequent career. Although his party in the county was in a vast minority, its members became strongly interested in his success, and ever afterwards remained ardently attached to him. In 1857 he was elected city solicitor, a position he held with credit to himself for several years. In 1858 he married a daughter of Wm. B. Fordney, esq., one of the leading lawyers of Lancaster. In 1866 he was the Democratic nominee for Congress from the Lancaster district.

In May, 1872, he was nominated at Reading by the Democratic State Convention as a delegate at large to the Constitutional Convention. He has served some nine years as a member of the Lancaster school board.

So admirably has he succeeded in his professional career, that he now ranks amongst those who transact the largest and heaviest legal business before the Lancaster bar, if, indeed, he be not the present crowning summit of success. There are but few instances of such a rapid rise in the profession as is exhibited in his career. As a lawyer engaged in a trial, Mr. Reynolds is quick, ready and strategical, and brings a dexterity to bear upon the management of his cases that often baffles his legal adversary. He has already grappled with the ablest attornies of Pennsylvania. But it is in his efforts before the jury where his abilities shine most conspicuous. Here, it is useless to prevaricate, he caps the climax. In his speeches he has command of language elegant and ornate, his unstudied sentences often presenting the roundness and beauty of the most finished composition. As a political speaker, he towers high above any other man in Lancaster county, and but few surpass him elsewhere. With the people he is remarkably popular, and but for his politics, his voice would be heard upon the floor of the national Congress.

RICHARDS, LUTHER, was born December 17th, 1809, in the borough of York, Pennsylvania. He removed, when a young man, to Lancaster, learned the printing business, and in 1834, in partnership with Geo. W. Hamersly, began the publication of the *Examiner and Herald*. This they published up till 1839, when they sold the same to R. W. Middleton. In 1851 he was elected register of wills of Lancaster county. Much of his time since he has been deputy register, which position he now fills.

RIGHTER, WASHINGTON, of Columbia, was born in West Chester, December 9th, 1799. He was for about three years a student of the West Chester Academy, the first institution of the kind ever started in that borough. He removed to Lancaster county in 1830. He had learned the tanning business in West Chester, and afterwards entered into partnership with his master for about four years. After coming to Columbia, he first started a currying shop, and afterwards, in 1834, engaged in the lumber business, which he has steadily pursued up to this time. He was elected clerk of the arphans' court of Lancaster county in the fall of 1842, and held the same for three years. He was never an aspiring politician, and the office he obtained was tendered him without solicitation. In business, Mr. Righter has been quite successful.

RINGWALD FAMILY. Jacob Ringwald, the founder of the family of this name in Pennsylvania, emigrated from Wirtemberg, where the family is still numerous, shortly before the year 1750. In an old family record, the origin of the name is ascribed to the incident of a remote ancestor being lost in a forest, from which he was rescued by persons attracted by his stentorian shouts. He made the "woods ring," and Ring-wald was applied to him as a cognomen. Jacob Ringwald, soon after his arrival in this country, was apprenticed to a blacksmith, at or near the present site of Bareville, Lancaster county, about four miles west of the town of New Holland, and in the immediate vicinity of the first settlement made in Earl township, by Hans Graff. At this period the district was already peopled by Mentzers, Kinzers, Rolands, Dillers, Seegers, Luthers, Sprechers, Weidlers and Bitzers families, which have since become numerous.

After the completion of his apprenticeship, Jacob Ringwald established himself as a blacksmith, in the same vicinity, and married Barbara Wagner, who, in the homely and industrious fashion of the time, assisted her husband in laying the foundation of his future fortune, by working the bellows while he fashioned the iron on the anvil. The sturdy blacksmith soon became well known in the community, receiving due honor for the zealous industry and piety with which he practiced to the very letter, the maxim often on his lips, the same couplet being a favorite saying among the Italians,

> Work as if you would live forever.
> Pray as if you would die to-morrow.

By perseverance and prudence, Jacob Ringwald steadily increased in wealth, and in a few years surpassed his neighbors, by becoming the purchaser of a farm near the eastern end of New Holland, which is well known for its fertility, and for a remarkably large and fine spring of water. He subsequently purchased another near Churchtown, both properties being selected with the wisdom of an accomplished judge of land, and with especial reference to their well-watered meadows—this being a point of great importance in the last century. Once during the Revolutionary war, a party of Virginia troops were encamped upon the New Holland farm, where Jacob Ringwald continued -to reside, and it is remembered, as an evidence of their imperfect equipment, that they were armed chiefly with spontoons, a home-made weapon resembling the Scottish halberd.

Of three children born unto Jacob Ringwald and his wife Barbara, the eldest, George, died in infancy; the second, Martin, born in 1763, lived to be the parent of eleven children; while the third, Jacob, born in 1765, was the father of fourteen sons and four daughters, these two brothers being the ancestors of the entire Ringwald family of Lancaster county. · Jacob Ringwald, the elder, the founder of the family, died about the close of the last century, his wife surviving him until the year 1805.

His eldest and surviving son, Martin, inherited and resided upon the ·Churchtown farm, near Churchtown; and the youngest, Jacob, inherited the property at New Holland, upon which he lived until 1825. At an early age he married Catharine Diller, a member of the numerous family of that name in Earl township. Living in an exclusively German neighborhood, and connected closely with them by bonds of blood and custom, Jacob Ringwald became imbued with the American spirit of progress. He battled strongly with the conservatism of his neighbors, and vigorously combated the popular disposition to perpetuate the exclusive use of the German language. A Lutheran church had been erected in New Holland, at least as early as the year 1748. As was general with this denomination, a parish school was attached, which was substantially free; for while all parents who were able to do so, paid for the tuition of their children, all were entitled to entrance, and the deficiency in funds was supplied by the congregation. For a long period the German language was exclusively used in this school, but Jacob Ringwald was an active advocate of the introduction of the English tongue, which innovation was accomplished in 1807. Under the impulse of the same feeling which prompted him to this action, he anglicized the family name to Ringwalt. Conscious of the defects in his own early education, Jacob Ringwalt turned his attention most intelligently and indefatigably to supplying such deficiencies, and his children still remember the habit of rising at a very early hour to secure leisure and quiet for reading and study before commencing the laborious avocations of the day. The Edinburg Encyclopedia, whose ponderous volumes were the grand storehouse of the learning of that time, was one of his favorite books, and in the scarcity of literature, was a complete library in itself. Many members of the Lutheran church at this period, were bitterly opposed to the threatened intrusion of the English tongue into the regular church services, and Jacob Ringwalt's earnest efforts to secure the advantage of English preaching once a month, excited such antagonism, that he finally and in consequence relinquished his membership in the Lutheran church and joined the Episcopalians. The Rev. Joseph Clarkson, as minister of the Episcopalian church, became a favorite friend and frequent guest at his house, and after him Jacob Ringwalt named his eighth son, Joseph Clarkson Ringwalt, who has been for many years a resident of Cincinnati, Ohio; a successful merchant and an exemplary citizen. Interested in all public movements, Jacob Ringwalt held the position of colonel of a regiment of militia, this form of military training being formerly very popular in Lancaster county. In 1811 he was elected to the State legislature, but this public service was not congenial to his tastes, and after serving one term he again devoted close attention to the varied avocations of agriculture for which he had a strong inclination, and in which his energy and intelligence won remarkable success. Notwithstanding the burden of a family, eighteen of his children reaching maturity, he rapidly acquired wealth. His children were sent to schools at Harrisburg and elsewhere, to acquire a more general education than was possible at home, while their father vigorously prosecuted an extensive business. His well-tilled lands and handsome buildings grew into such value, that he was offered for them what was considered a very large sum in those days ; but shortly after, he became one of the sufferers in the disastrous monetary revulsion of 1817, and his property was sold under most unfavorable circumstances. He then rented a portion of the former estate and continued to reside upon it for several years. Jacob Ringwalt subsequently abandoned this farm in Lancaster county, (which was then rented for a short time by his son Samuel), and removed into Cumberland county. In this new home, when about sixty years of age, he assumed the management of the immense estate of Judge Duncan, comprising sixteen farms of several hundred acres each he himself residing upon and reserving the product of the splendid property known as the "Judge Watts farm," long famous for having the largest barn in the United States. Jacob Ringwalt continued in these successful agricultural employments until he was accidentally injured in the prosecution of his labors; his health subsequently failed, and he died December 24th, 1828, in the sixty-third year of his age.

Catharine Diller, his wife, survived him, dying in 1858, and being the mother, grandmother and great-grandmother of one hundred and two descendants. His second, son Samuel, already mentioned, was at one time deputy sheriff and brigade inspector of Lancaster county, whence he removed to Downingtown, Chester county, where he still resides, devoting his great energy to agriculture, which is, in that district, in a very advanced condition.

The eldest surviving and youngest sons of Jacob Ringwalt, viz: Samuel and Lewis Ringwalt, were both actively engaged in the war of the rebellion, the former having served as Gen. George G. Meade's brigade quartermaster, and received the highest encomiums from the hero of Gettysburg for his gallantry and efficiency. Lewis Ringwalt being a member of Sheridan's celebrated cavalry, having been in forty-two skirmishes and engagements, was killed near Winchester, consistently ending a brilliant and courageous career in bravely defending an ambulance of wounded men.

ROATH, EML. DYER, was born October 4th, 1820, in the city of Lancaster. His father was a mechanic; ("his great-grandfather, Philip Brenner, was from Baden, and an early settler along Chicques creek, now in East Donegal township, and owned a large tract of land.") At the age of four years his father died; his mother, after the death of his father, moved with her family of four sons to the village of May-town, East Donegal township. After having somewhat qualified himself, he taught school from 1846 to 1854, was a member of the first teachers' institute held in Lancaster, January, 1853, and having settled in Marietta borough in 1857, he was nominated and elected a member of the Legislature. In 1861, when the tocsin of war sounded throughout the land, his military ardor rose, and applying to Governor Curtin, he received orders to raise a company for service; succeeding in this, he named his company "Union Fencibles," being composed of men from different counties, joined the 107th regiment of Pennsylvania volunteers, Col. Zeigler; he marched to the front with 98 men, always engaged in active service with his regiment, and participated in the following battles, viz: Cedar Mountain, Rappahannock Station, Thoroughfare Gap, second Bull Run, Chantilly, (took command of regiment;) South Mountain,[1] (second in command;) Antietam, (second in command,) slightly wounded; Fredericksburg, (brigade charged rebels out of their works;) below Fredericksburg, two days under fire; Chancellorsville, May 3d and 4th, 1863, (left in Wilderness on skirmish line, with five companies surrounded with rebels,

[1] While scaling the mountain, General Duryea rode up and remarked, "Captain Roath, will you let those vagabonds enter your State, desecrate your firesides, and enslave you?" The reply was, "No, never; we would rather die freemen; three cheers for Pennsylvania," which was given with a will. The General then asked: "Will the colors of the Keystone go to the top?" Being answered in the affirmative, he proposed three cheers for the same, which made the mountain echo amidst the discharge of musketry; the Fifth Reserves, Col. Fisher, and others, took up the cheering. The day ended with a glorious victory, and a happy meeting on the mountain top.

but eluded their grasp;) Gettysburg, July 1st, 2d and 3d, took part in first day's fight under the lamented Reynolds; and in the famous charges on the left, second day (took command,) and third day, in centre; Cemetery Hill, detailed to support battery, (wounded first day;) the crossing at Rappahannock, August 1st, 1863, commanded right wing; Mine Run, commanded advance guard, &c., three days; Spottsylvania Court House, North Anna, Bethsaida, "reinforced skirmish line on Richmond road, and took command, charged and retook a strong position of the enemy, and compelled them to withdraw the battery that made such terrible havoc by enfilading our lines;" Tolopatomy, Shady Grove Church, White Oak Swamp, had charge of the skirmish line, nine companies, repulsed the enemy on their advance without support, complimented from commanding General; Norfolk and Petersburg Railroad, June 17 and 18, 1864, took railroad and drove enemy into fort, afterwards blown up; Weldon Road, August 18 and 19, 1864, on the the 19th, after having sharp fighting on the advance, was taken prisoner, and after remaining in the prison pens of Richmond, Salisbury and Danville, over six months, was exchanged and sent to Annapolis; honorably discharged by the War Department, March 5, 1865; after expiration of service, was breveted Major, Lieutenant-colonel and Colonel, for meritorious service. Returning to his home in Marietta borough, he was again elected a justice of the peace; in 1866, was again nominated and elected a member of the Legislature.

ROBERTS, ANTHONY E., was born in Chester county, Pa., October 29th, 1803. On his father's side he is of Welsh descent, and on that of his mother, German. His early opportunities for the acquisition of learning being limited, his attainments in this particular were confined to the common branches of an education, but such as he was enabled to possess himself of, he has known admirably how to apply to practical life. He began his career in life by becoming a clerk in a store in New Holland, which position he filled for several years. In this situation he may be said to have laid the foundation of his success, as therein he made the favorable acquaintance of a large number of the people of the county of Lancaster, and his pleasant and engaging manners made him hosts of friends of both parties. While serving as clerk, he was frequently the representative of his party in the county conventions, and thus he came to form the acquaintance of the leading men of his party, and, indeed, of the whole county.

In 1839 he was nominated and elected high sheriff of Lancaster county, it being his first effort for the position. He discharged the duties of the office with success, and by his amiable manners still continued to add recruits to his hosts of friends all over Lancaster county. He early became one of the active Anti-Masons of the county; and even when the party was on the wane, his standing with its staunch leaders was always excellent, as he was believed ever to have been true to the principles of the organization. In 1843 he was, therefore, nominated by the Anti-Masons as their candidate for Congress in opposition to Jeremiah Brown, but his party being on the decline, he suffered a defeat. He had entered into the mercantile business in New Holland, in partnership with Elijah McLenegan, and this business he still prosecuted by his subordinates when official business required him to dwell in Lancaster. In 1849 he was appointed by General Taylor marshal of the eastern district of Pennsylvania, which office he filled up to the coming in of the Pierce administration in 1853. It was during the time that Mr. Roberts was marshal, that the exciting trials occasioned by the Christiana riot came off in Philadelphia, and upon these occasions he showed himself an efficient officer in the discharge of his duties. In 1854 Mr. Roberts was nominated by the American party as a candidate for Congress, and was elected; and after serving two years was again elected for a second term. During his first congressional term, he served as a member of the building committee. Mr. Roberts has been a member of the Lancaster school board, and has filled many other honorable positions in the gift of the people.

The success of Mr. Roberts in life, may be attributed to his remarkably genial and friendly disposition, as few surpass him in this particular. He is, besides, one of the most industrious, diligent, and energetic workers in any enterprise in which he may engage, that is to be found, perhaps, in Pennsylvania. His handsome improvements in Prince street, near his residence, amongst which "Roberts' Hall" may be mentioned, will long perpetuate his name in Lancaster city and county, and his public as well as private record will, for years to come, be evidence of the manner in which politeness with industry can, in free America, rear one from indigence and obscurity, rank him amongst the fortunate as regards possession, and enrol his name high upon the temple of fame.

ROBERTS, JOHN, a member of the Legislature in the years 1801, 1802, 1803, 1804 and 1805.

ROBINSON, JOHN, elected State Senator in 1831.

ROGERS, MOLTON C., for many years a prominent member of the Lancaster bar. He was a native of Delaware, and son of Gov. Daniel Rogers, of the same State. He graduated at Princeton College, New Jersey, and afterwards studied law at Litchfield, Connecticut. He removed to Lancaster, and was admitted to the bar in the year 1811. He soon took rank amongst the leading members of the profession, and that at a time when the bar was distinguished by men of first class ability. He was married to a daughter of Cyrus Jacobs, an iron-master of Lancaster county. In 1819 he was elected State Senator over Emanuel Reigart, receiving 2094 votes to 2088 for his competitor. Upon the election of J. Andrew Shultz, as Governor of Pennsylvania, Mr. Rogers was selected as Secretary of the Commonwealth, and on the 15th of April, 1826, he was commissioned by the Governor one of the Judges of the Supreme Court of Pennsylvania, a position he held up to 1851. Judge Rogers possessed intellectual powers of a high order, and therewith united great personal amiability as also general scientific and literary culture. As a jurist he was fearless and incorruptible, dignified in his demeanor, and his sense of right was acute in the highest degree. He was ardently devoted to the great principles of the Democratic party; but, upon the breaking out of the rebellion, he lent the weight of his influence in favor of the war for the restoration of the

Union. He died in Philadelphia, September 27, 1863, in the 78th year of his age.

ROHRER (JOHN'S) FAMILY. John Rohrer was born in Alsace, Germany, (lately a part of France), in the year 1696. When about the age of fourteen, the scourge of religious persecution drove his father and his family from his native land; and John being sent back to obtain and bring the family goods, was captured and lost sight of his parents entirely. He found his way to England, where he studied veterinary surgery, and afterwards sailed for America and settled in Lancaster county. After some years residence in his new home, and having acquired some real estate, he in 1732 married Maria Souder. All this time he had lost sight of his parents. Being in Philadelphia, and hearing of the landing of a vessel he started for the landing, and one of the first of the passengers whom he met, turned out to be his father. John immediately recognized his parent, but the latter did not know his son. His mother had died and his father was married again, and had two or three sons by his second wife. They were destitute of means and expected to be sold for their passage money. He paid the demands, brought his father and his family with him, and aided his half brothers to property near Hagerstown, Maryland. John Rohrer had four sons, viz: Martin, Daniel, John, and Christian; and four daughters, viz: one married to a Houser, one to a Smith, one to a Bachman, and another to Peter Miller. His third son, John, was a member of the Legislature in the years 1818, 1819–20.

ROHRER, JACOB, elected County Commissioner in 1815.

ROHRER, JOHN, elected Clerk of the Orphans' Court in 1839.

ROLAND, HENRY, elected County Commissioner in 1821.

ROLAND, JOHN H., elected a member of the Legislature in 1856.

ROSS, GEO., JR., son of George Ross, sr., was a staunch patriot in the Revolution, and for sometime Vice President of the Supreme Executive Council. In 1791 he was commissioned by the Governor, register of wills and recorder of deeds, which offices he held for eighteen years. He was known amongst the citizens as "*der Waisenvater*."

*ROSS, GEORGE, was born in New Castle, Delaware, in the year 1830. His father, the Rev. George Ross, of the Episcopal church, was a man of considerable ability and of rare classical attainments, and early perceiving that his son gave evidence of aptitude for study, he determined upon furnishing him an education that would fit him for any position in society. He was accordingly placed under instructors, and was not long in laying the foundation of a fine education, especially in his acquisition of the languages, in which he particularly excelled. By the age of eighteen he had made such advance in learning, that he was deemed amply qualified to enter upon the study of law, and he prosecuted it under the intructions of his elder brother, John, a lawyer of good standing in the city of Philadelphia; and as soon as he had finished the regular course of reading then prescribed for students, he was admitted to the bar. Finding that the ranks of the profession were at that time filled in the city of Philadelphia, he determined to try his fortune in some interior portion of the country, and for that purpose chose Lancaster, at that time near the limits of civilization. He settled in Lancaster about the year 1751. It was not long after his becoming a citizen of this latter place, that he married Miss Ann Lawlor, a lady of a most respectable family; and devoting himself zealously to the pursuits of his profession, he soon obtained a lucrative and increasing practice. Not long after this settlement at Lancaster, he was made prosecutor for the King, and discharged the duties of this office with eminent success.

Actively engaged in the pursuits of his profession, he does not seem for some time to have taken much part in political affairs, and the first notice we find of him in this connection, is his election as a representative to the assembly of Pennsylvania, in which he took his seat in the year 1768. Of this body he continued to be reëlected a member until the year 1774. During all the time he remained a member of

*Sanderson's Biography of the Signers of the Declaration of Independence, pp. 523 and 528.

the assembly, he merited and obtained the utmost confidence both of his colleagues and of his constituents. Whilst a member of the assembly, Mr. Ross seems to have given particular attention to the condition of our intercourse with the various Indian tribes settled within the State, or wandering near its borders. But it was not long till Mr. Ross was destined to act as the organ of the assembly in more important affairs than in quarrels about the maintenance of a petty garrison, or the aggression of a few hostile Indians. He had for a long time seen with that deep indignation that arises in the breast of a freeman, the arbitrary proceedings of the British government, and felt convinced that a general coöperation among the several provinces was necessary to secure their liberty. The resolutions of Virginia and of the other States, proposing the convention of a general congress of all the American colonies, was music to his ears. They were not, however, received in the assembly of Pennsylvania until it was on the eve of dissolution, as it was the opinion of the majority that whatever measures might be adopted, should proceed from a future assembly who would meet fresh from their constituents and representing their sentiments. Mr. Ross, nevertheless, was appointed on a committee to draft a reply to the speaker of the house of delegates of Virginia, and in so doing took occasion to express the cordial feelings he entertained. " The assembly of Pennsylvania," he says, " assure your honorable House that they esteem it a matter of the greatest importance to coöperate with the representatives of the other colonies in every wise and prudent measure which may be proposed for the preservation and security of their general rights and liberties; and it is highly expedient and necessary that a correspondence should be maintained between the assemblies of the several colonies. But as the present assembly must in a few days be dissolved by virtue of the charter of the province, and any measures they might adopt at this time rendered by the dissolution ineffectual, they have earnestly recommended the subject matter of the letter and resolves of the House of Burgesses of Virginia, to the consideration of the succeeding assembly."

In the month of July following, it was unanimously resolved to appoint a committee of seven members, on the part of the province, to meet the delegates of the other colonies at such time and place as might be generally agreed upon; and Mr. Ross was elected one of the members of this committee. He was also, by a singular coincidence, at the same time appointed to draw up the instructions under which they and himself, as one of them, were to act; these, however, are very properly simple and general in their terms, leaving them in a very great degree to be adopted, such as future circumstances might require. Under these instructions Mr. Ross took his seat in Congress on the 5th of September, 1774, and remained a member of that body until January, 1777, when he obtained leave of absence on account of indisposition and retired. His conduct met with the warm thanks and approbation of his constituents, and of this honorable evidence has been preserved in a resolution passed by a public meeting, held in the borough of Lancaster, which is as follows:

Resolved, That the sum of one hundred and fifty pounds, out of the county stock, be forthwith transmitted to George Ross, one of the members of assembly for this county, and one of the delegates for this colony in the Continental Congress, and that he be requested to accept the same as a testimony from this county of their sense of his attendance on the public business, to his great private loss and of their approbation of his conduct.

Resolved, If it be more agreeable, Mr. Ross purchase with part of the said money, a genteel piece of plate, ornamented as he thinks proper, to remain with him as a testimony of the esteem this county has for him, by reason of his patriotic conduct in the great struggle for American liberty.

Mr. Ross, however, declined accepting this liberal and honorable present, stating to the committee in so doing that his services were overrated by his fellow-citizens; that in bestowing them he had been impelled solely by his sense of duty, and that every man should contribute all his energy to promote at such a period the public welfare without expecting pecuniary reward. The occupations of Congress did not, however, prevent Mr. Ross from continuing his duties as a member of the Provincial Legislature, where we find his name recorded among the zealous political leaders of the time. Early in the year 1775 Mr. Penn, the governor and proprietary of the province, sent a message to the assembly, referring to the peculiar situation of the colony, and though couched in mild and conciliatory language, evidently meant to repress, if possible, the mode of proceeding which had been pursued by the union and coöperation of all the colonies. It was the universal custom at this period, for the assembly to reply at once to the messages of the governor, and on the present occasion it, of course, obliged the members of the House to express their opinions, and to decide at once whether the plan hitherto pursued should be retracted, or whether they should firmly stand by Congress and support its measures. The talents of the political leaders of the day were called out, and they exerted themselves in several long debates in favor of their several opinions. Mr. Ross was an able speaker, and he urged the continuance of decisive measures, with all the weight of his talents, character and influence; and he and his friends so far succeeded as to obtain the appointment of a committee coinciding in their views, and of which he was a member. This committee presented as their report an answer to the governor's address, in the following terms : " We are sincerely obliged to your honor for your attention to the true interests of the people over whom you preside, at a time when the disputes between Great Britain and the American colonies are drawing towards an alarming crisis ; and we agree with you that in all cases wisdom dictates the use of such means as are most likely to obtain the end proposed. We have with deep concern beheld the system of colony administration, pursued since the year 1763, destructive to the rights and liberties of his Majesty's most faithful subjects in America, and have heretofore adopted such measures as we thought were most likely to restore the affection and harmony between the parent State and the colonies, which it is the true interest of both countries to cultivate and maintain, and which we most sincerely wish to see restored. We must inform your honor, that a most humble, dutiful and affectionate petition from the delegates of all the colonies, from Nova Scotia to Georgia, is now at the foot of the

35

throne, and we trust in the paternal affection and justice of our most gracious sovereign, that he will interpose for the relief of his greatly distressed and ever faithful subjects in America. We assure your honor, that the House will always pursue such measures as shall appear to them necessary for securing the liberties of America, and establishing peace, confidence and harmony between Great Britain and her colonies." On the presentation of the report another violent debate arose, which lasted for ten days, when it was carried by a majority of twenty-two to fifteen voices.

In the summer of 1775 the Legislature found that measures more vigorous than resolutions were necessary, and they determined at any rate to make preparation to meet the consequences of their previous measures, whatever they might be. To this end they appointed Mr. Ross and several of the leading members of the Assembly, a committee to consider of and report such measures as might be expedient to put the city and province in a state of defense. This committee after deliberating a few days, brought in a series of resolutions approving of the association of the people for the defense of their lives, liberty and property, providing for the pay of such of them as should be engaged in repelling any hostile invasion of the British troops, and recommending the several counties of the province to collect stores of ammunition and arms. To carry their plans better into effect, they appointed a general committee of public safety for calling forth such of the associators into actual service when necessity requires, as the said committee shall judge proper for paying and supplying them with necessaries while in actual service, for providing for the defense of the province against invasion and insurrection, and for encouraging and promoting the manufacture of saltpetre, which said committee were authorized and empowered to draw orders on the treasurer thereinafter appointed for the several purposes above-mentioned. Of this committee, which became for some time, as it were, the executive organ of the government, Mr. Ross was a leading member, as he was also of another important committee, that of grievances. Besides these duties relative to the war, he was appointed with two other gentlemen, to prepare rules and regulations for the government of the forces of the province which might be raised.

When the proprietary government was dissolved and the general convention substituted for the previous Legislature, Mr. Ross took his seat in it also as a representative for Lancaster county. He was, within a few days after its organization, appointed on a committee to prepare a declaration of rights on behalf of the State, and chairman of two others of much importance—that of forming regulations for the government of the convention, and that for preparing an ordinance declaratory of what should be high treason and misprision of treason against the State, and what punishment should be inflicted for these offences. Indeed, in all legal matters, Mr. Ross at this period stood deservedly high. Before the Revolution he was among the first of his profession; and in the change which that event had produced in its component parties, as well as its forensic character, he still maintained the same rank. These changes were, indeed, very considerable; subjects of higher importance than those which commonly fall to the lot of provincial judicatures were brought forward; motives sufficient to rouse all the latent energies of the mind were constantly presenting themselves. The bar was chiefly composed of gentlemen of aspiring minds and industrious habits; and Mr. Ross found himself engaged among men with whom it was honorable to contend and pleasant to associate. Mr. Wilson, who had practiced with great reputation at Carlisle; Mr. Biddle, from Reading; Governor Morris, occasionally and sometimes; Mr. Reed, till he was chosen a member of the Chief Executive Council; and Mr. Lewis, of Philadelphia, in conjunction with Mr. Ross, formed an assemblage of powerful and splendid talents which might have coped with an equal number of any forum in America. The whole faculties of this bar were soon put in requisition for the prosecutions which were commenced against some of those accused of being adherents of the British cause. The popular excitement against them was high, and their defence appeared to many a service of danger; but the intrepidity of the bar did not allow them to shrink from the conflict, and Mr. Ross, and Mr. Wilson, especially, embarked all their talents, zeal, and professional reputation in the cause of those who were thus accused.

The last public employment in which Mr. Ross was engaged, was that of a judge of the court of admiralty for the State of Pennsylvania, to which he was appointed on the 14th of April, 1779; and while on the bench he was esteemed a learned and impartial judge, displaying sound legal knowledge and abilities, and great promptness in his decisions. He did not, however, long occupy the station he was so well calculated to fill, as he died suddenly in the month of July following, from a violent attack of the gout. Of his character little remains to be said beyond what has been already detailed. In his domestic habits he was kind, generous, and much beloved; in his professional career, zealous and honorable; as a practitioner, always active and patriotic; and he seems to have earned the praise bestowed upon him by one who knew him, as "an honest man and upright judge."

ROSS, JAMES, son of George Ross, sr., raised in 1755 the first company in Lancaster, in Col. Thompson's regiment, of which he was made captain, and marched to Cambridge for the defence of the liberties of his country. He rose to the rank of lieutenant-colonel of the eighth Pennsylvania regiment, with which he fought in the memorable battle of the Brandywine. In the battles of Long Island, Trenton and Germantown, he bore a conspicuous part. He was appointed judge in the territory of Louisiana. He died August 24th, 1808, in the 55th year of his age.

ROSS, WILLIAM BIRD, was elected County Commissioner in the year 1817, and in 1821 was appointed Clerk of the Quarter Sessions.

ROWE, BENJAMIN F., was elected Sheriff of Lancaster county in the year 1857.

ROYER FAMILY. Sebastian Royer emigrated from the Palatinate to America about the year 1720, bringing with him four sons. Two of his sons being young men grown, decided to settle in Montgomery county, from whom the families of this name in Montgomery and Chester counties are descended. Sebastian Royer and his two younger sons settled in Elizabeth township, Lancaster county. He was a Lutheran by persuasion, and being a widower, married again. His wife was a member of the German Reformed church, and he donated a couple of tracts of ground, one for the erection of a German Reformed church and the other for a Lutheran church. The churches erected upon these tracts (the Brickerville churches), stand to this day. His son John inherited the old homestead property, sold it and crossed the Susquehanna river, where his descendants are numerous in Cumberland, Franklin, Huntingdon and adjoining counties, and also in the State of Maryland. Samuel Royer, a member of the reform convention in 1838, and John Royer, a member of the Legislature from Cambria and Somerset counties, in 1842, belonged to this family.

AMOS ROYER, the youngest son of Sebastian, settled in Ephrata township, and was the founder of the Royers of Lancaster and Lebanon counties. He had four sons, viz: Daniel, Philip, John, and Christopher. Daniel had four sons, viz: John, Jacob, Joseph and David. John and Jacob settled in Lebanon counties, and left sons; Joseph emigrated to the State of Ohio; David remained in Lancaster county on a part of the old homestead, still possessed by his only heir, Samuel, now an old man. John, son of Amos Royer, remained on part of the old home property (on which is built the Royer meeting-house), and left numerous descendants in the county. Christopher, his brother, settled in West Earl, on the farm of Christian Rupp, and leaves numerous descendants in Lebanon county and elsewhere. His brother, Philip, settled in Manheim township, and had five sons, viz: Joseph, Benjamin, Jonathan, Abraham and Philip. Joseph remained on the old homestead, and had three sons, viz: John, Joseph, and Daniel. John had five sons, viz: Jonas, Cyrus, Daniel, John and Henry. Jonas lives in Lebanon county; Cyrus, in Providence township; Daniel, near Napierville, Illinois; John, in West Earl; and Henry on the old home farm. Joseph, one of the three sons of Joseph, has three sons, viz: Israel, Tobias, Joseph R., and lives in Lancaster city. Daniel, his brother, has three sons, viz: Reuben, Martin, and Jonathan, in Warwick township. Benjamin, son of Philip, had two sons, viz: Daniel, and Benjamin.

Daniel had one son, Samuel, living in Ephrata township, and who has four sons, viz: Phares, Isaac, Abraham and Milton; and Benjamin has a son in Ephrata township. Jonathan, son of Philip, settled in Leacock township, near Intercourse, leaving a son, John, whose family survives him. Abraham, son of Philip, settled on Mill creek, and leaves descendants. Philip settled in Cocalico township, and left sons, whose descendants live near Reamstown. Isaac Royer, of Ephrata township, and his brother Reuben, are grandsons of John Royer, of Mill creek, Lebanon county.

RUTTER, NATHANIEL, a member of the Legislature in 1818 and 1819.

S.

SAMPLE, DR. NATHANIEL W., oldest son of the Rev. Nathaniel W. Sample, was born at Strasburg, Lancaster county, Pa. He was instructed by his father in the classics, as he for many years had been in the habit of instructing a few young gentlemen as students in his house. He studied medicine with Dr. Duffield, of Strasburg, and began the practice of the profession in his native town. After practicing the profession for a few years in Strasburg, he removed to Paradise, and bought the farm on which he lived for a long time. Here he lived and practiced his profession for many years. He held a high rank as a member of the Free Masonic fraternity. He died at Gordonville, aged 80 years.

SAMPLE, REV. NATHANIEL W., was a native of York county, Pa., and a graduate of Princeton college, New Jersey. He graduated during the Revolution, and studied theology at Princeton. He first located as a clergyman at Strasburg, and preached for the Presbyterian congregation of Strasburg, Leacock and Octoraro. He married a lady of Chester county, named Elizabeth Cowan. He was an excellent classical scholar. He left five sons and three daughters. He died at the advanced age of between 83 and 84 years, and lies buried at Leacock.

SANDERSON, GEORGE, is a native of Cumberland county, Pennsylvania. In 1836 he became editor and proprietor of the *American Volunteer*, the old Democratic organ published at Carlisle. He continued to publish the paper until 1845, when he relinquished it to take charge of the post-office in that borough, tendered to him by President Polk. In the meantime he held the office of prothonotary of Cumberland county for three years and nine months, from 1839 to 1842—first by appointment, under Governor Porter, and subsequently elected by the people. In 1849, upon relinquishing the post-office at Carlisle, he removed to Lancaster and became proprietor and editor of the *Lancaster Intelligencer*, the old Democratic organ of Lancaster county. He continued his connection with this paper until 1864, a period of fifteen years. In 1859 he was elected Mayor of the city of Lancaster, and continued to hold the office for ten years and nine months, having been elected for nine consecutive terms. In October, 1869, he retired to private life. Always devoted to the principles of the Democratic party, and adhering to its organization in prosperity and adversity, he nevertheless secured not only the confidence of his own political friends, but to a large extent the good will and respect of his political opponents.

SAUNDERS, ISAAC, was a member of the Legislature in the years 1757, 1758, 1759, 1760, 1763 and 1764.

SCHAEFFER, EMANUEL, was born February 27th, 1793. Having lost his father when young, his mother and her children became a part of the household of his maternal grandfather, John Miller, an eminent citizen of Lancaster, once high sheriff of the county, and also a member of the State Senate. At the age of fifteen the subject of this notice was apprenticed by his grandfather to learn the saddling and harness-making business. After the expiration of his apprenticeship, he worked at his trade in the capacity of a journeyman, and having saved from his earnings about one hundred dollars, he began business upon his own account in Lancaster. When about twenty-five years of age he married, and his wife dying seven years afterwards, he entered into marital relations the second time. In 1841 Mr. Schaeffer was appointed by Governor Porter one of the associate judges of the courts of Lancaster county, which office he held for five years, when he was reäppointed by Governor Shunk, and discharged his duties with great fidelity for four years more, making his aggregate term of service as associate judge, nine years. In 1841 he was elected president of the Lancaster Savings Institution, a position he held for some years. He served as president of city councils for thirteen years. Besides these positions, Mr. Schaeffer was frequently chosen to fill various offices of trust and responsibility, all of which he discharged in such a manner as to reflect much credit upon himself and render entire satisfaction to the public. Mr. Schaeffer was an active supporter of the temperance cause, and during the whole of his life adhered strictly to the principles of sobriety, honesty, and the proper observance of religious duties, which resulted in that success and prosperity which he enjoyed. From the organization of the Church of God, in the city of Lancaster, he was an elder and annually reëlected. He was the superintendent of the Sabbath school belonging to that church for many years, and also a delegate to the east Pennsylvania and general elderships for a number of years. He died November 13th, 1864, aged 71 years, 8 months, and 16 days.

SCHAUM, BENJAMIN, elected Commissioner of Lancaster county in 1808.

SCHWARTZ, CONRAD, elected County Commissioner in 1805.

SCOTT, ABRAHAM, a member of the Legislature in the years 1781, 1782 and 1783.

SCOTT, ALEXANDER, was a member of the Legislature in the years 1797, 1798, 1799 and 1800. He was also elected to the State Senate in 1792.

*SCOTT, MAJOR JOHN, son of Samuel Scott, was born at "Scott's Manor,"[1] in the year 1749–50. At the time of

---

[1] Scott's Manor was a name given to a large tract of land taken up and patented probably as early as 1740, by Samuel Scott, an original settler in Little Britain, and the father of John Scott. The mansion

* Contributed by Charles H. Stubbs, M. D.

the breaking out of the Revolutionary struggle with the mother country he was a young man, and it appears that he did not enter the service in the first years of the war. The contest for freedom becoming protracted, and for a time the final success of the Americans under Washington doubtful, John Scott, like many other patriots of that time, resolved to leave his rural pursuits and join the army. At the age of twenty-seven he recruited a company of militia, composed chiefly of his neighbors—the yeomen of Little Britain—and marched it to Lancaster. He was elected captain, and his company entered as part of the second battalion of Lancaster county militia, formed in the year 1777.

James Watson was elected Colonel of this battalion; James Porter, Lieutenant-colonel, and Dorrington Wilson, Major. It consisted of eight companies, numbering, rank and file eight hundred and five men. John Scott commanded the first company, and consequently acted as senior captain. This battalion was ordered to the front immediately after its formation, and took part in the principal battles fought in the Middle States. Captain Scott remained in the service during the war, was present and took part in the battles of Brandywine, Germantown, and several engagements near New York and on Long Island. For bravery he was promoted to the rank of Major. After the close of the war he was honorably discharged, and returned to the Manor, which he inherited upon the decease of his father. Here he spent the remaining years of his life in superintending and improving his estate. He died at an early age, on the 1st of February, 1796, in his 47th year. His remains were interred in the southeast corner of the graveyard attached to Little Britain Presbyterian church. Over the grave his son and daughter have erected a handsome marble obelisk, seven feet in height, resting on a broad, flat, limestone base. On the west side is the following epitaph: "Major John Scott, an officer under Washington during the Revolutionary war, who distinguished himself at the battles of Long Island,

house erected by him, stood near the site of the present residence of Samuel Scott, a great-grandson of the settler. The farms of N. Davis Scott, Samuel Scott, and several of the Wrights, of Little Britain, were originally parts of this manor.

White Plains, Brandywine, Germantown, &c. Died February 1, 1796, aged 47 years." On the east side: "Erected by William and Eleanor Graham Scott, October 17, 1845, in memory of their departed friends."

SELDOMRIDGE, JOHN, elected Prothonotary of Lancaster county in 1863.

*SEYBERT, REV. JOHN. In many respects the subject of this memoir was a very remarkable man. As regards firmness of will and rigid self-denial he probably stands unrivaled. Indefatigable activity, faithful, disinterested and self-sacrificing devotion for the dissemination of what he regarded as the truth, were peculiarly marked features of his character. Unlettered and untaught as regards the technical rules of science, his natural good sense and discriminating judgment supplied in his career the want of early advantages, and rendered him one of the ablest theologians of his time and country. His father was a native of Germany, and came to America during the Revolution, with the British army, then a youth of but fifteen years of age. At the close of the war he chose to remain in this country, and for this offence was imprisoned in Lancaster in default of one hundred dollars commutation money. A man by the name of Shaffner, commiserating the condition of young Seybert, paid for him the hundred dollars, on condition that he should serve three years in his employ as a tailor. After the termination of this period of service, he married a young woman named Susana Kreutzer, whose father when crossing the ocean to America, had found a watery grave amidst the deep waves of the Atlantic. By industry and economy Henry Seybert, the father of the subject of this sketch, acquired some property, and died in March, 1806, leaving a farm and some considerable amount of money.

John Seybert, the subject of our notice, was born near Manheim, Lancaster county, Pa., July 7th, 1791. He was the oldest of four children, all of whom were sons. When he was about thirteen years of age his parents became the subjects of religious conviction, and his mother being a woman of very tender sensibilities, was the first to yield to

*Contributed by John B. Good, esq.

her feelings, but it was not long till the father also followed, and from this time their house became the principal resort of the Ministers of the *Albright Society*, now more generally known as *Evangelical Methodists*. It was under the influences that thus surrounded him that young Seybert first felt the workings of God's spirit in his heart, but at this time, however, no permanent impression seems to have been made, for as he himself says: "His love of levity and vanity was still too strong." Indeed, at this time, it is said that his parents regarded him as the most perverse of all their children; his strong will and firm independence seeming in their eyes wickedness of the deepest dye. At the age of ten years he began going to school, and continued his attendance during the winter months of every year, until he acquired a fair knowledge of both English and German. His father also sent him to a Lutheran clergyman as a catechumen, with the design of having him confirmed as a member of that church. He says that at this time he and the other catechumens were very wicked sinners, who were guilty of all manner of sins and wickedness. For some reason or other he was never confirmed as a member of the Lutheran church. He may, perhaps, have regarded himself as too vile a sinner, for he believed that the bad company in the school and among the catechumens, made him still worse than he otherwise should have been. He was now thirteen years of age, and was passionately fond of the fascinations of sin, which he says he committed with the greatest zest.

At the age of fourteen, when his parents had already changed their religious views, he frequently felt the influence of the Spirit striving with him, but he always deferred his conversion, still thinking that there was yet plenty of time, and thus no permanent effects towards a regeneration were produced. During all this time good and evil seem to have waged a terrible conflict in his soul. When under religious influence he felt penitent, but evil with him still held the upper hand; and when amongst his youthful companions, he would, against better knowledge, commit sins for which conscience afterwards had to suffer many pangs of anguish and regret. His father having died in 1806, his mother became a follower of the celebrated George Rapp, left her children and lived in Rapp's colony, called "New Harmony," near Pittsburg, Pa., leaving her family to take care of themselves as best they could. His mother used every persuasion to induce her sons to follow her into her new relationship, but John, the oldest of them, manifested at this time, though but sixteen years of age, such independence of will as is rarely found to be possessed by one of his age. Though he never could be induced to follow her, but frequently visited her, and whilst she lived tendered her every mark of filial affection. In 1810, when he was nineteen years old, he was brought under conviction, through a sermon of Rev. Mr. Betz, and after a protracted struggle committed himself to God. He became a member of the Evangelical Association (German Methodists), in which he was soon selected as a class leader and public exhorter. One of his classes was in Manheim, and the other in Mount Joy, Lancaster county, Pa. In 1819 he entered the ministry as a local preacher, and the year following set out as an itinerant.

His literary and scientific attainments at this time were of the most limited character. He had little other attainment, save being able to read and write in the most plain and humble manner. But he was in possession of an indomitable will, and his untiring energy and never flagging industry, together with his clear thoughts and common sense, soon compensated for lack of education. He rapidly improved as a pulpit declaimer, and it was not long till friends and enemies became convinced that John Seybert was by no means a man of ordinary ability. He was, nevertheless, the subject of many privations, and of the most bitter persecution, and that on the part of those from whom better things should have been expected. To us it seems almost incredible that a man whose energies are enlisted in behalf of the welfare of his fellow-men, should meet with so much opposition, and often, indeed, with brutal treatment. Among his bitter persecutors were some who stood high in the church, but whose vile treatment of him were no doubt in a great measure influenced by envy at his rising reputation. John Seybert was always scrupulously plain and simple in his dress. He never wore boots, but always brogans. In his diary he mentions, that at one time he was traveling in a heavy continuous rain, which drenched him thoroughly ; his brogans were filled with water, and yet he adds, " such things did not discourage me." On account of the faithful discharge of his duties as a minister, his advancement in the church was rapid. In June, 1822, he was elected deacon, and in the same month, three years later, was made a presiding elder. He always kept a diary, in which he noted down a full synopsis of his labors as an itinerant preacher, as well as his experiences of inner life, his hopes and his fears, his joys and his sorrows. In the earlier years of his ministry he was much troubled as to his being *divinely* called to preach the Gospel of Christ. Whenever his brethren in the ministry conferred a new mark of confidence upon him, or promoted him to some new position in the church, he invariably in his diary expresses great distrust and diffidence ; but generally consoles himself with the reflection, that it was not his own, but the judgment of the brethren that prompted the step, and that consequently he was not personally responsible, as it was done without his request or solicitation.

There is in the earlier part of the minutes of his diary, a feature that forcibly strikes the attention of the reader. He hardly pays any attention to the political divisions of the country, such as townships or counties ; he simply mentions the name of the families whose hospitality he enjoyed, and little more than this is noted by him. The geographical localities he passes over in silence. He speaks of rivers, mountains, and valleys, as these were objects that plainly presented themselves to his vision ; but of the imaginary lines that divided townships and counties, he gives little or no mention. They, perhaps, did not occur to his mind. But this is not the only instance that this really great man appears simple as a child. All his energies were directed to one point, and that was the glory of his Divine Master ; all else was, in his opinion, folly and vanity, and hence worthy of but little attention.

He was elected bishop at the seventh session of the general conference of the Evangelical Association held at Millheim, in Centre county, Pennsylvania, commencing March 25th, 1839. There were at this time only eighty traveling preachers connected with the church, of whom thirty were present as delegates to the conference. His election to the bishoprick took place on the second day of the session, at about five o'clock in the evening, and he was the unanimous choice of all the clergymen in attendance at the conference. It is noteworthy the great simplicity that characterized the clergymen of that early day, and the economical habits that they practiced; and conspicuous amongst the early pioneers, Bishop Seybert deserves special mention. His habits were so simple, and his wants so few, that he required little else to supply his wants, save the merest necessities of life. As an example of his economical method of traveling, the following instance may suffice: He traveled from eastern Penn-sylvania into the interior of the State of New York, a dis-tance of three hundred miles, at an expense of $2.83½, board-ing and fare included. His path through life never was one strewed with flowers, but he had ever his own difficulties with which to contend. Amongst these the following may be cited as illustrative of the obstacles which he was required to encounter. On the 7th of August, 1840, he attended a camp-meeting on Turkey Hill, Lancaster county, and was considerably annoyed by the conduct of some ill-bred men who were in attendance. Of them he thus speaks: " These creatures did not behave themselves at all like human be-ings; they were, if human, some of the Turkey Hill brutish men, who either never had any sense at all, or left it at home with their oxen, horses, and sheep; for they walked about with heads devoid of all reason ; they jolted each other about, and made use of such vulgar and profane language that every decent person was ashamed of them."

During the first four years of his official term as bishop, there were three of his conferences—the East Pennsylvania, West Pennsylvania, and Ohio. At each of these he presided as bishop; beginning with the East Pennsylvania conference he reached that of West Pennsylvania in April, and the one held in Ohio in May. In 1844 the Illinois conference was organized, but by that time another bishop had been elected, who shared the labors of the office with him. The new bishop was Rev. Joseph Long, who was elected in 1844. The two bishops divided the work between them, Bishop Long presiding at the sessions of the Pennsylvania conference, and Bishop Seybert at those of Ohio and Illinois. While engaged in the incessant labors of his office he visited in August, 1845, the churches of his denomination in Upper Canada. Here the people were much surprised at his plain dress, his child-like simplicity of manners, and to hear the unadorned and unstudied style of his address. They expected to hear a bishop, most necessarily of great consequence as well as of exterior display, and whose preaching would far transcend the intelligence of plain people. But in this they were very agreeably disappointed, for in Bishop Seybert they found a faithful follower of his Divine Master, who endeavored to be the servant of all.

On account of the sickness of his co-adjutant, Bishop Long, in the spring of 1846, he was required to preside at the sessions of both the Pennsylvania conferences as well as those in the West. On the 4th of July of that year he happened to be in Mount Carmel, Illinois, and in his diary notes some reflections which he indulged in as regards the observance of the national holiday. He says that the children of this world early began the celebration of the day with drinking, dueling, profanity and wild cheering. He adds, however: "I also got on my feet, hurriedly visited nine families in the morning, then shaved myself, greased my shoes and put on clean clothes, and then traveled thirty miles that day." From the above extract it is perceived that he used grease for his shoes instead of boot-blacking, an article he seems never to have used, this being categoried by him in the list of luxuries.

One instance of the charitable feelings of Bishop Seybert is thus detailed: On a cold day in the winter of 1846, while traveling in Ohio, he met a constable who was hauling a weaver's loom on a sled. Having entered into conversation with the officer, he learned that he had levied on the loom for a debt of little over four dollars; that the owner of the loom was a poor weaver, who depended on his trade for the support of a numerous family. The bishop listened patiently to the end of the story, and then declared that this case was *too hard*, and asked the constable whether he would return the loom to its owner if he paid the debt and costs. "O, yes," said the officer in reply, "that is all I want." Upon which the bishop at once paid the money, and the constable returned the loom to the poor weaver, who was very much surprised as well as heartily thankful to this eccentric stranger for his act of kindness. The weaver afterwards became a member of the bishop's church, obtained the position of class-leader in the same, and afterwards the bishop and other clergymen frequently preached sermons at his house.

He attended the general conference of his church at New Berlin, in Union county, Pa., and on the 22d of October, 1847, was reëlected bishop, this making his third term in the episcopal office. During the year 1850 he refused to accept any salary at all, as he regarded it the year of jubilee of the Evangelical Association, it being the 50th year since the denomination was founded by Jacob Albright, in the county of Lancaster, Pa. It was his intention to accept nothing at all after this as a salary; but he was censured by others for this, as it was considered the setting of a bad precedent, and he therefore yielded so far as to accept the salary, but disposed of it at his discretion for benevolent purposes. About this time he changed his mode of traveling on horseback to a dearborn wagon. At all events, in the spring of 1850 he attempted to ford the Lycoming creek, above Williamsport, Pa., with a dearborn wagon, at a time when the stream was much swollen, and he narrowly escaped finding a watery grave. Henceforth he was much more cautious in venturing to cross a stream of water. In 1852, at the general conference held at Pittsburg, Pa., he was reëlected for the fourth time to the episcopal office. From May 1st to June 19th, 1853, he preached a series of sermons in the State of New York and Upper Canada. His appointments were all made in advance of his arrival for a thousand miles, and he punctually supplied all of them at the very times that had been specified. On September 24th, 1855, at the general conference, he was for the fifth time elected bishop, which occasioned still deeper feelings of humility to rise in his soul, and he again formed new resolutions to labor with industry and faithfulness in God's cause. On the 11th of September, 1856, he met with an accident at Lincoln, Stark county, Illinois. His horse ran off, upset his carriage, and threw him upon the ground with great violence, and from this fall he was very severely injured. He alludes in his diary to this accident in the following language: "There was great danger that my old and weary body, which was become frail and weak through preaching 10,000 sermons during the last thirty-five years, had entirely broken down; for I find that the hardships incident to the itinerant ministry have impaired my strength. The Lord has, however, helped me again in this misfortune. To Him be praise forever."

About this time Bishop Seybert presided in the West Pennsylvania conference, where he took occasion to speak very earnestly of the duties of traveling preachers, and with much warmth expressed his disapprobation of the conduct of those who had forsaken the itinerancy and settled down to enjoy an easy life. "As for me," he said, "it is my intention to die in the field; when I can no longer preach every day, then I will preach four times a week; if that won't go any more, I will preach twice a week; and if I cannot preach any more twice a week, I'll preach once; I will die on Zion's walls." In 1858 he wrote in his diary: "What a happy man I am in my 68th year; I am at present well almost every day, and in good spirits; my sense of hearing is very acute, and I frequently read without spectacles, and if necessary, would try to preach three times a day. Glory to God." On October 13, 1859, he was elected bishop for the sixth time. In politics Bishop Seybert was always a Democrat, yet towards the institution of slavery was exceedingly hostile. He ever felt disinclined to travel in territory where slavery was sanctioned by law. Whenever he returned from a slave State he thanked God for the deliverance from the accursed soil. He believed that the principles of the Democratic party were right, but that slavery did not belong to them; the evil one had sown these tares in the field of Democracy. On the 18th of December,

36

1860, he preached for the last time. His journal stops with the 28th of the same month. He stopped with a man named Isaac Parker, near Bellevue, Sandusky county, Ohio. Being asked concerning the cause of his weakness, he merely spoke of having a bad cold. He rested on a lounge, and occasionally read his favorite authors, viz: Hiller, A'Kempis and Tauler. He also regularly read his Bible lesson every day. About an hour before his death he related that he had a dream, and in his dream that he came to a place where there were many preachers who were all glad to see him, and he desired to greet all by shaking hands with them, but that the number was so great that he had not yet had time to do so before he awoke. An hour later no doubt his dream was realized, in meeting an innumerable company of the redeemed in heaven.

Bishop Seybert died January 4, 1861. When the near approaching symptoms of death made their appearance, Mr. Parker, at whose house he was lodging, went out to call some of the neighbors that they might be present when the spirit of the aged pilgrim would take its departure. His son remained alone with him in the room. The weary wayfarer sat upon his lounge, his hands folded like those of a child in prayer. All at once he broke the solemn silence by saying: "How terrible must death be to a wicked person." Then having paused for a few moments, he again remarked: "Death commences below," at the same time laying his hands lower down on his body, "and proceeds upwards, and when he comes to this place," placing his hand upon his heart, "then it is all over with us." Thus I also shall sometime fall asleep. Here his voice stopped; he sunk on the lounge, and while young Parker stood by his side, he gently fell asleep and his spirit took its flight to the mansions of the blessed.

SHAW, ANTHONY, who emigrated from Ireland and settled within the limits of the Friends' meeting, at Sadsbury, was a man of considerable ability, being well educated, and remarkable for his piety and his many virtues, and was a worthy and serviceable member of the denomination of Friends at the time that the Sadsbury monthly meeting was first established.   He was elected a member of the Legislature for the years 1740–41–42–43.   He was appointed a commissioner and justice of the peace for Lancaster county in the year 1738, and the ancient documents in Sadsbury and Salisbury attest his abilities as a writer, a scholar and an upright and conscientious man.

SHAEFFER, BARTRAM A., was born in Lancaster county in 1824, and at an early age removed to Ohio, where he received his education.   Having returned to Lancaster, he began the study of law in the office of George Ford, esq., and was admitted to the bar in the year 1847.   Interesting himself considerably in politics, he was soon honored with the confidence of his party, and was returned as a member of the Legislature in the year 1850, and also in 1851.   Acquitting himself with credit, he was elected to the State Senate in 1857.   He was also chosen attorney for the Pennsylvania railroad company, a position he held for several years.   Upon the organization of the militia in 1858, he was appointed major general of the division composed of the counties of Lancaster and Chester.   When the rebellion broke out, he immediately tendered his services, and was appointed as aid on the staff of General Keim, of Berks county.   He served in this capacity for six months, being with General Patterson's division in the Shenandoah valley. His health and eyesight failing, he was compelled to give up military service and return home.   He was for some time engaged with C. S. Kauffman, of Columbia, in the iron manufacture.   He died in 1864.

SHELLEY, ABRAHAM, was elected a member of the Legislature in the years 1846–47.

SHENCK, HENRY S., was elected Register of Wills in 1869.

SHENK, MICHAEL, a Commissioner of Lancaster county, elected by the Republicans in October, 1804.   He was a citizen of Conestoga township, and an active and useful citizen. He died October 18th, 1806.

SHENK, RUDOLPH W., was born in Conestoga township, Lancaster county, Pennsylvania, on the 4th of October, 1834. His parents were Christian Shenk, (now deceased) and Mary

Warfel Shenk, and his ancestors were among the earliest settlers of Lancaster county. He attended school at Litiz, under Prof. John Beck, from 1849 to 1851. In 1852 he entered the academy at Erie, Pa., and in 1854 entered Dartmouth College, where he graduated in 1858. He read law and was admitted to the bar in November, 1859. At the breaking out of the rebellion he enlisted in Co. F. (Lancaster Fencibles) Captain Emlen Franklin, first regiment Pennsylvania volunteers, and served until the expiration of their term of enlistment. In August 1862 he was appointed Major of the 135th regiment of Pennsylvania volunteers, and served with the same until it was mustered out of service at the expiration of its term of enlistment. He was appointed deputy marshal of the Ninth district, Pennsylvania, in June 1863, and was elected to the Legislature in the years 1864–65. He is engaged in the practice of his profession, and is a member of the firm of Bair & Shenk, bankers, of this city.

SHERER, JOSEPH, was a delegate from Lancaster county to the the convention which framed, in 1776, the first Constitution of Pennsylvania.

SHIPPEN, EDWARD, was one of the leading citizens of Lancaster borough for many years before and at the breaking out of the American revolution. He held most of the county offices, as prothonotary, register, recorder, &c., from the year 1753 up to the commencement of the revolution. He was one of the committee on correspondence appointed at a meeting held in Lancaster, June 15th, 1774, to correspond with the committee of Philadelphia, which had been constituted to obtain an interchange of sentiment among the people of Pennsylvania with reference to united action in opposition to British encroachment. At a meeting of this committee, consisting of Edward Shippen, Geo. Ross, Jasper Yeates, Matthias Slough, James Webb, William Atlee, William Henry, Ludwig Lauman, William Bausman and Charles Hall, held July 2d, 1776, Edward Shippen was chosen president of the committee. He had been chief burgess of the borough of Lancaster for some years, and was acting in that capacity in 1763, when the Conestoga Indians were massacred by the Paxton rangers. Edward Shippen, with other of the leading citizens, were attending church at the time the work of destruction was going on, and before they were able to reach the scene, the Paxton boys[1] had again mounted their steeds and left the town.

[1] *Massacre of the Conestoga Indians :* The massacre of the Conestoga Indians by the Paxton boys, enacted within Lancaster county, is one of those events that attained a historical importance second to none that ever transpired in the county limits. It is one of those scenes of history that to be understood requires a resume of facts generally lost sight of. Pennsylvania having been settled by the Quakers, it can readily be supposed on account of the persecutions they endured in England that this class of people would flock into the new asylum opened up by William Penn, in considerable numbers. The result was that they obtained control of the State government for many years; most of the State and county officers were members of this persuasion, except in the most western parts of the settlements. The majority of the assembly were Quakers, and, indeed, their policy shaped the affairs of the State nearly up to the commencement of the Revolution. The Scotch-Irish, a numerous body of early settlers, were found mostly upon the borders of the settlements ; and being a bold, daring, and adventuresome class of people, they were encouraged by the government to choose their homes in those localities, as being the best adapted to buffet Indian collision. After the breaking out of the conspiracy of Pontiac, in 1762, the tide of Indian warfare began to rise in the west, and during 1763 the border settlements of Pennsylvania became the scenes of the most appalling desolation and distress that had ever yet been witnessed in those regions. It would be a lengthy task, and revolting to explore through all the details the horrid monotony of blood and havoc presented in the history of Indian brutality and carnage brought upon the white settlers of Pennsylvania at this doleful period. The settlements were filled with the wildest dismay and horror. The people, such as could escape, left their homes in consternation and fled in thousands to the settlements further east. Lancaster county was filled with refugees who had escaped for their lives, leaving the settlements one vast charnel receptacle, filled with the bones of their murdered relatives and kinsmen.

The scene presented in some of the settlements, beggars description. Ranging parties who visited in bodies the sights of desolation, discovered with unspeakable horror in the depths of the forest, the half consumed bodies of men and women still bound fast to trees where they had perished in fiery torture. Here lay the lifeless trunks of fathers and brothers who had fallen in an unequal contest, striving to resist the surging wave of Indian fury; and there, rolled in a common mass, were the mangled corpses of mothers, sisters and children, whose blood the tomahawks of the savage had drunk. It was a sad but maddening sight. A wail of agony rose to heaven over the scenes of desolation; but a resolve of revenge was then formed bitter, burning and unquenchable revenge, that retaliation should be obtained for such fiendish cruelties. The back woods rangers, who visited the scenes described, swore a solemn

SHIPPEN, HENRY, was captain of the company that marched to Baltimore in 1814, in which were James Buchanan, Jasper Slaymaker and others. He read law in the office of James Hopkins, but his tastes being of a military oath of vengeance never to sheath their sabers ere the heart's blood of their assailants, the savages of the forest, was spilled. An eye witness who saw the desolation that followed in the wake of Indian aggression, said: "The Indians had set fire to the houses, barns, corn, hay, and in short, to everything that was combustible, so that the whole country seemed to be one general blaze. The miseries and distress of the poor people were really shocking to humanity, and beyond the power of language to describe. Carlisle was become the barrier, not a single individual being beyond it. Every stable and hovel in the town was crowded with miserable refugees, who were reduced to a state of beggary and despair; their houses, cattle and harvest destroyed; and from a plentiful, independent people, they were become real objects of charity and commiseration. It was most dismal to see the streets filled with people in whose countenances might be discovered a mixture of grief, madness and despair; and to hear, now and then, the sighs and groans of men, the disconsolate lamentations of women, and the screams of children who had lost their nearest and dearest relatives. On both sides of the Susquehanna, for some miles, the woods were filled with poor families and their cattle, who make fire and live like the savages." *Conspiracy of Pontiac,* p. 382.

The Scotch-Irish, in whose settlements it was that this desolation reigned, implored the government of Pennsylvania to aid them in resisting Indian aggression. But "the Quakers, who seemed resolved that they would neither defend the people of the frontier nor allow them to defend themselves, vehemently inveighed against the several expeditions up the Susquehanna, and denounced them as seditious and murderous. Urged by their blind prejudice in favor of the Indians, they insisted that the bands of the Upper Susquehanna were friendly to the English; whereas, with the single exception of a few Moravian converts near Wyoming, who had not been molested, there could be no rational doubt that these savages nourished a rancorous and malignant hatred against the province. But the Quakers, removed by their situation from all fear of the tomahawk, securely vented their spite against the borderers and doggedly closed their ears to the truth. Meanwhile the people of the frontier besieged the Assembly with petitions for relief; but little heed was given to their complaints." *Conspiracy of Pontiac,* p. 391-8. It was well ascertained that at least two thousand persons had been killed or carried off from the settlements on the border. This loss was one that the Scotch-Irish population had to endure. Goaded to desperation by their long continued suffering, they were divided between rage against the Indians and resentment against the Quakers, who had yielded them cold sympathy and inefficient aid. They complained fiercely that they were interposed as a barrier between the rest of the province and a ferocious enemy, and that they were sacrificed to the safety of men who

cast and not succeeding to his expectation, he made an effort to obtain a situation in the army, but was unsuccessful. He removed to Huntingdon and practiced law there for some years. He married a Miss Elizabeth Evans, of Sunbury.

looked with indifference on their miseries and lost no opportunity to extenuate and smooth away the cruelties of their destroyers. They declared that the Quakers would go further to befriend a murdering Indian than to succor a fellow countryman.

It is not difficult to conceive the depth of feeling that would exist in a community situated as were the Scotch-Irish at that early period. They had besought aid of the Assembly in vain. They had also asked that the Indians living in the interior of the white settlements be removed, as they regarded all those professing friendship as spies and harborers of their enemies. To all these requests the Quaker Assembly turned a deaf ear. The Quakers clung to their policy of non-resistance, and left the borderers to shift for themselves as best they could. The rancor that rose on the part of the Scotch-Irish towards the Quakers and their policy was of the bitterest kind. Never was hatred more deep and general than on the Pennsylvania frontier at this period ; and never did so many collateral causes unite to inflame it to madness. It was by no means confined to the vulgar. Magistrates, and even the clergy shared it, and it is not surprising that it found a vent. In the Manor of Conestoga, about five miles from Lancaster, was a small band of Indians, chiefly of Iroquois blood, that had resided there since the first settlement of the province. These Indians William Penn had visited and made treaties with them, which had been ratified by subsequent governors. They had remained on terms of friendship with the English. The community had greatly decreased in membership, and no longer numbered over twenty individuals. These were clustered together in miserable huts, and were in the habit of gathering a pitiable subsistence by beggary and a petty merchandizing amongst the white settlers of the country around them. The men spent most of their time in fishing and hunting, and loitering around in idleness. In their neighborhood they passed for innocent vagabonds.

Among the Scotch-Irish, on the contrary, they were looked upon as spies ; and as guilty of giving shelter to scalping parties, and even in aiding their enemies in their depredations. That they were not altogether wrong in their opinions was proven by a mass of testimony ; though the treachery may have been confined to one or two individuals. The exasperated frontiersmen were not in a mood to discriminate between the innocent and guilty. They did not think these Indians should be permitted to occupy a position where they would have it in their power to do them injury. They belonged at least to that hated race that had brought so much misery upon themselves and their countrymen. A body of rangers, whose headquarters was the little town of Paxton, on the east bank of the Susquehanna, became noted about this time for their zeal and efficiency in defending the borders. John Elder, a Presbyterian clergyman of great worth and piety of character, had

Afterwards, through the influence of Molton C. Rogers, Secretary of State under Governor Shultz, he was appointed President Judge of the court of common pleas of one of the western judicial districts. He died March 2, 1839.

influenced the formation of this band, as it became necessary to have of them guards around the church while he was engaged in the performance of divine service. This band of rangers was composed of the best men in the community ; they were orderly and upright citizens, as the Rev. John Elder himself testified. One of their principal leaders was Matthew Smith, a man of influence and popularity amongst his associates, and one by no means destitute of culture, and yet who at the same time shared a full proportion of the general hatred against the Indian race, and suspicion against the band at Conestoga.

About the middle of December a scout called upon Smith and informed him that an Indian who had been committing depredations in the neighborhood had been tracked to Conestoga. Having communicated this to five of his companions, they armed, mounted and set out for the Indian settlement, where they arrived in the night. Smith dismounted from his horse and crawled forward cautiously until he saw, or imagined he saw, a number of armed warriors in the cabins. He returned, and related this to his companions, but fearing that they were too weak to attack the party, returned with all speed to Paxton. Their blood being now up, they determined to extirpate the Conestogas. Messengers were sent in all directions, and on the following day fifty armed men, chiefly from Donegal and Paxton, assembled at the place agreed upon. They set out with Smith as their leader, and arrived at Conestoga before daylight on the morning of the fourteenth. As they neared the place they perceived the light of a fire in one of the cabins, and having fastened their horses, they cautiously advanced towards the light. An Indian, having heard the noise of their footsteps or voices, advanced to see whence the noise came. As soon as he came near, one of the men, fancying that he recognized him, exclaimed with an oath, "He is the one that killed my mother," and firing his rifle brought the Indian to the ground. With a general shout they now all rushed forward and closed the career of all the Indians they could find. There were but six of them, the remainder, in accordance with their vagrant habits, being scattered about the neighborhood. They closed their vengeance at this place by burning all the cabins, and set out for home by the dawn of day. The morning was cold, and snow was falling and covered the ground to a considerable depth. They were met by a man named Thomas Wright, who somewhat struck by their appearance, began a conversation with them. They freely, and without compunction, told him all they had done. Proceeding some distance further they began to scatter around amongst the settlers in order to obtain some food for themselves and horses. Several of them rode to the house of Robert Barber, a prominent settler, near Wright's Ferry, who seeing the strangers shaking the snow from their blanket coats, invited them to enter, and caused refreshments to be set before them. Having remained a short time seated

SHIRK, HENRY, was elected County Commissioner in 1810, and reëlected again in 1819.

SHOCH, SAMUEL, of Columbia, was born in Harrisburg on the 28th of May, 1797. His opportunities of education around the fire, they remounted and rode off through the snow storm. Whilst they were in the house, a boy belonging to the family had gone out where the horses were standing, and coming in reported that he had seen a tomahawk covered with blood hanging to the saddle of each, and also a gun belonging to one of the Indian children. Barber at once suspected the truth, and having given information to his neighbors, a company of them started off to the Indian settlement, where they found the cabins in ashes and the charred remains of the slaughtered Indians. While they were there the sheriff of Lancaster county with a party of men arrived at the place ; and the first object of that officer was to send through the neighborhood and gather up the Indians that had escaped—fourteen in number. The survivors as soon as they learned the fate of their friends were in great terror for their own lives, and earnestly begged protection. They were brought to Lancaster, amidst the greatest excitement, and lodged in the county jail, a strong stone building, and one which was deemed sufficient to afford the amplest protection.

News of the massacre was immediately sent to Philadelphia, upon the hearing of which the governor at once issued a proclamation denouncing the act, and offering a reward for the arrest of the perpetrators. But in the excited state of public feeling at that time arrests were out of the question, as resistance would have been offered to any force that might have been sent into the Scotch-Irish settlements. Nothing daunted by the Governor's proclamation, the Paxton rangers determined to complete the work they had begun. In this determination they were incited by a prevailing impression that one of the Indians that had found protection at Lancaster had murdered the relatives of one of their number. They despatched a spy to learn the condition of affairs at Lancaster, and upon his return they again assembled at the usual rendezvous. On this occasion the leader of the party was a Lazarus Stewart, a young man highly esteemed on the borders for his heroic qualities and chivalrous deportment. Early on the 27th of December the party, about fifty in number, left Paxton on their work of death. About three o'clock in the afternoon, armed with rifle, knife and tomahawk, they rode into Lancaster at a gallop, turned their horses into the yard of a public house, and proceeded forthwith to the jail. In a moment the doors were burst open and they rushed in. The Indians were at the time in a small yard adjacent to the building, and surrounded by strong walls. Hearing the noise and alarmed by the sight of armed men in the doorway, two or three of them grasped billets of wood in self-defence. This show of resistance doubly maddened the foremost of the party, and rushing forward they fired their rifles amongst the Indians, huddled in a corner. The tomahawk soon ended the struggle, and the "Quaker pets," as they termed them, lay weltering in their gore.

The magistrates being in church, attending the Christmas service,

were limited to the schools of that place and the West Nottingham academy, in Cecil county, Maryland, under the presidential care of the Rev. Doctor Magraw. In 1814, when the British army destroyed the capitol at Washington, which had been postponed from the twenty-fifth, a messenger suddenly appeared at the church door, and in broken exclamations was heard to say : " *Murder—the jail—the Paxton boys—the Indians.*" The assembly broke up in disorder, and Edward Shippen, the chief burgess, hastened towards the scene; but before he could reach it, all was over, and the rangers had remounted and were galloping from the town. The sheriff and the coroner had mingled with the rangers, and as their enemies alleged, aided and abetted them in their work of destruction, but they contended that they were endeavoring to save the Indians. The people crowded into the jail to gaze at the dead Indians, and when their curiosity was sated they gathered their bodies together and buried them not far from the town. There their bones reposed until the railroad was being made through the city, when they were disinterred by the workmen. The massacre of the Indians occasioned a vast clamor when it reached Philadelphia, and the Governor issued another proclamation, probably to allay Quaker feeling, for he could not but have known that nothing else would be gained. It would have been madness to attempt to make any arrests of parties engaged in the transaction ; and the best evidence that all thought so is, that no attempt was made until years afterwards, when all the excitement had died away.

This event of history can be regarded justly in no other light than as an exhibition of the pent up rage against the Indians for the atrocities committed on the white settlers, and partially out of vengeance towards the Quakers, because of their unaccountable attachment to the Indians in preference to the whites, as it was regarded. It can not, and should not be viewed as the work of a vulgar mob. It was none such. It was simply the reflex of the public opinion as it existed amongst the settlers on the borders. Would any of the rangers who perpetrated the deed have been punished by a jury of their Scotch-Irish neighbors had these been placed on trial? They had the power to punish them, if they had the will, but this was wanting. Did Lazarus Stewart, or Matthew Smith sink in public estimation for the part they had figured in the transaction? Let the history of those days answer the question. They received the endorsement of high character and standing from the leading men on the border, clergymen and others. We should endeavor, therefore, to place ourselves in imagination in their circumstances before passing too harsh a judgment upon them. That the Quakers should condemn them is not strange. Does not every violent party man, condemn those of the opposite party? So in this case. The Quakers formed the one party in Pennsylvania, and which, at this time, they governed, and they endeavored to decry their opponents, the Scotch-Irish, for their sanctioning the Paxton massacre. Feeling became intensified, because the event was seized by one party for the injury of the other. Party rage gave the transaction its historical importance.

he volunteered and served three months in the army under the immediate command of Captain Richard M. Crain, of the Harrisburg Artillerists. He was employed two years as clerk in the land department at Harrisburg. In 1820 he was admitted to practice law at the bar of Dauphin county. In 1835 he was elected Clerk of the House of Representatives, and in 1837 was made secretary to the convention to amend the Constitution of the State of Pennsylvania. In 1839 he was appointed cashier of the Columbia Bank and Bridge Company, which afterwards became the Columbia National Bank, of which he still has charge. He at one and the same time served as President of the following companies and organizations, viz: the Common School Board in Columbia; the Columbia and Marietta turnpike road company; the Columbia and Chesnut Hill turnpike road company; the Columbia and Washington turnpike road company; the Columbia water company, and the Columbia gas company; and, also, as treasurer of the Reading and Columbia railroad company; director of the poor of Lancaster county, and of the Wrightsville, York and Gettysburg railroad company, and trustee of the Normal School, at Millersville; likewise cashier of the Columbia National Bank. He has also served a term as county auditor of Lancaster county, and fills most of the above posts at the present time. He has also been president of the old Columbia public ground company.

SHREINER, MARTIN, was born in Lancaster, January 23d, 1767. His father, Philip Shreiner, emigrated from Germany at an early day, and bought the property yet owned by Martin Shreiner, the grandson of the original proprietor. Martin Shreiner, the subject of this notice, learned the trade of a clock-maker with John Eberman, grandfather of Peter G. Eberman, esq. He was an apprentice of Mr. Eberman at the time the latter manufactured the old town clock. He began and carried on his business in the same place now occupied and owned by his son. He continued in this business up to 1829, and then began the manufacturing of engines. In 1818 Martin Shreiner was elected by the City Councils, one of the first street regulators of Lancaster, and was reëlected to this position in 1819.   One of the first engines manufactured by him, was that made for a hose company of Lebanon.   The Sun engine and hose company, one of the two oldest fire companies in Lancaster city, having used their engine from 1798 up till 1829, determined upon procuring a new one.   Martin Shreiner was employed by the company to build an engine at an expense not to exceed eight hundred dollars.   In December, 1830, the following appears upon the minutes of this company : " The committee appointed to procure a new fire engine from Martin Shreiner for this company, reported that they had received the same from Martin Shreiner, which engine upon fair trial, fully answered the expectation of the company as to beauty and excellence of workmanship and power of throwing water, and that it had been placed in the engine house at the disposal of the company."

In the year 1829 Martin Shreiner and Peter Reed were elected on the Anti-Masonic ticket, directors of the poor of Lancaster county.   He was for many years an active and influential member of the City Councils, and in 1832 he was one of the committee who were instrumental in having the Columbia and Philadelphia railway brought through the city of Lancaster.   In 1834 he built the celebrated " American fire engine" with two chambers, eight and a-half inches in diameter, which at its first trial forced the water to the ball of the Lutheran steeple, two hundred feet high.   He afterwards re-built the Middletown, Lititz and Columbia engines.   He was a member of the Lutheran church, and it was greatly through his influence that the German Lutheran church, in Vine street, was erected in 1826.   About the year 1836 he laid out and established the first cemetery in Lancaster, which bears his name ; and because no restriction was imposed as to the interment of persons of color therein, the late Thaddeus Stevens chose it as his last resting place. The cemetery was beautifully ornamented by the care of the venerable patriarch in life, and his monument now is one of the chief places of interest within its enclosure.   He died February 14th, 1866, at the ripe age of 97 years and 22 days.

SHULTZ, DAVID, was born in Dauphin county, Pennsylvania, May 28, 1805. His education was limited, having had no early advantages. He learned the hatting business with Jacob Ziegler, of Harrisburg, and traveled for several years in the capacity of journeyman. He moved to New Holland in 1824, and in 1829 began business for himself, which he continued up to 1852. He became an active politician, and frequently filled minor trusts in the gift of the people. He often represented his.party in the county conventions. He was appointed in 1847 the first mercantile appraiser in Lancaster county, and was twice reappointed. In 1852 he was elected treasurer of Lancaster county, and held the same for two years. After moving to Lancaster in 1852 he carried on the hatting business in the latter place up to 1856. He next entered into partnership in the banking business with Hiester, Henderson and Reed. The firm name was John K. Reed & Co., and it continued up till 1861. In 1862 he moved west upon a farm, and was engaged in agricultural pursuits till 1866, when he sold his farms and returned again to Lancaster, where he has since been living, chiefly in retirement.

SHULZE, JOHN ANDREW, was a native of Lancaster (now Lebanon) county, Pa. He was educated for a clergyman, and filled the pulpits of several Lutheran congregations for some years, during the early part of his manhood, but he was obliged to relinquish them in consequence of some physical affection which disabled him from frequent speaking. Sometime afterwards he took up his residence in the borough of Lebanon, and he soon became somewhat prominent as a politician of the Democratic school. After Lebanon became formed into a separate county he received the appointment of prothonotary, the duties of which he discharged for a number of years. In 1822 he was nominated as the Democratic candidate for the State Senate, and triumphantly elected. In 1823 he was elected Governor of Pennsylvania, over Andrew Gregg, the Federal candidate, by nearly 26,000 majority. In 1826 he was reëlected to the same office, without recognized opposition, receiving nearly 73,000 votes out of 75,000 polled. It was during his administration that the system of public improvements was commenced, and if his prudent and cautious recommendations had been followed by the Legislature, to finish one line of canal before commencing another, the commonwealth would have been saved from a large portion of the debt which afterwards weighed so heavily upon her citizens.

To Governor Shulze belongs the credit, which is usually accorded to his successor, of having been the first to advocate a general system of education. In his message of 1828 he said: "The mighty works, and consequent great expenditures undertaken by the State cannot induce me to forbear again calling attention to the subject of public education. To devise means for the establishment of a fund, and the adoption of a plan, by which the blessings of the more necessary branches of education should be conferred on every family within our borders, would be every way worthy of the Legislature of Pennsylvania, and attention to this subject at this time would seem to be peculiarly demanded · by the increased number of children and young persons who are employed in manufactures. The establishment of such principles would not only have the happiest effects in cultivating the minds, but invigorating the physical constitutions of the young. What nobler incentive can present itself to the mind of a republican legislator, than a hope that his labor shall be rewarded by insuring to his country a race of human beings, healthy and of vigorous constitutions, and of minds more generally improved than fall to the lot of any considerable portion of the human family." Far from a brilliant statesman who could sway the multitude by his eloquence, Governor Shulze, nevertheless, possessed administrative ability which enabled him to preside over the affairs of the commonwealth with credit to himself and satisfaction to the public.

Few Governors have left the executive chair with as large a share of personal popularity and carrying with them into retirement less personal and political animosity towards them than did the subject of our notice. Conservative in all his views, honest and straightforward in all his acts, he commanded the confidence of the people and never abused it. His was not a brilliant, but a judicious, faithful and useful career. Unable to agree with all the measures of his party, he had the integrity and the independence to array himself against anything he conceived to be wrong. He was educated in the Jeffersonian school of politics, and was, therefore, in feeling and sentiment, an old school Republican. He favored all the conservative Republican measures, of which Jefferson, Madison and Monroe had been the champions. With his old party friends he came to differ, however, on the question of home protection, and after his retirement from office he became affiliated with the Anti-Masonic party in sentiment. He was in 1839 chosen one of the Senatorial electors of the Anti-Masonic party. After his retirement from office in 1829 he removed to Lycoming county, where, in consequence of some unfortunate investments he lost all he had saved, and became exceedingly poor. He thereupon removed to Lancaster, at which place he continued to reside in quiet retirement until his death, which event occurred November 19, 1852. He lies buried in Woodward Hill Cemetery, Lancaster city, and a handsome monument erected in honor of him by his numerous friends, points out to the visitor his last resting place. *Requiescat in pace.*

SHUMAN, JACOB A., was born in Manor township, Lancaster county, in the year 1814. Losing his parents at an early age, he hired himself out for a short time to work upon a farm, but at the age of fourteen he apprenticed himself to learn the coopering business with one of his uncles. Upon the expiration of his term of apprenticeship, being but seventeen years of age, he started on a trip to the west, footing it over the Alleghenies to Pittsburg. He stopped a short time in that city and worked at his trade. From that place he proceeded to Cincinnati. Arriving there at a time when the cholera was raging, he had a severe attack of this disease and barely escaped with his life. After an absence of two years, he returned to his native home and began work at his trade for his old master. About this time an event occurred which proved the turning point in his career. A cousin of his own, who was engaged in teaching school, died after a short illness. During his cousin's illness, and at his request, Mr. Shuman took charge of his school, and after his death, at the request of the citizens of the district, he continued the school. His career in teaching was from that time up to 1845, almost continuous; all his leisure, however, was devoted to study. In 1844–45 he was nominated and elected by the Whig party of his native county, as a member of the Legislature. He proved himself in this position a creditable representative, was watchful of the interests of his constituents, and merited their approbation and esteem. After the expiration of his term of services in the House of Representatives, he continued teaching and also engaged in agricultural pursuits. About 1850 he abandoned teaching entirely, and now devoted his whole attention to farming. In 1854 he was elected a member of the Senate of Pennsylvania. As a senator, he was modest and unassuming, and rarely obtruded himself upon the attention of the Senate unless a question was pending that immediately affected the interests of his constituents.

*SLAYMAKER FAMILY. Mathias Slaymaker, (originally in German *Schleiermacher*,) the ancestor of the family in this county, was a native of Strasburg, Germany, and emigrated to this country about the year 1710. He and his family settled on a tract of about 1,000 acres, known as the "London Lands," situated in Strasburg, now Paradise township, which he purchased from a company called the " London Company," and built a log house or cabin close to a large spring on the farm, and near the residence of the late Wm. Eckert, in said Paradise township; a large portion of the said 1,000 acre tract being still in the name. He left two brothers in Germany, one of whom, a clergyman, was Secretary of Legation from his government to the Court of St. James; afterwards Charge d'Affaires to the same place. The other was a major in the King of Prussia's *tall regiment.* Matthias Slaymaker had an excellent German education, and in person was remarkable for his almost gigantic stature and great strength, as were also his sons, which qualities in those primitive times commended them to their neighbors, and won the respect of the Indians, who were then numerous in the neighborhood. He gave the name to Stras-

*Contributed by Nathaniel E. Slaymaker, esq.

burg township, and contributed greatly towards the permanent settlement and improvement of the county, which was then "back-woods," and inhabited by Indian tribes. He died at an advanced age, and lies buried at the old Leacock Presbyterian church, in Leacock township, which has been the burying-ground of almost all his numerous descendants for six generations. He left five sons, Lawrence, Matthias, John, Henry and Daniel; and two daughters, Margaret and Barbara.

LAWRENCE SLAYMAKER joined a company of pioneers going west, and was not afterwards heard from.

MATTHIAS SLAYMAKER purchased that portion of the aforesaid 1,000 acre tract, belonging at present to his great-grandsons, Jno. M. Slaymaker and Nathaniel E. Slaymaker, esq., the latter at present and for many years past secretary and treasurer of the Lancaster County Mutual Insurance Company.

DANIEL SLAYMAKER and his descendants owned the land now belonging to Uriah, Keziah and Levina Eckert.

JOHN SLAYMAKER, one of said sons, and father of the late Capt. Jno. Slaymaker, of Paradise township, was a soldier in Braddock's army at the age of twenty-two years, and took part in the disastrous battle of Braddock's field. He was also captain of a company in the Revolutionary war, and after his return home was chosen county commissioner, which ended his public service. He died in 1798, aged 65 years.

HENRY SLAYMAKER, another of said sons, was an active and conspicuous Whig during the Revolutionary war, being among the first in the neighborhood to take his stand with the Republic. Being a magistrate at the time, he administered the oath of allegiance to those who espoused the cause, and was prompt in suppressing any efforts on the part of the Tories at insurrection, and in punishing them for furnishing the British army horses and provisions. After Mr. Hubley became incapable of trying causes, Henry Slaymaker, being then the oldest justice in the county, was appointed principal judge of the courts of Lancaster county, and presided one year. He assisted in clearing the ground on which the old

37

jail in Lancaster was erected, and the present site of Fulton Hall; and was a delegate to the convention for framing a constitution of the State of Pennsylvania, which met at Philadelphia, July 15th, 1776.

AMOS SLAYMAKER, a son of Henry, also served in the Revolutionary war as ensign of the company commanded by his uncle, Captain John Slaymaker, before mentioned, and was a member of an association for suppressing the Tories in the eastern end of the county, at the head of which was Colonel James Mercer. He was a magistrate for many years; county commissioner in the year 1800; a member of the House of Representatives in 1810–11; and afterwards of the Senate of Pennsylvania from 1806 until 1810; and a member of Congress of the United States from 1814 until 1815, at which time he, with a number of others, lent their credit to the government, by endorsing for it when in financial difficulties. He and his two brothers, Henry and Samuel, were proprietors of the great stage line of Reeside, Slaymaker & Co., from Philadelphia to the west, before the time of railroads. He died in 1835, aged 85 years. He left six sons and four daughters; one of his sons, Jasper, was a leading member of the Lancaster bar, and the first prosecuting attorney of the Mayor's court. He also served two years in the State Legislature 1816–17 and 1817–18, and died at the age of 39 years.

JONATHAN S. SLAYMAKER, a son of Samuel R. Slaymaker, late of York county, Pa., and grand-nephew of Amos Slaymaker, before mentioned, was captain of a company in the 2d Iowa regiment in the late civil war, and was killed at the taking of Fort Donelson, where he showed exemplary bravery.

SLOKOM, SAMUEL, was elected commissioner of Lancaster county in 1865. He has acted for many years as justice of the peace of the county. The following is from the pen of one knowing Mr. Slokom for years: " Samuel Slokom is a man of strong practical sense, and as a business man has few superiors. He possesses great force of character and wonderful energy, and is an untiring worker in whatever he undertakes. His judgment in matters of every-day life is greatly superior to the average of men, and is so recognized among those who know him. He is strong in his likes and dislikes ; is a warm and devoted friend, and a bitter enemy. Without any brilliant talents, or superior cultivation, he is a gentleman of unusual intelligence and ability. His intuitive knowledge of human nature is one of the most marked features of his character, and has, no doubt, been an important agency in his career."

SLOKOM, THOMAS, son of Isaac Slokom, was born in Virginia, and removed to Lancaster county about the year 1798. The ancestors of Isaac Slokom were amongst the first settlers of the Wyoming valley, but removed thence to Virginia, prior to the Indian massacre in that colony. Thomas Slokom married a descendant of Jacob Miller, of Strasburg township.[1] He was an enterprising and useful man in his day and generation. He erected the " Red Lion Hotel," in Sadsbury township, and made many other useful and valuable improvements. He was the father of Samuel Slokom, late commissioner of Lancaster county.

SLOUGH, MATHIAS, was an active Whig of the borough of Lancaster, about the period of the Revolution. He was an innkeeper, and kept tavern at the southeast corner of Centre Square. The house, when kept by Slough, was erected of what were called "saw-bucks," or cross-pieces, and the interstices were filled with bricks. He was a man of considerable worth, and had sufficient taste in that early day to give his family a good education. His daughter Fanny, was an accomplished pianist, and her sweet music often attracted crowds in the evenings to listen to the harmonious melody of her strains. One of her favorite pieces was " The Rose Tree in Full Bloom." In that day there were but few pianos in Lancaster. Mathias Slough was coroner in 1763, and it was he who held the inquest upon the bodies of the Conestoga Indians, killed by the Paxton boys. He

[1] Jacob Miller was born in the year 1663, and emigrated to Pennsylvania, and purchased a large tract of land in Pequea valley (now Strasburg township). The warrant bears date October 10th, 1710. Jacob Miller's son Samuel, was the first child born in the Swiss colony. Henry Miller, one of the descendants of Jacob Miller, was a member of the convention that framed the constitution of Pennsylvania.

was in 1776 appointed, by the assembly of Pennsylvania, general agent for the province of Pennsylvania, to provide the necessary clothing and accoutrements for the troops ordered to be raised for the service of the province. He also had command of a Lancaster battalion in the years 1776–7. He was a member of the Pennsylvania Legislature during the years 1774, 1775, 1777, 1780, 1781, 1782 and 1783.

SMILIE, JOHN, was a native of Ireland, and came to America when a young man, shortly before the outbreak of the Revolution, but in what year we cannot ascertain. He settled in Lancaster county, Pa., and at once espoused the cause of American liberty. He rapidly acquired the confidence of his co-patriots, and soon became a leader in the resistance which they resolved and executed against the tyrannies of the King and Parliament. Being one of the committee of safety of Lancaster county, we find him in June, 1776, a member of the Provincial Conference of county committees of Pennsylvania at Philadelphia, which declared formally the sundering of the ties which hitherto bound the colony to the parent power, by resolving "to form a new government for this province, upon the authority of the people only." This conference called and provided for the convention which framed our first State constitution—that of 1776. In 1778, and again in 1779, he was elected one of the representatives of Lancaster county in the Assembly, of which he was an active and useful member.

Having married Miss Janet Porter, a daughter, we believe, of Col. Thomas Porter, a distinguished citizen of Lancaster county, he was induced in 1780, to seek a home in the west for his rising family. In that or the subsequent year, he removed to Fayette, then Westmoreland county; and after looking round for a time, eventually bought an improvement from old Joseph Huston, on the north side of the Yough river, about five miles below Connellsville, where he settled and where he henceforth resided until his death. He perfected his title to the tract—about 400 acres—in 1786.

Mr. Smilie's energies and good sense soon gave him prominence in Fayette county. In 1784 he became the first elected member of the Assembly from Fayette county, and was reëlected in 1785. In 1789 Mr. Smilie was, with Albert Gallatin, chosen to represent Fayette county in the State convention which framed the Constitution of 1790. In 1790 Mr. Smilie and John Hoge, of Washington, were elected the first State Senators from the district composed of Fayette and Washington counties. The term for which he was elected was four years; but having in 1792 been elected to the third Congress of the United States, which was to meet in December, 1793, he resigned the last year of the Senatorial term. In 1798 Mr. Smilie was again elected to Congress. In 1801 Fayette and Greene were made the Ninth district, from which Mr. Smilie was successfully returned in 1802, 1804, 1806, 1808, 1810 and 1812. He died in the city of Washington while attending the second session of the twelfth Congress, on the 29th of December, 1812, and was on the 31st interred with the customary honors, in the Congressional Cemetery, where his remains yet repose, designated by one of the uniform monuments which Congress erects to deceased members, even though their bodies be removed.

SMITH, ABRAHAM HERR, was born in Manor township, Lancaster county. His maternal grandfather, Abraham Herr, was the father of Benjamin Herr, familiarly known as "the King of the Manor." His father, Jacob Smith, was an ingenious millwright, and erected a number of flouring mills in Lancaster and York counties. He died in the year 1819. The ancestors of our subject, on both sides, came from Germany, on the Rhine, at the time of the Mylin and Herr emigration in 1710. They early became members of the Methodist church. Our subject received the early rudiments of his education at Lititz, under Professor Beck; next attended Haddington college, near Philadelphia, and graduated at Dickinson college, Carlisle, in the year 1840. He immediately began the study of law in the office of John R. Montgomery, and was admitted to the bar October 10th, 1842. He at once began the practice of his profession, and soon succeeded in establishing himself in a remunerative practice, which steadily increased until it has become one of the most lucrative in Lancaster county.

In 1843 he was elected to the Legislature of Pennsylvania, and reëlected in the following year. During his service in that body, he was the author of the bill providing for the payment of the interest on the State debt, a measure at the time essentially necessary to preserve the credit of the commonwealth. For two years preceding this time, the State instead of paying the interest upon her bonds, had issued certificates bearing interest, called "domestic credit scrip." This policy of compounding the debt, he deemed ruinous to the public credit, as the effect of it had been the sinking of the value of the bonds to 33 cents on the dollar, and repudiation had been openly advocated upon the floor of the House of Representatives. When the bill came up for passage, Mr. Smith being asked by his colleagues whether he would vote for it, and replying in the affimative, added: "*Is it not right?*" "Certainly," they replied, "but it will be very unpopular, and will ruin any man who will vote for it." Mr. Smith then remarked that he "would vote for it, and have nothing to do with consequences." Accordingly he warmly advocated the bill, and it became a law, and from that time the interest on the bonds was promptly met, the bonds rose to par, and are now selling above that, and have been for years. He also advocated the sale of the public works, which also became a law. It was he who introduced the bill for the abolition of the Mayor's court,[1] which, after being vetoed by the Governor several times, was finally passed and received executive sanction. He favored the abolition of this court, deeming it a useless expense upon the county; and the business transacted in it has, since its abolition, been

[1] The Mayor's court was composed of the aldermen of the city of Lancaster and a Recorder appointed by the Governor, who presided as president of the court. The jury for the trial of causes was selected from the citizens of Lancaster city, and a district attorney appointed by the Governor, who prosecuted the pleas of the city. There were twelve jurors empanneled for the trial of each case. There were also a grand jury. The Mayor's court held quarterly sessions, the same as the Quarter Sessions, and had criminal jurisdiction over all cases occcuring within the city, except the highest grade of felonies. The expenses of this court were borne by the county, except the salary of the recorder, which came from the State treasury. His salary was $600. George M. Kline, esq., at present one of the ablest lawyers of the Lancaster bar, was at one time district attorney of the Mayor's court.

more conveniently disposed of in the court of Quarter Sessions. Mr. Smith also refused to sanction the renewal of the district court [1] when it had expired by limitation, and this was also abolished.

In 1845 he was elected to the State Senate, serving one term therein. Whilst a member of this body he favored the enactment of the married woman's act, passed in 1848. He also favored the passage of the law which made the common school system obligatory upon the districts of the county, and doing away with the triennial election, which permitted the voters of every district to accept or reject the system every three years. He regarded this as one of the defects of the school system, which required to be changed. He was ever strongly devoted to rigid economy and governmental reforms, wherever the same could be effected; was a steady and faithful attendant at his post of duty, (scarcely an hour absent during the whole period of his service); and with patient attention and scrupulous fidelity watched the interests of his constituents. Since the close of his legislative career, he has sedulously devoted himself to the practice of his profession. In politics he is devoted to the principles of the Republican party, and was an abolitionist in sentiment long before the consolidation of the anti-slavery elements into that organization. As a student at Haddington college, he wrote an address for exhibition exercises so strongly anti-slavery, that the faculty declined to permit its delivery.

As a lawyer he is well read in his profession, and is very successful in the trial of his cases in the courts below, and also in the supreme court. In short, he ranks amongst the ablest in his profession.[2] Besides, he is altogether conscientious in his professional career, and will decline a case unless his support of it can be based upon the broad principles of justice.

[1] The district court was a court of concurrent jurisdiction with the common pleas, over which one judge alone presided.

[2] It should not be forgotten that in the Biographical History of Lancaster County the sketches have chiefly been confined to individuals who have filled certain official positions; and as regards such as came thus within the programme, they have in a few cases been spoken of as their deserts seemed, in the author's opinion, to merit. In very few instances,

SMITH, CHARLES, was a leading member of the Lancaster bar in his day, and was admitted in 1787. He was an ardent Federalist and a bitter opponent of the Republican principles of Jefferson. He was elected a member of the Legislature in the years 1806, 1807 and 1808. In 1816 he was elected to the State Senate of Pennsylvania. In his legislative capacity he ranked amongst the ablest men in the Senate and House of Representatives and bore a conspicuous part in the proceedings of the Legislature. He was appointed to and served as president judge of the ninth judicial district. He resigned this position in 1820, and accepted the president judgeship of the district court of the city and county of Lancaster. He married a daughter of Judge Jasper Yeates, of the Supreme Court. He was the builder of the residence near Lancaster, known as Hardwicke.

SMITH, E. K., was elected a member of the Legislature in the year 1863. He is a banker of Columbia.

SMITH, FREDERICK, was elected Sheriff of Lancaster county in 1863.

*SMITH, JOHN BLAIR, the fourth son of the Rev. Robert Smith, was born at Pequea, Lancaster county, Pa., June 12th, 1756. In very early life he evinced a great thirst for knowledge, and an uncommon facility for acquiring it. At the age of sixteen he was admitted to the junior class in Princeton college, New Jersey, and graduated under the presidency of the distinguished Dr. Witherspoon in 1773. He was one

however, was this attempted, and but of those of whom personal knowledge enabled him to form an estimate. In the bulk of cases he ,felt himself incompetent for this task, and left the sketches with a simple statement of facts. In the treatment of those so sketched, as already stated, it is not intended to unjustly elevate them over and above others equally worthy, who find no place in the history, but simply to express the truth, as near as may be, concerning the person so delineated. There are able members of the professions, and other intellectual men of whom no biographies appear in the work, inasmuch as they have never filled such official positions as brought them within the category of characters originally proposed to be sketched. All deserving a place in the history of the county could not be treated in a six-hundred page octavo, and no safer line of demarcation seemed feasible than that of official designation.

*Sprague!s Annals of the American Pulpit, vol. 3.

of a class of twenty-nine, fourteen of whom became Ministers of the Gospel, and three, Governors of States. His elder brother, Samuel Stanhope Smith, having become the head of the rising institution in Prince Edward county, Va., under the care of the presbytery of Hanover, the subject of this notice went, at his suggestion, in the early part of 1776, to join his brother as an assistant teacher, and at the same time to prosecute his theological studies under his instruction. Having gone through his several trials, he was licensed to preach by the Hanover Presbytery on the 29th of April, 1778. He was ordained at Prince Edward Court House, on the 28th of October, 1779. At the same meeting of the Hanover presbytery, his brother having received an invitation to the chair of moral philosophy in Princeton college, New Jersey, asked leave to resign the presidency of Hampden Sydney college, and also his pastoral charge; both of which requests were granted. John Blair Smith was immediately chosen to succeed him as president of the college; and in the following spring, he also became his successor in the pastoral office. About this time Mr. Smith married a daughter of Colonel John Nash, of Prince Edward county, a lady distinguished alike for her accomplishments and piety. When Mr. Smith first entered the pulpit, he attracted much attention, yet he was by no means so popular as his brother who had preceded him; but before he left the State, he is said to have been more attractive and powerful than any other clergyman of Virginia from the time of Samuel Davies. The times in which he began his services in Virginia, were anything but favorable to the progress of religion and high spiritual attainment. The State, and that very part of it, had been invaded by the British; and the minds of the people were occupied chiefly about their own safety and their country's independence. Mr. Smith was an earnest patriot, and withal, was a man of great activity and courage. The college suffered much in consequence of the war. Its resources were exhausted; and the youth that had been pursuing their education, were in the service of their country.

After the ratification of peace it was some time before

religion and literature began to revive. About this time the Methodists began to pass through the country, and their preaching had the effect of winning many from the ranks of the Presbyterians. In 1786 or 1787 they came within the bounds of Mr. Smith's congregations, and he himself seemed henceforth to become imbued with their zeal and ardor in the gospel, and a fresh impulse was given to his religious feelings and ministrations. He began preaching with a vigor and enthusiasm that soon produced visible effects. An extensive revival of religion ensued, which spread through the college and the whole adjacent country. Mr. Smith entered into the work with such glowing zeal, and his preaching was so powerful that he was continually solicited to extend his labors, and to places more and more remote from his residence. Some of his friends began to think that he was less attentive to the concerns of the college than could be desired; and this was the more felt as the institution, being without funds, was required to depend for its support on the fees of the students. Feeling it his first duty to preach the gospel, and perceiving that he could not give that attention to the college that was required, he determined to resign the office of president of the institution, and give himself wholly to the work of the ministry. This resolution he carried into effect in the year 1789, and at the same time he bought a farm in the neighborhood and retired to it. In April, 1791, he was appointed by his presbytery one of the commissioners to attend the general assembly in Philadelphia. During the meeting of the assembly he was invited to preach in the Third or Pine Street Presbyterian church, which was then vacant and looking out for a pastor. So acceptable was his preaching, that the congregation were called together, and a unanimous call was extended to him before he left the city, which he conditionally agreed to accept. When this became known to his Virginia congregations, they were greatly distressed, and did all in their power to divert him from his purpose. He felt, however, that his removal would add to the sphere of his usefulness, and he resigned his pastoral charge and removed to Philadelphia in the autumn following, and was installed over his new charge in December. In 1795 the degree of Doctor of Divinity was conferred upon him by his Alma Mater. In the same year Union college, at Schenectady, New York, was founded, and Dr. Smith chosen its president. He accepted the appointment, and for three years presided over the infant institution with great credit and success. He then returned to his former charge in Philadelphia, and was formally reinstated among them in May, 1799. The following extract from a letter written by him to Major Morton, of Prince Edward county, Va., discloses the reason of his last change: " I suppose that my return to my former charge in Philadelphia, will excite some surprise among my friends. However, it can be explained upon a very natural principle, without ascribing it to fickleness of mind. It is simply because I prefer being pastor of a congregation, before being president of a college; and I think myself better qualified for the former than the latter; and because I have regained that health and strength, the want of which only prevented me from staying in Philadelphia when I was there. It is true that I shall run a great risk, in the present circumstances and prospects of the city; but it is equally true that my post would have been there, and I should have had my chance with the other citizens, if the want of health had not compelled me to remove." " the Trustees of the college have accepted my resignation in a manner very respectful to me, and have directed that my portrait be taken and preserved in their hall. They insist upon my staying till after the commencement, next May, though I wish to go about the beginning of April." On his return to Philadelphia he was cordially greeted, not only by his own congregation, but by a large part of the intelligent people of the city. Their joy was destined soon to be turned into mourning. About the middle of August he was attacked with the yellow fever, and died on the 22d of the same month, one of the first victims of that terrible pestilence.[1]

[1] When the constitution of the United States was submitted to the consideration of the people, Patrick Henry, the great orator of the Revolution, offered himself as a candidate for representative of Prince Edward county, in the State convention; and he appointed a day to meet the people of the county at the Court House, to show the defects

SMITH, Rev. Sampson, a native of Scotland, who emigrated to Lancaster county before the Revolution. He was pastor of the Presbyterian church, at Chestnut Level, and also taught an academy for many years. He was struck by lightning while sitting by his window engaged in reading the bible, and instantly killed.

SMITH, Samuel, was a member of the Legislature in the years 1737 and 1738.

*SMITH, Samuel Stanhope, D.D., L.L.D., was born March 16th, 1750, at Pequea, Lancaster county, Penna. His father was the Rev. Robert Smith, a distinguished clergyman of the Presbyterian church, who emigrated from Ireland and established, and for many years superintended, an Academy, which supplied many able and excellent ministers to the denomination with which he was connected. His mother was Elizabeth, daughter of Samuel Blair, and sister of Samuel and John Blair, all of whom were among the most prominent clergymen of their day. The son, at a very early period, gave indications of possessing a mind of no common order, and the parents determined to give him the best advantages within their reach for cultivating it. When quite young he began the study of the languages in his father's school, and as his father had employed some of the most

of the constitution, and the grounds on which he opposed it. Dr. Smith, who was a great friend of the constitution, had made his arrangements to be present at the meeting, and defend it against his attacks; but being called away at that hour to visit a sick friend, he employed a man to take down Mr. Henry's speech in short-hand, for his (Dr. Smith's) benefit. Within a week or two from that time, there was to be a public exhibition in college hall—an occasion always sure to draw together a large assembly. When the day arrived Patrick Henry, who lived in the neighborhood, came with the rest, little dreaming of the rod that had been prepared for him. One of the best speakers among the students came forward upon the stage and delivered Henry's phillipic against the constitution, almost exactly as he had delivered it at the Court House. Another immediately followed with a speech prepared by Dr. Smith, in which he had put all his energies in defense of the constitution. There was no intimation given that the two speeches were not written by the individuals who pronounced them. Henry was not a little annoyed by the procedure, and at the close of the exercise gave Dr. Smith to understand, in no equivocal terms, that he felt that an unfair advantage had

*Sprague's Annals of the American Pulpit, vol. iii.

accomplished teachers from abroad as his assistants, there was perhaps no school in the country, at that day, that furnished better advantages for becoming thoroughly grounded, especially in the classics. The only language allowed to be spoken in the school-room, was Latin, and whoever uttered a word in the mother tongue, was marked as a delinquent. Young Smith made the best of his opportunities, and was distinguished for his improvement in every branch to which he directed his attention. In his sixteenth year he was sent to Princeton college, entering the junior class, in which he immediately took rank amongst the best scholars. Shortly afterwards Dr. Witherspoon arrived from Scotland, and assumed the presidential chair of the institution, while the subject of our notice was an undergraduate. Before he had completed his eighteenth year he had received the degree of bachelor of arts, under circumstances the most honorable to his talents and acquirements, and the most gratifying to his ambition. During his collegiate career Mr. Smith came near making shipwreck of his religious principles, in consequence of his intimacy with Mr. Periam, the senior tutor, who had embraced Bishop Berkley's theory, denying the existence of matter. He became for a time an enthusiastic advocate of these opinions, insomuch that his friends began to have the most serious apprehensions that he had become a permanent accepter of the idealistic theory. When, how-

been taken of him. Dr. Smith contended that he had no cause of complaint, unless his speech had been unfairly represented; and in that case he declared himself ready to make any amends in his power. Henry said that was not the ground of his complaint; for the young man certainly had taken his speech down with great accuracy; but he thought it was indelicate and improper that he should be placed in such circumstances before the audience, without any intimation having previously been given of what was intended. Dr. Smith replied that Colonel Henry knew it was his intention to have replied to him, when he spoke at the Court House, but was providentially prevented; that he had then spoken for public effect, and his speech became public property; that all that he could reasonably require was, that it should be fairly reported; and if that had been done, he could not see that he had any just reason for complaint. Henry, however, was not at all satisfied, broke off all intercourse with him from that time, and would never hear him preach afterwards, though he had previously been one of his constant hearers.— *Letter of Rev. William Hill.*

ever, Dr. Witherspoon arrived from Scotland, he brought with him the works of several distinguished Scottish philosophical writers, particularly Reid and Beattie, the influence of which was quickly perceptible in bringing back this gifted young man into the regions of common sense.

After taking his degree at Princeton, he returned to his father's house, and spent some time partly in assisting him in conducting his school, and partly in vigorous efforts for the higher cultivation of his own mind. He read the finest models in polite literature and the most accredited authors in intellectual and moral philosophy. He also occasionally tried his hand at writing poetry, but he was not much flattered by the result of his efforts; and he seems to have abandoned his devotion to the muses on the ground that "*poeta nascitur non fit.*" He had not been long in this new sphere of labor before he was invited to return to Princeton as a tutor in the college, especially in the department of the classics and belles letters. This position he accepted and filled from 1770 till 1773, discharging his duties in connection with the institution with exemplary fidelity and great acceptance, and all the while he was pursuing a course of theological study in reference to the ministry. About the close of his tutorship he was licensed to preach by the presbytery of New Castle. As his health had suffered not a little from severe affliction he determined, previous to assuming the responsibility of a stated charge, to spend some time as a missionary in the western counties of Virginia. When he reached that part of the country, he received a most cordial welcome from many Irish Presbyterians who had settled in that section. It was not long till his captivating oratory and exemplary deportment rendered him an almost universal favorite. Persons without distinction of sect or of rank, flocked to hear him; and those who had been entranced by the eloquence of Davies, seemed to feel as if another *Davies* had arisen. So powerful an impression did he make, that some of the most wealthy and influential persons soon set on foot a project for detaining him there as the head of a literary institution, and in a short time the funds requisite for establishing such an institution were subscribed. The necessary buildings were erected, and the seminary was subsequently chartered by the Legislature under the name of Hampden Sydney college. The new college being at length nearly ready to commence its operations, he returned to the North and formed a matrimonial alliance with the eldest daughter of Dr. Witherspoon. He then returned to Virginia and took upon himself the double office of principal of the seminary and pastor of the church; and the duties of each he discharged in such a manner as to fulfill the highest expectations that had been formed concerning him. But the new labors were more than his constitution could endure; and after three or four years, a slight bleeding at the lungs admonished him to take at least a temporary respite from his burdens. By the advice of friends he resorted to the watering place among the western mountains, then acquiring considerable celebrity under the name of the "Sweet Springs." A residence at this place for a few weeks caused the unfavorable symptoms in a great measure to disappear, so that he returned to his family with his health in a good degree renovated.

At this period (1799), he was invited to the chair of moral philosophy, at Princeton; and notwithstanding his strong attachment to the infant seminary in Virginia, (of which he might be considered the founder), the prospect of a more extended sphere of usefulness in connection with his *Alma Mater*, induced him to accept the appointment. Upon his arrival at Princeton, however, a most unpromising state of things presented itself. The college itself was in ruins, in consequence of the uses and abuses to which it had been subjected by both the British and American soldiers, during the previous years of the Revolutionary war. The students were dispersed and all its operations had ceased. Mainly by the energy, wisdom, and general self-devotion of Mr. Smith, the college was speedily reörganized and all its usual exercises resumed. For several years Dr. Witherspoon, though retaining the office of president, was engaged as a member of Congress in the higher affairs of the nation. Owing to the fact that Dr. Witherspoon some years afterwards became, in a great measure, disqualified for the duties of the office of

president, being affected with total blindness and many other
bodily infirmities, the great weight of care as to the management of the institution devolved upon the subject of this
notice; and it is not too much to say, that it was indebted
for no small degree of its prosperity to the increasing vigilance, the earnest efforts and the distinguished ability of
Mr. Smith. In 1783 he was honored with the degree of
Doctor of Divinity from Yale college; and in 1810 the degree of Doctor of Laws was conferred upon him by Howard
University. In 1785 Dr. Smith was elected an honorary
member of the American Philosophical Society, in Philadelphia—an institution distinguished not only for being the
first of its kind, in the order of time in the country, but for
numbering among its members many of the most brilliant,
profound and erudite minds of which the country could
boast. The same year he was appointed to deliver their
anniversary address; and he met the occasion in a manner
which of itself would have conferred lasting honor upon his
name. The object of the address was to explain the causes
of the variety in the figure and complexion of the human
species, and to establish the identity of the race. It was
published in the "Transactions" of the society, and was subsequently published in an enlarged and improved form in a
separate volume. With this work his reputation as a philosopher, both at home and abroad, is in no small degree
identified. In 1786 he was associated with several of the
most distinguished and venerable men in the Presbyterian
church, such as Witherspoon, McWhorter, Allison, Ewing,
&c., in preparing the form of presbyterial government, which
continues to the present time. His comprehensive views,
and intimate acquaintance with all the forms of ecclesiastical
procedure, eminently qualified him for the important service.

Upon the death of Dr. Witherspoon in 1794, Dr. Smith
succeeded to the honors and full responsibilities of the office
which his death had vacated. Besides being highly popular
as the head of the institution, he had now acquired a reputation as a pulpit orator which rendered it an object for many,
even from remote parts of the country, to listen to his
preaching. His baccalaureate discourses particularly, which

were addressed to the senior class, on the Sabbath immediately preceding their graduation, were always of the highest order, and it was not uncommon for persons to go even from New York and Philadelphia to listen to them. One of his most splendid performances was his oration delivered at Trenton, on the death of Washington; the occasion roused his faculties to the utmost, and the result was a production of great beauty and power. In 1779 he published a volume of sermons, which were regarded as an important contribution to that department of our country's literature. They are characterized rather by general than particular views of evangelical truth, by a correct, elevated, and perhaps somewhat elaborate style, by occasional bold and eloquent apostrophes, and by many stirring appeals to the heart and conscience. In the spring of 1802, when the institution was at the full tide of its prosperity, the college edifice was burnt, together with the libraries, furniture and fixtures of every description. Indeed, all was gone except the charter, the grounds, and the naked walls of brick and stone, together with the exalted character of the seminary and the commanding reputation of its president. After the first stunning effect of the calamity was over, it was the general sentiment of all, that the necessary funds must be raised to rebuild the edifice and sustain the institution. Dr. Smith made a collecting tour through the southern States, and returned in the following spring with about one hundred thousand dollars, which, with liberal collections made in other parts of the Union, enabled him to accomplish vastly more than he had ventured to anticipate. This was his crowning achievement. He had won new honors, and gained many new friends. The college was popular and prosperous, and numbered two hundred students. New buildings were soon erected, and several new professors were added to the faculty. From this period Dr. Smith bent all his energies towards the management of the institution, and it continued year by year to rise in public estimation. But the advance of bodily infirmities were making visible progress in the case of the distinguished head of the college; and in the year 1812, in consequence of repeated strokes of palsy, he became too much

38

enfeebled to discharge any longer the duties of his office. He, therefore, at the next commencement, tendered his resignation as president, and retired to a place which the board of trustees provided for him, and there spent the remainder of his life. For several years he occupied himself in revising and preparing for the press some of his works, but at length disease had made such havoc with his constitution, that he was scarcely capable of any mental labor. After a long course of gradual and almost imperceptible decline, he died August 21st, 1819, in the 70th year of his age. His published works are the following: An essay on the causes of the variety of complexion and figure of the human species, to which are added strictures on Lord Kaimes' discourse on the Original Diversity of Mankind, 8vo., 1787. Sermons, 8vo., 1799. Lectures on the Evidences of the Christian Religion, 12mo., 1809. Lectures on Moral and Political Philosophy, 12mo., 1812. A comprehensive view of the leading and most important principles of Natural and Revealed Religion, 8vo., 1816. Sermons, to which is prefixed a brief memoir of his life and writings, 2 vols., 8vo., (posthumous,) 1821.

SPENCER, WILLIAM, a citizen of Strasburg[1] borough, was elected County Commissioner in the year 1861.

SPRENGER, J. J., a citizen of Lancaster, somewhat reputed as an American traveler. In 1857 he visited and traversed a large portion of Europe. In 1859 he was appointed consul at Dresden, and was afterwards transferred to Venice, where he remained until 1862. He has traveled over a large portion of America, and in 1871 made his third trip to Europe, passing through England, France, Germany, Switzerland, Belgium and Spain. In the winter of 1869–70 he lectured in many places on "Steaming across the Continent," and during the winter of 1871–72 on "Reminiscences of a tour through Spain and Portugal." Mr. Sprenger is a man of an enterprising character, and endowed with considerable intellectuality.

[1] When Dr. Joseph Priestly, the celebrated philosopher, first emigrated from England to America, in 1794, he settled and lived for a short time in Strasburg, Lancaster county. He lived in the house now owned by William Spencer, ex-commissioner, for about six months. He removed thence to Northumberland, Pa., where he lies buried.

STAUFFER, BENJAMIN M., was elected Register of Wills in 1854.

STAUFFER, CHRISTIAN, elected County Commissioner in 1813.

STAUFFER, CAPT. WM. D., is a native of Lancaster county. Upon the breaking out of the rebellion he enlisted as a private soldier in Co. B., first regiment Pennsylvania Reserves, served all through the struggle, and was discharged as captain of Co. H., 195th regiment Pennsylvania Reserves. In 1869 he was elected Prothonotary of Lancaster county, succeeding Col. Wm. L. Bear, who filled the same office for three years.

STAUFFER FAMILY. John Stauffer and his brother Jacob emigrated to America from Germany about the year 1740. They were mere boys, John being not more than 12 or 15 years old. They started from Philadelphia to Lancaster on foot. While traveling along they came up with a farmer driving in a wagon. He, seeing that they were boys and must be hungry, threw some bread on the ground, which the boys eagerly picked up and ate. When they arrived in Lancaster they found the town to consist of only a few houses. They then traveled to the neighborhood of Litiz, where they lived until grown up, when John married a daughter of John Martin Amweg. He then settled about 3 miles north of Manheim, where he bought a mill on the Big Chiques creek, at present in the possesion of Moses Light. When the Revolutionary war broke out he refused to take up arms, having conscientious scruples, being a member of the Mennonite church. The officers searched the mill for him; he, however, made his escape to the hills. They finally gave up the chase and left. In 1778, on the 15th of November, was born his son, Martin Stauffer, who is still living, having just entered his 94th year, and is with his daughter, Mrs. Henry Snavely.

STAUFFER, JACOB. The subject of this memoir was born in Manheim, in the county of Lancaster, Pa., on the 30th day of November, 1808. He received a common country school education, and was early put behind the counter by his father, who kept both store and tavern, during his minority. He manifested quite a taste for drawing and painting in his youth, and great fondness for military display. A retired graduate of West Point, boarding with his father, took quite an interest in him, and gave him lessons; indeed, almost a regular West Point course. Owing to this, Col. Jacob Hostetter appointed him adjutant, May, 1825, of the 18th regiment Pennsylvania militia. He subsequently was elected first major, and on the expiration of Col. Hostetter's term, young as he was, he was almost unanimously elected colonel, without an effort on his part. After attaining the age of twenty-one he left his native village for Philadelphia, and made the acquaintance of the elder Sulley, Inman, and others, artists and engravers, and took lessons in oil painting and drawing. But, as his father did not approve of his course, and having no resources to sustain him while acquiring proficiency as an artist, he got a clerkship, first in the counting house of Mr. S. Eckstein, and afterwards in the recording office of Philadelphia, during which time he took to himself a wife. After spending a few years in Philadelphia, he removed to his native village, where he opened a store, and subsequently introduced the first printing press in Manheim, adding a job office to his mercantile pursuit. Having devoted much of his studies to medicine and botany, he gradually sold off his stock of goods and entered more especially into the drug business. He exchanged his Manheim property for one at what was then called "Richland cross-roads," in 1840, now incorporated in the borough of Mount Joy, at which place he also introduced the first printing press, as well as a lithographic press, and the art of taking daguerreotypes. These various pursuits were insufficient to keep him fully employed, so that he devoted much of his time to botany and natural science. His great love and facility of illustrating plants, insects, &c., occupied much of his time, and it is surprising to behold the immense number of illustrations, many very life-like and admirably drawn and colored, so that it is difficult to find a plant or insect that he has not figured. He was called on for writing agreements, deeds, specifications, and to make drawings for his neighbors. He was a useful member in the council and school board, as

well as in the church and Sabbath school, during his stay at
Mt. Joy. He wrote quite a number of articles for various
monthlies, on subjects connected with agriculture, botany,
and entomology especially, embracing much original matter,
and generally well received and highly appreciated.

It was during one of his botanical rambles he made the
discovery of the parasitism of a certain plant known as the
Comandra umbellatta, as also of several species of *Gerardia*,
being in frequent correspondence with Professor A. Gray, of
Harvard University. The Doctor published the result of
this discovery in Silliman's Journal, vol. xvi, No. 47, p. 250,
for Sept., 1853. He also received a highly complimentary
letter from Professor Joseph Henry, of the Smithsonian
Institute, with a donation of many valuable publications to
which he became entitled under Mr. Smithson's will. He
was urged to publish his figures, with a description, by
Prof. Gray. He accordingly set up the type in pamphlet
form, of his own manuscript, made the drawings on stone
and lithographed and printed the illustrations and letter
press, and stitched the same, without the aid of any other
party. Rev. Dr. Morris, of Baltimore, to whom a pamphlet
was sent, in answer acknowledging its reception, observed
that "he knew of no other *savan* except Mr. Sturm, of Nurem-
berg, who could write, set up, illustrate and print his own
work." One of these pamphlets is on file in the Academy of
Natural Science of Philadelphia, of which he has for years
been a corresponding member. His oldest son started the
Mount Joy *Herald*, in 1854, assisted by him, in which there
are weekly articles on botany, illustrated by neat wood cuts,
drawn and engraved by himself, giving much valuable and
interesting information, drawn from an extensive library of
botanical works. He wound up his affairs at Mount Joy
and moved to Lancaster in the spring of 1858, devoting his
time more especially to the procuring of patents. As a
solicitor he was quite successful, and no doubt stimulated
the inventive faculties of many by the announcement of
patents procured through his aid.

During the first few years, he had his office in the library
rooms of the Lancaster Athenæum, of which he had the

charge, but this he was forced to abandon, as his business increased to such a degree that he could but now and then write articles for the press; yet, being called upon, he would respond; so that to enumerate the monthlies and weeklies in which his articles appeared, would form a lengthy list; suffice it to say, that without any pretensions, and too apt to depreciate his own acquirements, his writings and illustrations are a proof of his industry, as the number would seem to require a lifetime alone to execute. In a letter from Prof. E. D. Cope, of Philadelphia, which came under the observation of the writer, he says: "Thee would have been encouraged in thy zoological studies, no doubt, in finding the number of species thee has added to the fauna of Pennsylvania;" then follows a list of hard names, hardly edifying if repeated. Very few of his most intimate friends have any idea of the extent of his labors; yet, it is acknowledged by all who know him, that he is well versed in almost every branch of science; and if a strange plant or insect is found, and a name wanted for it, you are usually advised to "go to Stauffer, he can tell you." His devotion to hunt and roam over the hills, valleys, swamps and by-ways, in search of something new, and when found, the habit of figuring it, of course, gave him opportunities for acqiuring a fund of information during a period of fifty years of study. On asking him why he never published a book, his reply was, "I first wished to know what I knew that was not known before," as a repetition of the old story was a species of drudgery for which he had no taste, however cunningly he might disguise it; "besides, such books as some men compile are no credit to them. I have purchased such, and found nothing new and no improvement on works previously written on the same subject; this has admonished me to be cautious." It is to be hoped that one of his sons will collect the numerous notes and observations scattered in manuscript in connection with his illustrations on various subjects, at no distant day. Either of them would be qualified for the task; his oldest son is a distinguished writer, while the youngest is a distinguished civil engineer, and has in charge the bridge now being built across the Schuylkill, South street, Philadelphia.

Mr. Stauffer has been three times married, and perhaps there are few men who have been more affectionate and devoted in their domestic relations. He is a man singularly disinterested and morally pure, practically recognizing the sanctity of the family union, as husband, father, instructor and friend. Few men possess a greater versatility of talent, and few have labored so long, so incessantly, and so little influenced by the desire of pecuniary reward. Few have been more willing to communicate what they know on any subject, without compensation, even where it has cost him much time and labor, and in many instances has drawn on his own pecuniary means. He seems to have labored much from a love of labor, and without seeming to be impressed with the idea that he had accomplished anything of very special merit. His ability to take up and adapt himself to almost any branch of science and philosophy, has, perhaps, produced that diversity which prevented the acquisition of that marked distinction, which would have resulted in recompense and fame in a special field. He seems to have lacked that love of gain which leads men to concentrate their energies in a special channel, for the mere purpose of *making it pay*. Always a man of limited means, yet he was habitually benevolent and liberal almost to a fault. When he desired and felt that he needed a book or an instrument to assist him in those studies and experiments to which his leisure hours were devoted, he never denied himself or caviled at prices, if the subject came within the limit of his pecuniary abilities; hence, he never was to any considerable extent a borrower, and accordingly has accumulated a large and valuable library of books, maps, charts and manuscripts, for a man in his circumstances. In common with frail humanity he may commit errors of the *head*, but those most intimately associated with him are loth to believe that he would wilfully commit an error of the heart, or that his word is of less value than his bond. Reasonably affable and social in his nature, he yet never was the man to obtrude himself where he had rational ground to suspect his presence would not be welcome or agreeable. Although peaceably and harmoniously inclined, yet when aroused he had the moral and physical courage to resist imposition; and in a tournament with the pen he has the faculty of detecting exposed points, and dealing effective thrusts, although it cannot be said that he is habitually controversial. He is firm in his moral and religious convictions, but not more firm than sincere, and does not seem to be solicitous as to whether his views are in strict accord with the most literal systems of popular ortho-doxy, although he does not profess to be heterodox. He is by no means a man of worldly aspirations, although not a recluse, or indifferent about what is going on in the world. He is one of the few men we find in society who are free from those prejudices which are engendered and fostered by religious, political and social clans, parties, sects and cliques; hence many of his warmest friendships are among those who differ with him radically in politics, religion and philosophy. Although he might tolerate on a civil plane, yet he could never affiliate with the impure, the obscene, or the profane; or for the sake of pleasing men alone, forget his higher rela-tions to his Creator.

STEACY, DAVID G., was born in Bart[1] township, Lancas-ter county, Pa., April 23d, 1824. His father, Benjamin Steacy, emigrated from Ireland in the early part of the pres-.ent century, and settled in Bart township. He was a man in humble circumstances, and raised a large family. He was simply a laboring man, and his son, the subject of this notice,

---

[1]William McClure was born in Scotland in the year 1698, and emi-grated to Lancaster county early in the last century, and was among the earliest and most respectable settlers of Bart township. His wife had emigrated with her friends from Ireland in the year 1734, and first set-tled at John Harris's Ferry on the Susquehanna, when Harris's house constituted the town of Harrisburg; but she having fled from the savages, finally settled in Lancaster county and was joined in marriage with William McClure, who purchased a large tract of land in Chester valley, most of which was held by his descendants for nearly one hun-dred years, and a part thereof is yet owned by one of his grandsons. He had three sons, viz: William, John and Thomas. William and John served in the army of the Revolution, and their team and wagon was engaged in the public service; one of them had his musket knocked from his hands by a ball, and his hat perforated with one or more bul-lets. After the war, they returned to their farms in the valley, where they spent the remainder of their eventful lives. John resided near a place called the Green Tree, and departed this life in the year 1838, aged

was obliged when but eighteen years of age to take charge of the family affairs and manage the same. He soon entered into speculative enterprises, having the favor of some men of capital and influence, which resulted in success. When young, he became noted for the interest he took in debating societies, and he gained some notice as a debator. He always took a lively interest in politics, first as an old line Whig, and afterwards as a Republican, of which party he is still a member. He has for many years stood amongst the leaders of this party in the county. He has ever been a great friend of the policy of American protection. In the fall of 1867 he was elected a member of the Legislature, and reëlected again to a second term in 1868.

STEELE, ARCHIBALD, a brother of Gen. John Steele, was a man of great intrepidity and resolute daring. Upon the breaking out of the Revolution he and a man named Smith raised a company in Lancaster county and marched to Boston, where they were organized into a regiment and placed under the command of Benedict Arnold. This was the regiment that made the celebrated march through the wilderness of Maine to Quebec, in the winter of 1775, which has ever been remembered as one memorable in the annals of American history. During this march Archibald Steele had the command of a party of men who were selected to go before

81 years, leaving six sons and one daughter, who are all living at the present time, the average of whose ages now exceeds 74 years. The family and descendants of William McClure have ever been considered as among the most highly respectable and influential members of the old Octoraro church, in the township of Bart. He departed this life in the year 1768, aged 70 years. His widow, who survived him for more than half a century, departed this life at the present residence of Joseph McClure (her grandson), in the year 1828, aged 108 years, 2 months and 29 days. Their descendants are still numerous and respectable in the neighborhood. Among their great-grandsons are Samuel, David, Thomas, Joseph, Robert Spencer and William McClure, of Bart ; and also Francis McClure, of Salisbury. Joseph McClure, who was elected a member of the Legislature in the years 1840 and 1841, is the youngest son of John McClure, and the grandson of William McClure, sr. He owns and occupies the old homestead, near the Green Tree, in Bart, and is a worthy and leading member of the community in which he lives, and of the Associate Presbyterian church, of which the Rev. William Easton, from Scotland, has been the pastor for more than 40 years.

the army and mark out the roads and crossing places; and on the arrival of the army at the St. Lawrence he was appointed superintendent of the crossing of the river. At the head of his company Steele marched with the army to the attack upon Quebec, but upon the fall of Gen. Montgomery the Americans retreated, and Arnold's division were all taken prisoners. He was badly wounded in the left hand, two of his fingers having been carried away by a musket shot. The following may be cited as showing the heroic daring of Capt. Archibald Steele: On one occasion as the Americans were crossing a river in bark canoes, these were filled to their utmost capacity with men, and Capt. Steele seeing no room in the canoe leaped into the river, rested his hands on the stern of the boat whilst one of the men therein sat upon them, and thus was he dragged through the floating ice to the opposite shore. When they reached the shore, life was almost extinct; the soldiers wrapped him in their blankets, and rolled him over the ground to infuse new life in him. On his return home from the Quebec expedition he met the American army in New Jersey, and was informed by Gen. Hand that two of his brothers, John Steele and Wm. Steele, were then serving with the army. Capt. Archibald Steele asked Gen. Hand if he thought his brother John would be competent to assume the command of a company (being but eighteen years of age.) Hand replied that he would warrant his qualification, and the commission was procured. Archibald Steele was afterwards appointed deputy quartermaster general, a position he retained for some considerable time. He was appointed by Washington colonel of a western expedition, but sickness prevented the acceptance of this command. He held for some time in Philadelphia his position of military storekeeper. He died in Philadelphia in 1832, aged 91 years. He had three sons in the naval service during the war of 1812 (George, William and Matthias), who were captured, taken to England, and there for a time detained as prisoners of war.

STEELE, GENERAL JAMES, son of William and Abigail Steele, was born in Sadsbury township about the commencement of the Revolutionary war. During the war of 1812 he was, for meritorious conduct, promoted to the rank of brigadier general. Prior to the war he had erected a paper mill on the east side of the Octoraro. His residence was on the Chester county side of the creek, while his store, with part of his family and most of his improvements, were on the Lancaster county side. He erected two cotton mills in Sadsbury township, about the year 1818. He was an enterprising business man. He was a Presbyterian, yet his wife and some of his family inclined to the Methodist faith. He died about 1840, at an advanced age. His son, Francis B. Steele, was appointed military storekeeper at the Falls of St. Anthony, in Minnesota, under the administration of President Jackson, in which State several of the family now reside.

STEELE, GENERAL JOHN, was born in Drumore township, Lancaster county, in the year 1758. His parents had emigrated from Scotland, and settled in that part of the county at an early day. His parents had designed him for the ministry, and with this end in view had placed him under the instruction of the Rev. Mr. James, a Presbyterian clergyman, and upon the breaking out of the Revolution he was reading divinity with the Rev. Mr. Latta. He immediately joined the American army as a private, being then but eighteen years of age, and at the age of nineteen, having shown his valor, he was given the command of a company. He continued in the service of his country during the whole of the Revolution. He received a severe wound in the abdomen at the battle of Brandywine, from the effects of which he came near losing his life. Upon the conclusion of the war of the Revolution he returned to civil life, having the fixed habits of military life and little qualified for business; and yet though one of his arms was disabled from a wound received in the service, he refused a pension when in his reach, and battled for the means of subsistence as best he could. In 1801 he was elected a member of the Legislature, the duties of which he discharged during one session. The following year he was nominated and elected by the Republican (Democratic) party State Senator of Pennsylvania. By virtue of the act of 15th of February,

1799, which seemed to preclude a Senator from occupying certain offices by appointment, the Senate declared the seat of General Steele vacant in 1803, and on the 16th of February, 1804, an election was ordered to fill the vacancy. His friends, however, believing that there was no valid constitutional objections to his taking his seat in the Senate, resolved to use their best efforts to secure his reëlection. He was accordingly elected Senator without any serious opposition, and was admitted to his seat. On the resignation of Robert Whitehill, Speaker of the Senate in March, 1805, General Steele was elected Speaker of that body. He was again, in December of the same year, the Republican candidate for Speaker of that body, but as his party was now in the minority he was not elected. Again in December, 1806, he was the candidate of his party for United States Senator, and tied Andrew Gregg on three ballots before the joint convention of the Senate and House of Representatives. An adjournment was now carried, and when the convention reassembled, his competitor, Andrew Gregg, was elected.

He was one of the commissioners who were appointed to adjust the damages sustained by the Wyoming sufferers at the hands of the Indians. He was, in 1808, appointed by President Jefferson, collector of the port of Philadelphia, a position he held during the remainder of his life. He died February 27th, 1827. The following is from *Poulson's Advertiser:* "On Wednesday last the flag of the custom house, and those of the shipping, in port, were suspended at half mast as a mark of respect to the memory of General Steele. He was an officer of the Revolutionary army, and served for many years as collector of the port of Philadelphia. In his death we are deprived of a useful citizen, whose character for integrity and benevolence will be long and deservedly remembered."

STEELE, WILLIAM, JR., son of William Steele, sr., was one of the early and staunch advocates of American independence. He was appointed one of the lieutenants for Lancaster county during the Revolution, and took an active and efficient part in the struggle. He was married to Abigail, a sister of Francis Baily, esq., of Sadsbury. After the close of the Revolution, he was appointed one of the magistrates of Lancaster county, a position he held until about the year 1812.

STEELE, WILLIAM, SR., was a prominent man among the early settlers of Sadsbury township. He obtained a warrant for a large tract of land west of the Octoraro, in the southern part of the township.. He was an influential member of the old Presbyterian church at Octoraro. He was chosen captain of one of the associated companies of the Lancaster county militia in the year 1756, at the time of the Indian and French war.

STEHMAN, JOHN M., a banker[1] of Lancaster, was elected a member of the Legislature in 1860. He was again re-elected to the same office in the years 1865 and 1866. He is also engaged in agricultural pursuits.

STEIGEL, WM. HENRY, generally known as Baron Steigel, was a native of Manheim, Germany. He emigrated to America and became associated with the Messrs. Stedman, of Philadelphia, who were Englishmen of great wealth, and who owned the land upon which the town of Manheim in

[1]There is no stronger evidence of the growing wealth of the people of Lancaster county, than the great change in its banking business, when we compare the past with the present. For a long time there were but four banks in the city, one in Columbia, and one in Marietta ; the latter was in existence but a short time, having to suspend operations. The oldest institution, theF armers' Bank, was incorporated in 1810; next the Lancaster Bank, incorporated in 1814, which suspended in 1856; the Lancaster County Bank, incorporated in 1841; and the office of Discount and Deposit, a branch of the Bank of Pennsylvania, which was compelled to wind up its business on account of the suspension of the mother bank in Philadelphia; the Lancaster Savings Institution, incorporated in 1835 or 1836 enjoyed, to a large extent, the confidence of the people, and had a heavy line of deposits, but was compelled to suspend in 1856; the next incorporated savings institution, was the Inland Insurance and Deposit Company, incorporated in 1854, which at one time carried a good line of insurance, but of late years has confined its operations more particularly to banking.

Private bankers now occupy a very prominent place in our financial circles, and this line of business was first started by George K. Reed and John F. Shroder, in 1850. Ever since that time Mr. Reed has been engaged in the banking business, and is now an active member of the old firm of Reed, McGrann & Co. Some years afterwards Reed, Henderson & Co. commenced operations; next John Gyger & Co., the firm now

Lancaster county is built. Steigel came to Lancaster county about 1758, and purchased from the Stedmans the one-third interest of a tract of 714 acres, and immediately thereafter built Elizabeth furnace, named in honor of his wife. He now laid out a town which he named Manheim,[1] in honor of his native city in Germany. The town was laid out as per plan of the European Manheim, which Steigel had brought with him from Germany. He built his chateau with brick, imported from England, and arranged it in the manner of a nobleman's castle. One of the rooms of his castle was ornamented with paintings representing an equestrian hawking party, of life-size figures. The antique and curiously wrought massive ceilings yet indicate the expense and labor bestowed upon the dwelling.[2] Over the old-fashioned fireplace are square plates of delf set in cement, representing landscapes. The baron lived in his wilderness home and sustained for a time the pomp and luxuriance of a nobleman. Upon the top of his castle was a balcony upon which a band of musicians would take their position and' play favorite airs as soon as the Baron's return home from a

dissolved. These have been succeeded by Bair & Shenk; Stehman, Clarkson & Co.; R. A. Evans & Co., the firm now dissolved; D. P. Locher & Son; J. B. Long; Diffenderffer & Bros.; Eshleman & Rathvon; and A. K. Spurrier & Co. In the county : The Farmers' Bank of Elizabethtown; Litiz Deposit and Columbia Deposit Banks, are also private institutions. After the passage of the National Banking law, all of the old State corporations were compelled to accept' its provisions if they wished to continue their circulation. It was also the means of starting up quite a number of new institutions. The following are the national banks in the county : Farmers' National Bank of Lancaster; Lancaster County National Bank; First National Bank of Lancaster; Columbia National Bank; First National Bank of Columbia; First National Bank of Marietta; First National Bank of Strasburg; First National Bank of Mount Joy; Union National Bank of Mount Joy; and Manheim National Bank. Almost every village in the county can now boast of its banking facilities.

[1] The land upon which Manheim is built was taken up in 1734 by James Logan, whose daughter married a Mr. Norris, and he sold it to the Stedmans of Philadelphia.

[2] The Baron's house was for years in the possession of John Arndt, a merchant of Manheim, not long since deceased, and who in repairing it made such alterations in it as leaves little to be seen that recalls the name of Steigel, save the room above cited with the paintings.

journey would be announced by the firing of a canon stationed some distance from the castle. In one of the upper rooms of his house or castle it was the Baron's custom to preach to his laboring hands on Sunday.

The Baron erected glass works to give encouragement to the inhabitants whom he desired to attract to his new town. These works for many years were carried on successfully by Steigel, and turned out great quantities of glass articles. He carried on both the glass works and the Elizabeth furnace for several years. He, however, exceeded in the end the limits of his ability in a financial point of view. He purchased the whole of the Stedman interest in the property, and being unable ever to liquidate the payments for the same he failed, and his property was all sold by the sheriff. He was also imprisoned for the debt in the Lancaster county jail, and an act of the Pennsylvania Legislature was, in 1774, passed for his relief and liberation. After his failure Steigel taught school in the German districts of Lancaster and Berks counties, and was somewhat supported by the iron-masters who came into possession of Elizabeth furnace, and who commiserated him in his misfortunes. He died in great indigence, and though his place of burial is unknown, yet he is thought to be laid somewhere east of Elizabeth furnace, near the line between Berks and Lancaster counties. Upon the breaking out of the American Revolution Steigel's aristocratic feelings led him to espouse the cause of King George, and one of his sons raised a company for the royal service. His company being severely pressed for provisions, young Steigel pledged his gold watch to a farmer for a bullock, and whether the story be mythical or not, his watch is yet said to be in the possession of a gentleman in Lancaster county.

STEINMAN, JOHN FREDERICK, one of the early citizens of Lancaster borough, and the ancestor of the highly respectable family of this name. He was a native of Germany, and emigrated from a small town near Berlin at an early day. He began the hardware business about the year 1762, at the place where his descendants have continued the same for one hundred and ten years. He was the first who began this branch of trade in Lancaster, starting it rather in the tinware line, and afterwards developing it into the regular hardware business. He had two sons, John Frederick and George M., the former of whom is yet living at the advanced age of eighty-three years. John Frederick Steinman, last named, was a leading and successful business man, and for many years an influential member of city councils and the Lancaster school board. General George M. Steinman, son of the latter, is one of the leading business men of Lancaster city, and a man of considerable intellectual capacity. He is besides, a man of inventive ingenuity, and the one who some years since invented for the city reservoir the plan which, by means of a floating ball, attached by a chain to the water pipe, prevented the mud and other filth from entering the pipes and being carried through the city. This was an invention which at the time was of vast utility. He served for many years as a member of city councils and as a member of the school board. In 1862 he was the candidate of the Democratic party for Congress in opposition to Thaddeus Stevens. He yet carries on the business started by his grandfather.

    *STEVENS, THADDEUS. When a man of peculiar qualifications is required to push the world onward towards the good time coming, when the lion and the lamb shall lie down together, and a little child shall lead them, Providence always furnishes an instrument adapted to the work. History is full of such cases. Sometimes the chosen one seems to come forth like Minerva from the hand of Jove, fully developed and equipped at all points for the work. At other times it would appear that a long course of vigorous training is required to fit the destined leader for his work. Moses spent the first forty years of his life in the most learned, the most luxurious, the most dissolute court then existing. In this period he learned to know men, their virtues, and their vices. Forty years more tending sheep in the solitudes of vast plains and rugged mountains, gave him leisure to think over, to fully comprehend the power and use of the knowledge he had before acquired. It was in this way he was

    *Contributed by Alexander H. Hood, esq.

made capable of becoming the leader and law-giver of the only people who retained the knowledge of the facts and principles on which only the highest civilization is possible: the law of the Eternal, Invisible, All-powerful Intelligence, which made and sustains the universe, material and spiritual.

In our own time we have seen numerous instances of Providential selection and preparation. No other man than Abraham Lincoln could have abolished slavery so effectually as he did. His slow, cautious mode of dealing with the question, prevented all hazard of failure from premature attempts. At the beginning of the war Grant never dreamed that he was the man destined to end the rebellion. Up to this time he had not been a prosperous man. Fortune, in almost every instance, seemed to baffle his exertions. Most probably it was from this very circumstance that he acquired that persistence of purpose which afterwards made his success so thoroughly complete.

Lincoln finished his alloted task, and in fire and blood was called to his reward. Grant still remains, because his distinguishing quality may be still further needed. Without the crowning victories of Grant, Lincoln's proclamation of freedom would have remained a dead letter. Without the reconstruction measures of Stevens, the South in a few years would, through the agency of its legislative bodies, have nullified all the good which the proclamation of Lincoln and the victories of Grant had given the nation power to establish. To give a history of this man as fully as can be done within the small space to which this article is limited, is the task which the writer has undertaken.

Thaddeus Stevens was born in the town of Danville, Caledonia county, Vermont, on the 4th day of April, 1792. Of his father but little is known, beyond the facts that he was a man of rather dissipated habits, and a great wrestler, able to throw down any man in the county. In the war of 1812 he enlisted as a soldier, and in the attack on Oswego received a bayonet wound in the groin, of which he died a few days afterwards. His mother, of whom he never wearied in talking, was a woman of strong natural sense and unconquerable resolution. Her maiden name was Morrell, and the great

40

object of her life was to give her sons a good education. In this effort she was successful. The eldest became a judge in Illinois; Alanson, the second son, was a practicing physician of high reputation at the time of his death. Another, the third of the brothers, became a farmer, and was a gentleman of intelligence and culture. Thaddeus, the youngest, was the one on whom she placed the greatest share of her affections. There was a valid, natural reason, for this. The boy, though healthy, was in some degree deformed. He had a club foot, and doubtless required greater attention than the others. . From the little that can now be gathered as to the relations between him and his mother, it is very clear that he was the Joseph of the family.

His first journey into the world was in 1804, when he went with his parents to Boston, on a visit to some relations. He very seldom alluded to this trip, though from what he did say about it, the inference to be drawn is, that he came to a resolution to become rich and live like the wealthy men did there. This resolution, however, seemed to have little effect upon his after-life, for there never was a man who cared less for money to be spent upon himself. It may be that it was at this time he began to understand that money was the power by which men were ruled, but it seems scarcely possible that one so young could have arrived at this conclusion. He was, however, a genuine Yankee, and in poor countries, like Vermont was then, taken in connection with his knowledge that all he could ever hope to be, must depend upon himself, it may be that it was then that some of the prominent characteristics of his nature were developed. That it was at this time he determined to make his mark in the world, is certain. The year after this, the spotted fever prevailed to an alarming degree in Caledonia. For miles around his home there was scarcely a family in which one or more were not stricken down. In many houses all were sick, and it was almost impossible to obtain help. In this state of things Mrs. Stevens turned nurse, and went to the help of her neighbors, taking young Thaddeus along with her. Among the families they visited there was no little suffering, and the recollection of this fact operated in after-life to make him always very kindly disposed to the sick and the poor. To such, up to the end of his life, when he knew of their wants, he was always a ministering angel. Often, it is true, he would rail at men for their vices, their want of industry and care, and yet it often seemed he was more kind to this class of persons than to those who had never been guilty of such imprudence. Many of his good works of this kind were done in secret, no one knowing anything about them except himself and the party benefited. Those who asked for his charity he never refused when he had money; when his pockets were empty, as was sometimes the case, he would never admit the fact, but justify his refusal by bringing forward the unworthiness of the applicant. Those who knew the real reason of his conduct, were often considerably amused at the seriousness with which he would lecture the applicant on such occasions.

That his father was a shoemaker is known, but he did not work steadily at the business. Thaddeus, though his opportunities were not great, had still a chance to pick up a little of the trade. Certain it is, that after his father's death, and perhaps before it, he made the shoes of the family, and perhaps some for a few of the neighbors. In his younger years, when first a candidate for the Legislature, he used to boast of being a shoemaker; and the writer has seen men who averred that they had worked with him in the same shop, but this was not true. Certain it is, that he never did anything of the sort in Pennsylvania.

During his early years Mr. Stevens was a most diligent reader of everything that came into his hands. Books, at that time, were not very numerous in Peacham, where he then lived. When he was about fifteen he tried the experiment of founding a library, which it is said still exists, having grown considerably in size since his day. About this time, like all Yankee boys who desire an education, he began to teach school, and, it is said, was quite a successful teacher. On September 11th, 1814, he was a student at Burlington college, for on that day he saw, with a spy-glass, the fight between McDonough and the British fleet on Lake Champlain. For some reason he did not graduate at this college, but at Dartmouth in the following year. Perhaps the following circumstance, which is taken from the relation of Stevens himself, may have had something to do with the change.

The campus at Burlington college was not enclosed, and the cows of the citizens used to enjoy it as a pleasant pasture ground. Before commencement, it was usual to give the people notice to keep their cows away till after commencement was over. The grounds were then cleared up, and everything kept in complete order till the exercises were ended and the students gone to their homes. It happened that among the citizens of Burlington was a man, "a stubborn fellow, whom," as Stevens said, "we shall call Jones." He would take no steps to keep his cows off the campus. One night, about a week before the day of commencement, Stevens and a friend were walking under the trees in front of the college, when they saw one of Jones' cows within the prohibited lines. They knew the cow belonged to Jones; they knew Jones let her go there in a spirit of defiance to the students. After some discussion, it was agreed to kill the cow.

Among the students was a young man who kept himself aloof from most of the others. In a word, he had the reputation of being decidedly pious. This young man had a room in an out-house belonging to the college, where in spare moments he manufactured many things out of wood, which he sold to the people of the town and to others. Among other tools, he was known to have an axe, and Stevens and his companion determined to use it in the execution of the cow. The axe was procured, the cow was slain, the axe returned, and the two avengers of the college dignity retired to rest. The next morning Jones was with the president making complaint about the death of his cow. An investigation was at once begun; blood was found on the axe of the pious, well-behaved student; he denied the charge, but as there was no evidence against any other person, he was threatened with a public reprimand and expulsion on the day on which he had expected to graduate with high honors. No doubt the young man suffered much, but Stevens and his associate suffered much more. They dare not inform against themselves, yet they could not see an innocent person punished for their misconduct. What was to be done? After many conferences, without any result, Stevens suggested that Jones was not a bad man, but rather a high-spirited fellow, who would help them out of the scrape if they would throw themselves upon his mercy. This they resolved to do. It was the night before commencement day, when they had their interview with Jones. They made a clean breast of it, and offered to pay twice the value of the cow whenever they should be able to do so. Jones listened kindly; told them not to distress themselves about the price of the cow, and said he would fix it all next morning. True to his word, about 9 o'clock Jones appeared just before the proceedings were to begin; told the professors that he was all wrong about the death of his cow, and that she had been killed by soldiers who were going down the river on a boat, and had no time to dress and remove the meat. This made all things right; the pious young man was not expelled, but honorably acquitted of the charge. Stevens and his friend were never suspected. Some years afterwards, when Stevens was rising in the world, Mr. Jones received a draft for the price of the best sort of cow in the market, accompanied by a fine gold watch and chain by way of interest. A year or two afterwards there came to Gettysburg, directed to Mr. Stevens, a hogshead of the best Vermont cider, and this was the end of the killing of Jones' cow.

It cannot now be ascertained with certainty what profession Mr. Stevens originally intended to adopt. In arguing predestination with one who is an Arminian, he evinced such an intimate acquaintance with the theological writers of the Calvinistic school, that the friend said: "Stevens, did you ever study with a view to the pulpit?" The answer was: "Umph! I have read the books." This is all that is known about it.

Mr. Stevens made his appearance in Pennsylvania, at York, about the end of 1815, where he obtained a situation as teacher in an academy, of which Dr. Perkins was the principal. Amos Gilbert, a very celebrated teacher, then residing at York, said that Stevens was at that time one of the most backward, retiring, modest young men he had ever seen, and that he was a remarkably hard student. This is the only fact as to the period of his stay at York the writer has been able to ascertain. Soon after leaving the academy he made application for admission to the bar at Gettysburg, but owing to the fact that he had not read law under the instruction of a gentleman learned in the law, for two years, as required by the rule of court, he was rejected. At that time Maryland admitted all applicants to the bar who, on examination, were found to be qualified. Mr. Stevens went to Bel Air, where the court was in session, and made application to be examined. The court, Judge Chase, of impeachment fame, appointed a committee, of which the chairman was General Winder. Stevens' description of the examination is well worth preserving:

Supper was over, the table was cleared off, and the clock said it was half-past seven. Stevens was, of course, punctual to time, and shortly after, the judge and the committee took their seats. "Are you the young man who is to be examined?" said the judge. Stevens replied that he was. "Mr. Stevens," said the judge, "there is one indispensable pre-requisite before the examination can proceed. There must be two bottles of Madeira on the table, and the applicant must order it in." The order was given, the wine brought forward, and its quality thoroughly tested. Gen. Winder began with: "Mr. Stevens, what books have you read?" Stevens replied, "Blackstone, Coke upon Littleton, a work on pleading, and Gilbert on evidence." This was followed by two or three other questions by other members of the committee, the last of which required the distinction between a contingent remainder and an executory devise, which was satisfactorily answered. By this time the judge was feeling a little dry again, and broke in saying: "Gentlemen, you see the young man is all right, I'll give him a certificate." This was soon made out and signed, but before it was handed over, two more bottles had to be produced. These were partaken of by a large number of squires, &c., who were there attending court, who, as soon as the examination was concluded, came in and were introduced to the newly-made member of the bar. "Fip-loo" was played then for a good part of the night. Stevens was then a green hand at the business. To use his own words, when he paid his bill the next morning, he had but $3.50 left out of the $45 he began with the night before.

He left early, rode fast, and while crossing McCall's ferry bridge, not then finished, he had a very narrow escape from death. His horse took fright, and would have fallen into the river with his rider, had it not been for the presence of mind of one of the men working on the bridge. He dined that day in Lancaster, at Slough's hotel, and while his horse was resting, walked from one end of King street to the other. He did not feel pleased with the town, and while thus engaged came to the conclusion he would go back to Gettysburg. That night he staid at York, and the next day began his legal career, with but few friends and very little money.

It was a considerable time before he obtained any business of importance, and he became quite discouraged. At a dance at Littlestown, he told a friend he could hold out no longer, that he would have to seek another location. A day or two after, a horrible murder was committed, and none of the prominent lawyers seemed willing to undertake the defence. Stevens was retained, and exerted himself to the utmost in behalf of his client, but without success. The man was convicted and executed. Many years after, Mr. Stevens said that he had been counsel for the defence in more than fifty murder cases, in all of which but one he had been successful, adding, that every one of them deserved hanging except the one that was hanged, who was certainly insane. This case brought Mr. Stevens a fee of $1500, and this was the beginning of his fortune.

Mr. Stevens rose at once to celebrity as a lawyer. He was up to 1831 engaged in nearly all the great cases tried in Adams, York, Franklin and Cumberland counties. During this period a large number of colored people, illegally held by persons claiming their services as slaves, were liberated by his exertions. When the law could not avail, he used to buy and set them free. At one time when coming from the

Hagerstown races, he stopped at a tavern, the landlord of which had been "cleaned out," and had no resource but to sell one of his *boys*. There was already a trader haggling about the price when Stevens arrived. The owner wanted $500, the trader offered four hundred. While this was going on, Stevens was so strongly impressed with the boy's resemblance to the landlord, that he called him aside and asked why he was going to sell the boy to a trader. The landlord said he did not like to do it, but he had been so very unfortunate at the races, that he must make a raise some way or other. Stevens, finding that the owner would rather not sell the boy, proposed to buy him for his own use. After talking it over, Stevens saying he would set the boy free at twenty-one years, a bargain was made for $350. When the bill of sale was being made out, Stevens asked what name he should give the boy? Observing the landlord looking confused, and red in the face, Stevens said, "Oh, I'll put your name in; these fellows always goes by the name of their owners." "I saw," Stevens remarked, "he was the landlord's own son, or I never should have bought him for $350." Stevens kept him about four years and then gave him a fair start to make his own living.

Until 1829 when the Anti-Masonic excitement swept over Pennsylvania, Mr. Stevens took but little part in politics. It no where appears that in the elections from 1817 to that period, he was in any degree prominent. The reason for this seems to have been, that being a Federalist, and the party going downward, he could not find a cause in which to exert his energies. He once told the writer, that the last intercourse he had with Buchanan, was at York, in 1827. They had both been engaged on the same side in the trial of a cause, and when the jury were out they walked down a lane some distance from the town and took a seat on the top-rail of the fence. Buchanan began the discourse by saying to Stevens, that now was the time for a man of ability to enter into politics, and suggested that Stevens would do well to come into the support of Jackson. Stevens answered by saying, that he saw the advantages of such a course, but for his part he was ashamed to forsake his old opinions, which he believed to be right, for the sake of joining a party in which he had no faith. This was the last time they met for many years. In 1867 they met at the wedding of Dr. Henry Carpenter, the friend of both. Stevens approached Buchanan holding out his hand. Buchanan turned aside as though he did not see the offer, and entered into conversation with some one he met as he turned. During all these years they had never met. A year afterwards both were in their graves.

In 1831 Mr. Stevens began his political career as a member of the Assembly from Adams county. The session was nearly over before he said anything which excited marked attention. He then made a speech reviewing the course of the Jackson party and its leaders, which at once placed him in the front rank of the ablest men of the State. This revelation of ability, with his strict adherence to his proclaimed principles, drew upon him the enmity of his opponents, and for many years he was the target at which their most venomous shafts were directed. The members of the Masonic order regarded him as little less than a devil incarnate. Democrats, not belonging to the order, were equally bitter against him. The deformity of his foot was seized upon to spread the idea of his connection with the prince of the fallen angels. Those who read the Democratic journals of that time, will see that no man was ever so foully abused. He was charged with all manner of evil, and men who said a word in his favor were regarded as little less devilish than himself. Such was his reputation up to 1835, when an attempt was made to repeal the school law, passed at the previous session by a nearly unanimous vote. The fact that it seemed to impose a new tax was seized upon by both parties, and each fearing the other might gain advantage by being foremost in its denunciation, made all possible haste to declaim against it. When the bill was called up in the House, it seemed as though no one would say a word in favor of the then existing law. Speech after speech was delivered in favor of the repeal, and the question was on the point of being put, when Mr. Stevens rose to speak. He was terribly earnest. All his powers were roused to the utmost. Those

41

who heard him, say he spoke like a prophet inspired by the truth and magnitude of his theme. In ten minutes it seemed as though all opposition to the schools was utterly vanquished. When the vote was taken the bill was defeated by a large majority. This speech placed the school system of Pennsylvania upon an impregnable basis. No man was ever afterwards heard to speak of its repeal. Ever since, it has been steadily growing in popular favor—indeed, at this time, but few recollect or know that it was ever bitterly opposed. Successive acts of the Legislature have brought it to the perfection it has now attained, and at this day it ranks in its sphere with the very best educational systems of the world.

But in 1835 there was no such thing as reporting speeches by phonography. There was not even a stenographer to be found in either house of the Pennsylvania Legislature. Some hours after its delivery it was attempted to report it from memory, but the written speech conveys nothing of the force and power of the words as they fell from the lips of the speaker. From that day forth Mr. Stevens was regarded by all intelligent people as a great man. Some hated him still, but no one was foolish enough to deny his ability.

During this same session, the committee to investigate Free Masonry, of which Mr. Stevens was the chairman and originator, made its report. At this day it would be quite a curiosity, but it had the effect to keep up the excitement for a year or two longer. At the election in 1835, in consequence of the split in the Democratic party, Joseph Ritner was elected Governor by a plurality of votes; the united vote of Wolf and Muhlenberg exceeding the number polled for Ritner by about twelve thousand. In 1836 General Harrison was nominated as the candidate for President in opposition to Martin Van Buren. During nearly the whole of this campaign, Mr. Stevens was unfavorably disposed towards the anti-Democratic nomination, and it was only after the State election had revealed how necessary it was for the salvation of his own party that Mr. Stevens yielded to the nomination a cordial support. Harrison's unexpected popularity, as developed in the election returns, made it apparent that by a union of all opposed to the Democracy, Pennsylvania might be carried by the opposition; and during the session of the Reformed Convention in 1837, this union, so far as the leaders of the various factions were concerned, was almost fully accomplished. In that convention, Stevens, for the first time in his life, came in contact with the most brilliant speakers and the most profound thinkers in the State, proving himself rather more than a match for the best of them. John Sergeant, Joseph Hopkinson, Joseph R. Chandler, Charles Chauncey, Thomas Earle, C. J. Ingersoll, James M. Porter, Walter Forward, John Morin Scott, and George W. Woodward, were the men who were always seeking for a weak spot in his armor, but could never find it. Those who were rash enough to make a direct attack upon him, always came out of the encounter damaged or completely overthrown. Those who now would like to take the intellectual measure of the man in his best days, should carefully study the debates of that convention, for the best talent of Pennsylvania was to be found on the roll of its members. Whether the changes made by this body in the fundamental law of the State, were improvements or otherwise is not yet fully settled. Further steps in the same direction must yet be taken to make us certain of its wisdom or its folly. Let the final verdict be what it may, it will never be known from the names of its makers appended thereto, that Mr. Stevens was its leading mind. The constitution, as amended, confined the right of suffrage to *white* males only. Mr. Stevens denounced this as a violation of natural right, as an act of the meanest sort of tyranny, perpetrated by cowards and fools, for the purpose of proving how low they could bend the knee to the "dark spirit of slavery." His name is not attached to the instrument. The record of the infamy of all its other members stands as objects of mingled detestation and pity to future generations. Thirty-four years have passed away since this act of tyranny was perpetrated. Stevens lived to see many of those whose signatures sanctioned the foul act, repent sincerely of their error. In the late copies of our Digest, the names are not attached to the constitution. No one of those who voted for the word *white*, now cares to be remembered as a member of the convention.

Such is the change time has wrought in the public mind. Soon after the adjournment of the Legislature in 1838, Mr. Stevens was appointed canal commissioner. This was done because it was believed he could so manage the public works as to make them a powerful engine in the reëlection of Governor Ritner. Never, perhaps, was there a more bitter electioneering campaign in Pennsylvania. No stone was left unturned on either side to ensure success. The newspapers of the day were full of libels, and a stranger, believing either side, would have thought the opposing candidates the greatest scoundrels that ever existed. Money was also used without stint. For nearly the whole summer ten thousand dollars were posted weekly by each side. A few days before the election, an officer connected with the collector's office at Philadelphia, came to Harrisburg and offered to bet a quarter of a million that Porter would be elected. The pockets of Ritner's friends by this time were empty. Stevens had spent, or bet at least one hundred thousand dollars, and was about at the end of his pile. The knowledge that Ritner's supporters were at the end of their financial scope, did more to defeat him than all other causes put together. The election came, and frauds of all kinds were resorted to by both parties. At this game the Democrats, from long practice, were far superior to their opponents. It soon became clear that Ritner had been defeated, but the Legislature was still in doubt. Both sides claimed that in Philadelphia all their members were elected. The return judges of that city and county split into two bodies, and each made their own return. The returns made by Ritner's friends came to Harrisburg, and were deposited in the secretary's office, in the manner prescribed by the law. The other set of returns were brought to the office by private hands, and the Secretary of State, Thomas H. Burrowes, refused to receive them. A day or two after this Burrowes published a short address, in which he counseled the defeated party to "treat the election as though it had not taken place, and in that attitude abide the result." What he really intended to say was, that Ritner's friends should not give up their bets, but his opponents interpreted it as a threat of revolution. This raised the blood of partisans on either side to fever heat. When the Legislature met, an immense crowd of bullies and roughs from almost every part of the State, filled the capital. The clerk read the returns as presented by both sides; both sides elected a Speaker, and both adjourned their respective followers, or as they were then called, Houses. In the morning it was feared there would be a terrible fight, but as an adjournment had been effected without violence, it was supposed that all things would go on peaceably. During the whole morning a rowdy from Philadelphia stood behind the seat of Mr. Stevens, with a dagger in his coat bosom, who swore that if the friends of Ritner attempted to eject the Democrats by force, he would kill Stevens. This desperado was watched closely by another of the same stamp, who, with a butcher knife, would have stabbed the first had he moved a step further towards his intended victim. It was a perilous time. Had the slightest assault been committed upon any one, no matter from what cause it originated, it would have produced a terrible scene of bloodshed. The crowd had come with a fight in view. No one cared to take the responsibility of striking the first blow. Its dispersion lifted a heavy burden from the hearts of all who desired peace.

The Senate met at three o'clock, and contrary to expectation the lobby was crowded to suffocation. It so happened that both parties had Senators to be sworn in, whose claims to seats were founded on returns known to be erroneous, but right upon their face. In this class was Senator Bell, from the Chester and Montgomery district. As he was entitled to his seat, in the first instance, there was no objection made. He was a Democrat; but when Hanna, a Whig, in similar circumstances, was about to be sworn in, a scene of the utmost confusion prevailed. The crowd broke over the lobbies, some of them got upon chairs and began to speak. Charles Brown, one of the Democratic contestants, was particulary vociferous, and so was Washington Barton. During all this time the Speaker, Penrose, kept his seat and tried to maintain order, but his efforts were in a great measure fruitless. It was now nearly seven o'clock. Stevens, who was in the hall, now attempted to leave, but could not make his way through the crowd. He went back to the fire-place, and while standing there was told by a friend, it was intended to kill him if he went out at the door. It was then suggested that he and Burrowes should leave by the window of the room, near the fire. This was done not to avoid danger, for he did not believe the story, but because there was no other means of egress. While going out of the window, the door of the room opening at the end of the lobby stood open, and they were seen by some of the crowd. Three persons, one of them with a large bowie-knife in his hand, ran out through the crowd, swearing he would kill the —— scoundrel yet. Had these villains not mistaken the direction of the window, there is very little doubt that both Stevens and Burrowes would have been murdered. For some days all was confusion, but on Sunday a considerable number of uniformed volunteers arrived from Philadelphia and restored order. For nearly three weeks the Stevens House met in a room at Wilson's, now the Lochiel House. This could not last; and the Senate agreed to recognize the Hopkins' House. For nearly the whole session Stevens absented himself from his seat. When the session was more than half over, the Democrats passed a resolution of expulsion, which was followed by an election, at which Mr. Stevens was reëlected by a large majority. He took his seat a few days before the end of the session, and remained there till its close.

In the great campaign of 1840, Mr. Stevens took a decided stand in favor of "the Hero of the Thames." For months before the inauguration of Harrison, it was understood throughout Pennsylvania, that Mr. Stevens was to have a seat in the cabinet. That Harrison had selected him for postmaster general, is known with certainty, but through the open opposition of Clay, and the wavering of Webster, the appointment was given to Mr. Granger. Stevens never forgave Webster for the part he took in this transaction; nor did he go into the support of Clay in 1844 till, through Harmer Denny, Clay made known to Stevens that, should he be elected, atonement would be made for past wrong. Had the urgent entreaties of Stevens and his friends in relation to General Markle, the candidate for Governor, been acted on,

Henry Clay would have been President of the United States. That Markle was known to be the fast friend of Stevens, lost him votes enough to ensure his defeat. This lost Pennsylvania to Clay, and that decided the contest.

Mr. Stevens closed his service in the Legislature of Pennsylvania with the session of 1841. His long continued attention to politics, and the large sums he expended, had materially impaired his fortune. In the summer of 1842 he came to the conclusion that Gettysburg did not afford an adequate field for his powers, and this induced his removal to Lancaster, in August, 1842. In the fall of 1843 he tried to reorganize the anti-Masonic party, but the effort was a failure. His course in 1844 has been already noticed, and from that time till 1848 he was quiescent in politics, though he was always keenly alive to what was going on in the country. During this period his practice was very remunerative, and from this and the sale of his Adams county farms, he brought down his debts to within what he considered a manageable limit. In 1843 he was in danger of being sold out by the sheriff. . In 1844 he paid interest on debts amounting to $217,000. In 1849, when he first went to Congress, he had reduced his debts to $30,000. On March 4th, 1853, when his first service in Congress ended, his debts amounted to about $60,000. What he was worth at his death, is difficult to say. It may have been $100,000, perhaps less than half of that amount.

When the free-soil movement began, he was favorable to its principles, though he supported Taylor with all his might for the presidency. In 1848, after a sharp contest with the opposing candidates for the nomination, he was named for Congress by the supporters of Taylor, and elected by a large majority. During the four years that he served at this time, he was recognized as one of the leading men in Congress, and enjoyed to a large extent the confidence of Gen. Taylor, who, though a slaveholder himself, was, without declaring it openly, opposed to the further extension of that evil; and it is very certain that it was through his adroit management California came into the Union as a free State. After the death of Taylor, Fillmore, in hope of a reëlection, and Webster, with the design of taking the wind out of Fillmore's sails, went down on their knees to the slave power, and gave it all it wanted, in the shape of the fugitive slave law. This law and all kindred measures Mr. Stevens opposed to the extent of his power.

In 1851, for the first time in many years, a fugitive slave resisted, with arms, the claim of his owner. About two miles from Christiana, Lancaster county, a number of fugitive slaves were hiding at the house of a colored man, named Parker. An elderly man, named Gorsuch, of Maryland, assisted by his son, and a deputy marshal from Philadelphia, named Kline, came to the house of Parker, about an hour before daylight. Gorsuch, the younger, with Kline, summoned the persons inside to surrender. To this it was replied, they would defend themselves, and at the same time the click of fire-arms was heard. Kline ran and hid behind a tree. Young Gorsuch went to his father and reported that an attack would be dangerous. The old man said it would never do to back out so, and started towards the house, his son following. Gorsuch hailed the house again, and on receiving a defiant answer, fired a pistol, the ball taking effect in the leg of one of the blacks in the house. This shot was returned by a volley, killing the elder Gorsuch. The firing alarmed the neighborhood. Castner Hanway and Elijah Lewis were the first to reach the place. These were white men and abolitionists. Their influence prevented further firing, and they assisted the younger Gorsuch to remove the dead body of his father to Christiana, the nearest railroad station to the scene of the fight. This occurrence raised the pro-slavery spirit to a flame, while all their toadies, far and near, seized upon it as a chance to show their devotion, not to be neglected. For a week no colored man could pass along the railroad without being arrested. Hanway and Lewis were taken to Philadelphia and tried for treason. In this trial Mr. Stevens, and John M. Read, now one of the judges of the supreme court, were the counsel for the prisoners. Judge Read's exhaustive argument on the law of treason, knocked the breath out of the prosecution, and Mr. Stevens was content with but a few words. The prisoners were acquitted, and from that day the fugitive slave law was a dead letter in Pennsylvania. The great merit of Mr. Stevens in this transaction, was in the bold, firm stand he took at the beginning. His defiant attitude kept up the courage of those who would otherwise have desponded. His share in the trial was not very conspicuous, but there were good reasons for the course he pursued. The great object was attained, and that was all he desired.

From 1853 till 1858 Mr. Stevens steadily pursued the practice of his profession, though at the same time taking part in the initiatory movements which resulted in the formation of the Republican party, he being one of the delegates from this district to the convention which nominated Fremont. In 1858 the necessities of the country required his presence in Congress, and, after a warm contest, he was elected by a large majority. He had scarcely taken his seat in that body, in December, 1859, when the first symptoms of the rebellion began to be developed. The south was preparing for an appeal to arms, while the north could not by any means be induced to believe there was any danger of a fight. During the whole summer of 1860, slaveholders were declaring that if a black Republican should be elected the south would secede, and Mr. Stevens was one of the very few men in the country who believed the southern leaders really intended to keep their word. Lincoln was elected, and even then, when the navy was on the other side of the globe; when the army was stationed in the very places most favorable for the designs of the traitors; and when nearly all our muskets and guns were stored in the arsenals of the south, scarcely any one believed that war was impending. In those critical thirty-seven days, from the inauguration of Lincoln till the attack on Sumter, Mr. Stevens continually urged upon those who had the power, to at least make some preparation for defence, but with scarcely any result. It was only after the first great act of the bloody drama had been closed, that people began to have some faint idea of the national danger. Even Mr. Lincoln and Secretary Seward thought that 75,000 men could make all things right in ninety days. Mr. Stevens saw the full extent of the danger, and always said that a million of men should be called out till the war was ended. After Bull Run had verified the correctness of his views, he was heard with attention; and though from his age and deformity it was impossible that he could be a combatant, no man in the country, in the field or out of it, exercised a greater influence or personally did more to place our immense armies in the field. Through all these bloody years, as chairman of the committee of ways and means, he was most emphatically the right man in the right place. Had he been younger and not deformed, his natural courage would have sent him to the battle-field at the firing of the first gun. Men, firm believers in the doctrine of special providence aver, that his lameness was a necessity ordained to keep him where he was. Without entering into any discussion on this point, it is enough to say, there were so many illustrations of the doctrine during the war, that to a thinking mind it is somewhat difficult altogether to deny the proposition.

The war ended, but the troubles it brought in its train stood out in such bold relief, that people only then began to have something like a correct idea of their magnitude. The south, though beaten and vanquished, was far from being in a temper to accept the situation as the fortune of a war brought on by themselves against their brethren. There was a debt of nearly if not more than three thousand millions, taxing the people and their posterity for many years to come. Besides this, there were four millions of emancipated slaves to be cared for, to be instructed and protected from the aggression of those who had formerly been their masters. Of the measures adopted to reconstruct the south, Mr. Stevens was the author. The whole general plan, though possibly not original with himself, was by adoption peculiarly his own; and though some modifications may have been made in Congress, yet the principal features of his measures were retained and were the means employed to govern the people of the section lately in rebellion until its several portions were again admitted as component parts of the Union, as States, members of the great family of communities forming the indivisible Republic.

During the whole period, from the beginning of the war

to the end of his life, Mr. Stevens was scarcely a day absent from his seat, and for the most of that time his labors were truly herculean. During the war, in times of peculiar adversity, when every body else seemed to lose heart, his indomitable energy, and his full assurance of final success, inspired with new life the hearts that were ready to give up the combat. After the disastrous battles of Fredericksburg and Chickamauga, he seemed more than ever determined to fight on, no matter how gloomy the prospect before the country. A single instance will show how contemptuously he treated those who even thought of the possibility of some sort of reconciliation with the rebels. A very distinguished journalist, a man then heart and soul devoted to the Republican cause, but at times rather doubtful of our ability to win, came to Washington, most likely at the invitation of President Lincoln, to talk over the matter as to the possibility of making a peace on some reasonable terms. At what conclusion he and the President arrived, can only be inferred from subsequent events; but it is certain that after leaving the White House, he called on Mr. Stevens. Here he unfolded his budget of statistics, &c.; spoke of how large the debt was already; how great it would become in a short time with gold at $2.80; how many lives had already been lost, and how many more would be sacrificed; that we never could succeed, and more of the same sort, ending: that "peace must be made in some way." Stevens heard it all patiently; was silent for a moment and then rising, said: " Mr. ———, every man in these United States has a constitutional right to make a d—d fool of himself." His visitor bundled up his papers and left at double quick.

Men will wear out, and Mr. Stevens was no exception to the general rule. When he left Lancaster for Washington, about the end of November, 1866, he was so feeble as to be unable to sit up in the car, and a bed was made for him on the floor. Those who knew his condition had great fear whether he could survive the journey. After his arrival at Washington he rallied, and during most of the session he remained comparatively well. At the adjournment he came home, and remained there till November, 1867, when he took his last journey to the capital. He then seemed much better than he had been for some time, and appeared very hopeful in regard to his health. Shortly after the opening of the session he made the only great mistake of his congressional career. By some strange perversion of reasoning, which took all his friends by surprise, he adopted the Pendleton idea of paying the national debt with greenbacks, and on one or two occasions argued strongly in its favor. That it was honestly entertained no one who knew him could doubt; but for a clear-headed, honest man to advocate practical repudiation, was something which most people could not well comprehend. But discussion was soon over. On the 25th of February, 1868, Mr. Stevens, with Mr. Bingham, appeared in the Senate and presented articles of impeachment against Andrew Johnson. The trial, of which Mr. Stevens was one of the managers on the part of the House, ended on the 26th of May. During all this time Mr. Stevens, so feeble as to be carried daily to the capitol in a chair, was always present attending to his duty. Nor, when the impeachment trial was over, did he fail to attend, but continued to appear almost daily to the end of the session, which closed on the 17th of July. Mr. Stevens was at this time too weak to attempt the journey to Lancaster. Every day he became more and more feeble, till at last, on the 11th of August, 1868, he ceased from his labors.

De mortuis nil nisi verum.

The character of Thaddeus Stevens was made up of contradictory elements. Nature designed him for one of the great men of the race, and so far as time and circumstances gave his powers opportunity to act, he fulfilled her intention. One of the most remarkable endowments, was that never-failing spirit of generous kindness, which made it his pleasure to do good to and confer benefits on all who came within his reach. His inherent liberality grew by continual practice, till it became almost one of the necessities of his being. No man, woman or child ever approached Thaddeus Stevens, worthy or unworthy, and asked for help, who did not obtain it when he was possessed of the means. His money was given freely and without stint, when he had it. And with this unbounded liberality was associated a strong feeling of pride, which but few of his most intimate friends ever suspected to exist. He never would confess to a want of money, no matter how straightened his circumstances. When in this condition, if contributions were solicited, he invariably either found some objection to the object, or to the person in whose behalf the request was made. The reason he gave to a most intimate friend for this kind of conduct, that if he told the truth he would not be believed, was plausible, but it was not the fact. The true reason was, that he preferred to have the reputation of harshness and cruelty, rather than be suspected of even occasional poverty. Beggars of all grades, high or low, are very quick in finding out the weak points of those on whom they intend to operate; and Mr. Stevens was always, but more particularly when he was a candidate, most unmercifully fleeced. This trait was the cause of injury to the politics of this county. Before he was nominated for Congress, no one here thought of spending large sums of money in order to get votes. Now, no man, whatever his qualifications, can be nominated for any office unless he answers all demands made upon him, and forks over a greater amount than any one else will for the same office. It is a most deplorable state of things, but the fact is not to be denied.

We have ascribed this profusion of liberality to an innate kindness of heart and a natural desire to do good to all with whom he came in contact. This is undoubtedly true; but Mr. Stevens was far too observant, far too good a judge of men's motives, not to know that he was almost invariably imposed upon. This knowledge led him to believe that nearly all men were corrupt and unfit to be trusted. As he grew old this feeling became stronger, and he came to regard the great bulk of mankind as mercenary creatures, only fit to be the tools of those who were strong enough, rich enough and skillful enough to use them for their own advantage. A man without some degree of selfishness in his nature, would be a poor creature. We all would like to win riches and honors. Honest men, as the world estimates honesty, struggling towards the prize they desire to obtain, feel bound to qualify themselves in all respects for the positions they seek, and at the same time they may be selfish enough to have no scruple as to the means they may use to push aside others having the same object in view. An honest man, qualified for any position in the Republic, and having the same estimate of mankind as Mr. Stevens, could not fail, in all things regarding his political aspirations, to be supremely selfish. It was not that low, mean selfishness which often accompanies small, feeble natures, but it was, within its sphere, the same kind of selfishness which induced a Napoleon or a Bismarck to sacrifice a million of lives to secure a favorite political object. Viewed in this light he was the very incarnation of selfishness. During the last twenty years of his life, there was no man living whose welfare, socially, financially and politically he would not have sacrificed, to obtain the end he had in view. Towards those who stood more immediately in his way, he sometimes expressed a degree of bitterness which minds less strong and vigorous than his own could but faintly appreciate. Nor was this state of mind incompatible with the kindlier feelings of his nature. To those of his friends who were sincerely engaged in helping him onward and upward, and who were not aiming at the same mark as himself, he was the best friend imaginable. No trouble or effort on his part was too great, provided it would serve them. And in numerous instances it was not always only on behalf of his friends his kind offices were exerted. Men who had treated him ill, who had slandered and defamed him, would often, upon submission, find in him a friend when they could find one nowhere else. Such men he looked upon as hungry dogs to whom bones ought to be given, whether deserved or not. He forgot their enmity, because he regarded them as below his resentment, and would not take the trouble to give them a kick when he had them in his power. This was only another phase of the natural kindness which, in spite of all the promptings of his judgment, often controlled his acts.

When the moral or mental constitution of any man displays unusual force, it is natural to expect that all his peculiarities should display a corresponding degree of strength. Growing out of the characteristics already mentioned, as their legitimate fruit, was a weakness which made him, in pecuniary matters, the victim of those whom he well knew were not worthy of his slightest favor. Of all men he was the most accessible to flattery. Any scamp with a smooth tongue, could soft-soap him all over, and the operation was most grateful to his feelings. And yet, though it pleased him to the core, he despised the men who laid upon his altar the incense of their praise. It may be that like most of men, he had some faith in the truth of what was told him in this way, but at the same time he knew the motives which induced the offering. He had not the power to deny the request which almost invariably accompanied the praise. At such times he was almost invariably angry at himself because he could not successfully resist the demand. It is true this process could never induce him to do an act wrong in itself, or injurious to the public interest, yet when his own funds were concerned, he could never muster up the courage to avoid the trap into which he would go with his eyes open. There is no doubt this failing, of which he was fully conscious, often gave him deep vexation; but he was not a man given to brooding over mistakes, or to waste time in regrets for any thing he ever did.

Another quality most strongly developed, was his unconquerable perseverance and determination to accomplish anything which he undertook. No matter how often defeated, he was always ready to "try, try again;" and this he would do when, to all appearance, he had not the slightest chance of success. One great object of his ambition was to be a Senator of the United States, and had he conceived the idea ten years sooner, there is little doubt he would have reached his aim. In this, perhaps, it was better for his fame he did not succeed. In no other position than the one occupied for the last ten years of his life, could he have done so much for the increase of his reputation, or the benefit of the cause in which he was engaged. That he never obtained his desire, was another verification of the undoubted truth : "Man proposes;" God rules.

The great results which flowed from this indomitable

firmness of purpose have never been attributed to their true source. From the beginning of the great conflict between the contending sections of the nation, till a very short period before its close, there were multitudes of people who were willing to make peace with the rebels upon their own terms. Even among distinguished men of the Republican party there were never wanting persons of weak backbones, who would at any time have been only too glad to have a chance to enter into some sort of compromise. Against all such his tremendous powers of invective and sarcasm were continually directed, not so much in speeches as in his general conversation. Whenever and wherever he detected the first symptom of backing down, the man who exhibited the weakness was soon made to feel uncomfortable; while to those who were but seldom troubled with such fits of despondency, he imparted a share of that perfect confidence in the ultimate triumph of the national arms, which was one of the most effective reasons of their final success.

Men of this description are not usually noted for their kindness and humanity, but with Mr. Stevens the bark was generally worse than the bite. To hear him speak of military men of all grades, who had during the war been derelict in duty, it might have been inferred he was extremely sanguinary, but such was not the case. During the war his good offices were often required to save men sentenced to be shot, and he never refused to invoke with success the kind feelings of President Lincoln, who was only too happy to have some person to intercede for the miserable delinquent. It is true, that in a speech in Congress, Stevens justified Juarez for shooting Maximilian, but it is very certain that had he been ruler of Mexico the fallen emperor would have been sent home safe and sound. There is no doubt that had Mr. Stevens been invested with the power of life and death, there would have been but few criminals executed. A woman's tearful face, or the wail of a child, was beyond his power to resist. This, in a ruler, might have been a great weakness, but in Mr. Stevens' position it was, doubtless, one of the most amiable traits in his character. Nothing ever pleased him better than to tell of his success with the President, on occasions like those above referred to. He never took the credit of success to himself, but always ascribed it to the goodness of Old Abe. Let us illustrate what has been said by introducing one of these stories: "A young fellow, from this county was to be shot for desertion. It was rather a hard case, and his mother, in great distress, called on me to help save him. I took her at once to the White House and introduced her to the President. On the road I told her to tell her story in her own way, which she did in such a manner as none but a mother could tell it. I said nothing. I saw by the President's eye it was all right. There was no use in my saying a word. While she was talking the President began to write. It was but a couple of lines, but it was effectual. Fearing a scene, I took her into the ante-room, telling her as we went along her son was safe. As soon as she fully understood it she broke out: 'Oh! this is the man *our* newspapers said was a brute and a devil. Why, he is the loveliest man I ever saw in my life! He is an angel! He does the work of the Almighty, and stands in his place on earth! I could worship him for his goodness—my poor Ben. is safe.'" No Democrat could be found in that family afterwards. "There was a great deal of desertion about that time. Some hard-hearted devils thought all should have been shot, but then I had nothing to do with that. It was Lincoln's business, and he did all those things as he believed to be right. He was a great man. In his place, perhaps, I would have done the same thing."

Of Mr. Stevens' religious views it is difficult to speak. His mind was so constituted that he was very incredulous as to anything in conflict with his own reason. But he was not altogether devoid of faith, for he was a fatalist in the strongest sense of the term. In this belief he was as firmly rooted as any follower of Mahomet could be. Those who knew him best find it exceedingly hard to believe that he ever gave an intelligent consent to be baptized in the Catholic faith. Still Mr. Stevens was not an immoral man. He was no scoffer, he was never profane, was strictly temperate, and in all things rigidly truthful. To say he had no vices, would be to exalt him far above the great mass of mankind.

42

In one respect, a man of his ardent temperament could scarcely fail to err—that he was the cold-blooded destroyer of female innocence, the heartless libertine, the hoary debauchee which his enemies in times of great political excitement represented him to be, is a most malicious lie. That he could, in any fair sense, be called a gambler, rests on no better foundation.

The intellectual powers of Mr. Stevens were of a very high order. His perceptions were quick, his reasoning powers strong and accurate, and his memory almost unrivalled. This last he always said was not a natural but an acquired faculty. This perhaps was partly true, though the foundation on which to build the superstructure must have been the result of his fine mental organization. He could remember all the evidence in the longest trial, and repeat all the important parts with surprising accuracy. At some period of his life he must have been a very hard student, for his knowledge seemed almost without limit. In reasoning upon a given proposition he scarcely seemed to think, his deductions coming as though by intuition. His illustrations were very seldom beautiful, but always apposite. They hit the nail square on the head, and made further blows needless. He could be exceedingly sarcastic, but he seldom employed this weapon without just provocation. He was too kindly disposed to use it in a manner not fairly legitimate. The same limitation could scarcely be extended to his wit, for that flowed out of itself, and had generally so much of good natured mirth in it, that the person against whom it was leveled could scarcely take offence. When the occasion required it, he was sometimes highly eloquent, but as a general thing it could not be counted as one of his characteristics. He was not a man of taste. Had no fondness for, and but little perception of, beauty in painting or architecture. There was but little of the imaginative about him. His mind was strongly practical, looking far more to the substance than to the outward adorning of things. For what is usually called "fine writing" he had a supreme contempt. Nothing worried him more than the "highfalutin" of the war correspondents, in their descriptions of battles.

"Confound the scamp," was his exclamation after the battle of Antietam, "why can't he tell us what they did, and leave us to think how it looked ourselves."

Another branch of this defect and of much greater importance, was his almost total want of creative power. He never originated anything, but he had the power, in wonderful perfection, of taking hold of other men's ideas, stripping them of every thing superfluous, leaving nothing but the useful and practical, and presenting them so clearly and forcibly to the world, that their importance was immediately recognized. So much was this the case, that every measure he ever brought forward in his legislative career, had its origin in the thought of some other man who, in nine cases out of ten, would be unable to claim its paternity in the new dress with which Stevens had invested it. It was from this power that most of his strength as a lawyer was derived. In citing authorities to sustain a legal position he would, in a few words, bring out the meaning of the judge who wrote it, much more clearly and far more forcibly than it had before presented itself to the mind of its author. This, together with the kindred faculty of seizing instantly upon the turning point of the case, without any regard to the quantity of legal rubbish accumulated around it, placed him in the very first rank of the greatest minds that ever appeared at the bar. This power of concentrating the force of his case in a few sentences, together with the perfect control which he had acquired over his temper, made him almost always successful. His tactics were to waste no strength upon the outworks of his opponent's case, but to attack the citadel at once. To sum up the whole in few words, it may be truly said, that the clearness of his mental vision, his innate reverence of right and love of justice, his wonderful powers of memory, analysis and concentration, his truthfulness, his perseverance, his thorough detestation of everything like trickery and meanness, his perfect fairness in all his business transactions, and his generous kindness to all, made him a man towering so high above the millions around him, that no one who intelligently studies his character, can fail to appreciate the magnitude of his greatness.

Thaddeus Stevens, in the prime of life, was a remarkably fine-looking man. None of his earlier pictures do him justice. Some of the oil pantings made towards the close of his life, are nothing but caricatures. The engraving, by Sartain, gives a very correct idea of his appearance when about fifty-five years old. The photograph by Eberman, taken when Stevens was seventy-three, is perfect. He was about five feet eleven inches high; clear, ruddy, smooth skin. His natural hair was chestnut, but he lost it from brain fever when about thirty-five years old, and afterwards always wore a wig. He had very fine teeth, was strongly built, but not corpulent; his appearance when the features were at rest, was very dignified. When young, he was a great lover of athletic sports, and could make a full hand at anything where swiftness of foot was not required. He was a splendid horseman, an excellent swimmer, and very fond of the chase. When a young man, he would occasionally take a glass of wine, but for many years of his life he abstained wholly from alcoholic drinks. That he possessed great courage, physical, as well as moral, is well known to all his intimate friends. Naturally obstinate and combative, he had so trained his mind as to despise all displays of pugnacity. When assailed with foul language, by dirty blackguards, as he often was about election time, he seldom took any outward notice of it, though he felt all such attacks very keenly. If he ever did reply to anything of this sort, it was in a single sentence by which the assailant was completely overthrown. His repartees were always far more damaging than any blow could have been; they were always put in such shape that the dullest man in a crowd could never fail to feel their force.

It has been already said, that he hated oppression and injustice in all its forms. This was the ruling passion, and exhibited itself in full force as he drew near his end. In the principal cemeteries of Lancaster it was stipulated, by charter, that no person of color should be interred within their limits. He had bought lots in both cemeteries, but when he received the deeds he sent them back, refusing to be buried in the grounds of either. Shreiner's cemetery, the smallest in the city, was free from this objection, and there he was laid to rest, within a few feet of the public schools, which his fearlessness and love for humanity established in Pennsylvania forever.

For the reason above stated, he ordered in his will the following should be inscribed upon his tomb:

"I repose in this quiet and secluded spot, not from any natural preference for solitude, but finding other cemeteries limited by charter rules as to race, I have chosen it that I might be enabled to illustrate in my death the principles I have advocated through a long life—equality of man before the Creator."

On December 17th, 1868, the House of Representatives met specially to express its respect for his memory. Men of all parties, in most eulogistic terms united to do honor to his name. Through the whole land it was felt that "a leader had fallen in Israel." Party rancor was for a time forgotten, and all men acknowledged the great value of his services to the country. Those who knew him best grieved most for his loss; but by none was he so sincerely mourned as by the millions whom his labors had elevated from slavery to freedom.

This imperfect memoir can be no more fitly ended than by quoting the concluding words of the eulogium delivered by Mr. Maynard, of Tennessee, on the occasion above referred to:

"As he was he will long be remembered. He has left his impress upon the form and body of the times. Monuments will be reared to perpetuate his name on the earth. Art will be busy with her chisel and her pencil to preserve his features and the image of his mortal frame. All will be done that brass and marble and painted canvas will admit of being done. The records of his official life will remain in your archives; our chosen words of commemoration will fall into the channels of literature. But the influence of a gifted mind, in moulding thought and giving direction to events, is not measured by words of commemoration or by official records. It is as measureless as the soul and enduring as time. Long after the brass and marble and painted canvas have disappeared, it will still remain transmitted from age to age and through successive generations."[1]

STONER, CHRISTIAN L., was born in the year 1823, at Millersville, Lancaster county, Pa. He learned the trade of a house carpenter in Lancaster city. He married Lizzie L. Hostetter, daughter of Col. Jacob Hostetter, in 1847, and in 1857 was elected Clerk of the Orphans' Court, a position he filled for three years.

STOEK, HENRY, elected Prothonotary in 1848.

STOEY, WILLIAM, elected a member of the Legislature in 1784.

STRICKLER, JACOB, was a member of the Legislature in the years 1797, 1798, 1799 and 1800.

STROHM, JOHN, was born October 16th, 1793, in what was then Little Britain township, in the county of Lancaster, and State of Pennsylvania, but in that part of said township which now composes Fulton township. His parents were of German descent; his father having been brought to this country from the kingdom of Wirtemburg by his parent when about eight years of age. The grandfather having died during the voyage, his remains were consigned to the rolling waves of the boisterous Atlantic. The widow with her small family (two sons and a daughter), were landed at Philadelphia, and finally settled in Strasburg, this county. The mother of the subject of this sketch was the daughter of John Herr, a Mennonite preacher, who was also the grandfather of another preacher, John Herr, better known as the founder of the New or Reformed Mennonite Society. She was of a religious disposition, and to her instructions and admonitions the subject of this notice attributed the foundation of that high appreciation of integrity and truth which has characterized his conduct during his whole life.

He was first sent to school when about four years of age,

[1] The above sketch of Thaddeus Stevens, being the production of an intimate friend and member of his own political party, the author of the Biographical History of Lancaster county desires it to be distinctly understood, that he is in no wise to be considered responsible for any sentiment or conclusion contained therein, or estimate submitted, regarding the deceased statesman.

and soon showed an aptitude for learning that few children of that age exhibit. But the schools of that period were of an inferior quality, and afforded none of the facilities now attainable in acquiring the rudiments of education. In the year 1804 his father purchased a farm in Strasburg township, and in the spring of 1805, when John was in his twelfth year, removed thereto, and from that time he was sent to school but a few months during the winter. Consequently, he received at school nothing but the ordinary instruction which farmers' sons of that period and in that vicinity usually attained. He was, however, very fond of reading, and improved every opportunity of acquiring a knowledge of men and things. From the time he was seven years of age, he read everything that came in his way, yet even in this way his opportunities were very limited. His father's library consisted principally of the Bible and Testament, and a few religious works in German, which he did not then understand, and some miscellaneous works picked up at sales. Amongst these was an old geography, giving a description of the various countries and divisions of the earth, an outline of the general principles of astronomy, the relative position of the planets, their courses in their respective orbits, &c. This book he studied carefully, and from it derived his first knowledge of many things previously unknown to him, and which proved highly useful in after life. His mother encouraged this avidity for reading, by borrowing such books for him as she could procure amongst her friends. Another means of acquiring information and storing his mind with useful knowledge, was found in the regular reading of a weekly newspaper to which his father was a constant subscriber. From this he obtained a knowledge of the leading events of the history of the world at the time, and became initiated in the politics of our own country in particular. In the beginning of the year 1809, at the solicitation of his teacher, he studied the theory of surveying, but did not practice it to any extent for near twenty years afterwards. About this time he commenced purchasing books on his own account, and all the money he could spare was invested in that description of property.

When about eighteen years of age Judge Clark, one of the associate judges of the county, who made his acquaintance at a public sale where he was clerking, wished to engage him as a teacher in his neighborhood, but his parents dissuaded him from accepting the offer. The following year he accepted a proposition ftom Christian Barr, of Bart, (now Eden township), to teach school for three months near Quarryville. He found the business irksome, and at the expiration of his term returned to his father to work on the farm. Here he remained for near three years, when he again accepted a situation as a teacher in West Lampeter township, upon the invitation of Christian Herr, of Pequea, who engaged to raise a school for him, offered him boarding at his own house, and remained his fast and ardent friend as long as he lived. In this neighborhood he remained as a teacher for five years, giving general satisfaction to his employers, and by a strict attention to business and uniform good conduct gained the confidence and esteem of all his acquaintances.

In 1817 he married the eldest daughter of John Herr, (limeburner), and commenced housekeeping in the neighborhood of his school. In 1821 he quit teaching school and commenced farming, as he always had a strong predilection for the occupation of a farmer. In 1830 his name was first brought before the public as a candidate for the Legislature, but his friends did not succeed in getting him settled on the ticket. The support he received encouraged his friends to bring his name forward the ensuing year, (1831), when he was settled and elected. The anti-Masonic excitement was then in full vigor, and Strohm was elected as an anti-Mason; but by prudent conduct and courteous demeanor he maintained his principles and those of his party, without unnecessarily giving offence to any, and enjoyed the good-will and esteem of many of the fraternity. He was reëlected to the Legislature in the years 1832 and 1833, and in 1834 was elected to the Senate for a term of four years, that being the extent of the Senatorial term under the old constitution.

In 1838 he was reëlected to the Senate for a second term of four years, making in all eleven consecutive years in which he was a member of the State Legislature, three years in the House of Representatives and eight years in the Senate. In 1842 he was elected Speaker of the Senate, the duties of which he executed with so much good judgment and impartiality, that there never was an appeal taken from his decision. In 1844 he was elected a member of Congress from his native county, and in 1845 took his seat in that body. In 1846 he was reëlected, his term expiring on the 4th of March, 1849, when General Taylor was inaugurated president. In 1851 he was the candidate of the Whig party for canal commissioner, then one of the most important offices in the State. The Democratic party proved too strong on that occasion, and his opponent, Seth Clover, was elected. In 1848 Mr. Strohm was one of the senatorial delegates to the national convention at Baltimore, when General Zachary Taylor was nominated as the Whig candidate for President; in 1852 he was a member of the national convention at Baltimore, which nominated Gen. Scott as a candidate for the Presidency, and in 1869 he was a member of the State convention at Philadelphia, which re-nominated Governor Geary for the office of Governor.

In his legislative capacity the subject of this imperfect sketch was more noted for assiduous attention to business and a watchful care of the interests of his constituents and the community at large, than for brilliancy of talent or oratorical display. He seldom addressed the legislative bodies of which he was a faithful member in a protracted argument, but gave his views in plain but forcible language; and if he did not succeed in convincing his audience of the correctness of his views, he left no room to doubt the sincerity of his convictions. During the eight years in which he was a member of the Senate, he was chairman of the committee on roads and bridges and of the committee on claims, and for several years stood at the head of both those committees; and such was the confidence placed in him by his compeers, that his reports and recommendations were generally accepted and his suggestions adopted. Plain and simple in his habits, he was at all times easy of access and disposed to accommodate, and to the extent of his ability serve any person that required his aid. His first wife died in 1832, and he remained a widower until 1857, when he married a widow Witmer, with whom he is spending the evening of his days in the quiet contentment of private life.

STROHM, JOHN, JR., was elected County Commissioner in the year 1867.

STUBBS, JEREMIAH BROWN, M. D., was born in Little Britain, (now Fulton) township, Lancaster county, Pennsylvania, on the 13th of April, 1804. He was the second son of Isaac and Hannah Stubbs, both descendants of early settlers in that neighborhood. Isaac Stubbs, his father, was a stone mason, and worked at the trade occasionally. He took more delight in perusing the contents of books, and in imparting to his children the rudiments of an English education, (at least as far as he was capable), than to accumulate wealth by a close adherence to his occupation or by any other manual labor.

When Jeremiah was three years old his parents removed to Harford county, Maryland, having purchased a small farm near the "Rocks of Deer creek." Here the family resided until the year 1821, when they returned to Lancaster county to reside upon a farm near Peach Bottom. This was jointly inherited by the father and mother. In all these paternal migrations the older children accompanied their parents, and rendered all the assistance of which they were able.

After the return of the family to Lancaster county, Jeremiah determined to commence business for himself, and with this object in view entered a mercantile establishment in the city of Baltimore. Disliking the business, in the course of a few months he returned home. Receiving the encouragement of his maternal grandfather, Jeremiah Brown, (of whom he always retained a grateful remembrance), he was induced to study and enter one of the learned professions. With no advantages of a preparatory education, other than instructions received from a kind parent, and the limited attainments obtained by a few years attendence at the public schools of an early period, he entered upon the study of medicine in the year 1824. He read under direction of Dr.

Vincent King, a well-known practitioner of southern Lancaster county; attended two full courses of lectures at the Jefferson Medical College, of Philadelphia, and graduated in the class of March 8th, 1827. Soon after graduating he located in the village of Rising Sun, Cecil county, Maryland, where he practiced his profession for nine years. During his residence in Cecil county, he was elected a member of the Medico-Chirurgical Society of Maryland. His membership of this body commenced September 9th, 1827. At that time a physician practicing in the State of Maryland, could not collect a fee unless he was a member of this medical organization, and no one became a member thereof unless he submitted to a rigid examination, and was recommended as worthy by a committee appointed for that purpose.

On the 25th of February, 1836, Dr. Stubbs was married to Rachel H., eldest daughter of Timothy Kirk, esq., of Oxford, Chester county, formerly a member of the Legislature of Pennsylvania, and then an active business citizen of that vicinity. Previous to his marriage he purchased the farm and good-will of Dr. John K. Sappington, of Little Britain, Lancaster county. Removing to this place he resumed the practice of medicine, which he continued with success to the time of his decease—a period of twenty-six years. For a long time after he located in Lancaster county, there was, with one exception, no physician in active practice within ten miles. In these early days of his medical career, his labors were unceasing and at times exceedingly arduous. Possessing a comparatively strong constitution and determined will, he was enabled to do herculean duty, practising his profession throughout a section of country many miles in extent.

On the 14th of February, 1844, he was elected a member of the Lancaster city and county medical society, and at one time was president of that body. He was elected to represent it as a delegate in the American Medical Association, and attended in this capacity its meetings at Boston, in 1849; Richmond, 1852; New York, 1853, and Philadelphia, 1855. In the fall of 1847 he was elected a member of the House of Representatives of Pennsylvania, by the Whigs of

Lancaster county, and was reëlected in 1848. During his first term he served on the committee of education, and in the second was placed on the committee of ways and means, and upon banks, besides several special committees. The House was strongly Democratic during the session of 1848; nevertheless Dr. Stubbs, by his plain and unassuming manners, made many friends and received numerous favors from his political opponents. During his service at Harrisburg, various expedients were devised by different members of the ways and means committee, to raise revenue to replenish the State treasury, and at the same time not increase the taxes of the working classes of the commonwealth. Being a member of the committee to devise means of revenue, he suggested the propriety of taxing the sales and manufacture of quack nostrums, which were then meeting with an immense sale throughout all parts of the State. For many years he was well acquainted with the fact, that thousands of dollars were made by charlatans, by imposing on the ignorant in medical knowledge. All honest trades and professions were taxed, but the manufacturer and vender of patent medicines went free. Receiving the assurance of a majority of the Legislature and the Governor, that to tax this class was just, he consulted with some of the learned of the profession and drew up a bill, which became a law. Its passage created a unanimous protest on behalf of all the semi-medical men, quacks and medicine venders in the State, and the vengeance of the whole fraternity was threatened against the author of the bill. In Lancaster county their influence was brought to bear against him, but availed nothing.

While a member of the Legislature, he took great interest in all subjects pertaining to the education of the children of the State, as well as to keeping up the standard of the profession of which he became in early life a member. For professional services rendered to half of the legislative body, he was presented with a handsome testimonial on behalf of the members of both political parties. Having served the customary two terms in the State Legislature, he returned to his farm and continued the practice and instruction of students of medicine. During his professional career, seven young men read under his direction and graduated. Of these only three survive. For several years previous to his death, Dr. Stubbs had frequent paroxysms of disease, that he was well aware would finally prove fatal. Nevertheless, he continued to work and study to the last. On the 4th and 5th of July, 1862, he was attacked with angina pectoris, but recovered and seemed to improve until the night of the 9th, when he had a relapse and died on the morning of the 10th, aged 58 years.

Dr. Stubbs was a member—by birthright—of the society of Friends ; but a few years after attaining manhood, by his own request, ceased to be connected with that society. No man was more familiar with the various tenets and doctrines advanced and believed in by different religious bodies. He appreciated works of a theological and scientific nature, was conversant with the scripture, especially those books attributed to Job and Paul, which he considered to far exceed the others in sublimity and literary excellence. In his opinion, the " Sermon on the Mount" with its golden rule, was sufficient in itself unto salvation; and to believe in and practice the truths there inculcated, was paramount to a blind adherence to the creeds of Calvin or Luther.

With him the moral law was the basis of true religion, and upon this he was willing to rest all hope of a peaceful hereafter. To the theory and science of medicine he was strongly devoted. A constant reader, he always kept pace with the progress of the age, and was ready to avail himself of all the recent discoveries in medicine and surgery, never permitting a remedy of value in alleviating human suffering to escape his notice. His varied and extensive reading on subjects appertaining to his profession, was attested by a valuable library of medical works.

Chirurgery, or that part of the science belonging properly to the surgeon, he did not fancy. His sympathetic temperment forbade it. His province or forte was the duties pertaining to the physician. Few men were better versed in etiology, or the causes of disease ; and in diag nosis he had few equals. To be familiar with disease sufficient to enable one to recognize it at all times, in its different phases, is one of the most difficult parts of the science.   In this Dr. Stubbs was an adept, and hence his skill and success in treatment. To him the oath of Hippocrates, and the code of ethics of the medical profession, were laws to be adhered to with a strictness bordering on Persian and Median tenacity.   To violate them, was a breach of professional honor not to be tolerated.

Quacks and medical pretenders of all descriptions met with no encouragement at his hands.   To younger members of the profession, he was ever willing to render assistance and counsel.   In his business transactions he was exact.   Starting in life poor, with few friends, and an abundance of envious relations, he made all he possessed.   An honest, poor man, never appealed to him in vain.   To him he would render needed assistance at all times.   He knew what it was to be poor and depend on others for aid.   In his latter years he often remarked, that it was a great source of consolation to him to know that he had repaid all favors ever extended to him, and to feel that he never knowingly took a cent of any one; and pecuniarily, he owed no man, living or dead.

STYER, DAVID, was elected County Commissioner in the year 1849.

SUMMY, AARON H., was elected a member of the Legislature in the year 1868.

SWARR, HIRAM B., was born March 9th, 1821, in Londonderry township, Lebanon county, and is a descendant of one of those early settlers of Lancaster county whom religious persecution drove from their native homes.   He was educated in the common schools of his district, afterwards went to Mr. Beck's academy at Litiz, and also to the academy at Germantown.   He was a student of the Abbeville Institute, near Lancaster, for some time.   Having finished his education before his arrival at the age of sixteen, he entered as accountant in a large commercial house in Philadelphia, of which sometime afterwards he became a partner, but with a growing dislike for the mercantile business.   Cherishing rather a fondness for the excitements of political life, in 1844 he abandoned commercial pursuits, and entered as a student of law, the office of Geo. W. and Levi Kline, of Lebanon, Pa., January 1st, 1845.   He was admitted to the bar April 1st, 1847. His strong attachment for his ancestral home, led him to select Lancaster as the place where he should pursue his profession, and on the 1st of May, 1847, he opened an office in Lancaster. Soon after coming to the bar he became active in politics, and in 1853 was chosen chairman of the Democratic county committee, a position he held upwards of ten years. He was a member of the Lancaster school board for a period of eight or ten years. Upon the death of Henry M. Reigart, postmaster of Lancaster, in the autumn of 1856 he was appointed postmaster in his stead, and in 1857 reappointed by Mr. Buchanan to the same position, which he held during the four years of his administration. Mr. Swarr has frequently been a delegate of his party to State conventions, and was a delegate to the national convention in 1856, when James Buchanan was nominated, and in this convention he acted a somewhat conspicuous part, this being required of him as the representative of the district in which the candidate for the Presidency had his home. He was afterwards a delegate to the national convention at Charleston, in 1860, and also, afterwards, at the adjourned convention at Baltimore, in the same year. He was in 1868 the candidate of the Democratic party for Congress in Lancaster county. During all the time he has been steadily engaged in the business of his profession, and has always secured the confidence of a very considerable and influential class of clients. He enjoyed the life-long confidence of James Buchanan, and stood so high in his estimation as a legal practitioner as to be appointed by him one of his executors, and also trustee for the execution of several important trusts created by the will of the late ex-President.

SWIFT, JOSEPH, was born January 14th, 1760, and was the progenitor of the Swift family of Lancaster county. His father, Joseph Swift, was a merchant of Philadelphia, of English descent, who was born June 24th, 1731, and died December 26th, 1806. Joseph Swift, sr. and William West purchased at sheriff's sale in 1772, the large farm of 374 acres, for £805, Pennsylvania currency, as the property of Robert Fulton, father of the distinguished Robert Fulton, and the same upon which the latter was born. Joseph Swift, jr., settled upon the property so purchased, and was a leading farmer in his day. His son, John W. Swift, yet owns part of the old Fulton farm, and occupies the house in which Robert Fulton was born.

T.

TAYLOR FAMILY.* Isaac Taylor, sr., was among the early settlers of Lancaster county, and according to his family tradition, was the son of Christopher Taylor, who emigrated from England in 1682, and purchased 5000 acres of land from William Penn before his arrival in the province of Pennsylvania. Penn'a Archives, vol. i., p. 41. He was a member of William Penn's first council in 1682. Isaac Taylor was born soon after the arrival of his parents. He was a surveyor, a magistrate, and a member of the assembly for the county of Chester, prior to the year 1722. He was arrested and imprisoned by the authorities of Maryland while surveying lands near the Maryland line. Colonial Records, vol. iii., p. 212. He was again appointed by the Executive Council, in the year 1726, to be a justice of Chester county. He was also appointed by the council, in the year 1718, one of the commissioners to lay out the old Philadelphia road from Conestoga to the Brandywine. He made the original surveys of a large portion of the land in the eastern and southern sections of Lancaster county. He surveyed the Christiana tract of 800 acres, in Sadsbury township, on the 27th of August, 1709, as appears by the records of the Surveyor General's office. He was the original patentee of a tract of land directly in the Gap, partly in Salisbury and part in Sadsbury. He erected the first stone house at the Gap, about the year 1747, which was built three stories high, and is standing to the present day. It is now owned by George H. Rutter, and kept as a hotel. He was a worthy and serviceable member of the society of Friends, and departed this life at an advanced age, in the year 1756.

*Contributed by Isaac Walker, of Sadsbury.

ISAAC TAYLOR, JR., son of Isaac Taylor, sr., was united in marriage in the year 1761 with Mary, the daughter of Thomas Bulla, sr., of Chester county. He resided many years at the residence of his father at the Gap, and was an esteemed minister of the gospel in the society of Friends, and served also as the clerk of the monthly meeting at old Sadsbury.

JACOB TAYLOR, grandson of Isaac Taylor, sr., was appointed by the yearly meeting of Friends in Philadelphia, about the year 1800, to superintend the civilization and education of the Cattaraugus Indians, in western New York, which office he filled with credit to himself and to the society for about forty years.

A daughter of Isaac Taylor, sr., was married about the year 1745 to Nathaniel Newlin, of Chester county, some of whose descendants in the fifth generation are: Isaac Walker, esq.; and Mary, the wife of Samuel Slokom, of Sadsbury; Deborah, the wife of Henry Pownall, of Bart; and Asahel Walker, of Lamborntown, Chester county, and their descendants.

THOMPSON, ANDREW, was elected a member of the Legislature in 1842.

U.

URBAN, LEWIS, was elected a member of the Legislature in the year 1843.

V.

VARMANN, HATTIL V.,* was born in Ireland, and was there united in marriage with Abigail, the daughter of William and Joan Sandwith, of Bellinauch, in the county of Wexford, where he was held in good esteem as a serviceable member of the church, from which place he emigrated (with his wife) to this country, and settled in the township of Lea-

*Contributed by Isaac Walker, of Sadsbury.

43

cock, in this county, in the year 1728, where he purchased 600 acres of land, and a meeting of worship was authorized by the society of Friends to be held at his house in the year 1732. He was on the first grand jury that was drawn for Lancaster county, and held various other public and private trusts, being a man of good education and possessed of rare abilities. He was the first clerk of the monthly meeting held at Sadsbury. He left no sons, but a number of daughters, who were intermarried into the most respectable families of Lancaster county, and their descendants are both numerous and highly respectable. He was the great grandfather of Judge Brinton, of Paradise. The old homestead, near Soudersburg, is still owned by another of his great grandsons, William Brinton, sr., of Sadsbury, in which township a large number of his descendants of the fifth generation now reside, including all that highly respectable family of the Brintons, and a number of the Pownalls, the Moores, and some of the Coopers, of Sadsbury.

VARNES, JOHN, was elected County Commissioner in the year 1844.

VONDERSMITH, DANIEL, appointed Clerk of the Orphans' Court in 1835.

VONDERSMITH, D. B., elected Associate Judge of the several courts of Lancaster in 1851.

W.

WADE, ANDREW, a citizen of Elizabethtown, was elected a member of the Legislature in the year 1849.

WALKER, ASAHEL, of Sadsbury township, was born at the Valley Forge, in the year 1746. He was the son of Isaac, and the grandson of Lewis Walker, who emigrated from the principality of Wales, about the year 1700, and purchased a large tract of land from William Penn at the Valley Forge, where, it was said, William Penn visited him the following year. He erected a commodious stone edifice thereon, at which a meeting of the society of

Friends was established in the year 1713. The same house was occupied by General Washington as his headquarters during the Revolutionary war, and although it has undergone repairs, it is standing as a part of the family mansion at the present time, 1872. The land is now divided into about ten farms, and is still held by his descendants. His grandson, Asahel Walker, was united in marriage with Ann, the daughter of the well-known James Moore, of Sadsbury, in the year 1769, and afterwards purchased a tract of land in Sadsbury which had belonged to his father-in-law, and which had been taken up by William Penn in the year 1700, while on his visit at the Gap, and which he had surveyed off for his own use. At the age of 66 years, he divided his land between his sons Isaac and Asahel, which is now owned and occupied by his grandsons, Isaac and Asahel C. Walker.

After thus adjusting his temporal matters, he retired from the cares of the world and spent the remainder of his life (over a quarter of a century), in promoting the cause of his Divine Master, and became a worthy minister of the gospel truths in the society of Friends. During no period of his life did he seek public distinction ; yet he had charge of various important public and private trusts for members of different religious persuasions, so that during his whole life he was truly a worthy and faithful member of the society, so that he may be classed with the good, and remembered with the just. He departed his well spent life in the year 1838, in the 93d year of his age.

His descendants are still numerous and respectable. Besides the Walkers are included some of the Moores, Pownells, Coopers, Linvilles, Ellmakers, Dillers, Worsts, Hersheys, Mrs. Pusey Barnard, Mrs. Mary L. Roberts, of Texas, the Sprouls, Houstons, and some of that ancient and highly respectable family of the Trouts, of the township of Bart. His youngest living grandson is the well-known Joseph C. Walker, esq., of the Gap, who was married in the year 1856 to Lucy H., daughter of Esaias and Sarah Ellmaker, of Earl township.

WALKER, CAPTAIN JOSEPH, of Sadsbury, was the son of John Walker who emigrated from Wales, and who was the original purchaser of a tract of land called the Avondale farm, in the year 1743. Captain Joseph Walker was a serviceable man in the Revolutionary war. He was first engaged in transporting arms and ammunition for the Continental army. He afterwards raised a company of militia in Sadsbury and Bart, of which company he was chosen captain, and was engaged in the service. Colonial Records, vol. xiv., p. 631. Dr. Michener's History, p. 397. After the war he was appointed one of the justices of the peace for Lancaster county, which office he filled with credit for the space of about twenty years. He also purchased and had patented the farm called McKeansville, now owned by Adam Rutter. The Avondale farm is now owned by Joseph D. Pownall, and by a recent survey and alteration of the line, this property is now in Bart. The descendants of Joseph Walker mostly reside in the southern parts of Lancaster county.

[1]WALKER, Isaac, was born in the year 1808, in Sadsbury township, Lancaster county. He was for some years engaged in the mercantile business, but latterly has followed agricultural pursuits. He is noted for his rare knowledge of matters pertaining to the early settlement of Lancaster and Chester counties, and has written considerably of the early local history of the southeastern section of the county. He erected, in 1872, a monument over the Penn Spring, at the Gap, in memory of the beneficent founder of the State of Pennsylvania.

WALLACE, John, was a member of the Legislature in the year 1822.

[1]Isaac Walker is a son of Isaac and Deborah Walker, a grandson of Asahel Walker, the first, of Sadsbury, and the great great-grandson of Lewis Walker, at Valley Forge; and also the great great-grandson of Andrew Moore the first settler at Christiana and Penningtonville, and who established the first meeting of the Friends at old Sadsbury in the year 1724, and also of Jeremiah Starr, one of the first settlers of New Garden, who was a prominent member of the Provincial Assembly in 1740, and of the well-known Guyon Miller, the first settler at Kennet Square. He is also the great great-grandson of Isaac Taylor, the first, who was a surveyor in the service of William Penn, and of his sons, proprietaries and governors of Pennsylvania; who made original surveys of a large portion of the land in the eastern section of Lancaster county and the western parts of Chester; who was also the original

WALTON, JOHN C., was elected a member of the Legislature in the years 1851 and 1852.

WARFEL, JACOB E., eldest son of John and Maria Warfel, was born July 21st, 1826. He early in life displayed considerable talent for drawing and painting, so much so that some of his work attracted the favorable attention of that eminent artist, Thomas Sully, of Philadelphia, who honored him with his friendship and gave him much valuable instruction. Mr. Warfel's prospects for honor and fame were very flattering, when his health failed, and after a protracted illness he died June 2d, 1855. He, however, had executed a number of valuable portraits, which now adorn the parlors of the fortunate possessors.

WARFEL, JOHN, was elected a member of the Legislature in the year 1842.

WARFEL, JOHN B., second son of John and Maria Warfel, was born in Paradise township, Lancaster county, September 19th, 1830. In early life he worked at the blacksmith trade. When twenty years of age he entered the Lewisburg University, and remained there two years. After this he taught public school, until the spring of 1854, when he commenced farming, and in connection therewith the practice of surveying and conveyancing. In 1855 he was elected a justice of the peace for Paradise township, and was reëlected in 1860. He also served for several years as district superintendent of public schools. In 1863 he gave up farming and resigned his several positions, to take an appointment in the pension office, at Washington, D. C. In 1865 he entered Columbia college, as a law student, and graduated

purchaser of all the land in the Gap, and erected the first stone house at that place, which is three stories high, and is standing and occupied at the present time, (1872) ; and who was also a magistrate and a member of the Provincial Assembly at different times, for the county of Chester from 1705 up to 1723. Isaac Walker is also the great-grandson of Nathaniel Newlin, who was a member of the convention which framed the old Constitution of Pennsylvania, and of Joseph Dickinson, one of the early settlers of Pequea Valley, who was joined in marriage with Elizabeth, the daughter of Guyon Miller ; also the great-grandson of the well-known James Moore, of Sadsbury, who emigrated from Ireland in the year 1723, and erected a large mill on the Octoraro, below Christiana, which is still standing and in use at the present time.

in the class of 1867. The same year he was admitted to practice in the supreme court of that city, and in the several courts of Lancaster county. In April, 1867, Mr. Warfel received the appointment of Assessor of Internal Revenue for the 9th Pennsylvania district, (Lancaster county), which position he continued to fill until removed, May 1st, 1869. The same year he was elected State Senator, receiving the largest popular vote of any candidate voted for at that election.

WARFEL, JOHN, son of Jacob and Mary Warfel, grand-son of Henry and Margaret Warfel, and great-grandson of George Warfel, one of the earliest settlers in Martic town-ship, and from whom, it is believed, all of the name in Lan-caster county have descended, was born in Strasburg (now Paradise) township, March 22d, 1788. His father died in 1810, and his mother afterwards married Henry Gara, from which connection H. S. Gara, esq., of Lancaster city, and the Hon. Isaac B. Gara, of Erie, Pennsylvania, were offspring. John Warfel married Maria Eshleman, daughter of Jacob Eshleman, of Paradise township. He was appointed recorder of deeds for Lancaster county in 1836, by Governor Joseph Ritner, and held that position for three years. He died May 25th, 1846.

WATSON, NATHANIEL, was elected a member of the State Senate in the year 1810.

WEAVER, PROF. ELIAS B., was born in East Earl town-ship, Lancaster county, February 1st, 1831. He is of Ger-man Mennonite ancestry, his father being Jonathan Weaver, a plain and unassuming farmer of his district. The subject of our sketch attended school taught by his cousin, John B. Good,[1] to whose suggestions it was chiefly owing that he early became animated with a thirst for learning. His father, having no idea of the advantages of education, did not favor anything in this direction, and he was instructed by his cousin in some of the advanced branches after the dismissal of the rest of the school, as a public prejudice existed

[1] John B. Good, esq., is now a member of the Lancaster bar, whose high sense of honor and scrupulous observance of his word are marked characteristics.

against the study of such. This even was shared by his father. But the industrious boy had the capacity, and with application (which he possessed in a remarkable degree) he made rapid progress and soon laid the foundation of a good English education. By the time he attained the age of eighteen or nineteen he made application to become the teacher of the same school in which he had obtained his instruction, and was successful. He continued teaching for several years, and expended considerable of his money so earned in the purchase of books, and thus laid the foundation of a library. Having made the acquaintance of J. P. Wickersham, at the first "Teachers' Institute," held in Fulton Hall, in January, 1853, he attended during the following summer as a student at the Marietta academy, then taught by the last named gentleman. After attending at this institution for some sessions, Mr. Weaver was chosen principal of the high school of New Holland, where he taught for some time. In 1855 he attended the first session at the Normal Institute, at Millersville, and in the spring of 1856 was elected assistant professor of mathematics in the Normal School at Millersville, then permanently established. This position he filled up till 1859, when he was elected professor of natural sciences in the same institution. This office he held up to the period of his death, which event occurred August 6th, 1863.

As a general scholar, Prof. Weaver had few superiors among the men of his years. He was able to read Latin, French and German, and had also acquired some knowledge of Greek. He was particularly at home in the German, and had read considerably of its classic literature; he had even essayed some translations of portions of celebrated German authors. But it was in mathematics that he especially excelled. Few men in our country understood mathematics better than he, or could solve more abstruse problems. As a teacher before his classes, he ranked amongst the most solid. Having clear ideas himself, he insisted upon his pupils acquiring a similar knowledge, and few teachers have been able to send forth students better versed in the branches of his department. He did not confine himself in his illustrations to the simple text-books, but was fertile in the presentation of anything that would in any wise make the subject of the lesson clearer to the apprehension of his pupils. He was ever himself a diligent student, and when he discovered anything new to his own mind, he was anxious to impart the same to his pupils. With his scholars he was ever a great favorite. His early demise was greatly lamented by the students and teachers of the institution in which he had so faithfully served as an instructor.

WEBB, JAMES, was a member of the Legislature[1] in the years 1747, 1748, 1750, 1755, 1756, 1757, 1758, 1759, 1760, 1761, 1762, 1764, 1765, 1766, 1767, 1768, 1769, 1772, 1773, 1774, 1775 and 1777.

WEBB, WILLIAM, was a member of the Legislature in the years 1790,[2] 1805 and 1806.

WELSH, GENERAL THOMAS, was for years a resident of Columbia, Lancaster county, Pa. He enlisted for and served with distinction in the war with Mexico. Upon the breaking out of the rebellion, he was among the very first who responded to the call of the President. He raised a company in the neighborhood of Columbia and was chosen captain of the same, and upon the organization of the regiment (the 2d Pennsylvania volunteers of the three months service) was elected lieutenant colonel. At the close of this service he again entered the field and was appointed colonel of the 45th regiment. This regiment was assigned to General Burnside's department, and took part in all the brilliant engagements of the campaign. In the engagements of South Mountain and Antietam, he commanded a brigade and displayed remarkable abilities for command on both these fiercely contested battle fields. To him has been accredited the honor of having turned the fortunes of the day at South Mountain. His soldierly qualities commended him to the attention of

[1] From the settlement of Pennsylvania up to the adoption of the constitution of 1789, the Legislature of the State was entitled the General Assembly.

[2] It is to be borne in mind that in enumerating offices held by individuals sketched in this work, the year of their election is generally given instead of that of their service.

General Burnside, and at his eager suggestion, as well as that of General Wilcox, he was appointed a brigadier general by President Lincoln. He was transferred to the west, his brigade accompanying him. He died at Cincinnati, August 14th, 1863. He proved himself a thorough soldier in every military position he occupied, and his promotion was one richly merited.

WHITE, HENRY M., was elected a member of the Legislature in the year 1860.

WHITE, WILLIAM, was elected sheriff of Lancaster county in the year 1824.

WHITEHILL, JAMES, son of John Whitehill, was a member of the Legislature in the year 1793. He served as a member of Congress from 1813 till 1814, when he resigned. He ;was a merchant of Strasburg, and a man of much influence in the community. He also presided for a time as associate judge of the courts of Lancaster county. He was reëlected to the Legislature in 1831.

WHITEHILL, JOHN, a citizen of Salisbury township, and a leading and influential man in his day. He was descended from Scotch-Irish ancestry. He was a member of the Legislature in the years 1780, 1781 and 1782. He also presided as associate judge of the courts of the county. He served two terms in Congress, from 1803 until 1807; he was again reëlected to the Legislature in the 1809.

WHITEHILL, JOHN, jr., was elected county commissioner in the year 1801.

WHITELOCK, ISAAC, was a member of the Legislature in the year 1772.

WHITESIDE, JOHN, a leading citizen of Lancaster county for many years. He was an influential Democrat, and was elected a member of the Legislature in the years 1810 and 1811. He served in the national Congress from 1815 till 1819. In 1821 he was appointed register of wills, which position he held for some time. In 1825 he was again reëlected to a seat in the Legislature. He owned and kept the Fountain Inn, in South Queen street, which for many years was the Democratic headquarters.

WHITESIDE, WILLIAM, son of John Whiteside, a member of the Lancaster bar, was appointed Register of Wills in 1830, an office he held for six years.

WHITSON, GEORGE, was elected Recorder of Lancaster county in 1860. In 1870 he was elected to the House of Representatives of Pennsylvania.

WICKERSHAM, PROFESSOR JAMES P., State Superintendent of public schools of Pennsylvania, was born in Chester county, where his ancestry have resided since the first settlement of that section of the State. Our subject was placed at school at an early age, and from a boy was noted for the rapid progress he made in his studies. After attaining a somewhat thorough knowledge of the rudimentary branches of study, he entered the Unionville Academy of Chester county, where he remained during six sessions. In this time he studied mathematics, natural science and history, as likewise the French and Latin languages. He now inclined in his mind to study a profession, but this not meeting the approbation of his father, the latter gave him the choice either to assist him upon his farm, or for the future to carve his course by the dint of his own exertions. The latter alternative was accepted, and shortly afterwards he engaged himself as an assistant teacher in the same institution in which he had pursued his studies, and for no other salary than the instruction he should receive. The following winter of 1841–42, he taught a country school at twenty dollars per month, and then returned to school himself, and thus he continued alternately teaching and studying until the year 1845, when he became principal of the Marietta Academy, Lancaster county, Pa. This position he obtained when but twenty years of age, and continued to perform the duties thereof for the period of nine years. In the year 1848 he married a daughter of Dr. Isaac Taylor, of Chester county. In 1854 he was elected the first County Superintendent of common schools of Lancaster county, and because he declined serving for less, received five hundred dollars more than any other superintendent in Pennsylvania. He immediately entered with great zeal into the work of elevating the schools of the county up to a higher standard of perfection.

Coming to perceive the advantages resulting from the association of teachers together in county institutes then budding into notice, he conceived the idea of enlarging this plan of teaching, and proposed to give instruction of this character for a period of some months at the Millersville Academy, then taught by M. L. Hobbes. This may somewhat be regarded as one of the inceptive steps which led to the establishment of the Normal school at this place. The movement thus inaugurated was steadily onward, and was gathering strength in its course, and in 1856 Professor Stoddard, the first President of the institution, was released from his charge, and J. P. Wickersham, our subject, chosen to succeed him as head of the first Normal school of Pennsylvania. He thereupon resigned his position as Superintendent of the schools of Lancaster county, and vigorously entered upon the discharge of his duties as President of the new Normal Pennsylvania college. This post he filled with efficiency up to the year 1866, when he resigned with the view of making a trip to Europe. Circumstances interposing, and his visit to the old world being delayed, he was in the meantime tendered by Governor Curtin, the position of State Superintendent of common schools, a position he accepted. He was again reappointed by Governor Geary, and his second confirmation by the Senate was unanimous, every one of the thirty-three Senators voting in his favor. This position he has continued to hold up to the present time.

During Prof. Wickersham's presidency of the Millersville Normal School he issued two volumes: one on "School Economy," and the other on "Methods of Instruction." The former of these was, in the year 1870, translated by the government of the Argentine Republic into the Spanish language, and established as a text-book in the schools of that Spanish republic. He was from the earliest inauguration of teachers' institutes one of the warm friends of this system of imparting instruction, and but few educators in the country have attended more of these and other meetings of like character. He has for years been recognized as standing amongst the prominent American educators, and at their county, State and national assemblages he has been repeat-

ˈedly honored by them with positions of rank and distinction. In 1868 he received the distinguished consideration' of being invited by Sarmiento, president of the Argentine Republic, to a position in his cabinet, to have charge of the educational interests of that country. This, however, he declined accepting.

Prof. Wickersham has ever been an industrious and indefatigable laborer in the cause of general education, and has been in the habit of writing considerably for magazines and newspapers, articles chiefly of an educational character. He has fine command of the English language, and pens an article in beautiful and rounded sentences, difficult to be excelled. He is, in short, a fine writer. As soon as he (as a partner,) came into possession of the *Pennsylvania School Journal*, in 1870, the improvement was immediately visible It rose to a scholarly rank at once, and has maintained this grade up to the present. At the last commencement of Lafayette college, Pennsylvania, the title of L.L.D. was conferred upon him.

WILEY, JOHN E., elected a member of the Legislature in the years 1869 and 1870.

WILEY, WILLIAM B., is one of the leading aldermen of Lancaster city, having filled this position from February, 1858. When young he learned the printing business with Thomas Feran, and in 1845 became publisher of the *Lancaster Democrat*, till he sold out to J. Forsyth Carter. From 1851 till October, 1855, he published the *Lancasterian*, which he sold to George Sanderson. He was the printer of the *Pennsylvania School Journal* from 1852 up to 1869, and in June of this latter year he began the publication of the *Lancaster Bar*. Mr. Wiley is endowed with considerable native capacity, entertains very liberal and enlarged sentiments of men and things, and possesses rare shrewdness and business sagacity.

WILSON, JOHN, was born in Amity township, Berks county, on 21st August, A. D. 1792. He died at Reamstown, Lancaster county, on the 28th day of October, A. D. 1854. On his mother's side, whose maiden name was Dehart, he was a descendant of the "Boone" family, to which,

"Daniel," the pioneer of Kentucky, gave celebrity. The subject of this sketch emigrated to Reamstown in the year 1814 or 1815, where he resided until his death. With no advantages of an early education, by industry he mastered most of the branches of a polite education. He was one of the first, if not the first, who opened an exclusively English school, and taught with great success for many years, not only school children, but young men and women, residing in that then almost entirely German region. In the year 1825 he was commissioned a justice of the peace by Governor Shulze, and at the same time commenced surveying and scrivening in all its branches, which he followed with success till his death. He, in addition, held many commissions of honor and trust from the Governors of Pennsylvania. He left a large family. He lies buried in the graveyard connected with the Reamstown Reformed and Lutheran church. William R. Wilson, son of the above, is a well-read and able attorney of the Lancaster bar.

WILLIAMS FAMILY. Robert, John and Thomas Williams, three brothers, were among the early and respectable settlers of Sadsbury township. They emigrated to this country when quite young, (whether with their mother is not fully known.) They were enterprising, industrious, and honorable young men. Robert and John Williams purchased about 500 acres of land in the year 1740, about one mile south of the Gap, from William Fishbourne, who had been appointed a member of Governor Gordon's Council in 1726. They were members of the old Presbyterian church at Octoraro. They divided the tract of land between them (Robert and John.) Robert afterwards purchased part of the Christiana tract, (known afterwards as the Murray property), and now owned by Lindley Brown, esq., for his brother Thomas, who was killed by a wild bear.

JOHN WILLIAMS built the old stone residence which is standing to the present day on the land of A. C. Walker, and which was afterwards the rendevous of the Doans and other notorious characters during the last years of the Revolution. He also built the old house, near the present residence of Isaac Walker, of Sadsbury township, which was afterwards the residence of James Knox said to be the grandfather of James K. Polk, President of the United States. John Williams died in the year 1747, and his tombstone bears the oldest date in the Presbyterian burying-ground at Octoraro. He left a widow and an only daughter, who was married to James Duff, and in the year 1759 they sold their property to James Moore and removed to Virginia.

ROBERT WILLIAMS retained his part of the land, in addition to which his son Robert purchased near 200 acres, that on which stood the ancient village of the Shawana Indians, the remains of which can be seen to the present day. His son, Robert Williams, jr., was married about the year 1765 to Grace, daughter of John Bell, of Colerain, and sister of Col. Patterson Bell and Montgomery Bell, of Tennessee. She was also the sister of John Bell, jr., said to be the father of John Bell, Senator of the United States, who removed to Davidson county, Tennessee. After the decease of Robert Williams, jr., and about the year 1792, was sold on his premises, the last African slave that was ever sold at public outcry in Sadsbury township, being a young female slave. She was exposed for sale in the barn-yard along with the stock cattle, and was purchased by Thomas Henderson, esq., for the sum of £50, and remained a faithful servant for Mrs. Henderson during the remainder of her life. The Williams family were among the first considerable money lenders of Sadsbury. Robert Williams, sr., held an obligation against Isaac Taylor, sr., about the middle of the last century for £200, and various other obligations on different persons. His grandson, the late John Williams, sr., secured a large distributive share out of the estate of his uncle Montgomery Bell, of the State of Tennessee, shortly before the late civil war, through the perseverance and assiduity of his friend and relative (grand nephew), John B. Livingston, esq., a member of the Lancaster bar. The Williams family have been noted for their honesty and consistent integrity in the community for one hundred and thirty years. James and Zachariah B. Williams, the great great-grandsons of Robert Williams, sr., are the present holders of the land, and reside on the property.

WITMER, ABRAHAM, was a member of the Legislature in the year 1791.

WITMER, DANIEL W., was elected a member of the Legislature in the years 1848 and 1854.

WITMER, JOHN, was elected commissioner of Lancaster county in the year 1847.

WITHERS, GEORGE, brother of Michael Withers, was a lieutenant in the Revolutionary army. He was born September 14th, 1747, and died May 23d, 1811. He was a farmer of Strasburg township. He left two sons and two daughters. Michael and George Withers, of Lancaster, are his sons.

WITHERS, GEORGE, a member of the Legislature in the year 1820, was born in West Earl township, in 1769, and died in 1829. His father was named George. He moved to near Reamstown when a young man, where he accumulated considerable property, yet in possession of his son, Curtis Withers. He was a man of considerable knowledge, and remarkable for his business talent. He had three sons, Curtis, John and George.

WITHERS, GEORGE B., a grandson of John Withers, read law and was admitted to the bar in 1822. He was a man of ability, and once held the office of prothonotary of Lancaster county. He was the Democratic candidate for the same office in 1839, in opposition to Zephaniah McLenegan.

WITHERS, JOHN, was a captain in Col. John Ferree's battalion, during the Revolution, and also a farmer of Strasburg township. He was born December 24th, 1729, and died December 24th, 1813.

WITHERS, MICHAEL,[1] was born March 4th, 1733. He was a gunsmith, and was employed by the government to manufacture rifles for the American army in the Revolution. He lived in Strasburg township. He was a man of influence and standing. He died August 18th, 1821.

WOOD, DAY, elected a member of the Legislature in the years 1864 and 1865. He died whilst serving as a legislator.

[1] It was chiefly through the instrumentality of Michael and George Withers that St. Michael's Lutheran church, in the borough of Strasburg, was built. They also furnished the said church with an organ, it being among the first procured for churches in Lancaster county.

WORK, Joseph, a member of the Legislature in the years 1783, 1785, 1786, 1787, 1790, 1791 and 1792.

WORLEY, Nathan, was born in Ohio, March 1st, 1819. He was early thrown with but a limited education entirely upon his own resources. In November, 1846, he removed from Ohio to Manheim, in Lancaster county, where he engaged in the mercantile business, an occupation he had followed for ten years previous. He has not grown rich, but has succeeded well as a merchant. About the year 1859 the question of building a railroad from Reading to Columbia was first proposed. Mr. Worley at once conceived the idea that Manheim should have the benefit of said road, although it was at least three miles north of the natural route. He took hold with a determination, and his conception was made a success. The people of the borough and neighborhood are now enjoying the benefits of his ideas put in practice. He was elected a member of the Legislature in the fall of 1861, and served one session. He is engaged in the mercantile business in Manheim.

WORRALL, Peter, was a member of the Legislature in the years 1747, 1748, 1749, 1751, 1752, 1753 and 1754.

WORTH, William C., was elected County Commmissioner in the year 1854.

WRIGHT, James, was a member of the Legislature in the years 1745, 1746, 1749, 1750, 1751, 1752, 1753, 1754, 1755, 1756, 1757, 1758, 1759, 1760, 1761, 1762, 1763, 1764, 1765, 1766, 1767, 1768 and 1770.

WRIGHT, James, jr., a member of the Legislature in the years 1821 and 1822.

WRIGHT, John, was one of the three first settlers who took up and settled the district where Columbia, in Lancaster county, now stands. He was born in England, and emigrated to Pennsylvania, settling first in Chester county, and afterwards made his way to Lancaster county. He was a Quaker by persuasion, and one of the active and enterprising men of his day. His name is intimately associated with all the earlier transactions of the county's history. He was a justice of the peace, and was the chief presiding magistrate of the justices' courts of the county for many years. He was one of the leading citizens who participated actively in securing the erection of Lancaster into a separate county, and to himself was the honor accorded of giving the name to the new county. It was named by him from his native county in England. He was one of the first members elected from the new county to the general assembly in 1729. He was afterwards elected in the years 1730, 1733, 1734, 1737, 1738, 1739, 1740, 1741, 1742, 1743, 1744, 1745, 1746, 1747 and 1748. His descendants are yet numerous in the county.

WYLIE, STUART A., was born in Lancaster city, January 25th, 1840. His father, David Wylie, was an humble cooper, who traced his descent from Scotch-Irish ancestry. Stuart A. was sent by his parents to the free schools of Lancaster, and being a boy of remarkable brightness, he far outstripped all his classmates in his studies, and graduated at the Lancaster high school at the early age of sixteen. Having taught school for a short time with great success, he next entered as an apprentice the *Inland Daily Times* office, and worked at case for a few months. In the meantime attention was attracted towards some articles written by him for the paper, and he was soon thereafter assigned the position of local reporter, which he filled for about two years. In this position he showed remarkable capacity, and was frequently complimented for his reports, and was on several occasions the recipient of handsome testimonials in appreciation of articles penned by him for the paper. On January 1st, 1859, S. A. Wylie & Co. began the publication of the *Inquirer* as a weekly paper, and afterwards consolidated therewith the *American Press and Republican*, purchased of Jacob Myers. In 1860 Mr. Wylie became sole proprietor of the enterprise, and from July 7th, 1862, until February 13th, 1864, issued likewise a *Daily Inquirer*. In 1861 he married Mary Amanda, a daughter of George Brubaker, esq. In 1868 he associated with him Ellwood Griest, and the firm continued the publication of the *Inquirer* up to the period of his death, June 12th, 1872.

In 1868 Mr. Wylie erected the largest printing establish-
44

ment[1] ever built in Lancaster, began business therein in February, 1869, and continued increasing and enlarging the same up till the day of his death.

Mr. Wylie was a remarkable man. As a business organizer and conductor, he ranked amongst those who are able to eclipse all their comrades and place themselves in the front column of the men of their epoch. In no sense did his capacities belong to an ordinary grade. He was extraordinary in every particular. He had a wonderful intuitive knowledge of men of all grades, and could measure almost at a glance any one with whom he came in contact, and assign their respective adaptabilities. As a writer, he wielded a ready pen; and as a speaker, he was able, upon any occasion, to acquit himself handsomely before an assemblage in a neat, appropriate speech that might seem to a stranger a studied production. In every particular, indeed, he exhibited rare ability. He could run the complicated financial machine of his vast business better than any subordinate, could attend to all the outside details, could canvass for business, as were this his allotted sphere, could make

[1] The *Inquirer* printing and binding establishment, erected in 1868, inaugurated in Lancaster, in the department of printing, a movement of activity not before witnessed in the State outside of Philadelphia, and equaled in but few places in that city. The idea of this mammoth enterprise was a conception of S. A. Wylie alone, and had time been spared him he would, in all probability, have rivaled almost the printing and publishing depots of Leipsic. Such was his ambition. His establishment employs in its different departments about, on an average, one hundred and sixty hands, and turns out an immense amount of work obtained from New York, Philadelphia, Boston, Baltimore, Chicago, New Orleans, and numerous other places. About nine weekly newspapers and twenty monthly periodicals issue from the establishment, besides millions of pamphlet publications, that are printed and put up for gratuitous or advertising circulation. The printing of books for Philadelphia and New York houses has already become an important feature of the concern. Twelve steam presses are kept nearly all the time in active operation, frequently running day and night. Often double sets of hands are employed. The system of stereotyping was introduced but a short time before the death of Mr. Wylie, and is now regularly prosecuted, the first of this branch of business ever established in Lancaster. The different departments of business are all regularly systematized, a foreman being placed over each, and those selected for the various positions were chosen with reference to their respective proficiencies in their several specialties.

estimates for contracts from $5.00 to $10,000 with amazing dexterity, and could, if need required, throw off his coat and equal if not surpass in the amount of work dispatched any employee in his service. He had a complete and accurate knowledge of the most minute details relating to the management, and execution of his vast and complicated printing and binding establishment, an enterprise of which, whilst living, he was the entire soul and manager. He was, in short, all combined, the most enterprising, successful, and intellectual business man of his years that the old inland city has ever yet produced.

Mr. Wylie as a citizen, was worthy of imitation. He was genial and bland, always in a good humor, and wore a smiling face for all. He was very affable and talkative, and no man ever saw him moody or morose. To all his employees he was ever courteous and kind, yet the proprietor's attitude was uniformly observed, forbidding undue familiarity. If occasion required, a sternness peremptorily demanded observance of duty, and quelled all indications of disobedience, or dismissal immediately followed. As a man, he was charitable and humane, and ready to extend a favor to any worthy object.

Y.

YEATES, JASPER,[1] was the most eminent lawyer in Lancaster before the period of the American Revolution. He was admitted to the bar in the year 1765. He took a very active part in all matters relating to the difficulties between the mother country and her American colonies, and was an ardent advocate of the Whig cause. He was one of the delegates from Lancaster county to the convention of 1787 which ratified, on the part of Pennsylvania, the Federal Con-

[1] Jasper Yeates, with Edward Shippen, and Smith, the three judges of the Supreme Court of Pennsylvania, were, in 1805, impeached before the Senate of Pennsylvania, but acquitted.

stitution. The other delegates from the county, were: Stephen Chambers, Robert Coleman, Sebastian Graff, John Hubley and John Whitehill. He was one of the committee of three with Thomas McKean and Judge Wilson who reported the form of the ratification, which is in these words: "In the name of the people of Pennsylvania, be it known unto all men, that we, the delegates of the people of the commonwealth of Pennsylvania in general convention assembled, have assented to and ratified, and by these presents, do, in the name and by the authority of the said people, and for ourselves, assent to and ratify the (foregoing) Constitution for the United States of America." In 1791 he was appointed a judge of the Supreme Court of Pennsylvania, a position he held with great credit during the remainder of his life. One of the series of State Reports was prepared by Judge Yeates, which confers great honor upon him as an author and a lawyer. He died March 13th, 1817, in the 73d year of his age. He was possessed of a clear and vigorous mind, and his opinions were bold. As a judge, he commanded the highest respect and deference. His decisions from the bench were clear, decisive and strongly indicative of a profound knowledge of the constitution and laws of his country. As a man of business, he was one of the most methodical. With him everything had its time and place. This trait was observable in all his transactions, whether of a domestic or public nature. He was kind and affectionate, of a cheerful and contented disposition, and correct and engaging in his deportment. In all the social relations he was truly amiable.

Z.

ZAHM, Godfried, was born November 10th, 1787, in Lancaster borough. When a young man he learned cigar making, and afterwards brush making, which latter business he carried on for upwards of fifty years. Mr. Zahm began life in humble circumstances, and by economy, industry and uprightness he accumulated a handsome independence and rose to the rank of the influential men of the day. Just prior to the breaking out of the war of 1812, by the advice of some friends, he invested largely in imported bristles. The subsequent embargo greatly enhanced their value, and this laid the foundation of his fortune. His strict integrity was early recognized, and before the incorporation of Lancaster as a city, having served as a collector, no bond was required of him. He was a member of the city councils for many years. He served in common councils for a time, and was a member of select council for twenty-three years, and during all this time was chairman of the finance committee, a position for which, by the common consent of all citizens of Lancaster, he was best qualified to fill. His sagacious shrewdness in financial matters earned for him the sobriquet of "Old Talleyrand." He was for twenty years a leading member of the school board. He was an early and ardent friend of the free school system, and was one of the first to advocate making the system compulsory upon non-accepting districts. He died universally esteemed and respected, March 9th, 1871.

ZAHM, MATHIAS, brother of Godfried Zahm, an aged and respected citizen, has been court-crier for nearly forty years. He was born August 17th, 1789.

ZECHER, CHRISTIAN, SR., emigrated from Germany and settled in Lancaster shortly after the close of the American Revolution. He was a tailor by trade, but did not follow it much after coming to Lancaster. He kept carts and horses, and by his industry secured a fair competence. He died aged sixty-two years. He raised eight children, all yet living: Christian, Frederick, Jacob, David, Lewis, Christiana, married to Brooks Campbell; Mary, married to James Campbell, and after his death to James Noble; and Catharine, married to Charles McLaughlin. Christian Zecher has for several years been the most industrious and efficient member of the Lancaster school board. He has also been one of the principal movers in the erection of the new market house,[1] at the corner of North Queen and Walnut streets.

[1] The new market house is now being completed, and its cost, it is believed, will reach $60,000.

ZELLER, JOHN H., was elected Clerk of Quarter Sessions and Oyer and Terminer in 1863. In 1866 Jacob M. Greider succeeded him in this office, and filled the same during his term of three years.

ZIMMERMAN, HENRY, (Carpenter), the progenitor of the numerous Carpenter family of Lancaster county, was a native of the canton of Berne, in Switzerland, and emigrated to this country about 1710. According to an old order of William Penn, the names of all persons to whom grants of land were made were Anglicised, and hence the name was changed to that of Carpenter. Henry Zimmerman was allowed to take possession of several hundred acres of land, provided he went sixty miles west of Philadelphia. The cause of his emigration was repugnance to persecution, and being a member of the German Reformed church his friends desired to force him to unite with those of their opinions in persecuting others. This did not seem to him as accordant with the spirit of christianity, and to escape this he resolved upon coming to America. To detain him his friends meditated seizing his wife, and thus they thought to prevent his going. She, however, resolved to follow her husband. He accordingly, in secret, obtained a small boat and fixed it upon the shore of the lake of the four cantons. They awaited a favorable opportunity, and finally left their home to escape, by means of the boat, forever from the land of their birth. Henry armed himself, and not in vain, with a sabre, for they were attacked on the road by four hussars, who wished to prevent their departure. Tradition says, with Salome clinging to her husband for protection, he successfully combated his four assailants, and succeeded in escaping, both himself and wife, in their little boat, to a more hospitable shore. Henry Zimmerman was a carpenter by trade, and going from Switzerland to England on his way to America, he was presented with a large auger and other tools by Queen Anne, to enable him to carry on his trade in America.

ZIMMERMAN, JOHN, ex-Mayor of the city of Lancaster, was born March 22d, 1798, two miles northwest of the city of Lancaster. When he was about eight years of age his father moved to Columbia, and thence to Soudersburg, where he died in 1813. In 1815 the subject of this notice came to Lancaster and entered the store of John Landis, as clerk. In 1822 he married Anna M. Schaeffer, a sister of Judge Schaeffer, deceased. In 1828 he was elected a member of city councils, and whilst a member moved the resolution to introduce water from the Conestoga into the city of Lancaster, pumped into a reservoir by machinery. He was afterwards, for a time, chairman of the water committee. He attended the first meeting held for the purpose of introducing the common school system into the schools of Lancaster. He was a great friend of the measure. He was for about 18 years a member of the School Board, 8 years of which he acted as secretary. He was city treasurer for 8 or 9 years, and in 1856 was elected Mayor of the city of Lancaster, and reëlected in 1857.

ADDENDA.

*HERR, REV. CHRISTIAN, an eminent and successful pastor and teacher in the Mennonite denomination of christians, was born on the 31st day of October, 1780, on the farm on which his son, Rev. Amos Herr, at present resides, situated in what is now West Lampeter township, bordering on Pequea creek. From this circumstance, and for the purpose of distinguishing him from others of the same name, (as the Herr family had then become numerous in that vicinity), his father, whose name was also Christian, either assumed, or had conferred on him by the neighbors the appellation of Pequea Christian Herr; the son assumed the distinctive appendage, and almost uniformly, except in private correspondence, signed his name "Christian Herr, jr., Pequea," until after the death of his father, when the junior was discarded, to be afterwards resumed by his son.

Tradition, which is fast becoming, if it has not already become history, informs us that about the year 1710 or 1711, a colony of emigrants, from Switzerland, effected a settlement on the north side of Pequea creek, which settlement was subsequently included in the limits of Lampeter township. These emigrants were mostly, if not all, members of the Mennonite church. Amongst them was John Herr, or as familiarly expressed in their native language, Hans Herr, as their pastor and leader, who brought with him five sons, who are the progenitors of the numerous and respectable family of that name in the county of Lancaster, many of whom still own and reside on the lands originally purchased from the proprietary government, by their ancestors, more than one hundred and fifty years ago. Christian Herr, the subject of this memoir, was one of the fourth generation from the above named Hans Herr. He had no brother, but six sisters, five of whom were married and one died single. He was brought up as a farmer, and received no education but what was obtained at our common country schools, which at best, in those days, was an imperfect knowledge of reading, writing and common arithmetic. But being of a sprightly disposition, and possessing an inquiring, contemplative turn of mind, and a retentive memory, by reading

* Contributed by Hon. John Strohm.

and study he improved his intellectual powers, and acquired a general knowledge of men and things superior to most young men of his class and age, which enabled him to aid and advise his neighbors and friends, who frequently consulted him in regard to matters of business. He was often employed in drawing instruments of writing in reference to the disposition of property, by agreement and by devise, and in the settlement of estates, and disputes and controversies amongst neighbors. These acquirements, connected with his kindness of heart and amiable disposition, made him very and deservedly popular amongst his associates and acquaintances. As an evidence of his good standing in the community in which he lived, it may be mentioned that, when yet a young man he was elected, in 1812, one of the commissioners for his native county, the duties of which he discharged with fidelity and ability. Had his ambition prompted him to aspire to worldly distinction he might have attained to higher positions. He was urgently solicited to accept a nomination for the Legislature, but refused. Politics and statesmanship seemed uncongenial to his tastes, and he withdrew from secular employments to exercise his talents and his energies in a higher and nobler field of action.

About the year 1817 he became seriously impressed with the sinfulness of man's natural condition, and the necessity of a Redeemer's grace. On a careful and prayerful perusal and study of the holy scriptures, and the elucidations thereof by learned and enlightened divines, he came to the conclusion that duty required him to connect himself with some religious denomination; and by withdrawing from and declining worldly honors, to enlist himself as an humble follower of his Lord and Saviour Jesus Christ. After a deliberate examination of the various creeds and professions that came within his knowledge and presented themselves to his mind at the time, none seemed to him more fully in accordance with the teachings of the holy scriptures, which he conceived to be the guide to all truth, than that in which he had been instructed from his childhood, and in which his parents and ancestors had been worthy members and communicants. In accordance with these views and impressions, he and his amiable and excellent wife became members of the Orthodox[1] (or old) Mennonite church. In this situation his meek and exemplary deportment did not escape the notice of his associates, and as an evidence of their confidence in his sincerity, uprightness of conduct and unaffected piety, he was appointed an elder in the congregation with which he worshiped. Pur-

[1]This word is used here to distinguish this denomination from those who call themselves the Reformed (or new) Mennonite society.

suing the even tenor of his way in a quiet and unobtrusive manner, attending sedulously to the various duties required of him, frequently visiting the sick and distressed, not only amongst those who belonged to the same congregation, but any who seemed to require his aid and advice, he performed many good offices and received the sincere thanks of many who profited by his disinterested exertions. In adjusting difficulties and reconciling controversies between those who ought to be friends, he was actively engaged, in which his good sense and earnest and impressive manner rendered him very useful; and many hard feelings and vexatious misunderstandings were allayed and assuaged through his intervention, and peace and harmony restored where distrust and suspicion, and in some instances falsehood and malice, had engendered discord and strife.

In the year 1835, as a further appreciation of his merits, he was, according to the rules and ordinances of the church of which he was a member, ordained a minister of the gospel. This opened to him a wider field of action and usefulness, and a corresponding increase of labor and fatigue. He soon obtained the reputation of being a fluent speaker, a sound, logical reasoner, and a fervent, earnest proclaimer of the truths of the gospel. Many who for years had been apathetic or lukewarm on the subject of religion, were awakened to a just sense of their condition, and, as a consequence, a considerable accession was made to the church under his ministration. He could not be called eloquent, attempted no flourishes of rhetoric, indulged in no flights of imagination, but his power lay in the simple, unassuming, but fervent and earnest manner in which he addressed his audience. This, together with the knowledge of his blameless life and unimpeachable character, carried conviction to the hearts of his hearers, when high sounding words, polished, elaborate sentences, delivered in a pompous and ostentatious style of action, would have passed them by as "sounding brass or tinkling cymbals." It now became his duty to preach at least one sermon on every Sabbath day, and not unfrequently he was called on two or three times a week to preach funeral sermons. In addition to those duties he had to give a portion of his time to visit the sick, so that his time was almost constantly occupied in attending to those duties, leaving him very little time in which to attend to private business. In 1831 he had the misfortune to lose his wife, who had for many years been the partner of his joys, and in sickness and sorrow his comforter and supporter. The writer of this article here claims the privilege of a slight digression, to pay a tribute of respect to the memory of one for whom he

entertained the highest regard. He remembers with gratitude the many kindnesses he received at her hands. He
knew her well, saw her in many difficult and trying situations, and never knew a lady of more equable temperament
and kind and obliging disposition. A loving and confiding
wife, she was a constant, unwavering friend, just and generous to her domestics and neighbors, and above all, a sincere
and devout christian. She was a daughter of Christian and
Barbara Forrer, of Conestoga township.

Some years subsequent to the decease of his wife, his children being nearly all grown up and married, he gave up the
management of his fine estate to his sons and took up his
residence with his eldest son, Benjamin; and having divested
himself as much as possible from all earthly cares, devoted
his time entirely to the duties of his calling. In the year
1840 he was elevated to the highest position recognized by
the church to which he belonged, that of bishop, successor
to Rev. Peter Eby, whose friendship and confidence he
shared, and with whom he had traveled many miles in the
discharge of the duties incident to their positions. Here
again the area and extent of his labors were augmented. It
became his duty to frequently visit other and sometimes
distant congregations, even beyond the limits of his native
county, and occasionally to other States. These labors, with
the pressure of advancing age, began to take effect on his,
not very robust constitution, and it was noticed by his
friends, and must have been felt and observed by himself,
that he was beginning to sink under the accumulated pressure of age, infirmity, care and labor; but he conceived it to
be his duty to continue in the service of his Lord and Master,
and impelled by love to his fellow-men, for whose benefit
those labors and inconveniences were exerted and endured,
he traveled and preached, exhorted, counseled and advised,
as long as he was able to move from place to place. Finally
his nervous system became relaxed, and he was scarce able
to walk; even his speech was affected by nervous debility, and
it was sometimes difficult for him to give utterance to words
intended to convey his ideas. Under these circumstances he
was compelled to refrain from public speaking, and for several years previous to his decease was unable to leave home;
yet he retained the faculties of his mind and conversed,
though not without difficulty, with such of his friends as
visited him. He endured his affliction with constancy and
resignation, his only lament being that he could no longer
attend to his duties in the church. His dissolution took
place on the 23d day of June, 1853. His funeral was attended by a large number of friends and relatives, as also of

neighbors and acquaintances, who deplored the loss of one so highly gifted, and who had been so eminently useful in his sphere of life. He was emphatically a man of peace. The tenets of his religion were non-resistant, and condemned war as sinful and not to be countenanced, aided or participated in by any of its professors. These likewise prohibited any of its members from engaging in any law-suit before the legal tribunals of the country, but directed all difficulties and controversies that might occur amongst the members of the society, to be referred to and adjusted by the brethren. To the spirit of those principles he gave his full assent, and so deeply was he imbued with the spirit of peace and concord that he deprecated even colloquial controversey, especially on the subject of religion, and avoided it as much as possible. But when duty seemed to require an effort in that direction, he was prompt and decided in maintaining his own views, yet always liberal and courteous to an opponent. Claiming the privilege of acting in accordance with the convictions of his own mind, he willing allowed to others the same liberty; and, whilst he sustained his own opinions with energy and perspicuity, he never rashly condemned others for entertaining a different opinion.

As a speaker he had a clear, agreeable voice, a good enunciation, and spoke deliberately, so as to be easily understood. His language was suited to the capacity of his audience, being the common idiom of the German population of Lancaster county, sometimes by way of elucidation interspersed with a word or words derived from the English. He was a sententious, forcible and logical speaker, which, with the earnest and feeling manner in which his sermons were delivered, rendered his preaching very effective. His style and manner were persuasive rather than denunciatory; he amplified on the unbounded goodness of God to his finite creatures, endeavored to awaken in their hearts a high sense of gratitude and love to that beneficent being, but failed not to warn them of the danger of persisting in disobedience to His commands.

Having experienced the inconvenience of a defective education, he felt anxious to give his children a better opportunity to improve their minds than had fallen to his lot in his youth. In the year 1815, not being able to get a competent teacher in the neighboring school, he employed a private teacher at his dwelling house for the benefit of his own children and those of some of his nearest neighbors. Subsequently, he succeeded in getting a better teacher in the neighboring school, and for many years took an active part in promoting the cause of education. In the management of his farm he was industrious, judicious and enterprising. By good judgment, industry, prudence and care, he augmented his paternal inheritance so as to leave a fine estate to his children. He raised a family of six sons, Benjamin, Elias, Christian, Joseph, Amos and Daniel, all of whom are married; and two daughters, Maria, who was intermarried with John Brackbill, and Ann, who was inter-married with John Herr, miller; all of whom reside in the vicinity of where they were born, with the exception of one daughter, Mrs. Brackbill, who is now dead. The sons are all respectable and thrifty farmers, who venerate the memory of their father, and evince a disposition to emulate the virtuous example which he left them; and what was probably most gratifying to him in his old age, his children all became members of the church in which he was so long a pastor and leader. Two of them, Benjamin and Amos, are preachers of the gospel; the former now occupy-ing the position that his father did during the last years of his life, that of bishop in the Mennonite church.

Such was the life and character of a man who in every situation discharged his duty with fidelity. An affectionate husband, a kind and indulgent father, an obliging and agreeable neighbor, a zealous and effective preacher, and a sincere and devout Christian.

HUBER, Jacob, elected Sheriff in 1848.

HUMES, James, elected Sheriff in 1809.

KLINE, George M., is one of the well-read and able at-torneys of the Lancaster bar. His mind is of an analytical order, and he possesses the faculty of grasping legal ques-tions and presenting them with clearness before the court and jury. He has ever been a close student, and without turning aside into political currents, has steadily devoted himself to the pursuit of his profession.

MILLER, David, elected Sheriff in the year 1833.

MILLER, Henry, elected Register of Wills in the year 1842.

POWNALL, Joseph D., elected a member of the Legis-lature in the years 1856 and 1857.

RHINE, Michael, elected Sheriff in 1800.

SHUMAN, Jacob B., elected Commissioner in 1864.

STUART, George, elected a member of the Legislature in the years 1730 and 1732.

WEIDMAN, George, elected Commissioner in 1807.

ERRATA.

On page 7, line 13, the word Dr. to be omitted.

On page 25, lines first and second, instead of Quarter Sessions and Oyer and Terminer, it should read Orphans' Court.

On page 39, line 9, instead of 1779 read 1799.

On page 115, John Buchanan was Commissioner in 1821, instead of 1824.

On page 117, in note, in line 22, instead of James read Wm. Hopkins.

On page 147, James B. Cowden was elected to the Legislature in 1850, and not 1853.

On page 182, in line 2 from bottom, instead of Martha read Martin E.

On page 237, Daniel Good was elected Commissioner in 1857, instead of 1854.

On page 285, line 9, instead of mother read grandmother.

On page 320, line 13, instead of three years read four years.

On page 333, instead of C. L. Kauffman read C. S. Kauffman.

On page 384, in line 3 from bottom, read motives instead of notions.

On page 395, line 10, instead of David Miller read John Miller.

On page 399, in foot note to James Moore, line 10, instead of 1708 read 1808.

On page 430, in sketch of William Noble, read 1833 instead of 1835.

On page 449, in line 11, instead of 1858 read 1868.

On page 450, in line 5, instead of Salisbury read Sadsbury.

On page 501, instead of John read Jonathan H. Roland, and instead of 1856 read 1857.

On page 561, in lines 12 and 13, instead of 1867 and 1868 read 1866 and 1867.